The Glorious Revolution in America

Also by David S. Lovejoy

David S. Lovejoy

The Glorious Revolution in America

HARPER & ROW, PUBLISHERS
New York · Evanston · San Francisco · London

Chapter 3 first appeared in somewhat different form in *Anglo-American Political Relations, 1675–1775,* edited by Alison Gilbert Olson and Richard Maxwell Brown. Published by Rutgers University Press, New Brunswick, New Jersey, 1970.

Chapter 6 appeared in somewhat different form in an article entitled "Equality and Empire: The New York Charter of Libertyes, 1683," in the *William and Mary Quarterly,* 3rd ser. XXI (October 1964), 493–515. It is printed here with permission of the editor.

FIRST EDITION

STANDARD BOOK NUMBER 06-012721-X

LIBRARY OF CONGRESS CARD NUMBER: 71-156533

For Elizabeth B.

Contents

Acknowledgments

Throughout several years' work upon this book, I have run up a series of debts to both individuals and institutions for help given to me in a variety of ways. It is difficult to know where to begin to thank appropriately these people, libraries, and archives. First on the list is the John Carter Brown Library at Brown University where my research began and where Thomas R. Adams, Librarian, and Jeannette D. Black offered their valuable knowledge and friendly advice. Also at Brown I had frequent aid from David A. Jonah and his assistants at the University Library, then the John Hay. To the staff of the Wisconsin State Historical Society I am indebted for several years of generous help from the librarians, earlier Benton H. Wilcox, now Charles W. Shetler, and particularly Ruth H. Davis, Josephine C. Harper, and Ellen Burke. At Northwestern University I found the same kind assistance, besides welcome encouragement from Professor Gray C. Boyce, then chairman of the History Department there. In Boston I remember with delight the guidance and hospitality of Mr. and Mrs. Leo Flaherty at the Massachusetts Archives, while an old and good friend,

Malcolm Freiberg, made my visit to the Massachusetts Historical Society rewarding and pleasant.

In Great Britain my obligations are many. A Fulbright Lectureship took me to the University of Aberdeen, presenting me an opportunity to continue my research at King's College Library and of a host of new friends with whom I could discuss it. Most of one summer was spent at the Public Record Office in London and the balance at the British Museum, the Library of the Society of Friends, and the Guildhall. At each of these I was cordially received and generously aided.

One of the happy conditions surrounding academic life at the University of Wisconsin has been a substantial granting of research assistance. In my experience this has come in several forms: research leaves and supplemental funds, summer grants, and graduate student assistants. I am particularly grateful to the following scholars, one time or another research assistants, who have made my task easier: Maxine Neustadt Lurie, J. William Frost, Robert M. Bliss, Jr., Laura Eldridge, and John W. Raimo. They have contributed in large and small ways to this study.

Professor William L. Sachse of the University of Wisconsin served in a special capacity by reading several chapters in manuscript and offering some very pertinent suggestions. John C. Rainbolt (once a research assistant) and Theodore B. Lewis, Jr., read bits and pieces here and there and over several years have discussed with me many of the problems dealt with in these pages in ways that were very helpful. James S. Leamon of Bates College kindly lent me his microfilm copy of the Livingston Family Papers in the Franklin D. Roosevelt Library at Hyde Park, New York.

The bulk of the writing was accomplished during the free time offered me by a Guggenheim Fellowship. This generous award allowed me to indulge a one-tracked mind in a single task. Helen Hull typed superbly a large part of the manuscript, winning my admiration and thanks. She was ably assisted by Laura Lehmann and Patricia Haen.

Lastly, I am grateful to my colleagues in the History Department at the University of Wisconsin. Serious teachers and scholars all, they have demonstrated continuously a love of learning and an ability to share it which are the heart of a great university.

D. S. L.

Madison, Wisconsin
March 1972

Abbreviations

A.A.S. *Proc.*	American Antiquarian Society, *Proceedings.*
A.H.R.	*American Historical Review.*
B.M.	British Museum.
BPCol. Wmsbg.	Blathwayt Papers, Colonial Williamsburg.
Cal. Treas. Bks.	*Calendar of Treasury Books.*
CSPCol.	*Calendar of State Papers, Colonial Series, America and the West Indies.*
CSPDom.	*Calendar of State Papers, Domestic Series.*
C.O.	Colonial Office Papers, Public Record Office, London.
Col. Recs. N.C.	*Colonial Records of North Carolina, 1662–1776* (1886–90).
Doc. Hist. N.Y.	*The Documentary History of the State of New-York* (1849–51).
H.M.C.	Historical Manuscripts Commission.

M.H.S. *Coll.*	Massachusetts Historical Society *Collections.*
M.H.S. *Proc.*	Massachusetts Historical Society *Proceedings.*
N.Y. *Col. Docs.*	*Documents Relative to the Colonial History of the State of New-York* (1853–87).
P.R.O.	Public Record Office, London.
Recs. Col. Conn.	*Public Records of the Colony of Connecticut, 1636–1776* (1850–90).
Recs. Col.R.I.	*Records of the Colony of Rhode Island, 1636–1792* (1856–65).
Recs. Mass. Bay	*Records of the Governor and Company of the Massachusetts Bay in New England, 1628–1686* (1853–54).
Toppan, ed., *Randolph*	*Edward Randolph: Including His Letters and Official Papers . . . 1676–1703* (1898–1909).

NOTE

I have tried to retain as much original spelling, punctuation, and arrangement of letters as possible in words, phrases, and passages quoted. On occasion changes were necessary to promote clarity and to conform to modern types.

To avoid confusion, dates are given according to the Old Style, Julian Calendar which Englishmen used until the middle of the eighteenth century. However, following modern practice, I have begun the new year with January 1 instead of March 25.

Introduction

This book is about England's American colonies in the latter half of the seventeenth century. It is less a study of colonial policy and navigation acts—although it would seem to begin that way—than about the colonists' responses to both of these, or more generally to the concept of empire which emerged in England after the Restoration in 1660. The focus of the book is upon events and ideas leading up to and climaxing in the colonial rebellions of 1689 which were provoked by both local crises and the Glorious Revolution abroad. It seeks to explain what colonists thought they were doing when they exploited the upheaval in England for their own peculiar purposes as well as to determine the meaning of the English Revolution for them as American colonists.

Historians have spent a good deal of effort already in describing the British colonial system in the seventeenth century. This is a side of the story one blinks at his peril if he wishes to make sense out of the colonial period of American history. We know less of what seventeenth-century colonists thought about themselves and their relationship to England. Such an inquiry is more easily answered for the eighteenth century and particularly for the period just before the American Revolution when colonists were forced by a number of circumstances to argue publicly their conception of empire and explain their connection with Crown and Parliament. In the seventeenth century colonial society was less sophisticated, less mature, less stable, and less reflective about itself and how it regarded its relation to government and people within the realm. Furthermore, communications between colonies and England and between colonists themselves were more primitive. For the most part each colony went along at its own pace, influenced by the nature of its surroundings, conditions, and needs, on the one hand, and by the emerging, yet fitful, colonial policy, on the other. One might conclude from this that colonists thought seriously about themselves and what they were doing only when their assumptions were sharply challenged by specific events as they were in the 1760's and 1770's. One is less likely to think, then, that American colonists in the seventeenth century came to strong conclusions about some of these same problems, since they had had less time to form habits and customs and assumptions about themselves and their connection with the realm. Furthermore, Crown, Parliament, and ministry after the Restoration had only begun to determine how they should implement what few ideas about empire were already current.

There were really very few precedents for an English empire. The rapid settling of new colonies after the Restoration, the regulation of trade and commerce by Parliamentary acts, and the attempt to extend royal control over governments and people were new experiences all around. Of course, colonial policy was based generally on concepts of what we now call mercantilism, but these were not precise in the seventeenth century and meant different things to different people. It was generally conceded in England that colonies existed for the benefit of the mother country, which could only mean some kind of subordination. At the same time colonists insisted that they were Englishmen and therefore ought not to be discriminated against because they happened to live outside the realm. Most charters establishing plantations overseas included statements which colonists believed assured them of the rights of Englishmen even though they might be thousands of miles from England itself.

No one had worked out the laws of empire in the first half of the seventeenth century. Since there were no hard and fixed rules, formulators of policy after the Restoration made them as they went along, and from these a colonial system emerged. At times the rules handed down by the planners clashed with the colonists' own interests and assumptions—even presumptions—about themselves and how they ought to be treated. New regulations, intensification and centralization of control often created uncertainty in the minds of colonists about what the bases for their settlements were. Besides policy from London, specific demands from proprietors and the Crown often upset local habits and suppositions, which led to further uncertainty. The period between the Restoration and the Glorious Revolution was a time of rapid development in English America, both economic and political, and its effect upon colonists was to force them to seek guarantees and assurances against what they believed were harmful "mutacons."

In view of the lack of maturity and sophistication in colonial society of the first century, it is surprising that after the Restoration several colonies and many colonists should make very explicit statements about their roles and what they believed were their rights in the emerging empire. No single challenge precipitated these reactions, but an accumulation of events and circumstances in both England and America and several decisions about colonial policy provoked responses which leave the historian no doubt about what colonists were thinking, who they thought they were, and what they regarded as their relationship to government and Englishmen at home. These statements were not all alike, since they were conditioned by local political, economic, and religious differences. Yet, when taken as a whole, they demonstrate that colonists in the latter half of the seventeenth century had come to some hard conclusions about the English empire and the meaning of their life in America.

The writing of early American history has certain built-in hazards peculiar to the subject—as do all historical periods, I suppose, given the nature of history. To American colonial history most significant of these is the American Revolution, that brute presence which, no matter how one interprets it, dominates almost the last half of the eighteenth century and spills many of its ideas over a good part of the nineteenth. Actually, at the outset the Revolution is an advantage to the historian of the earlier period, if for no other reason than it tells him when to stop, for it destroys the principal vehicle on which he hangs his story. But the disadvantages are more complicated and not easily avoided. The worst of these is the unmistakable fact that the colonial period of American history came to a violent end in a bloody revolution. So impressive is this historical truth that it is a frequent temptation, often unconscious, to let it color one's interpretation of, even attitude toward, the course of events, the development of ideas, which precede it. It is difficult sometimes not to read back into the colonial period conceptions, ways of thinking, even words and phrases of the Revolutionary era which do not belong there. To give the early period this kind of gloss is like reading the end of a detective novel first in order correctly to interpret the intricate plot in light of the conclusion.

I have tried to avoid this danger. To write the history of the colonies with one eye on the Revolution is grossly unfair to the first century and a half of American history. It is a period which richly deserves to be read, understood, and appreciated on its own terms. In writing this book one of the problems was to adhere to my own warning without at the same time bending over backwards and robbing the period of its rightful significance in the overall course of history. When I write that colonists in the 1670's and 1680's reacted to events and ideas sometimes in a fashion similar to that of their grand and great grandchildren in the 1760's and 1770's, am I guilty of reading the sources back to front? I think not. Rather, I conclude from the similarity that a knowledge of the colonists' problems in the seventeenth century is a necessary step toward an understanding of the American Revolution—not the other way around. Further, if colonists of the earlier period expressed certain ideas about empire which their descendants echoed at a later time, I conclude that these ideas are not only old but fundamental to English colonial society and ought to be sought where they originated, in the history of the seventeenth century. This is not special pleading, I think— only an argument for a truer perspective.

What were the circumstances, then, which provoked American colonists after 1660 to settle upon a set of principles which they regarded as fundamental to existence in the empire? What were these principles which defined their role and the rights and liberties they believed they could count on as English subjects living outside the realm? And what connection existed between these assumptions and the rebellions of 1689 which catapulted several colonies into crises second only to the conflict of 1776? These are some of the questions this study seeks to answer.

1   "An Affayre of State": Trade and Commerce

The Restoration of Charles II offered Englishmen splendid opportunities to expand dominions overseas. The settling of new plantations after 1660 was part of an overall economic expansion which, in addition to planting people in America, involved English merchants, courtiers, and promoters in mercantile ventures as diverse as extracting furs from the shores of Hudson's Bay and Negroes from the coast of Africa. Charles's restoration made it possible for an increasing number of interested Englishmen to devote attention to matters of colonies and trade. Around the throne gathered an influential group of noblemen and merchants who helped to shape colonial policy for the next generation. Although this group of well-placed individuals did not share precisely the same ideas about what ought to be done, they agreed generally that colonies in America existed for the benefit of England and for the benefit of those whose money and time were invested in particular colonial schemes and chartered monopolies of trade.

The names of this group are not hard to find, since they keep popping up on membership lists of chartered companies and as proprietors of colonies in America. Several appear, too, among the committees and councils of trade and plantations which were appointed during the 1660's and 1670's to administer the business of the expanding empire. First on most lists were James, Duke of York, and Prince Rupert, Charles's brother and cousin, respectively, whose associations with the several councils and chartered companies were almost identical. James was also sole proprietor of the colony of New York after its conquest from the Dutch in 1664. Outside the royal family, most prominent among the courtier-promoters were Anthony Ashley Cooper (later Earl of Shaftesbury), William, Earl of Craven, George Monk, Duke of Albemarle, John, Lord Berkeley (brother of Sir William Berkeley, already governor of Virginia and a proprietor of Carolina), Sir George Carteret, and Sir Peter Colleton. These well-established gentlemen were in positions whereby they might not only help to formulate colonial policy, but they might help formulate it according to their own colonial and trading interests.[1]

Within a generation after the Restoration the number of colonies in America doubled. With the exception of New Hampshire, the new colonies—the Carolinas, New York, New Jersey, and Pennsylvania—were proprietary grants, given by the King to favorites and others to whom Charles was obligated in getting back his throne. With these grants went a good deal of power, and although the courtier-promoters probably shied away from the authority boasted of by the Lords Baltimore over Maryland, each charter, Pennsylvania's excepted, fitted the proprietors with considerable control over both government and soil. During the same period the Crown also chartered several trading monopolies, most conspicuous being the Hudson's Bay Company and the Royal African and Royal Fishery companies. Each conferred specific

1. Each of the above individuals was a proprietor of Carolina; a member of both Royal African and Royal Fishery companies; except for Berkeley a charter member of the Hudson's Bay Company; and except for Albemarle a proprietor of the Bahamas (although his son was). Moreover, all were members of Parliament—Colleton not until 1681; Shaftesbury was a Privy Councillor at two different times; all but Colleton served at one time or another on at least one of the committees or councils of trade and plantations (Shaftesbury, Carteret, and Berkeley were on most of them); Craven, Carteret, and Berkeley were original members of the Lords of Trade appointed in 1675; and Berkeley and Carteret were proprietors of New Jersey. In addition, Edward Hyde, Earl of Clarendon, was a member of both councils for trade and plantations in 1660 and a proprietor of Carolina. For this information I am indebted to Professor John C. Rainbolt of the University of Missouri. Formerly a research assistant at the University of Wisconsin, he made a detailed listing of the imperial interests of more than one hundred individuals of the Restoration period.

rights respectively for trade in furs, slaves, and fish in particular areas; charter members and investors included the same group of people who were closely connected with other major economic enterprises of Restoration England.

Along with settling new colonies in America, and as part of the strong economic interest in overseas planting and trade, was a drive to regulate the products and commerce of new and old colonies to England's exclusive advantage. This was attempted by acts of trade and navigation, the laying down of a regulatory policy which was experimental at the outset but by the mid-1670's was fairly fixed in principle and aim. As the value of colonies increased, or seemed to increase, formulators of policy intensified and centralized it, pursuing political as well as economic ends. As a result a number of settlers became convinced that what they had accepted as a necessary part of being colonists was gradually subverting their rights as Englishmen in America.

Englishmen's heed for colonies overseas became more intense after 1660. It was then that circumstances and opportunities seemed to dictate a drive for economic development and expansion. Among some the interest was new; to others, particularly merchants, it was a legacy from the Commonwealth period when a start was made toward a closer watch over colonies and their trade. Probably no one disagreed with the purposes of the Navigation Acts of 1660 and 1663 which stated ideally that

The Trade of the Plantations is, by several Acts of Parliament, confined to England: whereby no Sugar, Tobacco, Cotton wooll, Indico, Ginger, Fustick, or other Dying Wood of the growth or manufacture of the Plantations may bee transported from thence to any other place than England; nor any European Commodities bee carried thither but what shall be shipped in England.[2]

It did not take long for the drafters of Parliamentary acts and those who agreed with them to realize that to state the ideal was only half the battle. There remained the task of implementing it into some kind of system and enforcing fundamental trade regulations before the "Empire of England" would take the shape most people hoped for.

Responsibility for trade and administration of overseas colonies, even for precise knowledge about them, was shuffled from council to committee and back again as it had been under both Commonwealth and Protectorate. Interested persons proffered "Overtures," suggesting means to gather the strands together toward more uniform control. "Instructions" demanded all manner of facts regarding "intrinsick value and . . . certain condition"; "Inquiries" probed ships and trade,

2. Additional Manuscripts, 15898, ff. 129–30, British Museum.

the colonists' "Complaints, their Wants, their Aboundance." The end
in sight, according to Thomas Povey, a well-known merchant and
adviser in London, was that the whole scheme of things might be
thoroughly understood,

> whereby a Ballance may be erected for the better ordering and disposing
> of Trade, and of the growth of the Plantations, that soe, each Place within
> itself and all of them being as it were made up into one Comonwealth,
> may by his Matie bee heere governd, and regulated accordingly upon com-
> mon and equal principles.[3]

By the late 1660's it was apparent that the cure for the expanding
problems of colonial regulation was more regulation, and the best
way to secure it was through permanent administrative organization
with power to order and dispose. Benjamin Worsley, who for twenty
years had had his eyes on the colonies and their development and no
doubt contributed to the drafting of the Navigation Act of 1660, put
his finger on the trouble in 1668 and wrote elaborately "About the Restoring of our Trade & improving ye Concerne of our Plantations."
Worsley worked closely with Shaftesbury, and it may be that his "Proposition" [4] was written at Shaftesbury's request, for the latter, besides
being a Privy Councillor, had been on all the Committees and Councils
of Trade and Plantations since 1660. Like Shaftesbury, Worsley had an
expansive view of the problems of colonies and empire, and in most of
his suggestions one can find a responsible, if not benevolent, regard for
settlers in America. Worsley's "Proposition" came straight to the point
when it declared that the plantations in America no longer depended
upon England but rather England upon them. Already the nation was
incapable of carrying on without the colonies' trade, he reported. As
expert as any Englishman in colonial matters, Worsley explained that
England's economic position was a good deal different from what it
had been forty years earlier when her woolen goods had sold all over
the continent. But the trade in manufactures had decayed; now it
was the plantations which must fill the gap, and this was fortunate,
since trade with colonies "swell[s]" not just one part of the nation but
would distribute itself far more equally for the benefit of many than
had the earlier exchange with Europe.

A plantation trade not only increased the nation's shipping and trea-
sure, wrote Worsley, but it increased the "Limitts also of oʳ dwelling."
It extended the "trade of one Clymatt after another" to England, and,

3. *Ibid.;* Charles M. Andrews, *British Committees, Commissions, and Councils
of Trade and Plantations, 1622–1675* (Baltimore, 1908), pp. 68–70, 102–3, 107–8,
123.
4. Shaftesbury Papers, P.R.O. 30/24/49/26, Public Record Office; C. M. Andrews, *The Colonial Period of American History* (4 vols., New Haven, Conn.,
1933–38), IV, 58.

what is more, it joined "the Countries themselves and the inheritance of them as well as theire trades" to His Majesty's territories and Dominions. By adding the "inheritance of them," Worsley went on, the nation establishes "a just foundaͨon for makeing of them in every age an affayre of State." With this accomplished, how much more important plantations will become than they were in their infancy! In other words, Worsley argued, England could not do much with plantations and their trade unless they were made an "affayre of State." The trades which remained to England could not be left to chance. A major defect in managing the plantations from the very beginning had been that they never were governed under any care, direction, or "regulation." No real order, method, or "Council" existed, and the lack led to serious inconveniences such as "glutts" and "druggs" without standards, limits, or prescription.

Englishmen too easily accepted the cotton and tobacco which the colonies naturally produced and the sugar, ginger, and indigo shown them by the Spaniards. Greater diversity and variety of colonial products, a better balance of commodities, would enrich England and improve employment. To increase the value of colonies, Worsley would encourage widespread movement of people there "so by how much yᵉ more any numbers of psons are incouraged to remove by so much is the name, honour, strength & magnificence of the nation increased." If the newcomers came not from the British Isles, they might come "yet out of New England as ye nursery of all into ye Rest of our plantaͨons," and one way to attract them would be to increase the variety of products the colonies produced.

Worsley's "Proposition" was a serious state paper whose suggestions looked forward to a concerted effort for improving the advantages of foreign plantations. And although these advantages would generally accrue to England, they were broad enough to include the people who did the work in America. Whether all Englishmen would agree with Worsley's suggested policies is not easily answered, but as he described them, they must have appeared almost beneficent and hardly arguable. The peopling and cultivating of plantations abroad, he warmly encouraged:

And that it is our wealth here that is properly increased ffor as much alsoe as by the multiplying of the English in those parts more familyes are provided for & raised to a better Condiͨon then if they had staid here[.] And that it is the Empire of England likewise that is hereby rendered the more August[,] formidable and Considerable abroad.

Granted Worsley's goal was ideal, his means of accomplishing it were more practical: there was need for authority; there was need for a council; there was need for power in the council to bring about regulation and a strict account of trade which would move England toward the end he had thoughtfully outlined.

At the time Worsley delivered his "Propositon," responsibility for the colonies fluctuated between two committees of the Privy Council, one for Trade and the other for Plantations. Shaftesbury was a prominent member of both; in fact, since the fall of Clarendon in 1667, he had been a dominant figure in managing colonial affairs.[5] It was under Shaftesbury that an elaborate set of inquiries was sent to the colonies in 1670 which elicited several replies, the most notable being that from Governor Sir William Berkeley of Virginia. An old hand as royal governor, Berkeley wrote frankly about his colony and its difficulties. He singled out for censure the Staple Act of 1663, which prevented colonists from trading directly with Europe, forcing them to exchange only through England. The restriction prevented Virginia from diversifying her economy and relieving herself of the burden of tobacco. What also bothered the governor was that Virginians obeyed the acts of trade, even the most destructive, "whilst the New England men break through and . . . trade to any place that their interest lead them." [6]

Berkeley's complaints did not force Shaftesbury and his council members to recommend a change in trade regulations. However, the first Earl had a reputation for flexibility at points where the acts of trade rubbed hard, and it was this characteristic which separated him from those who followed as overseers of plantation affairs. Shaftesbury was as much a believer in trade regulation as the next man, and he believed, too, in the centralization and intensification of policy which was just beginning, but he continued to lend a leniency to enforcement which was a part of his expansive and balanced view of a colonial system.[7]

The Crown put some of Benjamin Worsley's ideas into effect in 1672 when it commissioned a joint council on Trade and Plantations with Shaftesbury as President. Diarist John Evelyn, a holdover from the Council for Plantations, was included, and the new council made Worsley its secretary and John Locke, still a student at Christ-Church, Oxford, its clerk. (The next year Worsley died and Locke replaced him as secretary of the joint council.) 1672 was a gala year for Shaftesbury, for during it he received his earldom and became Lord

5. E. E. Rich, "The First Earl of Shaftesbury's Colonial Policy," *Transactions of the Royal Historical Society*, 5th ser., VII (London, 1957), 47–70.

6. William W. Hening, ed., *The Statutes at Large: Being a Collection of All the Laws of Virginia, from the First Session of the Legislature, in the Year 1619* (13 vols., Richmond, Va., Philadelphia, 1819–23), II, 516.

7. See again Rich, "The First Earl of Shaftesbury's Colonial Policy," pp. 47–70.

Chancellor. Despite involvement in the affairs of empire and settlement of colonies, Carolina and the Bahamas, Shaftesbury remained a politician and a good one, as the next decade would show. But political know-how apparently did not acquaint him with Charles II's secret dealings with France and the Treaty of Dover until 1673, at the very peak of his career. Once aware of Charles's deception, he promptly moved into opposition against the King by supporting the Test Act. Straightaway he was dismissed as Lord Chancellor and from the Privy Council, undermining at the same time his commanding position over colonial policy. Owing to Shaftesbury's demise and to the resignation of the Earl of Arlington, Secretary of State, both strong advocates of the joint council, the King revoked the council's commission the next year. Contributing to the dissolution, according to Thomas Povey, was the council's lack of executive authority, which rendered it sometimes slow and ineffective, a weakness Benjamin Worsley earlier had hoped to overcome in favor of decisiveness. The upshot of the change was that responsibility for the affairs of empire shifted to a special committee of the Privy Council which Charles established in 1675, a committee known from that time as the Lords of Trade. The Earl of Shaftesbury was not a member.[8]

The policies of the Lords of Trade reflected a more narrow view of the value of colonies than had the earlier councils under Shaftesbury's leadership. Even before his joint council gave way to the Lords, there appeared during the early 1670's tendencies toward greater restriction and more practical demands upon overseas dominions. The Navigation Acts did not seem to improve much the total value of goods exported from England to the plantations in the 1660's, but the value of products sent to the mother country from the colonies increased by about £121,000 between 1663 and 1669.[9] Doubtless it was the growth in the amount of goods coming to England from America that encouraged members of the House of Commons to demand higher duties on these importations. The House debated an increase in tobacco customs during November 1670. Although some members argued for an additional sixpence duty, three-pence rise was settled upon,

8. E. S. De Beer, ed., *The Diary of John Evelyn* (London, 1959), pp. 554–55; Rich, "The First Earl of Shaftesbury's Colonial Policy"; George L. Beer, *The Old Colonial System, 1660–1754* (2 vols., New York, 1912), I, 253–55; Memorandum by Thomas Povey in Andrews, *British Committees*, p. 112; W. L. Saunders, ed., *Colonial Records of North Carolina* (10 vols., Raleigh, N.C., 1886–90), I, 222–23; W. Noel Sainsbury *et al.*, eds., *Calendar of State Papers, Colonial Series, America and the West Indies* (42 vols., London, 1860–1953), *1675–1676*, #879; hereafter referred to as *CSPCol.*; Winfred T. Root, "The Lords of Trade and Plantations, 1675–1696," *American Historical Review*, XXIII (1917), 21–41.

9. Sloane Manuscripts, 2902, f. 118b, B.M.

not without strong words against any increase at all. The arguments of the opposition tell us a great deal about the value to the Crown of the tobacco trade and colonies generally in 1670. Sir John Knight revealed that tobacco alone yielded "seven-score thousand pounds per annum" (£140,000) which made up one-third of the whole of English customs. It afforded Bristol 6,000 tons of shipping, half of the ships belonging to that port. Already the duty was so high and the price so low as to force a good many skippers to leave their tobacco at the Customs House for want of money to settle with the King. Knight argued further that levying the new duty would spoil the trade and the King's revenue with it. And as if colonists did not pay the Crown enough in tobacco customs, Knight reported that the King gained five pounds a head "by every man that goes into the plantations." Whether many members of the Commons had contemplated before the cost of empire to the colonists, it was here revealed in striking terms. Had it not been that the bill included an additional duty on sugar, it doubtless would have become law. But the House of Lords turned thumbs down on any increase in sugar taxes, an indication that West Indian planters had strong representation in the upper house, an advantage the tobacco colonies, Virginia and Maryland, did not enjoy.[10] Fifteen years later, with a new King on the throne, Parliament went out of its way to please him and increased the duty on both tobacco and sugar, providing James II with a tidy new revenue at the colonists' expense.

The Lords of Trade took over the ordering and administering of colonies and trade in 1675. They found circumstances more in their favor than had Shaftesbury's council at its inception three years before. Early in the year of Shaftesbury's fall, Parliament passed the third Navigation Act, which laid the groundwork for a regulatory system easier to come to grips with than that faced by the joint council. The Navigation Acts of 1660 and 1663 were full, sweeping phalanxes of legislation, or at least thought to be when they were enacted. They assumed for England a monopoly of the empire's trade by confining it to English and colonial shipping and earmarking several colonial products for delivery at English ports or those of her colonies and no other place. With only a few exceptions all European goods destined for the plantations had first to go to England, where they were re-shipped aboard English vessels bound for America, leaving in England the profit of exchange and other benefits accruing to a mart and

10. Leo F. Stock, ed., *Proceedings and Debates of the British Parliaments Respecting North America, 1452–1727* (5 vols., Washington, 1924–41), I, 362–68, 370 n.

staple. In the dozen or so years following enactment of the trade laws, a number of experts had opportunity to see just how they worked and what their strong and weak points were. By the early 1670's most agreed that the system itself was good if it could be adequately enforced. Benjamin Worsley was one among many who admired the scheme but recommended more regulation to overcome the difficulties already apparent.[11]

As the experts and advisers in England scrutinized the acts to see where they might be improved, colonists in America scrutinized them to see where they could avoid them. Despite the fact that the Act of Enumeration (1660) hit the tobacco colonies hardest of all, since restricting tobacco to the English market drove down the price, Governor Berkeley insisted that Virginians toed the mark as far as the laws were concerned. New Englanders were the culprits, he claimed, and there were others who agreed with him. In Massachusetts John Hull, the godly goldsmith, confided to his diary in 1664 that Boston had entertained "near one hundred sail of ships, this year, of ours and strangers, and all laden hence." True, the Staple Act was only a year old at the time, but it is clear that the Bay Colony had not made an auspicious beginning of its career as a member of the empire.[12] Colonists received goods, then, directly from Europe. The Crown felt cheated of its revenue, but there was little to do about it without royal officers on the spot with authority to prevent it.

The second violation of the Acts of Trade was more complicated. New Englanders had been trading with tobacco planters in Virginia and Maryland for years, carrying their tobacco from the Chesapeake to England and ports of Europe. Once Albemarle County was settled in what later became North Carolina, small New England vessels adeptly pierced the difficult reefs and shoals which guarded Albemarle Sound, waters unnavigable for larger ocean-going ships from England. What tobacco the farmers of Albemarle did not send north to Virginia (usually a small amount owing to a local customs duty), they traded to New Englanders upon whom they became dependent for manufactured goods. New England vessels often loaded Chesapeake and Albemarle tobacco, carried it to Boston or another northern port— supposedly satisfying the Act of 1660 which demanded that all colonial tobacco be shipped to England or another colony—and then took it directly to markets in Europe. There they avoided the English customs duty and in the long run probably helped to keep up the price in

11. Worsley, Proposition, Shaftesbury Papers, P.R.O. 30/24/49/26.
12. Hening, ed., *Statutes*, II, 516; "Diary of John Hull," American Antiquarian Society, *Transactions and Collections*, III (1857), 214.

London. Of course, it took a little imagination on the part of New Englanders to argue that the letter of the law was satisfied, but they were up to the challenge. In England the conclusion was that both letter and spirit were violated; the King lost revenue, and Europeans bought tobacco cheaper than Englishmen, who were deprived also of reexporting it to the Continent at a profit.[13]

To eliminate the advantages of the broken voyage, Parliament responded with the Plantation Duty of 1673. The third Navigation Act placed a customs duty on all enumerated articles (one penny per pound on tobacco; five shillings per hundredweight on sugar) carried from one colony to another when the captain had not left bond in England to return them there. Labeled an act "for securing and improving the plantation-trade to Virginia, and other places," the Plantation Duty, it was frankly admitted, was "to turn the course of trade rather than to raise any considerable revenue to His Majesty." [14] To see that the colonists played the game according to the rules, the Commissioners of Customs—a new board, conveniently created just two years earlier as a division of the Treasury—appointed collectors and surveyors in all the southern colonies, including the Islands. New England's turn came later, but in 1673 the emphasis was on the colonies where enumerated articles originated, for the duty was payable where the commodities were loaded. Plantation governors received orders about swearing in the new officers, and the Commissioners of Customs sent elaborate instructions to the collectors, directing them in infinite detail about customs houses, deputies, bonds, keeping accounts, compensation for themselves and the surveyors, *and* their duty to enforce the other Acts of Trade as well as the new duty.[15]

By late November 1673 the Customs people in London had made

13. *CSPCol.*, *1675–1676*, #721, #787, #900; *ibid.*, *1677–1680*, #747, #1305; *Col. Recs. N.C.*, I, 232, 242–43, 257, 286–87.

14. 25 Car. II, c. 7, *Statutes of the Realm*, V, 792; Stock, ed., *Proceedings*, I, 398–400, 399 n.; William A. Shaw, ed., *Calendar of Treasury Books, 1660–1718* (32 vols., London, 1904–57), IV, *1672–1675*, p. 705. The Plantation Duty was never by itself a moneymaker. From Michaelmas 1676 to Michaelmas 1677 it produced £803 2s. 8d. When William III replaced James II, he received a report informing him that he could count on about £700 per annum from 25 Car. II. Sloane Mss. 2902, f. 117; Harleian Manuscripts, 1898, ff. 1–1b, B.M. For conflicting, or maybe just confusing, figures see Add. Mss. 8133c, f. 237. The Act's significance, of course, although it brought in little revenue, was that when enforced it channeled enumerated goods to England and increased the customs there. See Report of the Commissioners of Customs, C.O. 1/47/103. For other details respecting increase in salaries, lading and bonding rules, etc., under the Act, see Add. Mss. 28089, ff. 30–33; *Cal. Treas. Bks.*, IV, *1672–1675*, 126, 437, 456, 659, 705.

15. Instructions to collectors of customs, n.d., Add. Mss., 28089, ff. 30–33; *Cal. Treas. Bks.*, IV, *1672–1675*, 424, 427, 451–52, 501, 521, 659, 824; Thomas C. Barrow, *Trade and Empire: The British Customs Service in Colonial America, 1660–1775* (Cambridge, Mass., 1967), pp. 12–14.

appointments in all the colonies from Maryland south. In 1674 they added New York and New Jersey to their list.[16] There was some shifting about in the next two or three years, for some appointees refused commissions and some were found incapable of performing the duties. Despite salaries, it may be that the new positions were not attractive to everyone, for collecting customs from shipmasters, upon whom one was often dependent, was probably neither easy nor popular.

There is no doubt that the Plantation Duty was a complicated piece of legislation. Differences of opinion arose about its interpretation on both sides of the Atlantic, and, as one might imagine, decisions were made in England's favor, tightening the law here and there as new questions occurred. A number of New Englanders were sure that once the duties were paid, shipmasters were free to take enumerated goods wherever they pleased. Attorney General Sir William Jones disabused them of this liberty, but there is good reason to believe that for some time afterward they preferred their own interpretation.[17] Three years after the act became effective, colonists learned that even if they paid the duties, shipmasters were obligated to give bonds pledging that they would land enumerated cargoes at another plantation or in England. Confusion about details continued; by 1684 New York traders and shippers were still wondering whether the duty which they paid in Virginia would be refunded if they actually landed the tobacco in England.[18]

London merchants trading to the colonies were among the first to object to the Plantation Act and did so even before it became effective. They pointed out that a good deal of sugar from the British West Indies went first to New England before arriving in England and that this trade was a key to the Islands' economy, since they were dependent upon New England for "boards, timber, pipestaves, horses, and fish," all necessary to carry on their business. Obviously the sugar merchants believed that any interference by means of a new duty would disturb the delicate balance of the sugar trade in which New England played a vital role. Moreover, the London merchants went so far as to point out to several members of Parliament, besides the obvious reasons for objecting to the duty, how impracticable it was

16. *Cal. Treas. Bks.*, IV, *1672–1675*, 498, 521; E. B. O'Callaghan and Berthold Fernow, eds., *Documents Relative to the Colonial History of the State of New-York* (15 vols., Albany, 1853–87), III, 221–22; hereafter referred to as *N.Y. Col. Docs.*

17. C.O. 5/903, pp. 89, 106; *CSPCol.*, *1675–1676*, #798, #814, #900; *ibid.*, *1677–1680*, #1305; R. R. Hinman, ed., *Letters from the English Kings and Queens . . . to the Governors of Connecticut* (Hartford, Conn., 1836), pp. 123–26; L. A. Harper, *The English Navigation Laws* (New York, 1939), p. 164.

18. *N.Y. Col. Docs.*, III, 352; *CSPCol.*, *1681–1685*, #1915.

"to tax those that had no members in their House." [19] If only for argument's sake, some Englishmen regarded the Plantation Duty of 1673 as a tax upon an unrepresented people. The complaint was not widespread in England.

Objections came from other directions. The farmers of the revenue in Ireland complained of their great losses by war and the "Plantation Act," since the new law discriminated against Ireland as earlier regulations had not.[20] In Boston Increase Mather listed it as one of the "designs" against New England, and Governor Berkeley, who lost no love over Bay colonists, pitied the people there owing to King Philip's War, which had killed off so many, ruined trade, and now this "new tax of 1d. per lb., which my officers rigorously exact from them." [21] When the Royal Commission in 1677 inquired about Virginia's grievances which had led to Bacon's Rebellion, two parishes complained bitterly of the new impost, one emphasizing that it sharply cut into the New England trade upon which their people depended for necessities, even food.[22] Robert Beverley, in his well-known history of Virginia, claimed that the Plantation Duty was one of the last straws which helped bring on Bacon's Rebellion. And there is no doubt that a principal cause of Culpeper's Rebellion in Albemarle County of Carolina the next year was the Plantation Act of 1673. Even more than Virginians, Albemarle settlers depended upon New Englanders to bring them manufactured goods and carry off their tobacco. The penny duty interfered with an established trade, that is, when it was collected, and upset a good many people around Albemarle Sound.[23]

The new act was not an isolated piece of legislation. It was both regarded and enforced in relation to the other acts, particularly the Staple Act of 1663, which outlawed the carrying of European goods to America except through England. The three of them, passed within a period of thirteen years, laid a basis for a system which the new Lords of Trade took over and implemented in 1675. Particularly helpful for getting at the business of enforcement was the Plantation Act, which required a scheme of oaths and bonds and authorized a pinpointing of collectors and surveyors of the Customs in several colonies.

19. *Ibid., 1669–1674*, #1059.
20. F. H. Blackburne Daniell, *et al.*, eds., *Calendar of State Papers, Domestic* (96 vols., London, 1865–1924), *1673*, 412; hereafter referred to as *CSPDom.*
21. "Diary of Increase Mather," Massachusetts Historical Society, *Proceedings* (1899, 1900), 2d ser., XIII, 340; *CSPCol., 1675–1676*, #859.
22. *Ibid., 1677–1680*, #118, #138; *Virginia Magazine of History and Biography*, III (1895–96), 38, #8.
23. Robert Beverley, *The History and Present State of Virginia*, ed. by Louis B. Wright (Chapel Hill, N.C., 1947), p. 76; *Col. Recs. N.C.*, I, 255, 257, 291–93, 309–11; Bernard Bailyn, *New England Merchants in the Seventeenth Century* (Cambridge, Mass., 1955), p. 151.

Appointment of customs officers afforded, too, a chance to initiate a system of patronage which would be useful to the Crown, although at the very outset, several appointees were more loyal to their colonial friends than they were to King and empire.

As a committee of the Privy Council, the Lords of Trade had a good deal more authority and prestige than the earlier councils. Once organized in the early spring of 1675, it lost no time getting to work. Several months before the King had announced its establishment to the plantation governors, the Lords commenced to make inquiries in England about colonial trade and on the basis of these inquiries to make decisions and stricter policy. Most of the questions were about New England, where as yet no customs officers resided and where weaknesses in the system were prevalent. Within a year after the first of May 1675 the Lords of Trade did more to tighten and centralize control over the colonies and their trade than ever had been attempted before or would be again until the last Navigation Act of 1696.[24]

The new program took several forms. A Royal Proclamation sent to all colonies in November demanded obedience to all the Acts of Trade and emphasized both the Staple Act of 1663 and the Plantation Duty recently enacted. Moreover, it commanded all governors and civil and military officers to assist the customs people in enforcing the acts and in their other duties. The Crown and the Commissioners of Customs dispatched circular letters to the governors outlining procedures and enjoining obedience. To the two oaths already demanded of governors before commencing their duties, a third was added for the "due execution of the Navigation Act." Hinged to this was the obligation to return copies of bonds taken respecting the Plantation Duty, whereby ship-masters pledged to return enumerated goods to England. And then they demanded a pledge from each governor that he would send home lists of ships which loaded these goods in his colony. Since the passing of the Act, the Lords had learned from the Customs House of "very loose and imperfect return of these bonds," and, for that matter, the lists of ships, some governors having sent home very few and a number none at all. In a third circular letter, dispatched in April 1676, the Lords described themselves as "very strict inquisitors" who would exact from governors "frequent and punctual account."[25]

If the experience of Richard Pidgeon was any precedent, colonists'

24. *CSPCol.*, *1675–1676*, #231, #546, II, #679; W. T. Root, "The Lords of Trade and Plantations," A.H.R., XXIII (1917), 20–41.

25. *CSPCol.*, *1675–1676*, #713, #872, #875, #879, #880; *Cal. Treas. Bks.*, IV, *1672–1675*, 852; *CSPDom.*, *1675–1676*, p. 505; W. L. Grant and James Munro, eds., *Acts of the Privy Council of England, Colonial Series, 1613–1783* (6 vols., London, 1908–12), I, #1078, #1080, #1171; hereafter referred to as *Acts of P.C., Col. Ser.*

ships and cargoes when seized could be tried in Admiralty Courts without juries or the common law, for that was the fate of his *Golden Phoenix* when he landed tobacco in Ireland, contrary to the acts. His was not a common occurrence, but Lord Treasurer Danby determined in March 1676 that "the matter is regularly within the cognisance of that Court and fit to be left there." This was an innovation hardly foreseen by the colonists, for courts of common law with juries ordinarily tried violations of the Acts of Trade in England and would continue to do so.[26] Just one month after Captain Pidgeon ran up against a Court of Admiralty, the Lords of Trade, still smarting under repeated reports of trade violations, resolved that instructions be given to captains of His Majesty's frigates "to seize offenders against the acts." [27] And yet in New England, which seemed to be the source of the trouble, there were as yet no customs collectors, nor were the governors specifically sworn to uphold the acts.

There were two reasons for this. First, New Englanders grew none of the enumerated commodities, and at the outset there seemed to be no need to fix officers there, since the collectors in the Islands and Albemarle, Virginia, and Maryland, where sugar and tobacco grew, would exact the duties before they allowed New England ship captains to clear their ports. Reports to the Lords of Trade increasingly pointed out that this was not the way things worked, for once the duties were paid, too often the goods went to Europe, where the captains took on cargoes which they sold in the colonies, violating the Acts of Trade both coming and going. The second reason grew out of an embarrassing apprehension on the part of the policymakers that New Englanders might resist customs collectors forced upon them. New England had won a noisy reputation for independence in the minds of most Englishmen at the time. Both Shaftesbury's council and the Lords of Trade found New England—and when they said New England, they meant Massachusetts—a sticky problem which, according to those who pushed the new policy, the government had not solved but ought to immediately.

The evidence which reached the ears of the Lords of Trade was overwhelming. New Englanders' trade was open to all parts of Europe. One report claimed that they looked upon themselves as a "free State." An English merchants' petition to the King prayed they be compelled to obey the laws, since the volume of foreign goods taken to the colonies had made New England the "great mart and staple" of the empire. The mercers and silk weavers of London told the Privy

26. *Cal. Treas. Bks.*, V, pt. I, *1676–1679*, 170.
27. *CSPCol., 1675–1676*, #898.

Council that they feared ruin by the New Englanders who easily carried silks and stuffs directly from France and Italy. The list of violations grew larger as time went on; so, too, did the estimate of money the Crown lost in customs while the trade continued.[28]

In January and February 1676 talk centered on the lack of customs officers in New England, and in March Lord Treasurer Danby made preparations for administering oaths to the governors there. In April the Lords of Trade called in the merchants who traded with Massachusetts and queried them about the abuses there. Some were "shy to unfold the mystery," while others affected ignorance, but the majority laid bare the widespread exchange of enumerated articles for European goods which they commonly sold in the colonies 20 percent cheaper than could the fair traders. The frequency and magnitude of the trade forced the Lords to waive any tenderness for the Bay Colony's feelings. They immediately recommended that commissions be sent the governors to swear execution of the acts; that the Commissioners of Customs appoint officers in New England to collect the duties; *and*, "in case of refusal to admit them, the other plantations be forbidden to trade with them." Lastly, the Lords asked for the assistance of the Royal Navy in seizing offenders.[29] Other means were discussed for dealing with the New Englanders, besides settling customs officers among them, one being that the King commission all men-of-war and any merchant ships which would accept commissions to seize any colonial vessels found in the straits trading contrary to the law and bring them to the Admiralty. Apparent, too, was the desire among some to levy a duty in all the other colonies "upon any goods from New England wch may bee had from England." Included in these suggestions was a remark which implied less apprehension about New England's independence than had obtained earlier if the government clamped down upon it. New Englanders could revolt to no other nation because they would "have not plantations to trade withall." [30]

It was probably Edward Randolph, more than any other individual, who brought home to the Lords of Trade the most critical view of New England. Randolph came to Boston in June 1676 ostensibly on proprietary business in New Hampshire but largely to spy out the success or lack of success of the Acts of Trade in Massachusetts. For the next year or so his letters and reports not only confirmed what the Lords of Trade already believed, but once back in London, he sug-

28. Capt. Wyborne's Account, 1673, *ibid.*, #721, #787, #797, #881.
29. *Ibid.*, #898; CSPDom., 1675–1676, 574; *Cal. Treas. Bks.*, V, pt. I, 1676–1679, 170.
30. Add. Mss., 28089, f. 3.

gested that the colony's sins were even greater than they appeared. A long talk with Governor John Leverett had demonstrated to Randolph that the King and Parliament obliged the people of Massachusetts "in nothing but what consists with the interest of that colony." They took no notice of the Acts of Trade and "have engrossed the greatest part of the West India trade whereby his Majesty is damaged in his customs above £100,000 yearly and this kingdom much more." [31]

But the King delayed appointing a customs officer in New England until the middle of 1677, a move which, it was explained, "for some weighty reasons hath been deferred intil now." The delay is puzzling. One might think the cause was King Philip's War, which had tied up New Englanders in a struggle against annihilation, but subsequent events discount such solicitude. Probably the delay stemmed from the ruckus caused by Bacon's Rebellion in Virginia, which upset most Englishmen who had anything to do with plantation affairs since it sharply reduced the customs. It was late spring 1678 before the Treasury and Customs Commissioners finally got around to naming an officer to collect the Plantation Duties throughout New England. At a salary of £100 a year and power to appoint deputies where he pleased, he arrived in Boston the next year, and Edward Randolph was his name.[32]

The historian can be grateful that the new Lords of Trade continued the practice of sending "Inquiries" to the plantation governors. The answers tell us a good deal about the colonies, although there is the suspicion that the governors sometimes reported what they believed the Lords of Trade wanted to hear rather than the facts as they stood. Nevertheless, responses to the "Inquiries" of 1675–1676—sent to New England in 1679—are an excellent source of all kinds of information: economic, political, religious, military, demographic, and, on the whole, descriptive. To the question, "What obstructions do you find to the improvement of the trade and navigation of the plantations within your government?" the Lords received striking answers, one or two of which may have come as surprises. Jamaica avoided a direct answer but suggested encouragement of trade with Ireland. Lord Baltimore came to the point respecting Maryland and remarked that the greatest

31. *Ibid.*, ff. 6–30; Robert N. Toppan and Alfred T. Goodrick, eds., *Edward Randolph; Including His Letters and Official Papers . . . 1676–1703* (7 vols., Boston, 1898–1909) II, 216–21, 265–68; Michael G. Hall, *Edward Randolph and the American Colonies, 1676–1703* (Chapel Hill, N.C., 1960), *passim; CSPCol., 1675–1676,* #1067, pp. 463–68.

32. *Cal. Treas. Bks.*, V, pt. I, *1676–1679*, 688–89; *ibid.*, pt. II, *1676–1679*, 983–84, 1023, 1089; Hall, *Randolph*, pp. 45 ff. Randolph was not first named for the job but was finally settled upon in 1678.

obstruction to trade there was "what the late Acts of Parliament . . . for Navigation have occasioned." He prudently added, however, that he did not expect their repeal "until it be for the Interest of England to remove them." [33] Among other obstructions, wrote Governor Simon Bradstreet of Massachusetts, including the "swamping of markets with English goods," was paying double customs on enumerated articles, once in the colonies where they were grown and again in England when delivered. Bradstreet added that the Lords of Trade might encourage them most of all by confirming their rights and privileges and "making them a free port." Plymouth, like Massachusetts, would be a "free port," too. Rhode Island and Connecticut complained of a lack of men of estates to carry on much trade anywhere, and the latter liked the idea of free ports also.[34]

The "Inquiry" directed to Virginia arrived when Governor Berkeley was up to his ears in Bacon's Rebellion. When the council got around to considering it after things had settled down, Berkeley had already returned to England, where he soon died. But for Berkeley's opinions the Lords of Trade had only to dig up his answers to the "Inquiries" of 1670. To the same question about obstructions to the improvement of the plantation trade in Virginia, Berkeley had blasted:

Mighty and destructive, by that severe act of parliament which excludes us the having any commerce with any nation in Europe but our own, so that we cannot add to our plantation any commodity that grows out of it . . . for it is not lawfull for us to carry a pipe stave, or a barrel of corn to any place in Europe out of the king's dominions. If this were for his Majesty's service or the good of his subjects, we should not repine, whatever our sufferings are for it; but on my soul, it is contrary for both.[35]

In 1679 Virginia had a new governor, Thomas, Lord Culpeper, and the Lords of Trade held him to a speedy answer to the heads of the inquiry. But Culpeper was slow in getting to Virginia, and it was December 1681 before he felt able to report on the state of the colony. Appalled by the oversupply of tobacco and the drastically low price the planters received for it, the new governor could only recommend free exportation of tobacco to Russia, that is, to a new market outside the empire. Virginians, he wrote, "want nothing but a vent." [36] The

33. *CSPCol.*, *1675–1676*, #800; William H. Browne, *et al.*, eds., *Archives of Maryland* (69 vols., Baltimore, 1883–1962), V, 268–69.

34. The Massachusetts and Plymouth answers to inquiries are in *CSPCol.*, *1677–1680*, #1360, #1349. For Rhode Island's, see George Chalmers, *Political Annals of the Present United Colonies* (London, 1780), pp. 282–84; J. H. Trumbull and C. J. Hoadly, eds., *Public Records of the Colony of Connecticut* (15 vols., Hartford, Conn., 1850–90), III, 294–300.

35. *CSPCol.*, *1675–1676*, #884; Hening, ed., *Statutes*, II, 516.

36. *CSPCol.*, *1681–1685*, #319.

Lords of Trade left no record of their reaction to Culpeper's suggestion.

Despite delays in the answers to "Inquiries," the Lords were more successful extracting useful information from the colonies than they were sometimes from departments of their own government whose reports would be helpful in determining policy and regulation. Expert planning demanded precise knowledge of the volume of trade and its breakdown between the plantations and the realm and back again. But it was some time before the Commissioners of Customs could produce the kind of information the Lords really needed. When asked in October 1680 for quarterly accounts of all exports, imports, and shipping, the Commissioners all but threw up their hands. They produced an account just the same, although it was a year in preparation. Along with it came an explanation that a listing of London trade alone for one year consisted of 1,300 leaves of parchment and that of the outports almost as many. What is more, the information was "promiscuously entered," and to break it down as the Lords requested "would take the whole time and labour of 4 or 5 clerks the year round for London only," let alone the outports. The next February the Commissioners reported they hoped that the Lords of Trade would not make a practice of requiring specific accounts of the exports and imports of the plantations, for the last one took the clerks three months to prepare and put them far behind in all their other duties. But it was just this kind of information the Lords of Trade needed if they were to capitalize on the momentum already generated in their first half-dozen years in the saddle.[37]

Political problems in England, such as the Popish Plot and the beginnings of the Exclusion Crisis, blunted somewhat the sharpness of the Lords' activities in the late 1670's. But the thorough start they had made and the precedents they set were striking indications of a change in attitude toward colonial policy over what had preceded. Shaftesbury's dismissal was followed by James, Duke of York's, increased interest and influence in plantation affairs, which no doubt had their effect. With the appointment of the Lords of Trade the earlier ideal of mutual dependence within the several parts of the empire, which Governor Berkeley could describe as for His Majesty's service and "the good of his subjects," gave way to a narrower conception of colonial dependence. With power and prestige, the Lords of Trade worked efficiently and vigorously to intensify policy and centralize regulation and control. The Board became a permanent active vehicle bent on a

37. *Ibid.*, #302; *CSPDom., 1680–1681*, pp. 71, 547, 564, 633; *ibid., 1682*, pp. 33, 87.

greater degree of subordination and dependency than the colonies had heretofore known.[38]

The Commissioners of Customs lent enforcement facilities at home and abroad. The Plantation Duty with its network of collectors and myriad of details laid the groundwork for a bureaucracy which would plague the colonists until 1776. Governors newly sworn and customs collectors in residence, Royal Proclamations, circular letters, fresh oaths, new bonds, lists of ships, and then admiralty courts and naval captains—all were enlisted in the drive to subject the colonists' trade to England's interest and the King's revenue. If colonists were generally unfamiliar with the meaning of empire before 1675, they doubtless were set straight after the establishment of the Lords of Trade.

What is surprising is not so much the change in attitude among those who called the turn, or that the plantation trade should become an "affayre of State," as Benjamin Worsley had suggested. After all, what was an empire for, even in its primitive stages, if not to benefit the mother country? What is surprising is how quickly ideas about empire froze hard, and that contrary opinion was considered rebellious, if not treasonable. A partial explanation, of course, is that the sovereignty of the realm was intricately bound up with control of empire, despite the fact that it was Parliament which had enacted the Navigation Acts. Royal colonies belonged to the King; those in the hands of others, such as proprietors, were placed there by the King and, as time would tell, were revocable despite royal charters. But what struck colonists was how quickly the structure of empire became rigid in the minds of those who administered it. Two examples of this attitude, both expressed in 1677, demonstrate the point. The Royal Commission, which the King sent to restore order in Virginia after Bacon's Rebellion, invited Virginians to list their grievances with the hope of ameliorating them. Lower Norfolk County people complained of the Plantation Duty in plain language and asked to carry their tobacco to any colony without paying the impost. The Commission labeled this "An extravagant Request" and insisted that it was "wholly mutinous, to desire a thing contrary to his Maties Royal pleasure & benefitt and also against an Act of Parliamt." Citterborne Parish in Rappahannock County also complained of the "Penny Impost" because it obstructed their supply of goods from New England. The Commissioners' response was simply "that it ought not to be Complayn'd of" since it was levied "to prevent the defrauding his Maties Customes."

38. See again E. E. Rich, "The First Earl of Shaftesbury's Colonial Policy," p. 70; W. T. Root, "The Lords of Trade and Plantations," pp. 20–41; A. P. Thornton, *West-India Policy Under the Restoration* (London, 1956), pp. 159–60.

The acts of King and Parliament were not grievances to be complained of but hard facts to be accepted as part of a colony's lot, no matter how oppressive.[39]

As secretary to the Lords of Trade, William Blathwayt had his finger on just about all of their business. In the 1670's he made himself almost indispensable to its activities and to the many colonial officers who found it necessary to work through him. His countless letters were read by governors, secretaries, councils, and others who were on the receiving end of decisions by the Lords of Trade, the King, and the Privy Council. In June 1677 he wrote to the governor of the Barbados that the "methods of Trade either established by the Laws of this kingdom or supported by the usefullness of them in the generall appear so sacred that an alteration . . . even upon the best suppositions & grounds, is become almost impractical and the attempt from whensoever it proceeds, very ungratefull." [40] It was as simple as that. The colonists might have grievances, but they could not be against the Acts of Trade, for these were already "sacred" and unalterable and "not to bee Complayn'd of." Trade policy by 1677 was not negotiable.

39. C.O. 5/1371/pt. II, 166b; *ibid.*, 153; *Va. Mag. of Hist. and Biog.*, III (1895–96), 38, #8.
40. Blathwayt Papers of Colonial Williamsburg, v. XXIX; hereafter referred to as BPCol. Wmsbg.

2 "An Affayre of State":
Government, Politics, and Religion

The vigor of the new Lords of Trade made itself felt also in England's political and governmental relations with the plantations in America. True, the two aspects of colonial policy were not separate, although no doubt most Englishmen would have agreed that the real business of empire was a profitable regulation of its trade. It occurred to some and in particular to the Lords of Trade that the chief purpose of policy might be accomplished more easily if the King and Council had a firmer grasp on the governments of colonies. Experience after the Plantation Duty, if it taught anything, demonstrated how necessary it was that colonial governments, despite their type and character, be made to further the cause of empire, not impede it.

Intensification of economic policy, then, easily spilled over into stricter demands upon colonial governments. Sporadic "Inquiries" gave way to demands for quarterly reports, or "journals of occurrences," for which governors were scolded when they were negligent or remiss. London was scoured for colonial laws and charters, and governors received urgent requests to submit all acts, past and present, to the Lords of Trade that they might better acquaint themselves with the "true constitution of each governmt." Delays were not tolerated; the Lords threatened to remove Sir Jonathan Atkins of the Barbados from his office if he persisted in his refusals and evasions. Further, they demanded frequent correspondence between governors and the King's ministers, commenting that a lack of it in the past had led to mischief, abuse, even rebellion, and "other unhappy effects." [1]

The most glaring example of use of the prerogative was the attempt in 1678 to apply Poynings's Law to the Crown colonies in America. Collecting information about plantations proved to the Lords of Trade and the Crown that colonies were expensive. The King's annual charge for Jamaica was £4,500, to say nothing of the thousands of pounds paid out for royal stores. This was hard for Charles to take, since difficulties at home dictated serious financial retrenchment, and at the same time Jamaica had the reputation of being very prosperous. In addition the assembly there was not always amenable to the King's wishes, and in 1677 word got around Whitehall that it "flew high and [was] in a fair way of treading, in time, the footsteps of New England." [2]

Parliament had enacted Poynings's Law in 1494 as a regulatory measure over the Irish Parliament, and the same scheme was applied to Jamaica in 1678. According to the new governor's instructions, the Jamaica assembly would meet only when the King permitted and then only to enact laws already drafted by the King from suggestions sent to him by the governor and council. In other words, the Jamaica assembly was left to vote only such laws as the King dictated and no more, certainly a comedown from its usual practice of originating laws and levying taxes like other colonies. For some time Jamaicans had looked "upon it as their Magna Carta" not to "have anything imposed upon them but by their own consents," [3] and so the assembly adamantly resisted. At one point the Crown threatened to scrap their legislature altogether if they did not succumb to the code of laws sent them. But the King backed down after his attorney general and solicitor general and several judges found it difficult to agree just what were the rights of colonists and under what conditions the laws of England

1. *CSPCol., 1677–1680*, #1183, #1221; Nicholas Spencer to Lords of Trade, May 13, 1682, BPCol. Wmsbg., v. XVI; *ibid.*, v. XXIV; Blathwayt to Jonathan Atkins, June 15, 1677, *ibid.*, v. XXIX; Memorandum to Atkins, Oct. 16, 1679, *ibid.*; C.O. 324/4, p. 46; C.O. 324/4, pp. 72–73; *CSPDom., 1675–1676*, p. 505.

2. Historical Manuscript Commission 79: *Lindsey*, pp. 109–10; H.M.C., *Ormonde* N.S., IV, 386; C.O. 324/4, pp. 41–45; Blathwayt to Culpeper, Sept. 2, 1680, BPCol. Wmsbg., v. XVII.

3. Quoted in A. P. Thornton, *West-India Policy Under the Restoration*, p. 151.

were in force in America if at all. Conclusions in England were not clear-cut about the matter. They were very clear in Jamaica, however, where the assembly stood its ground: the "new model" was unconstitutional and its people "would not be governed as the Irish." Jamaicans had the bold idea that they lost no rights or privileges when they settled in the Crown's dominions. What the King wanted most of all was the guarantee of a permanent revenue in Jamaica which would relieve the exchequer of supporting the government. A compromise settlement included a bill which prolonged the revenue for twenty-one years, and Poynings's Law was dropped. When it was applied the next year in Virginia, just after Bacon's Rebellion, the outcome was in several ways different.[4]

Governor Sir Jonathan Atkins feared Poynings's Law might be tried next in the Barbados. An exchange between him and Secretary Blathwayt in London went a long way toward explaining the significance of the Jamaica experiment. Atkins told Blathwayt plainly that the new scheme would ruin the plantations, for no government could remain steady when "subject to such mutacons." What he meant was that whittling away at legislative powers, changing governments from one form to another, could only undermine them and render them helpless. Blathwayt's answer was what one might expect from a secretary of the Lords of Trade. Far from designing the ruin of the plantations, the Lords' aim through the new scheme was "to make all Governments Steady and subject to the least mutacons possible."[5] A wobbly foundation, on the one hand, was what Atkins feared and believed would spell decline. Blathwayt agreed, but, on the other hand, believed a tight-fisted control of colonial governments was the only means to ensure a basis which would spell success. If the issues were not drawn, they were better defined. Steadiness of government was admired on both sides; approaches to it, however, were very different.

4. The correspondence, petitions, instructions, etc., describing the attempt to introduce Poynings's Law into Jamaica are voluminous. See Leonard W. Labaree, ed., *Royal Instructions to the British Colonial Governors, 1670–1776* (2 vols., New York and London, 1935), I, 125; Blathwayt letters to the Earl of Carlisle and others between 1678 and 1680 in BPCol. Wmsbg., vols. X, XXII, XXVII, and XXX. Many official documents are in Bryan Edwards, *The History of the British West Indies* (4 vols., Philadelphia, 1806), I, Appendixes No. IX, 295, No. X, 296–97, No. XI, 298–99, No. XII, 299–304, No. XVI, 306, No. XIX, 310–18, No. XXIV, 323–24, 331, No. XXVI, 325, No. XXVII, 325–26, No. XXVIII, 326, No. XXXI, No. XXXIII, 330–31, No. XXXV, 331–32, No. XXXVI, 332–33, No. XXXVII, 333–34, No. XXXIX, 334–35. See also Leonard W. Labaree, *Royal Government in America* (New Haven, Conn., 1930, reprinted, New York, 1958), 219–22. For response to Poynings's Law in Virginia, see ch. 4 below.

5. See letters of Oct. 17, 1679, and Jan. 17, 1680, BPCol. Wmsbg., v. XXIV.

Patronage

Already the Plantation Duty had fixed a network in all the colonies of collectors, surveyors, and their deputies whose appointments depended upon the Crown. Edward Randolph was, without doubt, the most notorious of these officeholders, and he soon had his work cut out for him in Massachusetts at a time when the Bay Colony defiantly went its own way without much regard for King or Parliament or Randolph. In 1674 the King appointed William Dyer collector of customs at New York,[6] a colony which his brother, Duke James, ruled over as proprietor. Dyer and Randolph were a lot alike, and the merchants of New York grew no more fond of one than did their counterparts of the other at Boston.

During the very same period another method was practiced for enhancing the Crown's authority in the colonies. The King frequently shifted offices from appointment by the governors to himself, thereby building up a system of patronage made up of secretaries, marshals, clerks, and registrars who were dependent upon the King and not the governors. As early as 1672 Sir Thomas Modyford of Jamaica complained about the practice which, he said, undermined authority and prevented his governing well.[7] By 1676 the custom had spread to the Naval Office in the Barbados, which Sir Jonathan Atkins found intolerable since he alone was responsible for obedience to the Acts of Trade, and he could not fulfill his duty if strangers, not dependent upon him, held the office. Secretary Coventry's answer to Atkins made it clear that the King and his Council were "of another Opinion," that the King wanted to become acquainted with those who filled offices in his colonies, and by appointing them directly he could better let them know that "they are not to govern themselves, but be governed by him."[8]

The Lords of Trade acted upon the governors' complaints and ordered an investigation, hoping to set up some rule to determine which offices the Crown should dispose of and which should be left to the governors. Nothing came of it, for doubtless the King would have his way.[9] In 1680 Governor Atkins was still complaining. Recently a stranger had approached him with a patent to be a "deputy's deputy" to two people he had never heard of before. He found it "very pre-

6. *N.Y. Col. Docs.*, III, 221–22.

7. *CSPCol., 1685–1688* (Addenda, 1653–1687), #2049, pp. 637–38.

8. *Ibid., 1677–1680*, #482, #1182; Coventry to Atkins, 1677, quoted in Beer, *Old Colonial System*, I, 271 n.

9. C.O. 324/4, pp. 71–72; *CSPCol., 1677–1680*, #1182, #1203, #1220.

judicial" to any government to have offices of trust in the hands of a pack of strangers. "Where there is no dependence," he concluded, "obedience seldom follows." The practice continued, and so did the objections. Sir Thomas Lynch and his council in Jamaica planned a court writ against one claimant who appeared out of nowhere with a patent "for fourteen of fifteen offices." [10] Lord Howard of Effingham wrote home that a governor in Virginia cut a small figure at best, and that it was "absolutely necessary" for some offices to depend upon his favor. Governor Kendall of the Barbados believed the King's muscling in on the patronage there brought his government into contempt. No sooner was an office vacant "than it is begged for by some one or other in England." Often, too, the patentees remained at home and sent deputies who shirked their jobs and waited for profits.[11]

No doubt the King wanted to keep an eye on the goings on in America, and it was easy to fall back upon methods which were the custom in England. The Lords of Trade had frequently reported that the Navigation Acts were not well obeyed in America, and doubtless the appointment of more King's men looked like a means to bring the colonists into line. But reducing the number of offices at the governors' disposal seriously threatened their authority and prestige at the very time they were expected to augment a more vigorous colonial policy. The King was hardly the winner, for the men on whom the burden of control rested found it more and more difficult to satisfy his demands. At this point it looked as if the new policy was working at cross-purposes.

Not so was the appointment of William Blathwayt, already secretary of the Lords of Trade, as surveyor and auditor general of His Majesty's Revenue in America. It was the Treasury people who put him on to it because they were aware of a general neglect in accounting for the revenue in the colonies. Although his auditing did not include proceeds from the Plantation Duty, it included every other channel of revenue due to the Crown. The Treasury warned all the governors about the new appointment, demanding their cooperation, and Blathwayt lost no time appointing deputies, another source of patronage. The royal colonies contributed to his salary of £500 a year, which, of course, came out of the revenue, as did the percentages pocketed by his assistants, but the jurisdiction of Blathwayt's auditorship included all the colonies, even Massachusetts, where Edward Randolph was his deputy. No more conscientious bureaucrat implemented colonial policy

10. *Ibid.*, #1362; *ibid., 1681–1685*, #1759.
11. Effingham to Blathwayt, Apr. 29, 1686, BPCol. Wmsbg., v. XIV; *CSPCol., 1689–1692*, #496.

than Blathwayt. As his duties increased, so did his several salaries, not the least of which was from his auditorship.[12] Professionals like Randolph, Blathwayt, and Dyer, by their constant attention to duty and detail, convinced American colonists that if the empire did not yet have limits, at least it had meaning for those who administered it.

Religious Policy

When Governor William Berkeley answered the inquiry from the Council for Plantations in 1670 about instruction in religion, he was sarcastically uncomplimentary to the clergy then in Virginia. Yes, the ministers were a well-paid lot, he wrote, but they would be better paid "if they would pray oftener and preach less." Like all other commodities from England, he complained, the colonies got the worst, although during Cromwell's "tiranny," many worthy men were driven to Virginia.[13] Before the Lords of Trade took hold of colonial affairs in 1675, little was done about religious improvement in America. There was some stir in 1673 when Charles II renewed the scheme to establish a bishopric in the plantations and named his man, the Reverend Alexander Moray, M.A., who was then rector of Ware parish in Virginia. Moray, it seems, was a former royal companion and had impressed the King with his pious work and good service; however, his appointment was delayed, and for the meantime the King ordered his Lord Lieutenant to confer upon Moray any available livings or preferments in Virginia until a bishopric became vacant.[14] The plan never materialized, but rumors of it continued for some time to come.

The same year the King appointed the Lords of Trade, Dr. Henry Compton became Bishop of London, elevated from the See at Oxford. From that time the new Bishop—through his office as a member of the Lords of Trade—took the colonies under his wing and promptly instituted an inquiry about whose religious jurisdiction they fell under. Partly through default of claimants and partly owing to an intense interest in improving the religious climate in America, Compton took upon himself, with the help of the Lords, a campaign to promote the Anglican Church in the plantations.[15]

12. See three letters from Blathwayt written July 4 and 6, 1680, BPCol. Wmsbg., vols. XXII, XXVII, XXVIII. Beer, Old Colonial System, I, 220–23; Thornton, West-India Policy Under the Restoration, p. 204; Root, "The Lords of Trade and Plantations," A.H.R., XXIII (1917), 21–41.

13. Hening, ed., Statutes, II, 517.

14. CSPDom., 1673–1675, p. 2.

15. "Report of the Right Reverend Dr. Sherlock on the Church in the Colonies, Feb. 19, 1759," N.Y. Col. Docs., VII, 360–63; Gilbert Burnet, Bishop Burnet's History of His own Time (London, 1857), pp. 261–62 and n. Arthur L. Cross,

Letters and complaints about "shameful neglect" of Anglican churches in America spurred the Bishop in his program. But doubtless the bitter report to the Archbishop of Canterbury from the Reverend John Yeo of Maryland precipitated action. Yeo deplored the state of religion owing to a lack of an established ministry. For 20,000 souls in Maryland there were but three clergymen who could pass muster in the Church of England. Several others who "run before they are sent" pretended to be ministers but lacked proper ordination. They succeeded only in sowing divisions among the people and were altogether useless in confuting Catholics and Quakers. Maryland needed an educated Anglican clergy to prevent the colonists from falling away to "Popery, Quakerism or Phanaticism." Yeo found Maryland a "Sodom of uncleaness & a Pest house of iniquity." [16] The Archbishop had heard of both Sodom and iniquity but not John Yeo. He was impressed, however, with the Maryland minister's zeal and the seriousness of his charges and laid the matter before Bishop Compton, already acknowledged as responsible for the Church in America.

From a number of sources the Bishop of London listed the abuses against religion in the colonies and the next year presented a "Memorial" to the Lords of Trade describing them. Virginia and Maryland bore the brunt of the criticism, but the Barbados and other places took a share. Governors failed to fill parish vacancies, and the King's right of patronage was not asserted in a number of places. When a parish fell vacant, the profits from it, instead of accruing to the next incumbent or being used for ecclesiastical purposes as in England, were spent by the colonists on themselves, and therefore they were reluctant to accept new clergymen when available. Instead of calling ministers for life, parishioners often hired them by the year and even by the sermon, denying them the security they ought to enjoy; and when they were paid in commodities, they got the worst of the tobacco crop and at inflated prices.[17] In Maryland there was no settled maintenance at all except among the Catholics, and their numbers were not above a hundred in the whole colony (a doubtful conjecture by the Bishop).

The Anglican Episcopate and the American Colonies (New York, 1902), pp. 24–25. For an excellent account of Anglican policy at this time, see Philip S. Haffenden, "The Anglican Church in Restoration Colonial Policy," in James Morton Smith, ed., *Seventeenth-Century America: Essays in Colonial History* (Chapel Hill, N.C., 1959), pp. 166–91. For Bishop Compton's relationship with the colonies, see Edward F. Carpenter, *The Protestant Bishop, Being the Life of Henry Compton, 1632–1713, Bishop of London* (London, 1956), ch. XIV.

16. *Arch. of Md.*, V, 130–32.

17. For Governor Effingham's experience with Bruton Parish vestry, Virginia, in 1680, see Bishop Meade, *Old Churches, Ministers and Families in Virginia* (2 vols., Philadelphia, 1897), I, 148–49.

Unlike England, vestries in America were powerful bodies which took over sole management of church affairs, exercising a good deal of authority over the ministers themselves. So great was their power that the Bishop of London felt obligated to move at a meeting of the Lords of Trade, and the King later ordered, that each minister be made a member of the vestry in his parish and a party to all business except determining salaries. In Virginia colonists broke their own laws by permitting unordained ministers to solemnize marriages. They were careless about imposing punishment for fornication which ought to make the parties' children illegitimate and therefore incapable of inheriting estates. Despite their assembly's law, they maintained no public burying ground but interred their dead profanely "in their gardens, orchards, & other places." Only in Virginia, the Bishop found, did the colonists make provision for overseas passage and other accommodations when the English Church sent ministers to them. The most frequent abuse was the presence and practice of ministers not in orders from a bishop in England.[18]

Actually the Bishop of London had no legal authority over ecclesiastical matters in the plantations, but the aggressive Bishop Compton was not long in acquiring it. Commencing in 1679 the royal governors received instructions enjoining them to give preference to no ministers but those who bore certificates from the Bishop. Special effort was to be taken about use of the Book of Common Prayer, celebration of the Lord's Supper, and the care of churches and maintenance of ministers. Increasingly the Lords of Trade accepted Compton's advice and persuaded the King to act upon it through instructions and commands. By 1685 the Bishop's ecclesiastical jurisdiction over the plantations was official, leaving to the governors only the disposal of benefices, granting marriage licenses, and probating of wills; all else, where the King's Church had established itself, was in the Bishop's hands, including the licensing of schoolmasters.[19]

Had the Bishop's power and the Lords of Trade's interest in religion been confined to the royal colonies, the government's religious policy would have affected only Virginia and the Islands. But Bishop Compton took it upon himself to care for Anglicans anywhere in the plantations. From Edward Randolph's reports it appeared that Anglican souls were most abused in Massachusetts. Not only did the Lords of Trade ask the Bishop to send a priest to Boston and appoint more when necessary, "as the Country shall be willing to maintain"—an optimistic

18. C.O. 324/4, pp. 48–49, 75; Col. Recs. N.C., I, 233–34.

19. Labaree, ed., Royal Instructions, II, 482–83; "Report of the Right Reverend Dr. Sherlock," N.Y. Col. Docs., VII, 360–63; Cross, Anglican Episcopate, p. 31 n.

assumption—but they also recommended that the King bring an end to discrimination against Anglicans in the Bay Colony and declare them to be as free there as anywhere, that is, to vote and hold office. At the same time Sir Edmund Andros, the Duke of York's governor of New York, learned that an Anglican priest was on his way there, and that any laws favoring independents must not apply to those who attended his church.[20]

When the Lords of Trade discussed in 1681 a draft of William Penn's liberal charter for Pennsylvania, the Bishop of London submitted a paper recommending that Penn be obliged by the patent to accept an Anglican minister when any number of planters asked for one. Moreover, the Lords of Trade directed the Bishop to draft a law for settling the Protestant religion in Pennsylvania. Penn beat down the move for an establishment, but the guarantee of a priest when twenty Anglicans should ask for him was included in the charter. Not until 1695 did the Anglicans form a congregation; shortly it became a thorn in the side of the Quaker colony, since its members repeatedly complained of Quaker control and sent home criticisms which found a friendly ear in the Bishop of London.[21] The government's solicitude for Protestant subjects in Maryland continued. Baltimore admitted very few of them to his council, and the Lords of Trade directed him to redress the imbalance in 1681. They required also that when the government sent arms to Maryland for defense, Protestants should have access to them, too, an expression of trust Baltimore's government was reluctant to honor.[22]

Virginia held a special place in the heart of the "Protestant Bishop," as he was called. When the King commissioned Lord Howard of Effingham new governor there in 1683, the Bishop ordered Bibles, Books of Common Prayer, Canon Law, and Tables of Marriages for Virginia—thirty-nine copies of each, even "39 books of the Thirty-nine Articles." He was better at ordering than delivering, however, for a year later "Mr. Povey" was still busy about the Bibles, and in June 1685 Virginia was still without them.[23] Compton took a more aggressive step toward control of the Church in America in 1689 when he appointed James Blair Bishop's Commissary in Virginia. Blair, a Scot, did not win all Virginians to his side, or all royal officials, for that mat-

20. Toppan, ed., *Randolph*, III, 36–38; Blathwayt to Andros, Feb. 10, 1679, BPCol. Wmsbg., v. III.
21. *CSPCol., 1681–1685*, #8, #30; Edwin B. Bronner, *William Penn's "Holy Experiment": The Founding of Pennsylvania, 1681–1701* (New York and London, 1962), p. 200.
22. *CSPCol., 1681–1685*, #256.
23. *Ibid.*, #1329; BPCol. Wmsbg., v. XIV.

ter, but during his twenty or more years as the Bishop's man in Virginia, he was responsible for bringing order and organization to the Church there, besides championing the establishment of the College of William and Mary.[24]

Bishop Compton was pleased with Charles II's regard for the souls of his subjects in the colonies, including the souls of Negro slaves. According to John Evelyn, the King resolved at a meeting of the Privy Council that plantation Negroes should be christened, a resolution he persisted in "which piety the *Bishop,* deservedly blessed him for." It made no matter that Charles at the same time argued "exceedingly" against "that impiety, of their Masters prohibiting [baptism], out of a mistaken opinion, that they were then *ipso facto* free." [25]

Both Charles and the Bishop of London looked kindly upon the migration of foreign Protestants to the American colonies and encouraged contributions for their benefit. Even before the revocation of the Edict of Nantes in 1685, one group of French Huguenots already in London laid plans for a voyage to the plantations and petitioned the King for use of ships of the Royal Navy to transport them to Carolina, where they might settle and produce wine, oil, and silk, all welcome in England.[26] Londoners opened their pocketbooks for the relief of the Huguenots who tarried there and in Canterbury, Dover, and other cities, pending the venture to America. By 1684 individuals, churches, and churchwardens had contributed almost £13,000, and a good deal of it came from the Bishop of London. Disbursements were made to the needy until arrangements could be made for their migration to the colonies. Had all the refugees planned to remain in England, the charity probably would have been less generous, but French Protestants once planted in the colonies could only contribute to the success of the empire, since they brought with them needed skills and might even become Anglicans. The largest group journeyed to Carolina over the next few years, but there was a sprinkling of Huguenots in most of the colonies, even Massachusetts. Besides the City of London, the churches elsewhere and a number of bishops were active on behalf of the refugees. Contributions continued to mount, reaching more than £63,000 by 1695. French Protestants often did make good Anglicans in America, and their influence was felt throughout the colonies.[27]

24. Carpenter, *The Protestant Bishop,* pp. 263–68.
25. E. S. De Beer, ed., *The Diary of John Evelyn,* p. 824.
26. Adm 1/5139, pp. 162–63, Public Record Office.
27. Ex-Guildhall Library Manuscripts, 279, 280, pp. 1–41, 75–79, among Miscellaneous Papers, Corporation of London, Records Office, Guildhall, London, E.C. 2; R. Mason to Blathwayt, Sept. 28, 1687, BPCol., Wmsbg., v. XII; Robert M. King-

Colonial trade, government and politics, and religion—each was subject, although in varying degrees, to some kind of control from England before the middle 1670's. From that time, and particularly from the establishment of the Lords of Trade, this control intensified, forcing colonial policy to take a definite turn toward centralization. Certainly at the outset the royal colonies, Virginia and the Islands, felt the changes more abruptly than the charter and proprietaries, for the King had only to act directly upon his governors and other appointees. But the reaching out of power and authority spread to all of England's colonial possessions; it knew no colonial boundaries. The acts of trade and navigation were the center of the system; they were the frame upon which control and regulation hung. During the 1670's the frame became more rigid as colonies increased in importance, as England's economic needs multiplied and became more apparent. The rightness and necessity of economic domination of the colonies affected also Englishmen's attitudes toward people and governments in America. Colored by the Restoration's emphasis on the Crown's prerogative, these attitudes supported inherent assumptions that colonies existed solely for the benefit of the mother country, and colonists and their governments, by their very definition, were subject to authority from London. Before 1660 few people on either side of the Atlantic had felt the need to fathom the limits of this authority. With the Restoration, with the increase in colonies and planters and their exports, as competition and relations with France and Holland became more aggravated, as Englishmen sought more economic security, those who called the turn in London found it expedient to find few limits to authority in America. With the help of the Lords of Trade, men like Blathwayt, Randolph, and William Dyer, and other officers in the King's employ, including royal governors, English authority was expanded in the colonies in ways it had not been before. Since earlier plantation affairs afforded few precedents, policymakers extended as they wished rules and regulations which benefited the interests of England. The extension of this authority affected at times the livelihood, the government, even the religion of American colonists. Confronted with changing demands from London, or what colonists called "mutacons," it was they who first defined the limits of authority, limits they based on their own assumptions, their needs, their increasing experience, which helped them to determine the meaning of empire on their own terms.

---

don, "Pourquoi les Réfugiés huguenots aux colonies américaines, sont-ils devenus épiscopaliens?" *Bulletin de la Société de l'Histoire du Protestantisme Français* (d'octobre–novembre–décembre 1969), pp. 487–509.

3 The Virginia Charter and Bacon's Rebellion

Virginia affords a splendid example of a colony which attempted in the latter half of the seventeenth century to define the limits of its relationship to the Crown and the mother country. It did so first in a drive to secure a charter in 1675. Like New York, as we shall see, Virginia's response to demands from abroad was in constitutional terms, and the content was dictated by its peculiar conditions. What makes Virginia's experience particularly striking is that in these same conditions, which provoked the struggle for the charter, lay also the causes of Bacon's Rebellion.

Just Rights and Privileges

Virginians confronted a number of problems after Charles II was restored to the throne in 1660. Chief among these was their tobacco economy; it suffered under surpluses which drastically pushed down the price the planter received for his crop. Parliament in 1660 aggravated the problem by forcing all colonial tobacco to England, where it became an even greater drug on the market. Governor William Berkeley, who found the Navigation Acts "Mighty and destructive" to Virginia's economy, preached diversification which he hoped would afford the colonists a better life and through broader economic efforts still serve the King.[1] But diversification was not easy, particularly because Virginia's climate and geography presented excellent conditions for tobacco. Moreover, once Virginians commenced production when the price was high, it was next to impossible, or at least seemed so, to give up and start over with other crops when money, land, time, and labor were already heavily invested. On top of this, revenue to the exchequer depended not on the price but on the amount of tobacco shipped to England, and as the colonial policy intensified in the middle 1670's under the Lords of Trade's guidance, the Crown became more and more dependent upon the annual tobacco customs. Berkeley was well aware of this and found it a difficult obstacle to overcome in directing diversification. Earlier the Crown had encouraged his efforts, but as customs mounted, royal support became increasingly disingenuous. By 1676 tobacco customs amounted to probably £100,000 a year, although several other figures, some higher, were mentioned. Revenue from the tobacco colonies alone was estimated at a third of all English customs in 1670.[2]

In arguing against restrictions, Governor Berkeley tried hard to impress the King with the colony's real value to the realm. In doing so he doubtless impressed yeoman farmers even more, for he reported about 1675 that Virginia and the King's revenue from it had increased to the point that "there is not one laborer here that does not pay the king five pounds sterling yearly."[3] Eight years earlier a member of

1. William W. Hening, ed., *The Statutes at Large . . . of Virginia* (13 vols., Philadelphia and New York, 1823), II, 515–16; Berkeley to Earl of Clarendon, July 20, 1666, Virginia 350th Anniversary Celebration Corp., Colonial Records Project, *Survey Report*, No. X, 53; *Newsletter*, Oct. 27, 1668, H.M.C. 25: 12th Report, App., pt. VII, *The Manuscripts of S. H. LeFleming* (London, 1890), 60.

2. Giles Bland to Sir Joseph Williamson, Apr. 28, 1676, and Bland's "State of Virginia, 1676," *Virginia Magazine of History and Biography*, 20 (1912), 352–53, 356–57; *CSPCol., 1675–1676,* #906; John D. Burk, *History of Virginia . . .* (4 vols., Petersburg, Va., 1804–16), II, Appendix, l–li; Stock, ed., *Proceedings and Debates,* I, 362 ff., for debate on tobacco customs. In 1689 the Lords of Trade and Commissioners of Customs reported that Virginia and Maryland tobacco paid £200,000 in customs. C.O. 324/5/120; John C. Rainbolt, "The Virginia Vision: A Political History of the Efforts to Diversify the Economy of the Old Dominion, 1650–1706" (unpubl. Ph.D. thesis, Univ. of Wisconsin, 1966), particularly ch. IV.

3. H.M.C. 22: 11th Report, App., VII, *Manuscripts of the Duke of Leeds* (London, 1888), p. 10; Stock, ed., *Proceedings and Debates,* I, 362 ff. In 1682 merchants in England argued that each white man's work in producing tobacco for a year was worth £7 to the King. *CSPCol., 1681–1685,* #768.

Berkeley's council had estimated that 1,200 pounds of tobacco was average for one man to produce in a year. If a planter received a halfpenny a pound for it (as he did in 1667), his total income for the year was fifty shillings, or two and a half pounds, out of which came taxes and other necessities. This was precious little for a poor man who had a family to keep, and it probably seemed even less when he learned that what he produced in Virginia paid the King five pounds each year in England. Profits were so small in the 1660's that Secretary Ludwell could "attribute it to nothing but the great mercy of God . . . that keeps (the poor people) from mutiny and confusion." [4] It is revealing to learn what the cost of empire was to those in Virginia who did the work.

Politically, Berkeley found ways to get along with Virginians, at least with the assembly, the people who made up the government, if not the people as a whole. Virginia boasted not a government of the people anyway, nor did it mean to. It was the "better sort" whom the burgesses increasingly represented and the very best who found a voice in the council. This was particularly true after 1670 when the assembly restricted suffrage to freeholders, that is, property owners, eliminating the propertyless freemen who had elected burgesses for some time. [5]

Berkeley and the assembly worked well together and saw eye to eye on a number of things. But placid relations between the governor and his assembly did not hide the growing uneasiness of Virginians as a whole during the 1670's, and doubtless the growing elite quality of the government was one cause. There were other causes, too, and some were vital to the well-being of large numbers of colonists. First, of course, was the price of tobacco, which had tumbled some time before and had remained generally depressed, despite attempts at diversification and even cessation of planting. The effect of low prices was universal throughout the colony and bore upon all levels of society, for all of Virginia was tied to a single crop.

The normal trade in tobacco at best was unrewarding, but war with the Dutch interrupted even this. In 1673 a squadron of bold Dutchmen sailed up the James River and without opposition burned six vessels laden with Virginia tobacco and made prizes of five more. All told, the loss in this one-sided engagement was 5,600 hogsheads, a sizable portion of the total production. [6]

4. Thomas Ludwell to Lord John Berkeley, 1667, quoted in Thomas J. Wertenbaker, *The Planters of Colonial Virginia* (Princeton, N.J., 1922), p. 90.

5. Hening, ed., *Statutes*, II, 280; L. G. Tyler, writing in 1900, believed that the "suffrage remained practically unchanged" despite the new law. *William and Mary Quarterly*, 1st ser., VIII (1899–1900), 81.

6. H.M.C. 25: 12th Rep., App., VII, 104.

Acts of God always had plagued Virginia, but they seemed to accumulate in the middle 1670's. The winter of 1674–1675 was particularly severe, destroying a good many cattle. As a result, food was dear until new crops provided more. There was "much distress for victuals," since the bad winter was followed by an extreme drought which played havoc with the Indian corn and spoiled provisions for hogs. In one plantation region a multitude of squirrels swept down out of the woods and devoured what corn was left and most of the potatoes. Reports circulated in England that Virginia's "condition is much worse than it has been for many years." [7]

Already suffering from a lack of food, Virginians were convinced that the Plantation Act of 1673, which placed a duty on intercolonial trade in tobacco, worsened conditions, limiting their outlets through New England. Yankee shipmasters were wary of the penny impost, and when they did not come to load tobacco, they did not bring corn and "other necessaries" more cheaply supplied than from other places.[8]

Taxes were burdensome, and this was universal, too. But the poorer sort believed they were the sufferers, for Virginia taxes were levied *per poll* at the colony, county, and parish levels. A Virginian paid taxes in proportion to the number of tithables he supported, family, servants, and slaves. Granted the large planter who kept more servants and slaves paid more than his humbler neighbor, the difference was not in proportion to relative wealth and ability to pay, since the size of one's holdings had no effect on the levy. The smaller farmers and poorer sort were sure that the tax system discriminated against them, and they were probably right, although maybe not as absolutely as they imagined.[9]

With Dutchmen marauding their coasts and Indians disturbing the frontier—a reverberation from King Philip's War in New England— [10] Virginians' taxes were raised abruptly in the 1670's to build castles and forts against invasion from the sea and attacks from the hinterland. The threat of war was unsettling enough, but an increase in taxes unevenly distributed, physical hardships, characteristic of early colonies anywhere, and then acts of a distant Parliament which con-

7. *CSPDom.*, *1675–1676*, pp. 85, 98, 134, 154, 342; *CSPCol.*, *1675–1676*, #707.

8. "Causes of Discontent in Virginia, 1676," *Va. Mag. of Hist.*, 3 (1895–96), 38, #8; *CSPCol.*, *1675–1676*, #707; C.O. 5/1371, pt. II, 153.

9. For an explanation of Virginia taxes, see Henry Hartwell, James Blair, and Edward Chilton, *The Present State of Virginia, and the College*, ed. by H. D. Farish (Williamsburg, Va., 1940), pp. 53–56; Giles Bland suggested a tax on land instead of polls in "The State of Virginia, 1676," *Va. Mag. of Hist.*, 20 (1912), 355–56, as did the Isle of Wight County in its grievances following Bacon's Rebellion, C.O. 5/1371, pt. II, 161–62.

10. *CSPCol.*, *1675–1676*, #707, #859; *CSPDom.*, *1676–1677*, p. 337.

fined their trade and seemed to force them for survival to grow more of the very crop which tended to suffocate them—all these and more created an uneasiness and uncertainty which Virginians found hard to live with in the 1670's.

While these problems were accumulating, Charles II contributed another which undermined further Virginians' confidence in what they were doing and sharply aggravated the uncertainty of the times. In the early 1670's they grew increasingly aware that Virginia belonged not altogether to them and the King as a royal colony but to two different groups of proprietors to whom Charles in feudal manner had granted rights to land over several years' time. The first gift, the Northern Neck, a long stretch of land between the Rappahannock and Potomac Rivers, a desperate and newly exiled Charles had granted in 1649 to several royalists, including John, Lord Culpeper, Sir John Berkeley, and several others. Virginia had gained these proprietors nothing during the Commonwealth and Protectorate periods, but upon the Restoration, with their King back on the throne, they had trotted out their patent for all to see and made preparations to exercise authority and collect quitrents. Despite some modification in 1669, the proprietors still enjoyed rights to divide the land into manors, to hold courts baron, to have markets and fairs, collect tolls, customs, fines, and other perquisites including quitrents.[11]

In the midst of their wondering and complaining about the King's generosity to his courtiers, Virginians were thunderstruck when Charles in 1673 granted to Lords Arlington and Thomas Culpeper, Lord John's son, the remaining part of Virginia to the south "with all rights appurtenances . . . jurisdictions . . . and royalties whatsoever." Again, this was not the right to govern, but who knew what it might become? It did include escheats and quitrents—these last in specie rather than tobacco—and a lot more.[12]

There is no doubt that granting away to proprietors land already settled and planted bred "infinite discontents" and "sad effects." Thomas Ludwell, one of Governor Berkeley's right-hand men, put it succinctly when he wrote home that he had "never observed anything so much move the people's grief or passion, or which doth more put a stop to their industry, than their uncertainty whether they should make a country for the King or other Proprietors." If the King had wanted to discourage his subjects in Virginia, he could not have hit

11. *CSPCol., 1669–1674,* #63, #145–#146; H. R. McIlwaine, ed., *Minutes of the Council and General Court of Colonial Virginia, 1622–1632, 1670–1676* (Richmond, Va., 1924), p. 296.
12. Hening, ed., *Statutes,* II, 519; Burk, *Hist. of Va.,* II, App., xxxiii–xxxv.

upon a surer way.[13] What *was* Virginia, and what right did people there have to their lands if the King could grant them away and allow proprietors to gobble them up? Were not colonists the King's subjects like any other Englishmen? Or were they in a class by themselves whose rights no one seemed to respect?

Jamestown was a busy place in September 1674 when the Virginia assembly met to discover some scheme which would protect Virginians from their enemies, the proprietors, or maybe even from their best friend, the King. The scheme hit upon was the appointment of an agency of three men to treat with the King and the powers-that-be for the purpose of buying out the proprietors and coming to terms with the English government about the rights of Virginians. In the fall of 1674 three agents, Francis Moryson, Thomas Ludwell, and Robert Smith, left Jamestown armed with petitions, letters, and instructions to commence their campaign in London against the proprietors and in behalf of Virginians' rights.[14]

Before and after the agents arrived in London, Governor Berkeley sent a barrage of arguments against the proprietors' claims, ranging from high principle to common horse sense. Virginians, wrote Berkeley, ought to "have something out of their sweat and labour to supply their necessities," and this they could not if the proprietors exercised to its utmost the authority included in their patents. As it looked to the governor, the proprietors' agents had begun already to "grind" the people and leave only "disorder" behind them. Besides Berkeley, most Virginians were apprehensive lest the proprietors seriously disturb the headright system, which worked in Virginians' favor, and insist upon the collection of quitrents heretofore spotty and paid in tobacco, not specie.[15]

Once in London, the Virginia agents had their hands full. First they negotiated with Lords Arlington and Culpeper and exacted their promise to reduce claims in the larger, southern grant to just quitrents and escheats. Then they petitioned the King, requesting letters patent which would allow the colony to incorporate—in order to buy out the

13. CSPCol., 1669–1674, #572; Berkeley to Treasurer Danby, Feb. 1, 1675, Va. Mag. of Hist., 32 (1924), 191–92; Fairfax Harrison, Virginia Land Grants (Richmond, 1925), pp. 60, 84, 124, 149–50; Fairfax Harrison, Landmarks of Old Prince William (2 vols., Richmond, 1924), I, 42–43; R. B. Davis, ed., William Fitzhugh and His Chesapeake World, 1676–1701 (Chapel Hill, N.C., 1963), pp. 39–46.

14. H. R. McIlwaine, ed., Journals of the House of Burgesses of Virginia, 1659/60–1693 (Richmond, 1914), p. 62; Hening, ed., Statutes, II, 311–12; CSPCol., 1675–1676, #602–#604.

15. Berkeley to Lord Arlington, Sept. 21, 1674, Burk, Hist. of Va., II, App., xxxiii; Berkeley to Danby, Feb. 1, 1675, Va. Mag. of Hist., 32 (1924), 191–92.

proprietors of the Northern Neck—and at the same time to guarantee Virginians the "future security" of their "rights, properties, and privileges." Either the assembly or the agents organized the latter request under ten "Heads" which accompanied the petition and which, the agents hoped, would form the bases of a charter.[16]

The original charter, granted to the Virginia Company of London, James I had revoked in 1624 when he took the settlement under his wing, making it the first royal colony in America. Since that time, except for the Puritan interlude, Virginia had functioned through commissions and instructions to its governors, a system which guaranteed the settlers very little and left them to the whim of the King, as the proprietary grants sadly demonstrated. Virginia, through her agents, now asked the King to approve a royal charter which would tie down the colony's relationship to the Crown and the realm and explicitly define the rights of Virginians and their place in the empire.

What did the Virginia charter draft contain? It granted to the assembly a very marked degree of local power and authority. It permitted the colony to incorporate for the purpose of buying out the proprietors of the Northern Neck. It assured the colonists immediate dependence upon the Crown, eliminating any middle authority such as present or future proprietors. The King promised not to grant away their lands in the future, and he confirmed to Virginians and their heirs forever all land possessed by them at the time. Headrights of fifty acres would continue; escheated land might be repossessed and enjoyed forever after compounding at a moderate rate in tobacco. The charter gave power to the governor and council to try all treasons, murders, felonies, and other crimes, with full pardoning power to the governor except in cases of treason and murder. What is more, it confirmed and ratified the power and authority of the Virginia assembly, reserving to the Crown only a review of its laws. Lastly, and probably most important, the charter guaranteed that no taxes or impositions would be laid upon Virginians but by the "Comon Consent of the Governour Concil and Burgesses," excepting only customs on Virginia's goods sent to England.

Confirmation of the authority of the assembly, an assurance of the rights of Englishmen, and a guarantee against taxation without consent were the heart of the new charter. The agents in negotiating in London argued that these would not alter the colony's government, for it had functioned for some time in this manner, but only with an apparent authority. All they asked for now was confirmation of a working system, the making of their own laws, as close to those of England

16. Petition, June 23, 1675, *CSPCol., 1675–1676,* #602, #604.

as conditions allowed, subject only to the governor's veto and review by the King. Taxation by consent was the custom in Virginia, practiced for more than fifty years. It was also one of the liberties of Englishmen, guaranteed by Parliament in England, a right which planters and their heirs ought "to enjoy by law." After all, the agents claimed, colonies were "but in nature of an extension or dilatation of the realm of England," and colonists should possess "the same liberties and privileges as Englishmen in England." In the Virginia Company charter James I had declared that settlers and their descendants should be regarded as "natural born subjects of England" as, in truth, the agents added, "without any declaration or grant, they ought by law to be." The first charter was revoked, to be sure, but James had promised a second which would renew the "former privileges of the planters." Although he had failed to grant it, since that time no King in England had ever imposed taxes upon Virginia without consent of the people there. By the new charter Virginians sought a guarantee of this right in black and white. Heretofore, the power to tax themselves was given only through instructions to their governors, which, the agents conceived, "ought to be confirmed under the great seal." And, too, they argued, other colonies, so much less deserving than Virginia, "New-England, Maryland, Barbadoes, &c. are not taxed but of their own consent."

The Virginia charter draft very clearly stated what one assembly in America believed were the rights of colonies and settlers—the rights of Englishmen overseas. Dependence upon the Crown had a specific meaning to Virginians. To be "unseparably affixt to the crown" guaranteed to them, they believed, "those just rights and privileges as were their due whilst they lived in England, and which they humbly hope that they have not lost by removing themselves into a country where they hazarded their lives and fortunes, so much more to the advantage of the crown and kingdom, than to their own. . . ." This was a declaration of equality, of equality within the empire, for Virginians felt themselves equal to the people who stayed at home as well as to other colonists in America as far as treatment from government was concerned. In addition, they believed they were entitled to quiet possession of their property, with the prospect of adding to it, without threat from alien proprietors with power to manage the land and collect quitrents. They believed their assembly was autonomous except for the King's right to review their laws, and there was no doubt in their minds that as Englishmen their rights included taxation by consent.

Life in the colonies was hard enough without encroachment upon it from home, intensifying the uncertainty, instability, and the hazards of living in a wilderness 3,000 miles from a government which attempted control but not responsibility. Indians, the Dutch, geography and climate, high taxes, the vicissitudes of a single crop, all were difficult to contend with, sometimes impossible, when the price of tobacco sank far below existence levels. At very least, the home government ought to treat Virginians as Englishmen and by so doing lessen the uncertainty of a frontier existence, not add to it. Legalize our relationship so that we may have a foundation upon which to build. Don't keep us guessing about our identity as colonists. Guarantee us our property and Englishmen's rights, make permanent and legal the system of government we have worked out over two generations of colonial life, and we will benefit the Crown as well as ourselves and increasingly so—that is what the assembly seems to be saying in the draft of the charter which attorneys, Lords, Councils, and King scrutinized and then approved during the winter of 1675–1676.[17]

His Majesty's royal colony of Virginia had made a very definite statement in defining the role of its government and people in the empire. As Maryland, New York, and Massachusetts would do later, Virginia in 1675 demonstrated in no uncertain terms that in the first century of colonization, a number of American colonists had decided who they were and what their relation was to the government and people at home.

Disappointingly, despite the several approvals, the charter got only as far as the Great Seal but not through, for there it was stopped for reasons which have never been adequately explained. In March 1676 both secretaries of state, Coventry and Southwell, made inquiries, and the next month the Lord Treasurer and Lord Chancellor brought the matter before the Privy Council, but they were unable to pry the charter loose. It was stopped in the Hanaper Office, probably by the King himself.[18]

Why the Charter Failed

Was Bacon's Rebellion the cause of the Virginia charter's failure? Probably not. It is almost certain that Charles II and his advisers

17. The "Heads" of the charter as approved by the attorney and solicitor generals are in Burk, *Hist. of Va.*, II, App., xl–xli. For the King's approval, see *ibid.*, lvi–lvii. For agents' explanation of "Heads," see *ibid.*, xlvii–lx. The completed charter draft is in *Va. Mag. of Hist.*, 56 (1948), 264–66. See also *CSPCol., 1675–1676*, #602, #603, #696, #697, I–II, #834.

18. *Ibid.*, #834, #835; *Cal. Treas. Bks., 1676–1679*, pp. 37–38; *Acts of P.C., Col. Ser.*, I, *1613–1680*, p. 661, #1074; Burk, *Hist. of Va.*, II, App., lviii–lix; C. M. Andrews, *Guide to the Materials for American History, to 1783, in the Public Record Office of Great Britain* (2 vols., Washington, 1912–14), I, 271–72.

had turned thumbs down on it before they learned of the rebellion in Virginia, news of which arrived in England some time in June of 1676. By this time the King had already changed his mind, and the Privy Council's order annulling the charter was dated May 31.[19]

The charter failed for other reasons. Although the Lords of Trade had agreed to it in the fall of 1675, they were very new to their jobs, having just been appointed, and may well have withdrawn their approval by the spring of the next year. They doubtless found the power and authority about to be given to Virginia at odds with their schemes to centralize and intensify colonial policy for England's advantage. More specific evidence supports this contention. When scrutiny turned into delay and delay into a complete halt in negotiations in the early spring of 1676, the agents sought reasons for the stoppage, hoping to beat them down with their arguments. But Moryson, Ludwell, and Smith found it very difficult to learn what the objections were and who their authors. In some manner, not explained in their letters, they discovered that one reason for the charter's failure was its supposed threat to the Navigation Acts, something the Lords of Trade would be very likely to notice. In response Ludwell and Moryson drafted a lengthy Remonstrance, reviewing the "Heads" of the charter draft in light of the Acts of Trade. They pointed out an obvious proviso which preserved "the power of the laws of navigation, and all future acts of parliament, of that nature. . . ." In other words, the charter itself excepted the Acts of Trade, and therefore, said the agents, there should be no argument about it on that score. True or not, it made little difference; by this time no one was listening.[20]

A more significant cause for the halt in charter proceedings was Thomas, Lord Culpeper, who doubtless had a hand in persuading the King and Privy Council to reverse their earlier approval of Virginia's bid for power. There is some indication that Culpeper and his friends made several objections to the charter, particularly to the right of Virginians to tax themselves.[21] But there were more personal reasons why Culpeper might oppose it. First, he was a proprietor of both grants, north and south, which the King had given away at two dif-

19. June 8, 1676, *CSPCol.*, *1675–1676*, #942; Giles Bland to Sir Joseph Williamson, Apr. 28, 1676, and Bland's "State of Virginia, 1676," both received in June 1676, *Va. Mag. of Hist.*, 20 (1912), 352–57; *Acts of P.C., Col. Ser.*, I, *1613–1680*, p. 661, #1074; Wilcomb E. Washburn, "The Effect of Bacon's Rebellion on Government in England and Virginia," Paper 17 from *Contributions from the Museum of History and Technology*, U.S. National Museum *Bulletin*, 225 (Smithsonian Institution, Washington, 1962), pp. 142–43.

20. *CSPCol.*, *1675–1676*, #602, #603; Agents' petition to Lord High Chancellor, n.d., Hening, ed., *Statutes*, II, 537; "Remonstrance against the Stoppage of the Charter," n.d., *ibid.*, 534–37.

21. Edward D. Neill, *Virginia Carolorum* (Albany, 1886), pp. 382–83.

ferent times, and although he had compromised with the agents and agreed to incorporation for purchase of the Northern Neck, there remained the right to quitrents for the huge southern grant. (In 1677 the agents were surprised to learn that Lord Culpeper still was pushing plans for reviving the business of the patents and some time later worked out a compromise with the King.) [22]

Second, and more surprising, Lord Culpeper already possessed a commission from King Charles to be *governor* of Virginia upon the death or removal of Berkeley. The commission was dated July 8, 1675. Throughout much of the time the agents were negotiating in London, Culpeper knew full well that he would be governor of their colony when Berkeley gave it up.[23] A strong charter propping up the authority of the assembly would have stripped a new governor of much of the power of his office. Culpeper, an outsider, was no Berkeley and could not possibly identify himself with Virginia and a strong faction in the council and burgesses as had Berkeley. What is more, an aggressive assembly with a good deal of room to move around in would be difficult for a proprietor to manage when it came to the issue of quitrents. Culpeper's best interests would be served in Virginia with the power of the prerogative behind him, not the chartered authority of an assembly confronting him. There were several reasons, then, for the charter's failure before the bloody news of rebellion reached the King's ear. If not cause of the charter's defeat, Bacon's Rebellion did prevent renewal of negotiations by the agents, for they found the King deaf to continued talks after the serious nature of the rebellion became common knowledge in London.

A Charter for Whom?

To attribute the drive for the charter wholly to political and constitutional principle would be sadly to misunderstand the assembly's motives and at the same time some of the causes of Bacon's Rebellion. Encroachment by proprietors with power to control the land could only damage the economic and political interests of those who had already won themselves places of power and profit. The Virginia charter, while guaranteeing the rights of Englishmen in Virginia, would have guaranteed also considerable power and control in the assembly, power and control which Berkeley and his people had acquired over years of experience and wielded for their own sakes.

22. Moryson to Culpeper, Apr. 14, 1677, *Va. Mag. of Hist.*, 21 (1913), 368; Commissioners for Virginia to Mr. Watkins, Apr. 14, 1677, *ibid.*, 367; Harrison, *Landmarks of Old Prince William*, I, 194.
23. *CSPCol.*, 1675–1676, #599; *ibid.*, 1677–1680, #308, #360.

Moreover, in the hands of Berkeley and his party, this power, through politicking, persuasion, and patronage, proved to be enormous, great enough to endanger local rights, strong enough to provoke rebellion in 1676.

Sir William and the agents, although they had kept pretty much to the high ground of principle in their arguments against the patents, were not blind to the proprietors' threat to the headright system. Legally practiced, headrights were an encouragement to immigrants, guaranteeing them land to commence life as colonists. At the same time, the custom rewarded with land older settlers who sponsored newcomers, helping in this way to increase population and extend settlement. When abused, the headright system presented several splendid opportunities for those already settled to acquire more property than the law allowed and greatly augment their estates. Who knew but what the proprietors would stick their noses into the system as it was practiced and alter Virginia's customs? A guarantee of headrights held a prominent place in the "Heads" presented by the agents in London and remained a significant item in the final form of the charter draft.[24]

An equally serious threat to Virginia's way of doing things was the proprietors' authority under the patents to collect quitrents on the land already settled. All land in Virginia was subject to quitrents paid to the King, for he was ultimate owner of the soil. Fortunately for the colonists, collection had been spotty. Actually, the Crown never saw the quitrents which Virginians paid, since as early as 1650, the King had given over the profit of them to Colonel Henry Norwood, an exiled royalist, who had come to Virginia the year before.[25] Collection, however, according to an old practice, was in the hands of members of the council who had been "Farmers" of the quitrents in their home counties for some time, and although "not a certain Place, yet it is a certain yearly Profit and Favor." Proprietary quitrents, strictly collected, would strike a telling blow at the colonists' pocketbooks, to say nothing of the councillors' income.[26]

Along with quitrents the proprietors were allowed escheats, too, taking the business out of the hands of Berkeley's favorites, council

24. Burk, *Hist. of Va.*, II, App. xl–xli; *Va. Mag. of Hist.*, 56 (1948), 265; Harrison, *Virginia Land Grants*, p. 35.

25. Add. Mss., 30372, f. 24b, B.M. "Enquiries to the Governor of Virginia," Sept. 20, 1670, Hening, ed., *Statutes*, II, 511–17; Beer, *Old Colonial System*, I, 193 and n.

26. Hartwell, *et al.*, *The Present State of Virginia*, pp. 26, 35; Philip Alexander Bruce, *Institutional History of Virginia in the Seventeenth Century* (2 vols., New York, 1910), II, 577–78; *Va. Mag. of Hist.*, 3 (1895–96), 42–47; Harrison, *Virginia Land Grants*, p. 150 and n. 89.

members Francis Moryson and Thomas Ludwell, two of the three agents, who had been mixed up in the matter of escheats for some time. The charter draft directed that the colony revert to its earlier practices, allowing Virginians composition of escheats at favorable rates.[27]

Suddenly, headrights, quitrents, and escheats were all subject to proprietary control, "in prejudice of many royall concessions and grants . . . " which the Virginia government and certain individuals had acquired by several means over the years. Not only did proprietary interference in these matters divest the local government of its "just powers and authorities by which this colony has hitherto beene kept in peace and tranquility . . . " but it cut deeply into the perquisites of office which successful Virginia officials had been pocketing for years. No wonder, then, that the assembly demanded in the charter draft a "dependence upon the crown," for such dependence in the past, despite quitrents, had been fairly easy to live with and profitable to a few in power. A liberal concept of empire, if written into a royal charter, guaranteed a very favorable share of self-government. It also assured concrete advantages to those who directed that government.

The very origins of the charter seem to have stemmed from an elite group already strongly entrenched in Virginia's government. Agents Moryson and Ludwell had come to Virginia as royalist veterans and exiles in the 1640's, Moryson with the King's commission in his pocket to command the fort at Point Comfort along with its profits. Governor Berkeley had warmly received them, and it was not long before each with the governor's help had firm positions in government and considerable land around them. Moryson was at different times speaker of the House of Burgesses, deputy governor during Berkeley's mission to England, and for several years a powerful member of the Virginia council. Ludwell, a distant relative of Berkeley, received his first grant of 500 acres in 1648 and by 1660 was the colony's secretary and a leading councillor. Their companion, General Robert Smith, also an army officer under Charles I, was an active Virginia landowner and became a council member in 1663. He served several times on commissions to treat with Maryland over cessation of tobacco planting and soon owned a good deal of land. All royalists, the agents to London were closely tied to Berkeley and owed him personally for their advancement and estates.[28]

27. Hening, ed., *Statutes*, II, 39, 56, 137; *Va. Mag. of Hist.*, 8 (1900–1), 241.
28. For Francis Moryson's career in Virginia before 1676, see "Colonel Norwood's Voyage to Virginia in 1649," William Maxwell, ed., *Virginia Historical Register*, II (1849), 121–23, 137; H.M.C. 70: *Pepys*, pp. 262–63; *Va. Mag. of*

During the winter 1675–1676, with negotiations going in their favor, the agents showed a boldness which must have surprised a number of Englishmen. Despite the liberal grant of power already in the charter draft, the agents had asked for more. Once the "Heads" were approved, probably sometime in the fall of 1675, the agents sent them back to Virginia in a report of their progress which at that point was encouraging. The agents explained to the assembly that they had "come very little short" of what they desired. What they had not been able to swing was a permanent incorporation. The obstacle here was the government's experience with Massachusetts, a corporate colony, whose virtual independence had antagonized for some time King, Council, and ministry to the point that they were desperately looking for a way to revoke the Bay Colony's charter. Therefore, the bold request for permanent incorporation smacked of Massachusetts and colored Virginia's demand with the same kind of independence, a stand it was politic to recede from. Convincing critics of their good intentions was difficult, for it was well known in London that the "New England disease is very catching." The result was that the charter limited incorporation exclusively to purchasing lands from the proprietors of the Northern Neck.[29]

At the same time, the agents had tried to incorporate Virginia in the name of the governor, council, and burgesses alone. But the Privy Council quickly substituted "commonalty" for "burgesses'" remarking that this was in "favor of the country, as being more called in law." This shift in wording may have been simply a legal point, but it offers some grounds to suspect that the agents represented the assembly

---

Hist., 8 (1900–1), 108, 167; *ibid.*, 12 (1904–5), 205; *ibic.*, 18 (1910), 413; Hening, ed., *Statutes*, II, 39, 56, 137; Richard L. Morton, *Colonial Virginia* (2 vols., Chapel Hill, N.C., 1960), I, 189, 278–79 n.; C. M. Andrews, ed., *Narratives of the Insurrections, 1675–1690* (New York, 1915), p. 102; Justin Winsor, *Narrative and Critical History of America* (8 vols., Cambridge, Mass., 1884–89), III, 148.

For Thomas Ludwell, see *Va. Mag. of Hist.*, 1 (1893–94), 174–76; *ibid.*, 3 (1895–96), 133, 156; *ibid.*, 8 (1900–1), 239, 241; *ibid.*, 12 (1904–5), 288–89; *ibid.*, 14 (1906–7), 267, 354; Hening, ed., *Statutes*, II, 39, 56, 137, 313; *Virginia County Records*, V (Mar. 1909), 83, 119. Thomas and Philip Ludwell were related to the Berkeleys through the formers' maternal great-grandfather, *Va. Mag. of Hist.*, 1 (1893–94), 174–75. Philip Ludwell, Thomas' brother, married Berkeley's widow soon after the governor's death, *ibid.*, 25 (1917), 88 n.

For General Robert Smith, see *Tyler's Quarterly*, IX (Apr. 1928), 288; *ibid.*, VII (1925–26), 63; *William and Mary Quarterly*, 1st ser., VIII (Jan. 1900), 184; *ibid.*, III (July 1894), 67; *Va. Mag. of Hist.*, 9 (1901–2), 46; *ibid.*, 19 (1911), 33–34; *ibid.*, 20 (1912), 360–63.

29. Agents' report to Virginia, n.d., Burk, *Hist. of Va.*, II, App., xxxvi–xxxvii; "Observations upon the several heads proposed by Mr. Secretary Ludwell and other gentlemen from Virginia," *CSPCol.*, 1675–1676, #403.

rather than the people and were very willing that *it* become the incorporated body, not Virginians as a whole. In inserting the change the Privy Councillors argued that such a grant ought not be given to an order of men which could be dissolved or discontinued, a statement in itself not very encouraging to the permanency of the burgesses.[30] Did the Privy Council suspect some kind of "grab" on the assembly's part and believe it necessary to preserve the rights of the "country," the "commonalty," an attitude it later took respecting Bacon's Rebellion?

The next year the collector of customs in Virginia, Giles Bland, indicated that the agents' support in the colony was confined to a smaller body even than the assembly. In a report to the Secretary of State, Bland referred once to the agents as "those Gentlemen who are Employed as Com'rs from ye Governor and Councell to his Ma'tie" and later to those persons "who were employed hence by ye Governor." This may have been simply oversight on the collector's part, but it is curious that in two references he should omit even a nod to the assembly as a whole, let alone the burgesses or the people.[31]

In their report to the assembly, the agents found it necessary to make two other explanations. One was about the King's power to review laws, which, the agents remarked, they could not reasonably object to since "it is a power due him" and insisted upon in England in order not to exclude the Crown altogether from authority in Virginia. That question of the King's veto needed comment hints that the agents arrived in London ready to suggest that the colony get along without it.[32] Lost somewhere in the shuffle was another clause limiting the King to a period of two years only to exercise his veto over an act of the assembly, the law being valid in the meantime. Doubtless the agents agreed to suppress this once they had sampled opinions of those in power.[33]

That Berkeley's hold on Virginia's government was great hardly needs proof. A governor of his stamp, after years of experience, knew what string to touch and how to use those about him to concentrate power into a solid faction. Berkeley was the " 'sole author of the most substantial part' of the government, 'either for Lawes or other inferior institutions,' " wrote Secretary Thomas Ludwell in 1666, and Ludwell

30. Burk, *Hist. of Va.*, II, App., xxxvi–xxxvii.

31. Giles Bland, "The State of Virginia, 1676," *Va. Mag. of Hist.*, 20 (1912), 355, 356.

32. Agents' report to Virginia, n.d., Burk, *Hist. of Va.*, II, App., xxxvii.

33. Agents' explanation of "Heads," *ibid.*, pp. 1, lii. The final draft of the charter did not include the two-year limitation upon the King. *Va. Mag of Hist.*, 56 (July 1948), 264–66.

certainly must have known, for he had been at Berkeley's side for a generation or more.[34] Although Hartwell, Blair, and Chilton wrote their *Present State of Virginia* several years later, they based their conclusions about government on a retrospective view of the colony's history. All the great offices in Virginia, they wrote, "were at first heaped upon one Man, and, which is stranger, continues so to this Day." The normal checks on these "very large Powers" had disintegrated, leaving the council in particular "at the Devotion of the Governor" and the ready instruments to advance what he desired.[35] Through various means he and the council had secured the support of a majority of the House of Burgesses particularly through the efforts of Robert Beverley, clerk of the lower house, who exercised great influence over the members. The government's restriction of the suffrage to freeholders in 1670 tended to reduce opposition, and by the time of Bacon's Rebellion Governor Berkeley and several members of the council, through a majority of the House of Burgesses, pretty much called the turn in Virginia. It was common knowledge then and now that the governor had not called an election of burgesses for some dozen years.[36]

The causes of Bacon's Rebellion were multiple and make most sense when examined on several planes of Virginia society. No one would doubt today that Indian war precipitated the rebellion which in turn laid bare other serious grievances apparent at parish, county, and provincial levels.[37] But most of these grievances the colonists laid at the door of Berkeley's assembly, the same assembly which fought hard to secure the charter in 1675.

Besides fear of the Indians, most grievances stemmed from the high cost of provincial government which seemed to benefit the colonists not at all. Increased taxes for protection against the Indians failed to produce a successful Indian policy. Taxes levied to build forts and castles along the coast were inefficiently—maybe corruptly—spent, and exposure to a seaborne enemy continued. The very cost of government

34. Quoted in T. J. Wertenbaker, *Virginia Under the Stuarts, 1607–1688* (Princeton, N.J., 1914), p. 136.

35. *The Present State of Virginia*, pp. 21–26.

36. *Va. Mag. of Hist.*, 1 (1893–94), 175–76; Hening, ed., *Statutes*, II, 280. For duration of the Long Assembly, see Wertenbaker, *Virginia Under the Stuarts*, pp. 135–36 n.

37. Bernard Bailyn, "Politics and Social Structure in Virginia," in James Morton Smith, ed., *Seventeenth-Century America: Essays in Colonial History* (Chapel Hill, N.C., 1959), pp. 90–115. For other recent discussion of Bacon's Rebellion, see Wilcomb E. Washburn, *The Governor and the Rebel: A History of Bacon's Rebellion in Virginia* (Chapel Hill, N.C., 1957), and Wesley Frank Craven, *The Southern Colonies in the Seventeenth Century, 1607–1689* (Baton Rouge, La., 1949), ch. X.

seemed exorbitant to colonists whose tobacco was collected each year to support it. Particularly galling was the 250 pounds of tobacco it took each day to keep a delegate in the House of Burgesses, which, it was generally agreed, met more often than necessary anyway. Some of these grievances were longstanding, but they were aggravated when the bloody Indian war commenced and taxes rose again. And then, in the midst of this bad feeling, the Virginia assembly levied an additional tax of fifty pounds of tobacco per tithable for two years' running to support the agents in their negotiations against the proprietors and for the charter. To colonists, already complaining that they derived no benefits from increased taxation, that their tobacco was taken for public causes, but neither improvement nor strict accounting followed, the additional tax to support the charter agency, despite its alleged rewards, was another overwhelming burden and pointedly so when news of the mission's failure reached Virginia.[38] But by this time Bacon's Rebellion was on in earnest.

When news of the rebellion sifted into England in the spring of 1676, the agents refused to admit that the outburst in Virginia had killed any hope of securing the charter. In fact, they desperately tried to use the Indian war and the rebellion to persuade the King that now, more than ever, Virginia needed the charter to allay their fears and settle their condition. How seasonable it would be if the King would apply the charter to the "present distractions," they declared! How hazardous in the present circumstances to refuse Virginians any part of it! Actually, the Virginia agents were in a very tough spot, for they could not admit in London that the upheaval in Virginia was a rebellion against the governor and assembly who had sent them to England in the first place and who had instructed them to extract a charter which would guarantee tremendous local power to that government. What possible chance would there be to reopen negotiations with the King if he thought that a great many people in Virginia were violently opposed to the very government the charter would confirm? And so the agents supported Berkeley and played down the scope of the rebellion. Not only had Virginians always been loyal to the Crown, they pled, but even now the trouble in Virginia had nothing to do with disaffection to the King's government in England *or* Virginia.

38. See County Grievances, C.O. 5/1371, pt. I, 151–52b, and pt. II, 149–208; also *Va. Mag. of Hist.*, 2 (1894–95), 166–73, 380–92; and 3 (1895–96), 35–42, 132–47; Burk, *Hist. of Va.*, II, 250; Giles Bland, "The State of Virginia, 1676," *Va. Mag. of Hist.*, 20 (1912), 255. The Commissioners arrived in Virginia in January 1677 with instructions from the King to reduce the amount of tobacco paid to legislators. By March 27, after constant urging, the amount agreed upon was 120 pounds of tobacco per diem, *ibid.*, 21 (1913), 240, 262, 265.

What is more, they claimed that the "better or more industrious sort of people" were not the abettors of the mutiny; rather, the cause was the "poverty and uneasyness of some of the meanest whose discontents render them easier to be misledd." Truly, this was "the sole cause and foundation of these troubles. . . ." The most effective way to bring Virginia to a "lasting obedience" was first to revoke "those graunts wch have and still doe soe much disturb theire mindes . . ." and then settle the people's "just priveledges and properties . . . on a sollid foundacon . . . ," in other words, grant the charter they had come over to secure.[39]

The tensions of the rebellion brought out more evidence of its causes. Although the county grievances, requested by the Royal Commissioners in 1677, were somewhat after the fact, their reiteration of complaints against the government pointed directly to the assembly and claimed it to be the primary source of the trouble. Again and again the counties asked questions about where the tax money went and why there was no accounting of it. Nansemond County put it succinctly: its people complained "against the great Taxes imposed these 3 or 4 years last past," and they know not for what.[40]

The most direct statement of this kind can be found in the grievances of Charles City County, whose complaints flatly blamed Sir William Berkeley for subverting the government. He had forced his will on the council and then assumed to himself the appointment of all civil and military officers and other places of profit, giving them to people who would carry out his designs. And then to bind them even more closely to himself and to attract others to his party, he permitted them locally "to lay and impose what levies and imposicons upon us they should or did please," which they "converted to their owne private lucre and gains." By these means the governor got the upper hand over a majority of the "men of parts and estates," and these were the very people whom the voters found necessary to send to Jamestown as their burgesses. Berkeley strengthened his authority over the people and deprived them of great quantities of tobacco which were "embezelled and consumed betwixt him and his officers." Ordinarily Charles City

39. Agents to [?], March 10, 1676, Burk, *Hist. of Va.*, II, App., lviii–lix; Agents to Virginia, *Acts of P.C., Col. Ser.*, I, *1613–1680*, p. 661, #1074; "Memorial of the Virginia Agents to one of the Principal Secretaries of State," n.d., Hening, ed., *Statutes*, II, 538–43; "Proposals most humbly offered to his most sacred Matie by Tho: Ludwell and Robt Smith for Reducing the Rebells in Virginia to their obedience," *Va. Mag. of Hist.*, 1 (1893–94), 433–35; Ludwell to Sec'y Coventry, Apr. 1677, quoted in George Chalmers, *An Introduction to the History of the Revolt of the American Colonies* (2 vols. bound in one, Boston, 1845), I, 161–62.

40. C.O. 5/1371, pt. II, 169.

people sent their grievances to Jamestown with their burgesses, but lately they feared their representatives had "been overswayed by the power and prevalency of the s^d S^r Wm. Berkeley and his councell," neglecting their grievances and using them to "putt under their Pyes." [41] Some counties refused even to submit grievances, while Berkeley remained in power, "so overawed & biassed" were they by him. The "general cry" of the country was that Virginia would never be quiet as long as he was governor and Ludwell secretary.[42]

Berkeley did remain governor for several more months and, once the rebellion was over, vindictively sustained his power by hanging a number of his enemies and confiscating their estates. A Maryland observer wrote home to Lord Baltimore in January 1677 that the coming warm weather could very well produce another swarm of Virginians who "may have as venomous stings, as the late traytr had." It could happen again, he commented, if the King did not settle Virginia's affairs, for certainly those in power could not do it. His next comment went to the heart of the problem: "There must be an alteration though not of the Government yet in the Government, new men must be put in power, the old ones will never agree with the common people, and if that be not done, his Majtie in my opinion will never find a well setled Government in that Colony. . . ." [43] At the time the King ordered a Commission to suppress the rebellion and investigate its causes, he ordered Berkeley home to answer for all the trouble.

After the governor's departure Colonel Herbert Jeffreys took his place temporarily, supported by the Commission and its troops. The same Maryland writer reported to Baltimore that if Jeffreys built on the "old foundations" neither he nor his soldiers could "satisfy or rule these people." If there was anyone in Virginia brave enough to stick out his neck, he wrote, the "Commons would immure" themselves in rebellion as deep as in Bacon's time.[44] About a month before Berkeley left for England, his Green Springs faction, again in control of the assembly, implored the Secretary of State in London to revive the business of their charter with the King. But the King's mind about the causes of trouble in Virginia was clearly expressed by the Privy Council when it flatly asserted "that the Rebellion of Virginia was occasioned by the Excessive power of the Assembly." [45]

41. Va. Mag. of Hist., 3 (1895–96), 135–36, 141–42.

42. Commissioners to Sec'y Coventry, Apr. 5, 1677, ibid., 21 (1913), 366; William Sherwood to Sec'y Williamson, Apr. 13, 1677, ibid., 367.

43. Jan. 22, 1677, Arch. of Md., V, 154.

44. CSPCol., 1677–1680, #263.

45. General Assembly to Sir Joseph Williamson, Apr. 2, 1677, McIlwaine, ed., Journals of the House of Burgesses, 1659/60–1693, pp. 98–99; Blathwayt to Earl of Carlisle, May 31, 1679, BPCol. Wmsbg., v. XXII.

Ironically, Charles II did grant Virginia a royal charter in 1676. But it fell far short of what was expected, and this was owing primarily to Bacon's Rebellion, which was a slap in the face to the prerogative. More telling, the rebellion reduced drastically the King's customs on tobacco, besides costing him dearly to send commissioners and troops. The new charter met several of the original demands respecting headrights, escheats, the governor and council's power to try cases of treason and murder, and significantly, confirmation of the colonists' land. At the same time it stressed the colony's dependence upon the Crown, a dependence the assembly had hoped to achieve but which now had a wholly different meaning. Without the other guarantees, so important in the earlier charter draft, there was little protection afforded the assembly of Virginia against the power of the Crown.

The most glaring omissions in the new charter were a confirmation of the authority of the colonial assembly, a guarantee to Virginians of the rights of Englishmen, and specifically the right to consent to taxes. Without these Virginians were very much in the same position as before. The King had confirmed their property but not their rights as Englishmen.[46] The charter Charles granted to Virginia in the summer of 1676 very clearly defined a royal concept of empire, a concept which simply viewed colonists as a subordinate people not equal in rights to Englishmen in England and not entitled to the same treatment from government. An empire was made up of superiors and inferiors, and the inferiors enjoyed only the rights the superiors were willing to give them. It was this kind of thinking which laid the basis for the Crown's attempt, shortly after Bacon's Rebellion, to exact a permanent revenue from Virginia and to dictate laws to the assembly in the manner of Ireland after Poynings's Law.[47]

Had King Charles granted to Virginians the charter the assembly sought, they would have won, in the agents' words, "those just rights and privileges as were their due whilst they lived in England," a position in the empire equal to that of Englishmen at home. Such a grant would have been contrary to the whole tenor of colonial policy as it

46. For the royal charter of 1676, see Burk, *Hist. of Va.*, II, App., lxi–lxii. The new governor, Thomas Lord Culpeper, may have been responsible for the weak charter. See Hening, ed., *Statutes*, II, 531.

47. For the business of Poynings's Law and a permanent revenue, see *CSPCol.*, *1677–1680*, #917; Abstract of Commissions, etc., Add. Mss., 30372, f. 24b; Culpeper to Blathwayt, June 15, July 8, 1680, BPCol. Wmsbg., v. XVII; Labaree, ed., *Royal Instructions*, I, 125; Order of the Privy Council, Oct. 30, 1678, *Va. Mag. of Hist.*, 24 (1916), 79–80; John C. Rainbolt, "The Virginia Vision: A Political History of the Efforts to Diversify the Economy of the Old Dominion, 1650–1706" (unpubl. Ph.D. thesis, Univ. of Wisconsin, 1966), ch. VII; Labaree, *Royal Government*, pp. 219–22.

emerged in the 1670's. But the new charter would have protected only the government of Virginia from an arbitrary King and Parliament. It would not have protected the people of Virginia from their own government, whose arbitrariness was altogether apparent at the time of Bacon's Rebellion. The charter of 1675 would not have eliminated the grievances which caused the rebellion. On the contrary, it would have aggravated them, for it placed additional power and authority in the hands of the very people against whom Bacon and his followers rebelled. By vetoing the charter and substituting a weaker document in its place, the King guaranteed Virginians their land, but he kept their government in leading strings. Given the conditions which obtained at the time, given the fact that in more than thirty years of rule Sir William Berkeley had fused a governing body which seemed to work first for its own ends and only secondly for those of other Virginians, one might argue that Charles II did a majority of Virginians a favor. What was good for those in government was good for all Virginians, or so the assembly seemed to reason in 1675. That it was not was painfully clear the next year. Berkeley and the assembly also reasoned that what was good for Virginia's government was good for the King in England, too. But they misjudged the King as they had Virginians. After vetoing the assembly's charter, Charles then blamed its members for provoking rebellion and destroying his revenue. While the violence and complexity of Bacon's Rebellion have obscured the significance of the Virginia charter, the principle of self-government, which the charter contained, has obscured the self-interest which lurked behind it.

4 Virginia Under Culpeper and Effingham

Government

If Bacon's Rebellion significantly altered conditions in Virginia, the changes were not immediately apparent. To be sure, Bacon was dead, and Berkeley left for England and soon died, too. But the Green Spring people retained a good deal of power, and this did not assure peace and quiet, since they frequently tangled with Colonel Herbert Jeffreys and the Royal Commission. Fundamentally, Virginia's two major problems were still its government and a surplus of tobacco. Although the consequence of rebellion bore upon the government, it did not touch the difficulties of a single-crop economy.

If anything, the government was less stable after the rebellion than it had been just before it. From 1677 to 1680 Virginians looked to four different governors for leadership. Berkeley was recalled early in 1677 but delayed his departure for several months while he attempted to settle the rebellion in his own way. Colonel Jeffreys assumed the governorship under terms of the Commission once Sir William had left.

He served not much more than a year; ailing from the summer of 1678, he died early the next year. From that time until Thomas, Lord Culpeper, arrived in 1680, the government devolved upon Sir Henry Chicheley, president of the council.[1] All the while Culpeper was actually governor with a commission in his pocket issued in 1675, but he was in no hurry to leave England for a number of reasons, mostly pleasure-loving, but some having to do with the Popish Plot and the beginnings of the Exclusion Crisis. With four governors in as many years, Virginians found little stability from the top to ease their uncertainty about where colonies and colonists stood in the scheme of empire, or more specifically, where to find a solid foundation for government and society and the tobacco business.

There were other causes of uneasiness, some of which affected several levels of Virginia society. Indian troubles again plagued the colony, and so did a fear of a second rebellion. The two difficulties had been related in 1676, and they were still. Complicating the problem was the presence of the King's troops who had accompanied Colonel Jeffreys' Commission. They were short on supplies and pay, and Jeffreys himself was apprehensive lest they take up with dissatisfied colonists and raise hell all over again.[2] According to another view, the King's soldiers were no help at all to Virginians, since half had died owing to rough treatment and an inability to adjust to colonial duty. Between Indians, on the one hand, and discontented colonists, on the other, to say nothing of hungry redcoats and a Royal Commission in their midst, Virginians found the years immediately following Bacon's Rebellion far from happy or conducive to a settled order of things.[3]

The King and ministry at home believed that the Virginia assembly had been responsible for Bacon's Rebellion. Earlier Bacon had charged that the assembly under Berkeley's thumb was oppressive and uncontrollable. Even Sir William admitted that the assembly was at fault in the eyes of a good many Virginians.[4] Maybe more serious to the Crown than even rebellion was the loss of tobacco customs, a revenue which had increased each year with an increase in the tobacco crop. The amount doubtless reached well over £100,000 at this time, but while hunter and hunted stalked and skirmished in the summer of 1676, few Virginians had time to raise tobacco, and the exchequer took

1. Coventry Papers, Add. Mss., 25120, f. 140, B.M.
2. Jeffreys[?] to Sir Joseph Williamson, June 8, 1678, *Va. Mag. of Hist.*, 5 (1897), 50–53.
3. Coventry Papers, Add. Mss., 25120, f. 136.
4. John C. Rainbolt, "The Consequences of Bacon's Rebellion: Some Suggestions" (unpubl. paper read at the annual meeting of the Southern Historical Association, Nov. 9, 1967), p. 24.

a beating. This, too, was blamed on the assembly. On top of a loss in revenue was the actual expense of the Commission and troops sent to Virginia, which cost the King plenty, losses all told which Charles could little afford at a time when he was depending upon secret subsidies from Louis XIV, paid to keep him from calling Parliament, which was Whiggish and opposed to James and to France.[5]

The course of events for the next few years was dotted with incidents prejudicial to the Virginia assembly, whose wings King Charles fully determined to clip. The campaign began during Colonel Jeffreys' short reign when he fired Philip Ludwell, one of Berkeley's faction, and several others from the council on orders from the Privy Council. Ludwell, a brother of Thomas, the agent, had repeatedly insulted the governor and Commissioners, who tried and convicted him of scandalous insubordination. Ludwell's impertinence and the notorious career of the rebel Bacon persuaded the King to extend the governor's power to suspend members of the council at any time. Besides a purge of the upper house, Jeffreys' regime attacked the burgesses, too, and stripped clerk Robert Beverley, another Berkeley favorite, of all his offices. In defense of the burgesses' rights, Beverly had refused to surrender the lower house's records to the Commission and paid hard for his stubbornness. Well begun under Colonel Jeffreys, the struggle for control of the government continued in the 1680's under the two royal governors, Culpeper and Effingham, who vigorously attempted to bring Virginia under the thumb of the Crown.[6]

The King had all he could do to get Lord Culpeper aboard ship and headed for Virginia. During the first two weeks of December 1679 Charles sent six orders to the new governor for embarking and finally threatened to appoint someone in his place if he did not immediately sail for America. The *Oxford* frigate had waited around so long for him in the Thames that the King ordered the charge for pilotage deducted from the governor's salary, which, by the way, Culpeper had persuaded the King to increase to £2,000 plus house rent.[7]

The year after the Privy Council attempted to impose Poynings's Law upon Jamaicans, it sent similar orders with Culpeper for Virginia.

5. Stock, ed., *Proceedings and Debates*, I, 412, 414; Adm 1/5138, p. 516; Adm 1/3547, p. 643, P.R.O.; *CSPCol.*, *1675–1676*, #1121; David Ogg, *England in the Reign of Charles* II (2 vols., London, 1934, reprinted 1963), II, 539.

6. *CSPCol.*, *1677–1680*, #453, #821; *Va. Mag. of Hist.*, 22 (1914), 365; 23 (1915), 152; 24 (1916), 77–79; 18 (1910), 6–20; Hartwell, *et. al.*, *The Present State of Virginia*, pp. 24–25; Wertenbaker, *Virginia Under the Stuarts*, pp. 213–14, 216, 219.

7. Adm 1/5139, pp. 186–203; C.O. 389/9, p. 18; Abstract of Commissions, etc., Add. Mss., 30372, f. 24b; Hartwell, *et. al.*, *The Present State of Virginia*, pp. 32–33.

These instructions explicitly directed the governor to call the assembly only when the King permitted. He might then present to it for approval only laws already drafted by the King and Council, laws which he and the Virginia council had suggested to the King in the first place. Once in Virginia, Culpeper surprisingly found little difficulty in persuading the assembly to enact the three laws he brought with him from the King. Actually two were beneficial, an act for naturalizing newcomers and a pardon for the residue of Bacon's rebels. But the third demanded a permanent revenue for the King's use in support of the government, that is, a grant to the Crown forever of two shillings on every hogshead of tobacco exported from the colony.[8] Why Virginia's response to Poynings's Law was so half-hearted is not altogether clear. Jamaica had adamantly opposed the new encroachment on the basis of Englishmen's rights, but the Virginia assembly, probably owing to Culpeper's bribes and pointed threats about quitrents and arrears, reluctantly gave in to the Crown. That the two-shilling tax was what the legislature had granted annually for some time anyway may have had something to do with its voting the money permanently. Luckily for Virginians the King did not push the arbitrary demand beyond the three laws. Distance made the procedure clumsy, and the Crown soon dropped it from the governor's instructions.[9] But the attempt would not have been made at all in either Jamaica or Virginia had it not been for Bacon's Rebellion, for which the government believed the assembly was to blame. At a meeting of the Privy Council in May of 1679 Shaftesbury, back in the whirl of things for a short time, argued that imposing laws upon Jamaicans would "drive away the Planters who claimed the rights of Englishmen and would not be governed as the Irish. . . ." But Shaftesbury stood almost alone on the issue, and a majority of the Council answered that it would be better to hamstring the legislature and lose a few planters than to give in to their independence and lose the lot of them. After all, the Council concluded, "the Rebellion of Virginia was occasioned by the Excessive power of the Assembly." [10]

This kind of thinking set the pattern for the regulation of colonies for the next few years. Already determined in the 1670's to restrict further the governments and trade of the colonies, King, Council, and the Lords of Trade saw Bacon's Rebellion and the assembly's recent arrogance toward the Royal Commission as overwhelming evidence

8. *Va. Mag. of Hist.*, 24 (1916), 78–80; Labaree, ed., *Royal Instructions*, I, 125; *CSPCol., 1677–1680*, #917; Culpeper to Blathwayt, July 1680, BPCol. Wmsbg., v. XVII.

9. Wesley Frank Craven, *The Colonies in Transition, 1660–1713* (New York, 1968), pp. 152–54; Wertenbaker, *Virginia Under the Stuarts*, pp. 229–31.

10. Blathwayt to Earl of Carlisle, May 31, 1679, BPCol. Wmsbg., v. XXXII.

that colonial legislatures with real power led to no good. Although the King gave up the plan to impose directly his will upon the two colonies according to Poynings's Law, the attempts in 1678 and 1679 were clear indications that Charles II and the Privy Council believed they could do what they pleased with colonial legislatures. Some Virginians, and maybe even the King, may have remembered that, had the charter of 1675 become effective, it would have protected the Virginia assembly from this kind of dictation. With no guarantee but a weak charter which emphasized their dependence upon the King, Virginians were vulnerable to all kinds of "mutacons," and there were more to come.

Tobacco

The other severe problem which all Virginians constantly faced was the colony's great dependence upon tobacco, whose price was disastrously low and production great. Culpeper, of course, was not the cause of the difficulty, but he certainly aggravated it, which provoked more unrest. Sir William Berkeley, in his many years as governor, had pled repeatedly the planters' side against the Navigation Acts and favored a cessation in planting to improve the price of tobacco. At the same time he had encouraged a diversification of their economy in order to get Virginians out from under the burdens of a single crop. But the governors who followed Berkeley lacked his devotion to what he believed in his own way was the well-being of Virginia. For he was a Virginian whether he was in Jamestown or London. Culpeper was an Englishman, although more frequently in London than Jamestown.

Culpeper had arrived in Virginia at a bad time. The year before tobacco was such a "drugg" that the Virginia crop matched what the colony had produced in the preceding three years. Ten thousand hogsheads were left behind when the tobacco fleet departed, and what is more, the very seasonable weather promised a bumper crop in 1680, double what was produced the year before. Culpeper encouraged large crops from the beginning in order to increase the customs. If only a vent could be found for this year's crop, he wrote, and a sufficient number of ships to fetch it, the King might clear £200,000 in revenue. Virginians did their part; it was up to the Commissioners of Customs and the Lords of Trade to "make it a Commodity." [11]

Most Virginians looked at the problem a little differently. By June

11. Baltimore to Barnaby Dunck, Nov. 24, 1679, *Calvert Papers,* No. I, Fund-Publication, No. 28, Maryland Historical Society (Baltimore, 1889), p. 319; Culpeper to Blathwayt, June 15, 1680, BPCol. Wmsbg., v. XVII.

of Culpeper's first year, the assembly was hot after him to help cut production, and the governor was at a loss how to answer it. The assembly took the question further and the next year petitioned the King directly. If there is not a remedy soon to bring up the price, they told His Majesty, they did not see how they could subsist much longer. The only way open to them, with the help of Maryland and Carolina, was to stop growing tobacco for a while so that the price might improve. (Virginians had often complained that overproduction occurred because Maryland and other places grew too much tobacco.) Since Governor Culpeper was about to leave for England on one of his periodic visits, the assembly entrusted its petition to him for presentation to Charles with the hope that he would order a cessation.[12]

Culpeper's efforts in behalf of the assembly were not aggressive. Some time later he met with the Lords of Trade, who called in also some expert witnesses, merchants and sea captains, for an inquiry into the low state of Virginia. It followed that the Lords of Trade had little interest in cutting production, and Culpeper did not press them, although one of the leading merchants trading to Virginia suggested that the only means he knew to raise tobacco prices was to raise less tobacco. There was a good deal of talk about the poverty of the people and the "great apprehension of a rising among the servants" owing to their many needs, particularly a lack of clothing, and even that "they may plunder the storehouses and ships." The Lords' sole response to this alarming news was to recommend immediately that the two companies of redcoats, already in Virginia, "be continued and well paid." [13]

What a good many people feared might happen did so in early May 1682. Again, as in Bacon's Rebellion, an accumulation of grievances and frustrations, uncertainty and poverty, forced otherwise peaceful planters to overt action, not against their government this time, but against the very crop which seemed to be their undoing. Although there were a number of grievances, ranging from an attempt to collect quitrents [14] to Culpeper's innovations against their government, the tremendous burden of tobacco and an inability to interest their governor and the powers-that-be in England in a "cessation" of its planting were at the heart of the violence. And then, Lieutenant Governor Chicheley prorogued the very assembly which many had hoped would order a halt to planting. On May Day "a sick brain'd people uneasy

12. *CSPCol., 1681–1685*, #186.

13. *Ibid.*, #275, #277.

14. For the quitrent problem and Culpeper's role, see Nicholas Spencer to Blathwayt [?], James Citty, May 29, 1682, BPCol. Wmsbg., v. XVI; *CSPCol., 1681–1685*, #319.

under the low and mean price of Tobacco" danced from plantation to plantation cutting and pulling up plants. They began in Gloucester County but soon spread their activity to several others and would have spread it throughout the colony had the government not finally suppressed it. By the end of May they had destroyed between six and seven thousand hogsheads—some said ten thousand.[15]

Culpeper, of course, was in England when the riots occurred. The King hurried him back to Virginia, once he learned of the disturbance, and ordered him to keep the ship which carried him if the tobacco cutting turned into outright rebellion. The planters continued their "May sport" off and on during the summer, often working at night to avoid detection by Chicheley's militia. The King's two companies of foot soldiers, or what was left of them, were not much help, since their restlessness and "mutinous tempers," provoked by cuts in their pay and a strong desire to go home, rendered them more liability than advantage in times of crisis. Culpeper arrived in Virginia late in December or early January, despite the King's order to sail on August 1 preceding. "I shall crowde with all the sayle I can make," he wrote, not in August but in October.[16]

Ironically Culpeper brought with him instructions to permit a cessation of planting if circumstances dictated. He never divulged these to Virginians, one reason being that the price soon improved, no doubt because of the plant cutting. He found that Sir Henry Chicheley had imprisoned a number of alleged plant cutters including Robert Beverley, darling of the House of Burgesses, who had been a thorn in the sides of the King's governors since Berkeley's departure. Several of the plant-cutting leaders Chicheley had either pardoned or let out on bail, among them the "greatest rogue of all." But despite strong rumors that Beverley was notorious in inciting the rioters, Culpeper could produce no certain evidence against him except "general Sauciness"; he was forced to give him up, not, however, without having him stripped again of all his offices. The governor was left holding a few common planters whom Chicheley's militia had captured. Compelled, he said, to make an example of them, he tried, convicted, and executed two for treason, basing his case with the council's consent on an old law of Elizabeth's time. A third, a nineteen-year-old, and "victim to the seduc-

15. Baltimore to Sec'y Jenkins, May 18, 1682, *Arch. of Md.*, V, 357–58; Baltimore to Blathwayt, Mar. 26, 1682, *ibid.*, 353; *ibid.*, 361–62; Spencer to Blathwayt, Middle Plantation, May 29, 1682; same to same, Aug. 12, 1682, BPCol. Wmsbg., v. XVI.

16. Spencer to Blathwayt, May 29, Aug. 12, 1682, *ibid.*; Nathaniel Bacon to Blathwayt, Aug. 26, 1682, *ibid.*, v. XIII; Culpeper to Blathwayt, Oct. 6, 1682, *ibid.*, v. XVII; Adm 1/5139, pp. 678, 682–83; *CSPCol., 1681–1685*, #613.

tions of others," he reprieved until he learned the King's pleasure. By May 1683 Culpeper had pardoned several himself through proclamation, "Beverley exccpted." Besides blaming Clerk Beverley, whom he could not prosecute, Culpeper found Chicheley largely at fault for his "weaknesses, or rather nothingnesses," in pardoning "the Lord knows who." But old Chicheley soon died, much to the governor's relief. A month later, and order restored, Culpeper was making plans to return to England "to propose certain things of great consequence." [17]

Governor Culpeper returned home once too often. After placing him under house arrest, the King commenced an "Inquisition" against him and seized his office, appointing Lord Howard of Effingham in his place. Even William Blathwayt had lost patience with Culpeper, for he had made a "HodgePodge" of his government. Virginia was in no better shape than when he arrived, hardly better than when Berkeley departed.[18]

Effingham, 1683–1685

Lord Thomas of Effingham, or maybe anyone, looked good to Virginians after almost three years of Culpeper. Lord Baltimore reported that the new governor was afforded "the best welcome the people of the Colony were able to give him," which may or may not tell us very much. But doubtless a good many colonists were happy to see him, even the council, who found the change a great satisfaction.[19] Effingham was a sophisticated Peer, knowledgeable of court ways in London, as was Culpeper, for that matter. Virginia really must have seemed a howling wilderness to one accustomed to polite society at home, for in comparison the colony was still "wild," a word frequently used by visitors to describe it. But the new governor found Virginians more agreeable than he had expected, at least at first.

At the time Effingham disembarked at Jamestown, Virginia had a population of between 70,000 and 80,000 people. Culpeper had estimated that of these 15,000 were servants and some 3,000 Negroes, a gain in the latter of about 1,000 over 1671. The remainder were free

17. Spencer to Blathwayt, Feb. 15, 1683, BPCol. Wmsbg., v. XVI; [?] to [?], May 9, 1683, *ibid.;* Culpeper to Lord Dartmouth, Mar. 18, 1683, H.M.C. 20: 11th Report, App. V, *Dartmouth*, I, 80–81; *CSPCol., 1681–1685*, #1258, #1269; *Va. Mag. of Hist.*, 3 (1896), 229.

18. Blathwayt to Thomas Lynch, July 18, 1683, and Mar. 3, 1684, BPCol. Wmsbg., v. XXIV; Blathwayt to Spencer, Sept. 8, 1683, *ibid.*, v. XVI; Blathwayt to Nathaniel Bacon, Sept. 8, 1683, *ibid.*, v. XIII; Sec'y Jenkins to Culpeper, Sept. 29, 1683, *CSPDom., 1683* (July–Sept.), p. 435.

19. Effingham to Blathwayt, Mar. 14, 1684, BPCol. Wmsbg., v. XIV; Baltimore to Blathwayt, Mar. 11, 1684, *ibid.*, v. XVIII.

men, women, and children. A newcomer to the Chesapeake region must have been struck first by three things: Virginia, in contrast to England, was "all one continued wood," the people were widely scattered, and they utilized, or failed to utilize, their land in a very wasteful manner. According to one shrewd observer, it was a place where "plenty makes poverty," for Virginians coveted vast pieces of land and spread themselves so thin that they could not possibly manage a hundredth part of what they owned. Somehow, though, they seemed to live at ease, yet scorned work and failed to improve what they had, leaving them "poor wth abundance." Virginia attracted few "schollars," and therefore each settler became himself half doctor, half lawyer, demonstrating a natural ability which certainly amused Englishmen. They were an "obliging, quick & subtile people" whose lack of books made them "read men ye more." If there was ignorance, there was also ingenuity among them; if there was "coveteousnesse," there was plenty of hospitality, although the latter often grew out of an unwillingness or inability to spend money. Inns and ordinaries were very expensive in Virginia, and a traveler avoided them if possible, which meant he presumptuously expected to lodge with strangers whose homes he came upon along the way. This "common impudence" had grown into such a custom that it made everyone seem liberal and generous.[20] Characteristics of the cavalier still obtained in Effingham's Virginia. The colonists' unwillingness to spend money did not impose upon the habit of playing cards all night and gambling away their pieces of eight. Strangers were struck with the military bearing of the council, whose members sat "officially in their boots and swords." [21]

Effingham soon learned that it was not enough to cut a good figure in Virginia. He had to convince the colonists that his standing at home was respected, too. Culpeper had been aware of this, and probably his frequent returns to London had something to do with keeping up the show. The King helped Effingham in this respect very early in the governor's Virginia career by sending him a man-of-war ketch which, besides adding to the look of things, doubtless helped prevent insurrection and discouraged pirates. It came in handy, too, in enforcing the Navigation Acts, particularly the Plantation Duty, which "not one in ten payeth," according to one of the council.[22] Culpeper had bleated about the need for a warship in Virginia waters for just these purposes,

20. *CSPCol., 1681–1685,* #320; J. Clayton to Dr. Borlase [?], James Citty, Apr. 24, 1684, Sloane Mss., 1008, f. 335, B.M.

21. Durand of Dauphiné, *A Frenchman in Virginia Being the Memoirs of a Huguenot Refugee in 1686,* trans. and ed. by Fairfax Harrison (Richmond, Va., 1923), pp. 51–52.

22. Nathaniel Bacon to Blathwayt, Aug. 26, 1682, BPCol. Wmsbg., v. XIII.

but he had not been successful and was forced to get along with a "little vessel." Then on top of this, Effingham's wife had her pick of a frigate or "so good a merchant man" for her passage to Virginia. The governor thought this splendid and sent Blathwayt his "harty thanks." After all, he wrote, "one is esteamed here according as they jud[ge] their Interest is there." Effingham's interest "there" was sufficient for the King to allow him also 500 tons of freight for moving house and a new home built in Virginia.[23]

With matters of prestige settled, Effingham turned to the business of governing. Although he had left England before Culpeper settled affairs with the King, it was not long before he could announce that Charles and the former governor had come to a compromise over the Southern Grant, relieving Virginians of the burden of paying Culpeper anything out of their taxes or the quitrents, which the King had graciously assumed and assigned to support of their government. But this was about the limit of the King's leniency toward Virginia; the assumption of Culpeper's grant and the quitrents bound Virginians closer to the Crown, for the colonists learned that the King was a jealous landlord. Quitrents were *payable* and, wherever possible, Effingham collected them.[24]

After Bacon's Rebellion Robert Beverley became a symbol of the burgesses', and often the whole assembly's, independence and resistance to the Crown's attack upon their authority. Beverley had been a strong member of Berkeley's Green Spring faction, and the assembly repeatedly elected him its clerk. For his defiance of Colonel Jeffreys' Royal Commission in refusing to turn over the assembly's records, the King had issued strict orders to exclude him from any place in the government; but Culpeper had found it would be a drastic mistake to do so after the burgesses and council separately and unanimously elected him clerk in 1681. Despite his orders, Culpeper accepted the election, claiming he had really "gained a point to the Crown," for in consenting he encroached upon the assembly's right exclusively to choose their own. Doubtless Culpeper believed his action left the door open for further expansion of the governor's power, next time maybe a veto. Following the tobacco riots Culpeper again stripped Beverley of his offices, but between the governor's departure from Virginia and Effingham's arrival in February 1684, the burgesses rewarded their former clerk and several others with lavish presents. The council had

23. Adm 1/5139, p. 870; Effingham to Blathwayt, Apr. 23, July 12, and Nov. 25, 1684, BPCol. Wmsbg., v. XIV; Add. Mss., 30372, f. 24b.

24. Spencer to Blathwayt, Feb. 23, 1684, BPCol. Wmsbg., v. XVI; Effingham to Blathwayt, Feb. 13 and 14, 1684, *ibid.;* same to same, Feb. 24, 1683, *ibid.*, v. XIII.

balked at the idea but finally conceded after the assembly argued "into the night." But old Chicheley, the lieutenant governor, a few days later vetoed the whole business, which further angered the burgesses. The Beverley affair caused lots of talk and took a good deal of time, but it brought up the vital question in Virginians' minds as to just whose man the clerk was and by what right he held his office. The question was not settled at the moment, but like other matters of power, this one, too, would end in the King's pocket, for as Charles's reign drew to a close, prerogative power increased in both realm and dominions, and under James it was extended even more.[25]

A royal governor's official ties to the King and Council were his commission and instructions. The latter could be public or private as the King wished. Public instructions usually were exposed for all to see, but the private often remained secret until they were absolutely necessary for the governor to win the King's point against a recalcitrant assembly. In their attempt to centralize colonial control the Privy Council and the Lords of Trade demanded periodic transmission of colony laws for inspection. Effingham arrived in 1684 with instructions to inspect and revise the laws of Virginia with the help of the council; if he found anything either in matter or in style which he thought ought to be "altered or retrenched," he should send to the King and the Lords of Trade a complete body of the laws and his suggestions for change. In the spring of 1684 the King altered these instructions by explicitly ordering Effingham not to consult the assembly about the revisions. The governor easily fell in with the plan to exclude the legislature, remarking that it would be troublesome to include it, for if done, the laws certainly would not be "so advantageous to ye Government as otherwise. . . ." [26] It would seem that discrimination against the assembly had become a set part of colonial policy. Although no one would accuse the King and Council and other policymakers of outright consistency, it is easy to conclude that a government in England which favored such an exclusive system of lawmaking did well to quash when it did the Virginia charter of 1675. For had that gone into effect, the course of Virginia history might have been different. The guarantee of an assembly and its functions as explained in the charter would have left little room for the "mutacons" of a Culpeper or an Effingham.

25. *CSPCol., 1681–1685*, #319, #1258, #1465, #1476; Letters between Blathwayt and Spencer, Feb. 23 and July 28, 1684, BPCol. Wmsbg., v. XVI; Labaree, ed., *Royal Instructions,* I, 169.

26. *Ibid.,* 165–66; Spencer to Lords of Trade, May 13, 1682, BPCol. Wmsbg., v. XVI; Blathwayt to Effingham, Apr. 3, 1684, *ibid.,* v. XIV; Effingham to Blathwayt, Aug. 28, 1684, *ibid.*

Lord Howard had other innovations up his sleeve, and instructions to back them up. In the name of efficiency and expediency, he hoped that he and the council together might levy small taxes against the people in order to save the expense of calling the whole assembly, for too frequent sessions had supposedly been a cause of Bacon's Rebellion. Berkeley had got away with the expedient practice in the early 1660's, if only for three years, but the burgesses had never liked it, and they were successfully adamant now against the governor's attempt in 1684 to do them out of a "say" in securing revenue.[27]

Another point of conflict was the appellate jurisdiction of the assembly at large. For many years this body had been the last court of appeal in Virginia and a protection, the burgesses said, against inadequate justice. Earlier Culpeper had been ordered to do away with the assembly's role in judicial procedures, which meant that a case tried in a lower court, after an appeal to the General Court (governor and council), could go then only to the King in Council 3,000 miles away, an innovation which by-passed the burgesses and outraged a good many people. But Culpeper had never pushed the reform, since he found it not politic at the time; given the need of a revenue bill, he was wise enough not to insist on both. It was left for Effingham to drive home the King's demand, and although the burgesses stood hard against the council's levying small taxes, they could never reverse the King's decision to circumvent the assembly and hear appeals in England directly from the governor and council in Virginia.[28]

The loss of appeals to the assembly was bad enough. Close on its heels came the King's decision to exercise the royal veto over Virginia laws in a much more determined manner than ever before and often by proclamation without so much as a fare-thee-well to the assembly. This was very cavalier treatment of a lawmaking body, and in May of that year the burgesses concluded that the assembly ought to petition the King for redress of these several grievances. The whole assembly debated for some time the burgesses' suggestion, but Effingham resisted it, believing that what they were asking was an insult to the Crown and prerogative. So the burgesses decided to go it alone and send a petition from their house directly to the King after the council withdrew its support owing to the governor's disapproval.

The burgesses' Address to the King in 1684 was a notable document.

27. Wertenbaker, *Virginia Under the Stuarts*, pp. 244–45.

28. Burgesses' Address to the King, May 22, 1684, McIlwaine, ed., *Journals of the House of Burgesses . . . 1659/60–1693*, pp. 228–30; Hartwell, *et. al.*, *The Present State of Virginia*, pp. 26–28; Wertenbaker, *Virginia Under the Stuarts*, pp. 241–42.

In it one finds a number of statements which clearly explain how these people felt about themselves as members of a colonial legislature. It indicates, too, why Virginians as colonists believed they ought to possess legal guarantees like the people in England, particularly respecting justice and lawmaking. One is constantly reminded that the charter of 1675, if it had not settled all of these issues, would have settled a number of them and given the colony something to stand upon as it tried to protect itself from the encroachment of the prerogative in an expanding empire. As for the appeal of cases, the King's command to ignore the assembly was "Grievous and Ruinous," the burgesses complained. It laid all matter of obstacles in the way of justice, owing to the great difficulties a colonist would meet in attempting to present the intricate facts of his case in England, to say nothing of the long delays and prohibitive costs. This was all the more grievous since appeals heretofore had met with "General Satisfaction" when considered by the assembly where governor, council, and burgesses sat as a supreme court. Probably the King ordered a change in the judicial procedure because the burgesses earlier had tried to cut down the council's role in the Virginia court of last appeal. For some time members of the lower house had complained that council members participated twice in court decisions, once with the governor as the General Court, and again as members of the assembly. Doubtless the burgesses would have liked to make final decisions alone and suggested they do so. But the King determined to settle the conflict by eliminating the burgesses' role altogether in court procedure, arguing that it was contrary to English practices.[29]

The second grievance covered by the burgesses' petition touched the royal veto. It clearly explained the equation which represented colonists in America and subjects in the realm, or more specifically in this instance, the Virginia government and corporations in England. But the burgesses led up to the demand of equal treatment by first describing in colorful language the sad lot of English subjects in America, primarily those in Virginia. Very openly they described for the King several facts of life in this "Melancholy part of the world." They pointedly reminded him that his income was double theirs from the tobacco their labor produced; that they and their ancestors, for their own livelihood, for the enlargement of his dominions, and the "advancement of his revenue," had left their native soil, risking their lives, to inhabit a barbarous country devoid of His Majesty's presence. Moreover, they were subject to the "Incursions Inroads, Rapines, Cruell Murthers, and

29. McIlwaine, ed., *Journals*, pp. 228–30; Hartwell, *et. al.*, *The Present State of Virginia*, pp. 26–28.

depredations, of a skulking Cruell, inhumane Barbarous Enemie," and they did all this with loyal and obedient hearts. But despite these prejudicial conditions surrounding colonists in America, the burgesses complained, they did not participate in as much of his royal grace as the King extended to most of the "Lesser, and most inconsiderable Corporations" within the realm. For such corporations had authority to enact laws for themselves, and the King had not been pleased to repeal or make them void. Virginians had enjoyed this grace from His Majesty until very recently when suddenly he vetoed several acts and statutes by proclamation in England. What is more, this was done without consulting the Virginia assembly, a practice not only contrary to "Ancient usage" but a violation of one of their laws already "printed by Allowance in *England.*" The burgesses asked the King to permit their laws in the future to remain in force until the assembly repealed them, or at least until the King received the "Grounds & Reasons" for their making them in the first place.[30]

According to the burgesses, colonists in America were as good as the people who stayed at home in England and without question ought to enjoy with them equal rights and privileges. Again this was a statement of belief in equality in the empire, something an English subject ought to enjoy regardless of where he lived. Denied a charter which would have guaranteed this equality, the burgesses hoped to secure it by appeal to the rights of Englishmen inherent in dependence upon, and allegiance to, the Crown. What the burgesses did not understand was that at the very time they laid their ideas before the King, corporation charters in England *and* the colonies were being subjected to close scrutiny and attack; several already had been annulled by the Crown and more challenged. Charles's increasing interest in lumping authority took long spurts in reaction to the republican arrogance of the Exclusion Crisis, and it was not long before the corporation of the City of London and several others were dissolved, to say nothing of the Massachusetts Bay Company in America. The burgesses were appealing to a conception of empire which did not exist, and, in fact, never really had existed, except maybe in the minds of colonists who did the work in America and a handful of Whig conspirators who were either dead or lately out of fashion.

The burgesses rounded off their petition with a complaint against quitrents, prefacing it with another description of their hardships owing to the low price of tobacco and their bloody troubles with the Indians. They asked that the proceeds from quitrents be applied to defense against the Indians and the colony's other public expenses rather than

30. McIlwaine, ed., *Journals,* pp. 229–30.

to uses apart from the welfare of Virginia. Not long afterward the King agreed to apply quitrents to the support of the colony, but trouble began all over again in 1686 when the governor demanded them in specie. When this scheme was finally beaten down, Virginians had to settle for double the accustomed rate (1d. per pound) in tobacco. By this time Charles II was dead, and it was James II who clinched the higher rate when he repealed by proclamation an earlier law which had established the more favorable ratio between tobacco and money.[31]

High-handed acts of the Crown in revoking old laws were just what the burgesses were petitioning against. They might better have saved their energy. While the lower house was completing the draft of the Address, word of it leaked to the governor, who promptly sent for the burgesses to come before him. Realizing full well that he summoned them only to dissolve their house, they hurriedly completed the document, signed it, and ordered Thomas Milner, their clerk, and William Sherwood, a member, to speed it on its way to Whitehall for presentation to the King. Charles II neither saw nor heard the petition; it bounced around several offices in London before coming to rest for a time with the Lords of Trade, who objected strongly to its content and "manner of presenting" and announced it unfit for the King's ears. William Blathwayt returned the petition to Governor Effingham along with the Lords' commendation for his having refused to transmit it to the King. To complete the humiliation of the House of Burgesses, the governor summoned its members and gave them a severe dressing down for what they had done. Not satisfied, Effingham fired Milner, the clerk who had signed the petition, and put another in his place, thus asserting the Crown's right to appoint clerks of the assembly. As for Sherwood, the governor peremptorily revoked his license to practice law in Virginia. In the first year of his reign, James II included in his instructions a second commendation of Lord Effingham's handling of the matter.[32]

Colonists, it seems, could not complain about the prerogative. Grievances were entertained by the King only when power was abused, that is, by others. Legitimate power, or the King's prerogative, expanded or exaggerated under Charles, could not be faulted even if it was arbitrary. When Charles City County people had explained to the Royal Commission the grievances which helped to cause Bacon's

31. *Ibid.*, p. 230; Wertenbaker, *Virginia Under the Stuarts*, pp. 245–46.

32. Blathwayt to Effingham, Dec. 9, 1684, BPCol. Wmsbg., v. XIV; Effingham to Blathwayt, Mar. 20, 1685, *ibid.*; *CSPCol., 1681–1685*, #1994; Hartwell, *et. al., The Present State of Virginia*, pp. 30–32, 42; Labaree, ed., *Royal Instructions*, I, 118; Wertenbaker, *Virginia Under the Stuarts*, pp. 242–43.

Rebellion, those which complained about the Plantation Duty were called mutinous and treasonable, for the Navigation Acts were "sacred" and an inherent part of Crown policy. The burgesses' petition, because it did not bear the governor's blessing, but more important, because it questioned the King's prerogative, was offensive and impertinent and was never presented. The early Virginia historians put it succinctly: "it appears plainly how fast the Door is shut against the House of Burgesses . . . ." [33] The Virginia assembly had little protection against a determined royal policy.

At the time the Virginia burgesses petitioned the King, they had no idea what was going on in the minds of Charles II and the ministry respecting colonial policy and colony charters, corporate and proprietary. Even Governor Effingham was in the dark about far-reaching changes which were already taking shape during the first year of his governorship. William Blathwayt explained a good deal to him in December of 1684 in answer to some questions about a boundary squabble between Virginia and Maryland. Effingham learned that the Potomac dispute was the least of Baltimore's worries, that the King was determined to make Maryland a royal colony, and if the proprietor refused to forfeit his government, the Crown would go to court to secure it. Moreover, Maryland was only one of many colonies whose original foundations were about to crumble; the King had already vacated the Massachusetts and Bermuda charters and was ready to combine parts of New England under one government. The Duke of York and William Penn had consented to surrender their governments to the Crown, and the proprietors of the Carolinas would soon fall into line. These measures, Blathwayt seemed to crow, "will bring about that Necessary union of all the English colonies in America which will make the King great & Extend his real Empire in those parts." [34]

Governor Effingham, as much a King's man as Blathwayt, quickly fell into the swing of things. In no time he made it known in London that if the Crown seized Maryland as a royal colony, he hoped the King would annex it to Virginia under him. His reasons for urging the consolidation did not speak very well for the King's new "real Empire" in America. Although he received a splendid salary (£2,000 per annum), he found Virginia the least profitable of any of the colonies, the "perquisites being very Inconsiderable." What is more, there was

---

33. Hartwell, *et. al., The Present State of Virginia,* p. 32.

34. See a series of letters between Effingham and Blathwayt in 1684 and 1685, BPCol. Wmsbg., v. XIV, particularly Blathwayt to Effingham, Dec. 9, 1684. Blathwayt sought from Effingham evidence that might be used in condemning both the Maryland and the Carolina charters. *Ibid.* See also C.O. 1/57/81.

little advantage in the way of trade which was spread out all over the lot; therefore, a governor who lived as he ought for honor of the King found very "little in ye bag at the years end." (Virginians would have agreed.) Effingham warmly solicited Blathwayt's assistance in effecting the surrender of Maryland to Virginia.[35]

With these changes going on at home, no wonder the Lords of Trade leaped to protect the King from the burgesses' challenge. At that moment colonial policy took a decided turn. The tendency toward centralization of authority over government and trade, which dated from the early 1670's, gathered sudden momentum; in 1684 it came to a resolution which affected every colony in America. Charles II's death early the next year failed to slow the process; instead, with James on the throne, it was accelerated. In the colonies its chief characteristic was arbitrary government with little respect for assemblies. Already Virginians had felt its force and, like other colonies where it was less subtle, had several reasons to suspect it.

Despite Virginians' faith in the aborted charter of 1675, had it survived it would have afforded few guarantees for them in the 1680's. Both Charles and James demonstrated little respect for chartered rights in either England or America. The only protection Virginians could muster against the will of the Crown was the political skill of the House of Burgesses. And although politically adept, the burgesses were faced with a determined royal governor who was backed by the prerogative. The conflict grew increasingly intense as the Crown of England dictated a colonial policy based primarily upon dependence and profit, a policy often contrary to the rights of Englishmen and colonial self-interest as Virginians had come to know them.

35. Effingham to Blathwayt, Mar. 20, 1685, BPCol. Wmsbg., v. XIV.

5 Maryland: Colonists' Rights and Proprietary Power

Maryland and Virginia had a lot more in common than a sharing of Chesapeake Bay and the Potomac River. Dependence upon tobacco was as much a part of one's existence as the other's, and with tobacco went all the difficulties which accompanied a staple crop. For Maryland's tobacco brought no better price in London than Virginia's; settlers of both colonies were familiar with poverty when the price plummeted under the burden of their combined harvests. Marylanders may well have fared even worse, for while both colonies paid customs to the King and supported their governments out of duties against exports, Lord Baltimore demanded further his due from every hogshead of tobacco which left the province.

Maryland, with some 20,000 inhabitants in the 1670's, was much smaller than Virginia in both population and square miles. But like Virginians the planters had spread out their settlement in order to live on the land and take advantage of the splendid waterways. Baltimore was embarrassed to call any of his settlements towns, let alone cities, but St. Mary's, the provincial capital, came closest in the English sense of the word. Most shipping resorted there first before visiting the planters' wharves, where the real business of the colony was transacted. St. Mary's was on the river of the same name which flowed south into the Potomac a few miles upstream from where the larger river joined Chesapeake Bay. In 1678 it measured about five miles along the river but spread back from the shore no more than a mile. All told, there were about thirty houses, none close together, and "very meane and Little" except for the proprietor's home and the few public buildings where the assembly and courts met.[1]

Convenient as scattered living may have been for raising and loading tobacco, it inhibited the growth of social institutions, such as schools and churches. Cecilius Calvert, second Lord Baltimore, kept a schoolmaster for his own children, but the remoteness of plantations discouraged the establishment of regular instruction which the province badly needed. Counties would never be subdivided into parishes or precincts, Baltimore commented, until it pleased God to increase the number of settlers, which in turn would force them to change their trading habits and live together in towns.

Besides education, religion suffered, too; at least Protestant churches suffered from the thinness of the people.[2] But the deplorable condition of religion, according to the Reverend John Yeo, was caused more by a lack of an established ministry than the manner which people settled the land. Yeo's reports home about the dearth of Anglican priests— he found only three in 1676 who conformed to the discipline of the Church of England—painted Maryland in very sorry terms. When the Bishop of London and the Lords of Trade queried the proprietor about the state of religion, he argued the blessings of toleration and claimed it the basis of the colonists' liberty, peace, and prosperity. But toleration did not help the thousands of unchurched people in Maryland who were not Catholic. The Bishop of London came up with the improbable estimate that Catholics numbered only one in a hundred, and that the remainder lived dissolute lives for want of a settled church.[3]

A problem in Maryland, not shared with Virginia, was a continuing conflict between Protestant and Catholic. And although the issue was

1. W. H. Browne, *et. al.*, eds., *Archives of Maryland* (65 vols., Baltimore, 1883–1952), V, 266–67.

2. Charles Calvert to Baltimore, June 2, 1673, *Calvert Papers*, No. I, Fund-Public., #28, Maryland Hist. Soc., 286; *Arch. of Md.*, V, 267.

3. *Ibid.*, 130–34, 260–69; C.O. 324/4, p. 48; *CSPCol.*, 1675–1676, #1105; *ibid.*, 1677–1680, #340, #348, #349; *ibid.*, 1681–1685, #252, #256.

often exaggerated, it was an enduring difficulty which made impossible a harmonious working arrangement between a government predominantly Catholic and a Protestant majority of settlers.[4] Baltimore did little if anything to encourage Protestants except to defend the colony's religious toleration. What he did do was to weight his government heavily with Catholics, way out of proportion to their number in the total population. Patronage followed religious lines, as did the granting of land, two very sore points with the local Protestant gentry. Moreover, nepotism gave the government not just a Catholic but a Calvert identity. Fat jobs went to the proprietor's favorites, many of them his relatives. For the most part Protestants were out of the running while fees and perquisites were soaked up by the few. As much for the money as the principle, the Protestants complained, and the Lords of Trade, fearing that Catholics would wholly dominate the proprietor's council and other official spots, at one time directed him to redress the balance and cease altogether his partiality to Papists. In the 1670's and 1680's Maryland's government had all the earmarks of an oligarchy with the proprietor's relations and coreligionists calling the turn.[5]

Three years after the Lords of Trade requested answers to inquiries about Maryland, Lord Baltimore furnished an account. It may be that he deliberately delayed his reply, for when he wrote in March 1678, he could report that Maryland was "at present in great peace and Quiett." Had he answered the request a couple of years earlier, he would have found it necessary to mention the Indian wars, Bacon's Rebellion next door, certainly the "Affair of the Clifts," and several other serious outbursts which his government luckily suppressed. Had the proprietor delayed his answer a little longer, say two or three years, he might have agreed, although reluctantly, with Governor Culpeper of Virginia that Maryland was then "in torment, and not only troubled with our disease, poverty, but in very great danger of falling in pieces." Probably Baltimore picked his time, but he had to look sharp to find it, for

4. For an exaggerated view of Catholic domination in Maryland and the determination of the proprietor to turn over the colony to the Pope, see *To the Parliament of England, the CASE of the Poor English Protestants in Mary-Land . . .* , n.p., n.d., John Carter Brown Library.

5. On the court which tried Josias Fendall, a chronic dissident, in 1681, two Calverts sat, one chancellor of the colony and president of the court, the other the colony's secretary; another judge was Lady Baltimore's brother, and still another had married the proprietor's stepdaughter, *Arch. of Md.*, V, 312; *CSPCol., 1681–1685*, #256. For descriptions of the oligarchy, see C. M. Andrews, *Colonial Period*, II, particularly ch. IX and note on pp. 376–78. See also Donnell M. Owings, *His Lordship's Patronage: Offices of Profit in Colonial Maryland* (Baltimore, 1953), *passim;* and Michael G. Kammen, "The Causes of the Maryland Revolution of 1689," *Maryland Hist. Mag.* (Dec. 1960), pp. 293–333.

the history of Maryland after the Restoration of Charles II—as well as before—can best be described as turbulent.[6]

In the same report home Culpeper gratuitously suggested that the trouble in Maryland was either that "Old Lord Baltimore's politic maxims are not pursued or that they are unsuited to this age." (The latter remark came with ill grace from a royal governor who was also a proprietor of a large part of Virginia and whose claims derived from royal patents loaded with medieval trappings and outmoded perquisites.) [7] By the 1670's a large number of Marylanders would have agreed that Baltimore's political ideas were indeed "unsuited to this age." They might, if pushed, have gone a bit further and insisted that the proprietor's whole conception of society in several essential parts was unsuited to English colonization in the New World.

Baltimore's "politic maxims" respecting Maryland stemmed from the first Lord's charter given to him by Charles I in 1632. Like several proprietary charters to follow, it gave the proprietor "free, full, and absolute power," patterned after that of the Bishop of Durham in England, to whom the Crown had given royal powers thought necessary in medieval times to protect the northern border of the nation from the warlike Scots. By the seventeenth century the actual authority, but not the form of the grant, had disappeared from contemporary patents in England; nevertheless, George Calvert succeeded in persuading the King to include not just the form but the authority, too, in the charter for Maryland. It allowed him the full extent of power the Bishop had ever enjoyed at Durham, likening Baltimore's wilderness circumstances in the New World to those of medieval bishops' on the borders, a comparison not very flattering to the Scots.

The Calverts were jealous of their roles as proprietary lords. They insisted upon implementing their power, giving it substance in such demands as oaths of fidelity, courts in their name, and a number of other rights and powers which even the King lacked in England, setting Maryland apart from corporate colonies like Massachusetts and Rhode Island and even a royal colony like Virginia.[8] As in other private colonies, the proprietor enjoyed the right, through his governor and council, to initiate all legislation, leaving the assembly only an "aye" or "nay" to bills from above, a restriction which led to sharp discontent and before long gradual change.

6. *Arch. of Md.*, V, 267; *CSPCol.*, 1681–1685, #319.
7. *Ibid.*
8. See Baltimore's charter in Samuel Lucas, ed., *Charters of the Old English Colonies in America* (London, 1850), pp. 88–97. See also Baltimore's comments upon his charter and rights, *Arch. of Md.*, I, 262–66.

Complicating the anachronism of the proprietor's absolute power in Maryland were other clauses in the charter which held out to colonists the rights of Englishmen and protection against laws which were repugnant to those of England. Doubtless Englishmen's rights were not as numerous or precise to seventeenth-century colonists as they were a hundred years later when their descendants revolted to preserve them, but they did have clear meaning for their time. They revolved around colonists' property rights and certain court procedures for their protection such as trial by jury; they included, too, a share in lawmaking and particularly the right not to be taxed without their consent through some system of representation. Like all Englishmen, colonists expected that governments, even proprietary governments, were limited by law against abuse of authority.[9] But smack in the middle of the same charter which supposedly guaranteed them these rights was a grant of absolute authority to the proprietor, a power he not only exercised but, they complained, he sometimes used cavalierly. Indeed, the charter was ambiguous; the two grants of power were irreconcilable. As it turned out, a guarantee of the rights of Englishmen proved a weak reed against the authority of a proprietor, and the history of early Maryland hinged on a continuing clash between these two charter claims. The proprietor emphasized his sovereign power, the colonists Englishmen's rights, and the difference was never resolved in the seventeenth century. When colonists' claims proved insufficient to resist the proprietor's authority, like Virginians they attempted to build up an independent power in the lower house, patterned after the House of Commons, as a check against him. When this, too, failed, they threw themselves on the mercy of the Crown, believing that a royal government under a king 3,000 miles away would afford them more of what they wanted than an arbitrary proprietor, often resident in the colony, who held in his grasp most of the strings of power. Although countless serious problems arose—the tobacco depression, Indian wars, the Catholic "conspiracy," and eventually an attack from London upon the charter itself—the central conflict between colonists' rights and proprietary power remained to aggravate the peculiar and ordinary burdens of colonial life and to be aggravated by them.

"The Publick Grievances of 1669"

As the Restoration had returned the English nation and dominions to the Crown, so the Crown returned Maryland to Cecilius Calvert, Lord Proprietor. Through his half-brother, Philip, and then his

9. Mattie Erma Edwards Parker, ed., *North Carolina Charters and Constitutions, 1578–1698* (Raleigh, N.C., 1963), pp. xix–xx.

son Charles as governors, he sought to restore control after a generation of uncertainty and turmoil, when often neither government nor
governed was sure of where each stood. The intentions of the original
proprietor as proclaimed in 1633 were to convert the Indians and augment His Majesty's "Empire and Dominions," besides promoting the
welfare of the settlers who ventured there. If pressed, Cecilius probably
would have come off that high ground in the 1660's, and if not ready
to forget altogether the earlier aims of Maryland, he might have admitted to his confessor that land and profit were now central to his
schemes.[10]

A clear indication of the conflict between colonists' rights and proprietary power came in 1669. Whether the lower house would have
proclaimed the people's grievances when it did, without the goading
of a militant Protestant minister, and a republican at that, will probably never be known. The Reverend Charles Nicholet was a Commonwealth Presbyterian who had made a reputation for himself among the
Maryland Protestants. In April of 1669 their deputies invited him to
preach before the lower house, and preach he did. Never, he told them,
was more expected of an assembly than the one in which they now sat.
Consider the poor people of Maryland, he charged, and how heavy
their taxes lay upon them. In approaching their legislative duties, he
asked, why did they not model their proceedings after the House of
Commons in England, where brave things had been accomplished?
Elected by God and man to their offices, they as representatives possessed a power commensurate with that of all Maryland colonists, and
a liberty equal to the people of England. If they did not proceed with
courage and make laws agreeable to their own consciences, they exercised no liberty at all, only a seeming liberty which they were better
off without.[11]

When members of the upper house learned the burden of Nicholet's
sermon, they branded it seditious and immediately summoned him before them. While on the carpet he testified that several of the deputies
had invited him to "stir up the Lower House to do their Duty," but
then quickly denied the charge when asked to divulge their names.
After fining him forty shillings and telling him to keep his nose out of
the government's business, the upper house, sitting as a court, forced
Nicholet to acknowledge before the deputies the error of his sermon
and crave the pardon of both the proprietor and the assembly.[12] The
Reverend Mr. Nicholet did not remain long in Maryland. After a brief

10. "Instructions to the Colonists by Lord Baltimore, 1633," C. C. Hall, ed.,
Narratives of Early Maryland, 1633–1684 (New York, 1910), p. 20.
11. *Arch. of Md.*, II, 159–60.
12. *Ibid.*, 160, 162–63.

stay in Virginia, not free of trouble, he journeyed to Salem, Massachusetts, where, among the Puritans, his talents were more appreciated. So much for Mr. Nicholet. But likening the authority of the lower house of Maryland to that of the House of Commons; equating the liberty of colonists with that of Englishmen at home; and encouraging the delegates to scale down the heavy taxes which burdened the poor—these constituted clear-cut sedition in Maryland. Whether the oligarchy's reaction was stiffer because Nicholet was a Protestant clergyman is a question only for speculation.[13]

Three days after Nicholet's humiliation the deputies presented to the upper house the "Publick Grievances of 1669" for joint action as a petition to the proprietor. For a solid week the houses discussed the grievances and the issues involved in their presentation—separately, jointly, by word of mouth, and through written messages. Before a resolution was found, the Maryland assembly had laid bare the fundamental difference of opinion about power and rights in the proprietor's government. The grievances numbered seven; several had to do with Lord Baltimore's authority and were therefore the crux of the argument. The lower house questioned the veto power over the assembly's laws and more especially the proprietor's recent use of it in voiding a number of acts passed to alleviate known hardships of the poorer settlers. Another accused the governor and council of levying a tax contrary to the charter, for it was without consent of the freemen. The balance of grievances scored "Privileged Attornys," arbitrary sheriffs, new officers, extraordinary fees, and "vexatious Informers."

The burgesses probably were unprepared for the response their grievances provoked. The upper house, made up of the proprietor's council and eight other favorites appointed by him, took great pains not just to disapprove of the grievances but to lecture the deputies on the facts of political life in Maryland. To question the veto power and the proprietor's appointment of officers was to challenge his rights in the charter given by the Crown. And did they want to quarrel with the King, too? There could be no grievances against the proprietor's prerogatives, for they were "royal Jurisdictions." To vote them grievances was "mutinous & seditious"; the deputies should raze these votes from their journal, for what they had done was an "Arraignment of the Proprietor, Governor, and Council."

13. In the spring of 1672 the church in Salem called Nicholet to assist John Higginson, son of the patriarch. After threatening a separate movement within the church, he was on his way back to England in 1675. For Nicholet's problems in Salem, see "Salem Town Records," Essex Institute Historical *Collections*, 42 (1906), 264–65; *ibid.*, v. 43, 267; "Diary of John Hull," A.A.S., *Trans. and Coll.*, III (1857), 238, 239; J. B. Felt, *Ecclesiastical History of New England* (2 vols., Boston, 1855–62), II, 565, 587.

The lower house at first refused to back down or even hedge. The grievances were "still Real & Publick"; their votes were not "mutinous & seditious," nor would they scratch them from their records; and, they charged, in dignified tones, the conduct of the upper house toward them was a "breach of Privileges" of their own. The last provoked another little lecture from the proprietor's people. Who were they to imagine that their house enjoyed such privileges, and least of all the privileges of the House of Commons as Nicholet had claimed? Their power stemmed from His Lordship's charter; if they infringed upon it, they destroyed themselves, for without the charter there was no assembly, and with no assembly there were no privileges. House of Commons, indeed! Their power was like that of London's Common Council, whose members, if they violated their charter, "run into Sedition." What is more, if they failed to raze their mutinous votes, the governor would dissolve the assembly.

The threat of dissolution and a close scrutiny of the charter persuaded the deputies to back down a little. God forbid they should equate His Lordship's rights with grievances, they told the upper house. But they said very plainly that they believed Lord Baltimore, out of his abundant grace and goodness, would not exercise his "just Rights & royal Jurisdictions" so as to grieve and oppress the good people of Maryland *if* he were to understand "that any of them in the manner wherein now Exercised are indeed so." Thus the need for a petition to him. It is a question whether the upper house realized the subtlety of the deputies' argument, but for the time being it accepted the hint that exercising the proprietor's rights might lead to "Aggrievance & Opression" and agreed to consult Lord Baltimore about it. The immediate conflict subsided when the deputies erased from their record three of the sharpest grievances, while the upper chamber voted not to engross in its journal the words "mutinous & seditious." After a week of turmoil both houses returned to work.[14]

There was no real winner. The proprietor's people had defended his prerogative, which in their eyes was the issue at stake and could not be compromised. The lower house, although unable to force a petition to Lord Baltimore, made very public the people's grievances. And although they could not, at the time, stick them on the proprietor, they subtly identified the governor, council, and upper house with arbitrary power. Maryland's colonists, like Virginians, were learning that power of the prerogative, whether royal or proprietary, was above question, even scrutiny. Execution of its power was not grievous according to the wielders of it. Only when prerogative power was abused could one

14. The "Publick Grievances of 1669" and debate appear in *Arch. of Md.*, II, 168–69, 174–84.

complain. The trouble in Virginia and Maryland was that there was no standard to gauge power except the rights of Englishmen, and to the King and proprietor these at best had little sanction outside the realm. After defeat of their charter in 1675, Virginians learned that the rights of Englishmen were only what the King said they were, while Maryland's people found their claim to these rights overwhelmed by the proprietor's absolute power in his patent. With governor, council, and upper house firmly in the proprietor's hands, the only vehicle for Marylanders to work was the lower house where the freemen were represented. One step toward realization of Englishmen's rights was an assumption of Parliamentary privilege in the lower house, equating it with the Commons and eventually its constituents with Englishmen at home. The "Publick Grievances of 1669" were a move in that direction. The Reverend Mr. Nicholet probably never learned how effective his sermon was, leading one to wonder further what he had said in Virginia before sailing north to Salem.

The next year the proprietor gave clear evidence of just how tough a job the lower house was tackling. In 1670 Lord Baltimore suddenly restricted the franchise to freeholders, not freemen as had been the custom for some time, by demanding as a property qualification for voting fifty acres of land or a visible personal estate of £40 sterling. In the same instructions to his sheriffs he directed them to permit each county to elect four deputies as usual, but added that only *some* of these would the governor summon to St. Mary's to sit in the lower house. As it turned out, he called only two of the four from each county, a paring of the legislature his opponents would not forget. In the early 1670's the deputies' field of maneuver grew considerably more narrow.[15]

"Affair of the Clifts" and "Complaint from Heaven"

It was not a lack of grievances which slowed the spread of Bacon's Rebellion across the Potomac River into Maryland in 1676. More likely it was lack of a Bacon among the aggrieved and at the same time the prompt and forceful action of Thomas Notley, who sat in the governor's chair while Charles Calvert was absent in England. Given half a chance, many Marylanders would have subscribed to Bacon's list of grievances, since high taxes, arbitrary and expensive government, undependable crops, and Indian "mischief" knew no boundaries.[16] What did occur in Maryland was small potatoes beside

15. *Ibid.*, V, 77–78.
16. *CSPDom.*, 1675–1676, pp. 5, 141, 204, 216, 290.

Virginia's explosion of 1676; nonetheless, grievances existed, and some of Lord Baltimore's "subjects" chose violent means to attempt a redress of them.

The "Affair of the Clifts" occurred in Calvert County, north of St. Mary's, between Chesapeake Bay and the Patuxent River. Late in August 1676, at the height of Bacon's Rebellion, some sixty men gathered under arms at Thomas Barbary's plantation near the river, and published at the head of their company a paper of grievances, having quieted their militia captain with "Gunns cocked & presented." At their head were William Davyes and John Pate, no rabble-rousers but "Laudable Characters," according to their adherents. When the council's messengers ordered them to lay down their arms and go home, promising pardon for all except the leaders, the company hoisted colors and defiantly marched off to the beat of their drums. The rebellion was short-lived; the government chased Davyes and Pate as far as New Castle on the Delaware, fetching them back to the "Clifts," where both were hanged above the Chesapeake in their own county. Some of their followers paid fines; most got off with pardons.

Their grievances and the "immunities and freedoms" they demanded had a familiar ring. The chief complaint was high taxes, the highest ever levied, 297 pounds of tobacco per poll, and because they were levied per poll they were therefore unequal, since poor man paid as much as rich. On top of this, freemen who lacked estates could no longer vote for representatives yet paid these high taxes like everyone else. For publishing this mutinous, seditious, and subversive statement of grievances by force, Davyes and Pate paid with their lives.[17]

Having acted, they said, to prevent further spread of Virginia's rebellion to Maryland, the governor and council then answered the alleged grievances with what they called a remonstrance to complaints. If the people of Maryland were not put off by the content of the council's answers—which is hard to believe—they certainly were by the tone of the remonstrance. For the council again used the occasion to lecture the people generally, and Davyes' and Pate's sympathizers in particular, on the limits Lord Baltimore had set for his government and province as established by the charter. Granted seventeenth-century English political and social theories were not liberal, let alone democratic, Lord Baltimore's conception of proprietary rule in Maryland was an exaggeration of all that was condescending and paternal

17. Thomas Notley to Baltimore, Jan. 22, 1677, *Arch. of Md.*, V, 153–54, 143–44; *ibid.*, XV, 127–29, 131–32, 137; *ibid.*, VII, 110; *ibid.*, VIII, 225–28; "The Beginning, Progress and Conclusion of Bacon's Rebellion . . . ," C. M. Andrews, ed., *Narratives of the Insurrections, 1675–1690* (New York, 1915), p. 36.

in English government and society. Much of what was outmoded in English political ideas the proprietor attempted to introduce and perpetuate in his colony. The governor and council, who were the proprietor's son and favorites, depended upon his patronage for places and fees and therefore constantly attempted to educate the colonists to a life ordered in the proprietor's way. They caught in their manner the lordly view of Baltimore's conception of things and tried to fix it upon people who were struggling at times merely to stay solvent midst huge crops of tobacco and in one piece against the Indians, to say nothing of keeping their farms free from the tax collector. Maryland *was* different from other colonies, for in no other were the fortunes of the people as closely tied to one man and his presumptions.[18]

In their remonstrance the governor and council played upon a number of strings: the ingratitude of the people, my Lord's "Paternal care"; the "sword of Justice"; the proprietor's power; the due preservation of his rights; and the people's just rights and liberties—in that order. Satisfaction of modest and reasonable requests was possible only if seconded by the "Quiett demeanour of the ffreemen." High taxes were the obvious result of an expensive war with the Indians, against whom the colony should have risen as one man, not, to the council's amazement, "runn into an Actuall Rebellion." The governor and council had a good deal to say about votes of the freemen who owned no property and whom the proprietor had deprived of suffrage in 1670. Apparently the complainers had forgotten, and the council was quick to remind them, that Lord Baltimore could summon assemblies whenever he pleased and in the manner which seemed to him most fitting and convenient; what is more, his new manner of calling assemblies was agreeable to the laws and customs of England. Here followed a little essay about the large number of property holders and freemen in England who could not vote but were taxed, really a defense of virtual representation in Parliament which would have delighted Thomas Whately and outraged Daniel Dulany (of Maryland) almost a century later at the time of the Stamp Act crisis. It was an argument, too, which demonstrated that the proprietary side could manufacture the equation between colonists in America and Englishmen within the realm when it proved advantageous, although the proprietary people were more apt to favor its negative value: what Maryland colonists could not do, Englishmen in England could not do either.

The clincher here was to demonstrate the irresponsibility of freemen without property. Was the "poore ffreeman" dearer to the freeholder than "himselfe his Wife Children & fortune," and will they put them-

18. For the remonstrance, see *Arch. of Md.*, XV. 137–40.

selves in his hands, he who owns nothing and can duck out from under the reach of the law as easily as he can change his clothes? Still, the governor and council promised to plead with the proprietor to restore the vote to freemen. The complaint against unequal taxes, that the poll tax forced poor men to pay as much as the wealthy, the council dismissed as a "peice of Sophistry." Clearly, they argued, the rich man pays for all his people, for every servant and slave he owns, and, moreover, Virginia and the West Indian colonies taxed the same way. Anyway, the proprietor could not alter the arrangement without consent of the assembly, which must have struck the burgesses as curious, since the proprietor had not hesitated to alter other arrangements of government without consulting anyone, let alone the burgesses.

As ardently as the governor and council wished to see the proprietor's and the people's rights preserved, they were resolved, they said, to see the laws obeyed. Look at Virginia, consumed by rebellion, they warned, "torne in peeces under the maske of publique Reformacon & ease from taxes." Reflect, too, upon the barbarous Indians "hovering over their heads." God wills obedience, and a reward for obedience may be an easing of taxes once His Lordship returns. But resistance to laws only arms the hand of justice; it forces governors to expensive means of protection and defense for the whole colony. And, the council added, Davyes and Pate's mutiny and rebellion already have swollen the charges of government beyond everyone's expectation.[19]

This was not the answer the late Davyes and Pate and their friends had hoped for. It promised no change. Redress of "Publick Grievances" through political action had been frustrated in 1669 by the authority of the proprietor and his supporters. Redress by force on a small scale was even less successful at the "Clifts" in 1676, for it resulted in bloody reprisal and condescending reemphasis of a paternalism which seemed decreasingly effective as a means of political and social organization in the New World. The only alternative was revolution, and in 1676 it was suggested, not yet violent revolution, not through force of arms, but by peaceful means, a sweeping change in Maryland's government, completely shifting its basis from one source of power to another.

The suggestion came in the form of a document, written in late 1676, and it followed shortly the governor's and council's remonstrance. What is most striking about "Complaint from Heaven and a Huy and Crye out of Virginia and Maryland," after one gets through the prickly and deliberate primitiveness of the language, is its biting attack upon the proprietor and government and the boldness of recommendations for improvement. The document is a puzzler, appearing naïve at first look,

19. *Ibid.*

but it is not long before one realizes that the author was a skillful propagandist whose blasts left few corners of Baltimore's government unsinged. He also was well acquainted with the course of events in Maryland for the last generation or so and betrayed a republican bias in his favorable references to Commonwealth men and the "illustrious and puisant" Parliament in England. Besides being a "Complaint," it was a petition to Charles II *and* Parliament. And for good measure, it was directed also to the Lord Mayor, aldermen, merchants, and citizens of London and "elsewhere in England, whose off spring wee are."

The grievances described in "Complaint from Heaven" were a lengthy accumulation. They ranged from the proprietor's alleged conspiracy in a notorious Catholic plot against the empire to his ruthless extraction of tobacco from innocent settlers—a quarter part of the people's livelihood. Prominent were the familiar complaints against taxes, fees, fines, and levies to maintain the oligarchy, stingy suffrage requirements, the paring of the deputies, and a lot more. The absolute power of the proprietor, "Complaint" declared, enabled him to set himself up as a prince in Maryland. The courts of justice were in his pocket, all writs and warrants were in Baltimore's name; even his coat of arms graced the courtrooms. Oaths of fidelity to His Lordship were demanded without a *salvo* to the King. Appeals to the Crown were either criminal or denied; "owr mouths are lokt up, and treathned with destruction iff wee stirr." He and the upper house dictated law to the deputies and by threats and deceit suppressed opposition. The impermanency of laws and the cavalier manner of vetoing acts, the "doeinge and undoeing," undermined any chance of "Estability" in government. Indeed, there was great uncertainty in Maryland. Like Virginians, the people lacked a firm foundation on which to stand as English subjects outside the realm:

And now pray where is the liberty of the freeborne subjects of England and owr priviledges in Maryland, the Lord proprietary assums and attracts more Royall Power to himselfe over his Tenants then owr gratious King over his subjects in Engld, and therefore charge the Lord proprietary with Breach of Charter, who gives him noe warrant to deal with the King's Majesty's subjects in Maryland so deceitfully. . . .

Deliverance could come only "from owr souveraigne Lord the King and Parliament out of England, which is the legal way."

The suggestion of an appeal to England tipped the writer's hand about what ought to be done to redress the grievances and rescue Maryland from the clutches of the proprietor and his party. It was a very simple solution: the King should seize Maryland and make it a royal colony, appoint a Protestant governor to rule according to English customs, respecting, at the same time, Baltimore's ownership of the soil and right to quitrents in tobacco at the standard rate. Throw open the suffrage to all freemen and allow their deputies by "free votes" to enact laws for the common good without "compellment and perswasion or interruption." Let the justice of the Crown *and* Parliament prevail forever. Permit each county to establish a Protestant church and a free school, both maintained by the people, "notwithstanding liberty of conscience." Maintain the government, its forts and garrisons, its little necessities for the general welfare from the present export duty of two shillings per hogshead of tobacco and any other fines and "Americaments" the assembly might enact. Lastly, let there be no doubt about the freemen's perpetual enjoyment of "gratious recours and appeale" to the Crown.

"Complaint" reminded the King of the considerable customs he derived from colonists' labor and industry. It suggested to the Lord Mayor, aldermen, and merchants of London just how much an active exchange of goods meant to Englishmen in employment, ships, and profit. These last arguments belie the vulgar simplicity of the earlier pages; their sophisticated logic and improved spelling demonstrate that these were no country bumpkins who guilelessly petitioned their King. A well-informed party with axes to grind was bent on depriving Lord Baltimore of his government with the hope that the Crown would make Maryland a royal colony, affording all the alleged advantages this change would bring to them and those who supported them.

The republican slant suggests as author of "Complaint" the name of Josias Fendall, or one of his gang. He had opposed the proprietor for some time, and would continue to do so, but never more than he had during the Commonwealth period when as governor he threw up a commission from Lord Baltimore and accepted one from the assembly. During the Virginia rebellion Fendall had kicked up another fuss in Maryland. It was expected every day, said Baltimore, that he would fall in with Nathaniel Bacon, and only the forceful acts of Governor Notley prevented it. Moreover, "Complaint from Heaven" was openly sympathetic to Bacon's cause.[20]

A strong party of Maryland people would gladly accept dependence upon the Crown through a royal government to get them out from

20. "Complaint from Heaven" is printed in *Arch. of Md.*, V, 134–52, and *CSPCol., 1675–1676*, #937. Wilcomb E. Washburn has found many errors in the Maryland *Archives'* transcription from the original in the Public Record Office. *The Governor and the Rebel*, p. 184, n. 33. C. M. Andrews claimed it was "very inadequately calendared" in *CSPCol. Colonial Period*, II, 349 n. For Fendall, see *Arch. of Md.*, V, 280–82; *CSPCol., 1681–1685*, #180, #351.

under a proprietor whose self-interest, they believed, dominated their colony. For Baltimore stood between them and their King, between them and the rights colonists ought to enjoy as Englishmen did in England. His government deprived them of the position, power, and profits they believed were rightly theirs but were now almost wholly absorbed by the proprietor's favorites. The crisis of 1676, for which they blamed Baltimore, seemed a strategic moment to demonstrate the depth and scope of their grievances and the direction reform should take. For Maryland's government was unconstitutional, given the colonists' conception of the empire and their place in it. This is what the author of "Complaint from Heaven" attempted to do. The crudeness and earthiness of the writing only underlined his determination to present the petition as a grass-roots appeal from an abused people.

Fendall and Coode

The Exclusion Crisis brought England to within an eyelash of revolution. On the heels of the Popish Plot, Shaftesbury and his Whigs came very close to turning over the government in their attempt to exclude Catholic James from the throne. Charles's recovery from illness, his prorogation of the Oxford Parliament, and the Whigs' ultimate inability to muster the necessary strength in the House of Lords eventually averted the crisis.[21] News of the upheaval spread to the colonies, where it was laced with rumor and exaggeration which seriously aggravated the uncertainty and uneasiness which surrounded their governments.

There was no dearth of news and rumor in Maryland. Christopher Rousby, collector of customs, was the proud owner of "several new books," recently arrived from London, which reported the business of succession and the progress of the Exclusion Bill. Across the Potomac in Virginia Governor Culpeper read tracts and newspapers on Exclusion politics sent to him by William Blathwayt, secretary of the Lords of Trade.[22] Where Josias Fendall and henchman John Coode got their news is no great matter. Probably Maryland of all colonies was the most easily upset owing to a general anxiety which prevailed and to the carryings on of a strong opposition party which was ready to play upon the people's fears to bring down the proprietary government. As

21. J. R. Jones, *The First Whigs: The Politics of the Exclusion Crisis, 1678–1683* (London, 1961), chs. 3–4.

22. Deposition of Mr. Lowe against Christopher Rousby, June 6, 1681, *Arch. of Md.*, V, 278; Blathwayt to Culpeper, Aug. 26, 1680, BPCol. Wmsbg., v. XVII.

usual the trouble began with an Indian skirmish and the fear of several more.

Josias Fendall rode high in Charles County during the spring of 1681. Between March and May he had broadcast that the King and Parliament were so at loggerheads that civil war was imminent. There soon would be no government or established laws in England; nothing was treason now, and one might say what he wished; and he and his followers could appropriate what estates they pleased with impunity in Maryland and Virginia. At another time Fendall outright accused the proprietor of treason and called the people fools to pay taxes. What is more, he said, he would bear them out for not paying them and they need not worry, for in a few years he would have more honor in the country than the proprietor ever enjoyed. At still another time he hinted darkly of the proprietor's conspiracy with the Indians and Catholics to destroy all the Protestants. That Fendall and Coode had suspiciously visited northern Virginia across the Potomac, where Fendall allegedly commanded great influence, made such statements ominous to an uneasy, frightened people. Toppling Baltimore's government would be simple, Fendall once remarked; only the proprietor and a handful of his lieutenants amounted to anything.[23]

John Coode also reflected the dangerously unsettled conditions in England and Maryland. He was as voluble as his friend Fendall and just as stimulating in his language, for he loved to "amaze the Ignorant and make sport with [his] witt. . . ." In May of 1681 at the house of another malcontent, Nehemiah Blackiston of St. Mary's County, Coode spoke freely "his own mutinous and seditious mind" and informed all within earshot that in four months' time no Catholic in Maryland could call a foot of land his own. Once while feasting and well "heated," he bragged of 10,000 men at his command and that he could "make it high-water or low-water" in Maryland as he pleased. He, too, strongly hinted that the proprietary government was deep in conspiracy with the Indians.[24]

Shortly Lord Baltimore decided that the countryside had heard enough of this kind of talk and ordered the two "rank Baconists" taken up. Colonel Darnell of the council seized John Coode in his bed-chamber, some said in the "dead time of the night," and dragged him off to prison. (Lord Baltimore had his hands full the next day when

23. Baltimore to Earl of Anglesey, July 19, 1681, *Arch. of Md.*, V, 280–82; Philip Calvert to Col. Henry Meese, Dec. 29, 1681, *CSPCol., 1681–1685*, #351; Philip Calvert, *A Letter from the Chancellour of Maryland*, 1682, John Carter Brown Library.

24. P. Calvert to Meese, Dec. 29, 1681, *CSPCol., 1681–1685*, #351; Trial of John Coode, *Arch. of Md.*, V, 329–32.

Mrs. Coode "hectored my Lord at a rate . . . never heard from a woman before.") Soon Fendall was rounded up along with several others for the sake of the colony's security.[25]

With Fendall and Coode under restraint the proprietor thought Maryland would again be at peace. It was not; the summer of 1681 became another peak of discontent. The very seizure of the popular figures was itself a major grievance, for it was believed to be a means for preventing their election to the assembly. Virginians, who felt free to comment upon the troubles in Maryland at any time, were sure that Baltimore's action would have an effect opposite to what was expected. Seizure would make the voters all the more determined to elect the prisoners; it might even provoke them to storm the jails in order to place their people in the legislature.

While Protestants expected to air their grievances at the forthcoming assembly in the middle of August, Baltimore hoped to submit to it his accusations against the ringleaders. Some Virginians fully expected the discontented colonists to "give ease to the matters themselves," if the assembly failed to satisfy them, for the inhabitants were "talking very loudly" against their government.[26]

It took some time before the assembly settled down to the normal business of the session, for square in the midst of the lower house sat John Coode, then free on bail and recently elected from St. Mary's County. The proprietor and the council found this more than they could stomach—that a man charged with such notorious offenses, including subversion of the government, should sit innocently as a member of the legislature. Here followed a very busy week of discussion between the two houses, the upper demanding Coode's suspension, the deputies refusing it, all the while arguing like good Parliamentarians their right and privilege to decide the fitness of their members. The upper chamber repeatedly sent down evidence of how "Debauchedly & Profanely" Coode had carried on in St. Mary's County and how utterly defiant he was of authority. Coode's colleagues stood adamant. They did promise, however, that Coode would appear at his trial.[27]

Coode and Fendall were tried separately in November of 1681 for

25. P. Calvert to Meese, Dec. 29, 1681, *CSPCol., 1681–1685,* #351.

26. Extracts of letters from Governor Culpeper, July 25, 1681, C.O. 1/47/36; *CSPCol., 1681–1685,* #184, #185, #195, #275; *Arch. of Md.,* V, 301.

27. *Ibid.,* VII, 112–16, 135, 39. According to one deposition, at the height of a confrontation with Baltimore's secretary in 1681, Coode declared that he cared not a fart for William Calvert or a turd for the chancellor or governor, "nor for God Almighty Neither." *Ibid.,* 137–38. As Michael G. Kammen has wryly remarked, "Coode was not overly awed by authority." "The Causes of the Maryland Revolution of 1689," *Maryland Historical Magazine* (Dec. 1960), p. 323.

mutiny and sedition against the government. The court found John Coode innocent, although the chancellor, Philip Calvert, gave him some sharp advice about guarding his tongue and loving his quiet better than his jest. Josias Fendall was not as fortunate. He was found guilty, and besides being banished from the colony, the court fined him 40,000 pounds of tobacco and kept him prisoner until he paid it. The judges made it a point to tell him that he came very close to having his tongue bored and an ear or two cropped for his offenses. Fendall's court numbered six judges, two of whom were Calverts, the proprietor's uncle and cousin; one was Lady Baltimore's brother, and another, although a Protestant, had married the proprietor's stepdaughter. The remaining two judges were Protestants. The exiled Fendall settled in Stafford County, Virginia, along the upper reaches of the Potomac in frontier country where government was never very solid. Friends of Baltimore watched him like hawks lest he slip back into Maryland and stir up the people all over again. He died there in 1687, while John Coode lived to fight another day. Poor George Godfrey, a justice of the peace and officer in a troop of horse, was condemned to death for attempting to raise a company of men in July to spring Fendall from jail. Not long afterward Lord Baltimore magnanimously commuted Godfrey's sentence to imprisonment for life.[28]

Fear of Contagion

The unrest which Fendall and Coode stirred into "mutiny and sedition," like Bacon's Rebellion, had deeper causes than mere dislike of proprietor and government. The years 1681 and 1682 were very bad years for tobacco farmers whether they lived in Virginia or Maryland. Virginians told the King about their troubles, for if some "speedy remedy" were not discovered, they could not much longer subsist, they said. Culpeper described Maryland as in "torment" and distraught with internal struggles besides the general disease of poverty like Virginia. Lord Baltimore complained to William Blathwayt that if an "expedient" were not soon hit upon, the depression would reduce the people of both colonies to "great straights," for they were "very bare." Virginia's "expedient" was a halt in tobacco planting, and its assembly, after petitioning the King to permit it, went ahead with plans to do so anyway in the spring of 1682. Expecting "motions" from Virginia asking Maryland's cooperation, Lord Baltimore hedged as before on every front. He doubted he and his council could enact such a law, lacking

28. For the respective trials, see *Arch. of Md.*, V, 329–32, 312–28, 332–34. For the court's relationship to the proprietor, see Andrews, *Colonial Period*, II, 376–77 n.

commands from the King; it might do some good, he ventured, but only if the King lost no revenue by it; furthermore, they would have to be certain that no other producers grew large quantities at the same time. To support his gingerliness he dug up an old Order in Council of twenty years before which expressly commanded no cessation and assumed it was still in force.[29] He would be a great loser by it, he told Blathwayt, but, of course, would yield if the King agreed.

In the spring of 1682 Baltimore abruptly shifted his attention from the King's pleasure and both their revenues to fear of another rebellion. Frustrated in an attempt to enact a halt in planting by Chicheley's prorogation of their assembly, Virginians broke out in riot in May of 1682. They roared through several counties, pulling up tobacco plants along the way, determined to stop production by the only means they could find. Baltimore alerted his "foot and horse" and placed them along the banks of the Potomac, ready to repel the landing of Virginia's "rabble," for once they destroyed Virginia's tobacco, they doubtless would have designs on Maryland's. Coming so soon after the turmoil of Fendall and Coode, Baltimore was apprehensive lest tobacco cutting turn into wholesale rebellion, to which Maryland was very vulnerable. During the summer old Chicheley managed to bring the Virginia plant cutters under control, quieting fears of rebellion, but not before destruction of several thousand hogsheads of tobacco. Luckily the proprietor was excused the embarrassment of refusing to negotiate a cessation. The price of tobacco improved toward the end of the year, and Lord Culpeper, once back from England, never felt it necessary to divulge his new instructions, which allowed a stint and would have forced him to seek Maryland's cooperation. So Baltimore's revenue remained intact, as did the King's.[30]

These were perilous times for a proprietor, even an absolute proprietor, and in May 1682 Lord Baltimore strongly felt the need of a vote of confidence in view of the "Malicious evill Reports" which his colonists were sending home about him. The best way to secure a "Declaration in Vindication of himself" and government was to order the assembly to give him one, and order he did. After all, the aspersions against him were "Notoriously false," he told the assembly, and certainly must appear so to the inhabitants of Maryland. The speaker of the lower house failed to catch the spirit of the proprietor's needs and

29. *CSPCol., 1681–1685,* #186, #319; *Arch. of Md.,* V, 352–53.

30. Nicholas Spencer to Blathwayt, May 29, 1682, BPCol. Wmsbg., v. XVI; Baltimore to Sir Leoline Jenkins, May 18, 1682, *Arch. of Md.,* V, 357–58; *ibid.,* 361–62; William Stevens to Philip Calvert, May 16, 1682, *ibid.,* 355–56; Jenkins to Baltimore, Aug. 10, 1682, *ibid.,* 370–71; Culpeper to Lords of Trade, Sept. 20, 1683, *CSPCol., 1681–1685,* #1258; C. C. Hall, ed., *Narratives of Early Maryland,* p. 417.

made bold to inquire whether His Lordship proposed the declaration to the deputies as "particular persons" or as the lower house of the assembly, for if it were the latter, the members ought first to consult together before they could put it to a vote. Outraged, the proprietor prorogued the assembly to the next October.[31]

Baltimore had support outside his family circle. As "private persons" several Protestant colonists, who doubtless had opposed the militant Fendall and Coode, were sympathetic to his appeal and drafted a declaration in defense of the proprietor and his government. We have a good life here in Maryland, they insisted, and enjoy all the liberties, including those of Magna Carta and freedom of religion, "whatsoever it be," as fully as any of His Majesty's subjects in America. Baltimore, they claimed, distributed his patronage impartially; half of the council was Protestant, as was a majority of both militia officers and justices of the peace. The declaration bore only twenty-five signatures. Still, it was clear that the dissidents in 1682 did not command the loyalty of all Maryland Protestants.[32]

The Rights and Privileges of Englishmen

When the upper house challenged John Coode's right to sit with the deputies, the two houses and the governor resumed their struggle over other issues. Some were old, some new, but most revolved around suffrage, representation, and the lower house's rights and privileges. By various means the deputies continued to drive toward a degree of stability and certainty, usually at the expense of the authority above them. Three years earlier they had appointed a committee on "Priviledges & eleccons" and drafted rules of order for their own use which they posted near the "Dorekeep." But in the summer of 1681 they went after the right to order elections for filling vacancies among themselves, citing the House of Commons as model. The conflict over who ordered by-elections again stirred up the problem of the number of deputies each county might send to the legislature. The deputies had deeply resented the proprietor's cutting their delegations in half and renewed their claim to a full complement of four. Frequently they criticized the proprietor for summoning only those whom he thought he could use for his own selfish purposes. In arguing their case the deputies repeatedly cited the customs and usages of the House of Commons as "the only Rule to walk by." [33]

Response from the upper chamber was sharper than usual, no doubt

31. *Arch. of Md.*, VII, 314.
32. *Ibid.*, V, 353–55; *CSPCol., 1681–1685*, #500.
33. *Arch. of Md.*, VII, 7–8, 17, 114–15, 117–19, 122–23.

owing to the tension of the time—rumors of rebellion, widespread discontent, the harangues of Fendall and Coode, and the skulking of Indians about their very farms and plantations. Chancellor Philip Calvert spoke directly to the lower house on instructions from Lord Baltimore and accused its members of assuming a power never before heard of in Maryland or in Virginia, the Barbados, or any English colony. Parliamentary precedents, he declared, were "impracticable in Foreign Plantations," and as an assembly they ought not to amuse themselves with things they did not really understand. After all, the King has power alone to dispose of his "Conquests" as he pleases; he is not tied to the consent of Parliament in disposing of them. Did they not understand that the Crown had granted the proprietor the power to make laws, and the proprietor under this charter had settled the manner in which the assembly would function? Once this was understood, they could all get back to the weighty affairs for which the assembly was called, the enemy Indians already "being in the Bowells of the Province." On condition the deputies returned to business, the proprietor agreed to issue writs to fill up the lower house with four delegates from each county *for this occasion only*. Once the Chancellor had spoken his piece, the deputies impertinently requested the message in writing.[34]

The deputies were extremely grieved. They did not understand why His Lordship found it a "Matter of Wonder" that the lower house chose to assert its rights and privileges on the basis of English rules rather than the "imperfect Proceedings" of Virginia and the Barbados. This was their inherent right, "yea and Birth right," though born in Maryland, by the very words of the proprietor's charter. But likening them to a "Conquered People" was even worse, and the deputies took it "very heavily." If "Conquest" meant that the people of Maryland were subject to arbitrary laws and impositions, then they believed the proprietor was the victim of strange, "if not evill Council"—a remark his Lordship thought "not very civil." Certainly, they agreed, the proprietor's charter gave him sufficient rights and prerogatives for an honorable government, but at the same time the Crown had reserved to the people of Maryland "the rights and Priviledges of English Men," and they insisted upon them.[35]

And so it went. Each side was very clear in its position and, despite the tensions, argued calmly and logically from opposite premises. It came down to the issue of the rights of Englishmen, and in the minds of the deputies, these were based on the Crown's legal relationship

34. *Ibid.*, 124.
35. *Ibid.*, 125–27.

with all Englishmen expressed in the charter, regardless of where they lived, and on Parliamentary precedents. Both of these, they believed, would protect their rights and also afford their government sufficient guarantees and stability. According to the upper house, Maryland colonists deserved the rights the proprietor wished to give them under the charter. Parliamentary precedents had no bearing on America, since the King and Privy Council alone were responsible for managing colonies; Parliament had no dominion over the plantations.

Despite the clarity of each side's argument, in several ways neither was right. Dependence upon the Crown did not guarantee the rights of Englishmen to anyone, as Virginians had recently learned. The lower house's use of precedents from the House of Commons was presumptuous, given the attitude of the proprietor and upper house and, of course, the people in England. Parliament did have a role in colonial policy, although it was not yet well defined. Furthermore, respect in England for the proprietor's charter, or any charter for that matter, was dwindling, as Londoners soon discovered along with colonists in Massachusetts. The proprietor himself soon felt the Crown's influence in this regard when Charles II asserted the prerogative particularly after the Exclusion Crisis of the early 1680's.

The assembly came to agreement over the immediate issues with neither house winning outright. The proprietor issued writs to fill vacancies on the basis of four delegates per county but only for the rest of the legislature's term. To future assemblies he would call only two, and the lower house agreed for the time being.[36]

No sooner had the two houses come to a working agreement over election writs and representation than they resumed the struggle over confirmation of the assembly's laws. Nothing, the deputies believed, contributed more to the stability of the government than the validity and continuity of the laws from which they expected safety and protection. Why were most Maryland laws only temporary? Why could not the governor give final approval of them when the proprietor was absent? Why did the proprietor often veto their enactments after his governor had agreed to them? In answer the upper house rang in the King's veto power over both Virginia's laws and those of newly established Pennsylvania, but the deputies, with the House of Commons in mind, were not impressed by local precedents. The best the lower house could manage was the proprietor's promise that in his absence he would declare his confirmation or veto of the laws within eighteen months of the assembly's vote, although he refused to let this conces-

36. *Ibid.*, 127, 134–35.

sion bind his successors.[37] Stability in government was not increased, nor was faith in the proprietor enhanced, when in 1684, returning from a visit to England, he vetoed by proclamation all the assembly's laws enacted six years earlier, excepting only those since repassed and agreed to when he was in residence. No wonder the deputies were uncertain about the "Estability" of their government.[38]

Besides the proprietor's prerogative and the rights of Englishmen, the Maryland assembly continued to argue over a host of smaller issues ranging from plural officeholding—a product of both favoritism and nepotism—to such details as the lower house's refusal to allow a member of the other to address it with his sword on. At one point the deputies resolved in pique not to pay out of the public account expenses to maintain the upper house, since the deputies alone were representatives of the freemen whose money was spent.[39] But these were less important than the major conflicts over sovereignty and power which had plagued the government and people of Maryland for a number of years and would continue to do so without letup until 1689. Guarantee of rights and of equality with people at home came hard in Maryland.

Baltimore's Trouble with the Crown

All of Lord Baltimore's difficulties did not stem from conflict within his government, from fear of Virginia, or from skulking Indians. In 1681 Charles II granted Quaker William Penn a handsome proprietary just to the north of Maryland, and not long after Penn took possession there commenced a contest over the boundary between the two colonies. Shortly after the first grant, Penn persuaded his good friend the Duke of York to give him additional land—to which the Duke held doubtful title—in what is now Delaware, affording Penn access to Chesapeake Bay. Baltimore already claimed the area as his own on the basis of his father's charter, giving him, he believed, all the territory between the Chesapeake and Delaware Bays. The struggle between proprietors was a long, strung-out affair with several dramatic moments, including a gala excursion on Baltimore's yacht. But negotiations on the spot between the two potentates grew less and less promising, even bitter. By 1684 both proprietors were back in London, where Penn had the advantage, for he was much better acquainted at court

37. *Ibid.*, 152–53, 160–61, 178–79, 181–82. In 1684 the assembly voted the proprietor three years' time to veto laws. *Ibid.*, XIII, 34.
38. *Ibid.*, 49, 108; *ibid.*, XVII, 253–54, 261.
39. *Ibid.*, VII, 222, 356–57, 414–16, 419, 573.

than his neighbor. Baltimore in the meantime sent Colonel George Talbot, one of his council and temporary governor, into the disputed region, where, said Penn, he built a fort and proceeded "barbarously" against the settlers, threatening to root out all "Quaking scismaticks." [40]

The Lords of Trade put off for some time a decision about boundary claims between Baltimore and William Penn. Much more pertinent business respecting Maryland came before the King and them than a dispute between two proprietors. A number of sharp reports from Maryland accused His Lordship and his officers of violating the Acts of Trade and obstructing His Majesty's collector of customs, who attempted to enforce the Plantation Duty. For some time Collector Christopher Rousby and Comptroller Nicholas Badcock had been at odds with the proprietor about the penny duty per pound of tobacco, and both royal officers found themselves very unpopular among Baltimore's people, since they made strong efforts to collect it. Harsh words passed; the proprietor charged the collector with stuffing his pockets with illegal duties, and Rousby accused Baltimore and his government of defrauding the King of his customs. Besides this, Rousby claimed that Baltimore wanted both his and the comptroller's job in order to give them to dependent relatives. The issue between them was a technicality in interpreting the act of 1673; the King and the Lords of Trade took Rousby's side and claimed that the proprietor owed the Crown £2,500 in tobacco customs.[41]

Trouble over the King's revenue could not have come at a worse time for Baltimore. He was already deep in the struggle to keep his original grant out of the grasp of William Penn, a favorite of the Duke of York, who had granted the lower counties to Penn in the first place. James had survived the Exclusion Crisis and despite some opposition would probably become king, since Charles could not live forever. But this was only the beginning of Baltimore's difficulties. To earn the King's displeasure by allowing favorites in Maryland to violate an act of trade and cheat the King of his customs was risky business at any

40. Baltimore to Blathwayt, Mar. 18, 1681, Jan. 2, 1683, and Mar. 11, 1684, BPCol. Wmsbg., v, XVIII; Penn to Duke of York, 2 12 mo, 1683 [1684], Papers relating to Wm. Penn, Penn Mss., 13, Library of the Society of Friends, London; same to same, 8th of 4 mo, 1684, ibid., 17; Arch. of Md., XVII, 222–24; Edward Randolph to Sir Robert Southwell, Jan. 29, 1684, Toppan, ed., Randolph, IV, 4–5. See also "Reports of Conferences Between Lord Baltimore and William Penn, and their Agents, 1682, 1683, 1684," in C. C. Hall, ed., Narratives of Early Maryland, pp. 407–48; Andrews, Colonial Period, II, 360–62, III, 294–97.

41. See several letters, etc., from Badcock, Rousby, Baltimore, and others in Arch. of Md., V, 258–68, 274–80, 286–310. For the King's reprimand to Baltimore, see ibid., 344–46, and J. Thomas Scharf, History of Maryland, from the Earliest Period to the Present Day (3 vols., Baltimore, 1879), I, 289.

time. To continue to do so at the very moment the Crown had seized the charters of London and Massachusetts in a prerogative fit and was casting hungry eyes on several more was downright foolhardy. Plans to "make the King great and extend His reall Empire" in America were well under way. Sensing what was to come, "Prince Pen" agreed to "Resign His Principalities," keeping intact, of course, his rights to the soil of Pennsylvania and, he hoped, the lower counties on the Delaware. The Crown's attack upon the charters was in full swing; none was sacred, least of all one which granted a proprietor like Baltimore absolute control.[42]

Then in late October 1684 Baltimore's deputy in Maryland, Colonel Talbot, the man who had scattered "Mr. Penns people" along the Delaware, killed the King's Customs Collector Rousby in a brawl aboard a royal vessel in Patuxent River before all manner of witnesses. News of the killing arrived in London in January.

The murder of Christopher Rousby was a bizarre affair, as were its consequences. Already hated by Baltimore's clique of officers and relatives for his officiousness as collector in Maryland, Rousby returned the compliment in his pointed letters home to the Commissioners of Customs. That Rousby was friendly with William Penn did nothing to enhance his position in the minds of Baltimore's people. A showdown occurred on October 31, 1684, when Talbot, Baltimore's deputy, and Collector Rousby met aboard His Majesty's ketch, *Quaker,* in Maryland waters. The ship's "Chyrurgion" described it simply: Colonel Talbot stepped up to Rousby, who was sitting across the table, and greeted him handsomely with a "God Damme you Sone of a whore you Dogg Rousby give me your hand. . . ." The collector vowed he would do nothing of the kind without better words, and the two struggled and fought. Talbot pulled a knife, "newly prepared and sharpened," according to one report, used it effectively, and Rousby rolled over dead.[43]

Captain Allen of the *Quaker* seized Talbot and sailed down the bay to Virginia, where he turned him over to Lord Effingham, new governor there. Clapped in irons, Talbot was outraged, not over imprisonment, but in being dragged out of Maryland. He calmed down sufficiently to petition Effingham, eloquently, in fact, explaining that he had

42. Philip S. Haffenden, "The Crown and the Colonial Charters, 1675–1688," *William and Mary Quarterly,* 3d ser., XIV (July 1958), 297–311, and (Oct. 1958), 452–66; Blathwayt to Effingham, Sept. 6 and Dec. 9, 1684, BPCol. Wmsbg., v. XIV; C.O. 324/4, pp. 165–66.

43. Rousby to William Penn, July 15, 1683, Papers relating to William Penn, Penn Mss., 11, Lib. Soc. Friends; Information of Edward Wade, Chyrurgion of His Majesty's Ketch Quaker, C.O. 1/56/90, III; *Arch. of Md.,* V, 428–30.

"through misfortune, and not designe, wounded one Mr. Christopher Rousby, and thereby haveing unfortunately been the Cause of the said Mr. Rousby's death." In more pointed language he demanded return to Maryland where the offense occurred. Effingham was uneasy about holding Talbot; he argued that since the crime took place aboard His Majesty's vessel, it came under his jurisdiction as vice-admiral, although he wrote home posthaste for royal instructions. No doubt his decision was dictated by Talbot's threat that "if he were on shore He would raise a Thousand Men for his further Revenge." After all, said Effingham, the King's authority in Maryland was not as strong as it might be. He was more successful in arguing the legality of trying Talbot in Virginia than in explaining to the Privy Council how the defendant, although "sufficiently Ironed," "Corrupted his Guards" and "leaped out of prison." Already embarrassed, the governor seized those he suspected of assisting him and threw them into jail, from whence, he lamented, "they are since likewise escaped." Effingham, of course, demanded Talbot's return from Maryland, where he had fled; the escapee eventually surrendered to authorities there who ignored the governor's request.[44]

The Lords of Trade took very seriously Talbot's "quality" and his threat to raise forces in Maryland if he could, to say nothing of his murder of a royal officer. They persuaded the King to order him home for trial. But Charles II died soon after the decision was made, and James, once he got around to examining the case, ordered the trial held in Virginia, charging Effingham, if the prisoner were found guilty, to stay execution until the King's further pleasure was known. Virginia did try Talbot, found him very guilty, and condemned him to hang but, of course, respected the King's command and held off execution. James's pleasure was to remain silent; Colonel Talbot died in bed of a fever in 1687.[45]

Determined to deprive the proprietor of his charter, the Crown sought evidence against it from every corner. It milked Virginians of what they could remember about border difficulties and Baltimore's pretensions to the Potomac River; it played upon Effingham's ambitions to add Maryland to his rule in order to secure information which

44. *Ibid.*, 428–30, 453; Talbot's petition to Effingham, C.O. 1/56/139; Effingham to Blathwayt, Nov. 25, 1684, and Mar. 20, 1685, BPCol. Wmsbg., v. XIV; Spencer to Blathwayt, Apr. 1, 1685, *ibid.*, v. XVI; *CSPCol., 1681–1685,* #1963.

45. Blathwayt to Effingham, Feb. 12, 1685, BPCol. Wmsbg., v. XIV; Lords of Trade to King, Ham. 31, 1685, C.O. 1/57/8; Order of Council, Feb. 25, 1685, Adm 1/5139, p. 1025, P.R.O.; *Acts of P.C., Col. Ser., 1680–1720,* #173, pp. 77–78; *Arch. of Md.,* V, 429–30, 453; L. W. Labaree, ed., *Royal Instructions to British Colonial Governors,* I, 361–62.

might be useful. Violations of the Acts of Trade were central to the case. Besides the letters of the late Rousby and Badcock, other royal officials chipped in what they could; William Dyer of New York and the ubiquitous Edward Randolph added choice bits about "so much tobacco" that never saw England but was "shipd off & not accounted for." Nehemiah Blackiston, one of Coode's cronies, took over the job of customs collector after the death of Rousby, and he complained of the same kind of interference from Baltimore's people that his predecessor had described. The proprietor denied the charges, but again the Crown chose to believe its royal officer. Blackiston had a good deal to say, too, about the proprietary men's complicity in Talbot's escape from Virginia and insisted that the principals in Maryland made no attempt to seize him and bring him to trial. Blackiston in his reports home made good use of the Rousby-Talbot affair as a "signal token" of the "ill and wicked carriage of things here." Offenses against the trade acts alone, thought some, were sufficient to bring down the charter. Others were sure that Talbot's murder of the collector would be the clincher.[46]

To a good many people in Maryland the charter and the proprietor were barriers between them and the King. Dependence upon the Crown in a well-ordered royal government would guarantee the rights and privileges they believed were the birthright of every Englishman. It would establish for them a place in the empire equal to that of other colonists and to Englishmen who lived in the realm. But colonial dependence in the eyes of Marylanders meant, too, a larger share in government than they had enjoyed before, a taste of its privileges and perquisites for those who felt discriminated against, for those who had struggled so long against the selfish demands of a proprietor and his clique of family and favorites. Dependence upon the Crown meant, besides Englishmen's rights, sufficient self-government to satisfy the ever present demands of self-interested colonists, demands which the proprietary government had no intention of recognizing.

At the same time the Kings of England, Charles and James, as part of their understanding of prerogative and their conception of empire,

46. Blathwayt to Effingham, Sept. 6, Dec. 9, 1684, BPCol. Wmsbg., v. XIV; Effingham to Blathwayt, Feb. 24, 1686, and Feb. 7, 1687, *ibid.;* Spencer to Blathwayt, May 9, 1686, *ibid.;* Dyer to Blathwayt, June 13, 1685, *ibid.,* v. IV; C.O. 1/57/81; Randolph to Southwell, Jan. 29, 1684, Toppan, ed., *Randolph,* IV, 4-5. For Blackiston's charges and Baltimore's defense, see *Arch. of Md.,* V, 436-41, 446-52. James II, after a few months on the throne, sent new instructions to all the colonies commanding a tightening of the Acts of Trade. Accompanying those sent to Baltimore were specific orders to take "particular care" in these matters. C.O. 324/4, pp. 165-66; C.O. 389/9, pp. 348-58.

demanded colonial dependence but of a different nature, one which Baltimore's government also frustrated. Theirs was a desire for a colonial relationship which would first augment the empire, its power and authority, its trade, and particularly the Crown's revenue. It would allow subject colonists in America only the rights and privileges the King wished to give them. Uniformity, control, subjection, and profit were characteristics of the emerging empire, particularly after 1675, and Baltimore's charter and government were obstacles to fulfillment of the Crown's policy.

Baltimore found himself between these two forces, both bent on his demise but for different reasons. In pursuing proprietary interests he denied the rights of Englishmen to his colonists; at the same time he frustrated Stuart schemes of a dependent empire. For a few months the attack upon the charter bogged down in 1685, owing to the death of Charles, the accession of James, and Monmouth's and Argyle's Rebellions, all of which distracted attention from colonial affairs. But once the kingdom was quiet again, the campaign against the charter quickened. The Crown soon secured a *quo warranto* against it, and although no judgment was reached in the short years of James's reign, proprietary prospects looked very dim. Dissident colonists in Maryland kept pace, in fact increased the tempo, in a colony "too ripe for disturbances." [47] After 1685 it was a question which of Baltimore's opponents would reach his goal first. The uncertainty and instability of Maryland's past were more a part of the scene than ever before. It would not take much to upset the tenuous balance.

47. Blathwayt to Effingham, July 8, 1685, BPCol. Wmsbg., v. XIV; [?] to Baltimore, Oct. 1687, *ibid.*, v. VI; Randolph to Southwell, July 30, 1685, Toppan, ed., *Randolph*, IV, 26–27; *Acts of P.C., Col. Ser., 1680–1720*, #193, p. 88; Order to Attorney General, Apr. 1687, in George Chalmers, *Political Annals*, p. 371.

6 New York and the Charter of Libertyes

A Ducal Proprietary

The latter half of the seventeenth century proved to a good many settlers in America just how unsettled and tenuous was their position as Englishmen outside the realm. A unique situation obtained in the colony of New York after the English conquest of 1664; the colonists' response to it explains something about the colonial mind and gives a clue to what one group of American colonists had concluded about the imperial relationship.

For some time New Netherlands had been a thorn in the side of good mercantilists in England and hungry colonists in America. Both saw their trade threatened, furs siphoned off to Holland, and the expansion of New England blocked by foreigners at New Amsterdam and Fort Orange (Albany). After the Restoration of Charles II in 1660 broader and better-defined ideas of the Atlantic trade emerged in the minds of the English King, Parliament, and the trading people at home and abroad. One of the early imperial schemes of the Restoration government was the conquest of New Netherlands. After Peter Stuyvesant reluctantly surrendered his settlements to the Royal Commissioners and their troops in 1664, King Charles gave the colony to his younger brother, James, Duke of York, to govern as he pleased.

The Duke's proprietary was large but scattered. It stretched beyond Dutch mainland claims to include Long Island, half of Connecticut, several islands off the coast of Massachusetts, Pemaquid in the province of Maine, all of what is now New Jersey, and part of what became Delaware. Instructed to be "a good husband to the Duke," a governor of New York had his hands full merely keeping track of what belonged to His Highness, let alone ruling his people and collecting a revenue. Like Virginia and Maryland, New York's boundaries were not agreed upon, least of all by its neighbors. Connecticut was the least amenable and adamantly refused to recognize the Duke's claims to that half of the Puritan colony west of the Connecticut River which New York's third governor, Edmund Andros, reported was usurped and still possessed by New Englanders. The boundary troubles with Connecticut continued for a number of years. Both Governors Andros and Thomas Dongan, who followed him, were anxious to resolve the problem by annexing Connecticut altogether, claiming that the settlers there were very willing to oblige. Edward Randolph, who knew the Puritans better than most royal officials, called this nonsense, for if Connecticut people joined hands anywhere, it would be with their fellow saints of Massachusetts.

New York also found difficulty supporting itself. The problem became acute after the Duke gave New Jersey away to proprietors Berkeley and Carteret, and the Delaware Country to William Penn. Revenue was thin in the 1680's, and annexation of Connecticut looked like a means of increasing it. Contrary to law, which awarded a trading monopoly to New York City, the Puritans on Long Island continued to trade directly with their friends in Connecticut and Boston. The exchange not only deprived the Duke's government of customs but cut the city merchants out of a lucrative trade in whale oil, one of the colony's principal exports. Andros may have talked about the "good Correspondence" with his neighbors in America, but it did not include Connecticut as far as boundaries and trade were concerned.[1]

1. "Answers of Gov. Andros to Enquiries about New York, 1678," E. B. O'Callaghan, ed., *Documentary History of the State of New-York* (4 vols., Albany, 1849–51), I, 89–90; hereafter referred to as *Doc. Hist. N.Y.* (1849). "Gov. Dongan's Report to the Committee of Trade on the Province of New-York, dated 22d February, 1687," *ibid.*, 150–51, 153, 159–66, 187; Sir John Werden to Dongan, Dec. 4, 1684, *CSPCol.*, 1681–1685, #1979; Dongan to Blathwayt, Aug. 22, 1687, BPCol. Wmsbg., v. XI; Randolph to Blathwayt, Nov. 23, 1687, M. G. Hall, L. H.

New York was a little smaller than Maryland in population and a good deal smaller than Virginia. Estimates in the latter half of the seventeenth century varied, however. The Dutch claimed 6,000 people there when they recaptured the colony in 1673 during the Third Dutch War. Neither Andros nor Dongan reported population figures during his governorship, but given the number of militia (2,000 in both 1674 and 1678), one can estimate total population at about 10,000. Some twenty years later, when the Earl of Bellomont governed, he reported 18,067 men, women, children, and Negroes in New York (the latter numbered 2,170). Since he broke the inhabitants down by counties, his report gave promise of accuracy. This does not leave us a precise figure, say, for 1685, but one might be safe in estimating the population at the time of James II's accession to the throne at something less than 15,000. New Yorkers lived in three principal towns, New York, Albany, and Kingston, in houses generally of brick and stone. The rest of the people inhabited country villages, living in farmhouses, "mostly new built," but not very large, usually two to three rooms to a floor. Although both English and Dutch farmed the land, there was no doubt that the Dutch were the great improvers of the soil.[2]

If the size of New York in number of settlers is not striking, their variety is. Besides the conquered and the conquerors, there were Germans—Jacob Leisler, for instance—Swedes, Jews, and Frenchmen, mostly French Protestants who had suffered severely from Louis XIV's treatment at home. For the most part the English were concentrated on Long Island, having moved from Puritan Massachusetts and Connecticut. By the middle 1680's they had increased sufficiently to complain of a want of land on the island, and some already had left it for neighboring colonies. Overpopulation was not a problem on the mainland, nor was immigration, for that matter, at least not of British people. Governor Dongan lamented that in the first seven years of the

Leder, and M. G. Kammen, eds., *The Glorious Revolution in America: Documents on the Colonial Crisis of 1689* (Chapel Hill, N.C., 1964), p. 93. For a discussion of New York City's trading monopoly, see Jerome Reich, *Leisler's Rebellion* (Chicago, 1953), pp. 48–49; and Lawrence H. Leder, *Robert Livingston, 1654–1728, and the Politics of Colonial New York* (Chapel Hill, N.C., 1961), pp. 57–58.

2. From *Address of the Burgomasters &c to Bencks and Evertsen, Doc. Hist. N.Y.,* I (1849), 689; "Answers of Gov. Andros, 1678," *ibid.,* 89; "Gov. Dongan's Report, 1687," *ibid.,* 149, 160, 161; "An Account of the Number of Inhabitants, 1698," *ibid.,* 689. Marcus W. Jernegan states New York's white population to be 16,000 in 1689. *The American Colonies, 1692–1750* (2d ed., New York, 1959), p. 217. Edward Channing used estimates by George Bancroft and Franklin B. Dexter to come up with the improbable figure of 20,000 for the same period. *History of the United States* (6 vols., New York, 1908–19), II, 222 n. The estimate from the number of militia is from Evarts B. Greene and Virginia D. Harrington, *American Population Before the Federal Census of 1790* (New York, 1932), p. 89.

1680's less than twenty English, Scottish, or Irish families had ventured to the colony. A few French Huguenots were filtering in, coming by way of England and St. Christopher's, and he rightly expected more since King Louis revoked the Edict of Nantes in 1685. Curiously, several Dutch families had lately disembarked, but they only helped to swell the large number of Dutchmen already settled. Dongan, who looked for any excuse to increase New York in size, population, and profit, claimed that the preponderance of foreigners over Englishmen was reason enough to annex Connecticut and reclaim New Jersey in order to keep an orderly balance. It may very well be that New York was not a popular place for Englishmen to settle after the Restoration. Anyway, immigration was meager, and some who did settle came under duress, "being ordered for transportation," as victims of the Conventicle Acts in England, which were aimed at dissenters and fell hardest upon the Quakers. Daniel Denton, who visited in the late 1660's, concluded that a lack of English settlers was owing to a dearth of information about the colony in England, a void he tried to fill with his *Brief Description of New York* published in 1670. In 1682 a group of Scots after inquiry gave up a scheme to settle in New York and chose instead Carolina, where they found the constitution more "accomodate." [3] This was probably a polite way of pointing out New York's unattractiveness owing to a lack of an assembly.

The variety of national origins in New York was outdone only by the number of religions and sects which flourished there, or seemed to flourish. The "most prevailing opinion" was that of Dutch Calvinists, who shared with the Anglicans the "Great Church" close within the walls of the fort at the tip of Manhattan. There were Dutch Lutherans, too, but they were fewer in number. Besides these there were French Protestants and an abundance of Quakers, some of the "Singing," some of the "Ranting," variety. Next came the Sabbatarians, the Antisabbatarians, and a number of Anabaptists, along with a handful of Jews and Catholics. On Long Island, besides Quakers, the Independents (Congregational) and Presbyterians were "Substantiall"; they supported the public worship of God through local taxes, just as they had in New England, although Dongan complained that he found it difficult sometimes to make them pay their ministers. Small in number was the congregation of the Church of England, whose minister for a long time was the Duke's chaplain, the Reverend Charles Wooley. All

---

3. "Gov. Dongan's Report, 1687," *Doc. Hist. N.Y.*, I (1849), 161–62; Newsletter to Roger Garstell, London, Oct. 19, 1682, *CSPDom.*, 1682, p. 485; Daniel Denton, *A Brief Description of New York* . . . (London, 1670), reprinted in Gowans' *Bibliotheca Americana*, 1 (New York, 1845), 22; A. M. to Sir George Campbell, Apr. 28, 1682, H.M.C., 34: 14th Report, App. III, p. 113.

told there were some twenty churches or meeting houses in New York, and in 1678 more than half were vacant for want of clergymen. Good ministers sent there, said Andros, "might do well & gaine much upon those people." Dongan was less sanguine about both ministers' chances and the souls of New Yorkers; "of all sorts of opinions," he commented, "there are some, and the most part of none at all." Most settlers brought up their children and servants to believe as they, except for their Negro slaves, whom they took no care at all to convert. But New York was tolerant, even friendly, in its religious heterogeneity. When William Penn visited in 1683, Governor Dongan "with his fine folks" joined him at meeting, and Dongan was Catholic and an Irishman.[4]

Governor Dongan and Quaker Penn might have agreed that religion rested somewhat lightly upon the shoulders of most New Yorkers, no doubt one of the reasons why Connecticut people resisted annexation. There were a lot of "Strangers," to be sure, but very few of "ill principles." Dongan thought the men generally a lusty, strong-bodied lot and their wives prolific. One old granny, still very much alive, was well known for her progeny, "from whose Loyns," the governor reported, there were "upwards of three hundred @ sixty persons now living." Daniel Denton found New Yorkers lusty enough, too, particularly when they responded, as any colonist might, to good weather, young company, and the bounties of nature. June was a great time for frolic, he wrote, when the country people rode out from their villages, carrying wine, sugar, and cream, to enjoy strawberries in "such abundance . . . that the Fields and Woods are died red." The fruits of June were not only toothsome, Denton continued, "instead of a Coat of Male, every one takes a Female upon his Horse behind him, and so rushing violently into the fields, never leave till they have disrobed them of their red colours, and turned them into the old habit."[5]

---

4. "Answers of Gov. Andros, 1678," *Doc. Hist. N.Y.*, I (1849), 92; "Gov. Dongan's Report, 1687," *ibid.*, pp. 186–87; William Penn to J. Anderdon, Philadelphia, 29 9th mo., 1683, Portfolio 31/95, Library of the Society of Friends, London; Bartlett B. James and J. Franklin Jameson, eds., *Journal of Jasper Danckaerts, 1679–1680* (New York, 1913), pp. 85–86. Several years later Charles Lodwyck confirmed Dongan's suspicions about religion when he wrote, ". . . as to Religion we run so high into all Opinions, that here is, I fear, but little reall." Charles Lodwyck to Francis Lodwyck, New York, May 20, 1692, Sloane Mss., 3339, f. 93b, B.M.

5. Dongan to the Lord President, Sept. 18, 1685, E. B. O'Callaghan and B. Fernow, eds., *Documents Relative to the Colonial History of the State of New-York* (14 vols., Albany, 1856–87), III, 364–65; hereafter referred to as *N.Y. Col. Docs.* "Gov. Dongan's Report, 1687," *Doc. Hist. N.Y.* I (1849), 150; Daniel Denton, *A Brief Description of New York*, pp. 3–4.

Governor Dongan sensed the strategic importance, both economic and military, of New York colony and can be forgiven his optimism, even boastfulness, in the 1680's. It was the center of all His Majesty's Dominions in America, he wrote home; "A Thousand ships may ride here safe from winds @ weather." [6] He was doubtless right, but such statements at the time must have lacked substance in colonists' minds when they remembered that Andros had reported a few years earlier that maybe ten to fifteen vessels traded there in a year's time. Ten years or so later the number of ships entering and clearing New York Harbor had almost doubled; most were owned in the colony, except for a handful from England, New England, and the West Indies. Trade between New York and Albany kept six or seven of the colony's vessels busy most of the year when the Hudson was free of ice.

Furs, whale oil, and foodstuffs made up the bulk of New York's export trade. The fur came down the river from Albany, where the Indians had brought it. Fur and whale oil found their way to England; so did tobacco, "when we can have it." New York's tobacco trade had taken a beating following the Duke's grant in 1682 of the lower counties to William Penn, for Delaware tobacco was subject to the Plantation Duty after that date and its charge cut down the trade. To the West Indies New Yorkers shipped their foodstuffs, primarily wheat (60,000 bushels in 1678), flour, and bread, but also beef, pork, and peas, along with lumber products and a few horses. Their vessels returned with rum, which paid the King a sizable duty, and molasses from which they made their own rum and paid him nothing. From the mother country the colonists imported a variety of manufactured goods for themselves and "blancketts, Duffells &c." for the Indians. Importations from England were worth about £50,000 in 1678. Pemaquid, the small settlement in Maine, exported fish to the West Indies and sent home ships' masts to England. The three principal trading towns were New York, Albany, and Southampton, the last the only port on the ocean side of Long Island. [7]

A chief characteristic of New York's economy was that a good deal of it was tied up in monopolies of one kind or another. Despite the varieties of nationalities and religions which made up the population of the colony, there emerged from this mixture over the years a

6. "Gov. Dongan's Report, 1687," *Doc. Hist. N.Y.,* I (1849), 160–61, 187; William Penn also recognized New York's potential, probably more economic than military, as "too considerable to ye Crown, to be layd aside." Penn to Earl of Rochester, Phil., 14th of 4th month, 1683, Penn Mss., 32, Lib. Soc. Friends.

7. Dongan to Blathwayt, Sept. 18, 1685, BPCol. Wmsbg., v. XI; "Gov. Dongan's Report, 1687," *Doc. Hist. N.Y.,* I (1849), 160–61, 187; "Answers of Gov. Andros, 1678," *ibid.,* pp. 90–91; Denton, *A Brief Description of New York,* p. 3.

wealthy group of socially conscious merchants and landowners who won commercial monopolies, large landed estates, and political privileges from the proprietary and then royal governors, at whose council boards several of them sat. Most of the advantages went to New York City, where the elite traders and manufacturers did business. The Duke continuously encouraged the city—where he stood the best chance of collecting customs—an indulgence which often worked hardship on settlers who lived elsewhere. Be "careful of the city," the Duke instructed his governors, insisting that they adjust the trade of other parts of the colony in its favor. Particularly put out by the special treatment were Long Islanders who would rather have carried their goods to their Puritan friends in Connecticut and Boston than to strangers in the city as the laws demanded. Bolting and packing of flour was one of the city monopolies, and it infuriated farmers who were forced by law to send their grain there no matter where they lived. Similarly, Albany traders enjoyed exclusive control of the fur trade, except that they were denied the right to ship furs directly overseas; instead they sent them down the Hudson to Manhattan, where the city merchants reshipped them abroad. Such a system discriminated against the small farmers and traders and ordinary city folk whose normal means of making a living were inhibited by the economic privileges accruing to a powerful group of emerging aristocrats.[8]

Although economic prospects improved as time went on (a precious understatement, given our knowledge of New York's later development), the colony's economy in the years before the Glorious Revolution was tenuous at best. No doubt one difficulty was the Duke's greediness in attempting to control so large an area and so scattered a people under one government, even an arbitrary one. The difficulty in bringing it off had something to do with James's willingness to part with New Jersey and eventually the lower counties on the Delaware, although both grants were opposed by his ambitious governors.

New York's policy toward the Indians and the French to the north was a matter of grave concern, demanding diligence, patience, and considerable expense. The French in Canada were imperial rivals—no doubt about that—but policy toward them was no isolated affair; it hinged on the Indians, principally the Iroquois, whose presence in

8. For attacks upon, and defense of, these monopolies, see petitions and reports from Albany and New York reprinted in Hall, Leder, and Kammen, eds., *Glo. Rev. in Am.*, pp. 86–91; Werden to Dongan, St. James's, Nov. 1, 1684, *CSPCol., 1681–1685,* #1915; Reich, *Leisler's Rebellion,* pp. 44–51; Leder, *Robert Livingston,* pp. 57–58; Bernard Mason, "Some Aspects of the New York Revolt of 1689," *New York History,* 30 (1949), 165–80.

New York was a formidable responsibility. In 1685 the Five Nations boasted between 2,000 and 2,500 braves capable of taking the war-path. (The French in Canada about this time numbered probably 17,000 in total population with some 3,000 men able to bear arms.) No seventeenth-century colonist, regardless of where he lived, had any misgivings about the Iroquois as the strongest and most warlike of the Indians met by the English. And although the Five Nations spent most of their time in or near upstate New York, their influence upon other Indians, even their occasional presence in war dress, was felt, the colonists believed, as far afield as the "South-Sea," the "North-West passage," and Florida. (Both New Yorkers and Indians may have disagreed over the precise location of each of these geographical points.) All other Indians who resided anywhere near them were "tributary" to the Iroquois in one way or another, and even the people of Boston, who claimed they owed tribute only to God, were careful to send them presents in acknowledgment of their favor and good will.[9]

Luckily the government of New York retained a calculated friendship with the Iroquois, who served as a buffer between English colonists and the French of Canada. Much of the friendship had its origin with the Dutch, who long since had learned its importance in keeping their tiny colony intact. One Dutchman made such a favorable impression on the Iroquois in his relations with their chiefs that they called him "Corlaer," or beloved, and soon transferred the honor to the English governors with whom they dealt. Had Governor Dongan a free hand, he most likely would have used the Five Nations more boldly in his ambitious plans to undo the imperial schemes of France and fashion an English monopoly of the fur trade. But James at home, before and after he became king, charged his governors to play safe with their rivals. Since they never could persuade the French to cease their trade with the New York Indians, the governor more prudently tried to discourage the Iroquois from it by making the English trade more attractive. Mark you, warned James, this must be accomplished "without shocking the Governor of Canada"; we must "avoid anything that may involve us in dispute with the French." This was the precarious path Dongan walked. Doubtless he was vaguely aware of both Charles's and James's secret relations with Louis XIV and the French King's subsidies to the English Crown during its serious disputes with Parliament. To ordinary colonists anywhere in America the policy

9. C.O. 5/1135/22; "Memoir Concerning the Present State of Canada, 1685," *Doc. Hist. N.Y.*, I (1849), 196; *ibid.*, 690; "Gov. Dongan's Report, 1687," *ibid.*, pp. 154–55, 158.

must have been a puzzle, even suspect, if they knew about it, particularly later when a Catholic conspiracy became so much a part of the settlers' thinking, and no more so than in New York, where a Catholic governor, who got along with the Indians, ruled during the 1680's for a Catholic duke who became king. On top of this, New York geographically was vulnerable at both ends of the river, as the Dutch learned in 1664 and the people of Schenectady in 1690. Although more rumor than fact, as we know today, a fear of conspiracy between Catholics and Indians mushroomed in New York, as it did in Maryland, once James was on the throne. One of its prime victims was Jacob Leisler, a virulent Calvinist and as anti-Catholic as they come. Conspiracy or no, Dongan was largely successful in keeping the French at arm's length and the Iroquois friendly, bragging at one time that upon any occasion he could bring on the run three or four thousand braves to his side—which would have been a considerable accomplishment, since the Iroquois at best could number only about 2,500 fighting men.[10]

The Inexpressible Burdens of an Arbitrary and Absolute Power

If a large Dutch population, a babel of languages and religions, a lucrative fur trade, and an eggshell diplomacy with both Indians and the French distinguished New York from other English colonies in America, so, too, did the Duke's government. Unlike other Restoration proprietaries—the Carolinas, Jerseys, and Pennsylvania—New York had no representative assembly. Virginia was settled in 1607, and its first legislature met within twelve years. Massachusetts had enjoyed an assembly from the outset, Maryland almost from the start, but not New York. There were several reasons for the omission. Under the Dutch States General, four successive directors, including Peter Minuit and Peter Stuyvesant, first and last, had ruled arbitrarily, each with a council alone, without the help of the colonists or their representatives. Since the Dutch had never had a legislature, supposedly they would not miss one, and they were a large part of the population.

Second, and probably more important as things turned out, Stuart monarchs were suspicious of elected legislatures. They had never had any great luck with them in England, and James in particular thought them a nuisance. New Yorkers had to be satisfied with what were known as the Duke's Laws, a long and detailed code of regulations

10. *Ibid.*, 154–56; Abstract of Commissions, etc., Add. Mss., 30372, f. 2, B.M. Werden to Dongan, Nov. 1, Dec. 4, 1684, *CSPCol., 1681–1685*, #1115, #1979.

borrowed from New England and arbitrarily adapted to proprietary circumstances with no mention of the rights of Englishmen or colonists' role as English subjects beyond the realm. Richard Nicolls, a member of the Royal Commission charged with the conquest of New Netherlands and the Duke's first governor, ordered a convention in 1665 at Hempstead, Long Island, where elected representatives from the settled areas close by accepted, not without some protest, the colony's first set of laws. One cannot call this meeting an assembly, although Nicolls and governors who followed did so, for it met only to approve the laws and then was dissolved. The Duke's Laws went into effect immediately, and the governor and council ruled with an appointed Court of Assizes to dispense justice. In 1665 the proprietary colony of New York was under way.[11]

Between 1665 and 1683 a good deal of protest arose against the handling of New York affairs. The lack of an assembly was a primary grievance, for it not only deprived most New Yorkers of a role in deciding how they were to be governed; it deprived them, too, of a means to strike back against the economic monopolies and special privileges that only a few enjoyed. Most of the protests originated on Long Island where New Englanders were concentrated. Their arguments were based first on Governor Nicolls' promise—allegedly made at the time of submission to the Commissioners—"of equall (if not greater) freedomes and immunityes then any of his Majesties colonyes in New England." To transplanted New Englanders, rights equal to or greater than those of other Yankee colonists must mean at the very least protection from arbitrary government by establishment of a representative assembly with the sole power to enact laws and levy taxes upon them. The Court of Assizes later denied that Nicolls had made such a promise and informed Long Islanders that nothing was "required of them but obedience and submission to the Lawes of the Government." [12] A more vigorous protest complained that the inhabitants were "inslaved under an Arbitrary Power," and that Nicolls exercised more authority "than the King himselfe can do." The gover-

11. See *The Colonial Laws of New York from the Year 1664 to the Revolution* (5 vols., Albany, 1894–96), I, 1–71. "Gov. Nicolls' Answers to the Severall Queries," [ca. 1669], *Doc. Hist. N.Y.*, I (1849), 88. Southold's deputies came to the convention armed with instructions from their town meeting demanding that no taxes be raised from them without their consent "in a general court meeting," but no regard was paid. E. B. O'Callaghan, *Origin of Legislative Assemblies in the State of New York* (Albany, 1861), p. 9. O'Callaghan's study appears also as "Historical Introduction" in *Journal of the Legislative Council of the Colony of New-York* [1691–1775] (2 vols., Albany, 1861), pp. iii–xxvii.

12. O'Callaghan, *Origin of Legislative Assemblies*, pp. 5–11; *N.Y. Col. Docs.*, XIV, 632.

nor labeled this slander and high treason and reminded the colonists that the English Civil War, the "Late Rebellion," began "with the selfe same steps and pretences." [13]

Besides petitions and high words, protests took other forms. In 1666 two constables in Southold, opposed to the arbitrary method of taxation, refused to do their duty, and the sheriff issued a warrant to levy fines upon them. In the same town there was outright refusal by several people to pay their rates, even by some of the overseers who had agreed to the making of them. Petitions and protests got Long Islanders nowhere, and they were branded "ill mynded people who take delight to breed disturbances and to infuse ill principles into the myndes of his Majesties good Subjects." [14]

In 1670, after Francis Lovelace had replaced Nicolls as governor, he and the council levied a new tax upon the inhabitants over and above the usual to defray the expenses of repairing Fort James on Manhattan. A Huntington town meeting led the way and denounced the tax because it deprived people of the "liberties of english men." Besides, the meeting complained, the people of Huntington were busy with their own problems and would receive no benefit from a fort in New York City anyway. Jamaica people called the tax contrary to the "Laws of the nation" and doubted that the governor's commission permitted it. Already they were paying a penny in the pound to support the government; if the governor and council demanded money for the fort, they reasoned, they could also demand "what ills we know not tell thear be no end." [15] Flushing and Hempstead, along with Jamaica, held several town meetings and drew up resolves protesting the government's demands. These resolutions eventually reached the governor and council, who pronounced them scandalous, illegal, and seditious, demanded that they be "publiquely burned," and ordered that the "principall contrivers thereof be inquired into." [16]

During the Third Dutch War, 1672–1674, the Dutch recaptured New York, and agitation, at least against the proprietor's governor, ceased for a time. Reestablishment of Dutch rule, however, did not stop the settlers of East Hampton, Southampton, and Southold from petitioning King Charles about grievances sustained from both English and Dutch governments. What they objected to was interference with

13. Richard Nicolls to John Underhill, May 7, 1666, *ibid.*, 580.

14. Governor's commission, Mar. 9, 1671, Victor H. Paltsits, ed., *Minutes of the Executive Council of the Province of New York* (2 vols., Albany, 1910), II, 524–25; *N.Y. Col. Docs.*, XIV, 578, 582, 584.

15. Charles R. Street, ed., *Huntington Town Records . . .* (3 vols., Huntington, N.Y., 1887–89), I, 163–64; Josephine C. Frost, ed., *Records of the Town of Jamaica, Long Island, New York, 1656–1751* (3 vols., Brooklyn, 1914), I, 47–48.

16. *N.Y. Col. Docs.*, XIV, 646; Paltsits, ed., *Min. of Exec. Council*, II, 485–87.

their whale fishery, first by "heavy taxes" under the English, higher than those in New England, without allowing them "any deputies in court," and then by arbitrary laws imposed upon them by the Dutch. The eastern Long Islanders claimed they had purchased their land thirty years earlier and that the land rightly belonged under Connecticut's patent whence most of them had come. If they could not be governed by Connecticut, they suggested the King make them a "free corporation," a very unlikely possibility to say the least. The petition got as far as the Lords of Trade and doubtless died there.[17]

In the Treaty of Westminster which ended the war, the Dutch agreed to return New York to the English. James dispatched Major Edmund Andros as governor to replace Francis Lovelace, who returned to England in disgrace and was cast into the Tower to await trial for failing to defend the fort at New York against the Dutch.[18] Agitation for an assembly continued. Andros gave the colonists no encouragement, but he did report to the Duke that taxes and customs might come easier if the colonists had a part to play in the way they were levied. The Duke, of course, wanted New York to pay its own way. He also wanted income from his colony through revenue from customs duties. After all, what was a proprietary colony for if not to profit its proprietor? James considered Andros' suggestions and agreed that the colonists' desire for an assembly was "in imitacon of their neighbor Colonies"; but he refused to go along with Andros' suggestion. Instead James commended Andros for discouraging any idea of an assembly.

Duke James gave several reasons for his refusal. It was outside Andros' instructions to grant an assembly, he said. There was no argument there. Redress against grievances was easily come by under the Duke's Laws as they existed; all the governor and council had to do was to rule according to the laws already set down. What is more, wrote the Duke to Andros, the Court of Assizes doubtless contained the same people who would be elected to an assembly anyway. Assemblies without proper restrictions "would be of dangerous consequence" and apt to "assume to themselves many priviledges which prove destructive to, or very oft disturbe, the peace of the government wherein they are allowed." Probably the Duke could have made no statements more clearly revealing his insensitivity to, and misunderstanding of, the colonists' sentiments and attitude toward government. A final remark did suggest that if Andros still believed an assembly would help, the Duke would consider proposals the governor might make.[19]

17. *CSPCol., 1669–1674,* #875 and #875, I.

18. *Ibid., 1675–1676,* #530.

19. Duke of York to Andros, Apr. 6, 1675, and Jan. 28, 1676, *N.Y. Col. Docs.,* III, 230, 235.

A specific incident in 1680 brought the whole issue to a head and indicated that opposition to arbitrary government was not confined to testy transplanted New Englanders. As one might expect, it was a money problem which precipitated this sharp turn in the history of the colony of New York. The Duke's customs rates and duties on trade ran for three-year periods, and the rates levied in 1677, out of which came the support for government, expired in November 1680. But just before the date of expiration, the Duke recalled Governor Andros to London to answer several charges, including one against the governor's handling of the revenue. Andros embarked for home without renewing the customs duties—leaving Lieutenant Anthony Brockholls in his place as deputy. When Collector William Dyer attempted to collect the customs, the merchants balked. Ships entered and cleared without paying rates. The council met but took no steps to continue the laws. Brockholls stood by helpless, watching the government's sanction crumble.[20]

Collector Dyer bore the brunt of the people's pent-up anger. They claimed that his attempt to collect the expired customs and the use of soldiers to assist him were violations of Magna Carta, the Petition of Right, several other statutes, and the honor and peace of the "King that now is." For maliciously exercising such "Regall Power," a grand jury formally charged him with being a "false Traytour" to the King and with subverting the "known Ancient and Fundamentall Lawes of the Realme of England." Once in court to reply to the charges, Dyer challenged the jurisdiction of the Assizes, claiming that both he and the court had commissions from the same source, James, Duke of York, and therefore the court could not try him. The court, fearing trouble with the Duke, agreed not to pursue the case but instead packed the collector off to England where he might be proceeded against as the Crown directed. In London, after the prosecutor failed to appear, the charges were dropped, and Dyer was advanced in His Majesty's service.[21]

20. *Ibid.*, 221–23, 246; Duke to Andros and Werden to Andros, May 24, 1680, *ibid.*, 283–84; O'Callaghan, *Origin of Legislative Assemblies*, pp. 12–13. Another reason for recalling Andros was the complaints against him from New Jersey for exacting duties on trade there. Blathwayt to Culpeper, Aug. 26, 1680, BPCol., Wmsbg., v. XVII. For a similar stoppage of customs in the Barbados, see Sir John Witham to Blathwayt, Aug. 8, 1683, *ibid.*, v. XXXV. Andros was exonerated. John West to Robert Livingston, June 6, 1681, Livingston Family Papers, General Correspondence, 1661–1695, Franklin D. Roosevelt Library, Hyde Park, N.Y.; *CSPCol.*, *1681–1685*, #1415.

21. Blathwayt to Richard Dutton, Sept. 17, 1681, BPCol. Wmsbg., v. XXX. For the proceedings against Dyer and the bill found against him, see *N.Y. Col. Docs.*, III, 288–89 and n. "Proceedings of the General Court of Assizes . . . October 6,

William Dyer's trial in New York got a number of people excited. The lack of power to collect the customs and Dyer's attempt to do so without authority intensified demands for an assembly. The outspoken discontent made it clear that if the Duke wanted money, he would have to allow a legislature. Long Islanders no longer fought the battle alone; evidence of bad feeling among the people was widespread.[22] The colony's Grand Jury, which had indicted Dyer, petitioned the Court of Assizes and summarized the protests of a good many when it complained of the insupportable burden which was thrust upon them all. In a very revealing document the Grand Jury explained that the burden could be removed only "by sitting us upon Equall Ground with our fellow Brethren and subjects of the Realme of England In our Neighboring Plantacons." The only way to do this, of course, was to place the government in the hands of a governor, council, and assembly elected by the freeholders. Only by this means could New Yorkers enjoy the good and wholesome laws of the realm. In a burst of eloquence the Grand Jury proclaimed: "Thereby wee may Bud Blossom and bring forth the fruites of a Prosperous and flourishing Government for want of which wee have Been (and yett are) in a most wythering and Decaying Condicon. . . ."[23]

The Grand Jury begged the Court of Assizes—which, if not a representative body, at least included settlers from several areas—to carry their case directly to the Duke and strongly urged sending a petition, which the Court agreed to do immediately. The Assizes' petition to James complained of "inexpressible burdens" and of the "arbitrary and absolute power" over the people which exacted revenue against their will. Even more forcefully than the Grand Jury, it hammered home the idea that English subjects, no matter where they lived, were equal as far as rights and treatment from government were concerned. Under present conditions as colonists they were "esteemed as nothing" and had "become a reproach" to their neighbors in the King's other colonies who, unlike New Yorkers, flourished under the protection of the King's "unparalleled form and method of government." What was prac-

---

1680, to October 6, 1682," New-York Historical Society *Collections,* XLV (New York, 1913), 11. See also *CSPCol., 1681–1685,* #155. John West to [Sir Leoline Jenkins], July 1, 1681, *ibid.;* Order of the Privy Council, Sept. 14, 1681, and Report of Sir John Churchill to Commissioners of the Duke of York's revenue, Nov. 28, 1683, *ibid.,* #225, #1415.

22. James Graham of New York linked the discontent during the customs revolt and Dyer's trial with the Exclusion Crisis and a fear of civil war in England. Graham to R. Livingston, June 8, 1681, Liv. Fam. Papers, Gen'l. Corresp., 1661–1695, F.D.R. Lib.

23. N.-Y. Hist. Soc., *Coll.,* XLV, 14–15.

ticable at home and in other colonies, that is, an "assembly of the people," was the "undoubted birthright" of all the King's subjects.[24]

Another incident occurred which pointed to similar conclusions about government. At Albany Collector Robert Livingston took John De Lavall to court in August 1681 for refusing to pay an excise on 510 gallons of rum he had unloaded and sold. At his trial De Lavall turned the court upside down by directing to it several searching questions. By what right did Livingston collect the excise, and, if by order of the governor, when did the King, Lords, and Commons give such power to the governor to levy taxes? If the excise was lawful, in what law could it be found? Not bound by the limits of a customs case, De Lavall asked, too, whether he and other colonists were considered "free born subjects of the king?" If not, he asked, "during which king's reign and by which act passed during such king's reign we were made otherwise than free?" These were touchy questions, and the red-faced court found it expedient to refer the case to the "supreme authorities" at New York.[25]

With the customs uncollected, government in New York seemed to be grinding to a halt. The colony was losing income needed for its support to say nothing of the money needed to pay what it owed to the Duke. Brockholls wrote to Andros in London describing how the merchants took advantage of the courts which were too frightened to carry out the deputy's orders. "Here it was Never worse," he declared, a government "wholly over thrown and in the Greatest Confusion and Disorder Possible." [26]

To add to Brockholls' worries, the Long Island towns grew increasingly restless. Several town meetings elected deputies and sent them to an extralegal convention at Huntington in late September 1681 where they consulted about their "Just liberties" and dispatched a petition to the deputy governor and Court of Assizes.[27] Brockholls and his court rejected the petition, reprimanded those who presented it, and sent them home with a warning to "Remaine in Quiett." The town meeting of Oyster Bay was not put off by such treatment and defiantly answered the court: "When the five men which ware the Representatives off longisland have Satisfacktion wee are willing to make payment of whatt Is Justly due as to the publick." [28]

24. *Ibid.*; John Romeyn Brodhead, *History of the State of New York* (2 vols., New York, 1853, 1871), II, 658.

25. A. J. F. Van Laer, ed., *Minutes of the Court of Albany, Rensselaerswyck and Schenectady, 1668–1685* (3 vols., Albany, 1926–32), III, 153–55.

26. *N.Y. Col. Docs.*, III, 289 n.

27. Benjamin D. Hicks, ed., *Records of the Towns of North and South Hempstead, Long Island, N.Y.* (8 vols., Jamaica, N.Y., 1896–1904), I, 385–86; John Cox, Jr., ed., *Oyster Bay Town Records* (8 vols., New York, 1916–40), I, 245–46; Street, ed., *Huntington Town Recs.*, I, 315.

28. N.-Y. Hist. Soc., *Coll.*, XLV, 17, 25; Cox, ed., *Oyster Bay Town Recs.*, I, 247.

Sometime before Dyer's unsuccessful attempt to collect the customs, Matthias Nicolls, secretary of the governor's council, sailed home to England to have a talk with the Duke. Nicolls was an old settler, having come to New York in 1664, and a very busy officeholder. What his mission was is not clear, but once in England he followed James to Scotland, where the Duke was in cordial exile during the Exclusion Crisis, and doubtless explained to him just what the colony's financial problem was. In view of the circumstances in New York, he may very well have pled directly for an assembly.[29]

There can be no doubt that James changed his mind about a New York legislature for financial reasons. The government's recent failure to collect the Duke's customs was the second blow to his revenue within the space of a year or two. Even after James in 1680 had given over East and West New Jersey to proprietors Berkeley and Carteret, New York had continued to levy customs duties on her neighbors' trade for revenue purposes. The New Jersey people complained, and James, in a surprise move, requested a legal opinion about his customs rights in New Jersey from Sir William Jones, former attorney general, prominent Whig lawyer, and a new member of Parliament in 1680. Shortly after Jones replied that James had no legal right to the customs of New Jersey, the Duke released fully both colonies to their proprietors. The loss to New York was estimated to be about one-third of its trade, with, of course, a consequent sharp decline in its revenue. This was not the worst of it. Jones's opinion cast great doubt, even among the Duke's commissioners, upon James's right to charge customs at all, even in New York. And, what is more, if he continued to do so, whether legally or illegally, he would likely drive his colonists across the river to New Jersey, where they would be free of his jurisdiction and his taxes.[30] It

29. Wait Winthrop to Fitz-John Winthrop, Dec. 19, 1681, M.H.S. *Coll.*, 5th ser., VIII (Boston, 1882), 424; Brodhead, *Hist. of N.Y.*, II, 335–36.

30. Werden to Sir Allen Apsley, Aug. 8, 1681, *N.Y. Col. Docs.*, III, 291; Mayor of New York to Werden, n.d., *ibid.*, 361; Blathwayt to Culpeper, Aug. 26, 1680, BPCol. Wmsbg., v. XVII; C.O. 1/57/119; C.O. 324/4, p. 231. For Sir William Jones's opinion, see George Chalmers, *Political Annals of the Present United Colonies* (London, 1780), pp. 619, 626; and Chalmers, *An Introduction to the History of the Revolt of the American Colonies* (2 vols. printed as one, Boston, 1845), I, 150. Extract of a Letter from the Mayor of New York, dated the 13th May 1685, *Arch. of Md.*, V, 444–45. Why James should neglect his own legal advisers and ask for an opinion from Sir William Jones, ardent Whig and a leader in the drive to exclude James from the throne, is not altogether clear. For a partial explanation, see John E. Pomfret, *The Province of West New Jersey, 1609–1702* . . . (Princeton, N.J., 1956), pp. 111–12; and *The Province of East New Jersey, 1609–1702* . . . (Princeton, 1962), pp. 121–23. See also Mrs. Schuyler Van Rensselaer, *History of the City of New York in the Seventeenth Century* (2 vols., New York, 1909) II, 203. Sir William Jones's stand against taxation without representation made him a champion among American colonists. See his opinion as attorney general respecting Virginia's attempt in 1675 to secure from Charles II a charter which would

was doubtless these brute facts and maybe Matthias Nicolls' persuasive arguments which helped convince the Duke that the only way to make New York worth his time and effort was to grant an assembly, on condition, of course, that the people there agreed to support the government and to pay off the arrears accumulated since the disturbances began. His intent, he wrote to Brockholls, was to establish a government with all the "advantages and priviledges" which other American plantations enjoy, and "in all other things as nere as may be agreable to the laws of England." He may or may not have been believed when he added: "I seeke the common good and protection of that countrey and the increase of their trade, before my advantages to myselfe in the matter." [31]

The Charter of Libertyes

James's new governor, Colonel Thomas Dongan, arrived in New York in August 1683 carrying instructions to call an assembly.[32] Dongan had not been off the boat very long before the people of East Hampton, probably unaware of the governor's intent, cornered him with a petition, citing fully all the arguments in favor of a colonial legislature. The arrangement made in 1664 between them and Richard Nicolls, they claimed, was a "compact" which they alone had fulfilled. They stressed what Long Islanders had tirelessly repeated: a wish for status equal to that of subjects in other colonies, claiming that their unequal condition deprived them of a fundamental privilege of the "English Nation." In short order the governor issued writs for an election of representatives.[33]

On October 17, 1683, less than two months after Dongan arrived, the first meeting of the New York assembly took place at Fort James. Long Islanders sent six deputies—two from each riding; New York City with Haarlem, four; Kingston and Albany (including Rensselaers-

---

guarantee Virginians the right to tax themselves, in John Burk, *History of Virginia*, II, App., xl–xli. See also Cotton Mather, *Magnalia Christi Americana* (2 vols., Hartford, Conn., 1820), I, 162.

31. Duke of York to Brockholls, Mar. 28, 1682, *N.Y. Col. Docs.*, III, 317–18; Werden to Brockholls, Feb. 11, 1682, *CSPCol., 1681–1685*, #413.

32. *N.Y. Col. Docs.*, III, 331–34. Dongan, a strong loyalist, had fought for the Crown during the wars with Parliament. He was attached to Charles's entourage in Paris in the 1650's. See passport from Charles, H.M.C., 14th Report, *Ormonde*, App., pt. VII, v. I (London, 1895), 11. Dongan's salary was £400. *CSPCol., 1681–1685*, #917. Compare Culpeper's of Virginia, which was £2,000.

33. East Hampton petition is found in Benjamin F. Thompson, *History of Long Island . . .* (3 vols., New York, 1918), III, 637–40. O'Callaghan, *Origin of Representative Assemblies*, pp. 14–17.

wyck), two each; Staten Island, Schenectady, Pemaquid, and the islands, each one. Eighteen in all, they were elected, directly or indirectly, by the freeholders, although in New York City, Pemaquid, and Schenectady the sheriffs "appointed" the freeholders, who in turn elected representatives. As to who these men were, one can be reasonably sure of the identity of only about half of them.[34] Probably a majority were originally Dutch and not English.[35] Yet the Charter of Libertyes is very much an English document, which strongly suggests that the six Long Islanders and the few other Englishmen present took the lead over their Dutch colleagues in the task before them. Far better known than the names of the members is what they accomplished, for the result speaks for itself.

Of primary importance was the Charter of Libertyes and Priviledges which the members drafted as a frame of government protecting in no uncertain terms the colonists' individual liberties, the rights of property, and the right to consent to their laws and taxes. Even a quick reading of the Charter impresses one with the colonists' desire to guarantee for themselves rights English subjects anywhere ought to enjoy, reminiscent of Virginia's attempt to do the same thing in 1675. Second, the very statement of these rights implied strongly that they had not enjoyed them under the Duke and his laws—that they, in fact, had been governed arbitrarily, setting them apart from His Majesty's subjects elsewhere.

First of all, the Charter set up a frame or structure, as the preamble stated, for the "better Establishing the Government of this province of New Yorke and that Justice and Right may be Equally done to all persons within the same." [36] Supreme legislative authority, under the King and the Duke of York, was to reside forever in "a Governour, Councell, and the people mett in Generall Assembly." Executive authority was lodged in a governor and council who were to rule "according to the Lawes." The Charter rescaled representation in the assembly by county, varying it from four deputies allowed from the city and county of New York to two from all other counties except Albany,

34. For the various methods of electing representatives, see the writs issued by Dongan in *ibid.*, pp. 16–17. For names of some of the delegates, see Marius Schoonmaker, *The History of Kingston, New York* (New York, 1888), p. 75; Van Rensselaer, *Hist. of City of N.Y.*, II, 259; J. W. Thornton, "Ancient Pemaquid: An Historical Review," Maine Historical Society *Collections*, V (Portland, Me., 1857), 263–64; A. J. F. Van Laer, ed., *Correspondence of Maria Van Rensselaer, 1669–1689* (Albany, 1935), p. 127; and Edgar A. Werner, *Civil List and Constitutional History of the Colony and State of New York* (Albany, 1889), p. 67.

35. John West to William Penn, Oct. 16, 1683, in Samuel Hazard, *et al.*, eds., *Pennsylvania Archives* (138 vols., Philadelphia, 1852–1949), ser. 1, I, 80.

36. The charter is in *Colonial Laws of N.Y.*, I, 111–16.

which might send three. Again the Charter explicitly stated that once these representatives met with the governor and council, they would forever be "the Supreame and only Legislative power under his Royall Highnesse." Bills approved by the legislature were to become laws and remain in force until vetoed by the Duke or repealed.

The framers of the Charter went out of their way to provide for the protection of individual liberties. The right to vote for representatives was guaranteed to the freeholders and freemen of any corporation, and the Charter defined a freeholder as anyone so understood according to the laws of England—a clear case of equality there. The article guaranteeing liberty of person, one of the most fundamental rights of Englishmen, came directly from Magna Carta, II, 39 and 40: "THAT Noe freeman shall be taken and imprisoned or be disseized of his Freehold or Libertye or Free Customes or be outlawed or Exiled or any other wayes destroyed nor shall be passed upon adjudged or condemned But by the Lawfull Judgment of his peers and by the Law of this province." From the Petition of Right of 1628 came a paragraph protecting New Yorkers from taxation without representation. Another defended property rights and smacked generally of both Magna Carta and the Petition. Other fundamental rights, such as trial by jury, no excessive bail, and guarantees against quartering troops in private homes in peacetime, were included—every one of which protected the colonists from arbitrary treatment and suggested that under the previous government they had been apprehensive of such rights.

Besides personal and property rights, the legislators wrote into the Charter provisions for a number of parliamentary privileges for their legislature, which would have allowed a remarkable degree of legislative independence and fortified it against encroachment from either Duke or governor. Triennial meetings were guaranteed, a right Parliament in England had had trouble securing only a few years earlier and then not honored by the Crown. Representatives were empowered to appoint times of their meeting and to adjourn from time to time and assemble again as they pleased. They were to be sole judges of the qualifications of their own members and could purge their house as they saw fit. Also assembly members and at least three servants each were to be protected from arrest going to and from and during their sessions. It is clear the New Yorkers thought of their legislature as a little Parliament and intended by such privileges to maintain its power, dignity, and prestige.

The longest section in the Charter was devoted to religion, and well it might be, since New York contained a heterogeneous population, each part of which maintained its own church. Long Islanders may well have been a little stiff-necked about the whole thing. Although they went along with liberty of conscience for Christians, which was, of course, a practical necessity as it had been earlier, they saw to it that the Charter confirmed the supported churches in their towns when two-thirds of each town meeting approved. Moreover, they got written into the Charter power to compel the minor third of each town to contribute to the church's support. Liberty of conscience for Christians, yes, but as far as the English towns of Long Island were concerned, the public worship of God would continue under majority control, and the ministers' salaries would come out of taxes as was the custom in New England. Long Islanders used the Charter to establish legally religious practices already in effect. All other Christian churches within the colony the Charter confirmed, generally allowing them to continue their privileges.

The Charter of Libertyes is strong evidence that a number of New Yorkers had a definite idea of the kind of government colonists 3,000 miles from the realm ought to enjoy. But the very liberal aspects of the Charter might lead one to believe that political and constitutional principles were *all* the framers had in mind when they drafted it. It would be wrong to assume that the New Yorkers had inquired into their unequal condition in the empire and drafted a charter to correct it only from a dispassionate love of principle, any more than Virginians had in 1675. New Yorkers were made aware of these inequalities by conditions which affected their peculiar interests, for such inequalities frequently cost them money, deprived them of economic opportunities they believed they were entitled to, or discriminated against them by denying them rights which other English subjects enjoyed. That New Yorkers should express their discontent about these inequalities in political and constitutional terms is what one would expect. This is the way political and constitutional principles usually evolve or develop. After all, English liberties protected property and economic opportunity as well as civil and human rights. Members of the assembly owned property, or they would not have been elected, and they represented people who owned property, people who could not otherwise have voted for them.

New York colonists were well aware that the power to tax was the power to control property, and the Charter placed this power in the hands of the new legislature. But even this guarantee, it seems, was not sufficient for colonists whose property heretofore had been subject to the whim of a proprietor. Before the Duke ever saw the Charter, the lower house had expanded the "Libertyes" of the constitution and tightened the representatives' grip on the taxing power. On the same day the Charter was agreed to, the assembly worded the first revenue act in a style which echoed the House of Commons' similar business. It was the "Representatives" of the province of New York, with the advice and consent of the governor and council, who gave and granted to the Duke the "dutyes and Customes hereafter Specified."[37] Although the Charter granted control over taxes to the legislature as a whole— governor, council, and deputies—the lower house, the freeholders' representatives, at the very outset, asserted the right to originate money bills, just as did the House of Commons.

Each settled area of the colony had its peculiar demands, and no doubt these were seriously considered by the deputies and councilmen who drafted the Charter and enacted laws under it. That the six Long Islanders looked to their own interests and found votes to support them is already evident in the Charter's confirmation of religious privileges. Even better proof of Long Island influence was the new legislature's immediate repeal of a law which had annually taxed Long Islanders' property to defray public charges. The reason given for repeal was that "provision is otherwise made" for the colony's income, and the provision, of course, was the new revenue law which taxed through customs and excise.[38] The shift of part of the burden of taxation from Long Islanders' real estate to the colony's trade certainly suggests that their interest was well served by the assembly.

No doubt there were differences of opinion among those who fashioned the Charter, and debates over its drafting must have reflected several definite points of view. But it must be remembered that it was acceptable to the council as well as the representatives of the freeholders. And Dongan's council was an appointed body of six whose careers in government hardly demonstrated a devotion to the rights of Englishmen and government by consent. Four of the six, including Brockholls, Dongan continued in office from 1686 to 1688, after the business of the Charter was forgotten; and, when New York joined the Dominion of New England, Edmund Andros appointed to his council five of the six, again including Brockholls.[39] It was against the likes of these, men who willingly accepted arbitrary roles as rulers of New York under both Dongan and Andros, that Jacob Leisler revolted in 1689, as we shall see.

The assembly which drafted the Charter *elected* Matthias Nicolls,

37. *Ibid.*, 116–17.

38. *Ibid.*, 124. See J. M. Neil, "Long Island, 1640–1691: The Defeat of Town Autonomy" (unpubl. A.M. thesis, Univ. of Wisconsin, 1963), p. 95.

39. O'Callaghan, *Origin of Legislative Assemblies,* p. 17; Werner, *Civil List,* pp. 363–64; *N.Y. Col. Docs.,* III, 543.

now back from his mission to Scotland, its speaker. Nicolls, a trained lawyer and very able public servant, was a prerogative man who had come to the colony in 1664 as secretary to the Royal Commission and supposedly helped to draft the Duke's Laws the next year. He had been hand in glove with Governors Nicolls, Lovelace, and Andros; in 1680 he was both secretary of the council and a member of the Court of Assizes. He headed Dongan's council in 1686 but died before Andros drew New York into the Dominion. Owing to his close relationship with the proprietary government and his score or more years in vital offices, Nicolls was doubtless the most influential member of the legislature of 1683 next to Dongan. It is probable that he was more responsible than any other individual for the form the Charter took.[40]

John Spragge, who served on Dongan's and later Andros' Dominion council, was appointed clerk of the assembly which drafted the Charter, and during the year the Duke commissioned him secretary of the colony.[41] The failure of Dongan himself to veto the Charter (for reasons to be discussed below) is even surer evidence that those who controlled the government of New York had their own reasons for cooperation.

If such men as these were happy with the Charter, men who were firm supporters of any government, regardless of its principles, it must have been for reasons closely related to their own interests. Or to put it another way: if the Duke of York had decided upon representative government for New York, albeit as a last resort to secure its financial support, then that government ought to represent the interests of those who held positions of power. These men would mold the Charter in such a way that their particular needs might be reflected in the government the Charter established. While the new legislature afforded New York colonists treatment equal to what they believed other colonists and Englishmen at home enjoyed, at the same time it gave a smaller group of insiders a splendid opportunity to conduct the affairs of New York for their own good. A number of Virginians had reached a similar

40. For pertinent information about Matthias Nicolls, see Thompson, *Hist. of Long Island*, III, 334–35; Brodhead, *Hist. of N.Y.*, II, 335–36; Leonard W. Labaree in *Dictionary of American Biography*, s.v. "Nicolls, Matthias"; *Minutes of the Common Council of the City of New York, 1675–1776* (8 vols., New York, 1905), I, 4, 19, 48–49, 66; VIII, 149; Andrews, *Colonial Period*, III, 116, 117. Andrews asserts that Nicolls was largely responsible for drafting the Charter of Libertyes. For a different view, see Van Rensselaer, *Hist. of City of N.Y.*, II, 263–64; and Charles B. Moore, "Laws of 1683—Old Records and Old Politics," *New York Genealogical and Biographical Record*, XVIII (1887), 61. Rosalie Fellows Bailey, *The Nicoll Family and Islip Grange . . .* (New York, 1940), p. 9.

41. Werner, *Civil List*, 363–64; *N.Y. Col. Docs.*, III, 543; *CSPCol., 1681–1685*, #919.

conclusion in 1675. The rights of Englishmen and colonial self-interest were peas of the same pod. But in New York the whole scheme would mean little if the Duke failed to go along.

The first step was to get the Charter past Governor Dongan, who, as proprietary governor, was responsible for the Duke's interests. Fortunately, this proved to be no problem, and the reason may be that one of the first laws passed by the new legislature presented Dongan with a handsome sum of money, equal to a penny in the pound on all real and personal property belonging to freeholders and inhabitants.[42] Stephen Van Cortlandt of the council, who informally represented the huge Van Rensselaer estate in the new legislature, suggested that his constituents not oppose the move, "as it is for the governor," implying that they could not afford to offend Dongan at this juncture, since the Van Rensselaers were seeking at that very time his confirmation of a land claim.[43] The gift to Dongan was probably not considered outright bribery by the colonists but rather a "suitable returne" for the "many great favours" conferred upon them by the governor. Following Dongan's approval, the Charter of Libertyes was published at the City Hall on the last day of October 1683 in the presence of the governor, council, and representatives, the "Inhabitants having notice by sound of Trumpet." [44]

The second step was to obtain the Duke's approval. The Duke had agreed to grant an assembly if the colony would contribute the necessary financial support of the government and make up the arrears. At its first session the assembly levied ample taxes to carry the government's charges, but in doing so it stated that the revenue act was in consideration of the gracious favors extended to the colonists by the Duke—the favors included, of course, his future confirmation of the Charter already drafted, which, they claimed, restored their rights.[45] For granting an assembly the Duke received a sufficient revenue; for granting a sufficient revenue the New Yorkers hoped to secure approval of their very liberal Charter which put control of government in the hands of their legislature. There was a good deal of risk in this transaction on the assembly's part, but Dongan's immediate acceptance of the whole business was certainly encouraging.

Once the Charter became effective and the revenue assured, New York seemed "very easy & complacent"; the province "promiseth great

42. *Colonial Laws of N.Y.*, I, 137–38; *Min. of Common Council of N.Y.C.*, I, 102; J. M. Neil, "Long Island, 1640–1691," pp. 94–96.
43. Stephanus Van Cortlandt to Maria Van Rensselaer, Nov. 2, 1683, Van Laer, ed., *Correspondence of Maria Van Rensselaer*, pp. 131, 132. See also pp. 7, 127.
44. *Colonial Laws of N.Y.*, I, 137–38; *Min. of Common Council of N.Y.C.*, I, 99.
45. *Colonial Laws of N.Y.*, I, 116–17.

Improvement," said William Penn. The scene then shifted from the Duke's colony in America to London and the English court. After James's commissioners, who handled his colonial business, suggested a few amendments respecting customs and several other minor changes, James, in October 1684, one year after the drafting of the Charter, signed and sealed it and sent it to the auditor to be registered with orders to dispatch it to New York.[46]

But this was as far as it got. Suddenly the Charter of Libertyes ran up against obstacles in England the New York colonists had neither knowledge of nor means to combat.

Despite the outcome, several things were very clear. New York colonists were vitally interested in the rights of Englishmen as they defined them, and the use of Magna Carta and the Petition of Right was proof that they knew them pretty well. New Yorkers demanded rights equal to what they believed other colonists enjoyed and saw no reason why these should not be equal at the same time to those of Englishmen at home. Although they were colonists of a proprietary government, like the people of Maryland, they made it known that they did not regard themselves subordinate or inferior to His Majesty's subjects anywhere. Their concept of empire demonstrated a strong belief in equality among its members as far as government, rights, and opportunities were concerned. And like Virginians, they hoped to fix the idea of equality with a permanent charter which would guarantee it to them and dispel the uncertainty they had lived with for so long. This was a bold interpretation of empire in 1683, particularly in view of the fact that the Crown, Parliament, and proprietor were only beginning to decide what rights colonists ought to have, and what they decided, we shall see, was a far cry from what New Yorkers assumed to be true.

46. Penn to Duke of York, Phil., 2d 12th mo., 1683, Papers relating to William Penn, Penn Mss., 13, Lib. Soc. Friends; List of Bills (or Acts) of New York to Mr Graham for him to get engrossed, C.O. 1/56/66; Werden to Dongan, Mar. 10, 1684, *N.Y. Col. Docs.*, III, 341; Duke of York to Dongan, Aug. 26, 1684, *CSPCol., 1681–1685*, #1847; Memorandum, Oct. 4, 1684, *ibid.*, #1885; *The Historical Magazine*, VI (1862), 233.

7 Massachusetts Bay: Purpose and Defiance

Covenant and Charter

The legal safeguards and guarantees which Virginia, New York, and Maryland struggled to obtain, the people of Massachusetts Bay assumed they possessed from the outset. The Bay Colony charter, for the most part an ordinary trading company patent, had become, in view of the Puritan mission, a holy document, sacred evidence of a covenant with God. Through ingenious interpretation and several strokes of luck, their charter left them, they said, virtually independent and isolated, the better to shield themselves against the ecclesiastical and political evils of England, free to get on with the purpose behind their settlement. Their success in extracting and then improving such a grant from the King was continued proof that God was with them. He had contracted with a Christian community and agreed to be its Jehovah, if its members lived their lives according to His word. The charter of 1629, which made the venture possible, became an integral part of the covenant between God and themselves. As such, it was to be defended at all costs, against anything, as Increase Mather explained, "inconsistent with the main end of their fathers' coming to New England." [1]

Massachusetts was recognizably different from Virginia in purpose and in organization. Its religious character found various expressions, all pointing to providential origin. It and "Virginia went not forth upon the same reasons nor for the same end," wrote Emanuel Downing in 1633. Virginians had ventured only for profit; the saints of New England were bent on two other designs: to satisfy a point of conscience and to bring the "Gospel to those heathen that never heard thereof. . . ." New England was from the start a plantation of religion, not trade, the Reverend John Higginson, son of one of the founders of Salem, wrote in 1663. "If any man amongst us make Religion as *twelve* and the world as *thirteen,* let such an one know he hath neither the spirit of a *true New England man,* nor *yet of a sincere Christian.*" [2] Behind the settlement of Massachusetts was a holy commitment, and the charter was its sign. As Virginians and New Yorkers and the people of Maryland sought guarantees upon which they could build satisfactory lives and an equitable political existence, Massachusetts looked to its charter and covenant as the joint foundation of its being which made possible a holy commonwealth. Unlike other colonies, Massachusetts was founded by a chosen people whose destiny was manifest, if not to everyone, at least to those who settled there.

The Puritans of Massachusetts Bay tried very hard to use the power granted in the charter to fulfill the responsibilities which their covenant and holy charge had laid upon them. From 1630 they had attempted to mold a church-state which conformed to God's word and law or what they interpreted both to be. Although church and state were separate entities, they were closely related, sometimes even overlapping in the colonists' conception of a godly community. At the same time, the Bay colonists were not utopian idealists. They did not believe human nature had undergone a sea change in coming to America over what they had known it to be in England, or that their experiment would be entirely free of sin and the ungodly. They were neither separatists nor perfectionists—although they had trouble with both in the early years. Most of their fellow colonists, they hoped, would adhere to the same peculiar beliefs as they. By placing responsibility for leadership, even voting,

1. *Hutchinson Papers,* M.H.S. *Coll.,* 3d ser., I (1825), 78.

2. Emanuel Downing to Sir John Coke, Dec. 12, 1633, H.M.C. 23: 12th Report, *Cowper,* III, 38–39; *The Cause of God and His People in New England* (Cambridge, Mass., 1663), quoted in J. B. Felt, *Ecclesiastical History of New England* (2 vols., Boston, 1855–62), II, 303–4.

upon church members alone, they might assure a large measure of peace and harmony and, more important, agreement about the proper civil and religious institutions necessary to promote a "due form of government" and the means of grace among them. This is what they were pledged to do with God's help, and therefore any obstacle to their purpose, such as Quakers, Indians, the King's Church, or even his colonial policy, was ignored or reduced if possible in the quickest and most effective way.

Sin was a fact which all communities and peoples had to contend with. Since sin threatened their covenant with God, it had to be exposed and punished whenever it reared its head, for a just penalty against sin registered the community's disapproval of it and kept the covenant intact. The Puritans' assiduousness in this activity has labeled them "their brothers' keepers," and so they were, for they searched out sin that they might deal with it and for very good reason. Wrongdoing which escaped justice implied consent to it; moreover, unless chastened, it brought punishment to the whole community, usually in the form of calamity of one kind or another which fell alike upon guilty and innocent. Seventeenth-century Massachusetts settlers recognized only too well the occasional calamities which befell them—the wheat rust, drought, fire, Indian war, customs collectors—as God's way of punishing them for transgressions not publicly redressed. Once the sinning was properly dealt with, the calamities ceased, and repentance and punishment evened the score between God and His people, restoring the covenant and harmony to the land. Puritan New England held no monopoly on these principles, for they were part of a broad framework within Protestantism; but among the saints of Massachusetts, the covenant conception of God's relationship with the community was probably more universally understood and obtained longer there than among their colonial neighbors.[3]

The divine circumstances and political conditions under which Massachusetts seemed to prosper bred confidence, sometimes independence, and often defiance of authority from abroad and meddling strangers among them. The founders' successful removal of the Company charter to America, out of reach of both King and Bishop, translated the document into a constitution and the corporation into a body politic. Freemen of the Company, if church members, became freemen of the country who elected deputies to sit in a lower house of the General Court. Company officers, also elected by the freemen,

3. Perry Miller, "From the Covenant to the Revival," J. W. Smith and A. L. Jamison, eds., *Religion in American Life* (3 vols., Princeton, N.J., 1961), I, *The Shaping of American Religion*, 322–68.

became governor and magistrates and sat as a council or upper house. Company bylaws were transcended into colony legislation for a whole people. The General Court assumed the role of a supreme judicature with final say and erected inferior courts for lesser matters.[4]

Most colonists in Massachusetts owned allegiance to the Crown of England. This was true as long as it did not interfere with the purpose of their colony, although Edward Randolph spread word at home that Bay Colony settlers believed they had established a commonwealth and, unlike other colonists, needed not to swear allegiance to anyone but their own government.[5] Other outsiders shared Randolph's conclusion about Puritan presumption. One of the chief arguments met by the Virginia agents in London against incorporating their own colony in 1675 was that incorporation of Massachusetts had been a mistake and led only to independence and antimonarchical and republican ideas.[6] Allegiance to the King in England, Bay colonists believed, was compatible with their mission as long as his power remained in England with him. In Massachusetts it had little sanction. "His Majestye [has] nothing to doe here," said Daniel Gookin from the Bench, "for wee are a free people of o^r selves." [7] All Bay colonists were not as convinced as Judge Gookin that this was true, any more than all of them believed that the colony itself was divinely conceived above and beyond the normal assurances of Providence. But a sufficient number devoutly believed both, and what is remarkable is not that they eventually lost out to the King but that they held out so long against him.

Reflecting this independent attitude, Bay colonists were not very friendly to strangers, particularly to those who failed to respect their religious principles. Quakers, whom they denied the name of Christian, were anathema and run out frequently with harsh laws and cattails lest they infect the colony with heresy and enthusiasm. We have no beggars here and only a few idle vagabonds, Governor Bradstreet explained, "except now and then some few Quakers from Rhode Island." [8]

4. The best account of the transition from trading company to colony government is in Edmund S. Morgan, *The Puritan Dilemma: The Story of John Winthrop* (Boston, 1958), ch. VII.

5. Merrill Jensen, ed., *English Historical Documents*, v. IX, *American Colonial Documents to 1776* (London, 1955), p. 238.

6. J. D. Burk, *Hist. of Va.*, II, App., pp. xxxvi–xxxvii, lii–liii.

7. Deposition of Nicholas Wardner, June 1681, M.H.S., Gay Transcripts, State Papers, II, 80, 81.

8. N. B. Shurtleff, ed., *Records of the Governor and Company of the Massachusetts Bay in New England* (5 vols., Boston, 1853–54), IV, pt. 2, 2–4, 19–20; Governor Bradstreet's Answers to Lords of Trade's Inquiries, 1680, *CSPCol., 1677–1680*, #1360; Bradstreet's Answer to a Quaker, *ibid., 1681–1685*, #1021, #1022; Massachusetts Archives, Ecclesiastical, 1679–1739, 11, 22a, State House, Boston.

The Friends' reliance upon an inward light was a spiritual presumption no self-respecting Puritan could stomach. Omnipotence would never share its sovereignty or condescend to deal directly with its creature.

Hardly less discriminated against than Quakers, although less violently so, were the Anglicans, who could never form a church in Massachusetts as long as the saints were in power. As a son of the King's Church, William Veasie of Braintree complained that he and his family were virtually cast out of the Lord's heritage, for in Massachusetts the House of God lay in waste. How many there were like Mr. Veasie would be hard to determine. He and Randolph insisted there were plenty who were silenced because they would not go along with Puritan ways. The orthodox majority constantly played down the number, and accordingly one gets the impression that there was little dissent from Congregationalism, and then only among evil persons.[9]

The Bay colonists were well instructed in the "Truth." The Gospel's right was paramount, said John Higginson, bringing liberty to all who professed it, all who walked according to its faith and order. "That which was contrary to the Gospel hath no right, and therefore should have no liberty." The Puritans' purpose in coming to New England was certainly not a toleration of other religions or of the heresies and idolatries of the seventeenth century in which they lived. In an almost laughable piece of understatement Governor Edward Cranfield of New Hampshire once explained to the Lords of Trade that the Puritans were "very diligent and devout in their own Worship, very tenacious of it." [10] By 1660 New Englanders had already taken on a character for which they would later be well known, a character one had to be wary of, but which their private arrangement with God helps to explain.

1660 and the Royal Commission

The Bay colonists took lightly the Restoration of Charles II. Their General Court, while acknowledging allegiance to the King, "asserted the liberty of the country, according to the patent," and defined themselves a civil body politic in fact and name.[11] The Royal

9. Journal of the Lords of Trade, Feb. 6, 1675, in Toppan, ed., *Randolph,* III, 36–38; Petition of William Veasie to Bishop of London, Nov. 25, 1684, C.O. 1/56, 88.

10. *The Cause of God and His People in New England,* quoted in Felt, *Eccles. Hist.,* II, 303–4; Cranfield to the Lords of Trade, Dec. 1, 1682, *CSPCol., 1681–1685,* #824. For examples of Puritan treatment of outsiders, see M.H.S., Gay Transcripts, State Papers, II, 77; Blathwayt to [?], Oct. 22, 168[?], Mass. Arch. CVI, Political, 246; *CSPCol., 1685–1688,* #267.

11. "Diary of John Hull," A.A.S. *Trans. and Coll.,* III (1857), 202–3; Hall, Leder, and Kammen, eds., *Glorious Revolution in America,* pp. 12–13.

Commission of 1664 came as a surprise to Massachusetts, as well it might when one considers its duties. With some 400 troops the Commission's ostensible task was to conquer New Netherlands from Peter Stuyvesant and the Dutch, a duty it accomplished with dispatch, but without much help from Massachusetts, for volunteers were hard to find. Besides the New York business, the Commission was instructed by the King, reflecting restrictive Restoration policies, to determine the "true state" of the colonies and to discover whether the colonists respected their charters and the Navigation Acts recently passed by Parliament. The King specifically wanted to know whether the government in Massachusetts had carried out several pointed commands given two years before which forbade it to discriminate against Anglicans and deny the vote to settlers not members of the Congregational churches. These were the Commission's public instructions, and if accomplished, they would have shaded somewhat the autonomy claimed by the General Court and enjoyed since 1630.[12]

The secret instructions, had they been successfully carried out, would have left the Puritan Commonwealth in shambles. They directed Colonel Richard Nicolls and his fellow Commissioners to ingratiate themselves with the principal settlers and through them persuade the government to seek a supplementary charter which would clip much of its authority. What the King really wanted was to wrest from the Bay Colony the election of its own governor and place his appointment and command of the militia in Crown hands. In the meantime, Charles believed that a step in the right direction would be for the assembly to be "so wrought upon" as to choose Colonel Nicolls governor and Colonel Cartwright major general over the militia.[13]

Had the King had at his disposal the craftiest and cleverest diplomats in all Europe, it is doubtful they could have accomplished what the commissioners set out to do in Puritan Massachusetts. But to send three military men, all probably selected by the Duke of York and none known for his tact, along with a longtime enemy of the Bay, Samuel Maverick, whom the colonists had run off the land some years earlier, and expect them to persuade the saints of Massachusetts to bow and scrape and subvert their own government is unbelievable. The consequences of the Commissioners' visit *were* believable, however, even predictable, for the colonists frustrated their unsubtle efforts at every turn, and the government, refusing to cooperate in almost every detail, declared the Commission's presence a flagrant violation of the colony's charter. Why are we imposed upon? asked John Hull,

12. Hull, "Diary," 212; *N.Y. Col. Docs.*, III, 51–55.
13. *Ibid.*, 57–61.

the godly goldsmith and mintmaster. Why does anyone in the King's name "seek the subversion of our civil and ecclesiastical politics?" Massachusetts had both divine and royal sanction. God, through the King, had committed the care of these people to their government. If they could have no confidence in their charter, wrote another Bostonian, they could have no "certainty" in their lives, their estates, houses, and lands, let alone the "free passage of yᵉ gospell," which was so much more dear to them than any other comforts "natural or civill." Massachusetts' strong reaction to Richard Nicolls and company was a simple matter of "self-preservation." [14]

The Commission received a more cordial welcome in Connecticut and Rhode Island than in the "Lord's vineyard." Each was on its good behavior, having received a liberal charter a year or two earlier. Plymouth, too, was hospitable, since it sought a patent to confirm its foundation and requested the good offices of the Commission in securing it. A few people in New Hampshire, then claimed by Massachusetts, did "violently oppose" them. But a number of settlers in the district of Maine, also claimed by Massachusetts, had sharp grievances against Puritan Boston and accepted the authority of the Commission and several justiceships of the peace under His Majesty. A couple of years later the Bay government turned these officers out by force, giving Edward Randolph still another charge against the Bay Colony as contemptuous of the King's authority.[15] The Commissioners were not very impressed by what they saw at Sheepscott River and Pemaquid in Maine, where there was no more than a handful of "mean" houses in the largest settlement. They found no government among the people there, most of whom had fled justice in other settlements, two very good reasons for appointing justices of the peace. No doubt a third was "That as many men may share in a Woman, as they do in a Boat," a very unpuritanical basis for the social organization of a fishing village.[16]

The immediate outcome of the Commission's visit to New England was not as unfavorable as the colonists feared. On the way home to England, Colonel Cartwright was forced to throw the Commission's

14. *CSPCol., 1661–1668,* #1002, #1021, #1024, #1089, #1090, #1171; *N.Y. Col. Docs.,* III, 87–88, 95–96, 139–40; *M.H.S. Coll.,* 4th ser., II, 284; Hull, "Diary," 216–17.

15. For the Commissioners' business in Connecticut and Rhode Island, see *Recs. Col. Conn.,* I, 439–40, and John R. Bartlett, ed., *Records of the Colony of Rhode Island* (10 vols., Providence, R.I., 1856–65), II, 90 ff. For Plymouth, see George D. Langdon, Jr., *Pilgrim Colony: A History of New Plymouth, 1620–1691* (New Haven and London, 1966), pp. 190–91. Jensen, ed., *Am. Col. Docs.,* p. 238.

16. George Cartwright to Lord Arlington, 1665, Egerton Manuscripts, 2395, f. 426, B.M.

reports and papers overboard to prevent their capture by the enemy during the Second Dutch War—obviously an act of God. Furthermore, the Dutch then captured the Commissioners. Of course, later reports leaked through by other means to King and Council, but for the time being it looked as if Massachusetts was vindicated in its forceful defense of the "Sanctuary." [17]

Independence and the Navigation Acts

The Reverend John Higginson no doubt thought he had taken the measure of New England when he described its origin as one of religion, not trade, and its people more devoted to God than their pocketbooks. Higginson would have had trouble proving his statement to Edward Randolph, or any of His Majesty's customs people who descended upon the colonies after appointment of the Lords of Trade in 1675. Despite religious cant, outsiders quickly saw that Bay colonists were no slouches in the trade business. Massachusetts had not only "engrossed the whole trade of New England," but was the "key" to the West Indian trade, an exchange which was vital to the Islands, English and foreign, but which deprived the Crown at the same time of thousands of pounds in customs. And this was not all; the colony's direct trade with Europe, both coming and going, was lucrative, cutting out English merchants and providing the colonists with continental goods cheaper than Englishmen could supply them, which again made hash of the customs service, to say nothing of the letter and spirit of the Navigation Acts. In so doing, it was commonly thought, Massachusetts, not London, would become the "great mart and staple" of the empire.[18]

Besides being largely illegal, Massachusetts' trade was distinguished by its volume. New Yorkers boasted fifteen to twenty ships trading in

17. *Ibid.; CSPCol., 1661–1668,* #1103, #1199, #1297; John Winthrop, Jr., to Henry Oldenburgh, Hartford, Nov. 12, 1668, M.H.S. *Coll.,* 5th ser., VIII, 104, 130; Thomas Hutchinson, *The History of the Colony and Province of Massachusetts Bay,* ed. by L. S. Mayo (3 vols., Cambridge, Mass., 1936), I, 215; Rev. S. Danforth's Records, *New England Historical and Genealogical Register,* XXXIV (Boston, 1888), 165; Nathaniel Morton, *New England's Memorial: or a Brief Relation* . . . (reprinted Boston, 1721), p. 219.

18. For an indication of the extent of illegal trade, see Col. Cartwright's Account of Massachusetts, "Clarendon Papers," *New-York Historical Society Collections* (1869), 86; "Narrative of Capt. Breedon," *CSPCol., 1677–1680,* #811; *ibid., 1675–1676,* #721, #787, #797, #881, #898; *ibid., 1677–1680,* #1305. Notes upon New England made Aug. 1676, Add. Mss., 28089, f. 3; *Cal. Treas. Bks.,* V, pt. I, *1676–1679,* 170; *ibid.,* pt. II, *1676–1679,* 983–84; Robt. Holden to Commissioners of Customs, June 10, 1679, *Col. Recs. N.C.,* I, 245–46; Gov. Cranfield to Blathwayt, June 19, 1683, BPCol. Wmsbg., v. I.

their harbor in 1678, while more than a dozen years earlier, John Hull had counted nearly a hundred at Boston in twelve months' time, both "ours and strangers." Most of "ours" were built there; the "strangers" were entertained contrary to the Acts of Trade. Edward Randolph estimated that by 1676 Massachusetts had built more than 700 ships of varying displacement, some as large as 250 tons, and claimed at the same time that there were thirty master shipbuilders in the colony. But Randolph often colored his reports about the colonies in his constant attempt to lay significance upon his own work and the people he dealt with. One can hardly believe that Massachusetts, New Hampshire, and Maine teemed with 150,000 colonists as he claimed in 1676—Massachusetts alone probably numbered about 40,000 at that time [19]—or that some thirty merchants were worth between ten and twenty thousand pounds apiece. The colonists' estimates were fittingly more modest. Agents in London two years later told the Lords of Trade that not more than twelve to fourteen Massachusetts estates reached £5,000 and less than half of these came to £10,000. According to Governor Bradstreet, a Bay colonist was counted a rich man if his estate went as much as ten or fifteen hundred.[20]

Massachusetts exported some of the same products as New York only more of them: furs, wheat, and other grains, beef, pork, peas, fish, and a variety of lumber products, including ships' masts. Indeed, shipmasters carried tobacco from Virginia, Maryland, Albemarle, and the islands, and often in violation of the Plantation Duty which since 1673 had demanded a penny a pound on tobacco when shifted from one colony to another before it reached England. For some time New England traders claimed that once the duty was paid, they were free to take the tobacco wherever they pleased. Fish and grain and much of their lumber products they traded in the West Indies for tobacco, molasses, and rum, or bills of exchange on London, where, of course, they ought legally to have taken the tobacco. Some of their lumber and provisions they shipped to the Atlantic Islands, from which they brought home Madeira and other fine wines fit for Puritan palates, for God's blessings were many to a covenanted people. Manufactured goods they imported from England but also the Continent, much to

19. Estimates interpolated from E. B. Greene and V. D. Hamilton, *American Population Before the Federal Census of 1790* (New York, 1932), p. 14. Stella H. Sutherland estimates that there were 48,000 people in Massachusetts in 1675. *Population Distribution in Colonial America* (New York, 1936), p. 31.

20. Hull, "Diary," p. 214; Andros, "Answers to enquiries," Apr. 9, 1678, *N.Y. Col. Docs.*, III, 262–64; "Edward Randolph's Answer to Inquiries, Oct. 12, 1676," *CSPCol.*, 1675–1676, #1067; Mass. Agents to Lords of Trade, July 2, 1678, *ibid.*, 1677–1680, #747; Gov. Bradstreet to Committee of Trade, May 18, 1680, *ibid.*, #1360.

Edward Randolph's and the King's dismay. Boston, Charlestown, and Salem were their principal ports, Boston primary, while Newbury and Ipswich handled a healthy local trade.[21]

According to New England's critics, Massachusetts regarded itself as a "free State" and its people as "neuters" in the business of empire. When Edward Randolph on his first visit to Boston in 1676 confronted Governor John Leverett with several European vessels then riding at anchor in Boston Harbor, the old Cromwellian blandly answered that the laws of King and Parliament had no bearing on Massachusetts unless they touched directly upon the colony's interests. The charter was sufficient sanction and gave their government sole legislative power over the people without an appeal to the Crown.

Granted the Acts of Trade were not popular anywhere in America, New England and Massachusetts—indistinguishable in most Englishmen's eyes—were by far the worst offenders against them, giving these colonies generally a bad name at Whitehall. Governor Berkeley of Virginia insisted that his people obeyed all the laws "whilst New England men break through" and ". . . trade to any place that their interest lead them." The mercers and silk weavers of London complained to the King that they faced ruin because New Englanders got their silks and stuffs directly from France and Italy "or other parts."[22] Numerous suggestions were made about bringing Massachusetts into line, several of them drastic, such as ordering men-of-war to seize violators and commissioning any merchantmen who were agreeable to run down offending vessels and bring them to the admiralty courts for trial. Two remedies the Lords of Trade acted upon immediately: new oaths imposed upon governors to enforce the Acts of Trade, and the settling of customs collectors in New England under the authority of the Plantation Act. If the colonists resisted, the next step would be to discriminate against New England altogether either by duties upon its trade with other colonies or by outright embargo.[23]

21. Andros, "Answers to enquiries," Apr. 9, 1678, *N.Y. Col. Docs.*, III, 262–64; "Mass. Answers to Inquiries," 1680, *CSPCol., 1677–1680*, #1360; "Randolph's Answer to Inquiries, 1676," *ibid., 1675–1676*, #1067; Robt. Holden to Commiss. of Customs, Boston, June 10, 1679, *Col. Recs. N.C.*, I, 245–46. For Massachusetts and Plantation Duty, see *Acts of P.C., Col. Ser., 1613–1680*, #1068, p. 657; *CSPCol., 1677–1680*, #1305; "Randolph's charges against Mass., 1683," Hall, Leder, and Kammen, eds., *Glo. Rev. in Am.*, p. 25; L. A. Harper, *The English Navigation Laws*, p. 164.

22. "Capt. Wyborne's Account, 1673," *CSPCol., 1675–1676*, #721, #881; Randolph's "Short Narrative," Hall, Leder, and Kammen, eds., *Glo. Rev. in Am.*, pp. 18–19; Berkeley's answers to inquiries, 1671, Hening, ed., *Statutes*, II, 516.

23. Notes upon New England made 1 Aug. 1676, Add. Mss., 28089, f. 3; Lords of Trade, Apr. 24, 1676, *CSPCol., 1675–1676*, #898; Charles Bertie to Comm. of Customs, July 17, 1677, *Cal. Treas. Bks.*, V, pt. I, *1676–1679*, pp. 688–89.

Despite frequent warnings, disregard of the Navigation Acts continued. Even as the attack upon the charter intensified, the colony government insisted that the acts had no force in Massachusetts until confirmed by its own authority. And this the General Court did only reluctantly. To subject themselves to Parliament's laws, said one defender of the trade, was an "uncouth matter at first but at length they denied y^m selves to satisfy his Matie. . . ." [24] Neither King nor Randolph was ever satisfied, and a cavalier attitude toward the Acts of Trade was foremost in the home government's charges against the Bay Colony. Probably in no other imperial matter did Massachusetts demonstrate more independence. And religion colored this, too; business and trade were worthy callings, as acceptable to God and one's fellow men as the many others that were open to Massachusetts people—"professions and mechanical arts of all kinds thrive well," said Randolph.[25] But at the very time they spoke of the merits of "church government" and the "integrity of life," said one of their critics, the Bay colonists practiced a "Legerdermain" in trade which was notorious. Having tinged their commerce with "Christian Policy," they made devotion a prime commodity and zeal their "cheef broaker." Now these two passed for "the grand Cheates of the world." [26] Not all Englishmen were impressed with the rights and privileges of the covenant. As colonial policy became more restrictive and rigid in the 1670's and 1680's, the King and the Lords of Trade, on the one side, and the saints of Massachusetts, on the other, became increasingly aware of the gap which separated their understanding of the role colonies and colonists played in the empire. Faith in the covenant and charter sustained a majority of the government in holding to its principles for a surprisingly long time in view of the strength of the attack against it, an attack which intensified in the waning years of Charles II's reign.

King Philip's War: Covenant, Sin, Calamity, and Independence

King Philip's War was a calamity which seriously tested the Bay people and their covenant. In the Pequot War of 1637, the last time the Puritans had girded themselves in the armor of God against the Indians, they had slaughtered a defenseless enemy with fire and lead in such volume that there was no doubt where "truth" stood. King Philip's War was different; the outcome was uncertain for almost

24. Philo Roy, Philo patris, Dec. 14, 1683, M.H.S., Gay Transcripts, State Papers, III, 6.
25. "Randolph's Answer to Inquiries, 1676," *CSPCol., 1675–1676*, #1067.
26. Robt. Holden to Comm. of Customs, Boston, June 10, 1679, *Col. Recs. N.C.*, I, 246.

a year, leaving some uneasy lest the forces of "truth" go under. Colonists outside New England might cite the Puritans' nasty treatment of the Indian, seizing his land, selling him firearms, as prime causes of the war, but the people and government of Massachusetts attributed it to the "sins of the Country," their "great backsliding" in things of the spirit. The "hand of God has been heavy on the land," they said, but He is "righteous in this scourge." As they cataloged their sins, which ranged from the wearing of periwigs and false locks to suffering Quakers to live and worship among them, they buckled down to destroying the Indians.

I told them, preached Increase Mather, who was blessed with early recognition of the "Symptoms of divine displeasure," that the day of trouble was near. I warned them, he said, that God would visit with the sword, that judgment was close at hand. And so it was, for Massachusetts bore the brunt of a cruel war which claimed thousands of killed and wounded, destroyed numerous villages and towns, cattle and estates, disrupted their trade, and put back for a generation normal expansion of the colony. Although Apostle John Eliot agreed that calamity followed a community's transgressions, that their sins had "ripened [them] for so seveare a scourge as yᵉ warre . . . ," only to him did it occur that maybe their sin was the way they treated the Indians in the first place. Maybe God deliberately was punishing His people to make them treat the Indians better, not worse, to do them justice, not cheat them of their lands. Moreover, justice, instead of oppression, might open the Indians' hearts to the word of God, a goal Eliot had tirelessly pursued for some time. Doubtless the irony of his prayer was lost on most of his contemporaries. No Puritan accepted calamity, no matter how devastating, without struggling against it. God was not with the Indians; He only used them as a tool to humble His people under a "mighty hand." They did battle against the enemy for the glory of God, the honor and safety of King and country, and for themselves, confident in their resolve to repent of their sins, renew the covenant, and defeat the Indians. The outcome was what any good Puritan might expect. The colony had publicized its sins, prayed for forgiveness, and then, after suffering humiliating defeats, with God's blessing had pummeled the hell out of the Indians until there was no chance of their recovery. Days of repentance and thanksgiving were solemnly proclaimed throughout the trying months of the war and as late as the end of 1676. The eventual victory did nothing to change the Puritan mind about the war, its causes, or the enemy.[27]

27. The most recent and best study of King Philip's War is Douglas E. Leach, *Flintlock and Tomahawk: New England in King Philip's War* (New York, 1958). For a contemporary estimate of the causes, see *CSPCol., 1675–1676,* #721, and

King Philip's War was clear evidence, too, of Massachusetts' independence and its people's pride, for despite serious losses, they refused
to seek the King's help. At least the colony was consistent in its attitude; any people who denied validity of the Acts of Trade, or a Royal
Commission's jurisdiction among them, could not go begging the King's
assistance against a heathen neighbor. Nor did they wish to, for aid
from home, in one way or another, would have subjected them to the
very interference they were trying to avoid. Anyway, whether they
wanted help or not, the King never offered it to them. Contrast the
English government's reaction to Bacon's Rebellion, which commenced
just before the war in Massachusetts ended. To Virginia Charles II
sent a commission and more than 1,200 soldiers to suppress the trouble
there and support the government. Granted conditions were not the
same—Bacon and his people rebelled against the King's governor—
the real difference in response is measured by each colony's value to
the mother country. Virginia tobacco paid the Crown £100,000 a
year in customs. Massachusetts annually cheated the Crown of an
equal amount, or so reports ran, although estimates varied.[28] Since they
had brought the Indian war upon themselves, they could bloody well
fight it themselves. And bloody well they did, although it took a good
deal longer than expected, and a lot more blood. That a whole colony
of English subjects was in danger of annihilation—compared with only
a small number killed by rebels in Virginia—never became an issue in
London. The lack of response seemed to some in Massachusetts absolute proof of their independence. Lord Anglesey, the colony's agent
and sympathetic friend in England, chided Governor Leverett for the
Bay Colony's reluctance to spread its miseries before the King. "You
are poor yet proud," he told him.[29] Proud they were, if not altogether
poor, but the war was a matter between God and themselves and, of
course, the Indians. The King had no direct role to play in it.

Massachusetts' willingness to go it alone did not necessarily represent the feelings of her allies, Plymouth for instance, whose people

---

Edward Randolph's report in *ibid.*, #1067. The Puritan view is in Shurtleff, ed.,
Recs. of Mass. Bay, V, *1674–1686,* pp. 59–63, 130–31; Massachusetts' Proclamation, Dec. 7, 1675, *CSPCol., 1675–1676,* #745; Gov. Leverett to Sec'y Williamson, Boston, Dec. 18, 1675, C.O. 5/903, pp. 90–91; Increase Mather, "Autobiography," ed. by M. G. Hall, A.A.S. *Proceedings,* 71 (1961), pt. 2, pp. 301–2;
Josiah Winslow to John Winthrop, Jr., Marshfield, July 29, 1675, *Winthrop
Papers,* pt. III, v. I, 5th ser., M.H.S. *Coll.* (Boston, 1871), 428. For John Eliot's
interpretation, see his letter to John Winthrop, Jr., July 24, 1675, *ibid.,* pp. 425–26.

28. Jensen, ed., *Am. Col. Docs.,* p. 238.

29. Lord Anglesey to Gov. Leverett, May 16, 1676, printed in Hutchinson, *Hist.
of Mass. Bay,* I, 262. For discussion of some of these points, see *ibid.,* pp. 261–63,
and Leach, *Flintlock and Tomahawk,* p. 243.

suffered, too. Had the King known of their "innocency," they told him, their "streights, and hazards," their sufferings would have moved his tender heart to help them.[30] Aid from colonies outside of New England was small at best. Governor Andros in New York claimed the New Englanders refused his help and at the same time ungratefully accused the people at Albany of supplying the Indians with firearms against them. What the people of Connecticut remembered most about Andros during the war was his attempt to push the Duke of York's claim to their colony west of the Connecticut River, and this while they were defending themselves from the Indians on two fronts. On July 8, with two sloops loaded with soldiers, Andros anchored at the mouth of the river off Saybrook, ready to make good his claim. Despite their concentration on the Indian menace, Connecticut people were prepared to meet any other menace, including the Duke's governor. With considerable clatter they mustered the militia and marched and wheeled through Saybrook for a couple of days until Andros wisely weighed anchor and sailed his troops back to New York, clearly the loser.[31]

The Time to Strike

Although Governor Andros was unsuccessful, his tactics appealed to others whose interest it was to bring New England into line in matters of government and trade. Momentum accumulated by the Royal Commission of 1664 for remodeling Massachusetts had lapsed owing to the Second Dutch War, the disastrous plague, and the Fire of London, all of which diverted attention from colonial problems and helped to dissolve even the best-laid plans.[32]

A second effort had to await a more auspicious time, and it had come in 1671 when the King appointed his new Council for Plantations which included Lord Culpeper, Lord Ashley (later Shaftesbury), the Earl of Sandwich, who was Lord President of the Privy Council, John Evelyn, and several others. Surrounded by atlases, maps, and globes, these people first met in May at the Earl of Bristol's home, and on the day they read the patent which appointed them, they got right down

30. C.O. 5/904, 7–9.

31. Andros, "Answers to enquiries," 1678, *N.Y. Col. Docs.*, III, 262–64; Dongan's report, O'Callaghan, ed., *Doc. Hist. N.Y.*, I (1849), 154, 187; *Recs. Col. Conn.*, II, 334–35, 342–43; Leach, *Flintlock and Tomahawk*, pp. 59–60, 176–77, 236–37.

32. John Whitty to Peter Carteret, Nov. 2, 1665, William S. Powell, ed., *Ye County of Albemarle in Carolina: A Collection of Documents, 1664–1675* (Raleigh, N.C., 1958), p. 10; Gideon D. Scull, ed., *Voyages of Peter Esprit Radisson . . . from 1652 to 1684*, The Prince Society, *Publications*, XVI (Boston, 1885), 244–45.

to business and inquired "in what condition New England was. . . ." Their conclusion: it was wealthy, strong, and independent in its "regard of old England." The Council was undecided—really of several opinions—about what the next step should be, and it shifted from one remedy to another. One suggestion was a "menacing Letter," but those who better understood the "touchy & peevish humor" of the Bay colonists opposed such a procedure.

In June the Council heard witnesses, including Colonel Cartwright, one of the Commission of 1664, who left them convinced that if policy would not subdue the New Englanders, force must. They spoke then of fortifying an island in the harbor and employing several of His Majesty's frigates as the best way to "curb Boston." But under the moderate guidance of the Earl of Sandwich the Council by July had come off its hard line and advocated peaceful means to "regulate this people and gett as much hand in theire government" as possible. Force would have the wrong effect, they now concluded; Massachusetts was already too militant and strong to be compelled to do anything. "Roughnesse" and "severity" toward its people would only make them desperate, Sandwich insisted, and provoke them to set up for themselves. The soft line soon disappeared, too; despite the Lord President's advice, the Council next hit upon sending a commission, much like that of 1664 but with determination to take a firmer hold. The King approved the plan, and a commission made ready to embark in the spring of 1672. But this was as far as the idea got; the serious difficulties surrounding the Third Dutch War forced the Crown to put aside its scheme until a better time. Again the saints of Massachusetts were saved by an act of God, or, one might say, the King of England was spared another insult from "peevish" settlers whose colony, according to Evelyn, had "become a Bank of money, and a magazine of men and arms." [33]

The conditions which obtained in 1671–1672, persuading the Council for Plantations to be circumspect in its handling of Massachusetts, had changed considerably by 1676. The Lords of Trade, a permanent committee of the Privy Council, had taken over colonial business from the Council for Plantations and pursued its tasks with more determination than had any committee or council in the past. Moreover, the worst offender, the colony most often out of line with the emerging restrictive policy, was then in the throes of a war for survival against

33. E. S. De Beer, ed., *The Diary of John Evelyn* (London, 1959), pp. 554–55, 556, 557, 566; *ibid.* (1955 ed.), III, 584–85; John Evelyn, "Expences in the First Plantation of New England," n.d., H.M.C. 70; *Pepys,* pp. 270–71; G. L. Beer, *Old Colonial System,* II, 253–54 and n.

the Indians. From as far away as Jamaica first came the suggestion that the best way to reduce independence among New Englanders was to settle the King's authority in Massachusetts in no uncertain terms, and the best time to do it was right then, since the people had their hands full fighting for their lives.[34]

In the midst of these difficulties, and as part of the new campaign, the Lords of Trade sent Edward Randolph to Boston in June of 1676. Ostensibly Randolph came to Massachusetts to press proprietary claims to New Hampshire and Maine which the saints had refused to honor, but he bore instructions from the Crown and the Lords of Trade to learn what he could of the colony's conduct, the better to sustain a regulation of its government. He saw immediately the opportunities offered to the Crown by the government's concentration on the needs of the war, and he promptly wrote home that the time was ripe, since Massachusetts was then on its knees. As Bacon's Rebellion helped the Crown to inaugurate a tougher policy for Virginia, so King Philip's War lent itself to those who hoped finally to yoke New England with the responsibilities of empire. Not all of Randolph's suggestions were followed; still, the English government's sustained attack upon the Bay Colony charter dated from Randolph's first visit.[35]

Even Randolph's modest estimates of war losses were staggering proof of the weakened condition of the colony: 600 killed (actually several thousand), 1,200 houses burned, 8,000 cattle slain, thousands of bushels of grain destroyed, and a money loss all told of £150,000. No questions were asked or suggestions made about what the Crown might do to help Massachusetts get back on its feet. Instead, Randolph requested that the King station three frigates and several armed ketches, well manned, in Boston Harbor, with orders to seize all Massachusetts' shipping and force obedience to the Acts of Trade. This would do more to bring these people to the Crown's terms in a week than all the orders of King and Council in seven years. A few months later he recommended that the fleet then in Virginia, which had brought troops to quell Bacon's Rebellion, return home by way of Boston and "settle that country" once and for all.[36] But the Crown was not yet ready to use the Royal Navy against Massachusetts.

34. Gov. Lord Vaughn to Sec'y Williamson, Sept. 20, 1675, *CSPCol., 1675–1676*, #673.

35. Randolph to Sec'y Coventry, June 17, 1676, *ibid.*, #953. The best account of Randolph is Michael G. Hall, *Edward Randolph and the American Colonies, 1676–1703* (Chapel Hill, N.C., 1960). For the first Boston visit, see ch. 2.

36. *CSPCol., 1675–1676*, #1067, #953; *ibid., 1677–1680*, #218. For aftermath of King Philip's War, see Leach, *Flintlock and Tomahawk*, ch. XIII, particularly p. 243.

As if the devastation of King Philip's War was not enough to convince the Bay Colony people that God was displeased with them, the unwelcome visit of Edward Randolph at the same time was still more proof that the colony had not lived up to its promise and covenant. For Randolph, besides spying on their government and trade, their churches, their treatment of Anglicans and Quakers, had brought to the General Court the King's command to dispatch agents to London to represent the colony in its conflict with Mason and Gorges over proprietary claims to New Hampshire and Maine. Once there, no telling what the King and Lords of Trade might demand in order to bring Massachusetts into proper "regard of old England." During the next few years the Crown laid siege to the Massachusetts charter, a siege which threatened to destroy the heart of the Bay Colony, the very being of the Puritan commonwealth.

The Massachusetts Position of 1678

Massachusetts had taken a bad beating in King Philip's War. Its people were not likely to forget or recover from the suffering and losses for a generation or more. The colony had little difficulty in finding excuses for not immediately sending agents to London. The war and its consequences made it impossible, they told the King, and then an "epidemical sickness" prevented the General Court from meeting, further delaying the choice of agents. These were "Notorious falsehoods," said Edward Randolph, when he heard them back in England. The war had ceased some time before he left Boston, he claimed, and anyway, Massachusetts had not suffered half as much as Plymouth and Connecticut, which caught the full weight of the Indian attacks—also notorious falsehoods. As for extraordinary sickness, he informed the King, two or three rich old men had the misfortune to die. The King testily ordered the General Court to meet immediately and appoint agents to come to London.[37]

William Stoughton, one of the "honored magistrates," and Peter Bulkeley, speaker of the lower house, finally embarked for England late in October 1676.[38] The next summer they met with the Lords of Trade and were confronted with Randolph's numerous "Narratives," "States," charges, and reports, all condemning Massachusetts, besides a board of Lords determined to make the Bay Colony dependent upon

37. Shurtleff, ed., *Recs. of Mass. Bay*, V, *1674–1676*, 106, 130–31; *CSPCol., 1675–1676*, #945, #1136, #1138, #1186.
38. Hull, "Diary," A.A.S. *Trans. and Coll.*, III (1857), 242; Hall, *Randolph*, p. 30.

the Crown. Stoughton and Bulkeley were not prepared for the demands made upon them, for an inquiry into Mason's and Gorges' proprietary claims was just the beginning of a long investigation which poked into more dark corners of the colony's business than the agents cared to discuss or their instructions permitted. The Lords of Trade with Randolph's help came up with half a dozen "Heads," actually demands for changes, which the agents relayed to Boston. The King made it clear he did not wish to destroy outright the charter; he wished instead that the agents agree to a "Supplemental one" which would set all things right that were then amiss. Some of the demands were stiffer than what a virtually independent province would care to accept, but they could be lived with as a compromise in order to forestall something worse. Renounce all pretended claims outside the boundaries of the patent; beg His Majesty's pardon for coining money; repeal all laws repugnant to the laws of England. Other laws ought to be remodeled, and all should be closely studied. The Navigation Acts must be "religiously observed." The agents claimed a lack of power to accept a regulation of the charter, and they were roundly condemned for acting like ambassadors. Did His Majesty have to treat with his own subjects as he would "Foreigners"? Besides all this, the King ordered his attorneys and solicitors general to scrutinize the colony's charter and to report how and where the Bay government had gone astray and slighted the sovereignty of the Crown. The August meeting ended with a resolve to fix a permanent customs officer at Boston to enforce the Acts of Trade.[39]

Massachusetts' immediate response to the "Heads" was to ignore them, except on one point, and even this was handled in such a way as to antagonize the board. Although the General Court enacted new legislation equivalent to the Act of Navigation, it prefaced the law with an explanation complaining ignorance of His Majesty's pleasure in that regard, an explanation the Lords of Trade flatly refused to accept. The "softness" of the previous summer was missing in the spring of 1678 when the Lords met again on New England business; the board thoroughly resented the Bay Colony's attitude and resolved to consider the whole New England business "from the Very Root." If neither persuasion nor command was effective, if no one in Massachusetts gave "countenance" to His Majesty's orders, then some of the Lords were convinced that nothing but a royal governor would bring the colony around. Furthermore, they were certain that a good many

39. Randolph, The Present State of New England, Add. Mss., 28089, ff. 6–20; Randolph, "Report," Jensen, ed., *Am. Col. Docs.*, pp. 237–38; Toppan, ed., *Randolph*, II, 277–80, 281–84.

Bay colonists were agreeable to such a change, a mistaken belief on the Lords' part, as far as numbers were concerned, but one fixed in their minds by Edward Randolph, who constantly described the colony as in the tyrannical grip of a Congregational minority. Having threatened the colony with a royal governor, the Lords requested the attorney general to examine further the colony's charter and the possibility of issuing a *quo warranto* against it.[40]

Agents Stoughton and Bulkeley were in an impossible position, almost naked in a London of enemies, most of whom could not have cared less about the sanctity of the "Lord's vineyard." Their situation was not eased when news got out that they had secretly bought the district of Maine from the descendants of Ferdinando Gorges, right out from under the nose of the King.[41] They tried as best they could to dispute Randolph's exaggerated charges and the more moderate objections by the King's law officers. Bravely, maybe foolhardily, they complained of the Navigation Acts which the Lords had been tightening for two years in order to improve the mother country's grip on the colonists' trade. The gap between points of view about Massachusetts' role in the empire was already wider than what two agents in London could possibly straddle. Aware of growing resentment in London and the dead seriousness of the King's demands, they advised caution at home: "God moderate you in your Assembly," they wrote to friends in Boston.[42]

The General Court appointed a committee which prepared answers to the charges by both the Lords of Trade and the law officers of the Crown. The Massachusetts defense of October 2, 1678, was a state paper of considerable significance, for it got to the bottom of the issues and publicized the Puritan colony's point of view about its purpose and rights as a godly commonwealth *and* an English colony, a combination not irreconcilable to most Bay colonists. Champions of the Virginia and New York charters and the dissenters of Maryland had similarly determined the meaning of colonial relationships on their own terms. Once pressed, each colony came down to hard-rock principle which best expressed its reason for being, its self-interested needs and assumptions. The covenant and charter were as fundamental to Massachusetts' existence as the rights of Englishmen were to her neighbors farther south. Yet reliance upon them was not at the expense of Englishmen's rights. Indeed, Bay colonists were beginning to discover that

40. *Ibid.*, 295–98.

41. Hall, *Randolph*, p. 42; H. L. Osgood, *American Colonies in the Seventeenth Century* (3 vols., New York, 1904, reprinted 1957), III, 325.

42. *CSPCol., 1677–1680,* #747; Mass. Arch., CVI, Political, 216.

these rights were related to the charter and covenant and might have value in justifying their traditional independence.

Besides its religious character, what distinguished Massachusetts from other colonies was its idea of royal and Parliamentary power. It may have come as a surprise to the Crown and the makers of colonial policy that the General Court of Massachusetts believed English laws were bound within the four seas and did not reach "Amerrica." Since Massachusetts people sent no representatives to Parliament, they never before understood that as subjects they might be "impeded" in their trade by laws of that body, a conclusion, they said, in no way reflecting upon their allegiance to the Crown. Once they learned—and very recently—of the King's desire to subject them to these laws, their Assembly had enacted them first, a procedure absolutely necessary to avoid an invasion of Bay colonists' liberty and property—doubtless another surprise to both King and Parliament. From now on they would enforce the acts, although they found them detrimental to their trade and development and an "abstraction" rather than an enlargement of the royal customs. Specific answers more sharply defined their understanding of the rights of colonists. Since they paid duties on several goods imported from other colonies (Plantation Duty), it seemed particularly hard not to have freedom to carry them wherever they pleased, a restriction which deprived them of a liberty enjoyed by their fellow subjects in England and a clear-cut case of inequality between Englishmen. Furthermore, duties paid on goods imported from England were no "custome" at all but really a tax on their estates like a penny in the pound.

Allegiance to the Crown, exemption from the Navigation Acts unless their legislature confirmed them, a desire to be treated equally with Englishmen when it came to the laws of Parliament, and a complaint against taxes on their imports without their consent—these added up to a very definite statement of what they believed their rights were in the empire. The position they described was a far cry from the conception of empire held by Englishmen in England. Furthermore, it was not much different from one Massachusetts and other colonies adhered to in 1774. But who in 1678 had heard of dominion status?

Massachusetts regretted that some of her laws were accounted repugnant to the laws of England. Although the charter forbade such acts, they had not appeared repugnant when the General Court drafted them, only different. The government promised to examine those objected to in London and to repeal any which offended *except*— and here the General Court, in spelling out the exception, again distinguished Massachusetts from all other colonies and defined the very character of the province—"except such as the repealling whereof will make us to renounce the professed cause of our first coming hither." [43]

On the same day the General Court defended itself against the Lords of Trade's charges, it wrote to agents Stoughton and Bulkeley in London, suggesting positive arguments to combat the English government's criticism. New Englanders had prevented the Dutch and the French from swallowing up the New World, thus keeping the greater part of it English; their trade alone paid into the exchequer annually £ 20,000 in customs. But of far greater value than these, they told the agents, dearer to them than their own lives, was the "interest of the Lord Jesus, & of his churches." This they must protect above all, for the "charter being under God" was their only security against the wickedness of their enemies who would like to do them in. Any concessions on their part, therefore, allowing "the least stone should be put out of the wall," would bring the whole tumbling down around their ears. The Massachusetts government stood by its covenant and charter, for these, laced together, were its guarantees against "mutacons" and subversion. They formed the fundamental principle on which the Puritans' conception of themselves and their colony rested: "for, as our grouing up to such an orderly setlement hath binn the genuine offspring of his majestys charter . . . so also the Lord hath binn pleased gratiously to oune his people here that have adventured their lives & estates into this howling wildernesse in the pursuance thereof." [44]

Agents Stoughton and Bulkeley were saved further embarrassment in London by the turmoil of the Popish Plot in the fall of 1678. The several murders and Titus Oates's revelations threw such a scare into high and low, monopolizing everyone's time "from his Majesty to the Constables," that no other public business was attended to, least of all colonial affairs. Soon the Lords of Trade excused the agents from further appearances and sent them home, not empty-handed, however. They carried with them explicit instructions to the General Court to send over two new agents within six months' time fully empowered to deal with any and all matters respecting the colony. A saddened and weary Stoughton and Bulkeley arrived home late in December 1679.[45] For more than two years the colony debated whether it would accede to the King's demands.

43. Shurtleff, ed., *Recs. of Mass. Bay,* V, *1674–1686,* 198–201.
44. *Ibid.,* p. 202.
45. See Secretary Coventry letters, Coventry Papers, Add. Mss., 25120, ff. 132–33, f. 134, f. 135, f. 138; Add. Mss., 15487, ff. 92–94; Blathwayt to Jonathan Atkins, Nov. 25, 1678, BPCol. Wmsbg., v. XXIX; Hull, "Diary," p. 246.

8 Massachusetts Bay: Demise

The Reforming Synod

Despite the terrible scourge of King Philip's War, the cycle of sin and calamity continued in Massachusetts, greatly upsetting those whose task it was to keep the public conscience. The punishment of war, it seemed, had not wholly satisfied God's justice. True, some of the earlier sins had been expiated. As far as they knew, "Marry Moor" and her friends had ceased their fornication; Alice Thomas had given over the keeping of a "brothel-house." Even the dancing school had been "put down." [1] Nevertheless, the war had hardly ceased when fire broke out in Boston, and although the "Lord sent much rain, moderated the spreading of it," He had not acted in time to save some fifty buildings left in ashes, including Increase Mather's North Meeting-house and parsonage. Not much later smallpox was discovered, brought by an English ship, and before it was over, about 180 colonists in Boston had died and another eighty in Charlestown in a year or more's

---

1. "Diary of John Hull," A.A.S. *Trans. and Coll.*, III (1857), 232; C.O. 5/903, p. 105; *CSPCol., 1675–1676*, #849.

time. It was clear to many that God's controversy with New England was far from over.[2]

Probably the disastrous fire and an epidemic of smallpox had something to do with calling the "Reforming Synod" in 1679. Still, other troubles, some less sharply defined, nonetheless serious, were certainly evident. King Philip's War had profoundly disturbed Puritan society, and not just as a bloody punishment of its people for sins committed. Despite determination among many to close ranks and go on, the devastation and its aftermath of related problems shook the confidence of a people who could not afford to doubt the success of perseverance. Some of the cockiness which earlier characterized their doings was gone. Massachusetts had sustained a blow which blunted somewhat the sharpness of its purpose and endeavor; the war unsettled a lot of people, adding new strains to a society which was not at full spiritual strength and was unable properly to exert control in the accustomed ways over its people.[3]

But this was not the worst of it. Having published their sins to the world, Bay colonists continued to commit them; in fact, according to the clergy, they had violated already the public vows and solemn promises made in the very crucible of war. Differences appeared among people and their churches; new meetinghouses were erected, and although on the pretense of worshiping God, they really laid groundwork, if not for schism and heresy, at least for dividing and weakening the community, undermining the proper establishment of churches "in one faith & order of the gospell." On top of these internal difficulties were the frightening developments in England, where the King's men challenged the sanctity of the charter, ignored the meaning of the covenant, and humiliated their agents. To restore their spiritual confidence, to save the community from further destruction and resist interference from abroad, the General Court, urged by the clergy, summoned a Synod to meet in September of 1679, "to enquire into the causes of Gods displeasure . . . and scripture expedients for Reformation." And then, as if to mock them, on August 8 fire again swept through Boston; having begun in an alehouse, before sunrise the next day it had "consumed the body of the trading part of the town." [4]

2. Hull, "Diary," pp. 242, 243, 244; M.H.S. *Proc.*, 2d ser., XIII, 411; Mather, "Autobiography," A.A.S. *Proc.*, 71 (1961), pt. 2, 302–3.

3. For the war's spiritual and other damage, see Perry Miller, *The New England Mind: From Colony to Province* (Cambridge, Mass., 1953), pp. 20–21, 22–23, 31–32; Leach, *Flintlock and Tomahawk*, pp. 243–44, 249–50.

4. Mass. Arch., Ecclesiastical, 1637–1679, 10, 196–98; Shurtleff, ed., *Recs. Mass. Bay*, V, 215, 213; Mather, "Autobiography," p. 305; Hull, "Diary," pp. 245, 246.

When the Synod met, God gave Increase Mather the opportunity to do some "peculiar Service." He preached on the first day of the meeting to the assembled elders and messengers, and throughout the proceedings deftly prevented the dragging up of old and controversial business, like the Half-Way Covenant, which certainly would have threatened their unanimity. At its close the Synod presented the usual catalog of sins to the government, sins which it believed were the "provoking evils" of the people, along with suggested remedies and reforms. Besides writing the conclusions of the meeting, Mather composed the "epistle dedicatory" to the General Court. Leaving no stone unturned, he persuaded his own congregation to renew its church covenant, believing himself instrumental in pledging his people to continued efforts in the way of their fathers.[5] Getting right with God through a "Reforming Synod" was not only good business against the effects of a community's sins, past and present; it was also good insurance against an ominous future.

Faction and Moderates

In 1679, despite internal weaknesses, the blackest threats came from abroad. One of them materialized shortly when Edward Randolph arrived again in Boston, this time as the King's collector of customs.[6] It was one thing to struggle against an enemy at Whitehall; it was something else again when the enemy had an agent (a spy, the Bay colonists called him) in the very heart of Boston. Randolph had given every indication of his intent when he visited the colony in the summer of 1676 during the Indian war. Governor John Leverett had stood up against him during his earlier visit, but Randolph's recourse was to send bitter reports home which became the bases of the King's case against the colony. Leverett was as stiff a fighter as any against encroachment upon the Puritan province; in fact, he became something of a symbol of the Bay Colony's independence. An old Cromwellian, he had been wartime governor of Massachusetts and always a formidable public figure. When it was rumored that the King might make some drastic changes in the colony, some people were certain that as long as John Leverett was alive the country would resist. Would his successor possess the same "spirit" or "interest" and "withstand the authority of Old England"? The colony had not long to wait for an answer. In the middle of March 1679 John Leverett "died

5. *Ibid.*, 246; Mather, "Autobiography," p. 305.
6. *Cal. Treas. Bks.*, V, pt. II, *1676–1679*, 983–84, 1023, 1089; Coventry Papers, Add. Mss., 25120, f. 144; Blathwayt to Peter Bulkeley, Whitehall, Oct. 21, 1681, BPCol. Wmsbg., v. IV.

about four o'clock on a sabbath morning." [7] Simon Bradstreet, already an old man and of more moderate and compromising temperament, replaced him as governor. With Leverett's death, leadership of the resistance slipped from the governor's office and came to rest elsewhere in the Bay Colony government.

No doubt a majority of the people who counted in Massachusetts supported a hard line of resistance—although often loyally, sometimes even politely—to the Crown's attack upon their government and charter. Critics might say that the Puritan oligarchy governed in its own interests, and they were probably right. The strength was in the people who adhered to the Congregational churches, and it was these who filled the principal places in government and the militia, believing for a variety of reasons that what they enjoyed was good and ought to be preserved. If the principle was a holy commonwealth, supported by their charter and covenant, a number of them had done well enough under the arrangement to want to keep it as it was, free of "mutacons," that is, free of political control from England and a regulation of their trade.

Of course, not all colonists in Massachusetts agreed with the principle or with resistance to the King who was attempting to change it. There were several causes for dissent: some colonists objected to rule by the saints on religious grounds; they desired the Church of England, or toleration, or just to be let alone. Some merchants outside the Puritan faction approved of the Navigation Acts, or at least of imperial control; maybe they wished to get along with the mother country, since they depended upon lucrative economic ties with England for their trade and well-being. Land speculators like Richard Wharton, of course, looked to the Crown for confirmation of their schemes and so sought harmonious relations, not turmoil. Some disagreed politically with the oligarchy and thought it unfair that the government discriminated against them only because they were not orthodox church members. Otherwise, as Englishmen they had every right to vote, they claimed, and furthermore, as colonists of economic and social prestige, they ought to enjoy influence in government commensurate with their status. It was one of the disenfranchised moderates who described their anomalous position this way with some bitterness:

It was pleasant to behold poor *Coblers* and pitiful *Mechanicks*, which had neither House nor Land, struting and making no mean Figure at their Elections; and some of the richest Merchants and wealthiest People stand by as insignificant Cyphers; or in the words of one of their own, who thought he

7. Samuel Nowell to Jonathan Bull, Sept. 25, 1676, M.H.S. *Coll.*, 4th ser., VIII (1868), 573; Hull, "Diary," p. 245.

characteriz'd them ingeniously, as so many Asses to bear the Loads that should be laid upon them.[8]

Still, the articulate dissenters were a minority, and so far they had been unable to crack the church-state commonwealth which Massachusetts supported. When Randolph called the old guard the "ffaction," he meant men like Leverett, Thomas Danforth, and, of course, Increase Mather. The more flexible Bay colonists he dubbed the "moderates," such as Bradstreet, Bulkeley, Stoughton, and Wharton, men who would doubtless accept a compromise with the King if they had to, if not complete surrender of their government, in order to improve their positions or maybe even survive. A third force was one Randolph himself adhered to, the prerogative men like Joseph Dudley, who took the Crown's side on all issues. Their number was small, but like Randolph's, their efforts persisted. The King's demand for more agents in 1679 aggravated the internal conflict as well as that between Boston and London; at the same time, it stirred up moderate men to play a stronger role. Noticeable, too, was a change in the faction's leadership and a shift in its center of gravity.[9]

Agents, Quo Warranto, and Declaration

For two years the Massachusetts government stalled about sending agents. Moderates could not imagine what the colony hoped to gain by refusing to obey the King's demand; they were apprehensive lest New England fare the worse for it. The King became impatient in the summer of 1680; he sent the colony a scolding letter and ordered the General Court to send agents in three months' time or he would go to court against the charter. In January of 1680 the Legislature sought advice from the ministers, who were only too happy to give it (a good example of the overlapping of state and church). Indeed, dispatch agents, said the churchmen, and give them scope enough to answer any complaints, for we are bound to obey the King. Anyway, sending agents in the past, through God's blessing, always has worked to our advantage by "lengthening out our tranquility." However, cautioned the reverend elders, take utmost care not to give them power to act in any way which might weaken the government or our charter as it was granted. God forbid that we ourselves should diminish the rights and privileges He has given us. But the dead of winter was no time

8. *A Short Account of the Present State of New England, Anno Domini 1690,* by N.N., n.p., n.d., p. 9, John Carter Brown Library.

9. A very useful breakdown and explanation of the political groups in Massachusetts at this time is in Theodore B. Lewis, Jr., "Massachusetts and the Glorious Revolution: A Political and Constitutional Study, 1660–1692" (unpubl. Ph.D. thesis, Univ. of Wisconsin, 1967), ch. IV and App. IV.

to send agents anywhere; no ship would sail directly for England until the spring, a further excuse for delay.[10]

It was another year or more—a very long winter—before the agents eventually chosen, Joseph Dudley and John Richards, set sail for London (May 30, 1682). Their instructions gave them no more power to agree to a regulation of the government than had those of Stoughton and Bulkeley six years before. The King declared their appearance "meerly Dilatory" and promptly ordered them to secure the necessary powers or suffer the consequences of a *quo warranto*. His chief legal officers already had given the opinion that Massachusetts' misdemeanors were serious enough for the Crown justifiably to go to court to revoke the patent.[11]

The times in England were more opportune for proceeding against the colony than hitherto. Difficulties of one kind or another had continuously prevented or interrupted a regulation, but in the early 1680's, as the Exclusion Crisis cooled, the path seemed more clear. In reaction to the several plots and Shaftesbury's and the Whigs' attempts to exclude James from the throne, Charles sharply asserted the prerogative in ways not felt by Englishmen in recent years. The charter of London was one of the first casualties, and the colonies felt the change, too, Massachusetts in particular.[12]

The tougher policy in London, reflected in the attack on charters generally and a crackdown on dissenters, had its effect for a time in Boston. Randolph was elated, for he thought he sensed a weakening of the faction. As if frightened by the success of the prerogative in England, Massachusetts people looked with less hostility upon Randolph's seizures of ships and even granted him a court to try them in. He looked forward to better times.[13] The thaw did not last. Despite the

10. Josiah Winslow to Blathwayt, July 2, 1680, BPCol. Wmsbg., v. VI; Blathwayt to Culpeper, Aug. 26, 1680, *ibid.*, v. XVII; Peter Bulkeley to Blathwayt, Jan. 8, 1681, *ibid.*, v. IV; C.O. 389/9, pp. 53–56; Hull, "Diary," pp. 247, 248; *CSPCol., 1681–1685*, #2.

11. "Diary of Noahdiah Russell," *New Eng. Hist. and Gen. Reg.*, VIII (1853), 54; Mass. Arch. CVI, Political, 268; Add. Mss., 15487, ff. 92–94; *CSPCol., 1681–1685*, #559.

12. David Ogg, *England in the Reign of Charles II* (2 vols., London, 1934), II, ch. 17; J. P. Kenyon, *Robert Spencer, Earl of Sunderland, 1641–1702* (London, 1958), ch. 3; *Bishop Burnet's History of His Own Time . . .* (London, 1857), pp. 390–91. The best explanation of the attack upon colonial charters is Philip S. Haffenden, "The Crown and the Colonial Charters, 1675–1688," *William and Mary Quarterly*, 3d ser., XV (1958), 297–311, 452–66. See also BPCol. Wmsbg., vols. I and IV, and particularly Blathwayt to Effingham, Dec. 9, 1684, in v. XIV.

13. Blathwayt to Thomas Lynch, Oct. 2, 1682, *ibid.*, v. XXIII; Abstract of Randolph's letter to Comm. of Customs, Boston, May 16, 1682, in Toppan, ed., *Randolph*, III, 166.

eventual decline in the fortunes of the Whigs in England, the faction in Boston was more influenced by them in the long run than by their opponents, so much, in fact, that Randolph and other critics of the Bay Colony were certain of a conspiracy "between the two factious parties in both Englands." The fanatics in London, he claimed, kept the Boston people stirred up; they sent them all kinds of radical literature and posted them on the Earl of Shaftesbury's doings. Before Randolph became accustomed to securing judgments against smugglers, the tide had turned against him. Once Boston people learned that the Grand Jury in London had refused to indict Shaftesbury for treason, and that he and his friends were cheered at the Old Bailey, there was no holding the New Englanders. Randolph's several seizures in 1682 were a dead loss, and his efforts slackened out of discouragement. The same thing happened in New Hampshire, where he tried his luck against the shipping there, but Shaftesbury's acquittal became a "leading precedent" for the jurymen, who gave their verdicts against the King with costs.[14]

As the Crown and its legal officers pushed closer to a *quo warranto* against the charter, the faction stiffened its resolve, not, however, with the unanimity it had earlier enjoyed. While Governor Leverett and the council had led the resistance in the late 1670's, by the early 1680's the lower house emerged as the center of strength with Increase Mather as its spiritual adviser. "The General Assembly [meaning the lower house] was the Cheif power at present," wrote moderate Governor Bradstreet, and until the King remodeled the government, no one could expect obedience or even justice. When it was suggested to the assembly that it alter the agents' instructions, allowing them to compromise with the King, the deputies circulated papers among the townspeople and gathered signatures opposing the change. Those who refused to sign were "stigmatized" as enemies of the colony.[15] While the General Court debated, the government in London made good its threat and brought in a *quo warranto* against the Company "for usurping to be a body Politick"; it dispatched Randolph to Boston with letters informing the colony of the proceedings. He appeared before

14. Randolph to Sir Leoline Jenkins, Apr. 16, 1681, *CSPCol., 1681–1685,* #83; same to same, 1682, *ibid.,* #781; *ibid.,* #870; same to same, June 14, 1682, Toppan, ed., *Randolph,* III, 160; Randolph to Sir Robt. Southwell, Whitehall, Jan. 29, 1684, *ibid.,* IV, 5; *ibid.,* I, 181.

15. Robert Mason to Blathwayt, Mar. 22, 1683, BPCol. Wmsbg., v. XII; "Wee are hugging our priviledges & franchises to death, & presse the dissolution of our Body politique," was Peter Bulkeley's way of expressing the lower house's stubbornness. Bulkeley to Blathwayt, Dec. 7, 1683, *ibid.,* v. IV; Cranfield to Lords of Trade, Mar. 27, 1683, *CSPCol., 1681–1685,* #1024.

the Court in October of 1683. Accompanying the writ was the King's "Declaration" to the colony government, more accommodating than the moderates had expected, but very clear that if the government would not compromise, the Crown would prosecute the *quo warranto* to its conclusion. The question in Boston, then, became whether to submit, an issue which provoked more unrest and drove a wedge between the two houses of the General Court. Once the writ was served, the King dismissed the colony's agents and sent them home.[16]

New Hampshire

The council and deputies in Massachusetts had split before. In fact, they had strongly disagreed a year earlier over incorporating the Navigation Acts into the colony's laws. When it came to a question of submitting to the King, the split was more crucial, although not altogether clear-cut. Forty-eight of the deputies succeeded in dragging a couple of the council over to their side, losing at the same time nine of their members to Governor Bradstreet and the moderates. Still very much in charge, however, the lower house hired attorney Robert Humphreys in London and voted £3,000 for his use to defend the charter, or even better, to engineer the King's pardon for their past offenses, leaving the charter intact.[17] There were strong reasons behind the deputies' stubbornness, besides the Whigs' example in London. They were all linked, some tenuously, to a conception of the Puritans' purpose, or at least to what still appeared to be their purpose after two or more generations of colonial life.

The goings on in New Hampshire certainly bore heavily on the turn of events. Robert Mason, a descendant of the original proprietor, for several years had been pushing his claims to the north, even to a part of Massachusetts between Salem and the Merrimac River. By the late 1670's the King had determined that Mason had a clear right to the soil of New Hampshire but not to the government of it. Since Massachusetts people had expanded into his territory, he might settle directly for quitrents and other proprietary rights by initiating court cases

16. Blathwayt to Mr. Green, Aug. 20, 1684, BPCol. Wmsbg., v. VI; Add. Mss., 15487, ff. 92–94; Mass. Arch., CVI, Political, 299, 322; Mather, "Autobiography," p. 307.

17. Hall, Leder, and Kammen, eds., *Glo. Rev. in Am.*, pp. 20–21; Randolph to Lords of Trade, 1683, *CSPCol., 1681–1685*, #1566, I; Joseph Dudley to [Blathwayt?], Dec. 1, 1683, BPCol. Wmsbg., v. IV; William Dyer described the split as between the General Court and governor. Dyer to Blathwayt, Sept. 12 [or 17], 1684, *ibid*. For William Stoughton's sympathetic view of the "distempered spirits," see Stoughton to Richard Streyton, Boston, May 5, 1684, Stowe Manuscripts, 746, ff. 89, B.M.

against them on the ground. But government over the people belonged to the King, who had reinforced the decision by making New Hampshire a royal colony in 1679. Sometime later he sent over as governor Edward Cranfield, who militantly supported Mason and his claims, much to the displeasure of Massachusetts, which had pretensions to the territory and control of the people, most of whom were good Congregationalists.[18]

Cranfield's short reign in New Hampshire hardly recommended royal government to Massachusetts. Before he arrived, a president, council, and deputies had managed well enough without a royal governor. Once there, Cranfield reestablished an elected lower house and an appointed council but never got along with either. The deputies fought against him over taxes and trade, the courts, even his commission, and over many other colony issues. The conflict between them at one point became so hostile that a handful of assemblymen and a number of townspeople openly revolted. Cranfield seized the ringleader, Edward Gove, and convicted him of treason but sent him to England for execution. (The King pardoned Gove and shipped him back to New Hampshire, much to the governor's chagrin.)[19] Cranfield's vindictive enforcement of the Navigation Acts frightened away even legal trade from the colony's ports. He pressed the King's Church on settlers who were overwhelmingly Congregational, demanding their clergymen administer both the Lord's Supper and baptism according to the Church of England. Once a flourishing colony, New Hampshire was now in a "miserable condition," lamented even moderate Bradstreet. "This makes our people dread the like condition." Cranfield's conduct, said another moderate, "hath much influenced all Councils" and hur-

18. Abstract of Commissions, Add. Mss., 30372, f. 3b; Blathwayt to Governor Carlisle of Jamaica (draft), May 20, 1680, BPCol. Wmsbg., v. XXII; Blathwayt to Andros, July 15, 1679, *ibid.*, v. III. Cranfield's Commission, May 9, 1683, *CSPCol., 1681–1685*, #453.

19. Abstract of Commissions, Add. Mss., 30372, f. 3b; Blathwayt to Carlisle (draft), May 20, 1680, BPCol. Wmsbg., v. XXII; Cranfield to Blathwayt, Jan. 10 and Feb. 20, 1683, *ibid.*, v. I; Robert Mason to Blathwayt, Mar. 22, 1683, *ibid.*, v. XII; Randolph to Blathwayt, Feb. 3, 1683, *ibid.*, v. I; Cranfield to Jenkins, Feb. 20, 1683, *CSPCol., 1681–1685*, #906, #952; *ibid.*, #954; Deposition of John Foullsam, Dec. 11, 1684, *New Hampshire Historical Society Collections*, VIII (Concord, N.H., 1866), 211–12; "Diary of Noahdiah Russell," Jan. 1683, *New Eng. Hist. and Gen. Reg.*, VII (1853), 58. See two detailed lists of Cranfield's "offenses"; Nathaniel Ware to King and Privy Council, ca. 1684, Nathaniel Bouton, *et al.*, eds., *Documents and Records Relating to the Province of New Hampshire*—often called *New Hampshire Provincial Papers* (39 vols., Concord, 1867–1941), I, 515–19, and "Articles of Complaint against . . . Cranfield," *ibid.*, 556–57; Cranfield to Blathwayt, Nov. 15, 1683, BPCol. Wmsbg., v. I; Robt. Mason to Blathwayt, Boston, Nov. 15, 1683, *ibid.*, v. XII.

ried the "inconsiderate almost into desperation." His carryings on shocked even Edward Randolph, who claimed that he was the chief reason the Boston people were so stubborn about their charter.[20]

The New Hampshire governor believed that his efforts to reduce the settlers to order and obedience were useless as long as Massachusetts was free to violate the Acts of Trade, defy the King, and carry on as an independent republic. And so he early joined the general attack upon the Bay Colony, hoping, of course, to be in on the kill. He made frequent visits to Boston—one lasted three months—spied on their government and trade, and "insinuated" himself into the counsel of those who could stomach him, not, indeed, the faction.[21]

Cranfield's attack on Massachusetts was as strong as any the Bay colonists had come up against and more bitter even than Randolph's. During his few years in New Hampshire, he wrote home constantly to the Lords of Trade, William Blathwayt, and the King's principal secretary about the evils of Massachusetts and their vicious effect on other colonies, primarily New Hampshire. Revoke the charter; call up the leaders of the faction to answer personally for their crimes; send a frigate to force their trade into legal channels; do not trust the government in any matter, for it will never keep faith. Even more virulently than he blasted the faction, he let fly at the Congregational clergy and Harvard College. The ministers he damned for stirring up the "vulgar" against King and Church. They had attacked the liturgy as a "superstition picked out of the Popish dunghill." No reform of Massachusetts or New Hampshire could commence until a new government regulated the clergy or replaced them with orthodox Anglicans. But this was not all or even the worst. There was no greater barrier to the King's interest in New England than the "pernicious and rebellious principles which flow from the College at Cambridge," where "half-witted philosophers" turn out either atheists or preachers of sedition. The King would get nowhere with New England until the charters were revoked and the college "utterly extirpated." Cranfield found the prevailing faction in Boston wholly disloyal to the King. But it did not act alone. He was convinced that a conspiracy existed between Whigs in England and the faction in Boston which, he charged, was fully aware of

20. Richard Wharton to Blathwayt, May 18, 1684, BPCol. Wmsbg., v. VI; Cranfield to Jenkins, June 19, 1683, *CSPCol., 1681–1685*, #1129; Bradstreet to Randolph, Dec. 8, 1684, *ibid.*, #1993; "Diary of Noahdiah Russell," *New Eng. Hist. and Gen. Reg.*, VII (1853), 59; Randolph to Bishop Lloyd, Whitehall, Mar. 1685, Toppan, ed., *Randolph*, IV, 17.

21. R. Mason to Blathwayt, Boston, June 19, 1683, BPCol. Wmsbg., v. XII; same to same, Jan. 10, 1683, *ibid.*, v. I; Cranfield to Lords of Trade, Jan. 23, 1683, *CSPCol., 1681–1685*, #906.

the recent evil plots against the King and Duke. If James became king, he believed the faction would turn off its allegiance altogether, backed again by its nonconformists and Whiggish friends in England.[22]

Cranfield wanted more than just power and authority. The colonists claimed he was a racketeer of the worst kind who had come to New England "for money" and was determined to get it. It was clear to many that his real ambition was to become governor of Massachusetts once it fell to the Crown. His schemes for its takeover were outright scandals in their raw greed. "Wee shall att least make 3000 lb." in settling Maine, alone, he wrote to William Blathwayt, besides another eight or ten thousand in Massachusetts from selling pardons and managing the fund collected for converting the Indians. Later he again solicited Blathwayt's help and held out promise of "some thousands of pounds" over and above what he had already hinted of. Cranfield could count on William Dyer, surveyor of the customs, who had several reasons for helping to gut Massachusetts, not the least of which was revenge for the "Murther of [his] Mother," a Quaker lady the Puritans had hanged in 1660. Dyer listed fourteen plums ready for plucking, once the charter was voided, with a combined income of £4,000. Already Bay colonists were aware of an increased cost in government if the King took over, and they were aware, too, of how many of these added costs would end up in the pockets of the Randolphs, the Dyers, and the Blathwayts. It was threats like these which stiffened the backs of the resisters even though the end looked unpromising.[23]

Edward Cranfield was King Charles II's governor of New Hampshire. Instead of intimidating the faction in Massachusetts, his violent attack strengthened it. If this was what was in store for God's people in the Bay Colony, if Cranfield was an example of a royal governor, if his administration was a sample of the Crown's regulation of government, then Bay colonists wanted no part of any of it. This was the

22. For a sample of Cranfield's letters, see his to Blathwayt, Jan. 10 and Oct. 5, 1683, BPCol. Wmsbg., v. I, and several more in *CSPCol., 1681–1685*, #906, #952, #1024, #1129, #1130, #1316, #1320.

23. William Vaughn to Nathaniel Ware, Portsmouth, Feb. 4, 1684, Bouton, *et al.*, eds., *Docs. and Recs . . . of New Hampshire*, I, 526; Cranfield to Blathwayt, Feb. 20 and June 19, 1683, BPCol. Wmsbg., v. I; William Dyer to [Blathwayt?], n.d. [ca. June 1684], *ibid.*, v. IV; Peter Bulkeley to Blathwayt, Boston, Dec. 7, 1683, *ibid.* In the 1630's Mary Dyer was an Antinomian friend of Anne Hutchinson. Later she became a Quaker and was banished from Massachusetts on pain of death. Upon her return the Bay Colony hanged her in 1660. See J. K. Hosmer, ed., *Winthrop's Journal* (2 vols., New York, 1908), I, 266–69; Emory Battis, *Saints and Sectaries: Anne Hutchinson and the Antinomian Controversy in the Massachusetts Bay Colony* (Chapel Hill, N.C., 1962), pp. 178–79, 270; Perry Miller, *The New England Mind: From Colony to Province*, p. 124.

thinking of the faction when confronted with the King's "Declaration" demanding compromise.[24]

Mather

We cannot surrender, said a majority of the General Court, "for it would offend God." [25] However reprehensible the political and constitutional consequences of submission might be, however evil the machinations of a royal governor, particularly if he resembled Cranfield, these, of course, were less threatening than what a resignation of their charter would do to their souls and to the covenant with God. What the Court resolved simply, Increase Mather said more elaborately with scriptural documentation. In late 1683 he marshaled his arguments and presented them to the magistrates, who distributed copies into many hands. To submit, to consent to "alterations," would be "inconsistent with the main end of their fathers' coming to New England." Their predecessors had stood firm; there was no choice but to walk in their steps. Although resistance would provoke "great sufferings,"

Better suffer than sin, Heb. 11. 26, 27. Let them put their trust in the God of their fathers, which is better than to put confidence in princes. And if they suffer because they dare not comply with the wills of men against the will of God, they suffer in a good cause, and will be accounted martyrs in the next generation, and at the great day.[26]

Early in January 1684 Mather attended a town meeting in Boston called to discuss the King's "Declaration" and the colony's answer. There are three versions of this meeting, each a little different. Mather related that the freemen asked his advice and he responded, emphasizing particularly scriptural precedents which supported resistance, such as the stories of Jephthah and Naboth, who refused to give away the inheritance of their fathers, and of David, who wisely chose to fall "into the hands of God rather than into the hands of men." If we refuse to submit, argued Mather, we keep ourselves in God's hands, and who knows what He may do for us? After citing the experience of London's charter and the misery of their New Hampshire neighbors, he closed his little speech with the plea that none would "dare to be

24. M.H.S., Gay Transcripts, State Papers, III, 6–7. Even Joseph Dudley saw the danger of New Hampshire's example. See Dudley to [Blathwayt?], May 4, 1684, BPCol. Wmsbg., v. IV. The best explanation of New Hampshire's bad example is in Theodore B. Lewis, Jr., "Massachusetts and the Glorious Revolution" (unpubl. Ph.D. thesis, Univ. of Wisconsin, 1967), ch. V.

25. M.H.S., Gay Transcripts, State Papers, III, 6–7.

26. "Arguments against relinquishing the Charter," *Hutchinson Papers*, M.H.S. *Coll.*, 3d ser., I (1825), 74–81.

guilty of so great a sin." This brought the freemen of Boston to tears, Mather said; they thanked him for his encouragement and promptly voted unanimously not to submit. Their vote had great influence on other towns, he has told us, many following Boston's example.[27]

A second version, found in a letter from Boston to Edward Randolph, insisted that before the voting took place, the freemen dismissed all the nonfreemen who were present, since the issue did not concern them. When asked by Samuel Nowell, a magistrate who presided, for a show of hands of those who favored giving up the charter, none responded. Then, holding up both hands, one freeman burst out, "The Lord be praised!" At this point, *after* the vote had been decided, Increase Mather rose and exhorted the freemen about Jephthah, Naboth, David, and then Ahab for good measure. If they submitted now, he told them, their children would live to curse them. Governor Cranfield's story of the town meeting, probably third or fourth hand at best, described Mather's speech as "insolent," that he excited the freemen to arms to defend their charter. There is "such a canker among the generality of the people," Cranfield told the Lords of Trade. Peter Thacher, minister at Milton, discussed the issues of the "Declaration" and submission with the freemen of his town, but it was probably not a very large gathering, since it met in Thacher's study. What they concluded was not recorded.[28]

As election day in the spring of 1684 approached, it was clear that the faction's work had been effective and the moderates and compromisers would take a beating. Joseph Dudley, who several times had attempted to persuade the colony to surrender, admitted that he and his friends had lost their reputations. Others put it more strongly and branded Governor Bradstreet, Bulkeley, Stoughton, and Dudley enemies to their country. (Each of these gentlemen had been a colony agent in England at one time or another and, it would seem, had returned to Boston more resigned than zealous.) As expected, the election on May 7 produced a number of changes; although the freemen reelected Bradstreet governor, they dropped Dudley and several other magistrates from the council. Offended, Stoughton and Bulkeley refused to serve although elected by "a bare number of votes." Randolph made a good deal of this in London, using Dudley's forced retirement as further evidence of the colony's stubbornness and disloyalty. Following the election, the new government sent another ap-

27. Mather, "Autobiography," pp. 307–8.
28. *CSPCol., 1681–1685,* #1589, #1683; "Peter Thacher's Journal," A. K. Teele, ed., *The History of Milton, Massachusetts, 1640 to 1887,* App. B (Boston, 1888), p. 653.

peal to London begging understanding, delay, and a change of heart, claiming the sole motive for their conduct was "meer conscience" of their duty to God and posterity.[29]

Scire Facias et Terminus

In London the legal machinery behind the attack on the charter clanked slowly and clumsily. Forced to work within the framework of London courts, the government's legal officers had a troublesome time pretending that the Governor and Company of Massachusetts Bay, like any English corporation, kept headquarters in the realm. The *quo warranto* was worthless, since Randolph delivered notice of it in Boston long after the time of the writ had lapsed. When the sheriff in London explained to the court why he was unable to return a summons, he posed a question which seems not to have occurred to anyone in England, although to a good many at Boston: Could he "take notice of New England being out of his Balywick?" It was a pertinent inquiry and cut through to the very core of the problems surrounding a colonial system whose bases, legal and otherwise, were unresolved and often appeared whimsical, short-sighted, and even fortuitous. No wonder the colonies, Massachusetts among them, sought guarantees against "mutacons." The sheriff's question might have been expanded in scope by thoughtful members of the Lords of Trade to something like this: Just what is a colony, anyway, who are its people, and what are their political and constitutional ties to the King, his government, the people and courts of England? No attempt was made to answer the sheriff's query or the larger one it stood for, except in a wholly negative way through court procedures. To get around the impasse, the then attorney general, Sir Robert Sawyer, suggested a writ of *scire facias* (do you cause to know) in the Court of Chancery against the Company, a welcome suggestion in London. Since the charter "seemed to intend their abiding here in England," the court issued the new writ answerable in London at Easter term, 1684. Although the colony's attorney Robert Humphrey attended, he did not plead. Judgment was entered for the King, but the court agreed, with the attorney general's consent, to set it aside if the defendant would appear and answer at

---

29. *CSPCol., 1681–1685*, #1589; Dudley to Blathwayt, Roxbury, May 4, 1684, BPCol. Wmsbg., v. IV; Richard Wharton to Blathwayt, May 18, 1684, *ibid.*, v. VI; Joseph Dudley to Mr. Sec'y Jenkins, May 7, 1684, M.H.S., Gay Transcripts, State Papers, III, 27–28; Robt. Humphreys to Gov. and Company, July 28, 1684, Mass. Arch., CVI, Political, 323, 326; Wm. Stoughton to [?], May 8, 1684, Stowe Mss., 746, f. 89b.

Michaelmas term.[30] In the meantime, notice of the new proceedings arrived in Boston, where the General Court met to consider them. Some pooh-poohed the *scire facias,* called it a "toothless creature," and placed their trust in God and the King's pardon. Instead of sending new instructions to the attorney in London, albeit too late, the Court sent an address to the King, unsigned and unsealed, full of the "howling wilderness," their suffering as "exiles," and something about their lack of a staple crop. Since the Company failed again to plead, there being no time to respond anyway, even if it had wished to, the earlier judgment in Chancery stood and was confirmed on October 23, 1684. Attorney Humphrey, doubtless happily rid of a hopeless case, wrote simply to Boston: "The Dye is Cast." [31] From that time the faction insisted that Massachusetts was condemned unheard and the charter wrenched illegally from their hands, an argument very useful later as things turned out.

The period between the death of the charter and the establishment of a new government was one of great uneasiness and uncertainty. Long before the colony was officially informed of the dissolution, a good many people, moderates particularly, were preparing for the change and making adjustments. The old guard, the "phanatics," Robert Mason called them, refused to believe that God would suffer them to fall into the King's hands; they continued their fasting and praying and pretended to govern under the charter. It was "a long dark winter," Joseph Dudley lamented, in which no one prospered; he was confident, however, that the King would not slay the righteous along with the villains.[32]

While the faction fasted and prayed, those less offended by the turn of events speculated about the future and how the King would remodel the government. Every man "doth new Mould [and] settle the world here in his Imagination as pleaseth him best," Dudley declared, and he was among them, hoping for "any office of tollerable profit" which

---

30. R. Sawyer to Mr. Wynne, May 13, 1684, Mass. Arch., CVI, Political, 322. For a résumé of the writ business, see Add. Mss., 15487, ff. 92–94.

31. Extract from a Letter from Boston, Sept. 15, 1684, M.H.S., Gay Transcripts, State Papers, III, 34; Address to King, Oct. 30, 1684, Mass. Arch., CVI, Political, 334–36; Attorney Humphreys to General Court, May 2, 1685, *ibid.,* 343–45; *CSPCol., 1681–1685,* #1902. For a slightly different version of the writ procedure, see Viola F. Barnes, *The Dominion of New England* (New Haven, Conn., 1923, reprinted, New York, 1960), pp. 23–24 and n.

32. Dudley to [Blathwayt?], Nov. 4, 1684, BPCol. Wmsbg., v. IV; R. Mason to Blathwayt, Oct. 20, 1684, and Jan. 26, 1685, *ibid.,* v. XII. The General Court recommended renewal of the covenant, too much neglected in most churches, and a return to the advice of the "Reforming Synod" of 1679. Mass. Arch., Ecclesiastical, 1679–1739, 11, 35a.

he could manage. Plans and rumors of plans circulated widely. Robert Mason of New Hampshire hoped the King would unite all of New England under a general governor who would arrive, he reported, with six men-of-war to set things straight.[33] Richard Wharton confirmed Dudley's contention that every man's scheme reflected his own interests. His proposals for a new government approximated what most Englishmen understood a royal colony to be, but also divulged an expansive conception of seventeenth-century empire and colonization. Wharton suggested that the King boldly increase the number of his subjects in America and make them serviceable, for a large population could only redound to the King's honor. Transplant to the colonies those who were burdensome in the realm, he said, and encourage at the same time discontented foreigners to join them. And why? ". . . heer is roome and accomodation enough for a million of men and materialls to Imploy all occupations and facultyes [,] and p portionable to the increase of people the land wilbe Subdued and Improved, wealth and trade increased and his Ma^tyes Power and Revenues augmented." But what was good for King and empire would also be good for Richard Wharton, who was a notorious land speculator, probably linked to more New England schemes than any of his contemporaries.[34]

In February of 1685 Charles II died. Catholic James acceded to the throne, hardly an improvement in the Puritan view of things, or so it appeared at the time. Since God did not seem disposed to act in the faction's behalf, there was a belated move toward conciliation. In May the General Court contemplated an address to the new King and a revision of the laws in order to put them more in keeping with those of England. Grudgingly it agreed to repeal several objected to three years earlier by the Crown's law officers, including the death penalty for Quakers who returned after banishment. But sharp differences between magistrates and deputies provoked the latter's move to divide the General Court and sit separately. The magistrates, however, refused to concur. Even the clergy became testy and could not agree whether the old government should sit until it had seen and judged for itself

33. Dudley to [Blathwayt?], Nov. 4, 1684, BPCol. Wmsbg., v. IV; Robert Mason to Blathwayt, Sept. 30, 1684, *ibid.*, v. XII.

34. Wharton warmly suggested annual shooting prizes—£5, £3, and £2 of the King's money. He claimed they would afford diversion and make loyal and good soldiers, besides keeping colonists from faction. See Richard Wharton's Proposals, M.H.S., Gay Transcripts, State Papers, III, 50–58; *CSPCol., 1681–1685,* #2033. Theodore B. Lewis, Jr., stresses convincingly the significance of land speculation as a motive behind the actions of a number of moderates and prerogative men. "Massachusetts and the Glorious Revolution," ch. VII and App. IV, p. 438.

the new governor's commission. The "people are very unesie here," was William Dyer's laconic remark.[35]

But who was the new governor? Not until the end of the summer was it generally known, after several bits of false news, that James had appointed Joseph Dudley, one of their own, temporary head of the new government. Already on the spot, he and his council-elect—most of them suggested by Randolph, including himself—jousted awkwardly with the sullen faction while waiting what seemed an interminable time for Randolph to arrive with the King's commands. Dudley took office in May of 1686 with a "very remarkable Comm[n]," for he became interim governor not only over Massachusetts but New Hampshire, Maine, and curiously, the Narragansett Country or King's Province, which Richard Wharton and a handful of speculators had been trying to steal from Rhode Island for some time.[36] Also "remarkable" was that the King had denied New Englanders a representative assembly on the advice of the Privy Council, but contrary to that of his attorney general. He would rule instead through the governor and council alone, an outright "revolucon," according to Richard Wharton and John Dunton. On top of this, Edward Randolph took one seat in the new government as secretary and another as register, besides a third at the council table. The "long dark winter" continued beyond its season.[37] At the final session of the General Court which gave way to Dudley, his council, and the beginnings of the Dominion of New England, a "Weeping Marshall-General" declared the adjournment. "Many Tears [were] Shed in Prayer and at parting," wrote Samuel Sewall.[38] The faction was beaten; Massachusetts belonged no longer to the covenanted people.

35. Samuel Sewall, *Diary*, M.H.S. *Coll.*, 5th ser., V–VII (Boston 1878–82), here cited by *Diary* volume: I, 71 and n., 72, 89, 90; Mass. Arch., Literary, 1645–1774, v. 58, p. 177; Dyer to Blathwayt, Boston, Dec. 30, 1685, BPCol. Wmsbg., v. IV.

36. Dudley to Blathwayt, Sept. 20, Nov. 2, 1685, *ibid.*; same to same, Boston, May 16, 1686, *ibid.*; Randolph to Blathwayt, May 17, 1686, *ibid.*, v. I; R. Wharton to Blathwayt, Apr. 8, 1686, *ibid.*, v. VI; Abstracts of Commissions, 1685, Add. Mss., 30372, f. 3b; *CSPCol., 1681–1685*, #2017; C.O. 5/785, p. 33. For the problems of the Narragansett Country, see ch. 11 below and Richard S. Dunn, *Puritans and Yankees, The Winthrop Dynasty of New England, 1630–1717* (Princeton, N.J., 1962), pp. 109–10, 159–60, 226–27, 234–35.

37. Minutes about the Laws of New England, C.O. 1/57/50; *CSPCol., 1685–1688*, #50, #357; *ibid., 1681–1685*, #1953, #2026; R. Wharton to Blathwayt, Apr. 8, 1686, BPCol. Wmsbg., v. VI; C.O. 5/785, p. 33; M.H.S. *Proc.*, 1st ser., XVI (1878), 102.

38. Sewall, *Diary*, I, 140.

9 His Majesty's Real Empire in America

Colonies are Contiguous to the Whole

The last few years of Charles II's reign were unsettling for Englishmen in both England and America. A number of the difficulties which confronted the colonists in these and the years which followed had their origins in England but reached out to America and frequently affected the turn of events. Central to England's turbulence was, of course, religion, Catholicism, the hard fact that James was a Catholic and at the same time rightful heir to the throne. Charles was only fifty in 1680, but he had been seriously ill before and he would be again, and each indisposition forced the nation to contemplate the real problems of succession. To some it was a simple question: Can a Catholic be King of England? To others it was a good deal more complicated. Although religion was the heart of the problem, it was not an isolated issue; accompanying it was a host of related matters, having to do with politics, the constitution, diplomacy, war, and, surprising to most Englishmen, the empire. Matters of moment which bore on the character of English government, church, and society affected colonists, too, whether Englishmen were willing to admit it or not. Three thousand miles of ocean were not enough to insulate colonists in America from ideas and events at home, good or bad. Colonists and colonies were sensitive creatures; it was the nature of the empire to make them so. Americans remained vulnerable to the winds of change in England and even in Europe longer than they liked to admit, certainly throughout the colonial period and well into the nineteenth century. Colonies, said a group of Barbadian planters, ought to be considered "contiguous, as if the Sea did not divide them"; they were no less a part of the whole than children who ventured abroad, endeavoring to serve the good of themselves and their family.[1] No doubt island colonies were most sensitive to changes at home, yet all colonies and colonists regarded themselves, in some ways at least, "contiguous" to the whole. Even Massachusetts, which prided itself on its independence, found that what occurred in England bore heavily on its livelihood. Revocation of the Massachusetts charter was very good evidence of just how dependent Bay colonists were upon English events and the power and policy of the Crown.

The several plots, bloody intrigues, and the business of Exclusion affected the American colonies a good deal more than Englishmen realized. Turmoil in England frequently played into the hands of colonists who had something to gain from disruption and an ability to use it to their own advantage. This was not as true of the Popish Plot as it was of later conspiracies; still, the babbling of Titus Oates and the actions of the government in response brought ordinary colonial business in London to a standstill, postponing, for instance, the treason trial of John Culpeper of Albemarle in Carolina and allowing the government of Massachusetts and its agents a needed, yet not really helpful, respite from the long struggle over the charter. In Maryland the "damnable and hellish plot" for "murthering the King" worked to aggravate anti-Catholic feelings against Baltimore and his oligarchy, for at one time it looked as if the proprietor himself might be implicated in the English conspiracy when his name appeared on a list of suspects. When the danger seemed past, Connecticut ordered a day of humiliation and publicly thanked God for peace and quiet, a good harvest, and the King's escape from the machinations of evil-minded men who plotted against Christ's kingdom in "our nation" "there and heere"—clearly a nod to the idea of contiguity and one nation even among New England Puritans.[2]

---

1. Petition of Planters of Barbados, Aug. 25, 1681, BPCol. Wmsbg., v. XXXV.
2. Sec'y Coventry's letters, Add. Mss., 25120, f. 132–33, f. 134, f. 135, f. 138,

Before reaction to the Popish Plot had run its course, before all the accusations and recriminations were in, the English nation was shaken again by a strong effort among Whigs and nonconformists to exclude Catholic James from the throne. Leadership fell to the Earl of Shaftesbury, a dominant figure in Restoration government. He had also been a maker of colonial policy since the late 1660's as a member of the Privy Council, of the separate councils of trade and plantations, and then as president of the joint Council of Trade and Plantations beginning in 1672. But Shaftesbury did not remain long in a commanding position over colonial policy after reaching the height of his career and favor with the King. Learning of Charles II's and James's secret dealings with France, he moved into opposition and was dismissed from his post as Lord Chancellor and also from the Privy Council. In 1675 the Crown by-passed the Council of Trade and Plantations, over which Shaftesbury presided, and lodged administrative responsibility for the colonies and their trade, as we have seen, in the new Lords of Trade, to which he was not appointed.

By the time he became deeply committed to excluding James from the throne, Shaftesbury had already spent more than a year in the Tower for stubbornly insisting that Parliament had been convened illegally and new elections were needed before it could do business. The Earl enjoyed a brief period of favor in 1679 when Charles, purely for political reasons, invited him back into the Privy Council, where he served as its Lord President. But his activities in support of the Exclusion Bill, his enthusiasm for the Duke of Monmouth as Charles's successor instead of James, and his superb control of the Whig party in opposition to Charles and the Tories brought about a second dismissal in October 1679. When he and his party strongly pushed Exclusion, Charles prorogued Parliament several times and, after moving it to Oxford to avoid Whig influence in London, dissolved it altogether. England was close to civil war. Officially Shaftesbury was out of court, but never before had his popularity been as great among Whigs and with the people; he became a champion of Protestantism and a celebrated defender of Parliamentary rights, and as such he was warmly regarded in America, particularly by nonconformists.[3]

So, too, was Sir William Jones, former attorney general, who resigned his office and entered Parliament as a strong Whig voice against

B.M.; *Arch. of Md.,* VIII, 228; *Recs. Col. Conn.,* III, 45–46 and n.; Stock, ed., *Proceedings and Debates,* I, 416 n.

3. For Shaftesbury's career in the 1670's and 1680's, see appropriate chapters in K. H. D. Haley, *The First Earl of Shaftesbury* (Oxford, 1968); J. R. Jones, *The First Whigs: The Politics of the Exclusion Crisis, 1678–1683* (London, 1961); E. E. Rich, "The First Earl of Shaftesbury's Colonial Policy," *Transactions of the Royal Historical Society,* 5th ser., VII (London, 1957), 69–70.

James. His maiden speech in Commons was at the Oxford Parliament, where he spoke vigorously for exclusion and skillfully managed the Whig debate. Owing to his splendid reputation—"the greatest lawyer in England"—he lent legality and prestige to the Exclusion movement, convincing a great many Englishmen that the "thing was safe and certain." [4] Earlier he had won an enviable name for himself among American colonists. As attorney general he had recommended that the King confirm the Virginia charter of 1675, which would have guaranteed Virginians the right to tax themselves. In 1680 he questioned the right of Duke James as proprietor of New York to exact a revenue of any kind from the colonists of New Jersey, an opinion which led the Duke to release fully East and West Jersey to their proprietors.[5]

To Crown and government Shaftesbury was a menace, not just for his persistent attack upon James but because of his huge following in and out of Parliament and his political strength in the city of London. Besides leading the Exclusion forces, he strenuously attempted to present the Duke of York to the grand jury as a recusant. In the summer of 1681 the Crown turned on Shaftesbury, as it had and would other prominent Whigs, and on the information of several people—"a parcel of lousy Irish knaves," said one report—seized and imprisoned him in the Tower on a charge of high treason. His "closet" was ransacked and several incriminating papers found, the government said, linking him to Titus Oates and a Catholic plan to destroy the Protestants, to say nothing of writings advocating the dumping of James. When Shaftesbury told the King he would like to be transported to Carolina, instead of standing trial, Charles answered only that he would "leave him to the law." This was the King's mistake, for such was Shaftesbury's power over the people and their sheriffs in London that a grand jury of loyal Whigs stubbornly refused to indict him.[6]

4. *A Collection of the Parliamentary Debates in England* (20 vols., Dublin, 1741), I, 387–90; Sir William Temple, "Memoirs," quoted in William Cobbett, *Parliamentary History of England, from the Earliest Period to the Year 1803* (36 vols., London, 1806–20), IV, 1208 n.; *Bishop Burnet's History of His Own Time* (London, 1857), p. 319 and n.; Jones, *The First Whigs*, pp. 138, 195.

5. J. D. Burk, *History of Virginia*, II, App., xl–xli; George Chalmers, *Political Annals*, pp. 619, 626; John E. Pomfret, *The Province of East New Jersey, 1609 1702* . . . (Princeton, N.J., 1962), pp. 121–23. Later Increase Mather in London used Jones's opinion on colony taxes as evidence of the illegality of the Dominion of New England. *A Vindication of New England*, in *Andros Tracts*, II, 77. Cotton Mather in *Magnalia Christi Americana* had nothing but praise for Sir William and his vigorous defense of colonial assemblies (2 vols., Hartford, 1820), I, 162.

6. Blathwayt to Francis Watson, July 6, 1680, BPCol. Wmsbg., v. XXVII; Privy Council Warrants, 1678–1682, P.C. 6/14, P.R.O.; *CSPCol., 1681–1685,* #325; *CSPDom., 1680–1681*, p. 661; H.M.C. 13: 10th Report, App., pt. IV, *The Manuscripts of the Earl of Westmoreland* . . . (London, 1885), 173; *Burnet's History of His Own Time*, p. 335; Jones, *The First Whigs*, pp. 191–94.

Londoners joyously celebrated Shaftesbury's release. It was expected that the dismissal would greatly encourage the "factious party" in Ireland, too. But who would surmise that colonists in America would make much of Shaftesbury's escape, or of the Exclusion Crisis, or the Rye House Plot against both Charles and James, for that matter? From New Hampshire to the Carolinas, numerous colonists responded in a variety of ways to the upheaval in England. Fendall and Coode in Maryland pronounced it civil war; since no government ruled in England, they said, there was none in Maryland either, and they could do what they pleased. Nothing, then, was treason, no need to pay taxes, and they might take for themselves what estates they wished. The discontented party was very close to rebellion, and had its leadership not dissolved, the crisis in England might have proved the spark to bring it off.[7]

Edward Randolph was convinced of a conspiracy between the "factious parties" in Old and New England and was shocked at the "scandalous papers" in defense of Shaftesbury which the Boston faction gobbled up, sent them by Whig friends at home. In both Massachusetts and New Hampshire he claimed he had lost court cases against smugglers as a direct result of Shaftesbury's discharge. The Londoners' cheers for the great Whig outside the Old Bailey were heard as far west as Boston and Portsmouth. Governor Cranfield of New Hampshire, always willing to think the worst of colonists, insisted that those who opposed the Crown in New England were well aware of the Rye House Plot against King and Duke; some time earlier, he charged, they had "let fall words," suspiciously forecasting "great troubles were like to be in England." Cranfield in good Tory fashion was all for searching the ministers' and laity's papers for treasonable letters he was sure they possessed and lamented only the lack of orders and power to commence the investigation. In New York, after Governor Andros' departure, the breakdown of government, the "present distractions," when colonists refused to pay the lapsed duties and imposts, were laid by some individuals to the great fear of civil war in England.[8]

7. Christopher Rousby to Robert Ridgley, London, Dec. 6, 1681, *Arch. of Md.*, V, 302–3; Lord Lieutenant of Ireland to Sir Leoline Jenkins, Dec. 6, 1681, *CSPDom., 1680–1681*, p. 605; Philip Calvert, *A Letter from the Chancellour of Maryland, 1682*, John Carter Brown Library; Baltimore to Earl of Anglesey, July 19, 1681, *Arch. of Md.*, V, 281; A Shipmaster's answers before the Lords of Trade, Oct. 31, 1681, *ibid.*, 301; Witness at Fendall's Trial, Nov. 15, 1681, *ibid.*, 320–21; Philip Calvert to Col. Henry Meese, Dec. 29, 1681, *CSPCol., 1681–1685*, #351.

8. Randolph to Jenkins, Apr. 16, 1681, *ibid.*, #83; *ibid.*, #559, #781, #870; same to same, June 14, 1682, Toppan, ed., *Randolph*, III, 160; Cranfield to Jenkins, Oct. 19, 1683, in John G. Palfrey, *History of New England* (5 vols., Boston, 1858–90), III, 415 n.; James Graham to Robt. Livingston, June 8, 1681, Livingston Family Papers, Gen'l Corresp. 61–95, F.D.R. Library.

The names of Pennsylvania and Carolina were drawn into the course of events in a different way. The Quaker colonists probably entertained their proprietor earlier than either had expected. William Penn was in hot water as usual, for he found himself torn between respected Whig friends, such as Algernon and Henry Sidney and Shaftesbury, whom he had eagerly supported, on the one side, and Charles II and Duke James, on the other. From the King he had just won his liberal charter, and James was about to grant him the lower counties on the Delaware. Algernon Sidney, less fortunate than his brother and Shaftesbury, suffered a martyr's death for the Whig cause. Henry soon found the "Dutch aire" bracing, while mounting tension in England hurried Penn off to Pennsylvania, earlier than he had planned, where he hoped to shield himself "from ye revenge of [his] enimys." He embarked for his new colony late in 1681. Of all dissenting groups Quakers were least likely conspirators; they came off pretty well— even the Duke admitted it—at a time when most nonconformists were looked upon with suspicion. Nevertheless, a year or more later, when conspiracy and intrigue were even hotter in England, Quaker Penn, whose friendship for the King and Duke was well known, was accused of being a Catholic, confessing it, according to one exaggerated report, on his deathbed at Philadelphia in 1683.[9]

About as much truth as there was in the report of Penn's death surrounded the rumor that Shaftesbury's interest in Carolina was a cover for the intrigues of Whig revolutionaries. A handful of Presbyterians, whom some accused of acquaintance with the Rye House Plot, "did pretend to goe for Carolina"—which may have been a code phrase for their business in England—but gave up talk of it when their scheme was discovered, all very tenuous, to say the least. Still, Carolina and even New Jersey were on people's lips at the height of the crisis. Directly after his trial, Shaftesbury spoke of the "pleasantness of Carolina" and claimed that if it were not for his duty to the nation he certainly would live there, where, according to his overseer, he owned the best plantation in the colony. But Shaftesbury never saw his "darling Carolina." To escape the consequences of the King's revenge, which his dismissal by the grand jury only whetted, Shaftesbury soon

9. William Penn to Henry Sidney, 1681, Correspondence of Henry Sidney, Earl of Romney, 1674–1691, Add. Mss., 32681, 209b, B.M.; Robt. Barclay to Robt. Gordon, London, June 28, 1683, New Jersey Historical Society, *Proceedings*, V, 40 (1922), 5; Penn to Duke of York, [Feb. 2, 1684], Papers relating to William Penn, Penn Mss., 13, Library of the Society of Friends, London; Margaret Lowther to Penn, Aug. 4, 1683, *ibid.*, Penn Mss. 24; Penn's death reported, Newsletter, Jan. 13, 1683, H.M.C. 63: *Egmont*, II, 126; Peter Karsten, "Who was 'Colonel Sidney'?: A Note on the Meaning of the October 13, 1681, Penn-Sidney Letter," *Pennsylvania Magazine of History and Biography*, XCI (Apr. 1967), 197–98 and n.

fled to Holland and died there "of the Gout in his Stomach" in January 1683.[10] Besides the mainland, in Jamaica and the Barbados the "ffanatics" and the "factious parties" in the assemblies were full of English talk during the uneasy time of the Exclusion Crisis. Monarchy was on its last legs, said a cabal of Barbadians who, according to their governor, were ready to set up a commonwealth as soon as may be.[11]

A number of the principles and ideas, which came close to exploding into revolution in England, were attractive to colonists in America whose discontent with their own circumstances and distrust of governments over them fed on the violent disturbances at home. If authority crumbled in England, as many believed it would—some that it already had—then sanction for government in the colonies would crumble, too, permitting opportunity for change which "factious" people might improve. A worse crisis in England might turn the trick in colonies where resentment and feeling ran highest. Colonies were "contiguous" to England and assumed they were parts of the whole. Their colonists were sensitive people, and infection at home was contagious.

Plantations are of the King's Making

The final years of Charles II's reign, punctuated as they were by intrigue, several tangled plots, and the Exclusion Crisis, left him bitter and inclined to reaction, even revenge. The villains were Whigs, dissenters, and corporations, particularly the City of London, whose sheriffs and juries had thwarted his will as in Shaftesbury's trial. The reaction went far enough to diminish even the influence of a middle-of-the-roader like Lord Halifax, who had not supported Exclusion but who preached a concept of limited monarchy and opposed the French influence at court. His sway in political affairs gave way under pressure to the Duke of York and his adherents, the Duke having been re-admitted to Council and Cabinet secrets shortly after the Rye House Plot. In the last three years of his life, Charles surrounded himself with an inner group of favorites, principally Lords Sunderland,

10. William, Bishop of Raphoe, to Ormonde, Aug. 15, 1683, H.M.C., 14th Report, *Manuscripts of the Marquis of Ormonde*, I, App., pt. VII (London, 1895), 57; Thomas Lynch to Blathwayt, Jamaica, June [2?], 1684, BPCol. Wmsbg., v. XXIV; Blathwayt to Baltimore, Feb. 9, 1683, *ibid.*, v. XVIII; Stock, *Proceedings and Debates*, I, 451 n.; *CSPDom., 1680–1681*, 597; Samuel Wilson to Shaftesbury, Mar. 7 and Dec. 21, 1683, Shaftesbury Papers, P.R.O. 30/24/48/101, 103.

11. Gov. Sir Richard Dutton to Jenkins, Barbados, June 14, 1681, *CSPCol., 1681–1685*, #141; Sir John Witham to Blathwayt, Barbados, Oct. 31, 1683, BPCol. Wmsbg., v. XXXV; Francis Watson to Blathwayt, Jamaica, June 12, 1682, *ibid.*, v. XXVII.

Godolphin, and Jeffreys, and above all Lady Portsmouth, who along with M. Paul Barrillon, the French minister, had the King's ear. This knot of advisers, often called the "French party," who admired the absolutism of Louis XIV's successful rule across the Channel, helped Charles steer an arbitrary course which resulted in more stringent policies toward the major issues of the 1680's. Charles died before the new plans had jelled, but sufficient momentum was generated to reorganize local governments and judicial procedures and to force a sharp turn in the direction of colonial policy.[12]

In England there was a fresh assertion of the prerogative. It was felt far and wide against town governments, by justices of the peace, in courts and juries, and anywhere the King might successfully aver his power in order to ensure control and loyalty. The government enforced rigorously old laws against Catholics, dissenters, and conventiclers; in Scotland troops hunted down covenanters like rabbits in the field. The Crown often went out of its way to punish plotters and schemers; paid informers enjoyed open season against them. The courts convicted Whigs right and left, executing several and scattering the rest; many escaped to Holland, where William of Orange failed to move against them. John Locke was among them, for he "belonged to the late Earl of Shaftesbury." He was ferreted out of his physician's place at Oxford, having "behaved himself very factiously and undutifully to the Government." Most effective was the crackdown on city corporations whose freedom heretofore meant Whig sheriffs and Whig juries who stood out against the King. Notorious was the loss of London's charter, which succumbed to *quo warranto* proceedings in October of 1683, just a year before that of Massachusetts. The King did not act alone, of course; with Tory servants he rode a wave of reaction which rolled over England after several years of resistance, defiance, and intrigue, all contributing to an unsteadiness and uncertainty of surprising proportions. A determined but sometimes wrongheaded Charles pretty much succeeded in overcoming the opposition by one means or another, including the prorogations and then dissolution of Parliament. In so doing he strengthened and centralized the Crown's control. There is a great change in affairs here, William Blathwayt wrote to Governor Dutton of the Barbados; the King has resolved to govern

12. David Ogg, *England in the Reign of Charles II,* II, ch. 17; J. P. Kenyon, *Robert Spencer, Earl of Sunderland, 1641–1702,* ch. 3; *Burnet's History of His Own Time,* pp. 390–91; E. S. De Beer, ed., *Diary of John Evelyn* (London, 1959), p. 745; [Lewis Innes?], *The Life of James the Second . . . Collected out of Memoirs Writ of his own Hand . . .* , ed. by Rev. J. S. Clarke (2 vols., London, 1816), I, 740.

by law and he intends to lose no part of his prerogative. In fact, rather than losing it, he extended it considerably.[13]

Least of all did Charles intend to diminish the prerogative in the colonies. A Whig might argue—if he dared raise his head after the recent purge—the rightful place of Parliament in governing the realm as a check upon the Crown, or maybe even instead of the Crown. But in America the King was supreme, more so than he had ever been before, or so it turned out as Charles's reign drew to a close. It may be that this was not an isolated view but one shared by many Englishmen, even Whigs, who seemed to show little interest in exporting their revolutionary doctrines to the colonies, Halifax excepted. In support of the Crown's role there, the Lords of Trade ironically relied upon Shaftesbury, whom they described, in another delightful example of seventeenth-century understatement, as "no great promoter of the Royal prerogative." For Shaftesbury, they insisted, firmly believed that "all plantations were of the King's making, and that he might at any time alter or dispose of them at his pleasure." [14] If Whiggism meant anything, it had meaning in the realm, not the dominions where the King called the turn.

If there were few checks against tightening the prerogative in England, once Charles's "revenge" crystallized, there were even fewer to its exercise in America. As if acting upon Shaftesbury's pronouncement, the Crown's plans for reorganization took a long stride with revocation of the Massachusetts Bay charter in October of 1684. In order to bring other colonial governments more closely under control, Charles began actions against Maryland, the Carolinas, both New Jerseys, Delaware, and Bermuda. James, Duke of York, and "Prince Pen" agreed to surrender their proprietaries to the Crown, the latter reserving right to the soil, of course, and it was not long before the King turned to other colonies thus far immune.[15] Enforcement of the Acts of Trade was tightened; an Order in Council instructed the navy again in its duties to seize offending ships; and at the same time the Crown severely restricted jurisdiction of colonial governors over naval officers and fleets, a paring of maritime powers unsettling to the gov-

13. For tightening the prerogative under Charles, see Ogg, *England in the Reign of Charles II*, II, ch. 17; Kenyon, *Robert Spencer*, pp. 100–6. For Locke's loss of position at Oxford, see Shaftesbury Papers, P.R.O. 30/24/47/22; Blathwayt to Dutton, Aug. 24, 1681, BPCol. Wmsbg., v. XXX.

14. *CSPCol., 1681–1685*, #1087.

15. For attack upon the charters, see Blathwayt to Effingham, Dec. 9, 1684, BPCol. Wmsbg., v. XIV, and again Philip S. Haffenden, "The Crown and the Colonial Charters, 1675–1688," *William and Mary Quarterly*, 3d ser., XV (1958), 297–311, 452–66.

ernors' authority, particularly in the West Indies.[16] The Lords of Trade
announced a stop to further proprietary patents in America—which
makes one wonder how Penn ever got away with his in the first place
—or any grant of power which might render the plantations less
dependent. On top of this there was discussion among the Lords of
Trade of a plan for Parliament to tax the colonies directly, since it was
already clear that they would never agree to lay sufficient taxes upon
themselves, an ominously prophetic observation to say the least.
"Thriving conditions" at home made it possible for the Crown to
exercise sovereign powers beyond the realm where they sharply altered
the course of colonial government.[17]

In November and December 1684, just after revocation of the Massachusetts Charter and three months before the King's death, Charles
and the Privy Council did some very serious thinking about the colonies in America. A major question before them, once the way was
clear to consolidate New England under one head—a plan dear to
many who had sought the defeat of Massachusetts—was what kind of
a government it should have. Ought colonists to retain their legislative
assemblies, or should they be told what laws they might have by a
governor and council as New Yorkers had been told since 1664? Discussion of this question in the Privy and Cabinet Councils explains a
good deal about Stuart conceptions of empire and how Charles and
James thought colonists ought to be governed.

It was Lord Halifax who brought the issue to a head when he spoke
very pointedly in defense of colonial assemblies at a Council meeting
in early December which both Charles and James attended. M.
Barrillon got wind of the whole business—he may have attended the
meeting—and reported to Louis XIV Halifax's argument. It was un-
questionable, said Halifax, that "the same laws under which they live
in England ought to be established in a country inhabited by Englishmen." He lectured the Council at length with a variety of reasons why
"an absolute government is neither so happy nor so stable as that which
is tempered by laws and sets bounds to the authority of the prince."
He ended his appeal with the plain declaration "that he could never

16. *Acts of P.C., Col. Ser., 1680–1720*, #162, p. 71; Adm 1/5139, pp. 798, 826.
The problem of the governor's jurisdiction over officers of the Royal Navy is discussed in a series of letters between Thomas Lynch of Jamaica and Blathwayt
from Mar. 3, 1683, to Aug. 16, 1684, BPCol. Wmsbg., vols. XXIII and XXIV,
mostly the latter.

17. Lords of Trade's answer to Robt. Barclay's petition about East New Jersey,
C.O. 324/4, pp. 84–85, 101; Memo on Plantations' Revenue, Sec'y Blathwayt,
n.d., BPCol. Wmsbg., v. XLI; Blathwayt to Thomas Lynch, Oct. 2, 1682, *ibid.*,
v. XXIII.

like to live under a King who should have it in his power to take at pleasure the money out of his pocket." But Halifax was opposed by all who heard him, especially Lord Jeffreys; when it came to a question of the King's prerogative, said Jeffreys, "whoso capitulateth rebelleth" —the very attempt to define the function of the sovereign was equivalent to revolution. Ignoring Halifax's appeal, the Privy Council resolved that a governor and council alone should rule New England, "accountable only to his Britannic Majesty." Halifax paid for his boldness, for the Duke of York used the occasion to undermine Charles's confidence in Halifax by arguing that it was dangerous to share secrets of government with a man so critical of the King's sovereignty. M. Barrillon reported to Louis that Lady Portsmouth and Sunderland were pleased with Halifax's defeat, and that both agreed that their plans, which aimed at eliminating Halifax and persuading the King to assert himself, were going nicely.[18] As liberal, even radical, as Shaftesbury and his Whig cronies were about reforming government in England, it was Halifax, the "Trimmer," who enunciated a colonial policy in 1684 which took as its premise the equality of English subjects no matter where they lived. What was good for Englishmen in England was good for Englishmen in America, too. James dismissed Halifax not many months after he became king.

The deliberations of Charles, James, and the Privy Council about colonial government laid the basis for the arbitrary Dominion of New England which united Massachusetts, New Hampshire, and Maine in 1685 under a temporary president and council. Plymouth, Rhode Island, and Connecticut were added to it the next year under a governor general.

Certainly, with this kind of thinking going on, there was little hope for New York's Charter of Libertyes, which James had approved earlier but which had never been sealed and returned to the colony. Charles died in February 1685, and James, who had even stronger convictions about the prerogative, succeeded him as King. In the meantime the Lords of Trade had decided to submit the New York charter to scrutiny, doubtless persuaded to it by the abrupt change in colonial policy and probably by James himself. The reappraisal resulted in what the scrutinizers called "Observations," and these clearly pointed out to all who read or heard them the true nature of

18. M. Barrillon to Louis XIV, Dec. 7, 1684, in Charles James Fox, *A History of the Early Part of the Reign of James the Second* . . . (London, 1808), App., vii–ix; Louis XIV to Barrillon, Dec. 13, 1684, *ibid.*, ix; H. C. Foxcroft, *The Life and Letters of Sir George Saville, Bart., First Marquis of Halifax &C.* (2 vols., London, 1898), I, 427–29.

the charter: that it granted to New Yorkers rights and privileges not just equal to those enjoyed by English subjects in other colonies but really greater than any colonists enjoyed. The observers agreed that under the charter inhabitants of New York would actually be governed according to the laws of England, not merely as close to them as their colonial conditions might permit. This was a "Priviledge" not granted to any of the King's colonists in America. Further, the words of the charter, lodging the supreme legislative authority in the governor, council, and the "People" met in general assembly, represented an innovation found in no other colonial constitution or patent. The observers pointed out several other differences. The governor was much too dependent upon the council, more so than any other governor in America—which may help to explain the New York council's willingness to approve the charter. Since the governor, council, and representatives were the supreme and only legislative power of New York, the observers asked, would not such power seriously "abridge the Acts of Parliament that may be made concerning New York?" Doubtless New Yorkers would have agreed that this was precisely the case.[19]

The New York charter, the government it established, and the differences between them and what existed in other colonies were fully and finally discussed at a meeting of the Lords of Trade on March 3, 1685, with James II, the Earl of Sunderland, and Lord Godolphin all present. The conclusion reached was simple and to the point: "His Majesty doth not think fitt to confirm the same." The government of New York, it was agreed, would "be assimilated to the Constitution that shall be agreed on for New England, to which it is adjoining." Two days later James II wrote to Governor Dongan announcing his accession to the throne and that New York was now a royal colony attached to the Crown. He ordered Dongan to hold the line as it was and to follow former instructions. Tell my subjects, he wrote, that the colony and its affairs are now committed to the Privy Council, and they "may shortly expect such a gracious and suitable return by the settlement of fitting privileges and confirmation of their rights as shall bee found most expedient for Our service and the welfare of Our said Province." [20] More than a year later the colonists learned just what James meant, for in May 1686 he wrote fresh instructions to Governor Dongan declaring the New York charter "disallowed . . . Repealed, determined and made void."

19. Journal of Lords of Trade, Feb. 28, 1685, *CSPCol., 1685–1688,* #37. For "Observations" on the New York charter, dated Mar. 3, 1685, see *N.Y. Col. Docs.,* III, 357–59.

20. *Ibid.,* 354, 357, 360–61.

The governor and council, however, were to continue the duties and impositions which were levied under the charter until they decided otherwise upon taxes sufficient to support the government. In addition, all other laws passed by New Yorkers under the short-lived government were to remain in force as long as they were not contrary to the governor's instructions.[21]

Whether New Yorkers believed they had been tricked is not known. Certainly it must have appeared to some that the Duke permitted an assembly so that it might vote funds on its own terms; and once it had done so, he abolished the legislature and retained the tax laws. But probably the Duke was not quite so bold-facedly disingenuous. The New York charter ran up against sharp Stuart reaction to Whiggism and republicanism, which had its certain effect on imperial policy. In fact, the charter was scrutinized for the last time at a crucial turning point in colonial policy which hinged on revocation of the Massachusetts Bay charter and the decision to unite New England under one government. Begun by Charles, the new policy was strenuously pursued by James once on the throne, and the result was the Dominion of New England, to which New York was added in 1688. With these plans materializing in London, no wonder James lost sympathy for the New York charter, which granted his colonists a status not only equal to that of other colonists but surely even more advantageous. What is more, if the Lords of Trade accurately understood the charter, it gave to New Yorkers the same laws Englishmen enjoyed. And all of this was to become fact at the very time the Crown had decided to seize most of the charters and to rule more than half of the American colonies with little or no regard for the rights of Englishmen, let alone Englishmen's laws. The Dominion of New England under Andros proved that colonists enjoyed only the rights a Stuart king wished to give them, and despite the efforts of New Yorkers, these did not include representative government.

With Massachusetts reduced to insignificance, the Bermuda charter vacated, New York settled again under arbitrary government, with *quo warranto* proceedings ordered for most colonies whose patents still stood out against the King, it was clear that the Crown was determined to subject the dominions to centralized control. Randolph spoke openly of the intention to bring all the colonies under one general governor. William Blathwayt was jubilant. These measures, he wrote to the governor of Virginia, "will bring about that Necessary union of all the English colonies in America which make the King great & Extend his

21. Instructions, *ibid.*, 370; James II's Commission to Dongan, *ibid.*, 378.

real Empire in those parts." [22] Charles II, the Duke of York, and their friends had brought matters both foreign and domestic to a point which was definable and comprehensible to orderly-minded bureaucrats like Blathwayt and Randolph who administered colonial policy. Both had worked for almost ten years to bring about this revolution in the colonies. From their point of view they could look with pride and satisfaction upon the new order of things and anticipate a peaceful administration of His Majesty's "real Empire" in America.

James II

James's accession to the throne was a good deal more peaceful than many people had expected. Recent reaction to Charles's troubles with Whigs and plotters redounded to James's advantage, and probably most Englishmen were relieved that the rightful heir succeeded to the throne despite his religion. Great numbers of loyal subjects thronged to kiss the King's hand within a few days of his accession. Such a change was a surprise to many, really "God's great mercie," said some, "and not a Whig to be heard of." Shortly after being proclaimed, James called a Parliament to get the jump on the opposition but also to secure the Crown's revenues, since half had ceased with Charles's death. Had he waited, he said, the malcontents would have demanded a Parliament and thus "gained the favor of the nation." His dispatch succeeded, for Parliament fell all over itself voting him money, more even than he had asked for, and although there was some talk of handing it out piecemeal, the Commons agreed to vote the revenues for life.[23] Included, despite strong opposition from the trading people, were increased import duties on tobacco and sugar, a move which did not get James's reign off to a very good start in Virginia, Maryland, and the islands.[24] In both realm and colonies James confirmed all officers in their positions until it was his pleasure to replace them; this included Halifax, M. Barrillon told Louis XIV, but "only for forms sake." James's pleasure with Halifax lasted only a few months, and in

22. Randolph to Philip Musgrave, Deal, Dec. 12, 1684, Toppan, ed., *Randolph*, VI, 166; Blathwayt to Effingham, Dec. 9, 1684, BPCol. Wmsbg., v. XIV.

23. John Dugdale to Sir William Dugdale, Feb. 10, 1685, William Hamper, ed., *Life, Diary and Correspondence of Sir William Dugdale* (London, 1827), p. 450; Sir John Dalrymple, ed., *Memoirs of Great Britain and Ireland* (2 vols., London, 1773), II, App., pt. I, 103; John, Lord Viscount Lonsdale, *Memoir of the Reign of James II* (London, 1857), p. 451; Robt. Southwell to John Percival, June 23, 1685, H.M.C., 63; *Egmont*, II, 155.

24. James II to Colonial Governors, June 26, 1685, C.O. 324/4, pp. 145–46; *CSPCol., 1685–1688*, #253, #444, #450, #459, #461; Effingham to Blathwayt, Nov. 14, 1685, BPCol. Wmsbg., v. XIV.

the meantime the King settled most important matters in "secret conferences" with Lords Sunderland, Rochester, and Godolphin.[25] Chief Justice Lord Jeffreys, another close adviser to the King, was soon very busy with other matters in the west of England.

Ironically, James II had the Earl of Argyle and the Duke of Monmouth to thank for helping him make firm his seat on the throne. In May 1685 Argyle landed in the Western Highlands with rebellion in mind but soon ended his career in Edinburgh Castle, where he lost his head. Monmouth was no more successful. From Holland with a handful of adherents, he came ashore in the West Country, where he claimed his legitimacy and right to the throne. He gathered more discontented Englishmen around him than Argyle ever saw of Scots in the Highlands, but the rising was pitiful in its weakness, attracting men of the "lowest Degree," said James, and many of them unarmed. James sent what troops he had to suppress the rebellion, and although the outcome was never really in doubt, he borrowed back six regiments lent earlier to William of Orange, three Scottish and three English, for James meant business. Twice during the summer wily Prince William offered to embark for England with his Dutch regiments to join in the task of subduing Monmouth, and twice James thanked him kindly, refused his generosity, and suggested politely that William's real duty was to stay where he was. Probably the last thing James wanted in 1685 or any time was William at the head of Dutch troops in England.[26] The rebellions could not have come at a better time for James; his popularity momentarily soared, winning him further support and dispelling apathy. The votes for funds in Parliament came easier with Monmouth fumbling about in the West. The new tobacco and sugar bill and one to attaint Monmouth of high treason arrived in the House of Lords together; they were passed on the same day, along with additional duties on wine and vinegar.[27] Monmouth lived only a little longer than Argyle; his life was ended abruptly in the Tower of London.

It was some time before colonists in America learned what Monmouth's Rebellion was all about and who had actually succeeded. Again, what colonists wanted to believe tended to color their understanding of the news, particularly when it arrived late, in bits and snatches, and often garbled. In Bermuda, for instance, where mutiny

25. M. Barrillon to Louis XIV, Feb. 19, 1685, C. J. Fox, *History of the Early Part of the Reign of James II*, App., p. xxi; James II to Colonial Governors, Feb. 6, 1685, C.O. 324/4, pp. 123–25.

26. James II to Colonial Governors, June 26, 1685, C.O. 324/4, pp. 146–48; Dalrymple, ed., *Memoirs of Great Britain and Ireland*, II, App., pt. I, 123–37.

27. *Journal of the House of Lords, 1685–1691*, pp. 42–43, 44; [John Oldmixon], *The British Empire in America* (2 vols., London, 1741), I, 394.

was rife since the loss of the charter, the news of the rebellion set the disaffected whispering; it was now or never, they claimed, for the Duke of Monmouth was the rightful heir—well, at least natural—a Protestant, too, and "the Pope was the whore of Babylon . . . drunk with the blood of the saints." A strict guard, however, set up by the governor thwarted a rising until word arrived of Monmouth's ignominious defeat and imprisonment. In Nevis the expectation was so strong that Monmouth would prevail that the governor ordered new fortifications to protect the island from the rebels.[28] Healths were drunk to the Duke in Maryland, to say nothing of treasonable words in his behalf spoken there, the Barbados, and several other places. New York was "pestered" with "malicious and factious reports," which spread false "alarums," most of them coming from Boston. In New Hampshire, two months before the landing, word spread that there was no King of England, that Monmouth was proclaimed and crowned in Scotland, and had dashed to Ireland to raise an army. As for the Duke of York, he was not yet crowned and there was question whether he ever would be. A little later, these same colonists declared Argyle's rebellion to be God's answer to their prayers and fasts; it would deliver them from bondage and preserve their churches.[29]

In Massachusetts Monmouth had more success for a time than he ever won in the West Country, but this was owing to the Bay Colony's peculiar circumstances. After the revocation of the charter it was another year before the new regime was established; in the meantime the old, with Governor Bradstreet at its head, diffidently carried on the functions of government, held elections, and proclaimed the new King, although "Cold & Heartlessly performed," said William Dyer. There was a good deal of sentiment among the faction for hanging on, hoping, no doubt, that God would smite their enemies and restore full control to His people.[30]

Who would head the new government was a matter of intense interest. The faction and most others heaved sighs of relief when they learned that it would *not* be Edward Cranfield. Several other

28. Two letters from Gov. Richard Cony of Bermuda to Blathwayt, both written on June 4, 1685, BPCol. Wmsbg., v. XXXVI; Cony to Lords of Trade, Jan. 3, 1686, *CSPCol., 1685–1688*, #533; For Nevis, see Randolph to Blathwayt, Deal, Nov. 19, 1685, BPCol. Wmsbg., v. I.

29. *CSPCol., 1685–1688*, #864, #1166, #1898, XXIII; Gov. Dongan to Sec'y Sunderland, Sept. 18, 1685, *N.Y. Col. Docs.*, III, 364–65; J. Spragg to Blathwayt, Oct. 3, 1685, BPCol. Wmsbg., v. X; Robt. Mason to Blathwayt, Aug. 20, 1685, *ibid.*, v. XII; Deposition of Joanna Chesley, New Hampshire, Apr. 30, 1685, C.O. 1/57/117,I; N.H. Hist. Soc. *Coll.*, VIII, 244.

30. William Dyer to Blathwayt, Eliza. Town, East N.J., June 12, 1685, BPCol. Wmsbg., v. IV; Dudley to Blathwayt, Sept. 20, 1685, *ibid.*

names were tossed about; Randolph mentioned Edmund Andros, but his guess was premature. By early 1685 it was pretty much settled that Colonel Percy Kirk was King Charles's choice for the job, a choice which sent shudders clear through the faction and moderates alike and even jolted Edward Randolph. Kirk, former governor of Tangier, was a notorious brute who supposedly would bring with him six or seven frigates and 5,000 men.[31] But Kirk never set sail for Massachusetts; once on the throne James II found plenty to keep the colonel busy in England.

The faction at Boston made its own sense out of being spared Kirk's governorship, or Increase Mather made sense out of it for them. At the very peak of their frustration in February 1685, when both natural and supernatural worlds seemed stacked against them, Mather, dejected in spirit, took the colony's burdens upon his own shoulders and spent a whole day in his study, fasting, meditating, and praying for New England's deliverance. After being more "moved and melted" before the Lord than usual, he arose, "joyful and cheered," convinced that he had been heard, and confident of God's "salvation." Two months later a ship arrived in Boston with the news of Charles II's death. Mather quickly calculated that the very day he had spent on his knees in prayer was the day of Charles's demise, "by whose death Kirk's coming . . . was prevented and New England was that day delivered." Had Charles lingered on a few more weeks, New England would have been ruined, for "Bloody Kirk" would have come and "made horrible slaughter."[32] There was hope; God was still with them, and working through the King of England no less, or so it seemed according to Mather.

Were they too easily discouraged? Had they misjudged their God? Certainly some thought so when rumors of Monmouth's Rebellion reached Massachusetts shores in the summer of 1685. Unfortunately, the rumors were all wrong, as wrong as they possibly could be. If half of what William Dyer described actually took place in Boston in response to the news, a good many people were convinced that Jehovah again had saved them from what looked like certain disaster. Dyer arrived in Boston on September 2, 1685, and found the city in a "hurly-burly" over the "Whigg News" which joyfully related the victories of both Monmouth and Argyle and that the former was now

31. Robt. Humphreys to Mass. govt., July 25, 1685, Mass. Arch., Political, CVI, 327; Wait Winthrop to Fitz-John Winthrop, Boston, Nov. 11, 1684, *Winthrop Papers,* M.H.S. *Coll.,* 5th ser., VIII, 447; Fitz-John Winthrop to James Fitch, New London, Jan. 28, 1685, *ibid.,* 300.

32. Mather, "Autobiography," A.A.S. *Proc.,* 71 (1961), pt. 2, p. 313.

King of England with the whole nation behind him. James, after "Tearing his haire," had fled Whitehall for shelter at Windsor until he could find a way to leave England. With the crown safely upon a Protestant head and liberty of conscience granted, the General Court ordered a day of thanksgiving. God, indeed, had delivered New England.

But the bloody truth was soon to follow: James on his throne, rebellion wholly suppressed, and the "Grand Traytors" executed. Then the "Seeming Saints" hung down their heads, looked "dampish & Cloudy," and postponed their thanksgiving. The real truth, said Dyer, had "quite knockt all the Brethe'rn hopes on ye head," and they shuffled off, claiming Monmouth was betrayed. Joseph Dudley put it a little differently; he spoke of the "perfect disappointment of the expectations" of some "evil-minded" persons in Boston.[33]

William Dyer told his own story about Percy Kirk's abortive debut into early American history. From Taunton in Somerset, where Kirk set up emergency headquarters immediately following Monmouth's defeat, there spread some startling news about the colonel's doings. After entertaining a couple of dozen local gentlemen at dinner, he hanged the lot of them from the wall to satisfy his popish cruelty. Not much later he strung up twelve or so more to a tavern signpost, and when the innkeeper complained, "seeming to be trobled," he hanged him alongside them. For these "gross misdemeanirs" Kirk was laid aside, quite out of His Majesty's favor. Gilbert Burnet corroborated most of Dyer's wild story, except that the men Kirk executed were hardly gentlemen diners, but his prisoners, captured during the rebellion, and "Kirk was only chid for it," wrote Burnet.[34] Business at home had delayed his departure for Massachusetts, finally quashing it altogether. Kirk's gory successes in Somerset—his licks before Judge Jeffreys' Assizes—damaged his usefulness as a colonial governor even over fractious Puritans.

After Monmouth's Rebellion James kept his troops encamped at Hounslow Heath for some time, besides refitting ships to improve the navy, wholly with the idea of making himself "still more master of his country." It pleased him considerably to be in a position to deliver bold and authoritative strokes. If Parliament balked at financing his doings, it would become more submissive, he said, when it learned how much he could do without its help, for James had resolved "not to

33. Dyer to Blathwayt, Boston, Nov. 16, 1685, BPCol. Wmsbg., v. IV; Dudley to Blathwayt, Nov. 2, 1685, *ibid.*

34. Dyer to Blathwayt, Boston, Nov. 16, 1685, *ibid.;* Burnet's *History of His Own Time,* p. 415; Richard S. Dunn, *Puritans and Yankees,* p. 226.

reign precariously." [35] The colonies felt their share of the royal diligence. Randolph was kept busy delivering *quo warrantos,* while governors received strong reminders of their duties respecting the Acts of Trade. And when this was not sufficient the Privy Council bore down again on the captains of His Majesty's navy in American waters with express orders to seize all foreign ships trading in the colonies.[36]

A colonial policy which had begun at the Restoration, had gathered momentum under the Lords of Trade, and had taken several strong spurts in the last few years of Charles's reign gave promise of fulfillment under James II. Despite sporadic movement, its goals, particularly in the late 1670's, were dependence, uniformity, centralization, and profit. Charters, new and old, were forfeit if the governments or the people they supported trespassed upon the prerogative, the nation's good, economic, political, religious, or upon the revenue. Separate colonies were a nuisance, primarily if they harbored idiosyncratic notions about trade, rights, government, assemblies, or religion. There was no colonial constitution but the governors' commissions and instructions from the King in Council. Colonial governments rested upon no guarantees but a dependence upon the Crown. The rights of Englishmen were bounded by the four seas and did not reach the colonists, whose governments were by grace not right. On this basis the Dominion of New England was established. Under these conditions, colonists in America set their faces against the reign of James II.

35. Dalrymple, ed., *Memoirs of Great Britain and Ireland,* II, App., pt. I, 169–72.

36. C.O. 324/4, pp. 141, 151–66; *Acts of P.C., Col. Ser., 1680–1720,* #183, pp. 81–82; Randolph, "A Short Narrative of my Proceedings," Toppan, ed., *Randolph,* IV, 189.

10 The Dominion of New England: The Bay Colony

Establishment of the Dominion of New England was the high point of the new Stuart colonial policy. Bringing the northern colonies together under one governor general would go a long way, it was hoped, toward solving problems of trade enforcement, political dependence, and defense against French and Indians. It was likely, however, that consolidating New England under one head, to which New York and New Jersey were later added (1688), was not the last of the Crown's plans for union, but that a southern dominion was in the King's mind, or at least, some kind of reorganization in the south which would force greater subjection and dependence upon colonial subjects. Just what the plan was the government never made clear, but such was its imminence that even colonists were talking about it, and Blathwayt, before Charles's death, attempted to infect Governor Effingham of Virginia with the glory of His Majesty's "real empire" in America.[1]

1. John Saffin to John Allyn, July 1687, *Recs. Col. Conn.*, III, 382; Blathwayt to Effingham, Dec. 9, 1684, BPCol. Wmsbg., v. XIV. See also Philip S. Haffenden,

While policymakers and King's men gloried over the Crown's successes in imperial consolidation, the people of New England, at least those who continued to honor covenant and charter as the two props of their holy commonwealth, sank deeper into disillusionment. Indian wars, royal commissions, heresy, sin, and customs collectors, most calamities they had suffered could be resisted by the faithful and usually subdued—so their experience had taught them. But a royal government, led first by a local turncoat and then by a royal army officer, both of whom were backed to the hilt by commissions which robbed the Bay colonists of their normal means of survival, these were calamities of a different nature. Although most colonists did not succumb spiritually to them, these misfortunes presented new and uncompromising evidence of God's continued controversy with New England. The helplessness of the "Citty upon the Hill" against the royal odds was humiliating to a chosen people. Sad, indeed, was the sight of respectable sons of the fathers queuing up for offices in the new government. Most of the councillors had been fingered earlier by Edward Randolph as loyal and safe, and Dudley's council, when it first sat in May of 1686, included a number of well-known churchmen and merchants: William Stoughton—chosen deputy president—Peter Bulkeley, John Usher, Wait and Fitz-John Winthrop (grandsons of old John the founder), several leading colonists from Maine and New Hampshire (Robert Mason for one), and, of course, Edward Randolph. Old Simon Bradstreet, his son Dudley, and Nathaniel Saltonstall, like true "New England men," boldly refused to serve, although named in Dudley's commission.[2]

Besides absorbing prominent members of the New England oligarchy, albeit moderates, the new government under both Dudley and then Sir Edmund Andros destroyed the accustomed order of things by which the Puritans had maintained supremacy and supposedly advanced God's kingdom. The assembly was gone; the governor and council legislated and taxed without the vote of elected representatives. Andros severely restricted town meetings, where freeman and freeholder alike had discussed local affairs and managed town business. Toleration undermined the ascendancy of Congregationalism, as did the outlawing of ministers' rates. Andros reorganized the militia, replacing with Anglicans a number of church members and respected

---

"The Crown and the Colonial Charters, 1675–1688," pt. II, *William and Mary Quarterly*, 3d ser., 4 (Oct. 1958), 463–66.

2. Sessional Papers, Council, C.O. 5/785, pp. 1, 4, 7, P.R.O.; Randolph to Blathwayt, Boston, May 29, 1686, BPCol. Wmsbg., v. IV; Dudley to Blathwayt, June 20, 1686, *ibid.;* Richard S. Dunn, *Puritans and Yankees*, p. 226.

leaders of society in the top ranks. Establishment of the Dominion left the "due form of government" in shambles; it severed the ligaments of Puritan society which had kept the covenant intact. "Ye foundation of all our Good things ware destroyd," the Reverend John Higginson of Salem lamented.[3] To lose the charter was bad enough; to lose also the institutional bases of the covenant was disaster.

With the charter gone and the framework on which the covenant hung seriously undermined, Bay colonists were forced to fend for themselves. Granted the covenant conception might live on in the hearts and minds of the faithful, it was no longer useful along with the charter as a shield against the "mutacons" of a king and his governor. Deprived of their accustomed props which God had sanctioned, the Puritan party shifted its defense from one chiefly religious to one primarily political, even constitutional, to a defense, eventually resistance, based on the rights of Englishmen. Recognition of these rights was secondary in their earlier struggle with the Crown; Bay colonists had hardly needed them, since, as virtually independent, they had carried on much as they pleased, confident in their charter and contract with God. A covenanted people for two generations had both the inclination and the power to control the community as they believed God directed, and control it they did on their own terms. After 1685 they were deprived of this power, and ironically they looked to the only guarantee available to them, one they had earlier denied to others who had disagreed with them. Luckily it was a guarantee, a set of political principles, whose time had come or was about to come.

Calamity was not calmly suffered even after 1685. Jehovah was not with Dudley or Andros or their oppressive councils. He merely used them as tools to punish the community which was not equal to its promise, not wholly faithful to its mission. Anyway, resistance to government which destroyed God's way and the gospel order was not sinful. Was not the charter illegally revoked and their government denied a fair chance to defend it? So reasoned the faction quietly while Dudley and then Andros, first somewhat gently, then with more determination, rearranged their lives and livelihood, taxed them without consent, revamped their system of justice, forced the Navigation Acts upon them, poked long noses into property holdings, and introduced the Church of England and all its vanities into their midst.

Forceful resistance was scanty, although there was plenty of foot-dragging on several accounts throughout the years of royal control. One of their own kind as governor was hazardous to begin with. Dud-

3. Sewall, *Diary*, I, 168; Higginson to his son Nathaniel, Salem, Aug. 31, 1698, Essex Institute Historical *Collections*, XLIII (Salem, Mass., 1907), 182.

ley had never been popular, and the old guard heaped abuse upon him when it got the opportunity.[4] His government was but four days old when former secretary Edward Rawson and some of the old deputies submitted a "paper" which sharply challenged the regime on fundamental grounds. Its justice appeared arbitrary; the council abridged the colonists' liberties of Englishmen in depriving them of consent to laws and taxes. Although Rawson and his people would remain loyal to the Crown, they said, they could never assent to the government as it was constituted. Dudley's council branded the paper "libellious" and called Rawson on the carpet, but no action was taken. He took his time, however, in handing over the colony's records to Secretary Randolph; it was almost a year before the new government secured them, and then only after it had "fetcht" them away from Rawson's home.[5]

Before Dudley's temporary government gave away to Andros in December of 1686, it met one crisis which might have blown up into rebellion had it been improperly handled. Lieutenant John Gould, a farmer, of Topsfield in Essex County, spoke roundly before his militia company at a "Riotous Muster," refusing to own the new government and offering his troops in support of the old. Tried and convicted of uttering treasonable and seditious words, he got off with a fine of fifty pounds plus costs and a bond against good behavior. Two weeks earlier Ipswich and Rowley in the same county had refused to observe the public fast appointed by Dudley and his council. But these seemed minor matters which promised little trouble.[6]

Disagreement between the Dominion government and most New Englanders centered on fundamental issues: taxation, land tenure, justice, trade, and, of course, religion, all of which bore heavily on the character of the society Puritans and other settlers had known for two generations or more.

Both Dudley and Andros had trouble all the way along in levying and collecting taxes. Despite the president's commission, he and his council suggested that a well-regulated assembly would make taxes come easier, and this was vital to the new government, since it presided over an empty treasury and a colony loaded with debt.[7] There was no response to the suggestion in England. Andros, like the King, had little sympathy for representative government. After all, the chief

4. Dudley to Blathwayt, June 20, 1686, BPCol. Wmsbg., v. IV.

5. Sessional Papers, Council, C.O. 5/785, pp. 16–17, 33; Shurtleff, ed., *Recs. Mass. Bay.*, V, 515–16; Sewall, *Diary*, I, 168.

6. M.H.S. *Coll.*, 3d ser., VII, 150–54; Sessional Papers, Council, C.O. 5/785, p. 48.

7. *Ibid.*, pp. 20, 24; President and Council to Lords of Trade, Oct. 23, 1686, C.O. 391/6, p. 21; R. Wharton to Blathwayt, June 5, 1686, BPCol. Wmsbg., v. VI.

characteristic of James's new policy was direct control and no funny business about consent of the governed. For a time the temporariness of Dudley's government was excuse enough for colonists not to pay ordinary taxes, let alone arrears; as a result, in a bare two months after taking office the council attempted to tighten the system.[8] Andros tried for a short time to get along with existing tax laws but found them woefully short of what he believed an honorable government needed. His council, however, was very sticky about increasing the amount and changing the bases of the levies. Andros' council included Dudley and a number of inherited incumbents besides Randolph, plus some new people from New York mentioned in the governor general's commission. Most of the New Englanders on the council were either merchants or land speculators or both, and therefore they had very strong ideas about the incidence of taxes. Some opposed increased duties, excises, and customs which bore on trade; others resisted new county rates on real estate. Most agreed on changing nothing, while several even objected to repassing tax laws already on the books. Captain Francis Nicholson, a newcomer to the council—he had come as commander of the redcoats who accompanied Andros—declared its members a cunning, self-interested, and obstinate lot who made money-raising a "hard matter" for the governor. New Hampshire's Robert Mason, who backed the Dominion on every vote, was appalled at the "downright opposition" Andros met with chiefly when the issue had to do with His Majesty's honor and revenue. Randolph, for once, showed greater understanding of the problem: "They have always accounted themselves a free people," he said, "and look upon this Act [new tax] as a clog to them and their estates." By the end of March 1687 Andros and his closest associates had hammered out a new revenue bill which they then bulldozed through the council despite an obvious majority against it. Andros was an army officer accustomed to following orders but unaccustomed to dissent from his own by subordinates. His handling of the Dominion council and New Englanders generally gave substance to William Penn's earlier opinion—a little gently expressed— that his fault was "sometimes an over eager & too pressing an execution of his power when provoakt." Dudley and company probably would have agreed with Penn and increasingly so as the governor general discussed less and dictated more the direction his government should take.[9]

8. Sessional Papers, Council, C.O. 5/785, pp. 39–40, 49–50.

9. For Andros' tax problems, see his series of letters to Blathwayt, Boston, dated Dec. 23, 1686, Feb. 3, Mar. 30, Aug. 17, Aug. 31, 1687, BPCol. Wmsbg., v. III. See also Francis Nicholson to Blathwayt, Boston, Feb. 7, 1687, *ibid.*, v. XV; Dudley to Blathwayt, Boston, Mar. 30, 1687, *ibid.*, v. IV; Robt. Mason to Blathwayt, Boston, Sept. 28, 1687, *ibid.*, v. XII; Randolph to Lords of Trade, Mar. 25, 1687,

Several towns in Essex County took a bold stand against Andros' tax of 1687, hoping, no doubt, to force him to call an assembly. Ipswich led the way in August by refusing to elect a tax commissioner, as the treasurer's warrant demanded, or to permit its selectmen to levy the new rate. A week later Topsfield people in town meeting followed their neighbors, and before long several other towns and individuals had agreed not to go along with the new tax. Their justifications in defying Andros were similar: they could be taxed, they said, only through an assembly; any attempt to levy rates without their consent infringed upon their rights and liberties as Englishmen, for it violated the statute laws of the nation. Andros moved quickly and arrested more than thirty of the insurgents, including the Reverend John Wise, who at Ipswich town meeting had stirred up the people to "Refractoryness and Disobedience" in contempt of the King's laws and his government in New England. Some of the accused were carried from Essex County to Boston, where they lay in jail awaiting trial, while others were kept prisoners in their home county for trial there. Once they saw that Andros meant business, several begged forgiveness and release from jail, promising speedy execution of the rate, but the governor general, after dismissing a handful, left the rest to the law and tried them before a special court of oyer and terminer made up of members of his council. Judges at the trial, Dudley, Stoughton, Usher, and Randolph, showed little sympathy toward the defendants, and the jury, eleven of whom were merchants, found them guilty in short order. Later the defendants claimed the jury was illegal since very few of its members were freeholders, and the charge, if true, indicated how far Andros was willing to stray from former Massachusetts judicial customs to get convictions against those who defied him. Penalties were stiff: the court fined John Wise £50, demanded surety of £1,000 for his future good behavior, and suspended him from the ministry during Andros' pleasure. Other defendants received similar fines, and one was stripped of his public offices.[10]

CSPCol., 1685–1688, #1195. *A Narrative of Proceedings of Sir Edmond Androsse and his Complices . . . 1691,* Andrews, ed., *Narratives,* pp. 242–43. Theodore B. Lewis gives an excellent explanation of the Dominion's tax difficulties in "Massachusetts and the Glorious Revolution" (unpubl. Ph.D. thesis, Univ. of Wisconsin, 1967), pp. 225–28. For Penn's opinion of Andros, see Penn to Blathwayt, Nov. 21, 1682, BPCol. Wmsbg., v. VII.

10. Documents describing the Ipswich tax revolt are in Thomas F. Waters, *Ipswich in the Massachusetts Bay Colony* (Ipswich, Mass., 1905), pp. 239–64, and Toppan, ed., *Randolph,* II, 40–49 n., VI, 307. For court proceedings, see *ibid.,* IV, 171–82. See also *The Revolution in New England Justified . . .* (1691), *Andros Tracts,* Prince Society *Publications* (3 vols., Boston, 1868–74), I, 81–87. M.H.S., Gay Transcripts, State Papers, III, 59–60; Andros to Blathwayt, Boston,

When Wise and his Essex County friends pled Magna Carta and the liberties of Englishmen in defense of their stand against an arbitrary tax, a member of the court, at one point during the proceedings, replied point-blank that they need not expect the laws of England to follow them to the ends of the earth.[11] Two very different conceptions of empire faced each other in the Boston courtroom in the summer of 1687. One of these was only lately appreciated in Massachusetts, since heretofore the Puritans who had dominated the government relied successfully upon their charter, covenant, and isolation, rather than upon the English constitution, for their sanction and guarantees. Moreover, these Englishmen's rights the Puritan oligarchy had frequently denied to colonists who dissented, politically and religiously, from the due form of government worked out and administered over more than fifty years of life in the wilderness. But in 1687, confronted with an arbitrary tax law and a governor general behind it, the rights of Englishmen looked attractive to a people who had little else to stand upon.

Colonists were Englishmen, they now argued, with rights and privileges equal to subjects within the realm. One of these, and one they were then contending for, was representative government in which colonists' liberties were guaranteed and protected. If an Englishman at home could not be taxed without his consent, neither then could a colonist, for Englishmen, no matter where they lived, were equal respecting treatment from government. Andros' court disagreed; its interpretation of empire was clear in James's commission and instructions to the governor, for these demanded colonial governments to the King's liking, whose existence rested upon royal grace, not on the subjects' but the King's rights alone to govern a dependent people as he chose. That colonists in Massachusetts had come lately to their conclusion and for self-interested reasons did nothing, from their point of view, to vitiate its validity as a theory of empire or of colonial government. Virginians, Marylanders, and New Yorkers had believed it all along and for self-interested reasons, too. As colonists, they were unable to carry out their conviction, since they, too, ran up against an authoritarian policy derived from an opposite point of view. Circumstances only lately brought a good many people in Massachusetts to see the

---

Sept. 28, 1687, BPCol. Wmsbg., v. III. After John Wise humbled himself and petitioned for relief, Andros let him preach again. Order dated Nov. 24, 1687, Toppan, ed., *Randolph*, II, 49 n.

11. *The Revolution in New England Justified*, in *Andros Tracts*, I, 81–82. Theodore B. Lewis has determined that the court's remark about English laws was made at a pretrial examination, not the trial itself, and came from John West, a New Yorker, who was deputy secretary to the council. "Massachusetts and the Glorious Revolution," p. 235 and n. 114, p. 246.

usefulness of an empire based upon equality as protection against the kind of government Andros imposed upon them. Without an assembly Bay colonists found political maneuver and delay impossible. Stubborn resistance against a tax measure proved even dangerous, as Ipswich and Topsfield and several other towns quickly learned. Robert Mason was certain the governor's prompt suppression would "terrify others," and it probably did, although Andros' heavy hand did not prevent occasional delay in payment. Nevertheless, there were no more Ipswich revolts over tax issues. The outburst north of Boston proved to colonists one thing, and that was, if the laws of Englishmen did not follow them to America, their penalties certainly did. To Andros the goings on in Essex County proved the danger of New England town meetings. His council shortly outlawed them altogether except for single occasions in May of each year whereby townspeople might elect selectmen, constables, and other necessary officers. It looked to many like a splendid way to prevent colonists from meeting together and discussing their grievances.[12]

Bay colonists were surprised to learn that revocation of the charter had voided their titles to land they lived and worked upon. Andros' instructions directed him to require all landowners to petition for royal patents so that each might hold his land directly from the Crown. There were certain advantages for the Dominion in this: fees and future quitrents would help support the government; repatenting would settle rival claims and confusion resulting from slipshod grants and Indian purchases. To Andros it was a necessary reform to remind colonists of their dependence upon the King, the ultimate owner of the soil. There was a good deal of hanging back by Bay colonists, who were stung by the government's charge that they were violent intruders upon the King's possessions, upon land some of them had owned for forty, even sixty, years. Andros was forced to bring suits against several of the larger landholders as test cases of the Crown's right, although men like Dudley and Stoughton voluntarily petitioned for patents and suggested others do the same. Samuel Sewall refused to budge until the summer of 1688 when the government served a writ for his Hog Island in Boston Harbor. Friends split in their advice to Sewall; he finally knuckled under rather than go to trial against the King, since several judges had informed him he would certainly be found guilty

12. Mason to Blathwayt, Boston, Sept. 28, 1687, BPCol. Wmsbg., v. XII; Andros to Lords of Trade, Boston, Apr. 4, 1688, C.O. 5/905, pp. 15–16; "Andros Records," A.A.S. *Proc.*, N.S., XIII, 478, 494, and n.; Sewall, *Diary*, I, 206; *Andros Tracts*, I, 80.

anyway if he went to court. Very little Andros did caused sharper resentment than his attempts to repatent the colonists' property and charge fees for the service, and this among a people whose fathers had conquered a wilderness and who had quietly inherited the land and defended it against the Indians.[13] In Maine titles were even more confused than in Massachusetts, owing to rival claims between descendants of Ferdinando Gorges and the Bay Colony government. Francis Nicholson found it a "hard task" to change colonists' minds, since they idolized their Indian purchases and the former government's vote of confirmation, neither of which had much weight with him or Andros. Nor were landholders in Plymouth Colony any more eager to surrender their claims to the government at Boston.[14]

On top of this the Bay colonists learned that common land, land not yet granted, and even land whose title could not be adequately proved in Andros' terms had passed to the Crown, and the governor might grant it as he pleased. Several portions Andros did assign to his friends, causing bitter reaction, particularly when it looked as if several choice parcels might fall to Edward Randolph, who was constantly on the lookout for a good thing. Andros' land policy was intolerable to most New Englanders; it cut deeply into rights quite as sacred to settlers as the charter. It could not be the King's intention, they said, to deprive them of their land, and James was soon to hear about it.[15]

New Englanders were no more pleased with the Dominion's system of justice than they were with its attack upon their landholding. Edward Rawson and his deputies had labeled Dudley's judicial plans arbitrary at the outset because they included no "certain determinate rule" for its administration.[16] But this was nothing to the fault they found with Andros' innovations, which went into effect not long after he arrived. Accustomed to their own way of doing things, most Massachusetts settlers were happy with a judicial system which recognized the laws of God before the laws of England. They took very seriously

13. *Ibid.*, 87, III, 20; Andros to Blathwayt, Boston, May 25, 1687, BPCol. Wmsbg., v. III; Sewall, *Diary*, I, 219, 220–21, 229, 231–32; Viola F. Barnes, *The Dominion of New England*, ch. VIII.

14. Nicholson to Blathwayt, Boston, Sept. 5, 1687, BPCol. Wmsbg., v. XV; "Proposal from the Grand Jury of the County of Barnstable for an Address to the King," ca. Oct. 18, 1687, *Hinckley Papers*, M.H.S. *Coll.*, ser. 4, V (1861), 167–68.

15. M. G. Hall, L. H. Leder, and M. G. Kammen, eds., *The Glorious Revolution in America* (Chapel Hill, N.C., 1964), pp. 29–30; Wharton to Wait Winthrop, London, Oct. 8, 1688, *Winthrop Papers*, M.H.S. *Coll.*, 6th ser., III, 17–18; Barnes, *Dominion*, pp. 194–99.

16. Sessional Papers, Council, C.O. 5/785, p. 16; Shurtleff, ed., *Recs. Mass. Bay*, V, 515.

the need to adjust the legal baggage and procedures brought with their fathers from England to the exigencies of wilderness and the demands of their mission and holy commonwealth. What Andros found upon arrival was in some ways shocking to his well-ordered mind. He introduced several changes supported by a commission which directed a remodeling of the colonists' legal system in such a way as to bring it as "consonant and agreeable" to the laws of the realm as circumstances would permit.[17] Granted any change would have met resistance from a people riveted in their ways, those the governor demanded bore upon colonists' rights as Englishmen in America.

A number of the complaints came out in the trial of the Essex County insurgents over the Dominion's taxes. Before Andros' time Massachusetts juries were made up entirely of freeholders chosen by local freemen, which meant that they were more than likely church members and therefore sympathetic to the Puritan cause. Under Andros, sheriffs appointed by the governor chose jurors, with the help of justices of the peace, directly from among settlers worth some thirty pounds apiece in personal estates as the only criterion.[18] They were not necessarily freemen, and therefore church membership had no bearing on the selection. "Packt and pickt Juries," the old guard called them, and it was a jury chosen in this fashion which soon found John Wise and his followers guilty of sedition. Owing to the centralizing tendencies of Andros' innovations, defendants were dragged often to Boston for examination and trial, as were the Ipswich rebels, and this caused considerable complaint from people forced to undergo the added expense of transporting witnesses and defending themselves far from their own towns and counties before strangers at Boston.

A committee of Andros' council—Dudley, Stoughton, and Randolph—revised the colony's table of fees about this time, including those of the courts, raising them all along the line—thirteen pages of fees altogether. Randolph absorbed a good many of them himself, since the first three listed affected him as secretary, registrar, and a member of the council. Fines were excessive, too, claimed colonists, convincing a good many that when their indigent oppressors needed money they hauled unsuspecting settlers to court in order to extract it. When John Wise and his party were taken up, they claimed the privilege of the Habeas Corpus Act which Shaftesbury and his Whig followers had persuaded Parliament to enact in 1679. Andros' court denied it to them,

17. Andros' Commission, June 3, 1686, Peter Force, ed., *Tracts and Other Papers Relating Principally to the Colonies in North America* (4 vols., Washington, 1836–46), IV, #8.

18. Barnes, *Dominion*, pp. 109, 115–16.

since Parliament had restricted its jurisdiction to the realm alone, a restriction one would like to believe the Puritan oligarchy had honored for the same reason earlier when it consistently denied the privileges of the act to those who opposed the Puritan government.[19]

Swearing on the Bible had been banned in Massachusetts almost from the start because it smacked of idolatry and Anglican custom. In his eagerness to establish English procedures, Andros introduced the English practice and met with all manner of objection. The government occasionally fined and even imprisoned individuals for refusing to lay hands on the Bible when taking oaths. To the general run of Puritans the new practice was foreign and therefore repugnant, but so also was Andros. According to Samuel Sewall the government was not always consistent in its demands. Randolph on occasion swore in people without "the Book," but most other officials insisted upon it, and Sewall lamented that two jurors who refused the oath went to jail rather than pay the 13s. 4d. the court fined them. In some instances the native judges were not eager to accept changes. Andros found a few of them so wedded to their ways that they could hardly admit the King's rights, as the governor saw them. William Stoughton was the worst of the lot, and the governor confessed he found it embarrassing to read the law to Stoughton and men like him who should have known better.[20]

Like taxation, matters of justice and courts and legal authority were fundamental issues to both Puritans and the government over them. At bottom the differences between them were a disagreement over the relationship colonies bore to the Crown and mother country. This was a question both were attempting to settle in their own ways: colonists according to their self-interest and customary practices which they had come to exercise under a charter government virtually independent of the realm, the governor general and his followers according to a fixed interpretation of empire in which dependence and the prerogative were primary. Were colonists guaranteed the rights of Englishmen? Were they subject to the laws of England? Could a royal governor in America demand of colonists more than the King could demand of Englishmen at home? These were questions seldom asked before, let alone

19. *The Declaration of the Gentlemen, Merchants and Inhabitants of Boston, and the Country Adjacent. April 18, 1689*, Andrews, ed., *Narratives*, p. 178; *A Narrative of The Proceedings of Sir Edmond Androsse and his Complices, ibid.*, 246–47. For fees, see C.O. 1/68/39; Geo. Purfrey to Blathwayt, Boston, Mar. 15, 1687, BPCol. Wmsbg., v. V. For habeas corpus, see Randolph to John Usher, Boston, Oct. 16, 1689, Toppan, ed., *Randolph*, VI, 307. Barnes, *Dominion*, ch. V.

20. *Andros Tracts*, I, 29; Sewall, *Diary*, I, 201, 208; Andros to Blathwayt, Boston, June 4, 1688, BPCol. Wmsbg., v. III.

answered. But they were asked and answered more shrilly as Andros' government expanded its authority in New England.

Another offensive change was Andros' enforcement of the Navigation Acts, and this was a grievance New Englanders could least complain about openly. A primary purpose of the Dominion, along with its improved defense and tight political control, was to force the northern colonies into line with the mother country's control of trade. Lacking a staple crop like Maryland and Virginia and the Islands, New Englanders, by carrying their own meager goods and those of others, had developed instead an elaborate system of trade, some of which fell outside the Navigation Laws and deprived the King of his customs. In addition, for a number of years, the Massachusetts government had denied that Parliament's Acts of Trade were applicable there unless repassed by the assembly. The Privy Council and Lords of Trade had disabused the colony of this idea before the charter was revoked, but no real enforcement occurred until the Dominion was established. Dudley and his temporary government of 1686 were not as helpful as Randolph had expected. One of the first acts of Dudley's council was to petition the Lords of Trade to waive the Plantation Duty for New England traders and allow the colony to reestablish its mint for coining money. These were presumptuous requests in Randolph's book, since he had listed violations of the trade acts and the minting of money as prime reasons for revoking the charter.[21]

Randolph got more cooperation under Andros, and it was not long before enforcement seriously contracted New England trade. Ports of entry were reduced to five: Boston, Salem, Piscataqua, New Bristol, and Newport. Once Randolph and his people brought charges, enforcement of the acts was left to an admiralty court which the governor general established. A special maritime court which tried trade violations was bad enough; but Andros appointed the colony's enemy, Robert Mason of New Hampshire, its presiding judge, which seemed even more unfortunate for a colony whose people had long made a living their own way from trade and the sea. On top of this, Andros cleaned out the pirates and made Massachusetts ports unhealthy for refitting their ships. Pirates were a chief source of hard money, which the colony had difficulty accumulating. A little harmless trade with a few buccaneers had never hurt anyone, the colonists claimed, but Andros was of a different mind, and their freebooting friends with cash on the line were sorely missed. Rigorous enforcement of Parlia-

21. Dudley and Council to Lords of Trade, June 2, 1686, Sessional Papers, Council, C.O. 5/785, pp. 24–25.

ment's trade acts was sufficient to "damp & Spoyl" their trade, they pointed out, and it reduced His Majesty's revenue at the same time. Less trade, fewer foreign coins in circulation, both these made higher taxes and larger fees come harder, oppressively so. Andros' economic reforms rapidly increased resentment not just among the faction but among a good many others, some of whom were now in high places but still merchants and businessmen.[22]

Liberty of conscience under the Dominion was another blow to what was left of the Puritan covenant and the institutional means on which it rested. The charter government had guaranteed the public worship of God and had protected the Congregational churches from interference and even dissent. With a mission as right and a covenant as strong as theirs, there was no need for other points of view, since truth was found in the gospel order of the established churches. Dissenters like the Quakers might look elsewhere or at least entertain the inward light only dimly. Religious self-righteousness and independence among the Puritans had fostered political and economic self-interest and independence which were subversive of English plans and schemes of a dependent and profitable empire. For ten years Edward Randolph, and more recently Edward Cranfield of New Hampshire, had hammered the point home that the clergy and the churches were the heart of seditious, even treasonable, religious and political attitudes which prevented New England from succumbing to the empire and its regulation. One purpose of the Dominion was to break the church-state relationship which was the backbone of New England's disloyalty. Liberty of conscience to dissenters would dissolve the exclusiveness of Congregationalism and its political by-products; planting and favoring the Anglican Church would dilute further the strength of the Puritan way, and the Church might even prevail, given proper encouragement.

Liberty of conscience was anathema to the covenanted people, but, as in the face of other calamities, they got along as best they could in spite of it. President Dudley, never a very strong leader of men, relied heavily upon his council, most of whom were moderate Puritans with no love of drastic change or the Anglican service. In fact, despite a few grievances against the old ways of doing things, most of these new officers, including Dudley, had a great deal to protect in both power

22. Samuel Sewall to John Ive, Boston, July 15, 1686, *Letter-Book*, M.H.S. *Coll.*, 6th ser., I (1886), 34; Andros to Blathwayt, Boston, July 11, 1687, BPCol. Wmsbg., v. III; *A Particular Account of the Late Revolution at Boston*, Andrews, ed., *Narratives*, p. 208; John Palmer, *An Impartial Account of the State of New England* (London, 1690), *Andros Tracts*, I, 41; *CSPCol., 1685–1688*, #1110.

and property against encroachment from abroad, and the council was a good spot to accomplish this. The Reverend Robert Ratcliffe, whom the Bishop of London sent to Boston as the first Anglican priest to reside there, found little enthusiasm in the government for his presence or upkeep. His appeal to the council for public support was ignored, and the result was an annual maintenance of fifty pounds contributed by his listeners alone. Three weeks before Ratcliffe's appeal Dudley's council had confirmed the contracts of all Congregational ministers. If the council had its way, the public worship of God would be sustained as before.[23] This was not what Randolph had expected, and before Dudley and his council were comfortable in their new seats of power, he was screaming home about "Insolencyes" and gross abuses, offering at the same time the curt suggestion that a new governor be given authority to license all ministers and force "this people" to build an Anglican church, besides contributing an "honourable maintenance" for its ministry.

Late in 1686 Randolph had changed his tune somewhat, for the news of Andros' imminent arrival frustrated the old faction which, he insisted, Dudley's council as stoutly supported as had the charter government before it. By this time Randolph had lost all respect for Dudley, who, he commented, "wind milles like has turned to Every gale." Church matters looked better to the secretary-registrar. Ratcliffe and the Anglicans had set up in the Town House, where they worshiped four times a week, twice on Sundays. Randolph counted 300 or 400 "Hearers"— hardly possible—and sometimes seven or eight children were baptized of a morning. Discouraging, however, was that there were thousands more Massachusetts people, men, women, and children, still unbaptized. Moreover, he, alone of the council, attended Anglican services, and only two or three of the King's Church enjoyed any public office, civil or military. Dudley's council, despite its earlier break with the faction, had held the line pretty well, and as Randolph had said, it was nothing more than the old government under a different name.[24]

Under Andros things were different. Like Dudley's, his commission dictated a liberty of conscience and favoritism toward the King's Church, but unlike Dudley, Andros intended to do something about both. Sir Edmund showed a good deal of vigor, so much so that the council members, accustomed to their own way under Dudley, were

23. Sessional Papers, Council, June 8, July 1, and July 12, 1686, C.O. 5/785, pp. 28, 38, 44; C.O. 391/6, p. 21.

24. Randolph to Dr. Wm. Sancroft, Boston, Aug. 2, 1686, Toppan, ed., *Randolph*, IV, 108–9; Randolph to [?], Boston, Nov. 20, 1686, Hudson's Bay Original Correspondence, C.O. 134/1, p. 23; Randolph to Lords of Trade, Mar. 25, 1687, *CSPCol., 1685–1688*, #1195.

rudely shocked to learn that they were nowhere near as successful with Andros. Finding the Town House "no wayes convenient," the governor general and the Anglicans borrowed the South Meeting House for their services, not without asking, of course. When permission was refused—"'twas agreed that could not with a good conscience consent that our Meeting-House should be made use of for the Common Prayer Worship," wrote Samuel Sewall—they took it anyway and continued to use it until the next year when they built King's Chapel of their own. Doubtless to embarrass him, the Anglicans suggested to Sewall that he donate a part of his large landholdings for the new structure. It was no surprise to anyone when he refused, confiding to his diary that he "would not set up that which the People of N. E. came over to avoid." Unable to secure a gift of land, Andros and his followers seized part of a public burying ground to build upon. By this time the governor had forgotten all notions of tact, if he ever had any.[25]

Puritan moderates struck hard in the council to continue the public support of their ministers through town rates, but Andros, warmly seconded by Anglicans and Quakers, wore them down. Rhode Island Quakers were delighted with a religious equality in the Dominion which put them on the same ground as the Puritan militants who earlier had run them out of Massachusetts and then hanged several who dared to return. The Reverend John Higginson found life in Salem very difficult when tax money for ministers' salaries ceased. The voluntary contribution promised for his support soon proved a "nontribution" from many of his parishioners.[26] With public support of the Congregational ministry denied them, the Puritan faction sank deeper into self-righteous resentment. What would prevent an establishment of Anglicanism, demanding they pay for its maintenance, maybe even attendance at its services? Andros' strong start in church policy made such slavery look possible. While liberty of conscience under Dudley was bad enough, it was something they could live with. Under Andros it looked more like persecution, for it seemed to promise not an equality of religion but a subjection of their own.

25. See again Andros' commission in Force, ed., *Tracts*, IV, #8; Andros to Blathwayt, Boston, Mar. 30, 1687, BPCol. Wmsbg., v. III; Sewall, *Diary*, I, 162, 171, 207; *Andros Tracts*, II, 44–45.

26. A.A.S. *Proc.*, N.S., XIII (1899–1900), 258; Randolph to John Povey, May 21, 1687, Toppan, ed., *Randolph*, IV, 163; Rhode Island Yearly Meeting, Aug. 27, 1686, London Yearly Meeting, Epistles Received, 1683–1706, I, p. 21, Lib. Soc. Friends, London. For this piece of information about Rhode Island Quakers, I am indebted to J. William Frost of Vassar College. John Higginson to son Nathaniel, Salem, Aug. 31, 1698, Essex Inst. Hist. *Coll.*, XLIII, 183; Barnes, *Dominion*, pp. 96, 125–26.

And what about Harvard College? Andros demanded the right to oversee its accounts after Randolph reported that Dudley and Stoughton had dipped their fingers into some of the funds as a means of preserving them, of course. The governor attended Commencement in 1687 and directed that the Anglican Ratcliffe sit in the pulpit during the ceremonies. Rector Increase Mather forestalled any unpleasantness, however, by monopolizing both morning and evening prayers. Luckily for the Puritan faction, the Dominion had no real designs upon the College at Cambridge, but who knew this in 1687? [27]

The sad conditions forced upon the Massachusetts colonists by Andros' religious and other policies kept Increase Mather and his family closeted on their knees most of the spring of 1687, praying for New England's deliverance. James II's Declaration of Indulgence, issued in April of that year, was, in Puritan terms, God's answer. No matter that the King's bold-faced courting of nonconformists, allowing liberty of conscience, and suspending the Test Act and penal laws was a cover to legitimatize Catholicism, the Puritan faction, or most of them, greeted it with thanksgiving and accepted it at face value as protection against discrimination by Andros and the English Church in New England. In their present plight the King's largess looked bountiful, for besides sanctioning freedom to worship as Congregationalists, the Declaration confirmed dissenters' property in England and the dominions, thus supposedly ending Andros' right to seize their land for the King and charge them fees and quitrents.[28]

Ironically, liberty of conscience in Massachusetts, proclaimed first by Dominion governors, was calamity at its worst, since it destroyed the Puritan grip upon the minds and hearts of its people. But liberty of conscience, proclaimed by a Catholic King of England throughout the empire, was a blessed deliverance from evil, since it sheltered the Puritan party from persecution and the King's Church which would destroy them.

So grateful were Mather and his fellow Puritans for James's Declaration that several ministers and churches, at Mather's suggestion, sent letters of thankfulness to the King, one of which was printed in the London *Gazette*. It made a favorable impression, Mather was happy to learn, correcting some of the misrepresentations the colony's enemies

27. Randolph to Blathwayt, Boston, Aug. 5, 1687, Toppan, ed., *Randolph*, VI, 225; Sewall, *Diary*, I, 181; Kenneth B. Murdock, *Increase Mather, Foremost American Puritan* (Cambridge, Mass., 1925), p. 180.

28. Mather, "Autobiography," A.A.S. *Proc.*, 71 (1961), pt. 2, pp. 317, 319–20, 326, 331; C.O. 5/904, p. 341; Andros to Blathwayt, Boston, Aug. 31, 1687, BPCol. Wmsbg., v. III; Michael G. Hall, *Edward Randolph and the American Colonies*, p. 117.

had circulated. Plymouth people sent one, too, full of self-deprecating expressions, lately believed effective in that small colony's uneasy struggle to avoid domination by either the Dominion *or* Massachusetts. Andros nipped plans for a day of thanksgiving in Boston, believing it too soon after the tax revolt at Ipswich for a public demonstration—thus another charge against him which James would soon hear about.[29]

Effusive letters were not enough for a king who had delivered New England from the maw of Anglicanism. Mather persuaded himself and a number of others that one of them ought personally to thank James II on behalf of the colony. The logical messenger was Mather himself, but he let God decide through a vote of his congregation, which dutifully chose him (*Vox populi, vox Dei?*). Edward Randolph believed he could spot a troublemaker and soon slapped a charge of defamation with £500 damages on the minister to prevent his bounding to England. By God's blessing the jury which heard the case contained only two "common prayer men" and it promptly cleared him. Randolph was left with costs of the trial. He tried again, but this time an intestinal disorder, or maybe its cure, providentially kept Mather locked up at home and hidden from the writ server, whereby he "escaped the snare." Then, after a close race with the arresting officers, he and his son Samuel were hurried aboard ship bound for London, where he remained for four years, busying himself with a good deal more than thanking James the King. In Increase Mather's hands lay the fate of the Dominion and the future of the Bay Colony.[30]

29. Mather, "Autobiography," pp. 320, 329. Plymouth's letter to the King began: "Great SIR! Our Wilderness Education doth not furnish us with Words sufficiently to express the deep sense. . . ." C.O. 1/65/6. Barnes, *Dominion,* pp. 126–27; Hall, *Randolph,* pp. 117–19.

30. Mather, "Autobiography," p. 321. Randolph charged Mather with writing a letter in 1683 to an English Congregational minister in Amsterdam accusing Randolph and several others of serious crimes. Mather claimed the letter a forgery. His proof was that the letter writer had praised the late Earl of Shaftesbury as a friend of God's cause and one who was assured of future happiness. Mather insisted he could not have written the statement since he had "never had a high opinion of that Gentleman," or of his prospects in this world or the next, and so the letter, he claimed, was forged, probably by Randolph. "High opinion" of Shaftesbury or not, *The Compleat States-man,* a biography of Shaftesbury, was sent to Mather in September 1683 from London, probably upon order. The letter to Amsterdam is in BPCol. Wmsbg., v. V. See Mather's denial in Mather to Dudley, Boston, Nov. 10, 1684, *ibid.* See also C. W. Tuttle, *Captain Francis Champernowne, the Dutch Conquest of Acadie* (Boston, 1889), pp. 296, 300. Hall, *Randolph,* p. 118; Murdock, *Increase Mather,* p. 126.

11 The Dominion of New England: From the St. Croix to Delaware Bay

Governor Andros' Dominion was more effective in controlling Massachusetts than it was the other colonies which the King included in his regime. Andros' power and authority were more easily felt the closer one kept to Boston. Plymouth, the provinces of Maine and New Hampshire, Rhode Island, and Connecticut were supposedly under his thumb, but subjection to his rule varied. That no concerted effort was made by Andros and his council to dragoon all New Englanders into submission was partly owing to a general recognition that Massachusetts, primarily Boston, was New England's center of gravity, and control there made it less necessary elsewhere. The other colonies, save perhaps Connecticut, whose foodstuffs Massachusetts needed, were simply not as important economically and politically, and therefore less effort was spent in bringing them into line. Distance, too, militated against continued regulation after initial surrender. Furthermore, response to Andros' government depended a good deal upon needs and conditions peculiar to each colony.

196

Plymouth, closer to Boston than most of the others, was pretty much helpless, since it was small and had no claim to legal existence, anyway. For some time it had sought a charter to give it sanction but found difficulty in interesting sufficient people with influence in England to push it, let alone funds to support the campaign. Despite religious and political convictions similar to the Bay's, the Old Colony was jealous of its independence and had always fought against absorption by the larger, stronger colony. It had succeeded, too, only to fall victim to the Dominion of New England, whose centralizing of control was upsetting, even frightening, to its settlers. Besides taxes and laws imposed upon them by Andros' council, Plymouth people saw their land subjected to repatenting and some of it granted out from under them to Andros' cronies. They saw, too, their land records gathered up and hauled away to Boston, the probating of wills (of estates over fifty pounds) snatched from their towns' jurisdiction and lumped in Randolph's office, where Plymouth people were forced to journey at great expense to legalize actions and then pay excessive fees. Grievances became sharp enough to provoke a petition to the King which included another futile request for a charter.[1]

New Hampshire and Maine, both thinly settled, were touched less by Andros' jurisdiction than other parts of New England. No doubt New Hampshire colonists were so happy to be rid of Edward Cranfield that Andros, miles away, seemed hardly a threat. Like Plymouth people they were greatly disturbed by the "private removal" of their records to Boston, and by sea at that, exposing them to great danger. They sent their clerk after them with a request that Andros allow him to continue his duties in Boston, looking after their records until they could be safely returned to New Hampshire, and not by vessel either.[2] Most upsetting to Maine settlers was the Dominion's plan to repatent their lands. Already distracted by "so many pretended titles" anyway, they resisted the move despite Colonel Francis Nicholson's insistence that the King was their "great Land Lord" and would be kindest of all to them. This did not much move landowners whose holdings had been purchased originally from the Indians and confirmed by an earlier Massachusetts government. But Andros' authority was meager in Maine until the Indian troubles commenced, when the settlers saw a good deal more of him. A handful of leading colonists from both New Hampshire and Maine were named to the council; except for Robert

1. See Gov. Thomas Hinckley's letter to Blathwayt, "Proposal for Address to the King," ca. Oct. 18, 1687, and Petition to James II, Oct. 1687, both in *Hinckley Papers*, M.H.S. *Coll.*, 4th ser., V (1861), 153–62, 167–68, 169–85.
2. Council of New Hampshire to President of Council of New England, Portsmouth, July 30, 1686, *CSPCol.*, *1685–1688*, #796, #1122, #1253.

Mason, they found it difficult to keep up with the frequent meetings at Boston.[3]

Rhode Island

Rhode Island was not mentioned in Andros' commission of 1686, although he bore instructions to demand its surrender and take its government under the Dominion's wing. All told, there were only nine towns within the tiny colony's borders, and it claimed about a thousand adult males, half of them planters and "about 500 men besides." None could properly be called a merchant, although several kept busy in "buying and selling." The trouble was, Rhode Islanders had little to sell except horses and provisions which they traded in the West Indies for island goods; moreover, they complained, they lacked "men of considerable estates" to carry on trade and fishing, and owing to this they believed their economy suffered.[4]

Besides being small and not very profitable, Rhode Island was distinguished from the rest of New England by its religious liberty and lack of political organization, both stemming from Charles II's liberal charter of 1663 and both very annoying to its neighbors. Connecticut had received a similar charter the year before, but the grip upon the settlers there of state-supported Congregational churches added a religious and even a political and social decorum altogether unknown in Rhode Island. What Rhode Islanders cherished as religious liberty and political freedom, staunch Puritans, east and west, bitterly described as licentiousness and anarchy and conspired at times to root out these dangerous and contagious infections so close to them. The New England Confederation or United Colonies, begun in 1643, was a union of Massachusetts, Plymouth, and Connecticut but not Rhode Island, which was never invited to join. Organized primarily for defense against the Indians, it proved, too, a useful tool to bring pressure upon Rhode Island to conform to the wishes of Massachusetts, particularly to cease its harboring of wild-eyed Quakers and to surrender lands allegedly owned by others. Rhode Islanders felt very sorry for themselves, owing to difficult relations with their neighbors, and well they might, for they were "despised" on several counts by colonists on either side of them.[5]

3. Francis Nicholson to Blathwayt, Boston, Sept. 5, 1687, BPCol. Wmsbg., v. XV.

4. Rhode Island's Answer to Lords of Trade's Inquiry, May 8, 1680, in George Chalmers, *Political Annals of the Present United Colonies* (London, 1780), pp. 282–84; *CSPCol., 1677–1680,* #1352.

5. For the Rhode Island charter, see John Russell Bartlett, ed., *Records of the Colony of Rhode Island* (10 vols., Providence, 1857–65), II, 1–21; *ibid.,* I, 374–80,

A chief bone of contention was the Narragansett Country—coveted farm and grazing lands west of Narragansett Bay—which Connecticut and Rhode Island both claimed by virtue of their charters. Rhode Island insisted its right superseded its neighbor's since its charter was of a later date; Connecticut argued that the Rhode Island charter was a mistake and that the grant of the Narragansett Country to Connecticut was the King's true intention. Complicating this already thorny disagreement was a series of purchases from the Indians beginning in 1659 of much of the same territory by the Narragansett Company (Atherton Company), a group of Massachusetts and Connecticut merchants and speculators, including John Winthrop, Jr., Simon Bradstreet, and Richard Wharton.[6]

Unlike most other New Englanders, Rhode Islanders had welcomed the Royal Commission of 1664 with the hope it would protect them from their grasping neighbors and do justice to them, the rightful owners, respecting the disputed territory. The Commission's decision was not popular among most of the claimants, since it determined that the area belonged to the Crown and thus named it "King's Province." However, it favored Rhode Island over the others and left the Narragansett Country under its jurisdiction until the King's pleasure was further known. Least of all did the Commission honor the company's claims, and at the same time it called the United Colonies' interference with Rhode Island on behalf of both Massachusetts and Connecticut a usurped authority.[7]

For almost thirty years the parties quarreled among themselves, despite the King's decision in 1679 to leave matters as they were, that is, to leave authority in Rhode Island. Owing to further discontent, Charles II commissioned a half-dozen colonists in 1683, headed by Governor Edward Cranfield of New Hampshire and including Randolph, Dudley, and Stoughton of Massachusetts, to chew over the evidence and come up with some kind of solution. The commission was notoriously sympathetic to the company and bitterly opposed to Rhode Island. It tried to meet deep in the Narragansett Country but was badgered constantly by Rhode Islanders, whose government claimed the meeting illegal and further that Cranfield and his group

---

421, 498–500; Address to King, July 3, 1686, *ibid.*, III, 193; Gov. Cranston to Sir Robt. Southwell, Aug. 1, 1679, BPCol., Wmsbg., v. XI.

6. For documents describing the controversy over the Narragansett Country, see *Recs. Col. R.I.*, III, 12–227, *passim*. See also Andros' Report, Aug. 31, 1687, *CSPCol.*, *1685–1688*, #1414; Richard S. Dunn, *Puritans and Yankees*, *passim*. John Winthrop, Jr., died in 1676.

7. *Recs. Col. R.I.*, II, 86–89, 93–95.

arrogantly refused to disclose their commission. In their report to the King the commissioners recommended giving jurisdiction of the Narragansett Country to Connecticut but ownership of the soil to the company of speculators. The rest of the report was a stinging criticism of Rhode Islanders, whose "riotous manner" prevented the commissioners from meeting anywhere within the colony's boundaries, in fact, had chased them off to Boston. Cranfield found Rhode Island people and their government as corrupt as at Boston "but much more ignorant," and he suggested as before a "thorough Reformation among them." [8]

Reform began two years later when the Crown issued a *quo warranto* against Rhode Island's charter, basing its charges on a list of misdemeanors carefully compiled by Edward Randolph. By the time he delivered the writ, its time had elapsed, but after Massachusetts' experience, few doubted that the charter would fall shortly through legal means unless the colony submitted. The next blow came when Joseph Dudley's commission wrenched the Narragansett Country out of Rhode Island's control and attached it to the Dominion of New England.[9]

Decisionmaking in Rhode Island was a democratic process. When it came to a question of what to do about the *quo warranto,* the government invited the "free inhabitants" to come to Newport and "give in their judgments" to the assembly. Newport was the largest town of the colony, crowded into the southern tip of a large island which choked the mouth of Narragansett Bay. Those who could not journey there were encouraged to send their "judgments" in writing. Once all who chose had spoken, the assembly determined what to do, and the decision was "not to stand suit with his Majesty" but to dispatch an address begging him to continue their religious and civil liberties according to the charter. It was promptly drafted and sent with a messenger to London. Preparing for the worst, for its probable demise, the assembly also voted what one might call a reversion of sovereignty to the several towns, sanctioning their frequent meetings for settling their own affairs, particularly the levying of taxes by majority vote, taxes heretofore imposed and scaled by the legislature. It was as if the colony government, now about to dissolve, was returning power and authority to the freemen themselves in their town meetings, a kind of Lockean contract in reverse, a return to a condition which had obtained before

8. *Ibid.*, III, 40–47, 128, 130–32, 139–49; Wharton to Blathwayt, Aug. 26, 1683, BPCol. Wmsbg., v. VI; Cranfield to Blathwayt, Aug. 27, 1683, *ibid.*, v. XII, and Oct. 5, 1683, v. I; John Greene to Blathwayt, Warwick, Sept. 29, 1683, *ibid.*, v. XI; Dudley to Blathwayt, Feb. 28, 1685, *ibid.*, v. IV; *CSPCol., 1681–1685,* #1316, #1252, #1253, #1988.

9. For the *quo warranto* proceedings, see *Recs. Col. R.I.*, III, 175–78; See Dudley's commission, Oct. 8, 1685, and Proclamation, May 28, 1686, *ibid.*, 195–98.

the first patent gathered the several towns of the colony together under one head in 1644.[10]

As in Massachusetts, a giving in to the Dominion was not a difficult adjustment for all Rhode Islanders to make, for the colony had its share of "moderates," too, several of whom were members of the Narragansett Company. Two weeks after the assembly sent its address to the King, one followed it, drafted by "certain inhabitants" who disassociated themselves from the assembly's vote, clearly demonstrating instead "their full and free submission, and entire resignation" of the charter powers. They made it clear to the King, too, that they were more than ready to accept offices in his new government. Three of the signers Andros eventually named to his council, and several others won positions under the Dominion in Rhode Island. A third petition followed the other two in the summer of 1686, this one from Rhode Island Quakers who told the King they could not "'in conscience bear arms, nor learn war any more,'" but they were willing to pay all necessary rates and duties for carrying on the Dominion's business. While all this was going on, Dudley and his council in the Dominion's name appointed justices of the peace, a militia commander, and constables for the Narragansett Country. Three weeks later a court was held there, presided over by four of the Dominion council, two of whom were proprietors of the Narragansett Company, which still laid claim to the whole area.[11]

James II accepted the Rhode Island petitions as complete surrender of the charter, which was probably a surprise to most of the colonists. He ordered Andros to assimilate the colony government, which the governor did shortly after his arrival. The assembly ceased to meet, and the colony took its place really as a county in the extensive Dominion. Andros chose seven Rhode Islanders to sit on the council, not all of whom actually served. As far as government was concerned, Rhode Islanders were no better off than other New Englanders except that they were farther from Boston than some.[12]

On June 14, 1687, the first General Quarter Sessions and Inferior Court appointed by Andros sat at Newport. It lost no time .in establishing itself, handling a variety of business from issuing licenses for victualers and alehouses to punishing bastardy. It levied rates for public charges, such as building courthouses and paying wolf bounties.

10. *Ibid.*, 190–94; Samuel G. Arnold, *History of the State of Rhode Island and Providence Plantations* (2 vols., Providence, R.I., 1894), I, 487.

11. *Recs. Col. R.I.*, III, 194–95, 197–98, 200–3.

12. C.O. 1/65/97; C.O. 389/9, p. 421; Andros to Rhode Island, Boston, Dec. 22, 1686, *Recs. Col. R.I.*, III, 219; *ibid.*, 220, 193.

There was little resistance to its authority. A handful of settlers balked at taking oaths before serving on the grand jury, but these were doubtless Quakers who for religious reasons had resisted oaths for some time. Each was fined 6s. 8d. in money or goods. Two Newport shopkeepers shunned a day of thanksgiving proclaimed by the governor and council. One of them, Samuel Stapleton, replied to the charge against him "that he was above the observation of days and times"— an answer which smacked of old Samuel Gorton's enthusiasm. At one point the constables in Providence at the head of the bay refused to call the inhabitants together to choose "Rate-makers." They were ordered to do so forthwith or collect the rates themselves, and as far as one can tell they eventually performed their duties. Not long after Rhode Island succumbed to the Dominion, Andros settled several Huguenot families in the Narragansett Country; several colonists resented the intrusion and mowed and carried off the newcomers' hay crop, not probably because they were French and strangers, but because they had settled in the disputed territory which Rhode Islanders hated to see dislodged from their jurisdiction. But none of these, including bastardy, looked like serious rebellion against the Dominion and its officers.[13]

It may be that the advantages of the new government outweighed its disadvantages. Union under Andros protected Rhode Islanders from what they called the tyranny of Massachusetts Bay and even the possible revival of the New England Confederation, both of which had humiliated, discriminated against, and encroached upon them for almost two generations. Further, Andros reviewed the dispute over the Narragansett Country and turned thumbs down on the claim of the company of speculators, a decision very much in the colony's favor. Moreover, the governor discouraged Connecticut's pretensions to the same area, determining that the Rhode Island charter of 1663 canceled Connecticut's claim of the year before. The Dominion guaranteed throughout a liberty of conscience which was an absolute necessity for a great majority of Rhode Islanders, since they already made up a potpourri of denominations and sects.[14] Their independent legislature and the right to elect all their officers were denied them, to be sure,

13. *Ibid.*, 227–28, 229, 231, 233, 234–37, 239–40, 241–44, 246–48.

14. Andros' warrant to survey, June 22, 1687, *Recs. Col. R.I.*, III, 225; Andros' Report, Aug. 31, 1687, *CSPCol., 1685–1688*, #1414. Andros allowed Richard Wharton, a member of the Narragansett Company, a patent for 1,712 acres of improved land in the Narragansett Country on which Wharton paid a quitrent. *Recs. Col. R.I.*, III, 225–26. For liberty of conscience, see Andros' Commission, June 3, 1686, and Instructions, Apr. 16, 1688, *ibid.*, 217, 251–52. Dunn, *Puritans and Yankees*, p. 245.

and they were taxed without their consent. But their loss of the accustomed ways of doing things was not as great to them as was the Puritans' defeat in Massachusetts, where religious as well as political order was turned upside down. At this point there was an advantage in being small and inconsequential, lacking both "men of considerable estates" and an extensive trade. Given its conditions, its local needs, and its relative unimportance, Rhode Island was better able to get along within the Dominion than Massachusetts, primarily because it was let alone. Without much interest in political theory or conceptions of empire, Rhode Islanders, it would seem, went about their business as usual, not as disturbed by the turn of events, and not as disturbing to the authority of the Dominion, as Bay colonists. Of later significance was the fact that the English courts had never annulled the Rhode Island charter.

Connecticut

For colonies with similar charters, dated but a year apart, Connecticut and Rhode Island hardly could have been less alike. Granted minor differences in the patents and contrasting geographical conditions, major differences stemmed from the character of the people who had settled each colony and their different religious attitudes. Most original Rhode Islanders were Massachusetts rebels of one kind or another, the likes of Roger Williams, Anne Hutchinson, Samuel Gorton, and later the Quakers. Many of them deeply religious, they found toleration necessary at the outset, and it became one of the peculiar traits of the colony. The charter of 1663 confirmed it, guaranteeing "full libertie in religious concernments" and a separation of church and state. The settlement of Connecticut, whose people were no less religious, was more an extension of Massachusetts Puritanism than a reaction to it, and it was natural for its colonists to support established churches there as they had earlier. New Haven Colony and the Hartford people were often at loggerheads before the union and even after it for a time, but the Connecticut charter of 1662 gathered them into one government to which they eventually became loyal. Moreover, they were overwhelmingly Congregational, and this gave them a homogeneity, as it did the Bay settlers, in their attitudes toward religion, government, and even Rhode Island. Like the Bay Colony, too, the covenant spirit obtained among a special people who were united in purpose and belief, while in Rhode Island a variety of religious principles and a loose political system wrought a colonial character different from its neighbors', one of independence, individualism, and religious radicalism. Each colony developed its own way on not very friendly terms with the other; by the eighteenth century one was known as the "land of steady habit," the other, the "licentious republic." [15]

Connecticut was a good deal larger than Rhode Island. In 1680 it boasted twenty-six towns in four counties and an adult male population of 2,500, more than twice the smaller colony. Most of the settlers were farmers—"we labour in tilling the ground"—who yearly sent their surplus crops of wheat, peas, beef, pork, some hemp and flax, to Boston, less frequently to New York, where they bartered for clothes and utensils whose prices they found excessive. Smaller amounts of provisions they loaded aboard their few ships bound for the Barbados and other West Indian islands in exchange for sugar and rum—"to refresh the spirits of such as labour in the extream heat and cold." Hartford, New London, New Haven, and Fairfield were the principal towns: New London was the chief port, with a harbor so commodious and convenient that a ship of 500 tons could easily ride close enough to "toss a biskit ashoare." Alas! despite their ports, they enjoyed only a little trade, and in the whole colony, it was said, there were but "20 petty merchants." After years of sweat and toil at their own cost in the wilderness, they complained that they had been able to secure neither leisure nor ability to develop a lucrative economy, and like Rhode Island they lacked men of estates who might venture abroad and attract trade.

Still, they boasted some good things, too. Connecticut paid its ministers well, between fifty and a hundred pounds a year, derived from public rates. Each town maintained its own poor, but there were not many settlers who needed public relief, since labor was dear— as much as 2*s.* 6*d.* a day for common laborers—and provisions were cheap. They never suffered beggars if they could help it, the governor informed the Lords of Trade, and when one was discovered he was bound out to service. When a vagabond traipsed through their land, abusing the people with false news, cheating and stealing—no doubt what vagabonds were supposed to do in seventeenth-century English society—he was promptly taken up and punished according to his offenses. Connecticut people were poor but loyal, the governor reported, but they had a hard time of it, and any "rays" of "favours" the King might send their way would be greatly appreciated.[16]

15. For the charters, see *Recs. Col. R.I.*, II, 1–21, and J. H. Trumbull and E. J. Hoadly, eds., *The Public Records of the Colony of Connecticut, 1636–1776* (15 vols., Hartford, Conn., 1850–90), II, 3–11.

16. The foregoing description of Connecticut comes from Governor and Council's Answer to the Lords of Trade's Inquiries, July 15, 1680, *Recs. Col. Conn.*, III, 294–300, and a covering letter, *ibid.*, p. 301. See also Governor to Commis-

Instead of favor the King sent Edward Randolph their way with a *quo warranto* against their charter. Corporate colonies with independent notions were a contradiction to James's whole scheme of empire. But Connecticut government did not collapse as Rhode Island's, at least not immediately. Several magistrates, including the governor, met with Randolph to discuss the business; instead of resolving to answer the writ, which had already lapsed, like several others Randolph peddled, they asked him by what right he served it. This got the Connecticut council off to a bad start with Randolph, who reported to Andros he thought the colony was indifferent whether it submitted or went to court against the King. He may have been right. What it preferred was to remain independent with maybe some minor changes in the charter, and this was the burden of the Address the colony shortly sent to James asking pardon for past mistakes and praying for confirmation of their former liberties without interruption.[17] Andros' commission of 1686 did not include authority over Connecticut, but his instructions did, and as soon as he arrived at Boston he began to act upon them to bring the colony into line.[18] Almost two years elapsed between the first *quo warranto* and final submission.

Attack upon the charter and the imminence of the Dominion split Connecticut government much the same as in Massachusetts. Although most colonies preferred to be left alone, there were a number of Connecticut moderates, mostly in the council, who saw which way the wind blew, including Governor Robert Treat and Secretary John Allyn. If the end was near, these people argued, if inclusion in the Dominion was inevitable, they ought to give in graciously to the Crown and make the best of the new situation. By an obedient surrender they might keep on the good side of both King and Andros and retain as many of Connecticut's rights and privileges as possible. At the same time, those in command under the old government, primarily the council, would doubtless keep some of their power by being first in line when Andros distributed offices. Opposed to this strategy, and primarily responsible for the delay in submitting, was another group whose strength lay in the house of deputies, although it was led by a councillor, James Fitch. It poked along, hoping the King would forgive

sioners of Customs, 1681, in R. R. Hinman, ed., *Letters from the English Kings and Queens . . . to the Governors of Connecticut* (Hartford, 1836), pp. 120–22.

17. Randolph to Southwell, July 30, 1685, Toppan, ed., *Randolph*, IV, 26–27; Randolph to Andros, Boston, July 28, 1686, *ibid.*, VI, 190; Hinman, ed., *Letters from the English Kings and Queens*, pp. 171–72; Connecticut's Address to James II, 1686, *ibid.*, 169–70; Andros' Instructions, see *Recs. Col. R.I.*, III, 218.

18. These points are clearly explained in Robert M. Bliss, Jr., "Connecticut, 1676–1708: The Institutionalization of the Organic Society" (unpubl. A. M. thesis, Univ. of Wisconsin, 1967), ch. II.

the colony's innocent mistakes and withdraw his legal action against the charter.

The upshot was a good deal of correspondence between Connecticut and the Dominion. "Pretended loyalty," but actions to the contrary, Andros called it. "Dilatory letters to gain time," commented Randolph. Advice was freely given, too. Joseph Dudley warned Connecticut people of their loss of a market and "ancient neighborhood" with the Bay Colony if they delayed their surrender. Fitz-John Winthrop of New London, already safe on Andros' council, argued that submission would not be a total loss, since the King could be counted on to protect their "civil enjoyments." [19] Friends in London thought that proceedings against the charter had ceased; they supported the notion that the colony ought not to surrender without a condemnation. Contrary advice came from Tory-minded John Saffin of Boston, one of the Narragansett proprietors, who had grandiose visions of a subordinate empire in which he would play a major role. All must give in to "immediate dependency and subjection" sooner or later, he wrote, and the sooner the better, for, regardless of events in England, things will never be the same again in America, and those who "stand out longest will fare the worst at last." [20]

Andros showed remarkable restraint, more than he ever demonstrated in Massachusetts, and this may have been owing to his fear of losing Connecticut to New York. Connecticut was in a stronger position than Rhode Island to play a waiting game, and this strength lay in the value of its trade with Boston, for Connecticut supplied food for a good many people in Massachusetts, releasing them to catch fish and build ships. Its loss would be a great blow to the Dominion, Andros argued; the Bay settlers were "generally but poor" and had suffered severely in King Philip's War, by two drastic fires in Boston, and owing to the "blasting of wheat." (He did not learn of these hardships from Randolph, who had always played them down.) The Dominion needed Connecticut's trade—"interwoven from the first settlements"—and its revenue, estimated by Randolph at £3,000 a year, to pay its way.[21]

19. See series of letters from Connecticut to Andros, January–March, 1687, *CSPCol., 1685–1688*, #1197; see also *ibid.*, #1195; Andros to Lords of Trade, Mar. 30, 1687, C.O. 391/6, p. 81; Dudley to Blathwayt, Dec. 23, 1686, BPCol. Wmsbg., v. IV; Fitz-John Winthrop to John Allyn, Boston, Jan. 13, 1687, *Winthrop Papers*, M.H.S. *Coll.*, 5th ser., VIII, 300–2; William Whiting to John Allyn, London, Mar. 12, 1687, *Wyllys Papers*, Connecticut Historical Society, *Collections*, XXI (1924), 292.

20. R. Wharton to Wait Winthrop, London, Nov. 17, 1687, *Winthrop Papers*, M.H.S. *Coll.*, 6th ser., III, 10; John Saffin to Sec'y Allyn, June 14, 1687, *Recs. Col. Conn.*, III, 382.

21. Andros to Blathwayt, Boston, Mar. 30, 1687, BPCol. Wmsbg., v. III; Dudley to Blathwayt, Mar. 30, 1687, *ibid.*, v. IV; Andros to Lords of Trade, Mar. 30,

Connecticut held off just long enough to give substance to Andros' apprehension. Furthermore, Governor Thomas Dongan of New York had wooed the colony from the west for some time. He hoped to annex it, as had a number of New York governors before him, including Andros, who attempted to seize it during the crisis of King Philip's War. Randolph, close to Andros, had already fallen out with Governor Dongan, who had been a rival for the governorship of New England; he claimed that Dongan desperately needed Connecticut since he had "so squeezed" the people of New York that they were hardly able to manage, and as many as could had left for other colonies.[22]

Connecticut had no intention of joining New York. Indeed, its people dreaded the possibility. But by the time of the third *quo warranto,* some of the more prudent and less bold settlers had gained the upper hand; the colony government wrote home again that if it could not remain independent, it would sooner throw in its lot with Massachusetts and the Dominion than New York. This time President Lord Sunderland of the Privy Council and the Lords of Trade accepted the admission as complete surrender and promptly ordered Andros to assume its government.[23] Not until late November of 1687 did the colony finally submit, and then only after Andros journeyed to Connecticut "well accompagnyed" by a retinue of seventy-five. This was one of the great processions of early American history, for the governor made his grand tour of southern New England an occasion to visit a number of towns under his government—Dedham and Attleboro in Massachusetts, Providence and Narragansett in Rhode Island. From there they rode southwest to Stonington and Norwich, Connecticut, and then northwest to Hartford, where the transaction occurred "without any Contest."

The charter, however, remained untouched, at least by Andros, for it was hustled off by Connecticut patriots and lodged in safety for a later time. Charter or no, the colony surrendered and took its place within the Dominion. Before departing for New Haven and Fairfield, Andros named Governor Treat and Secretary Allyn to his council, both of whom seemed very willing to serve. Andros and his party traveled as far west as Greenwich and then back along the coast of Long Island Sound, everywhere greeted by the "principalest men," who readily

1687, *CSPCol., 1685–1688,* #1197; Randolph to Sunderland, Mar. 25, 1687, *ibid.,* #1195.

22. Dongan to Blathwayt, Nov. 24, 1686, Feb. 21, Apr. 11, 1687, BPCol. Wmsbg., v. XI; Dongan to James II, Mar. 2, 1687, *CSPCol., 1685–1688,* #1159; Randolph to Blathwayt, Nov. 23, 1687, Hall, Leder, and Kammen, eds., *Glo. Rev. in Am.,* p. 93.

23. C.O. 391/6, p. 69; C.O. 389/9, pp. 438–39; An Account of the Several Grants and Charters for the Plantations in America, C.O. 1/65/97; *CSPCol., 1685–1688,* #1301, #1308.

accepted commissions as justices of the peace and officers in the militia. The King never went to court against Connecticut's charter but accepted instead the colony's submission to his governor. The next year Connecticut and Rhode Island were named in Andros' second commission, which extended the Dominion even beyond New England.[24]

But the burden of Andros' government was a good deal lighter in Connecticut than in Massachusetts. Instead of ruling directly, he worked through the colony's officers, primarily Secretary Allyn, whose persuasiveness with both Andros and Randolph blunted several of the sharper edges of Dominion power, leaving considerable authority in Connecticut hands, where it had resided for some time. Because much of the power remained where it was, those without it, particularly the group of old deputies, were as uneasy under Dominion rule as they had been in the years preceding it, an uneasiness which later events aggravated.[25]

New York and New Jersey

King James added New York and New Jersey to Andros' Dominion in the spring of 1688. This was probably not what Governor Dongan had in mind when he sought help from the Crown, although he must have looked upon the annexation with some relief, since he had never been able to make ends meet in New York. Demands upon the colony's revenue were great. The northern frontier at Albany was exposed to the French in Canada, who renewed their efforts with a show of force to win the Iroquois and the fur trade to Louis XIV. James as Duke of York had never been successful in making New York support itself; the assembly under the Charter of Libertyes in 1683 had no time to show what it could—or could not—do before it was dissolved when James became King. Dongan believed that the Duke never should have given up the lower counties along the Delaware to William Penn. Like Andros before him, he regretted the loss of East and West Jersey, which James finally released to their proprietors after it became clear he had no business charging customs duties there. Even the people of Pennsylvania gave him trouble, for they were soon tapping beaver sources along the upper reaches of the Susquehanna River, preserves heretofore within Albany's orbit. If they were not stopped,

24. Andros to Blathwayt, Boston, Nov. 28, 1687, BPCol. Wmsbg., v. III; Albert C. Bates, "Expedition of Sir Edmund Andros to Connecticut in 1687," A.A.S. *Proc.*, 48 (1939), 276–99; Andros' Instructions, Apr. 16, 1688, *Recs. Col. R.I.*, III, 248–54; Dunn, *Puritans and Yankees*, pp. 242–43.

25. *Ibid.*, Robert M. Bliss, Jr., "Connecticut, 1676–1708," pp. 40–44.

Dongan lamented, New York government could not maintain itself, and there was a good chance the practice would depopulate New York City, to say nothing of Albany—doubtless a slight exaggeration.[26]

As a result of financial disappointments in his own government and increasing defense needs against the French threat, Dongan coveted Connecticut, its militia and revenue, as well as New Jersey. He put on a spirited campaign to bring about their annexation to New York, suggesting at one point that Connecticut would be worth £100 a year to Secretary William Blathwayt as Auditor General of Revenues in England if it could be accomplished. The New York government already owed Dongan a good deal for what he had borrowed and spent in its behalf—at one point he pawned his own silver plate to keep the establishment going. When he learned that Andros had added Connecticut to the Dominion, he immediately suggested that New York and New Jersey go along with it. There seemed to be no other way to hold things together and to support a strong front against the French, who had become increasingly bold, stirring up Indians heretofore loyal to the English and building forts and palisades on English territory, particularly at Niagara. Dongan was an aggressive soldier of the King; despite his Catholicism, he was full of ideas about joining the Indians in campaigns against the French in order to protect the frontiers and keep the fur trade healthy. Dominion forces would be a great help toward solving New York's problems, although Andros' aggressiveness was not as keen as Dongan's at the outset.[27]

Dongan was not the first to suggest that the King extend the Dominion of New England to include his colony and New Jersey. In fact, the Lords of Trade had discussed the possibility as early as 1685. But the suggestion was a good one, and James ordered Andros to act upon it in the spring of 1688. A union of all the English dominions from "Delaware-bay to Nova Scotia," Blathwayt chimed, "will be terrible to the French." [28] The plans did not include Dongan, however, who surprisingly was relieved of duty. Doubtless he had expected the same or a new command under Andros; instead, the King commissioned Colonel Francis Nicholson, already a member of the Dominion council,

26. See notes 41 and 42 below.

27. For Dongan's difficulties in New York, see a series of letters from him to Blathwayt between Sept. 13, 1686, and Oct. 24, 1687, BPCol. Wmsbg., v. XI; Dongan to Andros, New York, Mar. 28, 1688, C.O. 1/68/44, I.

28. *N.Y. Col. Docs.*, III, 357. For annexation of New York to the Dominion, see warrant, Mar. 25, 1688, C.O. 389/9, p. 466, 467; CSPCol., *1685–1688*, #1674; Instructions to Andros, Apr. 16, 1688, *N.Y. Col. Docs.*, III, 543–49; Blathwayt to Randolph, Mar. 11, 1688, in Thomas Hutchinson, *History of the Colony and Province of Massachusetts-Bay*, ed. by L. S. Mayo (3 vols., Cambridge, Mass., 1936), I, 316 n.

as deputy to Andros, who eventually established him in New York. Curiously, Dongan remained in the colony and retired to his extensive estates on Long Island, doubtless persuaded to stay by what he owed and was owed. He was followed by bitter remarks from Randolph, who insisted that he had impoverished the people of New York, had left them shamefully undefended, and was responsible for the disgraceful diplomacy with the French governor which fomented serious trouble between the two nations. This was little thanks to a governor whose fur trading and French and Indian policies were admired and copied by New York governors for several years to come.[29]

Annexing New York was no trouble for Andros, since it was already a royal colony, and all it took was publication of his new commission there to bring it around. This called for a visit, and in the summer of 1688 he and Randolph and their party proceeded to New York, where they remained for some time, long enough to celebrate the birth of the Prince of Wales, which they learned about in October. Andros was well known there, for he had been the Duke's governor for several years in the late 1670's. There seemed to be no dearth of prospective officeholders; he found his time "crowded with bisenes & people coming to [him]" for appointments as civil and military officers. His commission named eight New Yorkers to his council; release of their names could not have surprised many, for they were already in government or had been. Five of the eight were members of Dongan's council when the Charter of Libertyes was drafted by the short-lived assembly of 1683, and six of the eight served Dongan after the Charter's demise. These were New York regulars, merchants and landowners, who were leading members of the oligarchy which had called the turn for some time and would again regardless of the form of government. One was mayor of New York City, and another had been a year or two earlier. Each had held at least one other office previously and most several; two were Catholic. Although the colony had moved through three phases of colonial government during the 1680's, from a proprietary belonging to the Duke of York, through a royal colony under James now King, to a subcolony in the Dominion of New England under

29. C.O. 389/9, pp. 417, 466, 469; Effingham to Blathwayt, Feb. 7, 1687, BPCol. Wmsbg., v. XIV; Dongan to Blathwayt, Oct. 24, 1687, *ibid.*, v. XI; Dongan to King, Mar. 2, 1687, *N.Y. Col. Docs.*, III, 423. For Dongan's later reputation, see G. M. Waller, *Samuel Vetch, Colonial Enterpriser* (Chapel Hill, N.C., 1960), p. 100; Douglas E. Leach, *The Northern Colonial Frontier, 1607–1763* (New York, 1966), p. 106. For Francis Nicholson, see Nicholson to Blathwayt, Boston, July 19, 1688, BPCol. Wmsbg., v. XV, and C.O. 389/9, pp. 431, 468, 469–70. For Randolph's remarks, see Randolph to Blathwayt, Philadelphia, Aug. 19, 1688, BPCol. Wmsbg., v. I, and same to same, Sept. 12, 1688, Hall, Leder, and Kammen, eds., *Glo. Rev. in Am.*, p. 96.

Andros, the council in New York showed remarkable consistency in its membership. Andros shifted some about where he needed them: John Palmer, a good lawyer, went to Boston; Lieutenant Anthony Brockholls fought Indians in Maine. The principal councillors who continued to reside in New York were Nicholas Bayard, Stephen Van Cortlandt, and Frederick Philips, all originally Dutch but well accustomed to English control. Next to Francis Nicholson, authority in New York was in their hands.[30]

The changeover in New Jersey was not as simple. What originally had been one colony was now two proprietaries since John, Lord Berkeley, had sold his half in the early 1670's. While New York was a royal colony which the King could do with as he wished, New Jersey had two patents, two groups of proprietors, and two representative governments with which to deal. These were not insurmountable obstacles for Andros, since the way had been prepared by writs of *scire facias,* initiated as early as 1685, a method of revoking charters found successful against Massachusetts. But there were proprietors and assemblies to consider, and Andros left New York for a time to do business in both halves of the colony. New Jersey people were familiar with Andros, too, for in both East and West they had tangled with him over customs and duties when he was governor of New York.[31]

In August of 1688 Andros and some of his councillors visited Burlington in West New Jersey, where they published the governor general's commission and swore in a number of settlers as justices and militia officers. There was no resistance; in fact, Andros reported, he was "Crowded by friends, and all sorts of Contrey people," which could mean several things, among them, that the colonists hoped to make a respectable settlement with Andros which would leave them in sole possession of their lands if not actually their government.[32] Again, given the circumstances, they may have been right, for West New Jersey was a long way from Boston, and its people, mostly Quakers, fared well under ordeal of the Dominion.

Colonists in East New Jersey had quarreled among themselves for

30. Andros to Blathwayt, Burlington, N.J., Aug. 18, 1688, BPCol. Wmsbg., v. III; same to same, New York, Oct. 4, 1688, *ibid.;* Randolph to [?], 1688, *ibid.,* v. I. For Andros' council of forty-two, see *N.Y. Col. Docs.,* III, 543; For councillors' previous positions, see E. A. Werner, *Civil List and Constitutional History of the Colony and State of New York* (Albany, 1889), pp. 363–64 and *passim.* E. B. O'Callaghan, *Origin of Legislative Assemblies,* p. 17; Andrews, ed., *Narratives,* pp. 117 n., 361 n. Anthony Brockholls and Jervis Baxter were Catholics. O'Callaghan, ed., *Doc. Hist. N.Y.,* II (1849), 32.

31. Randolph to Lords of Trade, Aug. 18, 1685, *CSPCol., 1685–1688,* #319; Andros to Blathwayt, Aug. 18, Oct. 4, 1688, BPCol. Wmsbg., v. III.

32. *Ibid.*

some time and with their government and proprietors. But their struggles with the governors of New York had equally complicated the history of the colony after it was separated from the West. When Andros was governor of New York, he had charged customs duties in the East and had interfered with its government in several other ways, but he had slackened off once the Duke released New Jersey completely to its owners. In 1683 the colony devolved upon a group of twenty-four proprietors, largely Scots, among whom were James, Earl of Perth, and Robert Gordon of Cluny. The next year they wrote a stiff letter to Governor Dongan, who had continued New York's pretensions across the Hudson, telling him they had no intention of surrendering their colony to him and would he please keep his hands off their proprietary. About the same time they sought the help of the Earl of Sunderland against "Master Penn's" intrusions along the Delaware River, intrusions, they claimed, which belied his Quaker "unconcernedness in the world." [33]

Further encroachment, when it occurred, came neither from Dongan nor from Quaker Penn, but from Andros and the Dominion in the summer of 1688. Before surrendering, the proprietors presented several strong demands which lead one to believe that proprietary colonies, particularly when their owners resided in England, were in better positions to deal with the exigencies of empire than were charter or royal colonies. When the King revoked the charters of corporate colonies, he seized both government and soil, as the colonists of Massachusetts had learned; in the case of royal colonies, he was sovereign over both anyway. When James revoked the proprietary charter of East New Jersey, he left untouched ownership of the soil, thus arming the proprietors with at least one lever to manipulate. Since they were to surrender their government to the King, they tried to make certain that rights to the soil would be protected and so petitioned for a patent which would list these rights in black and white. A new patent ought to include, they told the King, liberty of navigation, fishing, trade, and free ports, primarily Perth Amboy, as were Boston and New York. They asked, too, that the King continue their privileges as manor lords, guaranteeing them quitrents and other manorial rights. They ought to

33. For East New Jersey's squabbles among settlers and with New York governors, see Andros to Blathwayt, New York, May 8, 1680, BPCol. Wmsbg., v. III; Thomas Budd and Samuel Jennings to [?], *ibid.*, v. VII. See also *CSPCol., 1681–1685*, #282, #1411, #1841; *CSPDom., 1684–1685*, p. 126; Gov. and Council to Deputies, Nov. 1, 1681, W. A. Whitehead, *et al.*, eds., *Archives of the State of New Jersey, 1631–1800* (30 vols., Newark, N.J., 1880–1906), I, 364–65; Richard P. McCormick, ed., "The Revolution of 1681 in East Jersey: A Document," New Jersey Historical Society *Proceedings*, LXXI (1953), 111–24.

retain their own council to deal with proprietary land matters and continue to choose freely their secretary, register, and surveyor. Beside wanting the courts at Perth Amboy left undisturbed, they very strongly urged that Dominion councillors and judges selected from East New Jersey be chosen from among themselves. The privileges which they requested—not actually demanded—were inseparably related, they said, to rights of the soil, and since they had surrendered only sovereignty in government, they ought to be confirmed.[34]

The Privy Council handled the proprietors' petition a good deal more respectfully than it had those of other colonies whose governments were about to be seized. Before determining the outcome, it directed Andros to use "all forbearance" in the affairs of East New Jersey. The proprietors came off very well in the negotiations and received just about what they had asked for, including Perth Amboy as a free port. They failed, however, to confine the King to their own membership for choice of Dominion councillors and judges. Indeed, they really lost in this regard, since no one from New Jersey, East or West, was invited to join Andros' council or his courts, while New York won eight council seats and several judgeships. Once the details were settled upon, the proprietors surrendered their government, receiving in return a new patent listing the privileges confirmed. It paid to be proprietors and to be in England where the negotiations occurred. East New Jersey took its place within the Dominion, and although none of its settlers had anything to say about governing the Dominion, the colony did not seem to be much the loser for its surrender.[35]

The Dominion Council at Boston

Not long after helping New Yorkers celebrate the birth of the Prince of Wales in October 1688, Andros and his party returned to Boston. The Dominion now stretched from the St. Croix River in the north, southwest beyond New Jersey to Delaware Bay. Andros ruled with a council at Boston, not all of whom were present. He governed most colonies through council members who resided in them, such as Robert Treat and John Allyn of Connecticut. Colonel Francis Nicholson, whom the King commissioned Andros' lieutenant governor in 1688, governed New York with the help of Nicholas Bayard, Stephen Van Cortlandt, Frederick Philips, and other members of the council there.

34. Proprietors' petition, May 4, 1688, C.O. 1/68/47, I.
35. Comments by T. Powys to Lords of Trade, July 6, 1688, C.O. 1/65/17; C.O. 1/65/18; Letter of surrender, July 6, 1688, C.O. 1/65/22; New patent, 1688, C.O. 1/64/48.

Maine and New Hampshire, having few councilmen among them, were left pretty much alone, as were East and West Jersey, which had none. Again, Dominion rule was strongest in Massachusetts; it was less burdensome at the extremities. No complainer, Andros let it be known he found his command difficult, primarily because it was so spread out and "thinly peopled." [36]

The council in Massachusetts, which Andros inherited from Joseph Dudley, did not work out as expected, either for Andros or for the councillors, and there were several reasons. Bay Colony moderates, whom Randolph had picked, found their influence with Andros very small in contrast to their successful manipulation of affairs under Dudley. There was considerable bickering. Randolph complained frequently to Blathwayt of Dudley's incompetence; Dudley informed Blathwayt of Randolph's "Choller"—mostly against Dudley; and Robert Mason kept Blathwayt well informed of all the council's difficulties, particularly the scandalous conduct of the "Trimmers," who unfortunately outnumbered the loyal people like himself. Randolph's bad temper stemmed mostly from his disappointment in the perquisites of office which he had eagerly anticipated under the Dominion. After a very good start the first year, when he absorbed the offices of collector, surveyor, searcher, secretary, and register, each of which was "very materiall," to please Andros he gave up the last two to John West, one of the governor's New York favorites, who was invited to Boston to assist him.[37]

West was not the only New Yorker Andros brought to the council in Massachusetts. Among others were John Palmer and James Graham, who had served under Andros when he was the Duke's governor of New York. They had been on Dongan's council, too, and held other offices—Palmer was a judge and Graham both attorney general and receiver general of the revenue. Not the least of Graham's recommendations was a note from the Earl of Sunderland, James's chief minister, suggesting to Andros that he find him a place in New England as soon as possible. These were the "abject strangers" whom the Massachusetts settlers found so objectionable, the "Yorkers" who soaked up splendid profits, but, even more offensive, looked down their noses at the Puri-

36. See instructions to Andros, Apr. 16, 1688, *Recs. Col. R.I.*, III, 248; Andros to Blathwayt, Boston, June 4, 1688, BPCol. Wmsbg., v. III.

37. *A Narrative of The Proceedings of Sir Edmond Androsse . . . By several Gentlemen who were of his Council . . . 1691*, Andrews, ed., *Narratives*, pp. 239–49; Randolph to Blathwayt, Boston, Aug. 5, 1687, Toppan, ed., *Randolph*, VI, 225; Dudley to Blathwayt, June 4, 1686, Aug. 29, 1687, BPCol. Wmsbg., v. IV; Mason to Blathwayt, Sept. 27, 1687, *ibid.*, v. XII; Thomas Treffry [?] to Blathwayt, Mar. 15, 1687, *ibid.*, v. V; Andros to Blathwayt, Boston, May 25, 1687, *ibid.*, v. III.

tans whatever their stripe, faction or moderate. These were the outsiders who became Andros' kitchen cabinet, an inner circle, with whom
he was content to do business often with high disregard for the rest of
them. In John Higginson's words, "Ye wicked walked on Every Side
& ye Vilest of men ware Exalted." Needless to say, they were very unpopular wherever they turned in Massachusetts.[38]

Richard Wharton, of all people, was one of the first to be alienated
from Andros and his strangers. No one had looked forward more to the
Dominion and "glorious empire" than he, unless it was Randolph. That
the governor had quashed the Narragansett Company's claim in Rhode
Island and thrown cold water on several other speculations to the
north had a great deal to do with his dudgeon. On top of this he was
the loser by about £2,000 in his "Trading Estate" from a "Grate fire" and
had turned his interest to promoting a copper mine at Woburn near
Boston. By the summer of 1687 Wharton had called it quits and
embarked for England to see what he could do to improve his claims
in both land and mining and if possible to get rid of Andros.[39] Lobbying in London made as strange bedfellows as politics; by early summer
of 1688, Wharton and Increase Mather had joined forces in petitioning
and pulling strings to undermine Andros and bring about his recall.

Defense

A chief purpose of the Dominion was to improve the colonists'
defenses against the French in Canada and their Indian allies. Its extension to include New York was part of the scheme, for the added troops
and larger revenues would help defend the frontier generally but also
the English fur trade, most of which was channeled through Albany in
partnership with the Iroquois Indians. Before Andros annexed New
York to New England, Colonel Thomas Dongan had been governor
there for five years; a good deal of his time was devoted to working
out a frontier policy which would encourage the fur trade for the bene-

38. Andrews, ed., *Narratives*, p. 117 n.; E. A. Werner, *Civil List*, pp. 363–64,
177, 180, 327; Sunderland to Andros, July 9, 1688, C.O. 389/9, p. 484; Andros
to Blathwayt, New York, Oct. 4, 1688, BPCol. Wmsbg., v. III; Higginson to son
Nathaniel, Salem, Aug. 31, 1698, Essex Inst. Hist. *Coll.*, XLIII, 182.

39. Besides Wharton's patent of 1,712 acres in the Narragansett Country from
Andros (see note 14 above), Dudley's council had done well by Wharton at
Pejepscott in Maine. Sessional Papers, Council, C.O. 5/785, p. 24. Wharton to
Blathwayt, Boston, June 5, 1686, BPCol. Wmsbg., v. VI; Andros to Blathwayt,
Boston, Mar. 30, July 11, 1687, *ibid.*, v. III; See Andros' Report on the Narra-
gansett Country, Aug. 31, 1687, *CSPCol., 1685–1688*, #1414, V. See again Hig-
ginson to son Nathaniel, Aug. 31, Essex Inst. Hist. *Coll.*, XLIII, 183–84. Bernard
Bailyn, *New England Merchants in the Seventeenth Century* (Cambridge, Mass.,
1955), pp. 173–74.

fit of Albany merchants and traders and the colony as a whole. At the same time Dongan attempted to keep the Iroquois friendly to England and protect the trade, traders, and Indians from French encroachment. It was not an easy task, but it was altogether necessary, since fur was the colony's chief export, and its exchange for English goods was the heart of the colony's economy. Furthermore, maintenance of the alliance between Englishmen and the Five Nations was as essential to checking the expansion of France as it was to promoting the fur trade.[40]

In attempting to carry out these broad plans in behalf of New York and the King's empire in America, Dongan was confronted with several difficulties. Near to home were the expansive schemes of William Penn, who very early in his career as proprietor of Pennsylvania had determined to plant a Quaker settlement high in the valley of the Susquehanna River. This was Iroquois country; although most of it fell within his patent anyway, Penn's plan was to buy a large chunk of it from the Indians out of courtesy. At the same time he hoped to cement an agreement which would make it attractive for them to do business with Pennsylvania rather than Albany. If Penn had been a loser geographically in acquiring access to the sea in the south of his patent— thus his boundary dispute with Lord Baltimore—he could have no complaints to the north, for he was blessed with a river system which begged the exploitation of the fur trade right out from under the noses of the Albany traders. For years the Iroquois had brought their pelts to the Hudson, and New Yorkers could think of nothing better than that they continue. Penn's scheme was to siphon this trade south by way of the Susquehanna and Schuylkill rivers to Philadelphia, isolating Albany altogether. It was to Thomas Dongan's credit as governor of New York that by a variety of maneuvers he was able to prevent this from happening; in fact, he and the governors who followed him delayed Pennsylvania's entry into the northern fur trade until the early years of the eighteenth century. But during Dongan's term of office, Penn's threats to New York's tenuous economy and to the alliance between English and Iroquois were a constant worry to him. Had Penn been successful, the course of New York's history would have been very different.[41]

40. Recent discussions of New York's frontier problems are Allen W. Trelease, *Indian Affairs in Colonial New York: The Seventeenth Century* (Ithaca, N.Y., 1960), and Douglas E. Leach, *The Northern Colonial Frontier, 1607–1763* (New York, 1966), pp. 106–10.

41. Dongan to Lords of Trade, 1687, C.O. 5/1135/114. A full discussion of Penn's threat to New York's fur trade is in Gary B. Nash, "The Quest for the Susquehanna Valley: New York, Pennsylvania, and the Seventeenth-Century Fur Trade," *New York History* (Jan. 1967), pp. 2–27.

By the 1680's the bulk of the peltry was no longer coming from the Iroquois territories but from areas farther to the west and north, near the Great Lakes, where the Indians who did the trapping were controlled by the French. In an attempt to capture and monopolize the trade of the Lakes region, the Iroquois attacked these western Indians with the intention of channeling the fur through their own territory to Albany. In retaliation the French, under both Governors De La Barre and, after 1685, the Marquis de Denonville, struck out at the Iroquois in New York, upsetting Governor Dongan's best-laid plans. French aggression cut into not only the English fur trade but the colony's revenues as well, and it strained the alliance with the Iroquois, who expected immediate help in their struggle from New York colonists. Moreover, defense against aggression was expensive, greater than New York could sustain.[42]

But the French attack presented a further problem for Dongan. For years Holland had been England's enemy; France was allegedly a friendly nation whose interest in America the English Crown was not prepared to challenge if it was not aggressive. Both Charles and James had charged American colonists to remain friendly with the French and not to assist the Five Nations in their quarrels with them. In 1686 England and France concluded a Treaty of Peace and Neutrality, and although it had to do primarily with mutual security and trade, it included an agreement which bound both nations to respect the other's colonies in North America.[43] What seemed perfectly clear and enforceable to James II and Louis XIV in Europe was not at all clear or enforceable to Governors Dongan of New York and Denonville of New France. The difficulty was the presence of a third party, the formidable Five Nations, whose tribes were stretched out between them and who were, of course, essential to either England's or France's success in the fur trade. English colonists insisted that the Iroquois were under the aegis of the English King; the French made no such assumption, regarding instead the Indians as outside the treaty's restrictions and fair game in imperial rivalry. The French are too crafty for us, wrote Dongan; they have taken advantage of the language of the treaty and by way of bribes and French priests, under the pretense of religion, have attempted to draw the Indians to the French side. When the

42. *Ibid.*, pp. 8–10; Dongan to Blathwayt, Albany, Feb. 21, 1687, BPCol. Wmsbg., v. XI; Stephen Van Cortlandt and James Graham to His Excellency, 1687, *ibid.*, v. IX.

43. Charles II's orders to Massachusetts, Aug. 25, 1684, C.O. 389/1, pp. 239–40; Orders and letters respecting the treaty, C.O. 324/4, pp. 236–37; C.O. 324/5, pp. 20–25; C.O. 5/1135/167–68; C.O. 1/64/8; C.O. 5/904, p. 341; *CSPCol.*, *1685–1688*, #1074.

Iroquois resisted, the French used force by building forts on Iroquois territory and by outright attack upon the Senecas, the Five Nations' chief warriors. Shortly, James gave permission to Dongan to repel the French if they interfered with the Iroquois and the fur trade, and he ordered Andros to support New York with Dominion soldiers in case of emergency.[44]

These were the defense problems which Andros inherited when he annexed New York to the Dominion, and they were doubtless very good reasons for the expansion in the first place. From this point the governor general of New England had time to worry about little else than the Dominion's military posture, which in turn was probably why so little attention was paid to East and West New Jersey. Andros had already reorganized the Massachusetts militia soon after he arrived in late 1686, replacing a good many officers, some of whom had refused to serve under him. Samuel Sewall, for instance, had returned his commission to Joseph Dudley the summer before. Shocked at the inferior and many unusable arms the Bay Colony militia carried about, Andros begged for a better supply and more ammunition and stores of war from England.[45]

While in New York, settling the government there in the summer and early fall of 1688, Andros learned of the serious incursions by the French against the Iroquois. He learned, too, of several reverberations these incursions caused along the frontier where Indians, stirred up by the French, attacked the English in poorly defended and isolated settlements. As early as August some stragglers killed both friendly Indians and colonists in the Connecticut River Valley. "Further mischeifs" at Caso Bay in Maine sent Andros hurrying back to Boston, stopping on the way at Albany and the Connecticut settlements where the depredations occurred.

In Boston Andros learned more startling news of Indian attacks in Maine at Saco River and North Yarmouth on the Royal River just up the coast from Falmouth. By early November Indians had burned two small towns on the Kennebec and Sheepscott Rivers, and New Englanders as far south as Boston, mindful of 1676, were in panic over fear of wholesale destruction. It was time to act. Andros' first choice for command was General Fitz-John Winthrop, who surprisingly declined the honor owing to poor health, he said. Piqued by the re-

44. Dongan to Blathwayt, Albany, Feb. 21, 1687, BPCol. Wmsbg., v. XI; C.O. 391/6, p. 71; Nash, "The Quest for the Susquehanna Valley," pp. 9–10; Barnes, *The Dominion of New England*, pp. 219–22.

45. Sewall, *Diary*, I, 168; Andros to Blathwayt, Apr. 4, Oct. 4, 1688, BPCol. Wmsbg., v. III.

fusal, Andros led 300 troops himself to Maine with more to follow.[46] With the governor general in the wilderness for four months the New England frontier was safer than it had been for some time or would be again for that matter. But Andros left Boston undefended, not against Indians and the French as much as against rumor and then news from abroad which were more harmful to him and the Dominion than French incursions could ever be.

While at Pemaquid in Maine, where by a variety of means he attempted to reduce the danger from the French and Indians,[47] Andros received James's proclamation and instructions of October 16, 1688. They warned him and colonial governors all along the line of an intended "great and sudden Invasion from Holland" against England. This was the governor general's first inkling of the momentous events which had already taken place in November at Tor Bay and in England generally. Back in Boston, good soldier Andros responded with a proclamation of his own on January 10, 1689, commanding the colonists to be on their guard against strangers who might invade New England.[48] At this point Andros knew no more of Prince William's intentions than the colonists. Nor did the Bay colonists at the moment see the outlines of what they later called a giant conspiracy, involving their governor general who had dashed off to the woods to deal mysteriously with the French and Indians.[49] It was a long winter for an uneasy people whose resentments had rapidly accumulated and intensified since the death of the charter. It would not take much more to start a number of them thinking about a remedy.

46. For Andros' preoccupation with defense measures, see a series of eleven letters to Blathwayt from Aug. 17, 1687, to Nov. 10, 1688, BPCol. Wmsbg., v. III; Dunn, *Puritans and Yankees*, pp. 251–52; Barnes, *Dominion*, pp. 227–28.

47. Andros to Blathwayt, Boston, June 4, 1689, BPCol. Wmsbg., v. III; *CSPCol., 1689–1692*, #1, #152.

48. James II's Proclamation to the colonies, Oct. 16, 1688, C.O. 324/5, p. 34; *CSPCol., 1685–1688*, #1910; Andros' Proclamation at Fort Charles, Pemaquid, Jan. 10, 1689, *ibid., 1689–1692*, #5; *Andros Tracts*, I, 75–76 n.

49. Some colonists were suspicious of Andros' activities. "It will one day bee known whence this war rose," wrote Joshua Moodey to Samuel Nowell in London. Nov. 19, 1688, M.H.S. *Coll.*, 4th ser., VIII, 372.

12 The Glorious Revolution in England

James

Increase Mather was fond of England. He had been there for an extended visit some time earlier, a visit which had stretched through Cromwell's time to the Restoration of Charles II, when he beat a hasty retreat to more friendly Boston. In late May 1688 he was back again with his son Samuel, age thirteen, and the weight of New England was on his shoulders. It was an exciting time to be in London, for Mather arrived when great events were beginning to happen, "God having ordered the season . . . so as was for the best." [1] Three weeks earlier James II had issued his second and stronger Declaration of Indulgence with a promise that Parliament (dead since 1685) would meet and confirm it no later than November. A week before Mather settled in London, the seven bishops, including William Sancroft, Archbishop of Canterbury, had petitioned the King, suggesting strongly

---

1. A principal source for Mather's agency in London is his "Autobiography," ed. by M. G. Hall, American Antiquarian Society *Proceedings*, 71 (1961), pt. 2. For the above quotation, see pp. 324–25. See also Kenneth B. Murdock, *Increase Mather, Foremost American Puritan* (Cambridge, Mass., 1925), chs. XIII–XIV.

that the Declaration was contrary to the statutes of Parliament and therefore illegal, as was the dipensing of laws. They asked the King not to insist that they publish the Declaration in their dioceses.[2]

James had already antagonized the Church of England in a number of ways, not the least of which was the first Declaration a year earlier. Then came his establishment of the Commissioners of Ecclesiastical Causes, which smacked of the High Commission Court of the early Stuarts. James used the new court to keep Anglican priests in line and further his appointment of Catholic officers, besides ordering it to carry forward the attack on Oxford and Cambridge. One of the Commissioners' first tasks was to suspend Henry Compton, Bishop of London, who had refused to discipline his clergymen in the King's behalf. Compton's jurisdiction over the city and diocese of London was placed in the hands of a second commission to which the King added responsibility for the Anglican Church in the dominions, a duty the Bishop had earlier taken upon himself. To anyone in the colonies who thought seriously about this change, it must have looked ominous, indeed, since it afforded a splendid means for the King to impose his religious policies on America as well as England.[3] James summoned the seven bishops before the Privy Council on June 8 for examination; beforehand he had denounced their petition as "a Libel that tended to stirr up Sedition & Rebellion." Furthermore, he explained, he had not dispensed with the laws as the bishops claimed, but only suspended them; votes in Parliament were not laws, anyway, for "if they had been, he had not been here at this time." [4] James's wit was sharper than his common sense. Despite near revolt over treatment of the bishops, they were sent to the Tower and shortly tried for seditious libel. London held its breath for the outcome. Indecision kept the jury overnight, but early on June 30 "Not Guilty" rang out through the city, where it was celebrated with bonfires in the streets.[5]

The very day the Court of King's Bench acquitted the bishops another seven weighty and representative Englishmen, including Bishop Compton of London, put their mark on history by inviting Prince William of Orange to England and the sooner he came the better.[6]

2. For the Declarations of Indulgence and the seven bishops' case, see Andrew Browning, ed., *English Historical Documents*, v. VIII, *1660–1714* (London, 1953), #16–#18, #149; See also *Bishop Burnet's History of His Own Time* (London, 1857), pp. 466–73 and notes.

3. *Ibid.*, pp. 430–31; C.O. 324/4, pp. 235–36.

4. Egerton Manuscripts, 2543, f. 270, B.M.; George N. Clark, *The Later Stuarts, 1660–1714* (2d ed., Oxford, 1955), pp. 124–26.

5. *Burnet's History of His Own Time*, pp. 469–72.

6. Letter of Invitation, June 30, 1688, Maurice Ashley, *The Glorious Revolution of 1688* (New York, 1966), App. C, pp. 201–2.

Between the bishops' petition and their trial, James's Queen, Mary of Modena, gave birth to a prince, and the fat was in the fire, for if the babe were accepted as a lawful heir—there was plenty of doubt surrounding the birth—moderates could no longer look forward to the King's death as an end to their troubles.[7]

Had she known of it, Queen Mary, blessed with a "supposititious" son according to her critics, might have been encouraged by the reception of the news in some of the American colonies. Although rejoicing was spotty, it burst out where one would most expect it. Andros and his loyal party were in the act of annexing New York to the Dominion when the announcement arrived there, and therefore that city joined Sir Edmund in a round of toasts, salutes, bonfires, huzzas, and just plain drunkenness—among His Majesty's troops, of course. The next day they more decorously honored the occasion in thanksgiving. Andros carried the good news to Albany a fortnight later and repeated the celebration, treating the "Jolly Dutchmen" to a roasted ox and barrels of "very stout beere . . . to drink or drown as they pleased." [8] Lord Baltimore ordered Maryland to take appropriate measures, and St. Clement's and Choptica Hundred in heavily Catholic St. Mary's County sent an obsequious address to the King describing their limitless joy in his male heir. Proprietor Penn had an uncommon interest in James's well-being, and he, too, directed his governor to order a day of thanksgiving which was soberly kept by Quakers who, along with Penn, were indebted to James for liberty of conscience. With Andros in New York, the Congregational churches at Boston gladly ignored the event and the governor general's orders for a public thanksgiving.[9]

In the midst of the whirling events in London, Increase Mather had his first audience with James II. Taxation without consent, arbitrary laws, the rights of Englishmen—who would have cared in James's court? But religion was something else again to a King who had proclaimed liberty of conscience in behalf of fellow Catholics and, to win their support, dissenting Protestants. Mather played his role well, or so he has told us; he presented the address of thanks from the Massachusetts churches, along with one from Plymouth, and then man-

7. Sunderland, etc., to William, Earl of Craven, June 10, 1688, *Records in the British Public Records Office relating to South Carolina, 1685–1690* (Atlanta, Ga., 1929), p. 265.

8. Randolph to Blathwayt, Oct. 2, 1688, Hall, Leder, and Kammen, eds., *The Glorious Revolution in America*, p. 98.

9. Address to King, Oct. 22, 1688, C.O. 1/65/77; *Arch. of Md.*, VIII, 40, 41, 44–45, 50; Governor John Blackwell to William Penn, Jan. 25, 1689, David Lloyd and Related Papers—Province of Pennsylvania, 1686–1731, Historical Society of Pennsylvania; Richard S. Dunn, *Puritans and Yankees*, pp. 247–48.

euvered the King into asking whether Sir Edmund gave "good satisfaction to his subjects there." The answer was that the people would be well satisfied if the governor stuck to the King's Declaration of Indulgence. Pressed by James, Mather reported that Andros had fined and imprisoned a number who scrupled to swear on the Bible; that all the churches in New England would have sponsored the grateful address he presented had not Governor Andros and his council discouraged them, one claiming they could not, without the council's leave, address the King; that when the good ministers of Boston proposed a day of thanksgiving to bless God for making James their King, Sir Edmund had summoned them and bade them keep it at their peril, and if they persisted, he threatened troops to prevent them.[10] Upon James's advice, Mather put New England's grievances into a petition which touched upon a good deal more than they had discussed face to face. It included a request to restore their earlier privileges—no colonist spoke to James about rights—such as a representative assembly, lawful taxation, equitable justice, and protection of property, privileges which had given colonists and their colony some claim to an equality with Englishmen at home. Several accounts tell us that it was Lord Sunderland who struck from this petition all references to an assembly, and after several drafts the address which finally reached James no longer looked like the one originally submitted. It asked only for a guarantee of liberty of conscience, confirmation of their property, including town commons, and a charter for Harvard College to prevent interference from the Dominion government.[11] Mather was aided, although he does not tell us so, by Samuel Nowell and Elisha Hutchinson, two former members of the Massachusetts council who had come to London before him. In July James graciously accepted their petition, pocketing it with the promise, "He would take care of that affair." [12]

10. Mather, "Autobiography," pp. 324–26, 329–30.
11. CSPCol., 1685–1689, #1860; Viola F. Barnes, The Dominion of New England, 232–34.
12. Mather, "Autobiography," pp. 329–30. For the various drafts of petitions and proposals, see CSPCol., 1685–1688, #1860, #1879. M.H.S. Coll., 4th ser., VIII (Mather Papers), pp. 114–16; Mass. Arch., Ecclesiastical, 1679–1739, 11, 44; H.M.C. 22: 11th Report, Leeds, App. VII. Samuel Nowell was an outspoken member of the Puritan faction in Massachusetts. Elisha Hutchinson had shown early signs of disenchantment with the Dominion when in 1686 he refused a commission from Joseph Dudley as captain of a foot company in Boston. He and Richard Wharton, who lent Mather a hand, too, were heavy investors in the Narragansett Company, which may explain their presence in London. Both petitioned for a charter to develop mines of copper and lead in New England. To ease its course, they included in their company the Lord Mayor of London and Daniel Cox of New Jersey, a colonial enterpriser par excellence. See Randolph to Lords of Trade, May 29, 1689, N.Y. Col. Docs., III, 582. Sessional Papers, Council, C.O. 5/785, p. 34; C.O. 5/896, pp. 5 and ff.

There was a second flurry of meetings with the King in the fall of 1688, while the pace of events in England quickened owing to Prince William's preparations in Holland. James had backtracked considerably during the summer in hopes of keeping his throne. One of his ploys was to seek closer ties with dissenting Protestants—with whom he associated Increase Mather—whose support he desperately needed against a growing number of enemies. To Mather, who complained again that the Declaration of Indulgence and its protection of dissenters were ignored in the colonies, James answered that he would take the "same care of New England as of England," and they may be certain of what he had promised. There was an ironic truth in the statement which went beyond his particular meaning, for James was perversely consistent in treatment of his subjects. For three years he had ruled England without Parliament, even dispensed with some of its laws; he had kept a standing army on Hounslow Heath; and he had forced Catholics into the army, the Privy Council, and the universities,[13] where they could not legally serve. Who was to say that Sir Edmund Andros' Dominion was not a reflection in America of this same arbitrary government? But who could deny that James believed in an equality of treatment between subjects in the realm and those in the dominions, an equality which colonists had demanded for some time, only to find that under James it was an equal sharing of arbitrary government, not the rights of Englishmen? And when it came to religion, James exhibited the same kind of consistency in dealing with his subjects, for the Declarations of Indulgence, he insisted, would be honored in the colonies as well as in England. Accordingly, the King assured Mather that liberty and property and the other benefits of his Declaration would be confirmed to them as dissenters. To this he added protection for Harvard College from possible Anglican attack. Mather was jubilant. But this was mid-October; it was the last audience he would have with James II.[14]

One wonders what Mather thought of all this. While liberty of conscience was a godsend to Boston Puritans under Andros, the dispensing (or suspending) of laws by the Crown, despite its ostensible liberality, was an insult to Parliament and the people of England and, given the issue, a slap in the face to the established church. It was to Mather's purpose to remain friendly with all sides, but he found this a difficult task in the London of 1688. He might speak of the royal Declaration to James and his loyal followers and discuss it with dissent-

13. J. R. Tanner, *English Constitutional Conflicts of the Seventeenth Century, 1603–1689* (Cambridge, 1928, reprinted 1960), pp. 253–54.

14. Mather, "Autobiography," p. 331.

ing London clergymen, but such talk was no way to win friends among strong Anglicans, or even Whigs, for that matter, bent on revolution and the ascendancy of Parliament over the King. A defense of Massachusetts or of colonies generally in 1688 was only half listened to by people who were much more interested in defending Englishmen's rights in the realm than in championing them in America. Mather's dilemma in London was that New England's needs had little meaning in the context of England's mounting political battle. Mather pled a colony's cause among people whose view of empire was very different from his own and the people who had sent him. And a revolution in England did not bear upon that view, as Mather soon learned. Given the circumstances, he was fortunate in succeeding as well as he did.

William

Despite the difficulties, Increase Mather made a number of new friends during his agency in London, and it was a good thing, for he needed all the aid he could get. Most helpful were the nonconforming ministers, who were also grateful for a liberty of conscience; he cultivated them openly, returning their kindnesses by preaching in their pulpits. William Penn, who was "great at Court," had little use for Edmund Andros and less for Francis Nicholson; he spoke to James in New England's behalf and advised the King to be kind to his subjects there, a favor which persuaded Mather, although dubious of Quakers, "to give mr Pen his due." He met a number of Catholics at court—for there were plenty about—who went out of their way to be courteous to him. Mather accepted but was not fooled by their attentions, since by this time the King had fallen out altogether with the bishops and the Anglicans. He drew the line, however, at the zealous Father Petre, the King's confessor and mentor and now a member of the Privy Council, who made several advances and intimated through Nevil Payne, the playwright, that he was prepared to solicit "kindnesses for New England." Mather gave him a wide berth; "it was next going to the devill for help," he said.[15]

When Mather was not seeking audiences with the King or cultivating the great ones at court and in Parliament, he was writing pamphlets. The first was aimed at refuting a recent charge that the Crown had revoked the Massachusetts charter because the colony threatened the trade and manufactures of England. The pamphlet defended the colony

15. *Ibid.*, pp. 325–26. For a description of Father Petre, see *Burnet's History of His Own Time*, pp. 429 and n., 464, 465, 468.

right down the line and included a plea to restore the charter; Mather saw it through the press probably in late September of 1688.[16] How wide an audience it reached is unknown, but it was probably not very extensive, since it competed against much more compelling reading. James's proclamation against a "great and sudden invasion from Holland" appeared before the end of the month. A few days later Prince William countered with a proclamation of his own announcing his intention "to go over to England with . . . a force sufficient" to liberate Englishmen and maintain the Protestant religion and a "free and lawful parliament." [17] Londoners were too busy with their own troubles to put their noses into *New-England Vindicated from the Unjust Aspersions.* In the middle of October Richard Wharton wrote home to Plymouth's Governor Hinckley excitedly describing the expectation of invasion and the government's last-minute attempts to stave off ruin by restoring the charter of London and all the other corporations, the agents boldly assuming the colonies were included. "Great revoluc̃ons seem to be hasteing," Wharton wrote; from them New England may find deliverance. And, he added, Mr. Nowell was dead.[18]

Prince William was as good as his word. He landed at Tor Bay in southwestern England on November 5 and had reached London by the middle of December, James having fled, or deserted, the legalists said. The revolution was well begun, although it took some time before a good many Englishmen learned to live with it. Some were puzzled, others timid; many were slow to go over to William, for firing a king, even a bad one, was serious business.[19] They needed the kind of encouragement given by a Scots preacher a few days after the invasion. When rebuked for a "smart sermon" in support of William, he replied to his bishop, "He y^t is afraid of a fart will never stand thunder," adding that "Courage as well as Cowardice are infecting." [20]

16. *New-England Vindicated from the Unjust Aspersions* (London, 1688), *Andros Tracts,* II, 113–123. Kenneth B. Murdock implies that it was published in early 1689. *Increase Mather,* p. 220.

17. Both declarations are reprinted in Maurice Ashley, *The Glorious Revolution of 1688,* App. D and E, pp. 203–6. See also C.O. 324/5, p. 34; *CSPCol., 1685–1688,* #1910; *Andros Tracts,* I, 75–76 n.; *Burnet's History of His Own Time,* p. 492.

18. London, Oct. 18, 1688, M.H.S., Prince Collection, I, 37. See also Wharton to Wait Winthrop, London, Oct. 18, 1688, *Winthrop Papers,* M.H.S. *Coll.,* 6th ser., V, 17–18.

19. Lucile Pinkham, *William III and the Respectable Revolution* (Cambridge, Mass., 1954), chs. 4–6; *Burnet's History of His Own Time,* pp. 493–522, *passim.*

20. J. Bonnell to [?], Dublin, Nov. 17, 1688, Stowe Manuscripts, 746, f. 106, B.M. The comment was improved, wrote J. Bonnell, "by giving it ye Scotch phrase & tone."

Despite the progress made in New England's behalf under James, agent Mather had to begin all over again with William. Of course, prospects in some ways looked better under the Prince of Orange, since part of the reasons for his replacing James, and for the Glorious Revolution for that matter, were questions of constitutional rights, and Whiggish rights at that. Moreover, William's Proclamation was strong in its condemnation of James's killing of charters; it labeled restrictions on the election of burgesses as null and void and called on all former magistrates unjustly turned out of their offices to resume their responsibilities. Mather was quick to presume that this meant the colonies, too, and the colonists, New Englanders, anyway, would lose little time, once they heard about it, in accepting the Proclamation "as a pattern, if not a precept." [21] Before William and Princess Mary, the elder daughter of James and a Protestant, were offered and formally accepted the throne from Parliament, Mather was busy lining up new friends and planning his campaign. While a good deal of time had been spent with James on religious matters, trying to force Andros to honor the Declaration of Indulgence and guarantee the rights of dissenters, with William he went to the heart of the matter and stumped for a restoration of the Massachusetts charter which, he believed, would solve the colony's problems once and for all. After all, according to William's own words, he had come to England to restore the charters in the realm, among other things, and why not in the colonies at the same time? They were all Englishmen and had suffered equally the arbitrary and unconstitutional burden of James, which now, through a Glorious Revolution, was over and done for.[22]

Mather, with Sir William Phips, a New England buccaneer who had lately joined the agency in London, followed shortly with a petition to the new King. Let the colonies, they pled, "share in the Comõn Deliverance of their Fellow subjects" by a restoration of their "antient Previledges" and a return of New England governments to their former magistrates in Massachusetts, Plymouth, Rhode Island, and Connecticut.[23] To the petition Mather and Phips added the charge that the *scire facias*, which had brought down the Massachusetts charter, contained a flaw and was therefore illegal. This tactic may have been a mistake. William turned over the matter to the Lords of Trade, who seriously questioned the charge, and with the help of Sir Robert Sawyer,

21. *The Case of Massachusetts Colony Considered* . . . (Boston, 1689?), C.O. 5/855, no. 4; *CSPCol., 1689–1692,* #133; *At a Convention of the Representatives of the Several Towns* (Boston, May 24, 1689), C.O. 5/855, No. 17, IV.

22. Mather, "Autobiography," pp. 327–28, 331.

23. *Ibid.,* p. 331; Feb. 18, 1689, C.O. 5/905, p. 77; *CSPCol., 1689–1692,* #18; *Acts of P.C., Col. Ser., 1680–1720,* #278, p. 124.

prosecutor of the case against the colony in the first place, pointedly concluded that the charter had been justifiably and legally voided, owing to the colony's several violations of it. The review of the charter business was stretched into an inquiry about what should be done with New England, an inquiry which extended beyond the immediate needs of Massachusetts, even New England, and the desires of Increase Mather and the agents for both. Defense of the empire was at stake, since war with France was probable, even imminent. Already the French and Indians from the north had attacked the Dominion's frontier, complicating strained relations between England and France since William's accession.[24]

In the short run, one result of Mather's petition was a significant victory for Massachusetts. If William should continue Andros in his governorship, the colonists might never get rid of him; the fruits of revolution would be lost and New England "undone." Because the future of New England colonies was under review, very probably leading to a return of the charters, Mather and Phips succeeded in persuading William to omit confirming instructions to Andros and orders to proclaim the new monarchs, although they were sent to all other colonial governments. To Mather this deed was worth his whole trip to England if he accomplished nothing more, and he wrote home to his friends in Boston about it. To Andros it was disastrous, for he found himself, in a time of momentous change, an uninstructed, unconfirmed governor amid a resentful people bristling with grievances.[25]

To help push the petition along and win sympathy in the Convention Parliament for the suffering colonists he had left behind, Mather published his second London pamphlet, probably in late January or early February 1689, *A Narrative of the Miseries of New-England.* Again he reviewed the recent tragic history of Massachusetts: the *quo warranto* and *scire facias* which wrongly wrenched the charter from the colonists; Andros' illegal commission which maintained over a "poor People" a "French government," taxing them without their consent, depriving them of town meetings, arbitrarily seizing their property, and leaving the country in a "bleeding state." And on top of all this, the "ill Conduct" of the present rulers had brought down upon them the "cruel Butcheries" of the French Indians, which led many to the frightening conclusion that there was a design afoot to deliver

24. *CSPCol., 1689–1692,* #25; C.O. 5/905, pp. 78–80. On Oct. 30, 1689, a final decision was made against the charter. *Ibid.,* 42–75; *CSPCol., 1689–1692,* #525.

25. C.O. 5/905, pp. 41–42; C.O. 324/5, p. 36; *CSPCol., 1689–1692,* #19, #20, #21; Randolph to Blathwayt, Boston, July 20, 1689, BPCol. Wmsbg., v. I; Mather, "Autobiography," pp. 331–32, 338.

the whole land into the hands of the French King. The Prince of Orange, alone, whom God had raised up, could relieve the oppressed people and prevent catastrophe. Before anyone concluded that this was all New Englanders wanted, Mather quickly added that since charters were restored in England, it was high time the same was done in New England. If it was illegal and unjust to deprive good subjects in the realm of their laws and liberties, then, according to "Justice and Equity," it was illegal to do so in the dominions.[26] Obviously this was not the time to argue in London the merits of the covenant with God or Massachusetts' mission in America, as Mather and the Puritans had done a few years earlier in defense of their charter and colony. 1688 was a revolution against a tryannical king whereby the rights of Englishmen had prevailed for *all* Englishmen over an unconstitutional and arbitrary regime. Mather based New England's case on a conception of empire rooted in an equality of treatment for the King's subjects everywhere, a conception shared by a good many American colonists in the latter half of the seventeenth century.

Respecting Massachusetts, the question in England, among those who thought about it, was whether the Glorious Revolution had actually guaranteed the rights of Englishmen to colonists, or any rights for that matter, other than what the Crown was willing to give them. Mather boldly lobbied from the assumption that the Revolution did just that; in fact, one can conclude from his argument that the Glorious Revolution did not as much win new rights for colonists as it confirmed old ones which they had once enjoyed but only lately an arbitrary government had snatched from them. The irony of this reasoning, of course, was that the Bay Colony was notorious for having denied these very rights to its own people. But this was before destruction of their charter. In 1680 at Boston, Increase Mather had been a provincial Puritan in America whose colony, in covenant with God and supported by a providential charter, had little need of Englishmen's rights or laws. Its leaders, like himself, trained in the splendid isolation of a virtually independent government and conditioned by their errand into the wilderness, could afford to turn their backs upon an emerging empire, or so they thought. In less than a dozen years they had learned differently, none as much as Increase Mather, who at the court of William III in London on the crest of revolution preached an imperial constitution which insisted upon an empire of equal parts, including Massachusetts. Time enough to shore up the covenant among

26. *A Narrative of the Miseries of New-England By Reason of an Arbitrary Government Erected there Under Sir Edmond Andros* (London, 1689), *Andros Tracts*, II, 3–14, and xviii.

the good people of the Bay Colony when he returned home. First, they needed a guarantee of ancient privileges upon which the covenant hinged in order to make it again the principal instrument of their godly society. But this was not part of the argument in London, for it had no bearing there.

Mather and Phips found unexpected support from the Bishop of Salisbury, Gilbert Burnet, who told them he would gladly go to bat in the House of Lords for restoration of the charter. Burnet's enthusiasm must have come as a surprise to the agents, for he explained to them his strong belief that there was a "greater sacredness" in New England's charter than in any of the English corporation charters to which they had likened it. The latter were mere "acts of grace" by a king, he argued; the charter of New England—and, of course, he meant Massachusetts— was a "contract between the King and the first patentees" who had promised him that they would enlarge his dominions at their own charge, provided they and their descendants were guaranteed the privileges agreed upon. Since they had performed their part of the bargain, it was a great injustice for the King to deprive their posterity of these same privileges.[27] Mather probably heard nothing more welcome during his four-year visit to England, and from the Anglican Bishop of Salisbury no less, whose reasoning smacked of the Revolutionary philosophy, not shared at the moment by all Englishmen, Dutch William included. Doubtless Mather remembered Gilbert Burnet longer than he Mather, for in *History of His Own Time* the Bishop unfortunately found room to mention neither Mather nor the charter, no doubt the price one paid for being a colonist, even the "Foremost American Puritan."

In part, Mather's petition was granted, enough of it, at least, for him to praise God for listening to his prayers, since William declared he would recall Andros. But not all of it, and it may very well be that he was sorry for the way he had commenced the business, since the Lords of Trade and the King in Council gave the inquiry a turn he and the agents had not expected. In their report to the King the Lords recommended sending another governor in Andros' place to proclaim the new monarchs and administer the colony until further orders, provided no taxes be raised by the governor and council alone, which doubtless meant the calling of an assembly. So far so good. Meantime, the Lords suggested that a new permanent government be established which would protect the rights and properties of New England settlers and at the same time reserve for the Crown a necessary dependence. This was vague, to be sure, but it hinted at a thoroughgoing change

27. Mather, "Autobiography," p. 327.

which would guarantee the colonists a right to tax themselves, if not the independence of the old charter. William accepted the Lords of Trade's advice and instructed them to draft a new charter for "New England," meaning again Massachusetts, not certainly the whole Dominion. But instead of appointing a temporary governor, William decided to send two commissioners, graciously giving the merchants and planters of Massachusetts then in London an opportunity to recommend one of them to the King.[28]

In Mather's view what looked like defeat of the Dominion was promising, but the prospect of a new charter was not. The old charter government, alone, could reestablish the colony on its original foundation, allowing it a fair share of the fruits of the Revolution. Frustrated at court, it seemed, Mather changed tactics and appealed directly to the Convention Parliament, where the consequences of revolution were boldly being worked out, not always to William's liking. Parliament had met as early as January 1689 and was very Whiggish in makeup. With the help of a number of his new friends, Mather succeeded in persuading the Commons to include New England in the Corporation Bill which the strong Whigs proposed to resurrect city and borough charters. There was a very good chance of its success,[29] for it was the Parliament of 1689 which passed the first Mutiny Act, the Toleration Act, and the Bill of Rights, constitutionally the heart of the Revolution.

The Whiggish mood of the Commons was not shared by William or by some of the English who had helped him take over the reins of government. In fact, the Corporation Bill went much too far for several who had given up their King and rallied to William and Mary; regardless of revolution, they were not ready to sacrifice prerogative power in favor of reforms which smacked of republicanism. Furthermore, some of these moderates were at the Plantation Office, where colonial policy was made and administered. Despite the unpopularity of James's domestic rule, which they had bloodlessly helped to overthrow, his colonial policy was admired on several accounts, particularly its expression in the Dominion of New England, which had unified and centralized imperial control and for the first time effectively administered colonies for England's benefit in matters of defense, trade, and government. Far from these people's minds was the thought that

28. *Ibid.*, p. 332; C.O. 5/905, pp. 78–80; *CSPCol., 1689–1692*, #28, #37.
29. Mather, "Autobiography," pp. 339, 340, 342–43. See course of Corporation Bill in Stock, ed., *Proceedings of the Debates*, II, 1–2, 4, 7, 8 n., and 15. For the Parliament of 1689, see George N. Clark, *The Later Stuarts*, pp. 144 ff.; Stephen B. Baxter, *William III and the Defense of European Liberty, 1650–1702* (New York, 1966), pp. 250, 255, 256.

the Glorious Revolution had changed the Crown's relationship to the colonies. Rule over the dominions was a Crown function; it always had been, and as far as many Englishmen were concerned, it would necessarily continue. Whatever the Revolution meant to Englishmen, it spread no farther than the shores of the realm, and the colonies were ruled as before. At least this was the thinking of the Blathwayts and other professional policymakers in the spring of 1689 who were appalled at the prospect of breaking up the Dominion and restoring old privileges to colonies just recently brought into line. The Whigs were getting out of hand and with their Corporation Bill were trying to turn New England into a commonwealth again where colonists would take up as before, coin money, laugh at the Navigation Acts, and shortly shake off all dependence. These men opposed the change in design, but were aware, too, such was the reaction to Stuart tyranny, that caution and foot-dragging on their part were dangerous. Nevertheless, they argued for continuity in colonial policy and a thorough airing of the true state of the colonies, especially in view of a war with France, before Parliament threw all to the winds and "irreparably damnified" the prerogative of the Crown.[30]

The differences of opinion over colonial policy and particularly over what to do with New England reflected the general ambiguity within the new administration in England. More surprising than the uncertainty of affairs, given the necessary confusion of a new government, was that the new regime found any time to consider the "foreign plantations." One reason was Mather's pressing the New England business at both court and Parliament. Another, and certainly ominous, was the imminence of war with France, and this, indeed, was related to the handling of colonies in America. The immediate prospect of war, which William reported to the colonies in the middle of April, took some of the wind out of Whig sails in Parliament. In April and May discussion about colonies intensified at court and among the Lords of Trade and Privy Councillors, particularly after May 7 when England actually declared war against France—although Parliament persisted in debating the Corporation Bill. With this turn of events, the Dominion of New England had a fair chance of survival primarily for reasons of defense. By the middle of May there was growing support to continue it besides talk of sending over another governor general to organize a united military front to oppose the French of Canada and Nova Scotia. Without a union of the northern colonies, the Lords of Trade told William,

---

30. For a sample of these sentiments, see [Sir Robert Southwell?] to Earl of Nottingham, Mar. 23, 1689, Hall, Leder, and Kammen, eds., *Glo. Rev. in Am.*, pp. 67–69.

the French might easily take over "that Dominion & Trade" which were so valuable to the Crown.[31]

But New England, New York, and New Jersey were not the only areas of colonial concern as the nation girded itself for war. To the south, Pennsylvania, Maryland, and the Carolinas, as proprietary governments, were all one step removed from the Crown's control, and they, too, were vulnerable in time of war. The Lords of Trade discussed the problem of the proprietaries over several weeks and came up with a surprising conclusion: that the proprietary relation to government in England was a matter for Parliament to consider. And specifically the Lords went on to recommend that the King instruct those members of his Privy Council who also sat in the House of Commons to move in that body that Parliament consider the present state of Maryland under Lord Baltimore and how that colony might be brought more closely under the Crown's control in the present circumstances.[32] It would seem that the effect of the Revolution upon colonial policy, in this particular, at least, was at once a continuation of centralizing control over colonies, similar to what had existed under both Charles and James, and a sharing with Parliament what heretofore had been exclusively the King's business.

By revolution Parliament had won a larger role in governing England, but it had also won the right to stick its nose deeper into colonial affairs than ever before. Mather's taking the charter business to Parliament was, indeed, a shrewd move, and he might very well have won had it not been for the war which altered the complexion of things in the spring and summer of 1689 and encouraged the continuation of a centralizing yet restrictive policy which had been characteristic of James's reign. Then, too, as 1689 wore on, Parliament became less Whig and more Tory in its outlook. The Corporation Bill, which was almost vindictive in its attempt to limit the political freedom of former officeholders and holdover Tories, although passed by the Commons, was stalled in the House of Lords and finally given up when William prorogued the legislature in early 1690.[33]

Thwarted this time by Parliament, Increase Mather turned back to

31. Lords of Trade, Apr. 26, May 2, 1689, C.O. 324/5, pp. 45, 47; Hampton Court, May 12, 1689, Mass. Arch. 1658–1751, XX, 26; *CSPCol., 1689–1692*, #69, #70, #75, #89, #90, #102; Baxter, *William III*, p. 251.

32. Lords of Trade to the King, May 2, May 18, 1689, C.O. 324/5, pp. 46–47, 50–51; *CSPCol., 1689–1692*, #102, #123, #124; *Arch. of Md.*, VIII, 100–1.

33. Mather, "Autobiography," pp. 340, 342–43; Stock, ed., *Proceedings and Debates*, II, 8 and n.; Clark, *The Later Stuarts*, p. 182; Baxter, *William III*, p. 256. The House of Lords voted to consider the colonies as distinct. See series of documents in H.M.C. 17: 12th Report, App. VI, *House of Lords, 1689–90*, pp. 422–32.

the throne for help in resurrecting the Puritan commonwealth. But William was overwhelmed by the necessities of war on the Continent and had little time to spend on colonial affairs. Anyway, by this time, circumstances had changed again with very strange news from Boston, arriving late in June and early July of 1689. Some of it came in letters from Edward Randolph, written, curiously, from the common jail.[34]

34. Mather, "Autobiography," pp. 343, 332; *Andros Tracts*, II, xx; Randolph to Lords of Trade, Common Goal, Boston, May 29, 1689 [received July 3, 1689], *CSPCol., 1689–1692*, #152. The Lords of Trade had a copy of the Massachusetts *Declaration* and a narrative of proceedings at Boston by July 16. *Ibid.*, #260, #261.

13 The Glorious Revolution in New England

The rule of James II hung as heavy over colonists in America as it did the people of England in 1688. For James was King in the dominions, too. His arbitrary government, the colonists believed, was reflected everywhere; in Andros' regime over all of New England, New York, and New Jersey; it encouraged the oppressions of Catholic Lord Baltimore and his oligarchy in Maryland; and Virginians felt it in the tightening of the prerogative under Lord Howard of Effingham. Not even Pennsylvania and the Carolinas, where the proprietors insulated colonists somewhat from the royal will, were free, for James was no friendlier to the proprietary form of government or to proprietors than Charles had been. His attack upon Baltimore's charter in Maryland, despite the proprietor's religion, was proof enough of that. The new policy strongly discouraged, even punished, idiosyncrasy and diversity among colonies. It ruled by commission and instruction, depriving colonists of consent to their laws and taxes, reflecting certainly in many eyes James's growing independence of Parliament and his dispensing of its laws. Breaking of charters was felt on both sides of the Atlantic.

In more than half of the American colonies, many offices of government, heretofore locally controlled, were now under Crown control.
Maryland had kept its assembly, to be sure, but it was increasingly
frustrated by the exercise of power from above which tied the hands
of the people's representatives. Whether subversion of liberties in
America was as clear to Englishmen in England as it was to colonists
is not the point. That colonists believed they were oppressed and were
denied these liberties was cause enough to anticipate means of change.
And James afforded them that, too.

Besides arbitrary government, but closely related to it, was the
King's Catholicism. Declarations of Indulgence may have pleased Increase Mather, English Catholics, and other nonconformists for the
time being, but they were not a policy which could long be maintained,
given the Protestantism of most Englishmen and the strong Anglican
Church which was part of the English establishment in more than just
an ecclesiastical sense. Protestantism was woven into the English character, socially and constitutionally. Liberty of conscience and religious
freedom made more sense in the colonies, where there was a growing
diversity of religion, although less in the south than the north. But in
overwhelmingly Protestant communities at home and in America,
freedom for Catholics was an ominous threat since it was pushed by
a Catholic King. It became more and more clear that James was seriously bent on supplanting Protestant institutions with those of the
Pope, and he did not shrink from defying Parliament, the Anglican
Church, and most Englishmen to do it.

Moreover, France across the Channel was Catholic, and its government under Louis XIV was absolute. To many Englishmen Catholicism
meant absolutism both religiously and politically. The revocation of the
Edict of Nantes, coming the very year of James's accession, was grounds
enough for English fears, for it was grave testimony to the perfidy of
a Catholic King, while the hounding of Protestants out of the land was
even clearer evidence of what a Catholic monarch was capable of
doing. Englishmen identified a popish nation with the very opposite of
English liberties. Colonists were Englishmen, too, and the lesson was
not lost upon them, particularly when their peace of mind was threatened by the French in Canada whose colonial government extended the
absolutism of Louis. Between the colonists and the Catholic French
were the Indians, to be sure, but their allegiance to the English was
not guaranteed—nor was the fur trade which the Indians engineered—
and the French lately were successful in utilizing Indians in their attacks upon the English in behalf of the French empire.

Andros and his party were devoted to Catholic James, and although

Protestants, their Anglicanism was suspect among staunch and jealous Puritans. In New York Catholic Thomas Dongan, formerly governor, remained in the colony instead of returning home, a stubbornness variously interpreted as time went on. In addition, several colony officers were Catholic, including a couple of militia captains whose retention by Lieutenant Governor Nicholson, along with a Catholic chaplain, was highly resented and not forgotten. And, of course, in Maryland, where the largest number of Catholics resided between the French in the north and the Spanish settlements in the south, Baltimore governed through an oligarchy which was substantially Catholic. With the French in Canada stirring up the Indians, exposing the frontiers of all three of these colonies to aggressive threats, new fears mushroomed among colonists already sullen and discontent with the governments over them.

Discontent fed, too, on the stifling of private and self-interested individuals and factions whose needs Stuart policy either ignored or failed to satisfy. An equitable imperial constitution, based on the rights of Englishmen, besides protecting their rights and liberties and guaranteeing them an identity and place in the empire, would afford colonists a substantial degree of self-determination which they could put to their own good use.

The Glorious Revolution in England was an unexpected but welcome jolt to most colonists in America, particularly to those who saw it as a means of escape from an uncomfortable dilemma. The Popish Plot, Exclusion Crisis, Monmouth's and Argyle's rebellions, all the recent upheavals in England, had shaken the foundations of the Stuart establishment, but none was successful, none was large enough in conception, for colonists to feel included—although several made the attempt. None was sufficiently popular or contained strength enough to force changes upon Stuart institutions—except maybe in reaction—by which Englishmen in England, let alone colonists, might benefit. The Glorious Revolution of 1688 was another matter; it got rid of one monarch and crowned two others. It was accompanied by popular support and promised several constitutional reforms which colonists were quick to appropriate, even exploit. For colonies were "contiguous," they said, and really "parts of the whole." Few Englishmen in the realm were convinced of this constitutional mateyness, and most were taken by surprise when colonists insisted upon a revolutionary role similar to their own.

Had news of 1688 come clear and straight to America, the outcome might have been different. About all the colonists had to go on at first was James II's declaration, warning of a sudden invasion from Holland,

and then on top of it came William's from The Hague, declaring his intention to sail to England and deliver it from the clutches of slavery and popery. Had the news which followed come directly, free of distortion, it might have dammed the spate of rumors which had spread throughout the colonies early that year, rumors which heightened the uncertainty of the time and sharpened grievances against arbitrary governments. The invasion of England from Holland was common talk among Jamaicans as early as December 1688. By the middle of January 1689 Massachusetts people had heard wild details of the campaign: an army of "120,000 men, equally composed of Frenchmen, Dutchmen, and Englishmen." [1] There was a dearth of shipping to Virginia in the winter and early spring of 1689, probably owing to the increased tension between England and France which shortly burst into war. But the "Joyfull nuse" of their being delivered from slavery supported the flagging spirits of Virginians in the middle of March, although it was another month or more before they were sure enough of the goings on to proclaim the new King and Queen at "James Citty." [2] By April 1 Quakers in Rhode Island were aware that Prince William was in command in England, but along with the news came the sad report that the new government had executed William Penn for being a Jesuit [3]—his second death in half a dozen years, both grossly exaggerated and both leaving him in the lap of Rome.

Official orders from William to the colonial governments suffered worse fate than news of the Revolution. As we have seen, Sir Edmund Andros in New England received no commands at all owing to the meddling of Increase Mather, who confidently expected the governor general's immediate recall and a restoration of the Bay Colony's charter which would dissolve the Dominion. Since Andros lacked orders,[4] none could be relayed by him to other colonies of the Dominion and particularly to New York, where Francis Nicholson and his small resident council sat uneasily at the head of a restless people. The delay was disastrous. Colonists became aware of revolutionary changes in England before their governments took notice. Lord Baltimore's messen-

1. George Reid to [?], Jamaica, Dec. 7, 1688, C.O. 1/65/90; John Pynchon to R. Livingston, Jan. 16, 1689, Livingston Family Papers, General Correspondence, 1661–1695, Franklin D. Roosevelt Library, Hyde Park, New York. Professor James S. Leamon of Bates College very kindly lent me his microfilm copy of a number of these papers.
2. Sarah Bland to Blathwayt, Mar. 16, 1689, BPCol. Wmsbg., v. XVII; Nicholas Spencer to Blathwayt, Apr. 27, 1689, ibid., v. XVI.
3. Newport, R.I., Quakers to London Yearly Meeting, Epistles Received, 1683–1706, I, Lib. Soc. Friends, London. Again I am indebted to J. William Frost of Vassar College for this piece of information.
4. C.O. 5/905, pp. 41–42.

ger, bearing orders for Maryland, had the misfortune to die before leaving England. It was several months before more orders arrived at St. Mary's, and they arrived too late to allay the suspicions of frustrated and impetuous colonists who, with a fair share of encouragement, read more wrong reasons than right into the crucial delay.[5] News of the Revolution first came unofficially in fits and starts; in this fashion it wore out the patience of the discontented. That it remained so long unconfirmed aggravated rumors of conspiracy. In less than four months after the middle of April 1689, major rebellions occurred in Massachusetts, New York, and Maryland. The other New England colonies promptly resumed their former governments; at the same time ripples of revolt came close to overturning Virginia and soon reached as far south as the Carolinas.

Massachusetts

Uneasiness and uncertainty were nowhere more apparent than in Massachusetts, where reaction to four lean years of Dominion rule was laced with fears of French and Indian hostility. Colonists pronounced worthless Sir Edmund's Indian campaign to Maine, "Hedging in the Cuckow's," they called it; it was highly suspect, too, in view of thickening rumors about English events and the threat of a Catholic conspiracy. In late March the buzzing became loud enough to bring Andros hurriedly back from Pemaquid, where he first had heard of William's invasion; accounts from Virginia and the Barbados strengthened earlier hints that the Prince of Orange was now "Comander in chiefe in England."[6] During the first week of April John Winslow arrived in Boston from Nevis in the West Indies bearing a copy of the Prince's Declaration from The Hague. When passed about, it spilled the news to the inhabitants, who saw Winslow seized and imprisoned for possessing "Seditious and Treasonable" papers—only for contemptuous behavior before a justice, said Andros' party, for which he was detained overnight and then released. But Andros said not a word, nor did he call a council meeting, inaction which convinced the people that he was suppressing news of welcome changes abroad. And then they remembered, too, that his last public act relating to England was

5. Baltimore to William Joseph, London, Feb. 27, 1689, *Arch. of Md.*, VIII, 114; Memorandum, Privy Council, Aug. 28, 1689, C.O. 324/5, pp. 71, 73; *CSPCol.*, *1689–1692*, #390.

6. *An Account of the Late Revolutions in New-England; in a letter*, by A.B., *Andros Tracts*, II, 193; "Andros' Report of his Administration, 1690," Andrews, ed., *Narratives of the Insurrections*, p. 232; Samuel Wyllys to Mary Wyllys, Boston, Apr. 8, 1689, *Wyllys Papers*, Conn. Hist. Soc. *Coll.*, XXI, 307.

the proclamation in January respecting James II's warning against a sudden invasion from Holland. These actions, or lack of them, along with succeeding momentous but unexplained events in England, seemed to plant Andros squarely in James's camp no matter what happened. When colony troops, left in garrison by Andros at Pemaquid, mutinied and worked their way homeward to Boston in the middle of April, an outburst was imminent.[7]

It came on April 18 and with a blast that was unmistakable.[8] On that morning inhabitants of Boston, or a good part of them, turned out into the streets; to beat of drums, they armed themselves and formed companies with the militia. First thing, they seized Captain John George of His Majesty's frigate *Rose*, as he came ashore, in order to prevent possible reprisal upon the town from her guns. Quick to respond and in an attempt to keep a damper on violence, a group of gentlemen met at the Town House with the task of managing the affair. As excitement and the number of armed colonists grew, Governor Andros agreed, after being summoned, to leave the fort and discuss matters at the Town House, where the group demanded his surrender and then imprisoned him. Off and on during the day the townspeople seized and jailed about twenty-five of his people, including Edward Randolph, John Palmer, James Graham, and anyone else who was still bent on opposing them. The gentlemen of the committee included a few merchants, several of the earlier charter magistrates, some of Andros' council, a handful of ministers, including agent Mather's son Cotton, and, of all people, an Anabaptist preacher, William Milborne. When Old Governor Bradstreet, then in his eighties, appeared for the first time to take his place at the head of the committee, he was cheered as a hero by the soldiers and populace who milled about the common.

7. *An Account of the Late Revolutions,* in *Andros Tracts,* II, 194; *New-England's Faction Discovered,* by C.D., Andrews, ed., *Narratives,* p. 257; Samuel Mather, *The Life of . . . Cotton Mather* (Boston, 1729), p. 42. For Andros' proclamation in January 1689, see ch. 11, n. 48; *Andros Tracts,* III, 145 n.; Viola F. Barnes, *The Dominion of New England,* pp. 241, 242.

8. The account of the early days of the revolt in Boston is taken from the following sources: John Riggs's Narrative, C.O. 5/905, pp. 85–87, and *CSPCol., 1689–1692,* #261; Extract of a Letter from Bristoll in New England unto Mr Mather and others, Apr. 29, 1689, C.O. 5/855, #2; Captain George's Letter to the Admiralty, June 12, 1689, C.O. 5/855, #15, and Andrews, ed., *Narratives,* pp. 215–19; List of those imprisoned with Andros, C.O. 5/905, p. 143; "Diary of Lawrence Hammond," Apr. 18, 1689, M.H.S. *Proc.* (1891–1892), 2d ser., VII, 149–50; Samuel Prince to Thomas Hinckley, Boston, Apr. 22, 1689, *Hinckley Papers,* M.H.S. *Coll.,* 4th ser., V, 192–96; *An Account of the Late Revolutions in New-England,* by A.B., *Andros Tracts,* II, 189–201; *New-England's Faction Discovered,* by C.D., Andrews, ed., *Narratives,* pp. 253–67; Nathaniel Byfield, *An Account of the Late Revolution in New-England, ibid.,* pp. 170–75.

All told there were more than a thousand colonists in arms by mid-afternoon, and more pouring in from Charlestown, so many, in fact, that the committee gentlemen only with difficulty managed to discourage the oversupply by signaling from Beacon Hill.

Sometime during the day a Declaration justifying the revolt was read from the gallery of the Town House. It rehearsed the familiar grievances against the Dominion government, from the illegal revocation of the charter, through unconstitutional taxes and appropriation of their lands, to the phony war in Maine—"we are again Briar'd in the Perplexities of another Indian War." And all these were described against the background of a monstrous popish plot, against which England had struggled for years, and now pure New England must battle, a plot to extinguish the Protestant religion forever and deliver them all to popery and slavery. Thus their "unanimous Inclination" under a "double engagement" to look to their own security. In compliance with the "Patterns" set for them in England, they seized upon "those few ill Men" who had been the "great Authors" of their misery. Hardly dashed off in the heat of revolt, the Declaration was a carefully written and eloquent document which was greeted with satisfaction by the hundreds who heard it. Those who did not, read it shortly in print.[9]

By the end of the second day, but only with the greatest reluctance, Andros was persuaded, on threat of bloodshed, to order surrender of both fort and castle, each meagerly defended by his troops. Ironically, it was Randolph whom the townspeople forced to carry the messages and arrange the capitulation—only to rub his nose in the Dominion's defeat, he said. John Usher's house first served as Andros' prison, but this hardly satisfied the country people, who in "rage and heat" insisted he be removed in chains to the fort, and they saw him delivered there that very day. Randolph, and eventually Joseph Dudley, who was shortly captured in Rhode Island while on circuit as a judge, ended up in the common jail; John Palmer, the other judges, and several officers spent the next few months close prisoners in the castle. There was little or no resistance; the actual turnover was complete in two days' time. "Through the Goodness of God there has been no Bloodshed," one of the bystanders wrote to Increase Mather in London. Out of the events emerged a Council of Safety, heavily weighted with merchants, who indecisively handled Massachusetts affairs for a month or more. It contained the fifteen gentlemen who had met at the Town House on April 18 and a good many more who willingly backed the revolt. At its head stood Simon Bradstreet, former colony governor, and a number

9. *The Declaration of the Gentlemen, Merchants and Inhabitants of Boston, and the Country Adjacent. April 18, 1689, ibid.,* pp. 175–82.

of other moderates, including several members of Andros' council, Wait Winthrop, William Stoughton, Samuel Shrimpton, William Brown, and Bartholomew Gedney. These last were lately alienated from the governor general's rule over a variety of issues but particularly their inability to control his government and his lack of sympathy for their schemes. It contained, too, some of the old faction, for former deputy governor Thomas Danforth, Elisha Cooke, and John Richards were among them.[10]

Edward Randolph several months later accused Increase Mather of encouraging the revolution from London through letters to Bradstreet and his son Cotton, at whose house, said Randolph, armed men met on the very eve of revolt. This would seem unlikely, since Mather in early 1689 was confident that King or Parliament or the courts were about to restore the Massachusetts charter. Under these circumstances rebellion would have been not only unnecessary but foolhardy. Randolph was earlier of another mind about the origin of revolt; when incorrectly informed of Mather's imminent success in London, he claimed the Bay colonists on April 18 "anticipated by force the favour that they would not wait to receive from England," a comment which implied he had not yet given Mather a prominent role in provoking the uprising.[11] This last pronouncement probably came closer to the truth. Bay colonists were indeed impatient, but for good reason, they believed. It was not yet clear to them that Mather was the cause of Andros' failure to receive official notice of William's success in England and of the Prince's orders confirming the governor and his officers in their posts until further instructions. And as far as the colonists were concerned, these orders might arrive at any time. The dilemma they faced, on the one hand, was a fear that Governor Andros might oppose the revolution in England and carry Massachusetts Bay for James II and Louis XIV and the Pope with the assistance of the French and the Indians of Canada. On the other hand, they were apprehensive lest Andros declare openly for the new King and be confirmed as governor, offering them no relief from his arbitrary government which had subverted their holy commonwealth. To forestall either possibility, they rebelled on April 18 and toppled the Dominion.

Lawrence Hammond, a Charlestown merchant, described the rebel-

10. C.O. 5/855, #2. For Committee of Safety, see Andrews, ed., *Narratives*, pp. 216–17 n.; "Andros' Report of his Administration, 1690," *ibid.*, 233 and n.

11. Randolph to Lords of Trade, Boston, Sept. 5, 1689, *CSPCol., 1689–1692*, #407; same to same, May 29, 1689, *ibid.*, #152; Randolph to Blathwayt, Boston, Common Goal, July 20, 1689, BPCol. Wmsbg., v. I. For Mather's confidence in restoration of the charter, see above, ch. 12.

lion glowingly in his diary: the people of Boston and the adjacent towns "did this day rise as one man" and throw off the oppresser. Stuff and nonsense, "Lyes and shams," charged Edward Randolph, who laid the blame squarely upon five or six ministers along with some "principall members" of their congregations, and several former magistrates who were the chief designers of the plot, into which, he added, they invited "God Almighty." [12] Whether the people "rose unanimously," whether the rising was "providentially done," were questions whose answers Edward Randolph and Cotton Mather, Joseph Dudley and Thomas Danforth could never agree upon. How much preparation went into the activities of April 18 will probably never be known precisely. Samuel Prince, then present in Boston, claimed he knew nothing of the outburst until the drums beat and he saw boys and men running with clubs and arms through the streets in the north end of town. There is no reason to doubt his word, as there might be that of the fifteen gentlemen who signed Andros' summons and declared that they were surprised by the people's sudden appearance in arms, "in the first motion whereof [they] were wholly ignorant. . . ." [13] Several accounts make it reasonably clear that the "sensible Gentlemen" of the town had met earlier and discussed, if not making a rebellion, at least managing one if it occurred. Peace in Boston in the few weeks immediately preceding had been tenuous, to say the least, given the strong apprehension about the French in the north and the return of the soldiers from Maine besides the unofficial news from England. The gentlemen were doubtful that peace could obtain much longer, although they had done what they could to promote it. Their best bet, they concluded, was to be ready to keep whatever took place under some kind of wraps. One account nicely managed an explanation: the responsible gentlemen resolved that if either the "outrageous madness" of their foes or the "impatient motion" of their friends provoked crisis, they would put themselves at the head of it. What this meant, of course, was that they were determined to prevent an attack upon the colony from Andros and the French. But they were just as determined to avert an unmanageable and bloody revolution on the part of the countryside which might upset more than the Dominion and leave them in a worse state than at present. The "sensible Gentlemen" kept the rebellion within manageable bounds—no bloodshed, no uncivil treatment of the

12. "Diary of Lawrence Hammond," M.H.S. *Proc.* (1891–1892), 2d ser., VII, 149–50; Randolph to Blathwayt, Oct. 28, 1689, Toppan, ed., *Randolph*, VI, 312–13.

13. Samuel Prince to Thomas Hinckley, Apr. 22, 1689, *Hinckley Papers*, M.H.S. *Coll.*, 4th ser., V, 192–96; Summons to Sir Edmond Andrews [*sic*], Apr. 18, 1689, C.O. 5/855, #17, III.

prisoners, except maybe Randolph, and no surrender to the country-side, although for a time there was little order as armed bands surged through Boston streets for a day or two after the seizure of the government. The Council of Safety, formed for emergency purposes to govern the colony, included the interested parties except, of course, Andros'.[14]

Curiously, no single leader emerged, either immediately or in the uneasy months to come. This was not Winthrop's, or Danforth's, or Cotton Mather's rebellion. Although Randolph accused several ministers, prominent church members, and a number of former magistrates of instigating and carrying out the plot, none lent his name to the uprising. Captain John Nelson, merchant and soldier, commanded the local troops and was prominent in forcing the surrender of both fort and castle, but leadership clearly did not fall upon him, possibly because he was suspected of Anglicanism and, Thomas Hutchinson tells us, sported a "gay, free temper"; [15] both certainly would have rendered him unfit to the faction. That the rebellion bears no specific name may be significant in itself. It might tell us that the leaders of the uprising wanted it remembered as a widely supported undertaking, a unanimous outburst of the "people" as the Declaration described and Mather and the agents contended in England. Therefore, it needed no name, only to be chalked up as the will of God.

Or it might tell us something altogether different. Maybe more likely, despite its wide support, two very different groups combined to bring it off, but for two very different reasons. First there was the faction, backed no doubt by most of the church people, the country-side, the ministers. Their object was a return to a godly government which satisfied the needs of a covenanted community with independent power to order society according to what they remembered of the Puritan mission as it had before loss of the charter. Second, there were the moderates—fading saints, a few Anglicans, and several un-churched—who had emerged under the charter government, often outside of it, often in opposition to it, owing to religious and political restraints, who had encouraged revocation of the charter, or at least not stood in its way. Some of these had accepted places in Dudley's and Andros' governments in order to control them in their own trad-ing and land-speculating interests. Failing this under Andros, they

14. See Samuel Mather's account in *The Life of . . . Cotton Mather* (Boston, 1729), p. 42; *Andros Tracts*, III, 145 n.; Hall, Leder, and Kammen, eds., *Glo. Rev. in Am.*, pp. 39–40; *An Account of the Late Revolutions*, by A.B., *Andros Tracts*, II, p. 195; Isaac Addington to Thomas Hinckley, Boston, Apr. 30, 1689, M.H.S. *Coll.*, 4th ser., V, 198; Thomas Danforth to Thomas Hinckley, Apr. 30, 1689, *ibid.*, pp. 191–92.

15. Quoted in Andrews, ed., *Narratives*, p. 173 n.

willingly combined with the faction to chuck the Dominion, trusting that a new royal government, in which they could vote and hold office, would allow them adequate power for their burgeoning needs in an expanding empire. Since motives behind it differed, neither group could comfortably claim the rebellion as its own, for each expected its own rewards. Their temporary bond was a strong desire to rid the land of Andros and his "creatures." Fear of a Catholic conspiracy, defense of the rights of Englishmen, and an opportune revolution in England first provoked and then justified their actions, as the Declaration explained.

Meanwhile, the Bay Colony got along as best it could. The Council of Safety called a convention of town representatives on May 2 who voted to resume the former government but not actually reinstate the charter, a nice distinction. On May 22 the colony held an election of deputies who from that time gathered as an assembly under former Governor Bradstreet and the council last elected in the spring of 1686, a procedure which gave the Tory-minded and opponents of the old government little means of dissent. Some of the uncertainty diminished the last week of May when two ships arrived at Boston with news happily confirming the success of the Revolution in England and the crowning of William and Mary.[16] But the upheaval was not yet over, and it would not be until Massachusetts was settled under a legitimate government which both the faction and the moderates could live with. King William was busy at home with James's Irish expedition and a war with France on his hands. Despite Increase Mather's indefatigable lobbying, it was some time before the King seriously turned his attention to America. Massachusetts revolutionaries had agreed long enough to form a huge majority capable of overthrowing the Dominion; once this was accomplished they saw fewer reasons for agreement, in fact, were at loggerheads for some time to come over the future of the colony.

Plymouth

It would be difficult to charge the settlers of Plymouth Colony with violent revolution. A more appropriate description would be the comment from a neighbor that, upon hearing of the Boston uprising, they quietly returned to their "former bottom." To be sure, by April 20 they had locked up a former secretary and Dominion councillor, Nathaniel Clark, to keep him out of mischief, but more alarming to them

16. *Ibid.*, pp. 218–19 n.; Capt. George's Letter to the Admiralty, June 12, 1689, *ibid.*, pp. 215–16.

than rebellion was an apprehension of invasion, strong testimony that a Catholic conspiracy and French threat were no idle fears at New Plymouth.[17] They soon resumed their "former way of government," explaining to the King that they believed they had good title to it "by Prescription," if no other, citing Sir Edward Coke, "that Oracle of the Law," as authority. They told William, too, that although they had had no hand in the violence at Boston, they eagerly accepted the benefits which relieved them of "Arbitrary, Tyrannical Invasions" upon their persons, lands, rights, and liberties. What they wanted and dutifully asked for was confirmation of their former liberties, especially in religion. They reminded the King that liberty of conscience was the prime purpose for settling their colony, the first in New England, where "wild beasts" and "wild men" had abounded when their fathers first arrived—probably William III's initiation into the elocution of the "howling wilderness." Humbly they left it to his "Princely Wisdom" how these ends might be met, either by royal charter or by act of Parliament, a choice William doubtless found difficult to appreciate.[18] (Colonial petitions immediately after 1689 included frequent references to Parliament, since colonists were not certain of the order of things in England and often gave more credit and responsibility to Parliament than William was willing to acknowledge.) The struggle for confirmation continued for some time and was settled only when the King determined what to do with Massachusetts. Meanwhile, Plymouth Colony continued as before; former Governor Hinckley took up the familiar reins, assisted by John Cotton, a "heady Independent" parson, quipped Edward Randolph from Boston Jail.[19]

Rhode Island

News traveled slowly in the seventeenth century, even news of successful rebellion against tyranny. Five days after the Bay colonists turned the Dominion government upside down, Rhode Islanders were asked to do something about their own. On April 23 Walter

17. "Reflections upon the Affairs of New England," *Wyllys Papers,* Conn. Hist. Soc. *Coll.* XXI, p. 326; Byfield, *An Account of the Late Revolution,* Andrews, ed., *Narratives,* p. 175, and n.; William Bradford and Nathaniel Thomas to Thomas Hinckley, Plymouth, Apr. 20, 1689, "toward night," *Hinckley Papers,* M.H.S. *Coll.,* 4th ser., V, 190–91, 200.

18. Address to William and Mary, June 6, 1689, C.O. 5/855, #13; C.O. 5/905, pp. 117–21; *CSPCol., 1689–1692,* #183. At least the new King was spared one rhetorical flourish on the wilderness theme which appeared only in a draft of the Address, for Plymouth people begged His Majesty to "cherish the parched plants of this great wilderness." *Hinckley Papers,* M.H.S. *Coll.,* 4th ser., V, 119.

19. Randolph to Blathwayt, Oct. 28, 1689, Toppan, ed., *Randolph,* VI, 312–13.

Clarke, last elected governor of the colony, addressed a call to "Neighbors and Friends," informing them of the seizing of Andros and the eclipse of his government. Owing to the "deplorable and unsettled condition" of the colony, Clarke suggested that "principal persons" of each town come to Newport before May 1, the usual election day under the old government, to consult about what ought to be done and whether they should insist upon their "ancient privileges and former methods" as many of the free people were bent on doing.[20]

But instead of just the "principal persons," a much larger number of voters flocked to Newport on May 1, 1689, enough to call themselves "the Assembly of freemen of . . . Rhode Island." They promptly saluted the "present supream Power of England," a clear indication that they were not certain what had happened there, and declared that, owing to the dissolution of Andros' Dominion, they were dangerously void of government. The best move they could make to keep the peace was to "lay hold of [their] Charter Priviledges" and establish officers according to their former station, not for the minute doubting that the charter, through grace and favor, would be confirmed to them. After all, they explained, theirs was a small colony, distinct from the others, which their predecessors had procured with great difficulty; moreover, they were a poor and distressed and persecuted people, a condition they would be happy to demonstrate if need required—but mercifully refrained from doing. After hedging against unfavorable reports sent home by "ill-affected people"—Rhode Island had its share of Tories and moderates—they prostrated themselves at "your feet," humbly confessing that they were ignorant of what titles to use in such an overture, not being "so rhetorical as becomes such Personages." [21] Rhode Island's revolution was not all talk, however. Spoiling for action against the Dominion, a dozen or more young militants, a few days after Andros' fall, boldly seized Joseph Dudley, who had taken refuge at Narragansett after learning of the rebellion while on circuit as a judge. They shortly packed him off to Boston, where he joined Edward Randolph in the common jail for a lengthy visit.[22]

Rhode Islanders were as uncertain about their own governor as they were about who graced the throne of England, for Walter Clarke, without prejudice, but for reasons not altogether clear, refused to serve them. The colony bumbled along without a governor for almost a year,

20. *Recs. Col. R.I.*, III, 257.

21. Declaration of the Colony of Rhode Island, May 1, 1689, C.O. 5/905, pp. 109–10; *Recs. Col. R.I.*, III, 266.

22. Extract of a Letter from Bristoll in New England unto Mr Mather and others, C.O. 5/855, #2; Byfield, *An Account of the Late Revolution*, Andrews, ed., *Narratives*, p. 174.

during which time little business was accomplished, but it took a good deal longer than that for King William—they eventually learned of his accession—to decide upon the colony's future. Despite the delay, once the government was functioning again, it did so on the basis of the charter of 1663.[23] Like Massachusetts and Plymouth, Rhode Island fell back upon the one foundation which offered it a familiar identity and position. Nevertheless, its course in the 1690's, like that of other New England colonies, was not smooth. One can be sure, at least, that the Colony of Rhode Island and Providence Plantations was not inhibited by a cumbersome bureaucracy or overbearing protocol.

Connecticut

Connecticut felt the effect of the Glorious Revolution and the overthrow of Andros more strongly than Rhode Island, since there was less unanimity among its settlers under the Dominion and about what ought to be done following its fall. James Fitch, who with the deputies had led the struggle in 1687 against surrender of the charter, quickly welcomed the upheaval in New England as part of the Glorious Revolution and as a means to accomplish his own ends. He took the lead immediately, again backed by the former deputies, and called for a new election in May 1689 within a few weeks of Andros' demise. Fitch's popular party, his opponents believed, was democratically, even dangerously, inclined; it strove by a new election to rid the colony of the old councillors, the moderates, who not only had frustrated the deputies' wishes under the charter but had accepted its surrender too easily and along with it comforting offices in Andros' government. Former Governor Robert Treat and Secretary John Allyn were chief among these moderates; despite their willingness to see the last of Andros and Randolph and the Dominion, they were not pleased with the prospect of a sudden election in May, manipulated by Fitch, which might easily sweep them out of the government.

When it looked as if Fitch's people would succeed in forcing an election, there emerged a third group, small in number but strong in voice, led by Gershom Bulkeley, a well-known Wethersfield physician and justice under Andros. Bulkeley was a Tory-minded, law-and-order man

---

23. *Recs. Col. R.I.*, III, 258–59, 260, 267–69; Samuel G. Arnold, *History of the State of Rhode Island* (Providence, 1894), I, 519; Petition, Jan. 30, 1690, C.O. 5/905, pp. 189–91; "Reflections upon the Affairs of New England," *Wyllys Papers*, Conn. Hist. Soc. *Coll.*, XXI, 326. Walter Clarke's unwillingness to serve as governor in 1689–1690 may have had something to do with his Quakerism. Whatever the problem, he had ovecome it by 1696, when he again became governor for a year. *Recs. Col. R.I.*, III, 312, 331.

of tremendous conviction who has left us the best, albeit biased, account of Connecticut's struggles during and after the revolution. Since they were no longer a "Body politick," Connecticut people could not possibly hold an election then or at any time, argued Bulkeley, until the King either confirmed the charter or settled a legal government upon them which permitted it. Until then they were still under Andros' commission; any action on their part contrary to it was rebellion and treason against the Crown and a usurpation over the people. Bulkeley demanded a continuation of the Dominion government until such time as the King commanded differently. Government was divinely sanctioned, and colonies could no more choose their own than they could their king.

Both Fitch and the moderates were repelled by such talk and continued their struggle over control of the government. Although Robert Treat and John Allyn were unable to prevent an election, by considerable maneuver they were able to dictate what the freemen voted for on May 9. Three alternatives faced the Connecticut voter as he marked his paper in town meeting: a continuation of government under Andros' commission; control given to a Committee of Safety until instructions arrived from England; or resumption of the former government which Andros had interrupted in 1687. Fitch's scheme for a fresh election never was posed. Connecticut's freemen, given only the three choices, voted, of course, for their old government under the charter, and the colony took up where it had left off two years before. Treat and Allyn and the other gentlemen of the old oligarchy returned to their familiar seats on the council, as did an angry James Fitch, although he was pretty much alone. To fill a vacancy, Fitz-John Winthrop, another Andros councillor, was invited to sit with them, but he surprisingly refused to serve.[24]

Bulkeley was outraged over what he called the "revolution." He lumped together both Fitch's people and the moderates, charging them with an attempt "to erect a democratical empire of and for themselves." They were usurpers who had overridden the King's will; without a taint of legality they had forced themselves upon the people.

24. For a discussion of Connecticut, I have relied primarily upon Gershom Bulkeley's two tracts, *The People's Right to Election* . . . (Philadelphia, 1689), *Andros Tracts*, II, 85–102, and *Will and Doom, or the miseries of Connecticut* . . . , Conn. Hist. Soc. *Coll.*, III, 69–269. Helpful, too, were Robert M. Bliss, Jr., "Connecticut, 1676–1708: The Institutionalization of the Organic Society" (unpubl. A.M. thesis, Univ. of Wisconsin, 1967), ch. III; Dunn, *Puritans and Yankees*, pp. 286–89; and Richard L. Bushman, *From Puritan to Yankee: Character and the Social Order in Connecticut, 1690–1765* (Cambridge, Mass., 1967), pp. 89–91.

Fitch must have resented inclusion with the Treats, the Allyns, and the old guard; although both sides agreed to resume the government, he and his party were boldly intent on running out the moderates at the next election. Fitch, whose primary interests were land speculation and popular power, had his own reasons for wishing to control the colony.[25] So, too, did his opponents, who endeavored to keep what they had enjoyed for some time at the head of Connecticut's government. But resumption of charter government was risky business, since it meant little unless the Crown confirmed it. For unconfirmed, it invited attack from dissidents of several kinds who did not find the old way of doing things to their liking. For many months to follow, Connecticut government struggled to persuade the King to restore the charter of 1662 and let the settlers continue as before.[26]

Still, in contrast to Massachusetts, the smaller New England colonies seemed to accept the Glorious Revolution with less a spirit of revolution than relief that a galling interruption had ceased. Samuel Wyllys found them "tolerably quiet the times considered," and although they were not without "discontents and murmurings," they were spared, in the two or three years which followed, the confusion, almost anarchy, of Massachusetts and the violence and bloodshed of New York.[27]

25. Bulkeley, *Will and Doom*, p. 151. For some of Fitch's activities, see *Recs. Col. Conn.*, III, *passim*, and particularly p. 456 n. See also John Wheeler's remonstrance to the General Court about the Fitch group's monopoly of power and offices in New London, town and county, May 8, 1690, *Wyllys Papers*, Conn. Hist. Soc. *Coll.*, XXI, 318–20. See again Bushman, *From Puritan to Yankee*, pp. 89–91.

26. C.O. 5/855, #52; Conn. Hist. Soc. *Coll.*, XXIV, 24–29, 37–39, 41; Hinman, ed., *Letters from the English Kings . . . to Connecticut*, pp. 188–91.

27. "Reflections upon the Affairs of New England," *Wyllys Papers*, Conn. Hist. Soc. *Coll.*, XXI, 326.

14 The Glorious Revolution in New York and Maryland

To Lieutenant Governor Nicholson in New York the overthrow of Andros at Boston could not have come at a worse time. But probably for any royal governor, no time was favorable for being on the wrong side of rebellion. By April 26, 1689, news of the goings on at Boston had reached New York, and Nicholson read a copy of the Massachusetts Declaration to his handful of councillors on that day. All told, Andros had appointed eight New Yorkers to his Dominion council in 1688, but he had taken several of them to Massachusetts with him, and they, of course, were imprisoned along with him in April, while Brockholls, the army officer and a Catholic, was seized by the soldiers at Pemaquid in Maine. Two other resident councillors in New York begged off from serving late in May, leaving only Nicholas Bayard, Stephen Van Cortlandt, and Frederick Philips available to do business in an emergency, and one occurred shortly.[1]

1. *CSPCol.*, 1688–1692, *Addenda*, #2734; Hall, Leder, and Kammen, eds., *The Glorious Revolution in America*, p. 107.

Reaction to the alarming news from Boston and Connecticut took several forms in New York. It began in early May in Suffolk County on the eastern half of Long Island where one might expect it. For years the settlers there had been at odds with the government and its restrictions upon their trade; they had hoped to separate themselves from the Duke's colony and join their Congregational friends in Connecticut, where a good many of them had originated, a wholly improbable dream given Governor Dongan's schemes for annexing Connecticut and New York's inability to pay its own way as it was. Boston's Declaration, announcing the revolt and imprisonment of Andros, startled Suffolk County people into a bold declaration of their own. They reviewed their longstanding grievances under arbitrary government and, citing the revolution in England and the turnover at Boston, agreed that duty to God dictated a securing of the colony's forts at New York and Albany against a "forraign ennemy" and placing them into hands they could trust. Besides demanding a return of tax money lately extracted from them, they encouraged the seizure of all enemies to public peace and prosperity and the "fundamental laws of our English nation."[2] As they had led the struggle for a charter in 1683 to guarantee their English liberties, Long Islanders led the way again in 1689 to protect the colony from a government which denied these liberties, particularly when both mother country and mother colony had set the pattern of revolt.

The New England disease spread quickly. The council might have kept the peace, it claimed, had not the "seed of sedition . . . blazed from thence to some outward skirts of this province." Setauket on Long Island had "shoocke" off the government by the middle of May, and a little later the council was alarmed by "uprores" in all parts of the colony, provoked, the members claimed, by the libelous reports from Boston. Actually, Francis Nicholson and his skeleton council were in no position to keep the peace, once New England had overthrown the Dominion. They had sat on the "strange" news of William's invasion of England, first heard by way of Philadelphia, since as long ago as early March in order to avoid tumult. Despite their government's silence, the colonists learned it by rumor and then fact from other colonies. Nicholson's source of official information had been choked off, first by Increase Mather's efforts in London and then by Andros' imprisonment at Boston. As April turned into May the council found itself more and more isolated from New York colonists, who under-

2. C.O. 5/1081/3; *CSPCol., 1688–1692*, #104. For an uprising among the Queen's County militia about this time, see C.O. 5/1081/3A; Hall, Leder, and Kammen, eds., *Glo. Rev. in Am.*, pp. 103–4; Jerome R. Reich, *Leisler's Rebellion, A Study of Democracy in New York, 1664–1720* (Chicago, 1953), p. 56 and n. 10.

standably suspected that Nicholson and his friends deliberately suppressed the news owing to loyalty to James.[3]

The council's control grew more and more tenuous for a variety of reasons. While the local and specific causes of Massachusetts' rebellion against the Dominion had accumulated only since the loss of the colony charter in 1684, New Yorkers' grievances, many of them, at least, were almost a generation old. The economy of the colony, although promising, had never paid off, a disappointment which explains its governors' reluctance to cut loose East and West New Jersey and the lower counties along the Delaware, to say nothing of Dongan's and Andros' attempts to annex Connecticut, primarily for its revenue. A successful frontier policy against the French and in behalf of the Iroquois was a financial drain, much greater than the colony could afford given its income. Hence taxes were high upon a people whose economy was out of joint and frustrated, said many, by the monopolies and favors granted to a small segment of the population which made up an oligarchy of privileged people, some of whom were continuously council members.[4]

Earlier the short-lived assembly of 1683, granted by the Duke but guided by the Charter of Libertyes which it had drafted, might have made it possible for more settlers to share the colony's economic benefits. Granted the council under Dongan had approved the charter along with the freemen's representatives, placing responsibility for government closer to the people doubtless would have improved their means of livelihood; at least in 1683 they thought it would. But the assembly under the new charter hardly won the chance to do much at all before it was quashed when colonial policy tightened as James became King; the government returned to its customary narrow form and personnel, consisting again of governor and council alone. The shift to the Dominion in 1688 did little to alter these conditions, for Andros invited most of Dongan's council to sit in his own, including Bayard, Van Cortlandt, and Philips.[5] And it was these people who ruled with Lieutenant Governor Nicholson in 1689, less those who had joined Andros at Boston in time for the explosion there. Besides economic troubles, fear of a Catholic conspiracy gripped many New Yorkers. This widespread

3. Hall, Leder, and Kammen, eds., *Glo. Rev. in Am.*, pp. 102, 105–6, 107; C.O. 5/905, pp. 81–84; *CSPCol., 1689–1692*, #121; "A Narrative in Answer to Their Majties Letter," *Doc. Hist N.Y.*, II (1849), 392–93.

4. See ch. 6 above and Lawrence H. Leder, *Robert Livingston, 1654–1728, and the Politics of Colonial New York* (Chapel Hill, N.C., 1961), pp. 57–58. Edward Randolph blamed Governor Dongan for New York's economic difficulties. See two letters from Randolph to Blathwayt, Nov. 23, 1687, and Sept. 12, 1688, in Hall, Leder, and Kammen, eds., *Glo. Rev. in Am.*, pp. 93, 96.

5. See chs. 6 and 11 above.

apprehension did not make the governing tasks of Nicholson and the council any easier, maybe impossible, after the news from Boston circulated. The Declaration there of April 18 was rich in imagery of the "bloody Devotees of Rome" and the "great Scarlet Whore," whose not so subtle vehicle for conquest was the Dominion of New England.[6] But New Yorkers needed no reminder from Boston of popish perfidy. They did not have to look very sharply to find Catholics in positions of trust in their own colony. After all, their former proprietor was Catholic, as was his Governor Dongan, who after being relieved by Nicholson in 1688 had never left the colony but busied himself at his estate on Long Island with who knew what scheming. Matthew Plowman, formerly the Duke's collector of customs and now the King's, was an avowed Roman, as were several royal officers at the head of Nicholson's troops. And the colonists were not of one mind about the lieutenant governor either; a "pretended protestant," they called him, whose closeness to James, like Andros, lent considerable suspicion to his activities.[7] Probably the fears aroused by the presence of Catholics in their midst, bad as they were, would have been less acute were it not for the spreading trouble with the French in the north. Albany, for all its importance, was wholly vulnerable to attack, and with its fall the road to the city was open to the aggressor, to say nothing of the rewards of the fur trade. William's invasion of England, James's escape to France and Louis, Nicholson's apparent reluctance to divulge any information about the Revolution and proclaim the new King and Queen, all of these in combination were more than many New Yorkers could stomach in the spring of 1689.

In view of worsening conditions Nicholson and his handful of adherents had little firm ground to stand upon in April and May. Seeking support, the governor wrote to Fitz-John Winthrop of New London, one of Andros' councillors from Connecticut, asking him to come to New York to consult about what ought to be done, for it was apparent that something should be done and promptly. Winthrop refused to join them, claimed he was ill or some such excuse, just as he would a few weeks later when Governor Treat and Secretary Allyn begged him to come to Hartford and help them head off Colonel James Fitch and his popular party from taking over the Connecticut government.[8] In

6. C. M. Andrews, ed., *Narratives of the Insurrections*, pp. 175–76.

7. A Declaration of the Inhabitants Soudjers, C.O. 5/1081/6; *Doc. Hist. N.Y.*, II (1849), 10; *ibid.*, 3–4; Hall, Leder, and Kammen, eds., *Glo. Rev. in Am.*, pp. 109–10.

8. Apr. 27, 1689, *Winthrop Papers*, M.H.S. *Coll.*, 6th ser., III, 497; Robert M. Bliss, Jr., "Connecticut, 1676–1708: The Institutionalization of the Organic Society" (unpubl. A.M. thesis, Univ. of Wisconsin, 1967), pp. 48–49; Richard S. Dunn, *Puritans and Yankees*, p. 288.

order to hold things together Nicholson desperately called a convention of his councillors, city officials, and captains of the militia, including Jacob Leisler, to knit together, he hoped, a stable body of leaders who might guide the colony through what looked like a rapidly approaching crisis. Within two weeks' time this group issued three proclamations which, if they meant anything, signaled to the inhabitants a state of panic in their government. The first ordered that all income from the customs, excise taxes, warehouse receipts, and similar forms of revenue be sunk into fortifying the city against threat of a French invasion, and that the city militia commence digging defensive works immediately with pick and shovel. Next came a proclamation against mutiny, sedition, and rebellion, followed eight days later by a similar document against rebellion and internal jealousies, which again encouraged defense against a foreign enemy. These last two Jacob Leisler signed as a militia captain along with Bayard, Van Cortlandt, and Philips of the council.[9] Meanwhile, several merchants refused to pay customs to the government on the claim that it lacked a legal foundation. Leisler was one of these, withholding duties on a shipment of wine then riding in the harbor because the collector, Matthew Plowman, was a Catholic and unfit to hold office since William's accession.[10]

A crucial disagreement on May 30 between Nicholson's redcoats and the city militia over posting a sentinel precipitated a violent argument. It ended with the governor's threatening to "pistol" a militia officer and an excited shout that he would rather set fire to the city than put up with more insubordination. The next day his inflammatory words, wildly exaggerated, rocked through the city. Most of the militia quickly defected and with little trouble seized the fort. After several days of uneasiness, Captain Jacob Leisler, a German from Frankfurt who had been twenty years or more a merchant in New York, emerged as commander of the rebel soldiers—or as an unsympathetic contemporary expressed it: after casting off the governor, "up Jump into the saddle hott brain'd Capt Leisller who has his hands full of worke about the City of Newyorke. . . ." Leisler would have agreed about having his hands full, since the immediate prospects of control were not promising. For several weeks his authority over the people, even the militia, was tenuous, although a sudden alarm over an attack by sea (falsely spread, said his enemies) brought five militia captains to his side and 400 colonists to pledge support. Election of a Committee of Safety which confirmed his leadership on June 8 was helpful, and in

9. C.O. 5/1081/3B–C; C.O. 5/1081/5; CSPCol., 1689–1692, Addenda, #2740.
10. "Council Minutes," Hall, Leder, and Kammen, eds., Glo. Rev. in Am., p. 106; A Modest and Impartial Narrative . . . of New-York (1690), Andrews, ed., Narratives, p. 322.

a few days Governor Nicholson fled to England to report the debacle, leaving New York to Leisler and his fellow rebels.[11]

Like Nicholson earlier, Leisler looked elsewhere for support and even approbation. He wrote to Connecticut and Boston, elaborately explaining his motives and almost begging for approval. He entertained observers from Hartford, including James Fitch, who consulted with "noble & Loyall Capt Leisler" about defensive needs and the disarming of Catholics.[12] To justify their actions Leisler and the militia, in a Declaration and then an Address to Their Majesties, harped again and again on the Catholic menace and the fear of betrayal to the enemy by their popish and tyrannical rulers. Willingly they awaited orders from their King, they said, having saved New York for him from James's people and the Fench in the spirit of the revolution in England. On June 22 Leisler and his militia companies proclaimed William and Mary before the fort and then again at the City Hall, where they marched when the mayor (Stephen Van Cortlandt) and the aldermen refused to do so without specific orders from the Crown.[13]

By the end of June the Committee of Safety was in good working order. Its members had elected a moderator and clerk, and with Leisler as captain of the fort and later as commander in chief of the province, they managed the colony for the rest of the summer. Besides commissioning a number of new officers, including a customs collector, they appointed a day of thanksgiving and reaffirmed the earlier claim "that ye taking & securing of the fort Is singely & Solely for their maties service," while they humbly awaited confirmation and orders from the Crown. When the Committee learned that England and France had declared war, it agreed to use the £773 12s. 6d. of customs money, seized earlier, to repair the fort, "keeping perfect acct." of the charges. About the same time Leisler formed an Association of Protestants which declared openly against all those who stood out against him

11. The action in New York is described in the following documents: "To the Governor and Committee of Safety at Boston" [June 4, 1689], Doc. Hist. N.Y., II (1849), 3–4; A Declaration of the Inhabitants Soudjers, ibid., p. 10; Depositions of Hendrick Jacobsen and Albert Bosch, ibid., pp. 11–13; "A Memoriall," ibid., pp. 55–56; ibid., pp. 7–8. But see also and compare A Modest and Impartial Narrative (1690), Andrews, ed., Narratives, pp. 323–29; and Colonel Bayard's Narrative of Occurrences in New-York, in N.Y. Col. Docs., III, 636–48. For Jacob Leisler, see Doc. Hist. N.Y., II (1849), Introductory; C.O. 5/855, #16; CSPCol., 1689–1692, #242.

12. Doc. Hist. N.Y., II (1849), 3–6, 14, 16–17, 20–22, 24–25.

13. Ibid., 10–11; Hall, Leder, and Kammen, eds., Glo. Rev. in Am., pp. 109–10; Order for proclaiming William and Mary, June 22, 1689, C.O. 5/1081/21; John Tudor to Nicholson, New York, Aug. 1689, CSPCol., 1689–1692, #365.

and his government and who continued to honor the illegal and arbitrary commissions of the "Late James II." [14] Although Leisler and the Committee slightly improved their grip upon the colony during the summer, the crisis did not subside, owing primarily to the strength of their opposition, which by several means they attempted to reduce. Little by little they succeeded in firing old officers and appointing new and in arresting and imprisoning the most militant opposers, except for some like Nicholas Bayard, who escaped to Albany, and Stephen Van Cortlandt, who remained "loose" but inconspicuous. It was an uneasy summer for those in command. Although they managed to control the city, some of the countryside was obstinate and slow to come around, particularly Albany, where the city government on the first of July happily proclaimed William and Mary (in both English and Dutch) but refused outright to throw in its lot with Leisler and remained outside his control for several months.[15] Nevertheless, the last support of the Dominion had gone under; but as it was with Massachusetts, King William was in no hurry to settle the business of New York, for who was Jacob Leisler, anyway?

In the summer of 1689 the people of Maryland knew as little about Jacob Leisler as the King. Both friend and foe of rebellion in New England and New York agreed that the overthrow of Andros' Dominion at Boston and the bold resumption of charter governments in Rhode Island and Connecticut went a long way to encourage revolt in New York and Leisler's rise to power. One would assume that the upheaval in Maryland, coming in the middle of July, was spurred by news of Leisler's success. Granted the people of Maryland had grievances heavy enough to provoke their own kind of response, knowledge of, and sympathy for, other colonists who rebelled under similar, oppressive circumstances would be at least an added impetus to revolt if not an excuse. There was plenty of time for news of the New York rebellion to reach St. Mary's and other Maryland counties, but, in fact, it seems that it did not. What the Protestants did under John Coode was probably innocent of encouragement from New York and even Boston, for it is reasonably clear that Maryland colonists knew nothing of either rebellion until some time after their own.

Between the continuing attack in London upon Lord Baltimore's

14. Proceedings of the Committee of Safety, June 27–Aug. 15, 1689, C.O. 5/1081/26, 28, 29, 46; CSPCol., 1689–1692, #352.

15. Stephen Van Cortlandt to Andros, New York, July 9, 1689, N.Y. Col. Docs., III, 590–97; same to Blathwayt, Aug. 1, Dec. 18, 1689, BPCol. Wmsbg., v. IX; Doc. Hist. N.Y., II (1849), 7.

charter in the 1680's and the swell of discontent in Maryland at the same time, it was a nice question which would topple the proprietary government first. James II continued his scheme to annihilate proprietaries in America, for he believed them increasingly prejudicial to the kind of empire he was molding in the New World, particularly to his customs, and he took steps to make private colonies more dependent upon the Crown. In April 1687 he ordered his attorney general to issue a second *quo warranto* against the Maryland charter, but before the court handed down judgment England and, primarily, James were overwhelmed by the events of 1688.[16] It is very possible that rising dissatisfaction in Maryland was an added impetus to James's and the Privy Council's attack upon the charter. Reports from Maryland and Virginia in late 1687 described both colonies as "too ripe for disturbances," and—prophetically—that seditious men in Maryland "will be very apt to pretend religion the better to carry on their evill Designs."[17] If Baltimore could not keep peace in his own colony, all the more reason to tuck it under the Crown. Like New York's, Maryland's grievances were longstanding, and as uncertainty intensified, long memories prevailed among those who carried the colonists' burden against the demands of the proprietor and his government.

Back in 1681, during Fendall's and Coode's uprising at the time of the Exclusion Crisis, Governor Culpeper of Virginia had gratuitously remarked that Maryland was in "torment" and that old Lord Baltimore's "politic maxims" either were not being pursued or were "unsuited to this age."[18] The appointment of William Joseph in late 1688 as president of the proprietary council in Maryland, really governor during the proprietor's absence, would seem an attempt by the present Lord Baltimore to prove right both of Culpeper's alternatives. Appropriately for the proprietor Governor Joseph was Catholic, but what appeared inappropriate for the time was his conception of an English colony and colonists articulated in his maiden speech and the demands which accompanied it before the fall session of the Maryland assembly. In more a sermon than an address, the new president reviewed for his hearers a stiff argument for the divine right of kings and governments. Power in the assembly, he declared, was originally from God; it descended through the King to His Lordship and finally to him and them in Maryland. He quickly followed with a demand, based on a duty to God, for new laws to suppress heinous and habitual crimes in Maryland, such as drunkenness, adultery, swearing, Sabbath breaking,

16. Effingham to [?], Virginia, Feb. 7, 1687, BPCol. Wmsbg., v. XIV; George Chalmers, *Political Annals*, I, 371.

17. [?] to Lord Baltimore, Oct. 1687, BPCol. Wmsbg., v. VI.

18. Culpeper to Lords of Trade, Dec. 12, 1681, *CSPCol., 1681–1685*, #319.

and several less exciting trespasses. Next came an order to prohibit the exportation of bulk tobacco from both Maryland and Virginia as a practice injurious to the King's customs. For some time colonists had claimed the sale of tobacco in bulk was favorable to the small Maryland planter, who had trouble enough as it was eking out a living in competition with the large producer. Hard on its heels came another demand, this one for passing (unanimously) an act of general thanksgiving to celebrate annually the birth of the Prince of Wales, James's heir, born on June 10 of that year. The president's speech closed with a curt reminder to respect the proprietor, a reminder charged with the command that the members swear a fresh oath of fidelity to Lord Baltimore without *salvo jure* to the King. But 1688 was a bad year for Englishmen brought up under the anachronism of divine right, whether they were Gershom Bulkeley, William Joseph, Lord Baron of Baltimore, or James II.[19]

Reluctantly the lower house agreed to pass new laws punishing whoredom and other moral lapses, not without informing the upper house that the trouble was not with the old laws but with the magistrates who failed to enforce them. Reluctantly, too, the deputies agreed to celebrate annually the Prince of Wales's birthday but added an amendment which limited the act to three years' time only or to the end of the next assembly. But despite the King's command and the president's urging to prohibit the export of bulk tobacco, the members refused outright, as did the Virginia burgesses, explaining simply that it was a bad bill, prejudicial both to the King's and proprietor's customs and particularly to the people of Maryland, who would be left with a good deal of rotting tobacco on their hands.[20]

Not as easily disposed of was the new oath of fidelity to the proprietor. The deputies refused it at the outset, and a struggle continued between the houses for several days, holding up all other business until it was settled. President Joseph did not ease the tension one bit when he equated fidelity with allegiance, and to refuse allegiance, he said, implied rebellion, a remark the deputies deeply resented. After a fruitless joint session, the president prorogued the assembly. While the house still sat unofficially, he pushed the oath on Speaker Kenelm Cheseldyne and the other members; after lengthy debate they took it but as separate individuals, not in legal capacity as a lower house, an evasion which satisfied the president and council for the time being and allowed the assembly to get down to work.[21]

19. *Arch. of Md.*, VIII, 41–43; *ibid.*, XIII, 147.
20. *Ibid.,* 181, 184, 186, 209. For conflict over bulk tobacco, see *ibid.*, 168–69, 174, 175, 198–99; *ibid.*, VIII, 45–46, 63.
21. *Ibid.*, XIII, 153–63; *ibid.*, VIII, 62–63.

The struggle over bulk tobacco and the oath, about which the deputies felt very strongly, stirred them to stew again about the people's other grievances, resulting in a grand review of them all which they presented formally to the upper house in late 1688. Most of the complaints the upper chamber had heard before—certainly an indication that they had not been alleviated. There were several new ones: exaction of exorbitant fees in specie, not tobacco, and an attempt to collect all the proprietor's rents and fines in sterling; arbitrary sheriffs who held colonists for trial without charges. Rights and privileges of the lower house were involved in the claim that it was denied the choice of clerks serving joint committees. Much time went into complaining of the proprietor's dispensing of laws, or parts of laws, which did not suit him, a practice which smacked of James II's treatment of Parliament. Crowning them all, old and new, was again the galling demand for an oath of fidelity to Lord Baltimore. The upper house half-heartedly responded to the complaints, explaining that if they were true, there were adequate laws to answer the needs of the people. Labeling the list a "grievous paper of pretended Agrievances," the council packed it off to the proprietor in London.[22]

In January 1689 news arrived of James's warning about a "sudden Invasion from Holland"; it was accompanied by orders to alert Maryland's defenses against a foreign enemy. The council's response was a startling proclamation calling in the public arms for repair by local gunsmiths at St. Mary's, Mattapany, and Patuxent, all in St. Mary's County, where the government was seated. In tense times and in face of French and Indian threats from the north, the council's move was looked upon with great suspicion. With how much more distrust would the colonists have regarded the proclamation had they known—and maybe some of them did—that the councillors decided, once the weapons were fit for service, they would distribute them "upon occasion . . . into such hands as shall faithfully serve" the King, the proprietor, and the countryside, decisions the council itself would make.[23]

Earlier Maryland colonists had complained that the proprietor stood between them and the Crown, denying them a relationship with His Majesty which was natural and beneficial to subjects elsewhere. The grievance took on even sharper meaning in February 1689 when the council peremptorily intercepted and sent to Lord Baltimore two "private papers" from Maryland people destined for the King. What it meant to live in the "Dominion of Right Honorable Charles Lord Baron

22. *Ibid.*, XIII, 171–73, 185, 187–88, 191–93, 203, 207; *ibid.*, VIII, 43, 61, 63, 64, 220–23.

23. *Ibid.*, 56–57, 65, 67.

of Baltimore" was becoming more and more clear to Marylanders. Oaths of fidelity to the proprietor, courts of justice in his name, a president who ruled by divine right, a council which governed arbitrarily in the proprietor's interest alone, these were more than English subjects ought put up with. And now petitions to the King were stopped, denying them access to the throne, the right of all Englishmen.[24]

March was a month of "greate uproar and Tumult." The trouble began with several bloody rumors picked up from the Indians, who claimed that some of the proprietor's "great Men," including Henry Darnall and Edward Pye of the upper house, had hired the Senecas to butcher the Protestants. The bloody deed was to be done before an expected fleet arrived from England; if it were not, once the ships were there, the Protestants were prepared to kill all the Catholics, for which they, too, had hired the Indians. There were accompanying rumors, equally wild, one that Englishmen were in revolt and had already cut off the head of the King. In a short week much of Maryland was in panic. The legislature was not in session, and the leading settlers were scattered about at their own businesses. Even the cool heads of respected men like Henry Jowles of the lower house were convinced of a conspiracy between Catholics and Indians. They begged the government to return the arms to the people and appealed as a last resort to William Digges, the only Protestant on the council, to help secure them all from the common enemy, that is, the Indians *and* the proprietor's government, for it had come to that.[25]

The gullibility of Maryland colonists is credible today only when one accepts the fact that many of them dearly wanted to believe the worst of the proprietary government, and a combination of circumstances encouraged it. For instance, in the midst of the "greate uproar and Tumult," the council prorogued before it met the April session of the assembly until October, a session the colonists had counted upon for redress of grievances and calming of fears and suspicions. One wonders how many knew that Henry Darnall had learned from President Joseph the "good newes" of James II's escape to France, for which Darnall heartily rejoiced and for "whose happy restoration" he most earnestly wished and daily prayed.[26]

William Joseph and several members of his council, Darnall, Digges,

24. *Ibid.*, 64–65; Sarah Bland to Blathwayt, Mar. 16, 1689, BPCol. Wmsbg., v. XVII.

25. *Arch. of Md.*, VIII, 70–76, 77–78, 82, 83, 84–85; *CSPCol.*, 1689–1692, #56; "Narrative of Coll. Henry Darnall . . ." in J. Thomas Scharf, *History of Maryland* (3 vols., Baltimore, 1879), I, 338–39.

26. *Ibid.; Arch. of Md.*, VIII, 62, 69, 88.

and Pye, consented to redistribute the public arms. Eventually they got the better of Henry Jowles's fears and those of men like him, many of whom had already armed themselves in the best way possible. After forming a committee, including Darnall and Digges and a dozen others, to which they invited Cheseldyne and Jowles, both burgesses, they traveled about the countryside, attempting with tremendous effort to track down the extravagant stories of Indian preparations. Their prompt report helped to settle the country; it insisted that a plot between Catholics and Indians was a "sleveless fear . . . fomented by the artifice of some ill-minded persons," not in Maryland but in Stafford County, Virginia. For their own malicious ends and with the help of a few like-minded people in Maryland who hoped to "raise the country," they had almost succeeded in provoking not just plunder and pillage but outright civil war. Luckily, by the end of the month the colony was largely free of the worst of the rumors; most of the people had put down their arms and returned to their homes, more settled in their minds about the future, at least for the time being.[27]

The committee which traced the origin of the March "Tumults" to Stafford County, Virginia, may have been looking only for a scapegoat, but it unconsciously had hold of a hotter piece of intelligence than it or the proprietor's government, or maybe even Virginia's, could handle. Colonists in Stafford County had been disaffected for some time and with good reason. The most western of Virginia counties and farthest from Jamestown, it lay in the Northern Neck between the Potomac and Rappahannock Rivers, the very area which Charles II had first granted away to a group of proprietors as early as 1649. Settlers of Stafford County had struggled against these proprietors frequently, and they were not altogether free of them yet, owing to James's recent assignment of the northern part of Virginia to Lord Fairfax.[28] A frontier county, its settlers always had been exposed to Indians, both Virginia's and Maryland's. It was in Stafford County that the Indian troubles commenced which set off Bacon's Rebellion, and it was to Stafford County—directly across the Potomac from Charles County in Maryland—that Maryland dissidents like Josias Fendall escaped when pro-

27. "Narrative of Coll. Henry Darnall," pp. 338–39; *Arch. of Md.*, VIII, 78–79, 80–82, 86–93.

28. For discussion of the Northern Neck see chs. 3 and 4 above. See also Add. Mss., 30372, f. 24b, and complaints against Virginia proprietors, July 26, Aug. 1, 1690, C.O. 5/1358, 25–28. In 1687 Thomas, Lord Culpeper, sold to George Brent of Virginia and three Londoners about 30,000 acres of the Northern Neck "in or neare" Stafford County, some miles distant from any settlement. Prospects were for building a town and fortifications and granting freedom of religion to settlers, James II having approved. C.O. 389/9, pp. 418–20.

prietary government was too hot for them. Since the river was narrower there than downstream near St. Mary's, there was more exchange between the two colonies than elsewhere, particularly of rumor and gossip.[29]

While Marylanders lived on the edge of upheaval, news of the Glorious Revolution reached Virginia in the middle of March 1689. There was a general reaction primarily because the accounts were garbled and uncertain, leaving a great deal to the settlers' imaginations. Before long it was noised about, chiefly from the "mouths of the Mobile," that there was no longer a King in England and therefore no real government in Virginia. Reaction was strongest in Stafford County, where discontent was rifest and the possibilities of rebellion most prevalent. It was led by a fiery preacher, John Waugh, and fortified by the same Indian rumors which had so upset people across the river, that the Senecas, massed by thousands, were ready to join with the Catholics to do away with the Protestants of both colonies on a day already fixed. As a result a number of settlers there were prepared not only to gather in arms and repel the bloodshed which they believed awaited them but also to "fly in the face of ye Government" of Virginia. Some, it was said, contemplated crossing over to Maryland, invited by the rebels there, in order to make the uprising a joint operation between the two colonies. Virginia's peace and quiet were indeed "for some little time very doubtful," to say the least. Of the northern parts, including Stafford, where disruptive rumors were sharpest, "matters . . . very pressingly" tended to a rebellion and a "great flame was kindled by the blasts of popular Breaths. . . ."[30]

Only by the vigilance, care, and prudence of Nicholas Spencer and the Virginia council—Governor Effingham was sojourning in England —were fears and panic partly quieted in Virginia late in March. Yet the uproar was not dampened altogether, for it cropped up sporadically like "Hydra's heads" until the last week of April when the happy news of the accession of the Prince of Orange to England's throne arrived along with strict orders from the Privy Council to proclaim him and his princess as the English King and Queen. The commands were promptly obeyed on April 27 at "James City"; orders were sent

29. T. J. Wertenbaker, *Virginia Under the Stuarts* (Princeton, N.J., 1914), p. 146; Andrews, ed., *Narratives*, pp. 13, 16 n.; Wesley Frank Craven, *The Southern Colonies in the Seventeenth Century* (Baton Rouge, La., 1949), p. 412.

30. Nicholas Spencer to Blathwayt, James City, Apr. 27, 1689, BPCol. Wmsbg., v. XVI; Spencer to Lords of Trade, James City, Apr. 29, 1689, C.O. 5/1358, 3–4; New-York Historical Society *Collections* for 1868 (New York, 1868), pp. 37–38; *CSPCol., 1689–1692,* #56; *ibid.,* #92; Fairfax Harrison, "Parson Waugh's Tumult," *Va. Mag. of Hist. and Biog.,* 30 (1922), 31–37.

immediately to all Virginia counties, where they helped to dispel the causes of uncertainty and tumult—except in Stafford.[31]

There the trouble burst out all over again. In early June a "Rabble of abt two hundred" rescued from the sheriff three settlers accused of "forgeing the pretended conspiracy" of Catholic and Indians against the Protestants. The trouble was a good deal deeper than uneasiness about affairs in England, for it appeared to set the poor upon the rich. Nicholas Spencer was convinced that the plotters' purpose was to plant the idea of conspiracy so firmly in the people's minds that they might use it as a cover to arm themselves and plunder and rob the men of property, in fact, make possession of a good estate "a Crime sufficient to have laid a man open to popular Rage." Moreover, the violent unrest had spread out of Stafford into Rappahannock County as well. No wonder Spencer was apprehensive. With Stafford County already in uproar, any disturbance, such as an explosion in Maryland, would uncork full-scale rebellion in Virginia, too. At the very time Governor Effingham was reporting smugly to the Lords of Trade in London that his colony enjoyed "full peace and plenty," Spencer and the council were fervently praying that Virginia might escape wholesale revolution. It did so, but barely, and again it was the prompt action of Nicholas Spencer and a small number of Virginia councillors who forceably suppressed what looked like outright rebellion in Stafford County. They seized the Reverend John Waugh and a handful of other leaders, and this turned the trick besides cutting off the source of rumors which had so upset the people.[32]

The difference between Virginia and Maryland in the spring and summer of 1689 was that the proprietary government proclaimed no king at all. Why, is not altogether clear. Earlier, on February 20, the Lords of Trade had instructed Lord Baltimore to order Their Majesties proclaimed in Maryland; the proprietor promptly dispatched a messenger, a Mr. Broom, who got no farther than Plymouth, where he suddenly died. Fearing that the message had miscarried, Baltimore sent a second a few days later which included a duplicate of the order. But on the tenth of June Nicholas Spencer reported from Virginia that Their Majesties had not yet been proclaimed in Maryland. Once in August and again in September Lord Baltimore was brought on the carpet to explain the delay, and each time he insisted he had sent the

31. Spencer to Lords of Trade, Apr. 29, 1689, C.O. 5/1358, 3–4; Spencer to Blathwayt, Apr. 27, 1689, BPCol. Wmsbg., v. XVI; O. Burton Adams, "The Virginia Reaction to the Glorious Revolution, 1689–1692," *West Virginia History,* XXIX (Oct. 1967), 8–9.

32. Spencer to Blathwayt, June 30 [20?], 1689, BPCol. Wmsbg., v. XVII; Effingham to [?], May 28, 1689, C.O. 5/1358, 1. See again Fairfax Harrison, "Parson Waugh's Tumult," pp. 35–37.

orders. Either Baltimore was lying or his messages and commands had reached their mark only to be ignored by his proprietary government. Had it voiced honestly its sentiments, it doubtless would have admitted a loyalty to James as did Henry Darnall a few months earlier, and as John Coode would frequently charge against the lot of them.[33]

When Virginia proclaimed the new English monarchs in late April, John Coode of Maryland, a member of the lower house and long an enemy of proprietary government, formed "an association in arms for the defense of the Protestant Religion," in behalf of King William and Queen Mary in Maryland.[34] Just what the organization purported to be at the time is not clear, since Coode and his "associators" were not immediately active, at least not ostensibly so. It may be that they deliberately refrained from action, giving the proprietary government a last chance to collect itself and decently perform its duty. As things turned out, it is more likely they bided their time only to perfect their plans. That they had plans for some time before they used them is fairly certain. Gerrard Sly, a Maryland merchant then in London, attempted about this time to dissuade Kenelm Cheseldyne, one of Coode's cronies and speaker of the lower house, from pushing further the "design" against the Maryland government. Sly was sure it was unnecessary; the Catholics, he said, would fall of their own accord, which doubtless meant that as a result of the revolution in England, the proprietor and his Catholic supporters would lose power in Maryland soon enough as it was. Whatever the reason, the Associators were quiet for several weeks, or at least seemed to be, although they certainly had not scrapped their plans.[35]

What rankled most was the government's failure to proclaim Wil-

33. *CSPCol., 1689–1692*, #25, #38, #390, #417, #422; Memorandum, Letter rec'd from Coll. Spencer, dated 10th June . . . C.O. 324/5, pp. 71, 73; *Arch. of Md.*, VIII, 67–69, 112–13, 114; John Coode to Earl of Shrewsbury, Sept. 22, 1689, *ibid.*, 123–24.

34. Francis Edgar Sparks, *Causes of the Maryland Revolution of 1689*, in *Johns Hopkins University Studies in Historical and Political Science*, 14th ser., XI–XII (Baltimore, 1896), 572; Justin Winsor, *Narrative and Critical History of America* (8 vols., Boston, 1884–89), III, 551. As far as I know there is only one description of John Coode, and this is by an enemy written ten years after the rebellion. In 1699 Coode was in trouble in Virginia, and Governor Francis Nicholson issued a proclamation ordering his arrest including this description: "He being of a Middle Stature a deformed person, his face resembling that of a Baboon or munckeys, Club-footed his feet Standing inwards one to the other and a Notorious Coward." H. R. McIlwaine and W. L. Hall, eds., *Executive Journals of the Council of Colonial Virginia* (5 vols., Richmond, Va., 1925–45), I, 419.

35. Mr. Bertrand to Bishop of London, Sept. 1689 [?], *Arch. of Md.*, VIII, 116. Gerrard Sly was John Coode's stepson. Andrews, *Colonial Period*, II, 378 n. B. Coode went to court against Sly before the revolution over an estate. M. G. Kammen, "The Causes of the Maryland Revolution of 1689," *Maryland Historical Magazine* (Dec. 1960), p. 324.

liam and Mary. Although the Catholic and Indian conspiracy had been proved pretty much a hoax by several leading colonists, including some of the lower house like Jowles and Cheseldyne, the fact that Virginians had declared for William, and Marylanders had not, allowed plenty of opportunity for discontented settlers to revive the scare and add to it the conclusion that orders for proclaiming Their Majesties must have arrived but were deliberately suppressed by an evil government. Toward the middle of June the Protestants were "rageingly earnest" for breaking out in favor of William and Mary, and threatened off and on to do so regardless of their government. It was this threat which had so frightened Nicholas Spencer and the Virginians at James City, where they had scarcely succeeded in quieting their own settlers. They were apprehensive lest the Protestants in Maryland go ahead on their own and "unhinge the whole Constitution" there, dissolving it altogether with drastic repercussions in both colonies.[36]

By July 16 the lid was off, and John Coode and the Protestant Associators marched on St. Mary's. What contained them until that date is a mystery, and maybe even what provoked them specifically at that time is, too. Probably news that Colonel William Digges and some of his people were turning the government buildings into garrisons, fortifying them against possibilities, did it. Anyway, Coode, having raised "men up Potomeck," with more from Charles County—which was directly across the Potomac from Virginia's Stafford—marched them to the capital. By the time they reached the State House, their number had swelled to several hundred. Colonel Digges prepared to defend the government but gave up to Coode when his men refused to fight. Immediately the Associators took command and seized the colony records. A counterforce under Henry Darnall and Nicholas Sewall on Patuxent River failed to materialize; although the officers rallied, their men accepted Coode's claim that he rose only to save the colony from the Catholics and Indians and to proclaim the new King and Queen. Expecting no danger from Coode and his followers, they would not stir in the proprietor's behalf.

Without enough men to defend the government, Baltimore's deputies tried two other diversions. They offered command of the colony's troops to Henry Jowles; he refused with a "very civill answer" and then joined Coode at St. Mary's as second-in-command of the rebel forces. Next they published a proclamation of pardon for all the rebels upon condition they lay down their arms and quietly disperse to their homes. This failed, too, for instead of reading it to his troops, Coode read a

36. Spencer to Blathwayt, June 30 [20?], 1689, BPCol. Wmsbg., v. XVII; *Arch. of Md.*, VIII, 112; *CSPCol., 1689–1692*, #194.

"defyance" which further enraged them against the government. With the help of "some great gunns," borrowed from a London ship in the harbor, the rebels lay siege to Mattapany, Lord Baltimore's manor house eight miles from St. Mary's, where most of the council had retreated, including President Joseph, who lay sick. After a "parlay," which Coode refused to hold in public as the council requested in the hope of convincing the settlers of their mistaken suspicions, and after such rebel "artifices" as a sudden report of Indians' destroying their crops and abandoning their towns in preparation for war, Mattapany capitulated to "prevent Effusion of blood." The Associators' demands were the terms of surrender on August 1; no Catholics in office, civil or military, according to Their Majesties' proclamation and the laws of England; a guarantee of safe return to their homes of all men in arms and garrison; and protection and just rights to the proprietor's people who surrendered, again according to the laws of England and the colony. From this point Lord Baron of Baltimore and his Catholic supporters ceased to be political figures in the colony of Maryland.[37]

Between the seizure of the State House and the siege of Mattapany, Coode and the Associators found time to publish a long Declaration, laying out their grievances and justifying their "Present Appearing in Arms." It missed none of the accumulated injustices and introduced several more; it emphasized heavily the Catholic conspiracy and added the alleged role of the northern Indians and the French who recently had gone to war with England. It pointed out specifically how Baltimore's government had denied the people of Maryland "a proportionable Share of so great a Blessing" as the "happy Change in England." It promised a full and free assembly and looked forward to a just and legal government—royal, of course—which would forever protect them from "Tyrany and Popery." Eight of the leaders signed it, including John Coode, Henry Jowles, and Kenelm Cheseldyne.[38]

Two days after Mattapany surrendered, the "Protestant Inhabitants" addressed William and Mary. They congratulated them on acceding to the throne and begged a favorable construction of their dutiful and truly loyal endeavors in Maryland. Despite every possible effort imaginable on the part of the proprietor's people, they explained, to choke off a proclaiming of Their Majesties, they had rescued Maryland from

37. "Narrative of Coll. Henry Darnall," in Scharf, *Hist. of Md.*, I, 338–39; *Arch. of Md.*, VIII, 107–8, 156; Beverly McAnear, ed., "Mariland's Grevances Wiy The Have Taken Op Arms," *Journal of Southern History*, VIII (1942), 405–7.

38. July 25, 1689, *The Declaration of the Reasons and Motives For the Present Appearing in Arms of Their Majesties Protestant Subjects In the Province of Maryland* (London, 1689), Andrews, ed., *Narratives*, pp. 305–14; *Arch. of Md.*, VIII, 101–7; *CSPCol., 1689–1692*, #290.

the Crown's enemies by force of arms but without bloodshed.[39] Good
to their word, Coode and his followers called a representative assembly
—*four* delegates from each county—which met the last week of August. It, too, addressed the King and Queen, assured that their success
in restoring the Protestant religion in England and civil rights and liberties to Englishmen was "graciously intended to be extensive" and
to reach Maryland and all other dominions. They begged again consideration of their grievances and the security of their religion, liberties, and rights under a royal Protestant government. In the meantime, they promised to persevere in defense of the same against all
comers.[40] Coode's government was fairly launched in late August 1689,
and the proprietary people stifled. Like the rebels in Massachusetts
and New York, Maryland's Protestant settlers, or most of them, governed themselves for some time until William decided what to do about
the surprising extension of his revolution to America.

Apparently the actual rebellion, which began with Coode's march
on July 16, owed nothing to Leisler's uprising in New York of May 31.
The two new governments corresponded frequently about common
problems such as seizure of escaped Catholics and defense measures,
but the relationship did not commence until late in September of 1689.
During the summer, while Leisler and his Committee of Safety were
attempting to consolidate control over New York, Coode and the Associators worked independently and seemed to be ignorant of the New
Yorkers' doings.[41] Massachusetts' example in overthrowing the Dominion had great effect upon Leisler's discontented people, but apparently
it failed to reach beyond New York, a circumstance which tells us
something about intercolonial relationships, or their lack, in the latter

39. "To the high and mighty the most illustrious Prince Willm & Mary . . . ,"
Aug. 3, 1689, *Arch. of Md.*, VIII, 108–10; *CSPCol., 1689–1692*, #315.

40. *The Address of the Representatives . . . in the Province of Maryland Assembled*, Aug. 26, 1689, *Arch. of Md.*, XIII, 231–32. The address was the first printed
document from a Maryland press. See Elizabeth Baer, comp., *Seventeenth-Century
Maryland, a Bibliography* (Baltimore, 1949), 132–33.

41. Two rebels' accounts of the revolt claim that Henry Darnall and Nicholas
Sewall set out for New York to secure help from Governor Nicholson five days
after they surrendered at Mattapany. At New Castle on the Delaware River they
learned of the rebellion at New York and Nicholson's flight to England, events
which had occurred almost two months earlier. See McAnear, ed., "Mariland's
Grevances Wiy The Have Taken Op Arms," 406–7; Leisler to the Assembly of
Maryland, Sept. 29, 1689, *Doc. Hist. N.Y.*, II (1849), 31–32, 43. Henry Darnall
claimed that John Coode prevented first their writing to Baltimore and then book-
ing passage to England, where they hoped to deliver their reports to the proprietor.
"Narrative of Coll. Henry Darnall," Scharf, *Hist. of Md.*, I, 338–39. For the Leisler-
Coode correspondence, see *Doc. Hist. N.Y.*, II (1849), 31–34, 36, 42–44, 181,
225–27, 229–30, 248–50.

half of the seventeenth century. Granted New York and New England were united—somewhat unnaturally—under Andros, and Long Island was a kind of bridge between Puritan rebels and their counterparts in New York, similar links did not exist between New York and Maryland, or if they did, they were not effective in 1689. One reason for the block was the Quakers of Pennsylvania, whose "disafected interest interposed betwixt N. Yorke & this place," said Coode; even the mail through Pennsylvania was undependable, Leisler added.[42]

Colonies' connections with one another were regional rather than general; they depended upon local trade, geography, even climate, and in some instances religion. New England, for instance—apart from Rhode Island—was bound loosely together through Puritanism which spilled over to Long Island, while Quakerism in Pennsylvania set it off from more orthodox colonies. Maryland was naturally drawn to Virginia, with which it shared, besides similar grievances, a tobacco and plantation economy, to say nothing of Chesapeake Bay and the Potomac River—although Baltimore claimed all of the last. Catholics aside, even in religion they were similar, since many Protestants in both colonies were Anglicans. Despite the dissimilarities in their governments, at least in kind and character, if not style and structure, Maryland, the smaller colony, was vulnerable to influence from Virginia.[43] It was from Virginia, not New York or Massachusetts, that Maryland settlers were first upset by rumors of the Glorious Revolution and in late April by the proclaiming of William and Mary, knowledge which so provoked Coode and the Protestants. Along with Stafford County's generous role in promoting the Catholic and Indian scare, the combination precipitated the rebels' move in the middle of July. But Maryland's rebellion was independent of what occurred in colonies to the north. Like them its people suffered intolerable burdens, they believed, under an arbitrary government; like them, too, the desire for a piece of the "happy Change" in England provoked the outburst. But the impetus stemmed from their fellow planters of Virginia who came within an eyelash themselves of overthrowing the government there and maybe would have, had the government not promptly proclaimed William King and had Governor Effingham, symbol of arbitrary power, been present at Jamestown.

Between April 18 and the middle of August 1689 newly crowned

42. Coode to Leisler, Apr. 4, 1690, *ibid.*, 225; Leisler to Coode, Apr. 9, 1690, *ibid.*, 229.

43. Maryland's Declaration of July 25, 1689, accused Baltimore's government of trying to make "Differences" between Maryland people and Virginians, whose "Friendship, Vicinity, great Loyalty and Sameness of Religion" they could rely upon in time of need. Andrews, ed., *Narratives*, p. 312.

William and Mary were presented with a number of colonial governments in America they were unaware they had lost. England's revolution was imported by its colonists before some Englishmen had accepted it at home. Presumptuous Americans moved rapidly to satisfy provincial needs by exploiting a revolution which occurred at an opportune moment. But William took his time before resettling their governments. Meanwhile, New England, New York, and Maryland limped along as best they could, rid for the time being of an arbitrary Dominion and a selfish proprietary. William's delay in accepting or condemning their "dutiful efforts" strung out the crisis and intensified the confusion.

15 Sanction and Justification

Search for Authority

Rebellion against authority in the American colonies, whether justified or not, did not dispel the uncertainty and uneasiness of those who rebelled. Similarly, neither those against whom rebellion was aimed nor the do-nothings who sat between the two camps found life easier or more certain. Yet in several ways the abrupt changes cleared the air; they forced leaders and followers to do some thinking about bases upon which they could build interim—maybe permanent—governments to serve until the King resettled their colonies on his terms or confirmed their present arrangements. Apart from attempts to justify what they as rebels had accomplished—and there were plenty—there was a good deal of talk and speculation about equitable foundations and workable guarantees for protecting rights and liberties, civil and religious, which they had rebelled to recover, or in some instances, discover. Besides footings in the English empire, the rebels searched, too, for ways to satisfy more selfish interests with which their schemes of security and guarantee were laced. In each case there was a falling back upon a previous condition or plan which either had worked to their satisfaction or might have worked under different circumstances. The Glorious Revolution in the colonies was less an attempt to kick over the traces and strive for a brave new world in America than it was a return to acceptable conceptions of empire which colonists either had lived with or had lived for in the past.

According to John Coode's people, had the Lords Baron of Baltimore stuck to the limits of their charter, as the colonists understood them, there would have been little need for rebellion. But Charles, third Lord Baltimore, more so than his father, had abused the charter, they complained, and with the help of family and fellow Catholics had arbitrarily and illegally governed Maryland in his own narrow interests and those of his relatives and close associates. Maryland rebels gave up, then, on a proprietor's charter which could be so easily subverted; their goal in rebellion was to repudiate the proprietor and fly to the Crown. Their plan was to submit Maryland to the King, who would remodel it as a royal colony, establishing the rights and liberties which all other English subjects supposedly enjoyed and which Maryland colonists had lacked almost from the beginning. A royal government would afford them, also, a degree of self-determination which could only be agreeable to ambitious settlers too long denied a role in colony affairs, a role including patronage and profits which any colonial government had at its disposal.

This was not a new proposal. It had been on many people's minds for several years, particularly since 1676, when it emerged at the time of the aborted rebellion at "the Clifts." "Complaint from Heaven," which followed the hanging of Davyes and Pate, strongly protested against a host of grievances and illegal abuses under Baltimore's government. It just as strongly pled for royal government in Maryland and a Crown-appointed Protestant governor who would rule according to the customs of England. Let the proprietor have his right to the soil and quitrents if he must, but allow Marylanders to live free of "compellment and persuasion or interruption." Permit the justice of the Crown and Parliament to prevail forever, and let there be no doubt about the settlers' rights to "gratious recourse and appeals" to the King.[1] In 1689 Coode and his people asked for no more, in fact, a little less, for the role of Parliament was dropped from their demands since old Commonwealthmen like Josias Fendall had faded from view.

It is curious that Maryland people placed so much trust in the King and royal government. Living as close to Virginia as they did, aware

1. See ch. 5. "Complaint from Heaven . . ." is printed in *Arch. of Md.*, V, 134–52.

of the fate of the Virginia charter of 1675 and the imposing of Poynings's Law upon the legislature a few years later, they should have
learned a lesson or two about the lack of restraint upon the King in
Crown colonies and direct use of the prerogative by such royal governors as Culpeper and Effingham. But royal government gave the appearance, at least, of certainty and stability, even consistency, which
Coode's people claimed Maryland lacked. By throwing in their lot with
the King they might better know where they stood, what they could
or could not expect, and they no doubt expected a more favorable
portion than heretofore allowed them. Despite Virginians' experience
across the Potomac, a royal government, even with its dependence
upon the King, looked promising to settlers who had lived under the
Calverts' rule for two or more generations. In their Declaration, in
their addresses and petitions to William and Mary, the Associators
begged for acceptance of what they had done and a prompt resettlement of their colony under the Crown.[2] They were aided in London by
an official prejudice against proprietary rule which was as much a part
of the new administration as it had been of the old.

Until notice of royal confirmation arrived at St. Mary's in the spring
of 1690, Coode and the assembly governed out of necessity, they said,
and legitimately, too, although they used a curious logic to substantiate
the claim. In contrast to his and Fendall's wild claims in 1681, Coode's
approach to revolution in 1689 seems legalistic, even conservative. The
hinge of the matter was William's proclamation of February, which
Maryland people eventually got a look at. One could argue, said
Coode, that there was no legal government in Maryland since the
proclamation disabled all Catholics, that is, most of the former government, and no new one had been established in its place. But if William's proclamation did not apply to Maryland because its disabling of
Catholics dissolved practically the whole government, then that part of
the proclamation which continued Protestant sheriffs, justices, and collectors in their posts did not apply either, and Maryland's customs officials could not function, since they held commissions from James,
who had abdicated. This, Coode said, was "unreasonable to imagine."
Therefore, the King's command did apply; Coode and his people had
substituted themselves for Baltimore's Catholics and carried on as best
they could. Out of His Majesty's needs and interests, then, government
continued; out of necessity Coode's government functioned in the
Crown's behalf. This was sanction, too, for holding courts without
specific order from the King, since the colony and the Crown's interest

2. For the Declaration and Addresses, see Andrews, ed., *Narratives,* pp. 305–14;
Arch. of Md., VIII, 108–10; *ibid.,* XIII, 231–32; *CSPCol., 1689–1692,* #315.

wholly depended upon trade which could not exist without courts. With authority of the King's name behind them, the Associators' assembly enacted ordinances and set up a civil and military administration whose officers proceeded according to former customs but also the laws of England and the colony. It was as simple as that. Any doubts in the minds of the Associators were dissolved when William's instructions, affirming Coode's temporary government, arrived at St. Mary's early in the spring of 1960.[3]

New York

Jacob Leisler's search for authority and sanction during the bitter struggle which followed rebellion in New York was more difficult than that of the rebels in Maryland or Massachusetts. While Leisler looked eventually to a royal government as Coode did in Maryland, more like the faction in Massachusetts with its covenant and charter, he looked first for some independent base of authority on which to establish his government until the Crown took New York in hand. Not satisfied, it seems, simply to fly to the King and his mercy, Leisler glanced in several directions for a foundation upon which he and his government might stand, all the while agreeing to submit to royal control when demanded. Only a few days after the militia companies took over the fort from Governor Nicholson, Leisler naïvely wrote to Connecticut expressing a wish that his colony might have a share of Connecticut's' charter, New York being in the same latitude, he said. He requested information about it and the rights it granted as if there might be some way to extend its jurisdiction westward. At the same time he announced that he and his committee soon would send an agent to England to secure some "priviledges," and doubtless he meant a charter for New York—more naïveté, given what we know of Virginia's similar quest a few years earlier and the Crown's continued reluctance to guarantee rights by charter.[4]

Leisler and his New York people had poor luck with agents in London. In August they dispatched Matthew Clarkson and Joost Stoll with instructions to petition the new government for a charter. Clarkson was of no use whatever, spending his time angling for a lucrative position

3. For the King's affirmation, see C.O. 324/22, pp. 205–6; *CSPCol., 1689–1692,* #731, #752; *Arch. of Md.,* VIII, 167–68. For Coode's argument, see his letter to Nathaniel Bacon, Feb. 8, 1690, *ibid.,* 169. For courts, see Beverly McAnear, ed., "Mariland's Grevances Wiy The Have Taken Op Arms," *Journal of Southern History,* VIII (1942), 407–8. Papers relating to the Associators' Assembly, 1689, *Arch. of Md.,* XIII, 241–47.

4. Leisler to Major Gold, June 2, 1689, *Doc. Hist. N.Y.,* II (1849), 14–15; Leisler to Gov. Treat, Aug. 25, 1689, *ibid.,* 25; *Recs. Col. Conn.,* III, 466–67.

back in New York. Stoll was a dram seller who had been very forward
at the time of the rebellion. Leisler had faith in him, so much so that
he discounted Governor Nicholson's presence in London, since he believed the King would hang the governor once Stoll described the
situation and presented Leisler's explanatory letters about what had
occurred. In November Stoll submitted a petition with accompanying
documents, listing the injuries New Yorkers had endured; he begged
the King's approval of the rebellion and asked for a charter to sustain
the colony along with authority to punish the disaffected. But this was
about as far as the campaign reached. Stoll, an ignorant, pretentious
man, made a very poor impression at court and doubtless did more
harm than good to the rebels' cause.[5] The next June Leisler's government sent Benjamin Blagge, whose capacity for negotiation was a cut
or two above Stoll's, but nothing constructive seems to have come of
his mission. All the while Nicholson and other opponents of Leisler
"made their advatages" in London at the rebels' expense so that Leisler's story was not distinctly heard there.[6]

Up to this time Leisler had had no encouragement from London
which offered the slightest confirmation or even recognition of his limp-
ing administration. But in early December 1689 there arrived in New
York an Order in Council commanding a proclaiming of William and
Mary and other instructions for carrying on. The packets were addressed to Governor Francis Nicholson, *or*, in his absence, to those
who for the time being preserved the peace and administered the laws
—Nicholson not yet having reached London when the order was dispatched in July. Leisler pounced upon the packets of letters and forci-
bly denied the old council's claim to them. He insisted they confirmed
the rebellion and his administration and later wrote to the King openly
explaining his actions in seizing them. From this moment Leisler expanded the activities of his government and widened its jurisdiction.[7]

December was the month of translation. Leisler assumed the title of
lieutenant governor and from that time sat in the governor's pew at
church "with a large red carpet before him." A council replaced the
Committee of Safety—four members from the city and county of New

5. C.O. 5/1081/55; *CSPCol.*, *1689–1692*, #365; Andrews, ed., *Narratives*, pp.
324, and n., 398 n.; *N.Y. Col. Docs.*, III, 629–32; Van Cortlandt to Nicholson,
Dec. 18, 1689, BPCol. Wmsbg., v. IX; Jerome R. Reich, *Leisler's Rebellion*, pp.
85–86.
   6. Leisler to Coode, June 27, 1600, *Doc. Hist. N.Y.*, II (1849), 268.
   7. *N.Y. Col. Docs.*, III, 605; Van Cortlandt to Frederich Flyps [*sic*], Dec. 13,
1689, C.O. 1081/81; Leisler to William III, Jan. 7, 1690, C.O. 5/1081/103; Van
Cortlandt to Nicholson, Dec. 18, 1689, BPCol. Wmsbg., v. IX; Hall, Leder, and
Kammen, eds., *Glo. Rev. in Am.*, p. 125; "Blagge's Memorial," *Doc. Hist. N.Y.*,
II (1849), 56.

York, one each from the other four counties so far under Leisler's rule. It included, too, Jacob Milborne, secretary, soon to marry Leisler's daughter Mary. At the same time New York City held a second election of mayor and aldermen; Leisler's crony Peter Delanoy was confirmed in the former post, having held it temporarily during the summer and fall. Besides proclaiming again Their Majesties, Leisler ordered a new seal for the colony and got down to the real business of governing. Opponents rejected his moves as further usurpation; Albany continued to ignore his regime, but Leisler carried on, insisting upon the legitimacy of his administration until the Crown should reorder the government.[8]

Even a temporary government needed money. Leisler and his council, lacking yet an assembly and probably doubting the legality of raising money without one, revived by proclamation and ordered enforcement of the customs and excise laws of the New York assembly of 1683, convened by Dongan under the proprietary. This move must have surprised even Leisler's friends, for why should he go so far out of his way to legitimatize a taxing power when New Yorkers had been taxed repeatedly since 1664 by a governor and council alone? Leisler's other deeds had not been timid; yet it appears he hesitated to call an assembly and doubtless because he was not yet in complete control of the colony. Albany still stubbornly remained outside the fold, and there were pockets of opposition in other places. Lacking an assembly of representatives and needing revenue for government, Leisler and his council, respecting the rights of Englishmen, fell back upon what they considered the last legal body which had taxed New Yorkers, the assembly of 1683, to which the Charter of Libertyes had given birth. The laws of this assembly, if not the assembly itself, remained in "good and full force," they said.[9]

The authority to tax was immediately challenged. Leisler's proclamations were torn down from the doors of the customs house and other public places as fast as he put them up, and a hostile declaration nailed in their stead, purporting to be from the "English freemen" of New

8. It was Milborne's brother, William, an Anabaptist minister, who sat with Cotton Mather and the committee of gentlemen at Boston on April 18 when they took over the rebellion there and demanded surrender of Andros. Bayard to Andros, Dec. 10, 1689, CSPCol., 1689–1692, #632. Stephen Van Cortlandt, mayor under the royal government, had scoffed at the new election at the Town Hall, where the rebels kept a guard at the door, he said, with "drawn Shord, that none but their owne gang should enter. . . ." Van Cortlandt to Nicholson, Dec. 18, 1689, BPCol. Wmsbg., v. IX; Doc. Hist. N.Y., II (1849), 45.

9. C.O. 5/1081/82; Doc. Hist. N.Y., II (1849), 50; E. B. O'Callaghan, ed., Calendar of Historical Manuscripts in the Office of the Secretary of State (2 vols., Albany, 1866), pt. II, 185, 188; CSPCol., 1689–1692, #641.

York. But Leisler and his council stood firm, demanding obedience to the law and condemning the "false Constructions" of the dissenters. They again rooted their authority in the act of the previous assembly and the charter from which it derived: the "Supreame Legislative" under the King—omitting the Duke—"shall forever reside in a Govenr Council & ye People met in general Assembly." This they broadcast to the people of New York; it was a direct quotation from the preamble of the Charter of Libertyes.[10]

By early spring of 1690 Leisler's control of New York had improved, Albany having succumbed to his rule for reasons discussed later. It was a more opportune time for an assembly to meet and carry on the colony's affairs, particularly its defense against hostile French and Indians. Again taking his sanction from the Charter of Libertyes of 1683, Leisler issued to each of the counties writs for elections empowering the inhabitants in King William's name to elect delegates for an April meeting. For the second time since 1664, New York could boast a representative assembly. It met twice in 1690 and probably would have the next year had not circumstances beyond Leisler's control seriously interfered.[11]

The search for authority was complex in New York; acceptable precedents were few. There was little to fall back upon but an aborted charter and assembly and the short-lived laws under them. At the same time, Leisler and his council, like Coode in Maryland, appealed to the Crown for confirmation of what they had accomplished and requested the establishment of a Protestant government in Their Majesties' names. Behind both appeals was a conception of empire which colonists believed any decent king ought to recognize and honor. Had there not been a revolution in England, too, a revolution whose very occurrence condemned the arbitrary policies of both Charles and James on which the government of New York had been based for some time? William would agree that there had been a revolution in England, but whether it affected America was a question he and Englishmen had not really asked.

Massachusetts Bay affords the best example of a reactionary goal in the revolution of 1689. Increase Mather had been lobbying intensely for restoration of the charter since his arrival in London in the late spring of 1688—although somewhat guardedly under James. Granted the moderates who had supported Andros but joined the revolution had no love for the charter or its revival, the majority of Massachusetts settlers, the countryside, under leadership of their ministers and the

10. C.O. 5/1081/89; *Doc. Hist. N.Y.*, II (1849), 50–51.
11. *Ibid.*, 283; O'Callaghan, ed., *Cal. of Hist. Mss.*, pt. II, 175.

old guard, understood the 1629 charter to be the foundation of their mission, the anchor of the covenant with God. They contemplated no other possibility than its restoration as the outcome of their overthrow of Andros. These people accepted the revolution in England and the accession of William and Mary as God's first steps toward returning the Bible Commonwealth to its former condition, "an undertaking through the wonder working Providence of Sions Saviour. . . ." [12] How could they not follow His lead and join together what evil men had put asunder, whereby they might live out their lives and their children after them, subject to the earlier relationship God had commanded? In their relative freedom with a virtually independent legislature, they might, too, continue to look lightly upon imperial regulations, such as the laws of trade and royal commissions, which they had accepted heretofore only insofar as they agreed with them. God had punished them for their waywardness; the calamities He had subjected them to had been almost catastrophic. But as always He had not really forsaken His people when He learned that they were truly repentant, and the end of their trial had come. Now they could pick up the pieces and carry on as before, or so it seemed to the faction and a majority of settlers in the summer of 1689.[13]

There was more agreement about tearing down the Dominion than about what to do with their sudden new freedom. A good deal of debate followed the events of April 18. Some were for declaring themselves a "Free-State," but the more politic, less presumptuous leaders like William Stoughton put a damper on this radical turn; in fact, he prudently threatened to abandon the cause altogether unless some degree of dependence upon the Crown was recognized. (Stoughton had been a colony agent in London and knew the ways of the imperial world.) Several others were all for erecting a military government; what they had won by the sword, they said, they ought to preserve by the sword. The appeal was limited, however, to a few and faded after the first hot days of rebellion. A timid few were for continuing under the Council of Safety until the new King commanded otherwise. A larger group supported a fresh election "by all the People" of governor, magistrates, the works. But according to one of the colony's critics, it was the ministers, apprehensive of losing their authority, who successfully talked the suggestion down and moved instead to resume the colony government as it stood in 1686, filling vacancies here and there from a list of the truly faithful. And then there were the Tory-minded like Nathaniel Byfield, whose argument smacked of Gershom Bulkeley's

12. C.O. 5/905, p. 115.
13. *From a Gentleman of Boston to a Friend in the Country*, by N.N. (Boston, 1689), C.O. 5/855, #5; Massachusetts Archives, Ecclesiastical, 1679–1739, 11, 45a.

in Connecticut. Massachusetts could not resume its former ways except by usurpation, since the old charter was null and void. Andros' regime was a legal regime, and Bay Colony people could not lay its authority aside, for even the worst of governments was better than none. The source of power and authority was the Crown, not the votes of even ten thousands. One other suggestion found its way into the debate: a request for a royal governor under the laws of England. A few moderates, a handful of Anglicans, and some former members of Andros' council helped support the idea, as did some settlers in Maine who had never been happy under the saints of Boston; but this was hardly a serious alternative when the opportunity to resume the former government appeared.[14]

Bay settlers overwhelmingly preferred a resumption of their earlier government, some even for the charter itself, but at least the government as it had existed before the Dominion. Arguments in its favor were varied and tell us something about what was going on in their minds. They ranged from sheer necessity, on the one hand, to an outspoken claim, on the other, that at the "present Juncture" the method of settling the government "lieth wholly in the Voice of the People." One good saint argued persuasively that the Massachusetts charter, after all, was really their Magna Carta, and without it they were wholly stripped of law. Since the laws of England were made for Englishmen alone, as was English common law—so uncertain that even the judges could never agree in construing it—they could not fill Massachusetts' needs. Anyway, before Sir Edmund's time both were unknown in Massachusetts. Had not the English courts revoked the charter illegally, against all reason, and should colonists now question full use of it once the power which kept them from it had disappeared? [15]

The most popular argument for resuming the government stemmed from the Prince of Orange's Declaration which spoke of a general restoration of English charters and liberties. To Increase Mather in

14. For the course of debate, see *From a Gentleman of Boston to a Friend,* C.O. 5/855, #5; Samuel Prince to Thomas Hinckley, Boston, Apr. 22, 1689, Andrews, ed., *Narratives,* p. 190; *A Short Account of the Present State of New-England, 1690,* by N.N., John Carter Brown Library, pp. 9–10; [Nathaniel Byfield], *Seasonable Notices to our Duty and Allegiance* . . . (Philadelphia, 1689); A Merchant in Boston to a Merchant in London, May 16, 1689, *CSPCol., 1689–1692,* #129; *An Account of the Late Revolutions in New-England* . . . by A.B. (Boston, 1689), *Andros Tracts,* II, 189–201; *The state of New England under the government of Sr Edmond Andros,* Andrews, ed., *Narratives,* pp. 234–35.

15. Declaration of the Convention at Boston, May 24, 1689, C.O. 5/855, #17, IV. See also Daniel Neal, *The History of New England* . . . (2 vols., London, 2d ed., 1747), II, 55–59; *The Case of Massachusetts Colony Considered in a Letter to a Friend at Boston,* May 18, 1689, C.O. 5/855, #4; *CSPCol., 1689–1692,* #133.

London, William had come to England primarily to restore the charters, all the charters, colonial as well as English, and Massachusetts settlers were very willing to oblige.[16] In Boston the Prince's Declaration became a "pattern if not a precept" for them; reinstating their charter privileges was "allowed and countenanced by the King," encouraged by his "motions" in England and "examples of the corporations" there. What better authority was needed for carrying on as before? [17]

Some changes, however, were suggested. A number of newly elected representatives, who came to Boston for the first meeting of the General Court the last of May, bore instructions from their townspeople to plug for an "Enlargement of the Freemen," that is, of the number who might vote for colony officers. Supporting the suggestion was a more specific request that the government willingly enfranchise settlers who combined sobriety and "some Interest in the Country by Estate," with not a word about church membership and sainthood, which had been the criteria until revocation of the charter. Charles II had been after the colony for some time to relax its suffrage requirements in favor of right-living Anglicans and other aliens in the Bible Commonwealth, but by one means or another the Bay Colony had thwarted his demand. Here came the same demand from within the colony. It was obviously a request to expand the suffrage to those with a stake in society, in the here-and-now and not the hereafter, a request which was favorably acted upon within a year. Whether the reform was a genuine democratic effect of the revolution or merely a sop to win support from the unchurched moderates and unregenerate opposition is not clear. Either way, or both, freemanship, as the old guard had known it, crumbling a bit before 1684, did not survive the revolution.[18]

In resuming their former government Massachusetts people fell back upon the familiar and the known. The covenant and charter were a substantial foundation which had supported them before and would again, they hoped. Tory and moderate opposition was helpless for the time being against a majority who salvaged what they could from the

16. Increase Mather, "Autobiography," A.A.S. Proc., 71 (1961), pt. 2, p. 331.

17. C.O. 5/855, #4; CSPCol., 1689–1692, #133; C.O. 5/855, #17, IV; C.O. 5/905, p. 115; Thomas Danforth to Thomas Hinckley, Apr. 20, 1689, Hinckley Papers, M.H.S. Coll., 4th ser., V (1861), 191–92.

18. Declaration of the Convention at Boston, May 24, 1689, C.O. 5/855, #17, IV; Neal, History of New England, II, 55–58; From a Gentleman of Boston to a Friend, by N.N., C.O. 5/855, #5. On Feb. 12, 1690, the General Court altered the law for admitting freemen by repealing the clause referring to ministers' certificates; it reduced the property qualification from ten to four shillings tax in a single country rate, and included as an alternative houses or land with an annual value of £6 freehold. Selectmen would certify to the General Court that the applicant was not "Vicious in Life." C.O. 5/855, #64.

founders' original mission and ideal, both tarnished a bit by experience, but still capable of attracting loyalty and devotion. "They are exceeding wedded to their own ways," a Boston merchant commented, "a very home-bred people, but exceeding wise and conceited in their own eyes." [19] Authority lay with the King, to be sure, but until he acted, they were comforted by their ancient privileges which God had sanctioned and which a Protestant King might be brought through God and Increase Mather to approve. News from England in early December 1689 was proof enough that Mather was holding up his end of the task. As early as the middle of August he had persuaded William to signify his "royal approbation" of their proclaiming him and his Queen. At the same time the King recognized their present care of the government and authorized them to carry on in his name until a new settlement was decided upon. On December 3 the people of Boston read the happy news in a broadside, proudly published by order of the governor, council, and representatives.[20]

Some uneasiness remained in Rhode Island and Connecticut, where charters were resumed. Rhode Islanders apologized to the King for acting without his approval; they pointed out to "Pater Patria Nostra" that their charter, although submitted to the late King, nevertheless "was not condemned nor taken from [them]." Connecticut people argued similarly; they never really had surrendered their charter to Governor Andros but merely had remarked that if they were to be annexed to New York or Massachusetts, they preferred the latter. Later, during an uneasy winter with no confirmation in sight, they admitted to William that they were not sure just what had happened to the charter under James; they were certain only that neither had they resigned it nor was it condemned. Both colonies, of course, begged confirmation; the immediate result was negotiation and delay.[21]

Justification: The Catholic Conspiracy

Most Englishmen agreed that William had come to England to rescue the nation from popery and slavery. In justifying the overthrow of established government in Massachusetts, New York, and Maryland, colonists argued repeatedly that they rebelled for the same reasons as

19. A Merchant in Boston to a Merchant in London, May 16, 1689, *CSPCol., 1689–1692*, #129.

20. King William to Gov. of Massachusetts, Aug. 12, 1689, C.O. 324/22, p. 67; Broadside, Boston, Dec. 3, 1689, C.O. 5/855, #53, II, X.

21. Rhode Island petition to William III, Jan. 30, 1690, C.O. 5/905, pp. 189–91; *Recs. Col. R.I.*, III, 258–59; Connecticut petition, Jan. 3, 1690, C.O. 5/855, #52; *Recs. Col. Conn.*, III, 463–66; Conn. Hist. Soc. *Coll.*, XXIV, 24–25; "Reflections upon the Affairs of New England," *Wyllys Papers, ibid.*, XXI, 326.

Englishmen. But the twin articles of oppression were not separate. Catholicism and arbitrary government tended to be synonymous in most Englishmen's minds, and evidence of one was good grounds for suspecting the other. Both were very evident in America as well as England, colonists claimed, and revolution against their perpetrators in the realm was reason enough for similar actions in the dominions.

That there was a monstrous Catholic plot to deliver England's colonies to the Pope, that there was a conspiracy hatched by James II and Louis XIV, willingly assisted by the Dominion officers, Lord Baltimore's oligarchy, the French in Canada, and the neighboring Indians, is not easy to accept today. But more important than whether there was actually a Catholic conspiracy is whether the colonists believed it to be true, and despite the leaders' clumsy use of the threat for propaganda purposes—and maybe because of it—there was indeed an honest and widespread fear that Protestant colonists were not safe in America under James's governors. The fear approached hysteria in Maryland, as we have seen; it was strong enough to convince many colonists in New York of its truth; and in Massachusetts it made a number of Andros' misunderstood deeds highly suspicious. James's flight to Louis's protection, the outbreak of war between England and France after William's accession, James's recruiting of troops in Ireland—he threatened to enslave the Irish and ship them to the plantations if they refused to fight [22]—his return to France once the game was up, all were further testimony to uneasy colonists of schemes to do them in.

One has only to glance at the declarations, addresses, petitions, and letters sent home to England to appreciate the universality of the threat: the seductive parading of the "great Scarlet Whore" in Boston, the rule of "bitter papists" in New York, or the yoke of arbitrary government, tyranny, and popery in Maryland. Nor did it die down after the initial outbursts of revolution, for it was needed to drive home justification for what they had done and were doing; at the same time it was kept alive by the French war and specifically the continued incursions from the north which upset colonists as far south as Virginia. If the charges lost some of their sting in Massachusetts after the dramatic effects of the Declaration had worn off, Bay settlers were reminded of the threat by rumors of French fleets off the banks, sent for by Sir Edmund, it was said, who had promised the delivery of New England to France.[23] On top of these came reports from Leisler in New

22. H.M.C., Report #37, *Ormonde*, N.S., VIII, 368.
23. "The Charges Against Sir Edmund Andros, Governor," Hall, Leder, and Kammen, eds., *Glo. Rev. in Am.*, p. 58. See a full treatment of the alleged plot

York, one warning of ambuscados and papist blades aimed at springing Andros from prison in Boston. Tories left in the Bay Colony, in and out of jail, had claimed all along that the Mathers spoke and printed scandalous words about common-prayer worship whereby they smeared Andros and the Anglicans in Boston as Catholics and idolators, all for the purpose of exciting rebellion.[24] If Massachusetts, as Judge John Palmer remarked, seemed less vulnerable to a Catholic plot than other colonies, the Bay settlers were unaware of it.

As anti-Catholic as were the Puritans, Jacob Leisler outdid them, probably as much from conviction as necessity during his rule. A true "Protestant Germanian," his own people called him, he was an "old Stander . . . of fervent Seale for the protestant Religion." Leisler was a staunch Calvinist and already well known in New York for his stubborn orthodoxy.[25] Besides driving out Matthew Plowman, James's Catholic collector of customs, Leisler, in the summer of 1689, while trying to consolidate his government, went after other Catholics and those "papishly affected" with the intensity of a purge. Unable to rely on justices of the peace in the city, Leisler sent for Gerardus Beekman of King's County on Long Island, who was kept busy taking depositions and hearing evidence in order to discover all he could about the depth of the plot and its schemers. Earlier, when Francis Nicholson replaced Thomas Dongan as governor, people like Leisler had breathed more easily; Dongan was openly a Catholic and, it came out after the revolution, among other suspected deeds, had attempted to establish a Jesuit college in New York "upon cullour to learne latine." The college soon vanished, since only a handful attended, including, Leisler was quick to point out, the sons of Judges West, Graham, and Palmer. But even Nicholson proved not to be "strong for true religion," and Leisler's people never forgave his permitting a Catholic chaplain to keep religious images in the fort on full display.[26] Once in possession of the government, Leisler and his people found Nicholson's Protestantism more than suspect, for like Dongan before him he had neglected

---

between Andros and the Indians in *An Account of the Late Revolutions in New-England,* by A.B. (Boston, 1689), *Andros Tracts,* II, 189–201. The charge does not appear in *A Narrative of The Proceedings of Sir Edmond Androsse and his Complices* (Jan. 27, 1691), written by several members of the Dominion council who joined the revolution. Andrews, ed., *Narratives,* pp. 239–49; Leisler to Gov. of the Barbados, Dec. 16, 1689, *Doc. Hist. N.Y.,* II (1849), 47.

24. Leisler to Gov. of Massachusetts, Oct. 22, 1689, *ibid.,* 38; *New England's Faction Discovered,* by C.D., Andrews, ed., *Narratives,* pp. 258–59.

25. Address to William and Mary, Aug. 17, 1689, C.O. 5/1081/48; Lawrence H. Leder, "The Unorthodox Domine," *New York History,* 35 (1954), 168–74.

26. C.O. 5/1081/50; C.O. 5/1081/64; *CSPCol.,* 1689–1692, #458; Leisler to Gov. of Mass., Aug. 13, 1689, *Doc. Hist. N.Y.,* II (1849), 23.

to keep the fort and other city defenses in repair. On top of this a helpful witness, Nicholas Browne, swore before Justice Beekman that earlier in England he had seen Nicholson at Mass in the King's tent at Hounslow Heath "on his knees before the altar in a Papist Chapel." More alarming were frequent reports and affidavits describing panic among the people on Staten Island. So apprehensive of massacre by Catholic hands, some were afraid to sleep in their beds at night; many had fled to the woods to protect themselves, while a number lay with their families in boats upon the river. Nicholas Bayard roundly denied the danger there, but a committee visited the island and found, if not evidence of a bloody plot and caches of arms as expected, at least a number of settlers paralyzed with fear, wretched victims of the rumors.[27]

Coode and Leisler swapped information about the whereabouts and extradition of Catholic escapees and problems of defense, convinced that their circumstances were "so alike" in view of the "common danger so equally threatening. . . ." Leisler traded intelligence with the saints of Boston and Hartford, too, discovering for them the "papisticall tricks" of their enemies and carrying on a "mutuall & neighbourly correspondence" in behalf of all the Protestants in America. If Leisler and his enemies in New York could not agree on the truth in the charge of a Catholic conspiracy as cause of the revolution, they did see eye to eye in scotching a second charge that a Dutch plot was behind it all. Dutchmen, numbering three-quarters of the inhabitants, as well as Englishmen, were on both sides of the conflict. A list of Leisler's councillors and associates certainly indicates that Dutchmen supported him; at the same time, his enemies took pains to point out that most people at Albany were Dutch and "manifestly against" Leisler.[28] New York rebels made little distinction between outright Catholics and those "papishly affected," which included anyone opposed to Leisler and his regime and particularly those, like Bayard, Philips, and Van Cortlandt, who clung to commissions issued by the former government.

Like Leisler, John Coode and his Associates kept constantly before the Maryland settlers the specter of Rome. This was not a difficult task, since they had had considerable practice dating from Josias Fendall's time and before. While Catholicism was a relatively fresh issue at Boston and New York, in Maryland the lower house and the anti-proprietary settlers had been complaining for years about the apparent

---

27. "Blagge's Memorial," *ibid.*, 55; *ibid.*, 27, 28–30; C.O. 5/1081/57.
28. Coode to Leisler, Nov. 26, 1689, *Doc. Hist. N.Y.*, II (1849), 42–44; Leisler to Gov. of Mass., Sept. 25, 1689, *ibid.*, 31; *ibid.*, 58; "Answers to Blagge's Memorial," Apr. 27, 1691, *ibid.*, 390; *ibid.*, 27 and *passim*.

hold of Lord Baltimore's coreligionists upon the government and more recently of the bloody plot cooked up between the proprietary leaders and the French and Indians. Coode's Associators were hardly comfortable in their assembly seats before they appointed a "Committee of Secrecy" to discover the truth of the charges, and discover it they did in no time at all. Not only did the committee report that the charges were justified, that the late popish governors had wickedly conspired to betray the Protestants to the French and northern Indians, but that even after the revolution there was still danger to the Protestants' lives, liberties, and estates from the malicious combinations of these proprietary Catholics bent on subverting and destroying their religion. Supporting evidence was President Joseph's prorogation of the assembly earlier in March lest the truth of these designs become public and the council's refusal to proclaim the new King and Queen, in fact, its downright denial of the sovereignty of William and Mary. (On the back of the committee's manuscript report in the Public Record Office, written in a different hand, is the following: "Memorandum notwithstanding [,] have often desired a proofe of the accusations this Comittee charged upon some of ye Lord Proprietarys Deputies yet the same could never be obtained or was anywayes made appear.") [29] Although Coode doubtless believed that Maryland of all colonies was most cruelly treated by Catholic overlords and stood to lose most by the evil conspiracy, he generously shared with Leisler and the saints of Boston his firm conviction that they were all its victims, that the "greate men" of Maryland, New York, and New England were themselves a "Caball" whose plot to capture all of English America was a significant part of a "great designe" of the "Popish world." [30]

No doubt John Coode out of habit would have assigned a leading role in the "great designe" to Catholic James, as would most Protestant Americans, but he and they may not have known just how close his propaganda came to the truth. Colonial Tories and other critics of the rebellions, even some of its sympathizers, never accepted seriously the threat of a Catholic conspiracy of either local or imperial proportions. Most historians since that time, while pooh-poohing the truth of the scare, recognizing all the while its fertile propaganda value, are quick to admit, as well they might, that men often act on what they believe to be true over what is actually true. Certainly the fear of a Catholic plot was effectively used, and no doubt it went a long way toward persuading a surprising number of settlers that they were in imminent danger and ought to turn their backs on the governments over them

29. C.O. 5/718/9; *Arch. of Md.*, XIII, 234–35, 240.
30. Coode to Leisler, Nov. 26, 1689, *Doc. Hist. N.Y.*, II (1849), 42–44.

before it was too late. What historians have not explained is just how seriously James intended, even in the heat of war, to continue his imposition of Catholicism upon the realm. More important, during his reign, had he meant to introduce it officially into the colonies in America as well?

Primarily to save his own skin, while still king, James had slowed the pace of his Catholicizing in 1688. By the fall of that year it was clear he already had gone too far and too fast, and a majority of Englishmen, although slowly at first, were led to encourage and then accept the Prince of Orange in their midst as the answer to their dilemma. But it was some time before James gave up the fight, and in the middle of it he attempted to enlarge the campaign by several strong pleas to Pope Alexander VIII for help in turning William out of England. A series of letters to Rome in 1689 and 1690, after he had fled the kingdom, gives some indication of what James intended, at least, of what was on his mind as the Crown of England appeared to slip from his grasp.[31] Granted he and his dwindling court would put the best face possible on his situation and intentions, his appeals to Rome are surprising in their grandeur of design and expectation of success— for both James and the Church. Since Alexander was new to his job, having replaced Innocent XI, who died in August 1689, he may have seemed a likely bet for support. James's appeals were based on what he called his remarkable gains for the Church already accomplished and several more on the brink of success, which Rome should be proud of and itching to support and continue. The entreaties, some written for James and Queen Mary of Modena by the Duke of Melfort, explained the Revolution in England to His Holiness. Its single cause was James's Catholicism and firm resolve to restore the Holy Church to the three kingdoms *and* the "Several Colonies of [his] Subjects of a Considerable extent in America." On the basis of military successes so far in Ireland, James wrote from Dublin, he would shortly establish the holy religion there and "in our other Dominions" as soon as they were restored to him.

The new Pope was treated to a lesson in European history, too. William of Orange had joined the Protestant Princes in the League of Augsburg in reaction to the advance of Catholicism, particularly

31. The series of letters is in the British Museum, Add. Mss., 38144, ff. 2–3, 3–4, 6–11, 18, 19–20, 22–23, 26, 30. Pope Alexander's letter is dated Oct. 16, 1689, from St. Peter's. James's was written at Dublin, Nov. 26, 1689. The rest are undated. A quotation from Queen Mary's letter to the Pope in 1690 is in Martin Haile, *Queen Mary of Modena* (London, 1905), p. 259. See also similar pleas from the Queen to Cardinal d'Este, Feb. 26 and Mar. 14, 1689, *ibid.*, pp. 242, 246.

James's success in converting his own people and the extirpation of Huguenots in France, a deed which had alarmed Protestants all over Europe, even in "Hell Itself." The League was a Protestant conspiracy whose only purpose was an enlarging of the bounds of heresy to the prejudice of the Catholic Church. Now, because of what James already had accomplished, because he had sought to obtain an "eternal crowne" for his subjects rather than an earthly one for himself, they had expelled him and his family from England "for the meer cause of their Religion." James, his deeds and plans, needed now the Pope's assistance to sustain the war against William before he fixed himself permanently in the usurper's role. Most necessary was peace among Catholic princes in Europe; the Pope must intervene in the conflict there so that they might be freed to aid the mighty effort in England and Ireland. In particular, peace in Europe would release Louis XIV and his armies to support James and the holy cause of Catholicism in his kingdoms.

As James's position worsened, the letters and memorials to Rome became more frantic. The Pope must remember, the Duke of Melfort wrote, that James II was no ordinary Catholic monarch, but a King who had returned the Crown of England to the "Lap of the Holy Church" and to the obedience of the "Vicar of Jesus Christ." He ought then to be looked upon as a great King, deserving every bit of assistance possible from the head of the Church he so ardently embraced. For James, in sustaining the faithlessness of friends, his soldiers' cowardice, a shocking imprisonment, the treason of his kingdoms, and the "Impiety of his Daughters," had suffered more than martyrdom, yea, even greater than that of "St. Thomas of Canterbury." The appeal finally came down to a question of money, and if the Pope could not send cold cash, could he send firearms: powder, lead, match, etc., "of which there are plenty in ye Arsenals of [His] Holiness." In a final effort, Melfort's memorial from the Queen asked directly how much money the Pontiff could spare and ended with the ominous prospect that not only would the Pope's public marks of protection shake soundly England's rebellious subjects, but that James's army, which contained exclusively zealous Catholics, would be encouraged in their fight to "run ev'n to Martyrdom"—and all this if the Pope through his assistance owned their cause as the cause of God and the holy religion. James's pleas elicited from Pope Alexander at least one reply in his own hand; it contained a message of "unexpressible grief" for the King's misfortunes; it spoke, too, of a promise to "implore of God" His comfort; and it opened and closed with an "Apostolical Benediction." After defeat by William at the Battle of the Boyne in Ireland, where he had the use of some French detachments, James fled again to France, leaving his kingdoms for the last time in July of 1689.[32]

It is difficult to determine today whether James's appeals to the Holy Father were only wishful thinking, or less politely, bravado, or cynically viewed, propaganda, or a combination of these. But that he, his Queen, and the Duke of Melfort repeatedly pled for support from the Pope, that French troops supported James in Ireland, and that he would redouble his efforts to convert his kingdoms and dominions were he to regain the throne, lend some substance, at least, to colonists' fears of a "great designe" of the "Popish world" against them. Had James succeeded against William, would Andros and Nicholson and Baltimore's people have denied his will?

Justification: A Shared Revolution Against Arbitrary Government

If colonists went out of their way to prove the threat of a Catholic conspiracy, they spent as much effort providing evidence of arbitrariness in the governments they overthrew. There was no end to such testimony; it was the burden of every explanation or description uttered by supporters of the rebellions between the days of rising and eventual resettlement of their governments, and in New York for several years afterward. "Slavery" was arbitrary treatment by government contrary to the rights of Englishmen, the laws of England, and the laws of the particular colony where the tyranny occurred. Massachusetts and New York began their protests with the illegal and arbitrary commissions of Andros and Nicholson over them, and the Bay settlers added an earlier step in the illegal revocation of their charter. New Yorkers never listed their sum total of grievances with the same formality as the rebels in Boston or Maryland. They spoke, to be sure, of subversion of their ancient privileges which in effect made them slaves,[33] but most of their justifications as we have seen, centered on their fear of betrayal to the Catholic enemy.

In justifying rebellion, Massachusetts and Maryland people trotted out their complaints anew and gave them full treatment. In Boston it was again the lack of an assembly; laws and taxes without consent, with full credit to the Ipswich rebels; a council of Andros' cronies packed with strangers and "lawyers"; arbitrary justice with biased,

32. Stephen B. Baxter, *William III and the Defense of European Liberty, 1650–1702* (New York, 1966), pp. 264–66.
33. Address of the Militia, June 1689, Hall, Leder, and Kammen, eds., *Glo. Rev. in Am.*, p. 109.

illegal juries and exorbitant fees, all violating New England "common law," to say nothing of the rights of Englishmen. It included, too, Andros' attack upon landed property, falsely in the name of the King; a deceitful Indian war in Maine which killed off the flower of their youth; and subversion of their precious institutions such as a publicly supported ministry, the sanctity of their churches, and frequent town meetings.[34] Old John Higginson, minister at Salem and son of one of the founders, explained the justice of the colony's cause to his son in a way the faction would have approved: by the "Exercise of an arbitrary Government," he wrote, "ye foundation of all our Good things ware destroyed, ye wicked walked on Every Side & ye Vilest of men ware Exalted." Such was the suffering and oppression of multitudes, he continued, that as soon as they heard the "Prince of Orange was Gone for England, ye Country Ros in Armes [and] Imprisoned ye whole Crew. . . ."[35]

In late June 1689 the Massachusetts Convention, which succeeded the Council of Safety, voted in a series of resolves separate charges against Andros and "ye whole Crew." The heaviest blast, of course, they dealt to Sir Edmund himself (although they doubtless hated Edward Randolph more, for his attack upon them seemed personal and deliberate). If any man, they resolved, conspires or attempts invasion or insurrection, or publishes rebellion against their Commonwealth, or treacherously or perfidiously attempts to alter or subvert their frame of government in a fundamental way, he shall be put to death. As authority the Convention cited "Numb. 16. 2 Sam. 3. 2 Sam. 20." They spared Andros' life, of course, although His "Arbitrary and Despotick power" did not deserve their mercy. Joseph Dudley, they claimed, had broken a capital law of the colony in subverting and usurping the government under an arbitrary commission and all contrary to the laws of England. Charges against Randolph were similar, labeling him an "evill Counsellor." Owing to the immensity of their crimes, none was "baylable."[36]

At St. Mary's in Maryland the list of grievances was longer, for they had accumulated over a greater period of time than in Massachusetts. The Declaration of July 25 picked up most of what the lower house

34. For example, see Massachusetts Declaration, Andrews, ed., *Narratives*, pp. 175–82, and *An Account of the Late Revolutions in New-England*, by A.B., *Andros Tracts*, II, 189–201.

35. John Higginson to Nathaniel Higginson, Aug. 31, 1698, Essex Inst. Hist. *Coll.*, XLIII (1907), 182.

36. The Convention levied appropriate charges against all of Andros' people whom they imprisoned. Resolutions of the Convention Concerning Sir Edmund Andros, Dudley & Randolph, June 28, 1689, C.O. 5/855, #21, II.

had complained about since Josias Fendall's time. What the Associators missed and a few more were added to the list early the next year in a major defense of Coode's Rebellion which was not published at the time. Called "Mariland's Grevances Wiy The Have Taken Op Armes," it was a frank explanation of charges against the government probably sent to Leisler in New York in order to acquaint him further with the causes of the Maryland revolution. It was less hard on Baltimore than on his deputies, who as councillors, as members of the upper house, and proprietary representatives, constituted a "third estate" which stuck its nose wrongly into every bit of colony business and in its attitude and actions was wholly inimical to the needs and interests of the people. The Declaration and "Mariland's Grevances" together were a minute dissection of Baltimore's government from the rebels' view and renewed the clamor of the discontented against the kinglike prerogatives of the proprietor ("Jus Regale"). They stressed his demand for oaths of fidelity without even a nod to the Crown and his refusal to honor the charter which guaranteed to colonists the same rights as subjects at home. Most objectionable were the uncertainty and temporariness of the laws, which kept the colonists unsettled and uneasy about their liberty and property, a state the proprietor aggravated by his cavalier vetoes and dispensing of laws at will. Many Maryland Protestants, who were an overwhelming majority, felt discriminated against in favor of Catholics, who held most of the profitable jobs and enjoyed rights denied the Protestants; they complained bitterly of plural officeholding by the proprietor's favorites and of biased judges or "dealers" who were also councillors and ruled and judged in their own causes. They heartily denounced the proprietor's cutting in half the number of representatives to the assembly from each county; fees and fines were exorbitant; those extracted from trade were taxes without consent; and appeals to England and the King were stifled. In spite of an assembly, the government represented not the colonists themselves and their needs but the selfish interests of the proprietor and his small band of Catholic relatives and friends. This was the "Injustice and Tyranny" under which Maryland settlers groaned.[37] Because of the threat of a Catholic plot and the oppression of arbitrary governments, because of conditions which a good many American colonists found intolerable, the revolutions of 1689 occurred.

37. For Maryland Declaration, see Andrews, ed., *Narratives*, pp. 305–14. McAnear, ed., "Mariland's Grevances Wiy The Have Taken Op Arms," 396–409. So confident was John Coode of the rightness of his cause and that of rebelling colonists elsewhere that he wrote home in defense of Leisler and his rebellion, telling Englishmen of the great service Leisler had done Their Majesties by securing for them "so considerable" a colony as New York. Coode to Leisler, Nov. 26, 1689, *Doc. Hist. N.Y.*, II (1849), 44.

In the minds of those who rebelled in New England, New York, and Maryland there was no doubt that they had proved their case against popery and slavery. Englishmen everywhere shared the horror of a Catholic regime, and who could say—but their critics—that the threat in the colonies was any less ominous than in the kingdom? To be virulently anti-Catholic was a solid English trait and had been for some time. But colonists in America shared also Englishmen's rights, they said, and their appeal to these rights was based on their understanding of the role they played in the empire, a role which in no way discriminated against them as Englishmen. Justification for this point of view rested on a belief that the colonies were part of the English nation, that it was really one nation, and that colonists in America participated as equals in the English revolution. There was no doubt about this in the declarations and addresses, memorials and letters, which spouted from America in 1689 and after.

In defending Massachusetts' overthrow of the Dominion, Increase Mather argued in the public prints in London that if the colonies of New England were not "*parts of England*," why did the English courts issue *quo warrantos* against their governments "as belonging to *Westminster in Middlesex*," or why was the tenure of their land settled in "free Soccage as of the Manour of *East Greenwich*"—questions, indeed, which no Englishman had ever thought about before. Andros' Dominion, itself, was an invasion of rights which the whole English nation laid claim to, said a Boston writer, and "every true Englishman must justifie" the colonists' dissatisfaction with it.[38] New Yorkers were even more expansive. Leisler's soldiers declared their expectation to "have parte" of the glorious deliverance procured by "so happy an instrument" as Prince William, since they long had groaned under the "same oppression" as people in England. Other New Yorkers spoke of reaping the benefits "of this most happy Revolution." Coode's Associators looked forward to a "proportionable Share of so great a Blessing," while some of their friends in Talbot County begged to participate in William's accomplishments with "fellow subjects" in their "native Country of England."[39]

As parts of the nation, then, and as equal sharers in the glorious events, American colonists could only imitate their cousins at home.

38. *A Vindication of New England*, in *Andros Tracts*, II, 77; *An Account of the Late Revolutions in New England*, by A.B., *ibid.*, pp. 191–92. See also Hall, Leder, and Kammen, eds., *Glo. Rev. in Am.*, p. 48.

39. *A Declaration of the Inhabitants Soudjers*, May 31, 1689, *Doc. Hist. N.Y.*, II (1849), 10; "Blagge's Memorial," *ibid.*, 58; Address of the Militia, June 1689, Hall, Leder, and Kammen, eds., *Glo. Rev. in Am.*, p. 109; Maryland Declaration, Andrews, ed., *Narratives*, pp. 310–11, 313; Talbot County petition, *Arch. of Md.*, VIII, 143–44.

Anyone who approved of the revolution in England must justify what occurred in New England, for it was "effected in compliance with the former." Surely colonists had only followed the "Patterns" set before them by the "Nobility, Gentry and Commonalty" in England. The only difference, the Massachusetts Declaration explained, was that patriots in England had proposed chiefly to prevent by revolution what Bay Colony settlers already had endured, and, Bradstreet and his council added, "under a like (if not worse) evill"—a nice touch.[40] New Yorkers found their actions "not only encouraged but invited" by William's and Parliament's declarations; it was "England's example," Suffolk County freeholders chimed.[41] They had acted on the Prince's "Directions," said a Bay colonist. Seizing the governor and his people, wrote another Bostonian, "was no more than was done in *England*, at Hull, Dover, Plimouth, *Ec*." [42]

A nation had rebelled against popery and slavery; these were glorious undertakings, promising success for the Protestant religion and the rights and liberties of English subjects. The revolutions in America were based on a conception of empire worked out some time earlier, which assumed that colonists were guaranteed equal treatment with subjects within the realm. Increase Mather's late appreciation of an empire of equals did not vitiate the principle upon which it was based: "No Englishmen in their Wits will ever Venture their Lives and Estates to Enlarge the Kings Dominions abroad, and Enrich the whole English Nation, if their Reward after all must be to be deprived of their *English Liberties*." [43] And this was what the revolutions were all about. When William landed at Tor Bay, he came as much to rescue colonists in America from oppression as he did Englishmen, maybe more so, since colonists were harder pressed, or so they said. Denied these rights, denied equal treatment, they rebelled to rediscover and preserve them both.

In Maryland and New York the search for authority and justification for rebellion were closely related; one depended upon the other, and both were grounded on the rights of Englishmen. This was not as true in Massachusetts, where a falling back upon the foundation of covenant and charter had less to do with traditional Englishmen's rights. Under covenant and charter Massachusetts had established for years

40. *The Revolution in New England Justified*, in *Andros Tracts*, I, 71; Massachusetts Declaration, Andrews, ed., *Narratives*, p. 181; Massachusetts President and Council to the King, May 20, 1689, C.O. 5/905, p. 111.

41. Hall, Leder, and Kammen, *Glo. Rev. in Am.*, pp. 109, 103.

42. *Ibid.*, p. 50; *The Revolution in New England Justified*, in *Andros Tracts*, I, 72.

43. *A Vindication of New England, ibid.*, II, 76.

its own authority in accord with its mission and not always in accord with English rights and laws. But in *justifying* rebellion, Bay colonists told another story. An appeal to the liberties of Englishmen, besides being respectable in view of the Glorious Revolution, was not only useful but really the only means left to clear the way for a return to the earlier foundation. The hope was that a government premised on the rights and liberties of Englishmen would afford sufficient self-determination to allow Massachusetts again to function as a Bible Commonwealth, this time ostensibly within the empire. But was Massachusetts really so different? Was this not true in the other colonies as well, at least in effect if not in religious emphasis? Coode's people in Maryland and Leisler's in New York welcomed the revolution and formed new governments based on Englishmen's rights, for they were a means to alter the tight distribution of power and profit from what it had been under the arbitrary claims of the oligarchies during the reigns of Charles and James. While the Massachusetts faction would use this power for its own interests, to return the colony to its earlier foundation, similarly Coode and Leisler would rearrange their governments to serve their own people's interests and needs instead of those of the oligarchies which had enjoyed control for so long. And this also was what the revolutions were all about.

16 Resistance and Dissent: The Ghost of Masaniello

The new governments in New England, New York, and Maryland did not lack opposition. It rose in a variety of forms and in varying degrees of intensity, ranging from violent resistance, on the one hand, to reasoned constitutional dissent, on the other, with considerable indecision between the extremes. The differences of opinion all added to a confusion, sometimes even chaos, which was characteristic of the interim governments from the early moments of rebellion to eventual settlement by the Crown. And along with opposition went a good deal of resentment which stemmed from loss of place, to be sure, but also from the alleged vulgarity and commonness in some instances of those who replaced them. It stemmed, too, from a disgust at the dishonesty and deception behind some of the wild propaganda on which the rebellions spread. The variety of reactions to the uprisings helps to define and explain them. Although there was, in throwing the rascals out, a sameness in motives from Massachusetts to the Potomac, there were also differences which, once examined, relate what occurred to peculiar causes not shared. Distinctions emerged which tended to set off New England from the rest, if not generally at least specifically. Rebelling colonists might share similar conceptions of empire and the roles of their governments in it, but they usually came to these conceptions for different reasons and often for different self-interested reasons.

Reaction to rebel government was severest in New York, where independent action in outlying settlements, such as Queen's County on Long Island and Albany up the Hudson, were difficult, sometimes impossible, to control. Except for Maine, settlement in Massachusetts was fairly compact along the seacoast, as it was in Maryland; distances were not great in either colony, even to the latter's eastern shore. Moreover, at Boston and St. Mary's the rebels had acted quickly and deftly, at least more effectively at the outset in either rounding up the opposition or silencing it than in New York. In Boston men who formerly held power were promptly jailed except for the few merchant councillors who abandoned Andros. In Maryland the rebels by force made listless most opposition from the proprietary people except that of a few who escaped to Virginia. In New York the rebels' job was not as easy, although slower accomplishment was not for lack of determination. Scattered settlements, the entrenched strength and political ability of the former regime, and the nature and temperament of Leisler's government, as well as of himself, seemed to encourage a stronger and more active resistance than rebels encountered elsewhere, north and south. For Leisler not only antagonized the Bayards, Van Cortlandts, Philipses, and others loyal to the Dominion, but he and his government eventually rubbed the wrong way a number of colonists, particularly merchants, who otherwise might have been his friends, colonists who early lent their support but later turned their backs on him.

While rebels spouted arguments about the rights of Englishmen, their victims argued, too, but from different premises. On what grounds, if any, was rebellion justified in the English mind of the seventeenth century? Political theorists of the time were pretty much agreed that only under certain circumstances was rebellion against a civil authority permissible. Only when the common, ordinary inhabitants *and* the landed, titled, and gentry, the well-to-do classes, joined forces against oppression and injustice was an uprising justifiable. What they meant was that the ordinary people, the rabble alone, could never rebel even in the face of injustice and tyranny. Not until misrule affected all the people, high and low, did seventeenth-century rules sanction rebellion.

By the end of the century Englishmen were accustomed to speak of

Masaniello's revolt at Naples as a classic example of an illegal and criminal uprising which never should have occurred. Naples was under the rule of Spain in the 1640's; the Spanish viceroy, through misgovernment and burdensome taxes, chiefly on food and which the nobility escaped through collusion, kept a strong and arbitrary hand on the people there. Quickly following an example set by Sicilians at Palermo, the common people of Naples in early July 1647 erupted violently in sudden reaction to a new, heavy gabelle on fruit, the principal food of the poor. From the uprising rose Tommaso Aniello, called "Masaniello," a peasant fish seller who, besides leading it, was its immediate instigator. Backed overwhelmingly by the armed common people, Masaniello in a few days was absolute monarch of Naples; his supporters freed prisoners, burned the excise houses, and plundered the nobles of their property, for the good of the cause. They forced the viceroy to grant broad concessions. With the bishop as witness, Masaniello and Duke d'Arcos signed a convention which abolished the gabelles, pardoned the rebels, and granted citizens of Naples several civil rights they had not enjoyed before. The viceroy proceeded to make a great deal of the peasant king, wined and dined him and his family in the palace, and lavished dignities upon him. After placing a gold chain around the fish seller's neck, the Duke ceremoniously confirmed him as captain general of the people of Naples.

But at the peak of his power Masaniello showed frightening signs of instability, even madness. His despotism fairly exploded; executions multiplied, 250 in all, many of them based, it seemed, on whim, others on his exalted idea of dispensing absolute justice. At the same time he inconsistently threatened to resign his great office, to abandon the rebels to their old rulers, humbly claiming he was an illiterate fishman and ought to remain so. Contemporaries explained that his frenzy and contradictions were the result of the tremendous strain brought upon him by his sudden translation, that the abrupt changes in his life and the excitement that went with them were too much for the simple peasant. As his ruthlessness increased, supporters commenced to abandon him and looked again to the Spanish viceroy to keep the peace. While recovering from a senseless bout with cruelty, Masaniello suddenly was assassinated by some of his own people. A butcher soon cut off his head, and after the mob dragged his body through the streets, they cast it into a ditch. The next day, however, angered by an arbitrary reduction in the weight of bread, the crowd repented its rash action of the previous day. Followers exhumed Masaniello's body, sewed on the severed head, and with great pomp and ceremony the city of Naples gave him a splendid funeral, "the common people crying him up for a Saint already." But with the leader's death the rebellion dissolved; an exhausted and demoralized Naples returned to its former obedience. And all this had occurred in nine or ten days in the summer of 1647.[1]

In the nineteenth century Masaniello's revolt became a romantic legend, a fit subject for heroic treatment in poetry, drama, and opera. Writers of his own century, however, looked upon his strange and violent career very differently. Rebellion of common people, the rabble, who had little to lose, even when they believed they were intolerably oppressed, was incongruous and inexcusable. Such outbursts could lead only to anarchy and confusion and would encourage openly oppressed people everywhere to attack the supreme powers over them. Common people had no knowledge of affairs of state or whether the common good might require grievous taxes, impositions, and even tyranny. According to the mistaken principle of the mob's seizing power, wrote John Locke, who had no real sympathy for the dregs of society, one might easily make Masaniello king who was but a fishman the day before.[2] Furthermore, said James Tyrrell, Locke's contemporary and popularizer, rebellions like Masaniello's made it easy for "Wicked, Crafty, and Ambitious men" to exploit the mob and through it to set themselves up for selfish reasons on pretense of establishing better government and more liberty. Common people had no business rebelling unless the "whole People," including the nobility and gentry, joined them and led them and then only against a tyranny that was "so evident, and general, and insupportable, that it is past all question. . . ." Wat Tyler and Masaniello were criminally mistaken, wrote Tyrrell, for they represented far less than the whole people. They and others like them were better off to suffer their oppressions in silence—waiting until the *"Mischief* be grown *general"*—than to put themselves into an immoral *"State of War"* against their governments. Masaniello's was the epitome of wrong-headed aggression by the *"meaner sort,* the Scum of the *People,"* who could not rightly judge the wrongs against them.[3] Under such circumstances rebellion was wicked and criminal. So Masaniello's own time looked upon his rebellion; it became a canon by which his century and the next judged resistance to established governments.[4]

1. Alexander Giraffi, *An Exact History of the Late Revolutions in Naples* . . . (London, 1664), trans. from the Italian by J[ames] H[owell].

2. John Locke, *Two Treatises of Government,* ed. by T. I. Cooke (New York, 1947), par. 79, p. 61.

3. James Tyrrell, *Bibliotheca Politica* (n.p., 1694), pp. 164, 182–83; Caroline Robbins, *The Eighteenth-Century Commonwealthman* (Cambridge, Mass., 1959, reprinted, New York, 1968), pp. 64. 75.

4. Surprisingly, Tom Paine utilized the ghost of Masaniello in *Common Sense.* In arguing for independence, he argued also to persuade American patriots of the necessity to draft immediately a constitution lest some Masaniello, some "desperate

By the latter half of the seventeenth century the legend of Masaniello had reached England's American colonies. The context in which his name was used had not been altered in passage. Governor William Berkeley seized upon it in 1676 to explain Bacon's Rebellion to Englishmen at home. He told the King that he was surrounded by rebellion "in every respect like to that of Massanello Except their Leader." Doubtless a gentleman's code of honor prevented Sir William from directly identifying Virginia's rebel with a peasant fish seller, for after all, Berkeley and Bacon were cousins by marriage, and the governor was responsible for appointing Bacon to his council the year before. Otherwise the pattern fitted, for, Berkeley declared, "Mr. Bacon hath none about him but the lowest of the people." [5]

Those against whom the rebellions of 1689 were aimed, particularly in New York and Maryland, found the figure of Masaniello and his revolt convenient weapons against Jacob Leisler and John Coode and their followers. Their use of him is helpful for an understanding of how the New York oligarchy and the proprietary people in Maryland wished the rebellions to appear to others and maybe even to themselves. Actually, the Masaniello smear served several purposes. It helped to present what occurred as constitutionally reprehensible, wholly outside the acceptable limits of political change. What is more, the old New York council and Baltimore's supporters in Maryland could hardly have hit upon a better way to damn the rebellions than to appeal to the class consciousness of their own times. The use of Masaniello painted Leisler, Coode, and their supporters with the attributes of the mob, the "Meaner sort," who had presumptuously usurped the roles of their betters.

The victims of rebellion played all the familiar notes which the mention of Masaniello presented them. The rebels were ambitious upstarts, meddlers in affairs where they had no business. Nicholas Bayard, who sprang from old Dutch and French families and was a nephew of Peter Stuyvesant, blasted Leisler's common background. He was unhappy "with the station nature had fitted him for, and placed him in"; "his soaring, aspiring mind" aimed constantly at "that which neither his birth nor

---

adventurer," take advantage of "popular disquietudes," gather together the discontented, and assume the powers of government, sweeping away the liberties of the people. Moncure D. Conway, ed., *The Writings of Thomas Paine* (4 vols., New York, 1894–96), I, 99.

5. "The Beginning, Progress, and Conclusion of Bacon's Rebellion, 1675–1676," C. M. Andrews, ed., *Narratives of the Insurrections*, p. 31; Merrill Jensen, ed., *English Historical Documents*, v. IX, *American Colonial Documents to 1776* (London, 1955), 586; Wilcomb E. Washburn, *The Governor and the Rebel* (Chapel Hill, N.C., 1957), pp. 17, 19.

education had ever qualified him for. . . ." And again, he was a proud person who exalted himself above "his brethren" and disdained even his own kindred "unless they will entitle him Lieutenant Governour." A "puny usurper," Chidley Brooke called him, who was infatuated with a taste of power. Coode and company were an "indigent people," "restless spirits," full of "malice, pride, and ambition." [6]

There was difficulty, however, in clothing Leisler and Coode as individuals in peasant garb. After all, Leisler had become a well-to-do merchant who had married into a prominent Dutch family. He was a German, however, and therefore an outsider to both Dutch and English in New York, and this helped support contempt for him.[7] More telling, his enemies frequently spoke of the "manifest irraconal & intollerable violence" of Leisler and his faction, of his "turbulent mind," his "mad and violent temper," which fitted better the Masaniello pattern.[8] Nor was Coode out of Maryland peasantry. A planter, an officer in the militia, he owned considerable land and sat frequently in the Maryland assembly. He had often been in trouble with the proprietary government but always managed to escape severe punishment, probably owing to his popularity, which once elected him to the lower house while his trial was pending for attempted rebellion.[9]

But if Leisler and Coode were not rabble themselves, they were rabble-rousers, or so their opposition claimed. Bayard's friends in New York and Baltimore's in Maryland went out of their way to broadcast the archrebels' followers as the vulgar and common. They were the "meane sort of people," and the "worser sort" who abetted Leisler; others described them as of "meane birth and sordid Educacon & desperate ffortunes," the "ignorant Mobile," the "most abject Comon people." In Maryland Coode's enemies spoke of the "long soard in the Rables hands" and the "profligate wretches" who danced to his tune. The innocent objects of rebellion in New York were, of course, the "Gentlemen," the "principall ffreeholders," and the "Considerable In-

6. [Nicholas Bayard], *A Modest and Impartial Narrative, 1690*, Andrews, ed., *Narratives*, pp. 327, 351; Chidley Brooke to Sir Robt. Southwell, New York, Apr. 5, 1691, *N.Y. Col. Docs.*, III, 757; Cecil County petition, Nov. 18, 1689, *Arch. of Md.*, VIII, 134–35; Richard Hill to Lord Baltimore, Sept. 20, 1689, *ibid.*, 122.

7. For Leisler's background, see Edwin R. Purple, *Genealogical Notes Relating to Lieut.-Gov. Jacob Leisler and His Family Connections in New York* (New York, 1877); *Doc. Hist. N.Y.*, II (1849), Introductory; Andrews, ed., *Narratives*, pp. 317–18, 334 n.; Lawrence H. Leder, *Robert Livingston*, p. 59; Jerome R. Reich, *Leisler's Rebellion*, pp. 58–60.

8. "Answer to Blagge's Memorial," *Doc. Hist. N.Y.*, II (1849), 390; *Nicholas Bayard's Narrative of Occurrences*, in *N.Y. Col. Docs.*, III, 636–48.

9. See ch. 5 above. See also Andrews, *Colonial Period*, II, 378, n. B; Michael G. Kammen, "The Causes of the Maryland Revolution of 1689," *Maryland Historical Magazine* (Dec. 1960), pp. 322–24.

habitants," while in Maryland they were "men of estates or men of note," the "best men," even the "best Protestants."

Exploiting the mob for sinister purposes was as criminal as rebellion itself. Enemies of Leisler and Coode piled up evidence in their propaganda of the rebels' manipulation of the common people for their own ends. Leisler was repeatedly accused of instigating the rabble against his opponents; he put notions into the "ignorant peoples heads," who were "deluded, infested, and poisoned thereby." He and his faction blindfolded the "ignorant and innocent people with . . . special and guilded pretence." And all this for their "particular ends," to reap some selfish advantage. Specifically, his enemies made much of the charge that Leisler had stirred up the trouble at first to avoid paying customs on a shipload of wine at anchor in the harbor. John Coode came in for the same kind of attack: he had "poisoned" the fools who followed him by the most absurd lies ever invented; he and his cronies persuaded the "poor silly mobile" to do their bidding and all to "shelter themselves from the law." [10]

If Leisler, Coode, and their rebellions were not quite Masaniellian in character by the century's standards, it was not for lack of effort on the part of their enemies in New York and Maryland. By the middle of 1690 Robert Livingston believed the charge had taken hold in England. While suffering under Leisler, he rejoiced at the appointment of his former governor, Francis Nicholson, as new governor of Virginia. It sharply demonstrated, he wrote, ' "how our massienello's . . . Proceedings are Received at Home." ' But, of course, all rebels are irresponsible, Nicholas Bayard scoffed: Leisler led a "drunken crue." "Most of those who appeared in Arms were Drunk," said a New York gentleman. "It's a pleasant thing to see the rascals in their Cupps," Peter Sayer wrote home to Lord Baltimore; "Coade calls himself Massinella, but vaunts he has outraigned him." [11]

Leisler and his rebels spent little time defending themselves against the charge of mob and rabble. He often spoke of the "people" as his supporters who had chosen him to lead them. Once he described his

10. The above comments can be found in a variety of letters and documents. For New York, see *Bayard's Narrative of Occurrences,* in *N.Y. Col. Docs.,* III, 636–48, *passim.* Andrews, ed., *Narratives,* pp. 320–54, *passim.* See also, "Answer to Blagge's Memorial," *Doc. Hist. N.Y.,* II (1849), 388–90, and "A Narrative in Answer to their Majties Letter," *ibid.,* pp. 391–93. Bayard to Blathwayt, Dec. 10, 1689, BPCol. Wmsbg., v. VIII. Not all who opposed Leisler were of New York's elite. After a riot protesting against his government, two of those arrested were Edward Buckmaster, a tavernkeeper, and Derrick Vanderburg, a mason. Andrews, ed., *Narratives,* p. 335 and n. For Maryland, see *Arch of Md.,* VIII, 118–22, 125, 126, 129, 130–31, 134–35, 136–37, 153–55, 158–59, 161, 188–90, 193.

11. Quoted in Leder, *Robert Livingston,* p. 72; *A Letter From A Gentleman . . . of New-York,* Andrews, ed., *Narratives,* pp. 363, 364; *Arch. of Md.,* VIII, 162.

enemies as "grandees," [12] but rebel propaganda was usually not loaded with the contempt of class like that of Bayard and others. That Leisler and his "people" were of a different sort from the oligarchy with different aims is apparent when one discovers who they were and what they did, or what they thought they ought to do, once they were in control of the government of New York.

True, there were plenty of artisans and ordinary people who supported Leisler and fought his battles for him. Nicholas Bayard and former mayor of the city Stephen Van Cortlandt frequently let the world know about the lowly occupations of his supporters. Cornelius Pluvera was a "poorman" who sold beer and rum at retail; Hendrick Cuyler and Henry Johne were bakers. Leisler's new sheriff, Johannes Johnson, was formerly a "Carpenters M****" (?) and George Brownson a surveyor. Van Cortlandt contemptuously called Abraham Gouverneur, whom the rebels made town clerk and later deputy secretary of the colony, a "boy" who lived "in our street." Leisler's new marshal was a bricklayer, and Gerrit Duyckinck earned his living as a limner and glazier (who with his father, Evert, gave rise to a dynasty of prize craftsmen and portrait painters of the next century). Joost Stoll, the man Leisler sent to England as an agent early in the rebellion, was a dram seller who Bayard claimed was not "worth a groat." (He was not worth much as an agent either, for he got nowhere in his attempts to explain the rebellion in London.) To paint Leisler as the old council wanted him to look, he needed a rabble around him, and Bayard and Van Cortlandt tried hard to supply it. [13]

What they did not say was that Leisler's council contained several substantial colonists, along with the artisans and ordinary people about them. It was sprinkled with a few professionals like Gerardus Beekman and Samuel Staats, who were both physicians. Peter Delanoy and Samuel Edsall were far from rabble, and so were some of Leisler's other supporters, Charles Lodwyck, for instance, who was a well-to-do merchant like Leisler himself, and Abraham de Peyster, a militia captain and a "gentleman of figure." [14]

Not as easily placed is Jacob Milborne, Leisler's second-in-command and son-in-law. He had had a spotty career in England—where he was born—the Barbados, and Connecticut, before settling in New York. There he had prospered moderately as merchant and part-time lawyer, although he ran afoul of Governor Andros during proprietary days. He

---

12. Leisler to Gov. Treat, Aug. 9, 1689, *Doc. Hist. N.Y.*, II (1849), 22.

13. Van Cortlandt to Nicholson, Dec. 18[?], 1689, BPCol. Wmsbg., v. IX; Andrews, ed., *Narratives*, pp. 324 and n., 325.

14. *Ibid.*, 324 n., 325 n., 340 n. 1. Lodwyck later defected along with several other merchants.

was in Holland at the time of the Glorious Revolution, and there and later in England he picked up numerous rumors about a Catholic conspiracy and New York's danger from the French. When he returned to the colony in August 1689, he threw himself whole-heartedly into the rebellion and was loyal to his chief throughout, taking on some of Leisler's arbitrariness and impetuousness, particularly in his attempt to force Albany to Leisler's side. According to Nicholas Bayard, Milborne was full of tales about the common people's role in William's success. The new King held his power owing to the people's electing him, he argued, and *"Vox Populi est vox Dei."* William was really the servant of his subjects, and Milborne preached that the revolution in New York was very much the same as in England. As far as circumstances permitted, Bayard tried hard to put Milborne, a man of "decayed fortunes," into the Masaniello camp, and he repeatedly spoke of him with contempt, which does not tell us very much, since he described all rebels that way.[15] Jacob Milborne's brother William was an Anabaptist minister in Boston, of all places, where he took part in the rebellion there and sat with the "sensible Gentlemen" at the Town House on April 18 when they forced Andros' surrender.[16] Although the Milbornes were not rabble, they certainly were not considered among the colonies' first families either.

Leisler's ranks, then, were laced with several prominent New York names, along with a sizable number from working, artisan, and farming classes. Doubtless the majority had less to lose by rebellion than the proprietary and royal favorites whose governments had benefited those who administered them. But they hardly fitted the Masaniello pattern.

John Coode was not wholly successful in painting the rebellion in anti-Catholic colors. If the number of complaints and petitions against his government is an accurate indication of dissent, one must conclude that a good many Protestants, besides the suppressed Catholics, opposed their liberator. Still, there was little sustained and violent resistance. There was plenty of disagreement, however. Some came from colonists who seemed altogether willing to accept the demise of Lord Baltimore as proprietor but not the rise of John Coode, whose government they found oppressive and distasteful. A number of these looked forward to a royal government and petitioned for it, as did Coode, for that matter. Others were ready to accept either William's settlement of the colony, whatever it might be, *or* a reestablishment of the pro-

15. *A Modest and Impartial Narrative, 1690*, Andrews, ed., *Narratives*, 335–36 and n.; Reich, *Leisler's Rebellion*, pp. 69–70.

16. See ch. 13 above. Andrews, ed., *Narratives*, p. 336 n.

prietor's rule, for, said a handful of petitioners in Calvert County, they had enjoyed many happy times under Baltimore when their religion, rights, and property were secure. Still others, and, according to the bulk of the correspondence left to us, maybe the largest number of dissenters, asked outright for a return to proprietary government and the "halcyon dayes" under Lord Baltimore. They had enjoyed the liberties of Englishmen then, as fully as subjects in the realm, a strong indication that they no longer believed they did so under Coode. On all accounts, the opposition made clear its disgust of Coode's upstart government, and Coode himself it accused of fraud and deception. He had taken up arms under pretense, and by a great hoax about French and Indians had frightened a good many colonists into rebelling with him and his accomplices.[17]

It was against these dissenters, substantial Protestants like Richard Smith, Sheriff Michael Taney, and Captain Richard Hill, that Coode's government moved with force, especially when those who refused to obey encouraged others to do the same. There were no pitched battles, but stubbornness increased when Coode's people yanked colonists from their homes, imprisoned some "contrary to all laws," and dragged others before the new assembly to answer for their actions. A number fled from their homes to avoid capture and while they were gone had their property seized. In some counties elections to Coode's assembly were slow and took place only because voters were awed by his troops. In Anne Arundel County, where settlers claimed not five Catholics resided, no elections were held for some time. The same delay occurred in one or two other counties, forcing the early assembly to meet without their burgesses. Coode's people, like Leisler's in New York, regarded all opposition as rebellion against Maryland's government and William III, and, again like Leisler, he and his followers were considered by a substantial minority as oppressors who ruled by the sword.[18]

It is clear that a number of Protestants, besides Catholics, were openly vocal about the false and vulgar character of the rebellion. It was they who looked upon Coode and his followers with contempt, charging them with deception, exploitation, ambition, malice, and self-interest of the worst sort. Leaders surrounding Coode were somewhat alike in background and position: Protestant landowners and planters, justices of the peace, and officers in the militia. For the most part they had been barred from the better places in government, although Cheseldyne was speaker of the lower house, elected, of course, not by choice of the proprietor. Most enjoyed more savory reputations than

17. *Arch. of Md.*, VIII, 114–22, 128–29, 130–31, 133–37, 153–55, 212–13.

18. *Ibid.*, 110–11, 118–21, 125, 126, 134–37, 147–49, 153–55, 181–82, 192–93; *ibid.*, XIII, 235–36, 237–38; *CSPCol.*, 1689–1692, #632.

Coode, who, while popular, was tainted with subversion by his earlier association with the infamous Josias Fendall.[19]

Coode lived with this doubtful reputation for the rest of his life. The sum total of his career affords little to damage the conclusion that he was a chronic agitator and perpetual malcontent who seldom failed by his uninhibited outbursts to stir up both friends *and* enemies. Some time after the rebellion Governor Nicholson looked back on Coode's doings in Maryland and wryly observed that it would be extraordinary if there were not such people as Coode in the American plantations— which tells us something about the governor's opinion of colonies and colonists. In affairs of government, he thought, Coode was a "diminutive Ferguson." (Peter Sayer already had likened another Maryland rebel to the same notorious republican plotter and supporter of Monmouth in England, while saving Coode exclusively for the Masaniello slot.) [20]

In point of religion, Nicholson went on, Coode was a "Hobbist, or worse." There was, indeed, some question about Coode's steadfastness in religion and in political principle. He was at home, it seems, in Anglican and Catholic churches and admitted to training in the priesthood of both. En route to England in 1690 he bragged to a fellow passenger that he could get on well enough in either Ireland or France since he "could make a popish Masse." Governor Nicholson at one time called him a "notorious coward" and claimed it was Coode's maxim during his numerous political struggles in Maryland that "if much dirt is thrown some of it will stick." Most incriminating evidence against his character and the integrity of his rebellion came from his enemies, to be sure. But Coode's own comments, if accurately reported, do not do much to enhance his character, including such remarks as: "God damn mee what I did was in prejudice or revenge to the Lord Baltimore." Maryland's revolt was no doubt rightly called Coode's Rebellion, for John Coode was its outspoken leader. It is likely that his followers were more attracted by his aggressive leadership than by his sterling character.[21]

19. For the backgrounds of these men, see ch. 5 above; Andrews, ed., *Narratives*, pp. 309 n., 313 n.; Michael G. Kammen, "Causes of the Maryland Revolution of 1689," pp. 321–27; Hester D. Richardson, *Side-Lights on Maryland History* (2 vols., Baltimore, 1913) II, 18–19.

20. Nicholson's observations are quoted in George Chalmers, *Political Annals,* I, 383, and Edward D. Neill, *Terra Mariae* (Philadelphia, 1867), p. 173. Andrews, *Colonial Period,* II, 378 n.; Peter Sayer to Baltimore, Dec. 31, 1689, *Arch. of Md.,* VIII, 161.

21. Andrews, *Colonial Period,* II, 378 n.; Kammen, "Causes of the Maryland Revolution of 1689," p. 323; *Arch. of Md.,* VIII, 210; H. R. McIlwaine, ed., *Exec. Journals of the Council of Va.,* I, 419; Chalmers, *Political Annals,* I, 383.

Coode, Cheseldyne, and Nehemiah Blackiston, three prominent leaders of the rebellion, had all married daughters of Thomas Gerrard, an old planter and curiously a Catholic within a Protestant family. Like Josias Fendall, Gerrard had opposed the proprietary for years, and some of his dissent rubbed off on his sons-in-law. When the overthrown Catholics and outraged Protestants complained about self-interested men who had turned the colony upside down, they meant these people along with Henry Jowles and a few others who manipulated affairs through cruel hoaxes, they said, and poisoned the minds of the ordinary people with their criminal lies.[22]

From the beginning charges of self-interest as a cause of rebellion were common. Although Coode and company were officeholders before the uprising, they improved their positions considerably once the government was in their hands. For instance, when the Associators' Assembly met in early September 1689, not long after the takeover, it appointed John Coode commander in chief of the province and assigned him military command of St. Mary's County, too. Control of civil affairs there went to Kenelm Cheseldyne with Coode and Nehemiah Blackiston as justices. Henry Jowles superintended both military and civil affairs in Calvert County. Coode became naval officer for the Potomac trade, responsible for its encouragement and the dispatch of shipping until Blackiston replaced him as collector in 1690. Andrew Abington, a close associate and an "ordinary keeper," became collector of Patuxent River and the bay district the same year. These posts were the most lucrative of the collectorships in the colony. Coode, Blackiston, Cheseldyne, and Jowles, at the outset of the new government, were four of a seven-man committee charged with "alloting, laying and assessing the publick leavy" of the colony and proceeded immediately, with the help of the sheriffs, to draw up lists of taxables.[23] Petitions to the King from both Kent and Talbot counties complained bitterly that delegates, sitting in Coode's Convention government, were quick to appropriate judicial places for themselves, all "to the terror" of the colony's more peaceful subjects.[24] From places of power and prestige in the rebel government, each of the leaders, Coode briefly, went on to splendid positions under the royal government, once the King decided to attach Maryland to the Crown.[25]

22. Andrews, ed., *Narratives*, pp. 309 n., 313 n.; Kammen, "Causes of the Maryland Revolution of 1689," pp. 321–27.

23. Papers relating to the Associators' Assembly, 1689, *Arch. of Md.*, XIII, 241–47; *ibid.*, VIII, 167, 192, 209.

24. *Ibid.*, 129, 133–34.

25. *Ibid.*, XIII, 251, 252; *ibid.*, VIII, 312; Randolph to Blathwayt, James Town, June 28, 1692, Toppan, ed., *Randolph*, VII, 373–85; Copley to Blathwayt, July 30,

As a result of the rebels' rise in government, particularly that of the four principals, charges of self-interest as primary cause of the rebellion increased in frequency. More than a hundred Calvert County Protestants insisted that the rebels had struck to "gratifie their own ambitions and mallitious designes," and it was not the first time that some of the ringleaders had tried to tear down the government. Of course, they were right in this last accusation, since Coode had been particularly visible in the disruptions of 1681 when he and Fendall laid their aborted plans and at a meeting in Blackiston's house. To Cecil County protesters the instigators were "certain discontented and indigent persons" who by their rebellion acted to protect themselves from prosecution.[26]

Governor Francis Nicholson in Virginia, who kept a wary eye on Maryland's doings, was more specific in his charges. He claimed that the new customs collectors in Maryland were hand in glove with the new government and not at all diligent in their duties. One, he knew, and others he suspected, were already indebted to the Crown. As a royal governor Nicholson took it upon himself to admonish the Maryland "Committee" to enforce the acts of Parliament and collect and account for the customs. At one point he ordered a captain of the Royal Navy, whose ship was on duty in Chesapeake Bay for just such occasions, to examine all vessels leaving Maryland with an eye in particular for violations of the Plantations Duty. Nicholson's intelligence reports had informed him that the Crown's customs was "very much defrauded" by great quantities of tobacco being carried from Maryland to New England, other colonies, Scotland, and several European ports and no duty paid. It came out later that the Plantation Act had taken a severe beating in Maryland under the interim government. Some twenty-five ships had left the colony in 1690 without even clearing, never mind paying the penny duty on each pound of tobacco. Besides losing his colony, Lord Baltimore was stuck with the royal customs arrears, which he tried desperately to extract from Coode and the rebel collectors.[27]

Probably more important to Baltimore than securing the King's customs was collection of his own, which was his principal source of revenue. He and James Heath, his agent in Maryland, claimed that

1692, BPCol. Wmsbg., v. XVIII; Kammen, "Causes of the Maryland Revolution of 1689," pp. 325, 326–27, 329.

26. *Arch. of Md.*, VIII, 130–31, 135.

27. C.O. 5/1358/21; *CSPCol., 1689–1692*, #1023; *Arch of Md.*, VIII, 209; H. R. McIlwaine, ed., *Exec. Journals of the Council of Va.*, I, 130; Blathwayt to Copley, Feb. 22, 1693, BPCol. Wmsbg., v. XVIII; George Slater to Blathwayt, Apr. 5, 1697, *ibid.*

proprietary duties on Maryland's trade were also sadly neglected, that besides failing to surrender these sums to the proprietor, Coode and his people embezzled the revenue and spent it on themselves. Nor would they allow Heath to superintend the collection or even inspect their accounts. On top of this, the rebel leaders, according to agent Heath, plundered and pillaged the estates of those who opposed them, even "good protestants," and imprisoned many who resisted.[28] Coode not only denied the charges but journeyed to London to do so personally before the Privy Council which investigated. The revolt, he blandly testified, was a peaceful affair; it was carried out in the King's service and was "managed without any Sort of Self Interest or Cruelty toward [their] Enemies or Oppressors." [29] As events turned out, his judges seemed to agree with him.

In justifying revolt in 1690, Coode laid heavier emphasis than before on the depressed conditions of Maryland colonists as a cause of rebellion. At the heart of their grievances were the "disability & poverty of a distressed people" long subjected to an oppressive and grasping government. While Coode's and his cronies' attacks on despotism and the subsequent seizure of the government satisfied their own constitutional complaints and maybe their personal ambitions, their actions, they said, coincided with the crying needs of a poor and suffering people. Sensitive to their poverty, Coode's assembly was solicitous of its people's pocketbooks. It maintained the government with as little cost as possible; the "publique leavy" was the least ever asked, the "smalest that ever was in the Province." For a distressed people the revolution, then, was a welcome release from a "long tirannick arbitrary" government. Tyranny was dislodged and the poor were comforted, or so Coode argued at home and abroad.[30]

Proprietary favorites could in part agree that the new government's tenderness toward the poor and distressed was indeed a welcome relief, as many could see. People in debt, Peter Sayer wrote home to His Lordship, "think itt the bravest time that ever was, no Courts open, nor no law proceedings, which they pray may continue, as long as they live." And the cause of it all, Sayer went on, was that "Our Masinella Coade had gott at the head of five or six hundred men." [31]

The only Maryland Catholics who dared show resistance to Coode

28. *CSPCol., 1689–1692*, #947, #948; *Arch. of Md.*, VIII, 189–90, 204–5, 211.

29. C.O. 5/713/4; *CSPCol., 1689–1692*, #792; *Arch. of Md.*, VIII, 212, 216–18, 219–20, 225–28.

30. *Ibid.*, XIII, 237–38; C.O. 5/713/4; *CSPCol., 1689–1692*, #792; Beverly McAnear, ed., "Mariland's Grevances Wiy The Have Taken Op Arms," *Journal of Southern History*, VIII (1942), 408.

31. Dec. 31, 1689, *Arch. of Md.*, VIII, 158, 161.

were those who had escaped to Virginia. These were the "papish rebellious grandees," as Leisler dubbed them,[32] men like Governor William Joseph and Councillor Nicholas Sewall, along with a couple of Catholic priests and William Digges, a Protestant, who was loyal to Baltimore throughout. Digges was originally a Virginian who had fled under a cloud to Maryland during Bacon's Rebellion. He had become a solid supporter of the proprietor, a member of his council, and a deputy governor charged with command of the State House at St. Mary's when it surrendered to Coode. Digges kept a residence in Virginia, where he took refuge once Coode was in the saddle, offering a convenient and much needed asylum to other proprietary favorites who had held the chief offices in the colony and whose careers in Maryland abruptly had come to an end.[33]

Had these people remained in Virginia and kept the peace, they might have met with little trouble from Maryland. The governor and council of Virginia were not very sympathetic to Coode's government or his demands for extradition of the refugees, described as traitors, tyrants, and, as we shall see, murderers by Coode. But Nicholas Sewall, Lord Baltimore's stepson, found it difficult to stay away from Maryland, so accessible by water; several times he visited his home on the Patuxent River, doubtless on private business but also in order to keep tabs on Coode's doings.

During one of these visits in early January 1690, John Payne, now royal customs collector for the region and a loyal supporter of the rebels, tried to board Sewall's yacht and was shot dead from close range by the vessel's defenders. Sewall himself was ashore during the fracas but was declared responsible for the murder by Coode and other Maryland rebels, since the shots were fired from his vessel. Two stories emerged from the incident. Coode and his government claimed that it occurred in the daytime and that Payne, carrying out his legal duties as collector in the King's name, was murdered in cold blood by enemies of William III and the rightful government of Maryland. Sewall and his backers insisted that Coode, as part of the conspiracy against the proprietor's government, had deliberately sent Payne to capture them and the yacht. Further, they said, Payne had tried to board the vessel between three and four o'clock of a cloudy night and refused to turn back when warned off by the ship's crew. As a result he was shot and it served him right. Both sides agreed the fire was

32. *Doc. Hist. N.Y.*, II (1849), 181.
33. See letters between Maryland and Virginia, C.O. 5/1358/13; C.O. 1/68/108; C.O. 5/713/10; C.O. 5/713/1; *Arch. of Md.*, VIII, 127–28; Andrews, ed., *Narratives*, 79 n.; *CSPCol.*, *1689–1692*, #888.

returned, wounding a couple of Sewall's men, one critically. Sewall's yacht quickly fell down the Patuxent for York River in Virginia, where he and his men resumed their asylum.[34]

The Protestant Association made a large ruckus of the incident and claimed that Payne's was the only blood spilled in the whole course of the revolution. Not much imagination or a very long memory was needed to liken the event to George Talbot's murder of the King's collector Christopher Rousby a few years before, and Sewall, like Talbot, was a deputy governor and a prominent member of Baltimore's council. As in the earlier killing there followed a legal hassle over which colony should try the defendant and his accomplices, and both governments wrote home to England for instructions. William III's new regime probably was even less fond of proprietaries than James's. It promptly took the accusers' side of the case, doubtless encouraged by a petition from Payne's outraged brother in England, who demanded that justice be done. William ordered trial of the "Papists Confederates" in either Virginia or Maryland, wherever the killing of Payne in "Execution of his office" had occurred.[35]

Twice now Baltimore's people had murdered a royal officer. Coode used both incidents to stoke his propaganda with the hope of winning to his cause the powers-that-be at home, and he was successful. By April 1690 the Lords of Trade were describing him as chief of government in Maryland in the Crown's behalf.[36] Coode had less luck in Virginia, whose government was lukewarm about recognizing the Maryland rebellion, particularly after Francis Nicholson's arrival in the spring of 1690 as governor. Hounded out of New York a year or so earlier, Nicholson bore no love for rebels. Eventually, however, his government rounded up the offenders and carried them to St. Mary's, where court proceedings commenced. Two years later Maryland found three of the defendants guilty of murder and executed one, John Woodcock, who had actually fired the fatal shot. But Nicholas Sewall, like Talbot before him, never faced trial, for it was repeatedly delayed and finally forgotten.[37] No doubt the murder of John Payne by the proprie-

34. Details of the shooting of John Payne are plentiful. See letters, depositions, reports, etc., in the following: C.O. 5/713/3, I, III, IV, V; C.O. 5/1358/14–15; BPCol. Wmsbg., v. XVII; *Virginia Magazine of History and Biography*, 9 (1901–2), 30–31; McIlwaine, ed., *Exec. Journals of the Council of Va.*, I, 109–10; *Arch. of Md.*, VIII, 163–66; 168–69, 170–72, 176–77, 178–79; *CSPCol., 1689–1692*, #725, #785, #787, #792.

35. C.O. 5/1358/19–20; *CSPCol., 1689–1692*, #833, #851, #852; *Arch. of Md.*, VIII, 173–76; L. W. Labaree, ed., *Royal Instructions to English Colonial Governors*, I, 362; BPCol. Wmsbg., v. XVII.

36. C.O. 5/713/7.

37. BPCol. Wmsbg., v. XVIII; Andrews, *Colonial Period*, II, 377 n.

tor's friends had something to do with the Crown's lenient response to rebellion in Maryland.

Opposition to Coode was strong in several parts of the colony and represented a substantial number of Protestants besides Catholics. Some may have been dissatisfied with life under proprietary rule but not sufficiently to chuck it for the likes of Coode and his people. Regardless of the opposition, Coode managed to remain on top, maybe owing to his earlier popularity but certainly to the forceful leadership which he and his followers exerted. And then the violence committed by the Catholic party against collector Payne redounded to Coode's favor despite his inability to bring to trial one of his chief antagonists. Those who opposed the rebellion may have taken some comfort in explaining it to themselves and Lord Baltimore as Masaniellian in style, although Coode and his fellow rebels, like Leisler and some of his, belied by their backgrounds much of the accusation. Yet their very defense of the affair testified that they looked to the poor and distressed, the "meaner sort," for support. In so doing they played into the hands of the Sewalls, the Diggeses, and the Sayers, who called them rabble-rousers and condemned them for criminally exploiting the discontent of the "poor silly mobile."

There was no Massachusetts Masaniello, catapulted out of his fishman's hut to lead a Congregational mob against the English viceroy. There was no Boston Bashaw, no Puritan Pasha either, to deceive the vulgar crowd and bend it to his selfish will. Edward Randolph tried hard to paint the rebellion in this familiar hue: "Here is a violent & bloudy zeal," he wrote, "stird up in the Rabble[,] acted & managed by the preachers." [38] Although Boston at times was far from peaceful during the rebellion and after, conditions hardly matched the accustomed pattern of illegal rebellion. Primarily this was true because there was no single leader, no Leisler or Coode, least of all a Masaniello, upon whom Randolph and his fellow prisoners could focus as the villain of the business. Cotton Mather, Simon Bradstreet, and Wait Winthrop certainly did not measure up as either vulgar fanatics or deceitful manipulators of the people. "Sensible Gentlemen" had put themselves forward at the precise moment on April 18, 1689, and successfully guided the affair. Randolph's "preachers" doubtless had their say and exercised influence upon their people as before, but it would be hard to conclude that they had provoked a rabble to rise against their betters. Whether Lawrence Hammond was right when he claimed the

38. Randolph to Blathwayt, July 20, 1689, Hall, Leder, and Kammen, eds., *Glo. Rev. in Am.*, p. 63.

people of Boston and the adjacent towns "did this day rise as one man" would be difficult to determine, but the circumstances seemed to support the conclusion. Surely the rebels and their supporters were an overwhelming majority in Massachusetts. One might almost say they were the "whole people," give or take a few Anglicans and Quakers here and there. But what rabble participated was quickly absorbed into a larger group of colonists from all levels, including the cream of society like the Winthrops, Bradstreets, and Mathers. Later in England the colony's agents insisted that the "country" brought the charges against Andros and his officers, not individuals like themselves. Hitherto historians have condemned the agents' failure to sign the charges against Andros and his people as a lack of nerve or confidence, telling evidence of their hypocrisy and the disingenuousness of the rebellion. This may be true, but one might argue as logically, as their counsel did, that the agents meant what they said and did not believe they were individually competent to sign charges against their oppressors when it was the "country," the whole people of Massachusetts, who had justifiably rebelled against tyranny in their King's behalf. Massachusetts colonists, like Englishmen at home, rebelled against James's arbitrary Catholic government.[39] Masaniello had no role to play in the overthrow of the Dominion. Historically it was another kind of rebellion and one which Bay colonists would not forget.[40]

39. Mather, "Autobiography," A.A.S. *Proc.*, 71 (1961), pt. 2, 340–41; Elisha Cooke to Bradstreet, London, Oct. 16, 1690, Hall, Leder, and Kammen, eds., *Glo. Rev. in Am.*, p. 71; Michael G. Hall, *Edward Randolph and the American Colonies*, p. 130.

40. Perry Miller suggested the idea of a new kind of revolution in *The New England Mind: From Colony to Province*, ch. XI. A more specific linking between ideas of 1689 and those of the 1770's is explained in Theodore B. Lewis, Jr., "Massachusetts and the Glorious Revolution: A Political and Constitutional Study, 1660–1692" (unpubl. Ph.D. thesis, Univ. of Wisconsin, 1967), ch. XIII, "The Revolutionary Tradition, 1689–1774."

17 Resistance and Dissent: War, Merchants, and Tories

New York merchants were a problem for Leisler. At the outset a number supported him, men like Charles Lodwyck, and well they might, for he was a merchant himself and appeared to share their interests. Before the overthrow of the Dominion he had led a peaceful revolt against paying customs duties to what he called an illegal Catholic government, and his defiance won him followers. Once he was in the saddle, however, merchants were quick to criticize his policies, and their grievances mounted, particularly in the spring of 1690. Much of their discontent was bound up in one way or another with the cost of defending New York. England had gone to war with France in May of 1689, and Leisler took seriously, if the merchants did not, the colony's vulnerability to attack by the French and Indians. His attempts to force Albany and Schenectady into the fold, for both political and military reasons, were bitterly resented by the merchants, primarily those involved in the fur trade. And then Leisler's tactics and the resistance he encountered led to tragedy for which both he and his opponents were probably to blame.

The strongest challenge to Leisler's regime came from Albany, more than a hundred miles up the Hudson River. Owing to the increasing threats from the French and Indians, leading citizens of Albany, in continued defiance of Leisler, established in August 1689 what they called a convention made up of the mayor, aldermen, justices of the peace, and military officers of both city and county. Its purpose was to organize defenses and direct public affairs until William III, to whom, like Leisler, they willingly gave allegiance, directed otherwise. But in early September, when "Eminent Danger" of invasion threatened them from the north, they swallowed their pride and asked Leisler to help them. Leisler refused any aid until they recognized his regime. Disappointed, yet determined, they turned to New England and managed the loan of about eighty soldiers from Connecticut, an act of generosity which enraged Leisler and commenced a bitter feud between his government and that colony's which lasted for some time, in fact affected the course of events for the next few years. Outflanked from the east by Connecticut troops, who could only reinforce Albany's stubbornness to remain separate and free of his control, Leisler sent some of his own forces up the river in early November 1689 under command of Jacob Milborne, despite the convention's strong protest and resolve to resist. According to Leisler and Milborne, the move was to share the burden of defense with their compatriots at Albany and Schenectady against the French. To Mayor Peter Schuyler and the convention it was a deceptive maneuver to seize the fort, take over the government, and carry off to New York the Albany leaders, an encroachment on loyal subjects as serious as any they might expect from the French and Indians.[1]

The little drama played out at Albany was not only frustrating but humiliating to Leisler and his cause. The convention was cordially adamant and refused altogether to give up the fort. Milborne tried several means to persuade them, even an eloquent appeal over the heads of the convention to the common people of both Albany and Schenectady near by, proclaiming Leisler's readiness to rescue them from slavery and popery and the illegal rule of Catholic James which, he claimed, the Albany convention still represented. When this failed

1. Albany Convention Records, *Doc. Hist. N.Y.*, II (1849), 92–93, 97–98, 113–14, 117, 122, 124–32; Van Cortlandt to Nicholson, Dec. 18[?], 1689, BPCol. Wmsbg., v. IX; Leisler and Council to Gov. Treat of Conn., Mar. 1, 1690, C.O. 5/1081/112; Bradstreet to Hinckley, Oct. 5, 1689, *Hinckley Papers*, M.H.S. *Coll.*, 4th ser., V (1861), 217–18; Lawrence H. Leder, *Robert Livingston*, pp. 62–63.

to budge them, he promised a freedom of trade and the right to bolt their own flour, promises which did not go down well at all with Albany merchants and the convention, made up, as it was, of leading citizens who supported the monopolies, in fact were party to them. The response from Albanians was not warming. At one point Milborne marched his troops right up to the fort where Mayor Peter Schuyler and his forces quietly waited. But Milborne was dissuaded from attacking it by the ominous presence of a company of Mohawks poised on an adjacent hill who threatened to intervene if he carried out his plans. One of the reasons for Albany's stubbornness in the face of Leisler's determination to bring it into line was a fear of what the change might mean to the delicate balance of relations with the Iroquois upon whom they depended as suppliers in the fur trade, to say nothing of their role as allies against the French. That the Mohawks appreciated Albany's tenuous position was evident in their silent threat to Milborne, who was forced to retreat and not very proudly. He was successful, however, in detaching a faction of the burghers from their loyalty to the convention with the help of Joachim Staats, whom a small party of Albanians was willing to accept as commander of the fort in place of Mayor Schuyler. But the convention had its way and insisted that Leisler's troops at Albany be under its command or go home where they belonged. Although Milborne left some twenty soldiers quartered privately when he drifted down the river to safer ground, the convention stood firm, keeping both Albany and Schenectady free of Leisler's control for the time being at least.[2]

Albany and Ulster collaborated in a protest against Leisler's attempted encroachment and published it with fanfare in the middle of January 1690. It blasted his grasping the government and denied his arbitrary, assumed power; his malicious promises to break open their trade and flour monopoly, they claimed, were deliberate attempts to delude the common people foolishly into rebellion.[3] Not many days later the Albany convention petitioned for help, not to Leisler this time but to William's royal governor "when he comes," giving him an earful of Leisler's "usurped Power." But Albany people told him, too, of their dreadful fear of a French attack, particularly since Leisler's "distractions" had muddled their defenses.[4]

2. *Doc. Hist. N.Y.*, II (1849), 113–35, *passim*; Van Cortlandt to Nicholson, Dec. 18[?], 1689, BPCol. Wmsbg., v. IX; *N.Y. Col. Docs.*, III, 636–48.

3. Letter of the Convention to Gov Slatir [Sloughter] when he comes, Jan. 20, 1690, Livingston Family Papers, General Correspondence, 1661–1695, F.D.R. Library.

4. *Doc. Hist. N.Y.*, II (1849), 52–53, 59; Albany and Ulster protest, C.O. 5/1081, 101A.

Albany's fears were justified. Count Frontenac, governor of New France, had been quick to exploit English disorganization after the Glorious Revolution. He longed to strike a blow against the rebelling colonies for James, the French King's friend and fellow Catholic, lending more substance to the colonists' fear of a Catholic conspiracy against them. With help of his military commander, Frontenac translated elaborate plans, agreed upon by Louis XIV's government, into an aggressive campaign against the English colonies in the winter of 1690. French determination to attack the rebel colonists had more behind it than love of James's Catholic rule. A strong wish to avenge their colony against the English followed the success of New York's governors, Dongan and then Andros, in persuading the Iroquois to accept dependence upon the English King. How deeply this affected the Five Nations is another matter, but the French regarded the Indian defection a blow to their fur trading and imperial plans in America. Moreover, they anticipated further English encroachment, not just upon the western Indians, from whom the French derived most of their furs, but upon Canada itself and very soon at that. French campaigns in the early 1690's were aimed both at winning back the allegiance of the Iroquois and forestalling an English invasion by crippling England's colonies, particularly by the capture of Albany and, according to Frontenac's military commander, New York City as well, with aid from the French fleet. Besides this, there were plans to deal the English costly defeats in the New Hampshire settlements and along the coast of Maine. Doubtless the three-pronged campaign called for concurrent attacks, but the eager French at Montreal, supported by a number of their converted Iroquois, got off first toward Albany about the first of February 1690. All told there were just over 200 in the expedition, almost evenly divided between Frenchmen and Indians.[5]

The French very dearly must have needed a victory over the English. In order to regain prestige in the eyes of the Indians and their settlers' confidence, they put up with the tremendous hardships of a midwinter campaign in country where severe cold and abundant snow made even survival hazardous, never mind a successful military offensive. Having tramped their way south from Montreal, Sieur le Moyne de Sainte Helene and his company switched plans a few miles short of Albany and turned toward Schenectady, a small trading village some twenty miles northwest of Albany. No doubt the abrupt change was owing to

5. For French plans, see "Papers Relating to the Invasion of New-York and the Burning of Schenectady by the French, 1690," *Doc. Hist. N.Y.*, I (1849), 285–302. Francis Parkman, *Count Frontenac and New France under Louis XIV* (Boston, 1880, reprinted 1966), pp. 187–89.

advice, maybe even threats, from the Indians, who scorned the French presumption in taking the larger, stronger settlement. The numbing cold of February 9 dictated an immediate attack, for delay would have been fatal to the intruders. They found Schenectady unguarded and the gates of the palisades open. Severe weather and internal disagreements about defense had sapped the strength of the inhabitants. The invaders quietly slipped into the village and took command, massacring in their beds whom they did not capture, sparing the few Iroquois there with whom they claimed no quarrel. After killing sixty men, women, and children and burning Schenectady to the ground, the French and Indians withdrew northward the next day with twenty-seven prisoners, five of them Negroes, and most of the village's horses. A handful of lucky survivors escaped during the night and in the wee hours of the morning trudged toward Albany to give the alarm. Albany sent a detachment, mostly Indians, after them; a late start and hard going made pursuit hazardous, but it managed to track down and destroy some of the stragglers, a few at the very outskirts of Montreal.[6]

Albany was terrified; doubtless it was similarly marked for destruction. The convention bitterly blamed Leisler for the catastrophe at Schenectady. Through his specious talk about rights and liberties and promises of breaking trading monopolies, he had destroyed the unity of the people there. Because of these promises, some of the inhabitants had refused to defend the village, foolishly expecting a change in their condition, and had prevented others from doing so. Robert Livingston claimed that Leisler had perverted the helpless victims by his seditious letters, which rescuers later found strewn and bloody in the streets of the village. Leisler's response to the Schenectady massacre was understandably different. The rebellious convention which denied his authority was still guided by loyalty to King James and Governor Andros and had refused his help which could have prevented the disaster. He blamed Connecticut, too, for earlier sending troops to Albany and thereby supporting the convention in its stubborn rebellion against his government at New York.[7] But the fate of Schenectady was more persuasive than Leisler's threats had ever been. Despite Livingston's appeal to Connecticut and Massachusetts for more help, Albany gave up to Leisler's government within a few

6. *Doc. Hist. N.Y.*, I (1849), 302–312; Short account of the sad massacre . . . , Liv. Fam. Papers, Indian Affairs, F.D.R. Lib.; C.O. 5/855, #40; *CSPCol., 1689–1692*, #826; Parkman, *Frontenac*, pp. 208–19.

7. *Ibid.*; C.O. 5/855, 80; Short account of the sad massacre, Liv. Fam. Papers, Ind. Aff., F.D.R. Lib.; Robt. Livingston to Andros, Apr. 14, 1690, *Doc. Hist. N.Y.*, I (1849), 309–10. See also pp. 311–12. For Leisler's story, see *ibid.*, pp. 307–9, 310–11.

weeks' time in the spring of 1690. Massachusetts warmly suggested the submission and cited the slaughter at Schenectady as a warning of what might occur if it did not. Leisler again sent troops up the river, where this time they replaced the former magistrates and took over the fort. The convention reluctantly accepted defeat; without outside support it had little choice in the matter. Following shortly the massacre at Schenectady, Leisler's control of New York was complete.[8]

Once Leisler believed the King had confirmed the new regime and particularly after the surrender of Albany to it, his government exerted itself more forcefully. But the very vigor of its leadership provoked reaction against him, primarily from the merchants, which eventually was his undoing. When his first assembly met on April 23, 1690, it promptly levied for defense purposes a colony-wide tax of three-pence in the pound on all real, personal, and "visible" property of the inhabitants, who, said Van Cortlandt, were "much against it." Already the merchants were disturbed by Leisler's levy the previous fall when he resurrected by proclamation the tax and customs system which the aborted assembly of 1683 had devised.[9]

The next day the government went even further to alienate the merchants. It was the assembly's determined action, more than anything else, which forced them to make a choice between Leisler and rebellion, on the one hand, and the economic advantages which New York City and Albany for some time had enjoyed, on the other. For years farmers of the countryside in the Hudson River Valley and elsewhere had been discriminated against by the proprietary and then royal governments which had forced them to transport their grain to the city, where it was bolted and baked and then marketed at home and abroad. From these processes the city millers and merchants took healthy profits, larger than they deserved, according to the growers. Long Islanders in particular resented the system which channeled their products to Manhattan instead of Connecticut and Massachusetts where old Puritan ties existed. But under Leisler this discrimination came to an abrupt halt. On April 24 the assembly broke the flour monopoly and guaranteed equal freedom for all New Yorkers to "boult and bake and transport" anywhere, anything they produced. "The onc

8. At a meeting of the Council in Hartford, Mar. 11, 1690, Liv. Fam. Papers, Ind. Aff., F.D.R. Lib.; The Governor and Council of the Massachusetts to Peter Schuyler, Esq . . . , Mar. 25, 1690, *ibid.*, Gen. Corresp., 1661–1698; C.O. 5/1081/113A; *CSPCol., 1689–1692, Addenda,* #2763; Van Cortlandt to Blathwayt, June 5, 1690, BPCol. Wmsbg., v. IX.

9. C.O. 5/1081/121; *CSPCol., 1689–1692,* #840; *Colonial Laws of New York,* I, 218; Van Cortlandt to Blathwayt, June 5, 1690, BPCol. Wmsbg., v. IX. For Leisler's earlier tax, see *Doc. Hist. N.Y.,* II (1849), 50.

place should have no more privileges than the other," the assembly insisted.[10] Taken literally, this act would have altered drastically New York's trading patterns beyond even the confines of the flour trade. It would have upset the precious Albany fur monopoly and spread the trade to other communities. With this idea in mind Leisler and Milborne had wooed the common people of Albany and Schenectady, hoping to bring them over to their side, with disastrous results as we have seen. But time ran out on Leisler, and the Albany trade remained undisturbed.

Breaking the city monopolies was enough to turn eager merchants away from rebellion even though they had backed Leisler earlier for other reasons. City merchants, particularly the less well-to-do, might not have appreciated the oligarchy which had selfishly called the turn in New York for so long, but to upset the system which brought most of the colony's trade to their doorsteps was not to be taken lightly. Three weeks or so after Leisler's assembly struck against the monopolies, thirty-six merchants got together and bitterly protested directly to King William and his Queen. The burden of their petition was simply that the "insolent alien" had destroyed their business. Some time later Governor Nicholson in Virginia echoed their protest and reported to the Lords of Trade that most English merchants had been forced out of New York by Leisler, thus ruining the colony's trade.[11]

Hard on the assembly's action in April came Leisler's "press" of provisions and materials in support of the war. This put the government at odds with many more inhabitants, again particularly merchants, who balked at forced contributions to William and Mary's cause against Canada, as the rebels insisted. When revenues fell short of defense needs, Leisler seized what the colony needed, or "plundered" the people, said Bayard and others. "Refractory" merchants stood by helpless while sheriffs broke into their cellars and warehouses on Leisler's orders to seize what they could find, although the government insisted that exact accounts were kept and compensation promised.[12]

Shortly after Leisler's assembly cracked the city monopolies, he and his government turned their attention to another task. Since the start of his regime, he had become increasingly sensitive to the problems of

10. *Colonial Laws of New York,* I, 218; Van Cortlandt to Andros, May 19, 1690, *N.Y. Col. Docs.,* III, 717.

11. *Ibid.,* 748–49. Several months later Governor Henry Sloughter reported the merchants' complaints to be "severally true." *Ibid.,* 762. Nicholson to Lords of Trade, Nov. 4, 1690, C.O. 5/1358, 32–33; Andrews, ed., *Narratives,* p. 350.

12. *Doc. Hist. N.Y.,* II (1849), 243; *Loyalty Vindicated from the Reflections of a Virulent Pamphlet* . . . (1698), Andrews, ed., *Narratives,* p. 388.

defending the colony from the French Canadians. Englishmen had more or less expected a war with France since William carried England into an alliance against the French King, and the Revolution itself had unhinged England's ties with Louis XIV which Charles and James had honored for a generation. But its outbreak certainly complicated circumstances for the colonies, whose interim governments lacked the stability, to say nothing of the money, to sustain the added burden. Moreover, European wars had a habit of extending to the New World, and the northern colonial frontier was dangerously exposed. Besides, war with France and Canada lent more substance to the paralyzing fear of a Catholic conspiracy which colonists, Leisler among them, were only too ready to believe. And then the disastrous raid on Schenectady gave pertinency to the whole danger which provoked Leisler to conclude that the problems of colonial defense fell primarily upon New York. He took upon himself the responsibilities of a soldier of the King, convinced that the colonies should carry their load in an imperial war against the French in Canada.

At Leisler's invitation commissioners from Massachusetts, Plymouth, and Connecticut met with him at New York City in late April 1690 to lay plans for some kind of cooperation, which would include the Iroquois, against the French. Colonies to the south were invited too, but they cordially begged off, claiming their own defense problems and their poverty prevented participation or contributions. From the convention emerged a master plan for the conquest of Canada which would strike a bold blow in England's behalf. At the same time, and maybe more important in colonists' eyes, they persuaded themselves that the best way to overcome a number of bad reports sent home and to secure a favorable hearing at court for their rebellions was to win the Crown a glorious victory against the French. But all this would cost money; in fact, it was already doing so, for the new tax of three-pence in the pound levied by Leisler's assembly was really to prepare New York's defenses. And merchants hated taxes like everyone else, maybe more so, since their trade was already undermined, or ruined, as they said.[13]

The threat of war with Canada provoked the arbitrary streak in Leisler. Already Nicholas Bayard and several others had marked him a harsh, overbearing man. Late in April 1690, like any royal governor,

---

13. For the Convention in New York, see a series of letters in *Hinckley Papers*, 232–33, 239, 247, 249–50, 250–52; Samuel Sewall, *Diary*, I, 317 and n., 318; Leisler to All the Westerne Governments, May 13, 1690, *Doc. Hist. N.Y.*, II (1849), 242; "Reflections Upon the Affairs of New England" [1691], *Wyllys Papers*, Conn. Hist. Soc. *Coll.*, XXI, 328; Leder, *Robert Livingston*, p. 71.

he peremptorily prorogued his first assembly when it displeased him. To William Penn's Governor Blackwell, who visited the city, he was a madman, "as arbitrary and tyrannical as any Bassa." Even the New England commissioners who helped to plan the campaign against Canada thought he carried "some matters too arbitrary." They thought him "earnest," however, in his design against the common enemy and had no hesitation about calling him "Governor"—to Coode he was "ye Honorble"—an honor he never won from Virginians or Quakers in Pennsylvania, or the people of Albany, for that matter, until after Schenectady was devastated.[14] As Leisler's responsibilities became greater, the charges of despotism against him grew sharper, accompanied by a decline in support, all of which convinced him the more of conspiracies and counterplots, to which he responded vigorously.

To officers of the old government and their adherents Leisler's whole rule was usurpation and his actions dictatorial. In turn, Leisler saw their criticism and resistance as disloyalty to the Revolution, King William, and, of course, to himself, and cursed them for Catholics or "papishly affected" villains still loyal to James. Since Leisler had the power, the consequences were severe: a seizing and imprisoning of opponents as traitors, sometimes without regard for the niceties of law. The Catholic conspiracy remained very strong in Leisler's and his followers' minds, and they related resistance in New York City to new French and Indian attacks on the frontier. Several sudden alarms and threats of a French fleet on the coast, later found to be false, were all the more reason for confining the field of maneuver of Leisler's enemies.[15]

All the rebel governments were by necessity cautious in their doings, apprehensive lest their enemies unite and recapture control. They watched the mails closely and were suspicious of arriving strangers, even departing friends. This was particularly true in New York, where the opposition was strongest and Leisler's aggressive leadership and impetuous nature provoked increasing mistrust and a falling off of loyalty. For some time the city was an armed camp, sensitive to any disturbance from outside or within. For example, in the summer of 1689, shortly after the rebellion, Leisler alarmed the whole town at the arrival of four Boston visitors who had failed to give the password. He mistook them, he said after jailing them, for a revengeful Andros

14. Benj. Bullivant's Journall, C.O. 5/855, #94; John Walley to Thomas Hinckley, Bristol, May 8, 1690, *Hinckley Papers*, 250–52; Gov. and Council of Mass. to Hinckley, Boston, Apr. 11, 1690, *ibid.*, 239; Coode to Leisler, Nov. 26, 1689, *Doc. Hist. N.Y.*, II (1849), 44; *ibid.*, 238, 282, 290.

15. See Leisler's correspondence, *Doc. Hist. N.Y.*, II (1849), 1–65, *passim*.

and Nicholson in disguise. Once searched, the newcomers' papers "told of their quality," harmlessly revealing them as two tutors and a couple of students on a jaunt from Harvard College. Leisler was indeed jittery.[16]

Not as harmless were his actions in the early weeks of 1690 when the fear of war and conspiracy against him intensified. Twice he seized John Perry, the "Publick Post," and searched his mailbags, claiming to discover "horrible devices" and "hellish designs" against the Protestants. Out of the seizures came a renewed determination to suppress conspiracy by arresting not just Catholics but all "disaffected persons," anyone, in fact, who had held a commission under former governors Dongan and Andros. Leisler "catched" his chief antagonist, Nicholas Bayard, and William Nichols, but Colonel Dongan, Stephen Van Cortlandt, and Anthony Brockholls eluded him, escaping to Pennsylvania or Maryland, Leisler believed. He spread the alarm to John Coode and requested their arrests in order to prevent their "wicked designe." By early March 1690 Leisler's government had jailed a number of colonists accused of conspiracy. By force and persuasion he managed also the surrender of about 150 civil and military commissions granted earlier by the royal government. Such success sharpened his will to "gett them all." With command of the militia more closely in his own hands, New York was much better able, he believed, to deal with subversion and, at the same time, to withstand the threat of French and Indians.[17]

In early June of 1690 opposition to Leisler reached a dangerous peak. In what began as a protest against the continued imprisonment of prominent New Yorkers, such as Bayard and Nichols, a group of about thirty militant burghers, including several merchants, accosted him in the street. Once the struggle began, the protesters violently complained of arbitrary taxes and illegal confinement of their friends. Although they insisted later they were unarmed, Leisler said one of his antagonists came after him with a "cooper's adze." A stroke of his cane square in the teeth of his assailant, plus the timely arrival of a handful of loyal New Yorkers and a few soldiers from the fort, drove

16. They were tutors John Leverett and William Brattle with students "Mr Emerson" and "young Mr Mackarty." George McKenzie to Capt. Nicholson, Aug. 19, 1689, M.H.S., Gay Transcripts, State Papers, III, 99–100; S. E. Morison, *The Intellectual Life of Colonial New England* (2d ed., Ithaca, N.Y., 1956), pp. 40–41. For Leisler's side of the story, see his letter to Gov. Treat, Aug. 28, 1689, *Doc. Hist N.Y.*, II (1849), 25–27.

17. See letters and orders in *ibid.*, 26, 55, 60, 62, 71, 181–84; E. B. O'Callaghan, ed., *Calendar of Historical Manuscripts in the Office of the Secretary of State*, pt. II, 193, 195; *A Modest and Impartial Narrative, 1690*, Andrews, ed., *Narratives*, pp. 350 and n., 353–54.

off the attackers. Hearing of the violence done their leader, the countryside rushed into the city in droves and out of revenge arrogantly quartered themselves for a couple of days in the homes of the city malcontents, many of them merchants, "committing divers Insolences" upon them. Leisler and the magistrates soon persuaded the country people to cease their looting and go home, but in order to prevent further disorders they seized more of the growing number of opponents, besides several who had led the assault on Leisler. Once the riot was over, Leisler claimed it was an outright attempt on his life. Nicholas Bayard later insisted that Leisler himself had unleashed the country folk and deliberately ordered them to descend upon the homes of good subjects, where robberies and abuses were notorious, solid evidence for Bayard of a Masaniellian revolt. The day after the riot Leisler peremptorily ordered all inhabitants to the fort to renew their allegiance to William III and declare their intent to defend the city. Delinquents were condemned as enemies to King and country with treatment promised accordingly. Imprisonment of opponents and sharp treatment of the protesters went a long way toward changing the minds of a number of city people who were hitherto sympathetic to Leisler.[18]

Later that year there was more trouble, this time in Queen's County on Long Island, a few miles east of the city. The grievances there were similar: high taxes, alleged oppression, and arbitrary government. Led by Major Thomas Willett, who had earlier participated in the assault on Leisler in June, a sizable group of men in Queen's County took up arms and militantly protested against the new regime. Leisler's council by proclamation granted indulgence to all who would give themselves up. Since none appeared to comply, the council declared them rebels and sent again troubleshooting Jacob Milborne with troops to put down the mutiny and arrest the leaders. At the same time Major Willett commenced a march toward New York with 150 supporters to make their demands known; he was met on the way by Milborne with twice that number of soldiers. Stopped in his tracks, Willett boldly asked why Milborne marched upon their lands. The deputy governor replied that he came to collect taxes from rebels and traitors. The front ranks exchanged "several high words" and a few blows, Milborne knocking down one of the insurgent captains with the butt of his musket. Sud-

18. "Blagge's Memorial," *Doc. Hist. N.Y.*, II (1849), 57–58; "Answer to Blagge's Memorial," *ibid.*, 390; Leisler to Coode, June 27, 1690, *ibid.*, 268–69. See also Lawrence H. Leder, "'. . . Like Madmen Through the Streets,' the New York City Riot of June 1690," *The New-York Historical Society Quarterly*, 39, #4 (Oct. 1955), 405–15. Leder has edited and printed here "Account of What Happened at New York, June 5–8, 1690," hitherto unpublished. For Leisler's proclamation, see *Doc. Hist. N.Y.*, II (1849), 264.

denly the government troops commenced firing; Willett's Long Islanders wheeled and retreated, claiming they had no orders to shoot. Luckily an oversized military coat of leather saved Major Willett from a serious wound in the back or even death. One of his men was not as fortunate, for he was killed, and a handful wounded. Milborne's soldiers plundered Willett's home and several other rich men's houses, but after occupying the rebel territory for a week or so, they returned to New York. Meantime, Willett escaped to New England. Several towns in the same county jointly and bitterly protested against the government's invasion, the illegal taxes, and the tyrannical usurpation by Jacob Leisler, or "Cataline," as they called him. Prominent on their list of offenses were the government's recent stripping of their estates and sequestering property.[19] But superior force had put them down, or "rule by the sword" as Bayard called it.

The military plan which emerged from Leisler's convention was much more expert in conception than in execution. The commissioners hatched a two-pronged attack, one arm by land, the other by sea and the St. Lawrence River, with Montreal and Quebec as targets. But Leisler failed to account for colonial jealousies and personal hatreds— his own included—to say nothing of inept commanders, contagious diseases, wilderness hardships, poor seamanship, and just plain bad luck, all of which combined to make the campaign a major fiasco. Of the 2,000 troops who marched on Montreal only a platoon of New Yorkers ever reached as far north as the St. Lawrence. Under Sir William Phips the Massachusetts fleet of thirty-two vessels and 2,200 men was tardy in sailing from Boston; it foundered on the rocks of the St. Lawrence and barely extricated only a fraction of its vessels. Landing parties were thwarted at every turn by the French, and disease took tremendous toll of both soldiers and sailors. Leisler accused Fitz-John Winthrop of cowardice in failing to push the 2,000 troops he commanded toward Montreal. When he jailed Winthrop on his return, outraged Connecticut men, through threats to Leisler, forced his release. The results of the campaign, besides hard feelings all around, were a burdensome debt—£50,000 for Massachusetts alone—and very few Frenchmen killed or taken or a foot of soil captured.[20] The advan-

---

19. *Ibid.*, 309–10; By the Lieut Govr and Councill, Nov. 3, 1690, Liv. Fam. Papers, F.D.R. Lib.; *CSPCol., 1689–1692,* #1246; C.O. 5/855, #128; John Clapp to Sec'y of State, Nov. 7, 1690, *N.Y. Col. Docs.,* III, 754–56.

20. Address of divers merchants, C.O. 5/855, #122. For Leisler's opinion of Fitz-John Winthrop, see Leisler to Sec'y Allyn, New York, Sept. 30, 1690, *Doc. Hist. N.Y.,* II (1849), 300–3; Nicholson to Lords of Trade, Nov. 4, 1690, C.O. 5/1358, 32–33; Howard H. Peckham, *The Colonial Wars, 1689–1762* (Chicago and London, 1964), pp. 34–38; Douglas E. Leach, *The Northern Colonial Frontier, 1607–1763* (New York, 1966), pp. 110–12.

tages which might have accrued to Leisler's New York and to New England from a successful Canadian campaign were hopelessly lost. Instead of unity in victory, there was left a lot of squabbling colonists.

At the outset of Leisler's rebellion doubtless a majority of New Yorkers accepted him and his regime as the legitimate authority in the colony. For instance, out of 223 males in Ulster County, halfway to Albany and west of the river, 189 willingly took oaths of allegiance to his government in September 1689. Six months later it was reported that the "generality of the People" acknowledged Leisler their lieutenant governor and commander in chief.[21] How many New Yorkers accepted him only through fear of the consequences if they refused is probably not determinable. The number of supporters shrank, however, as his government gathered momentum and purpose. For it taxed and legislated, destroyed monopolies, and went to war; it asserted itself in behalf of King and country, according to Leisler. To its enemies it became more arbitrary, even despotic, satisfying only its leaders' "ambition and malice."

Despite the overwhelming support of the overthrow of Sir Edmund Andros, resistance to the new government in Massachusetts had sting to it. Most of the violence subsided after the first two or three days of rebellion. Trouble came not from the royal party, of course, for most were in jail, although Andros himself created some excitement when he attempted to escape disguised as a woman. Resistance came chiefly from several former officeholders not jailed and a few Anglicans, often the same people, who refused to accept the rebellion, finding its every detail illegal and mutinous. Thomas Graves of Charlestown, across the river from Boston, had been a judge under Andros and was a troublemaker. A legalist like Gershom Bulkeley in Connecticut, he eloquently refused to recognize any government which lacked sanction from the new King and Queen. Boston magistrates tried to jail him but backed off when Charlestown men and several from neighboring towns threatened to pull down the jailhouse if they dared. A couple of months later he and a dozen friends petitioned the King in good Tory fashion. They asked for a government of English laws and declared flatly to William that there had been no need for revolution in Massachusetts.[22]

Worse off than the Tory legalists was the small group of Massachusetts Anglicans. Nurtured under the Dominion's wing, they found

21. "A Rool of the Names and Surnames," Ulster County, Sept. 1, 1689, *Doc. Hist. N.Y.*, I (1849), 279–82; Deposition of Robt. Sinclair, *ibid.*, II, 402.

22. C.O. 5/855, #40, II, III; C.O. 5/855, #43; C.O. 5/905, pp. 185–88; C.O. 5/855, #59; *CSPCol.*, 1689–1692, #743.

life after 1689 almost unbearable. Under the old charter they had been outcasts, denied the sacrament and other sacred rites, yet were forced to attend Congregational churches without being members. In fact, they protested, under the faction's laws not one-tenth of the colonists had been convenanted members of the colony's churches, to the great shame and scandal of the Christian religion. It was Governor Andros and his Dominion, they claimed, who had rescued them from arbitrary treatment by their Puritan enemies. Yet, despite building King's Chapel and enjoying their own Anglican services, they still had sustained the malice, scorn, countless affronts, and indignities from the majority who charged them with idolatry and popery. Then came the rebellion whereby the new government again oppressed thousands but particularly the Anglicans, whose chapel was threatened with destruction, its windows broken, besides an actual hindering of their minister in his holy duties. What the Anglicans feared most was a confirming of the old charter, and, according to Cotton Mather's letters from his father in London, renewal looked very likely. The higher the rumors about restoring the charter, the more bitter the attacks upon the Anglicans, most of whom were convinced that should Massachusetts legally return to its old government, the Puritan faction would tear down their church.[23]

The new government's reaction to dissent was uneven, to be sure, but the more it got away with the more severe became its procedures, particularly against its enemies. Charles Lidgett, whom the rebels had imprisoned with Andros, somehow managed to publish a pamphlet, probably printed in Philadelphia, "reflecting on the Government." Lidgett was a Charlestown Anglican and well-to-do merchant who had helped found King's Chapel under Andros. Besides this, he was notorious for accepting from Andros a piece of the common land in Charlestown and by court action actually took possession. Once sent for, Lidgett claimed his pamphlet was "only a matter of argument" and did little harm. The court thought differently. Although the government already was holding him without charge, it bound him over under £500 bond to answer for both pamphlet and his future behavior. Treatment of other dissidents was no less severe.[24]

By late 1690 the new government felt strong enough to control dissent even among its friends. Benjamin Harris, a bookseller and coffee-

23. C.O. 5/905, pp. 177–81; Extract of a letter from Samuel Miles, Nov. 29, 1690, C.O. 5/855, #124; An Ingenious Merchant of Boston . . . writes to his friend in London, Feb. 6, 1691, *ibid.*, #3.

24. *Ibid.*; Samuel Worden to Thomas Hinckley, Boston, Nov. 14, 1689, *Hinckley Papers,* p. 224; Viola F. Barnes, *The Dominion of New England,* p. 195; Andrews, ed., *Narratives,* p. 173 n.

house proprietor, supplied Boston with its first newspaper, *Publick Occurrences,* to keep the townspeople informed of what was going on. But after one printing it never saw light again, since Harris had failed to secure a license, and, as Samuel Sewall added, the news sheet contained a passage which was critical of the government. A week later the governor and council published its disallowance of Harris' efforts, and the next day, to bolster support for the interim administration, Cotton Mather sent around a "very sharp Letter." Boston, under a temporary government of saints, was not yet ready for a public newspaper, least of all one which gave "much distaste" to authority.[25]

Virginia's new governor, Francis Nicholson, was apprehensive about the strange goings on in the northern colonies, and well he might be after his flight from New York. In the summer of 1690 he dispatched Colonel Cuthbert Potter with a bagful of inquiries addressed to prominent colonists in Pennsylvania, New York, and New England in order to determine the "certainty of things." At both Philadelphia and Elizabeth Town Potter delivered numerous messages and discussed affairs with several refugees who had recently escaped from New York. Well aware of Leisler's security measures, Colonel Potter sneaked into New York City after leaving his papers aboard a vessel in the harbor. After dark he had little trouble in getting the letters ashore and promptly delivered a number of them to "Gentlemen" there. These were the "honest Gent," of course, friends of Nicholson and therefore Leisler's enemies, who were quick to unburden themselves to Potter about the deplorable "state of affairs." They eagerly awaited the arrival of Colonel Henry Sloughter, already commissioned by King William as new royal governor of New York but maddeningly slow in taking up his post.[26]

Colonel Potter's reception in Boston was much less cordial. Although he managed to deliver a good many letters to Nicholson's correspondents there and in Cambridge, Charlestown, and Salem, eventually he was seized and subjected to many indignities: his portmanteau broken into and emptied, even his "pockets and breeches" searched, besides a forced appearance before the council. Governor Bradstreet had already given him a pass which should have smoothed his path in the Bay Colony, but it is clear the old governor was not in control of several militant councillors who gave the colonel a detailed scrutiny.

25. Sewall, *Diary,* I, 332–33; Carl Bridenbaugh, *Cities in the Wilderness* (New York, 1938), pp. 130–31.

26. Nicholson to Coode, Aug. 1, 1690, *Arch. of Md.,* VIII, 198; "A Journall and Narrative of a Journey made by me Cuthbert Potter from Middx in Virginia to Boston in New England," in Newton D. Mereness, ed., *Travels in the American Colonies* (New York, 1916), pp. 3–11.

Bradstreet tried to explain that because of the war with the French and present preparations of the fleet for the campaign against Quebec, the government was forced to take extreme caution against several seditious people who had managed to distribute "scandalous papers" about the town. Hardly satisfied, the resentful Potter claimed that the council stopped several of his letters and after reading them arrested one of his friends and fired another, the public notary. Other associates of Potter fully expected to be called to account for what they had written.

Later Potter reported that the people of Massachusetts were "generally much dissatisfied." Those he spoke to blamed all their sufferings on the new government, including the "great losses" in Maine after the demise of Andros' Indian protection. A good many colonists, he went on, who earlier had supported the rebel government were now its "inveterate enemies." Obviously Colonel Potter had sought out the "honest Gent" in Massachusetts as he had in New York. Probably his report of large supplies of Canary and Spanish wines he had seen, even sampled, in Boston and Salem was closer to the truth. In the latter port, one ship captain bragged freely of a recent voyage to Spain, where he had sold tobacco at a great profit, an admission which supported Randolph's and Nicholson's charges that Massachusetts merchants had returned promptly to their old tricks at the expense of the Acts of Trade.[27]

None of the rebel governments could afford to be careless about their opposition. There were strong feelings against the new regimes all along the line, no doubt stronger in New York than in Massachusetts, given the nature of the rebellions. Like Leisler, John Coode was certain that his enemies were deep in plans to subvert his government, but from what one can gather he anticipated less trouble from the unhappy Protestants—although he seized and read their mail—than the Catholics, the "Popish politicons," from whom he expected bloody reprisals. Collector Payne's murder, he said, was a startling example of what might occur. Maryland's government was obligated, he and his followers explained simply, to suppress all disloyal practices.[28] What rebel leaders feared most was a linking of plans against

27. *Ibid.*; "Diary of Lawrence Hammond," M.H.S. *Proc.* (1891, 1892), VII, 155. For other letters "broke open," see Abstract of a Letter from Thomas Cooper to John Ellis in London, Boston, Apr. 2, 1690, C.O. 5/855, #78.

28. Richard John to Samuel Groome, Sept. 27, 1689, *Arch. of Md.*, VIII, 126; Cheseldyne to Commissioners of Somerset County, Oct. 18, 1689, in Clayton Torrence, *Old Somerset on the Eastern Shore of Maryland* (Richmond, Va., 1935), p. 343; See Cheseldyne's and Coode's letters to Leisler, Nov. 26, 1689, Apr. 3, and May 19, 1690, *Doc. Hist. N.Y.*, II (1849), 42, 211–12, 226.

them. Their precautions were detailed yet not altogether effective, but neither was Tory effort at collaboration.

Several times during and after the rebellions dissent from the new governments took constitutional and legal form. It ranged from simple argument against any change which had no origin in the Crown to reasoned and sophisticated discussion of empire and the colonies' place in it. To some rebellion was wrong because it smacked of treason; to others it was evil because it was sinful. The most learned discussions were those which probed the meaning of empire; these Tory arguments began not with colonists' rights, as had so much of the colonial revolutionary literature, but with the King's sovereignty and power over realm and dominions.

No Gershom Bulkeley emerged in Maryland to rock Coode's government with a *Will and Doom*. Still, Protestant individuals, who challenged the interim government, often used similar arguments along with the charge that the new regime denied them the laws and privileges of Englishmen. Their duty was to God, the King, and Lord Baltimore, they said: the latter's power in Maryland was derived legally from the other two, and they revered it, making them incapable of submitting to any authority which came not by way of the Crown.[29] When Michael Taney, sheriff of Calvert County under the proprietor, balked at calling an election of burgesses, he was dragged out of his home and into jail and then forced to appear before Coode's assembly to answer charges of rebellion against the King. Taney refused outright to submit to Coode's authority, claiming he was a freeborn subject of England's King and Queen and expected full benefit of all the laws which protected the lives and estates of loyal Englishmen. When Coode's people placed Richard Smith, Jr., in the same predicament, he, too, proclaimed his birthright and demanded to know what law of England or Maryland he had broken. Smith rang in Magna Carta, on the one hand, and the Court of Star Chamber, on the other, and asked where were the privileges of Englishmen which guaranteed subjects like him from imprisonment and judgment contrary to the common course of law. Taney and Smith remained in jail.[30]

Although they found Coode's Rebellion anything but glorious, most Protestant opponents of it happily accepted the Revolution in England and looked to William and Mary as their sovereigns. Most, but not all, not Richard Hill, a Scot from Anne Arundel County, who had been troublesome to Coode since the beginning of the rebellion. Captain

29. *Arch. of Md.*, VIII, 114–18, 130–31.
30. *Ibid.*, 120–21, 149–51; Petition to King, Nov. 20, 1690, *ibid.*, 212–13.

Hill warned friends near home not to be hasty in serving William before they were certain he *was* King in England. What was more, if he were King, Hill claimed, it certainly had not come about by "faire play," law, or justice. It was high treason, then, to proclaim him as their sovereign, and he could prove it by "good Law"—at which point he burst into "Lord Cooke." Despite Coode's proclamation against Richard Hill and the efforts of a posse ordered to bring him in "alive or dead," the fugitive escaped to Virginia, after hiding in the woods while his house was searched, fields destroyed, and ship seized. By the time Governor Nicholson got around to apprehending him, slow as usual in aiding the rebel government, Hill was safe on board ship bound for London, no doubt to determine who *was* King in England anyway. Peter Sayer, a strong Catholic and the Calverts' close friend, managed to stay free despite his habit of drinking James II's health and regularly damning Protestants in both England and America for several years to come.[31]

There was little political theory behind statements that Leisler was a usurper and ruled arbitrarily the colony of New York. In fact, one must look carefully through the sources to find the niceties of constitutional objection to the rebel government there. As far as opponents to his rule were concerned, Leisler and his people had "Committed barefaced and open Rebellion"[32] and were, therefore, dead wrong in everything they did. When constitutional arguments were used in opposition to Leisler, they were usually against arbitrary imprisonments which violated due process of law and abused men's persons.

An exception was an elaborate constitutional objection to the new government's taxing power. Leisler's early authority for taxing the people of New York, although honest, was at best tenuous, since it was a convenient resurrection of a defunct charter and laws passed under it in Governor Dongan's time. At the same time arguments by those who challenged his authority were in their main thrust downright hypocritical, although they contained smatterings of truth, to be sure. First, claimed Leisler's critics, the tax law in question and the charter of 1683 on which it was based were never approved by James as Duke or King and therefore never effective—a charge which was not altogether true, since the Duke had confirmed the tax levy and the charter but failed to return the latter to the colony when he ascended

31. John Hammond's testimony, July 15, 1690, *ibid.*, 181–82, 196–98; *ibid.*, XIII, 237–38. For Peter Sayer's loyalty to James II, see *ibid.*, VIII, 560–62. Francis Edgar Sparks, *Causes of the Maryland Revolution of 1689*, in *Johns Hopkins University Studies*, 14th ser., XI-XII (Baltimore, 1896), 578.

32. "A Narrative in Answer to Their Majties Letter," *Doc. Hist. N.Y.*, II (1849), 393.

the throne. Second—and here was a nasty dig—the law was enacted under a Catholic governor (Dongan) and now by the rebels' own revolutionary principle "*ipso facto* null and void." Moreover, the tax law when passed was only a *quid pro quo* for the Duke's approving the charter and therefore had no bearing whatever on the present situation.[33] So far they were partly right. Under Leisler the charter and the laws which followed it had no official sanction except what rebel colonists wished to give them as equitable bases for governing.

But if his antagonists believed Leisler subverted his own principles in taxing as he did, their arguments made a shambles of what they had loyally defended for some time. It was primarily Nicholas Bayard, their spokesman, who marshaled the constitutional arguments against the new government. The real irony came when he threw up Magna Carta and the Petition of Right to Leisler's council, whose "Pretended act" of taxation violated both, he said. By subjecting New Yorkers to taxes without their consent, Leisler and his government denied them the fruits of the Glorious Revolution which all English subjects ought to share. His arbitrary rule distinguished between subjects in the dominions and those in the realm, a distinction which not only violated the rights of Englishmen but was even a travesty upon the very charter they cited as their authority. Bayard's was a disingenuous charge but difficult to answer. By early 1690 he, too, it seems, had accepted the Revolution in England and for really the same reason as Leisler a few months earlier: to rid the colony of a government which ruled arbitrarily, contrary to Englishmen's rights.[34]

Had Leisler's government discovered a propagandist like Bayard or Increase Mather, it might have made clear to New Yorkers that this very equality of treatment, an equality between subjects in England and colonists in America, was what Leisler was trying to preserve, or, more the pity, establish for the first time in New York. It was for these reasons among others that he and his followers had revolted against the likes of Nicholas Bayard and Stephen Van Cortlandt, their friends, and against a colonial regime which had governed and taxed since 1664 without a fare-thee-well for the rights of Englishmen. Bayard willingly and profitably had served both proprietor and King; in fact, said Leislerians, he had been a "complying tool all King James's Arbitrary Reign." [35] Despite his warm loyalty to a colonial government

33. This revealing statement helps to confirm the partisan nature of the Charter of Libertyes of 1683 and the assembly which drafted it. See ch. 6 above.

34. C.O. 5/1081/85; *CSPCol., 1689–1692,* #642; [Nicholas Bayard], *A Modest and Impartial Narrative, 1690,* Andrews, ed., *Narratives,* pp. 321, 341–43; *Colonel Bayard's Narrative of Occurrences in New-York,* in *N.Y. Col. Docs.,* III, 636–48.

35. *Loyalty Vindicated from the Reflections of a Virulent Pamphlet . . .* (1698), Andrews, ed., *Narratives,* p. 382.

which for a generaton had defied Englishmen's rights, Bayard accepted suddenly the constitutional principles of the Revolution in England, along with their pertinence in the colonies. But in the spring of 1690 it was a question of who called "tyrant" first, and Leisler had the jump on his opponents for the moment. Bayard was dragged off to jail, and the others would have followed had they been captured. The government persisted in levying and collecting taxes according to the 1683 law until the new assembly met in April 1690, further testimony, said Leisler's enemies, of "rule by the sword."

Judge John Palmer in Boston would have called Bayard a hypocrite. Palmer was an English-trained lawyer, and like Bayard his colonial experience was in the government of New York under James as Duke and King. He had been a member of Andros' government there and later sat on Dongan's council. When Andros formed the Dominion of New England, he invited his New York friend to join him in Boston as both councillor and judge. Palmer enjoyed Andros' confidence and became one of the inner circle of advisers whom the Puritan faction and jealous moderates alike abhorred and called "Haters of the People." Like the rest of Andros' retinue, Palmer was clapped into jail at the outset of the rebellion and released only when the Bay Colony government packed the whole crew off to England some fourteen months later. Whiling away the empty hours in prison, Palmer wrote a pamphlet about the goings on in Massachusetts; next to Gershom Bulkeley's *Will and Doom* it was the best piece of writing to come out of the Revolution. As one might expect from an Anglican lawyer, locked up in the Castle at Boston, Palmer's *Impartial Account* was a bitter attack upon the saints of Massachusetts and their moderate supporters.[36] It was a point-by-point refutation of the Bay Colony's Declaration of April 18, 1689, and challenged with learning and wit just about all the rebels' assumptions. In his struggle against Leisler in New York, Nicholas Bayard had recently succumbed to the idea that colonists in America should share the liberties of the English nation, or so he said. Palmer was of a different mind; he argued consistently a Tory theory which reflected his legal training and political experience in both New York and Boston, a theory of empire which distinguished absolutely between subjects at home and abroad. Palmer reduced his theory to a "certain Maxime": ". . . That those Kingdoms, Principalities, and Colonies, which are of the Dominion of the Crown of England . . . are subject to such Laws, Ordinances, and Forms of Government, as the Crown shall think fit to establish." New England and all the colonies in America were in that category. Settlers migrated to the colonies

---

36. *An Impartial Account of the State of New England* [London, 1690], in *Andros Tracts*, I, 21–62.

with the King's leave only; they were dependent upon his favor alone and enjoyed only the rights he was willing to give them. Certainly the Crown had granted charters and permitted assemblies, but again they existed only by grace and favor, and what the Crown gave it could take away, as Massachusetts had painfully learned in 1684.

On this basis Palmer applied his "certain Maxime" of empire to Massachusetts' claims in the Declaration and found them wanting, of course. That the King's courts revoked illegally the colony's charter and that both Joseph Dudley and Edmund Andros held illegal commissions were, therefore, nonsense. By the same logic, John Wise and the Ipswich rebels who protested against taxation without consent were not denied the privileges of Magna Carta and other Englishmen's liberties since, as colonists, they were not entitled to them in the first place. Palmer's answer to the charge that the Ipswich rebels were denied a writ of habeas corpus (enacted by Parliament in 1679) was simply that Parliament had "particularly" limited it to the "Kingdom of England." He scoffed at New England common law as a defense of the Bay Colony's peculiar oathtaking, sans Bible; he dubbed it *"rara Avis in Terris,"* and anyway, it was repugnant to the laws of England. For some time, he argued, Parliament, besides the Crown, had discriminated against colonists. The Acts of Trade had never favored them or enlarged their rights, but on the contrary had restrained and burdened them "beyond any in England." Simply stated, colonies were "much differenced from England." Seldom had the colonists' inferior position been as baldly described.

This difference was so much a fact that colonists had no grounds for complaint, let alone rebellion. Here Palmer demonstrated the same insensitivity which had greeted colonists' questioning of prerogative power at other times, whether it was proprietary in Maryland or early New York, or royal in Virginia and under the Dominion. Colonists could call arbitrary no government which they were obliged to submit to by law. Lord Baltimore had said as much to his burgesses of Maryland, as did governors like Culpeper and Effingham to Virginians and Duke James to New Yorkers. Prerogative power could never be illegal; it could not be challenged or made an object of negotiation by colonists whose governments existed out of grace not right.

Since colonists in America were on a wholly different footing from subjects in England, there could be no parallel between the recent events in England and those in Massachusetts as Bay colonists had claimed. The one was justifiable, legally accomplished, peaceable, avoiding "Confusion and Disorder"; the other was arbitrary, willful, chaotic, and without law or reason. "Betwixt their Condition and ours,"

Palmer wrote, "there can be no Parity." Having destroyed for his own purposes any constitutional principle the Bay colonists might stand upon, Palmer called the overthrow of Andros' government a self-interested and false move, a using of Their Majesties' names to cover selfish designs which burst from a hatred of the Acts of Trade and a suspicion of any government established from England. To call their uprising a duty to God, as did the Declaration, was preposterous. "Is not Rebellion, as the Sin of Witchcraft?" for both are rebellion against God.[37] A Catholic conspiracy was "Ridiculous and Incredible." Who could have effected it? "There were not Two Roman Catholics betwixt this and New-York."

Subjects who settled colonies overseas were not Englishmen at all in a legal sense. Englishmen in the realm enjoyed rights and privileges which simply did not extend to colonists in America. As colonists they were subject to the whims of the Crown, not the guarantees of the English constitution. Palmer was very clear and reasonable in his Tory argument. But he was in jail in Boston. Increase Mather read the *Impartial Account* in London, where it was published in 1690. His answer was simple and concise and bears repeating: "No Englishmen in their Wits will ever Venture their Lives and Estates to Enlarge the Kings Dominions abroad, and Enrich the whole English Nation, if their Reward after all must be to be deprived of their *English Liberties.*"[38] There were probably very few people in New England who agreed with John Palmer, and most of those who did were locked up with him.

37. Gershom Bulkeley had written similarly in *Will and Doom:* "Rebellion against the king is a mediate rebellion against God, and is like the sin of witch-craft." Quoted in Perry Miller, *The New England Mind: From Colony to Province* (Cambridge, Mass., 1953), p. 154.

38. *A Vindication of New England* . . . in *Andros Tracts*, II, 76.

18 Resettlement I

Not long after the Revolution in England Sir William Temple described King William III as a prince of great firmness who spoke little but thought much.[1] William's American colonists might have agreed, but they probably would have added that if William thought a good deal, it was not about them. One of the ironies of the Revolution was that Englishmen in England believed it was their revolution alone, and colonists should not presume it had meaning outside the realm. "The King is dead; long live the King" may have been a slight exaggeration if one dealt strictly with the facts, but the idea ought in substance to be good enough for colonists in America, for what bearing did events in England have upon colonists 3,000 miles away? That Englishmen in England, William III included, were surprised at what occurred in America is good evidence of their regard, or lack of it, for colonists and colonies and of what they understood the relation between England and America to be. Despite the constitutional changes which

1. "Diary of Lawrence Hammond," Feb. 15, 1692, M.H.S., *Proc.* (1891, 1892), 2d ser., VII, 160.

accompanied the Glorious Revolution in England, the Crown's role in imperial matters was not altered officially. The American colonies were still the King's business and would remain so theoretically, at least, until 1776. To most Englishmen, imperial affairs remained about the same whether James or William ruled. While several colonies underwent severe jolts in the spring and summer of 1689, followed by a trying period of anxiety and confusion, imperial responsibilities in the hands of men like William Blathwayt continued under the new government in England without much of a hitch. Revenues, including customs duties, were toted up and continued for the new King; colonial shipping was carefully allotted owing to the hazards of war on the high seas. Experts published essays on the American trade; entrepreneurs petitioned the King for commercial charters and monopolies. And Edward Randolph, first in Boston and then in England, continued to report violations of the Acts of Trade and to lay plans for a tighter colonial administration.[2]

William was a very busy king in the early months of his reign. With pressing demands upon his time in England, Ireland, and on the Continent, he was slow to bring about a settlement of the colonies which had overturned their governments. The delay, of course, added substantially to the instability which characterized their interim regimes. News of England was scarce in Boston and New York and often misleading. Hungry for accurate accounts of what had occurred, and particularly for acceptance of what they had done, colonists were frustrated by instructions and odd bits of news which managed to cross the Atlantic, information often unrelated to their immediate, sometimes acute needs. One wonders what John Coode's reaction while chasing Catholics was to the King's circular letter which asked colonial governors to help in obtaining a variety of plants and shrubs for the royal gardens. Or what Jacob Leisler, beset by countless problems in New York and desperate for confirmation of his government, made of the news that the Bishop of London was scurrying about the city looking for Anglican priests to fill the pulpits at Newtown and Esopus, besides an "ingenious Schoolmaster" for the city of New York. In the

---

2. A Paper Setting forth the Publick Revenue . . . payable to their Majesties from the 25th of March 1689 . . . , Harleian Manuscripts, 1898, ff. 1-1b, B.M.; Petition from Merchants Trading to New England, Sept. 1690, C.O. 1/68/7; C.O. 324/5, p. 150; H.M.C. 17: 13th Report, App. V, *House of Lords, 1690–1691*, pp. 73–74; *Sir Dudley North, Discourses upon Trade* [London, 1691], ed. by Jacob H. Hollander (Baltimore, 1907); Daniel Cox, Petition to King for Patent to develop area . . . , Apr. 24, 1690, C.O. 5/855, #87. For Randolph, see *ibid.*, #110. J. H. Plumb discusses the continuity in administration during the Revolution. *The Origins of Political Stability: England, 1675–1725* (Boston, 1967), ch. I.

midst of their turmoil the King charged New Yorkers with the promotion of the Indian trade while encouraging Massachusetts people to convert Negroes and Indians to Christianity.[3] These were difficult times in all the colonies but particularly so where temporary government rested uneasily on the heads of rebels like Coode and Leisler and on a self-conscious coalition of Puritans and moderates in Massachusetts.

New York

Jacob Leisler's government had poor luck with the new regime in England. Increase Mather handled Massachusetts' affairs in London with a good deal of skill. Maryland's rebels had the anti-Catholicism of the Glorious Revolution behind them in their dealings with William and the Lords of Trade. But Leisler sent a dram seller to London, and Joost Stoll spent as much time calling attention to his own role in the rebellion as he did negotiating for a charter and seeking confirmation of New York events. Matthew Clarkson had accompanied Stoll; if he was officially Leisler's agent, he gave no time to the job but busied himself in securing a place in William's new plans for New York.[4] Late in June of 1690 Leisler dispatched Benjamin Blagge to London along with the promise to send shortly his son-in-law, Jacob Milborne, as co-agent. (London was spared the lobbying of Leisler's deputy, who stayed home to fight against the French.) Blagge lacked either ability or opportunity to repudiate Francis Nicholson, whose reports, along with those of others, had succeeded in prejudicing William's people against Leisler.[5] As early as September 1689 the King had appointed a royal governor for New York. He was Colonel Henry Sloughter, who had the good fortune to welcome Prince William to England early enough to become a favorite. The colonel was soon convinced that the colony lacked a government and already a "Rable" controlled it.[6] Tories like Stephen Van Cortlandt and Nicholas Bayard rejoiced at the news of his appointment and wished him Godspeed. But they were

3. *CSPCol., 1689–1692*, #402; C.O. 5/1081, 74; C.O. 324/22, p. 418; L. W. Labaree, ed., *Royal Instructions to British Colonial Governors, 1670–1776* (2 vols., New York, 1935), II, 465.

4. *CSPCol., 1689–1692*, #365; *N.Y. Col. Docs.*, III, 629–32; Andrews, ed., *Narratives*, pp. 324 and n., 398 n. C.O. 5/1081/68, 70.

5. Leisler to Coode, June 27, 1690, *Doc. Hist. N.Y.*, II (1849), 268.

6. Shrewsbury for King to Attorney or Solicitor General, Sept. 1, 1689, C.O. 324/5, pp. 1023–34; C.O. 324/22, p. 85; Marquis of Carmarthen to Earl of Nottingham, Sept. 11, 1689, H.M.C., ser. 71, *Finch*, II (London, 1922), 245; Sloughter's proposals for New York, Oct. 28, 1689, C.O. 5/1081/67; *CSPCol., 1689–1692*, #521.

disappointed, as probably were many others who by this time were sick of confusion and mistrust and hoped soon for a stable regime which would straighten matters out. Colonel Sloughter, then commanding troops on the Isle of Wight, had the devil's own time getting away from his post owing to the war with France and a strong reluctance to leave England. It was not until the spring of 1691 that he finally arrived in New York.[7] The delay was crucial, for it contributed to Leisler's undoing.

Governor Sloughter's troop commander, Major Richard Ingoldesby, sailed into New York's harbor late in January 1691. Well ahead of the governor, he brought with him an imperiousness which matched Leisler's and a conviction that the interim government was a usurpation. There followed for the next six weeks a struggle over power which was reflected sporadically in vicious exchanges, even violent skirmishes. Ingoldesby demanded surrender of the fort where Leisler and three to four hundred men soon retreated with more straggling in every day, but he adamantly refused to show his commission as authority to do anything. Leisler, equally proud, kept the fort and damned the major's disregard of his governorship and command, although he insisted he would turn the colony over to the King's governor once he was certain of his arrival. Sharp differences between the two commanders divided New York into armed camps.[8]

Leisler's stubbornness was bound up with his conviction about the revolution. From his point of view New York was in a precarious position. In fact, it had continuously suffered since the beginning of James's reign, given the constant danger from French and Indians in the north *and* from the "disaffected" within the colony who, he believed, were popishly tainted and had never accepted him or the Glorious Revolution. Leisler did not confine his suspicion to opponents in New York. It spread to Englishmen in high places, and this distrust he had impressed upon Joost Stoll, the agent he sent to London in the early months of the rebellion. Among the several documents Stoll submitted in behalf of the colony was a petition which asked for confirmation of what Leisler had done and for a charter like "the citty of Boston." But the petition included an impertinent, even insulting, request which revealed Leisler's profound suspicion and anxiety, to say nothing of ineptness.

7. Van Cortlandt to Blathwayt, Dec. 18, 1689, BPCol. Wmsbg., v. IX. See series of letters from Sloughter to Blathwayt and others, the last dated Nov. 27, 1690, from the Isle of Wight. *Ibid.*, v. VIII. Sewall, *Diary*, I, 342–43.

8. *Doc. Hist. N.Y.*, II (1849), 320–26, 328–30, 340–45; Dudley to Blathwayt, Mar. 17, 1691, BPCol. Wmsbg., v. IV; Van Cortlandt to Nicholson, Apr. 6, 1691, *ibid.*, v. IX.

It boldly asked that only "loyal and faithful persons" be appointed to the principal offices in New York. If the King had already chosen a governor and other officers, the petition asked that their appointments be reviewed in order to determine without question their loyalty and good will to the people there. Doubtless Leisler was hoping to ensure appointment of a governor who would be sympathetic to the rebellion. The strange request probably reflected Leisler's apprehension lest the King reappoint Francis Nicholson, or someone like him, who would immediately fall in with Leisler's enemies, the likes of Bayard, Van Cortlandt, and Philips.[9] According to Leisler, loyalty meant loyalty to the revolution as he saw it; it meant allegiance to William and Mary and to himself as an interim governor who had saved New York from James, the Catholic French, and from Bayard and the other traitors. What Leisler did not know was that two months before Joost Stoll presented his petition to the Lords of Trade, the King had commissioned Henry Sloughter governor of New York, not Nicholson, whom he sent to Virginia. And long before he embarked for America, Colonel Sloughter had determined who was right in New York, and it was not Leisler.[10]

When Major Ingoldesby came ashore with two companies of redcoats, Leisler was suspicious. When he claimed he was Sloughter's commander and issued a proclamation offering his protection to New Yorkers from people prejudiced against the King and Queen, Leisler was outraged. Yet the major condescendingly refused to divulge his authority. In the few weeks between Ingoldesby's arrival and Colonel Sloughter's appearance, Leisler was convinced of an outright conspiracy against his government. The major promptly allied himself with the old council, that is, Leisler's enemies whom, it turned out, the King had recently appointed to the new council under Sloughter: Bayard, Nichols (both still imprisoned), Van Cortlandt, and Philips. To these were added Joseph Dudley, whom the Massachusetts rebels had overthrown along with Andros, and Thomas Willett, the man Leisler's troops under Milborne had suppressed earlier in Queen's County and had come very close to killing. On top of this, Matthew Clarkson settled down as secretary to Sloughter, demonstrating the success of his negotiations in London for a lucrative position in the new government of New York.[11]

9. "Report of Joost Stoll to Shrewsbury," Nov. 16, 1689, *N.Y. Col. Docs.*, III, 629–32; *CSPCol., 1689–1692*, #567.

10. *Ibid.*, #271, #274; C.O. 324/22, p. 85.

11. Sloughter's instructions: C.O. 324/22, pp. 212–21; Clarkson's appointment, *ibid.*, p. 1020; *CSPCol., 1689–1692*, #658; *Doc. Hist. N.Y.*, II (1849), 358.

Ingoldesby, Clarkson, and the old-new council worked hand in glove until Governor Sloughter arrived. Their propaganda explained that New York was in danger of violent attack from Leisler's fort, and to defend the city Clarkson summoned the militias of outlying towns to join the redcoats in defense of the people. Even Connecticut troops were requested, which must have been the last straw for Leisler. He and his soldiers fought back with proclamations and protests, warning the same people of the danger from Ingoldesby's intentions, all the while nurturing anew the fear of a Catholic conspiracy whose principals were James II, the French in Canada, and the "papishly affected" among them whom Ingoldesby villainously encouraged.[12]

By the middle of March a showdown was inevitable. Leisler believed the fort was under siege, that the major and his troops were determined to root him out by force. Ingoldesby and the council insisted that the fort was about to explode in attack upon the city. Each side claimed the other commenced the violence. A large cannon which Ingoldesby's men had trained upon the fort blew up in the crew's faces as they prepared to fire, killing several of them. Leisler's soldiers spent a day or more sporadically firing upon suspicious movements within range of the fort's guns, killing half-a-dozen colonists, wounding several more, and destroying a good deal of property. In the middle of the chaos Governor Henry Sloughter arrived; on March 19 he published his commission and demanded surrender of the fort.

There followed two days of tragic misunderstanding and more suspicion on both sides. Jacob Leisler welcomed Colonel Sloughter by message but tactlessly sent Joost Stoll to identify him as the rightful governor since Stoll had caught a glimpse of him once in England. All the while Major Ingoldesby demanded the fort and threatened to storm it without waiting for Leisler's niceties. When Stoll convinced Leisler that the King's governor was actually in New York, Leisler dispatched Jacob Milborne and Peter Delanoy to greet him and arrange terms for handing over the fort. It was Sloughter's turn to be outraged; he claimed the King negotiated terms with his enemies, not his subjects, and promptly seized Milborne and Delanoy. During the two days of parlaying, Leisler refused surrender three times; each delay added to the seriousness of the charges against him. When he finally relinquished his command, he was doubtless persuaded to it by his restless soldiers, whose resolve the seizure of Leisler's envoys had undermined. At an appropriate moment they dropped their arms and all 350 of them marched out of the fort into the streets of the city. Sloughter seized and jailed Leisler and his council, throwing him into the very

12. *Ibid.*, pp. 332–34, 335–39, 340–45.

cell and irons vacated minutes earlier by Nicholas Bayard, whom the governor had released to take a seat at the council table. Sloughter immediately appointed a court of oyer and terminer to try the ringleaders, and New Yorkers spent the first peaceful night in their beds for some time. Leisler's rebellion was over.[13]

Massachusetts

Increase Mather had plenty of help during his several years of lobbying and negotiating in London. Although Samuel Nowell died before the Revolution, Richard Wharton, the entrepreneur, had joined Mather early in his negotiations with James. But Wharton wore himself out in his vigorous promotion of a mining scheme back in Massachusetts and died in London just after William accepted the throne. At various times Mather had the aid of other Bay colonists who visited London. Consistently helpful throughout the whole period was Sir Henry Ashurst, a wealthy merchant who shared the colony's nonconformity in religion and remained a good friend for years to come. Ashurst was a member of Parliament and well acquainted among people who were in positions to help Mather and the colony.[14] At the very time Massachusetts shipped Andros, Dudley, Randolph, and the rest of the prisoners back to England, the colony dispatched two more agents to work with Mather: Drs. Elisha Cooke and Thomas Oakes, both old-guard members of the Puritan faction, bent on restoration of the old government, and none of this nonsense about a new charter. Mather may have seen eye to eye with them back in the days of the Dominion, but he had come a long way since 1688. A practical, shrewd man, he was quick to appreciate what was and was not possible in the early months of William's reign. His sights were still high, and he pushed every opportunity, whether at court or with Parliament, to

13. The last days of Leisler's regime are described in the following: Dudley to Blathwayt, Mar. 17, Apr. 6, 1691, BPCol. Wmsbg., v. IV; Dudley to [?], Apr. 6, 1691, *ibid.*, v. XV; Van Cortlandt to Blathwayt, May 7, 1691, *ibid.*, v. IX; Van Cortlandt to Nicholson, Apr. 6, 1691, *ibid.*; Thomas Watson to Nicholson, Apr. 8, 1691, *ibid.*, v. VIII; Bayard to Nicholson, Apr. 26, 1691, *ibid.*; Sewall, *Diary*, I, 342–43; Samuel Worden to Hinckley, Boston, Mar. 30, 1691, *Hinckley Papers*, 282–84; *Loyalty Vindicated*, Andrews, ed., *Narratives*, pp. 248 n., 391 and n., 392; Chidley Brooke to Robt. Southwell, New York, Apr. 5, 1691, *N.Y. Col. Docs.*, III, 757–759.

14. Richard Wharton reported Samuel Nowell's death in a letter to Thomas Hinckley, Oct. 18, 1688, M.H.S., Prince Collection, I, 37. John Higginson to Nathaniel Higginson, Salem, Aug. 31, 1698, Essex Inst. Hist. *Coll.*, XLIII (1907), 183–84; Increase Mather, "Autobiography," A.A.S. *Proc.*, 71 (1961), pt. 2, p. 327; Andrews, ed., *Narratives*, pp. 272–73.

salvage for Massachusetts as much of its former independence as possible, but his approach and means, with Ashurst's help, demonstrated an experience and sophistication which Cooke and Oakes sadly lacked.[15]

The agents met a number of disappointments in the spring of 1690. Already the King had prorogued Parliament, preventing further consideration of the Corporation Bill which Mather hoped would include the colonies.[16] Soon after the new agents arrived, the whole team appeared before the Lords of Trade, where Andros, Dudley, and Randolph, their former prisoners, faced them. By this time the Whig ascendancy had leveled off somewhat, and it became increasingly difficult to paint Andros as an enemy to his country. In addition, counsel for Andros and his friends constantly forced the Massachuetts agents into defensive positions where they were uncomfortable and frustrated. Particularly annoying was the Lords of Trade's embarrassing inquiry about why the charges against Andros and the others were not signed by those who submitted them, or by anyone, for that matter. The agents had hesitated to add their signatures since, among other reasons, they would be vulnerable to reprisal if all were not proved. Their attorney, Sir John Somers, argued before the Lords that the agents could not properly sign the complaints. They personally did not bring the charges but rather spoke in behalf of the "country," the people of Massachusetts, who as a whole overthrew Andros in the same way the "people" in England, rising as one man, had revolted against James. The argument appeared to impress several of the Lords, even the Lord President, who had been particularly hard on the agents. At the moment Mather must have felt a good deal of satisfaction in realizing that Massachusetts' rebellion seemed to be accepted in high places as an integral part of the Glorious Revolution, really a confirmation of his recent argument that there was a basic equality between Englishmen in England and Englishmen in the colonies, at least in Massachusetts. But there was something fishy about the agents' victory. Easy acceptance, it seems, of the idea of parallel revolutions was a simple concession for the Lords to make at the time, for it really cost them nothing in their dealings with the colony. Given the rise of Tory sentiment in the spring of 1690, it was no time to stir up the embarrassing question of loyalties respecting James and then William or where censure or praise was due for adhering too long to James or running too fast with William. The Lords listened politely (although

15. Hammond, "Diary," pp. 151–52; Agents' instructions, Jan. 24, 1690, C.O. 5/855, #54; Mather, "Autobiography," pp. 324–45, *passim.*
16. Mather to Hinckley, London, May 24, 1690, *Hinckley Papers,* pp. 254–55.

not at first) to the Massachusetts agents and then reported what they pleased to the Crown. But the agents' failure to sign the charges offended the King, Mather learned, and several newly won friends to New England were "extremely scandalized" by it. To the agents' dismay their former prisoners soon were invited to kiss the King's hand, and in a day or two William released them. Uncomfortable rumors spread that Andros would return to Massachusetts as governor.[17]

The agents' next encounters with Andros and Randolph were even more frustrating. These, too, occurred before the Lords of Trade, who in late May summoned before them a number of people interested in New England in order to discuss the settlement of government there. The audience was not altogether friendly to the agents' cause, for the summons included Joseph Dudley and John Usher, both earlier jailed in Boston, and Governor Henry Sloughter, who had not yet embarked for New York. The day was climaxed by Sir Edmund Andros, who again put the agents on the defensive. He presented a paper which described in painful detail what shambles the rebellion had made of his New England defenses against the French and Indians: forts deserted, soldiers debauched and sent home, and the country destroyed by the enemy. Before the agents could present publicly an answer to Andros' charges, the Lords summoned them again. This time Edward Randolph seized the floor and delivered a "large complaint" against Massachusetts' violations of the Navigation Acts since capture of the government. When Randolph sat down, two Commissioners of the Customs gave "long harangues" describing the interim government as no different from the charter government as far as obeying the Acts of Trade was concerned. New Englanders, they charged, would never conform to Parliament's laws until the King sent a governor to make them behave. The agents immediately drafted answers to Randolph's charges but again were deprived of any chance to offer them publicly, although they cooled their heels several times in outer offices, answers in hand, waiting an opportunity. So ended the first round of negotiations, and Massachusetts had little to show for it.[18]

17. Mather, "Autobiography," 340–41; Increase Mather, *A Brief Account concerning Several of the Agents* (London, 1691), Andrews, ed., *Narratives*, pp. 276–97; Elisha Cooke to Simon Bradstreet, London, Oct. 16, 1690, Hall, Leder, and Kammen, eds., *The Glorious Revolution in America*, pp. 69–72; "Reflections Upon the Affairs of New England," *Wyllys Papers,* Conn. Hist. Soc. *Coll.,* XXI (Hartford, 1924), 327.

18. Summons to several persons connected with New England, May 29, 1690, C.O. 5/855, #104; Cooke to Bradstreet, Oct. 16, 1690, Hall, Leder, and Kammen, eds., *Glo. Rev. in Am.,* pp. 73–74.

For the next year or more discussion of terms continued. Chief obstacles were the King's frequent absences from London and the reactionary sentiments of Elisha Cooke and Thomas Oakes. The new agents often disagreed with Mather and Ashurst, insisting that the agency continue its efforts through court action if necessary to restore the former charter. Mather had accepted the obvious fact that the old charter was dead and that the King and his officers would do nothing to revive it, even if they could. The only alternative, which Mather and Ashurst worked for ceaselessly, was to extract a new charter which would give Massachusetts colonists as many of their ancient rights and privileges as possible and maybe a few more.

It was a long and drawn-out procedure. Increase Mather constantly sought new friends and advisers who might prove helpful, including the Archbishop of Canterbury. While the King was in Holland, Mather spoke with Queen Mary, who seemed pleasantly disposed toward New England and commented sympathetically on its "bad condition." Several times during the King's London visits, Mather won audiences and argued his cause. Besides stressing the colonists' exceptional love for Their Majesties and their forwardness in proclaiming them in 1689, he painted the Canadian expedition as a "noble undertaking" and reminded the King how much New Englanders had done to enlarge his dominions. Moreover, they were like to do the same again, given the proper encouragement.[19]

Increase Mather again changed his tune in defending Massachusetts. As necessity required, he had shelved the earlier charter-covenant argument in favor of the rights of Englishmen and the philosophy of the Glorious Revolution. In 1691, when negotiating for a new and ample charter, his argument, or the basis of his argument, shifted back, if only slightly, toward the old stand. Colonists ought to enjoy the rights of Englishmen, to be sure, but all colonies were not alike, Mather claimed. Massachusetts was different, distinctive; the King ought to consider the circumstances of the people there in the same way he had considered the differences between his subjects in England and Scotland after the Revolution. For New Englanders were Congregationalists, and therefore a governor whom the King might think very proper for any of the other colonies would not suit the people of New England. Mather claimed his pressing the King on this issue had a bearing on the outcome of the negotiations which at that point were coming to a determination. But for Mather, the King would have lumped Massachusetts along with the rest of the colonies,

---

19. Increase Mather has left two accounts of his negotiations. See "Autobiography," pp. 333–35, 336, and *A Brief Account concerning Several of the Agents,* in Andrews, ed., *Narratives,* pp. 276–97.

and it would have emerged from the Revolution with no better government than what other colonies were granted. Mather later recorded
these facts in his autobiography "conjecturally, but as that which is
indubitably so." [20]

The Bay Colony was not like other colonies; its very nature was
different, therefore entitling it to distinct privileges which Mather
was determined to secure. Colonists in America were English subjects
who enjoyed all the rights possessed by Englishmen in the realm. But
one colony, at least, was unique, and with this uniqueness went peculiar privileges. As Mather saw the colony's circumstances in 1691, the
rights of Englishmen were not enough, for Massachusetts was still
covenanted with God, which entitled its people to a special relationship. Cooke and Oakes would have insisted that this distinction be
recognized by restoring the old charter. More realistically, Mather accepted the facts of life in William's reign but hoped by astute bargain-
ing to endow a new arrangement with the providential distinction the
colony deserved.

There were disadvantages to negotiating in behalf of Massachusetts.
One was that the colony had nothing really to stand upon in its campaign to extract a liberal charter from the Crown. That Increase Mather
realized this is apparent in his attitude toward the government then
attempting to keep the peace back home. Besides chiding old friends
in Boston for being stingy with money to support his agency, he criticized them for not actually reassuming the old charter in 1689 after
toppling Andros. Mather argued that had the colony boldly revived
the charter itself, they all would be in a stronger position in 1691. What
he meant was, having not done this, and having explained to the King
in 1689 that they would not reassume the charter, his people put the
colony and themselves entirely into the King's hands to do with as he
pleased. And Mather in the spring of 1691 was about to learn the
King's pleasure. Since William came to England to restore charters
revoked by James, in America as well as the realm, said Mather, the
colony's reassuming the charter government would have been justified,
and maybe the King, true to the Revolution, would have let them continue it. On this point Mather seems to have agreed with Cooke and
Oakes, although the argument was a little ungrateful and a little late.
In fact, the argument was a little disingenuous on Mather's part.[21]

One might argue another way as some did. Had Massachusetts surrendered its charter in 1683, as Connecticut and Rhode Island did three

20. "Autobiography," pp. 335–36, 341.

21. Mather to Hinckley, London, May 24, 1690, *Hinckley Papers*, p. 255;
Mather, *A Brief Account*, p. 292; Cooke to Bradstreet, Oct. 16, 1690, Hall, Leder,
and Kammen, eds., *Glo. Rev. in Am.*, p. 74.

years later to Andros, there probably would have been no court judgment against it. Reassumption would have been a good deal easier, even legal, had the charter not been revoked by an English court. Because there were no judgments against the Connecticut and Rhode Island charters, there was little difficulty in taking them up again at the time of the Revolution, and both colonies proceeded to do just that.[22] But Mather could not argue this tack since he had led the crusade against surrender—better to fall into God's hands than the King's, he had preached—thus forcing revocation by court action which the Crown, the attorney general, and the Lords of Trade claimed in 1691 was legal and irrevocable.[23] Mather would have liked a stronger basis on which to negotiate, for he found the colony *was* firmly in the hands of the King, who could do with it as he pleased. The Glorious Revolution may have altered the constitution in England, but regardless of how much he presumed, Mather again and again came up against the hard fact that revolution had not really changed the status of colonies. What guarantees he might win for Massachusetts would be purely the King's gift, not a colony's right.

Given these circumstances, the fact that Mather won so much is a tribute to his negotiating ability and perseverance. The results were striking evidence that the colony was distinctive. Negotiations intensified in the spring of 1691 and continued through the summer. Mather and Ashurst did most of the business but no doubt received plenty of advice—not always helpful—from Cooke and Oakes, who continued their stubbornness. Sir William Phips was in London also, and he doubtless lent credence to the colony's claim that it had helped to enlarge the King's dominions against the French. After all, Phips had led a successful, although minor, campaign against Port Royal, although the less said about the details of Quebec the better.[24]

Mather fought doggedly to retain as many of the advantages of the old charter as possible and a few more. The colony suffered a quick defeat the last of April when William finally decided a main point: the Crown would appoint the governor, a major change from the freemen's annual election of him under the old government.[25] The Lords of Trade

22. See Thomas Hutchinson's discussion of this point, *History of the Colony . . . of Massachusetts-Bay*, I, 286–87. For Rhode Island and its charter, see C.O. 5/905, pp. 189–91; *Recs. Col. R.I.*, III, 258–59, 293–94; *CSPCol., 1689–1692*, #746. Connecticut Petition, Jan. 3, 1690, C.O. 5/855, #52; *CSPCol., 1689–1692*, #686; R. R. Hinman, ed., *Letters from the English Kings . . . to Connecticut*, pp. 189–91.

23. See ch. 8 above.

24. Mather, "Autobiography," pp. 335, 337.

25. C.O. 5/905, pp. 269, 270–71; Add. Mss., 34712, f. 218, B.M.; Robert Harley to Sir Edward Harley, June 2, 1691, H.M.C. 29: 14th Report, App. II, *Portland III* (Harley Mss., I), 467.

and the Crown's law officers took it from there; they drafted a document which Mather found was not commensurate with William's earlier promises. When he complained to the King's ministers that he could not consent to it, that the draft infringed upon Massachusetts' liberties and privileges, their answer was anything but encouraging. Echoing the Crown's side of the argument in the earlier charter struggle, the ministers testily answered that they did not think the colony's agents were "Plenipotentiaries from another Sovereign State." Furthermore, if the agents did not accept the proposals, the Crown would settle the matter in its own way. Mather and Ashurst persisted politely and were able to restore negotiations to a more manageable calm.[26]

As late as the end of July the agents were still holding out for a surprisingly large chunk of power in the General Court. For instance, in their objections to the Crown's proposals, they made it clear they wished the assembly itself to choose the judges, sheriffs, and justices of the peace, not the governor and council. Although the charter draft permitted the lower house to elect the twenty-eight councillors with consent of the governor, the agents asked for sole power of election in the house. Furthermore, they objected to the governor's veto of the assembly's bills, complained about the time allowed the King to confirm or veto their laws, and boldly disagreed with a liberty of conscience for all Christians but Catholics. The agents presented their objections on July 29; the next day, doubtless after consultation and some hard thought, they reduced them to two, insisting still that the General Court choose the judges, sheriffs, and justices, and that the house alone elect the council, that is, *without* the governor's approval. These last two were sent immediately to the King for determination.[27]

On the last day of the month Lord Nottingham offered some strong advice to William on these two crucial points. He explained that the Lords already had made all the concessions possible consistent with the King's sovereignty. If the King gave in on these two demands, by the first he would relinquish the whole administration of justice, and by the second he would invite a "copartnership in the government." The result would be very little dependence upon the Crown, since punishments and rewards would be lodged in the colony's hands. Furthermore, the draft as it was gave more power and privilege to the colony than any other plantations in all the dominions ever pretended to. Already the concessions to Massachusetts would set precedents which would attract all kinds of bold demands from other colonies. Notting-

26. Mather, *A Brief Account,* pp. 283–84.
27. Agents' objections, C.O. 5/905, pp. 277–81.

ham went on to tell the King that the issue of Massachusetts' charter was not a dispute between parties in England, and then added revealingly, unless it was between those who loyally supported the King's "just authority" and those who little by little would steal it away. William was not a man to slight the prerogative. Ten days later he announced that by no means could he accept the agents' objections. The next day Mather and his crew gave up the fight and agreed to the government's proposals. He tells us that the widespread advice he sought impressed upon him the need to accept what was offered. Any other action—Cooke and Oakes still pressed a court case—would doubtless leave them with nothing.[28]

The new Massachusetts charter was dated October 7, 1691.[29] It was a remarkable document. Other royal colonies, like Virginia, New York, and soon Maryland, enjoyed assemblies only through the King's commissions and instructions to their governors and therefore were subject to the King's pleasure. Besides guaranteeing an assembly the Massachusetts charter permitted the lower house to elect the council, subject to the governor's approval, of course. This was a unique twist in the constitution of Crown colonies and eased considerable authority out of the hands of the governor. True to his earlier promise, William invited Mather and the agents to suggest the first governor and a number of the council. According to Mather this was wholly owing to his earlier persuading the King that New England was different from other dominions and deserved peculiar privileges. The agents chose Sir William Phips, who had lately become a member of Mather's congregation back in Boston—baptized by son Cotton in 1690. The choice suited the King, since Phips, a military man, could plug holes in the colony's defenses. Besides picking William Stoughton as Phips's deputy, Mather submitted councillors' names also, deftly selecting a variety which represented, he thought, a safe group of both moderates and old Puritans.[30]

The charter, of course, contained several items which the agents had hoped to avoid. The King retained his right in the future to appoint the deputy governor and secretary, and through the governor to select judges, sheriffs, and justices of the peace, although the assembly elected all other officers of the colony. Gone was the possibility of religious

28. Nottingham to the King, July 31, 1691, H.M.C. 71: *Finch III*, pp. 187–88. See three letters between Nottingham and Viscount Sydney, Aug. 10, 11, and 20, 1691, *ibid.*, pp. 199, 202, 220; C.O. 324/22, pp. 328–53.

29. *Ibid.*; Hall, Leder, and Kammen, eds., *Glo. Rev. in Am.*, pp. 76–79.

30. Mather, *A Brief Account*, p. 294 and n.; Mather, "Autobiography," p. 337; "Mr. Bullivant's Journall of Proceedings . . . ," M.H.S. *Proc.*, XVI (Boston, 1879), 105; Richard S. Dunn, *Puritans and Yankees*, p. 264.

discrimination in voting rights, since the charter introduced a system of suffrage tied to property, equating in this way Massachusetts' with English practice. The charter guaranteed liberty of conscience to all Christians but Catholics, which liberalized considerably religious customs over what the Puritans earlier had insisted upon. The King kept both the governor's veto and his own over assembly bills, but he accepted a three-year limit on his own time for review.

Midway through the charter there appeared a very broad statement granting Massachusetts colonists all the liberties and immunities of free and natural subjects equal to those enjoyed within the realm. This was doubtless pleasing to a good many, although a little thought on the subject might have stirred up a variety of feelings. The same statement was planted in the colony's original charter of 1629, a guarantee to the King's subjects which the Bay Colony itself had denied to many of its inhabitants, Quakers and Anglicans for instance. The fact that Massachusetts had abused these rights was one reason for the charter's revocation in 1684. Still, in 1691, it was a necessary statement; its assumption was at the very heart of both Mather's defense of the colony's revolution and his negotiations for restoration of rights. Such a guarantee was basic to a colony's existence, as Virginia, New York, and Maryland had maintained for some time, although unsuccessfully. But to this basic assumption Mather had added several extras which reflected the Bay Colony's differences. The remarkable thing is that he got away with it.

As a kind of subplot running through the drama of negotiation was the question of what to do with Plymouth. The Old Colony had much less leverage in England than most, since it had never had a real charter incorporating it, and it was too poor to support an agent of its own in London. At the time of revolution it had resumed its former government like Connecticut and Rhode Island despite the pleas of a handful that it lacked a right to do so. In 1690 the Bay government sent to London the Reverend Ichabod Wisewall of Duxbury in Plymouth Colony to aid Increase Mather, and he served as an unofficial voice in the smaller colony's behalf, doubtless with some instructions from Thomas Hinckley, Plymouth's old governor. But Wisewall became suspicious of both Mather and Sir Henry Ashurst, convinced that neither had really put himself out for Plymouth and probably would not in the future.[31]

31. Hammond, "Diary," pp. 151–52; Ichabod Wisewall to Hinckley, July 6 and Nov. 5, 1691, Hinckley Papers, pp. 285–86, 299–301; George D. Langdon, Jr., Pilgrim Colony: A History of New Plymouth, 1620–1691 (New Haven, Conn., and London, 1966), p. 237.

There were several alternatives for the disposition of Plymouth. The bulk of its people hoped for a charter which would establish for all time their separateness, whereby they could go about their business as before but with some guarantee of security for the years to come. But New York, eager as it had always been to expand its jurisdiction, had eyes on Plymouth, and while still in London, Governor Sloughter succeeded in having the colony joined to New York, at least on paper. When Increase Mather got wind of the annexation he persuaded the powers-that-be to revoke it and, in order to protect Plymouth, included it in the Massachusetts proposals. Ichabod Wisewall was outraged and claimed the Old Colony would curse him for it. Obligingly Mather undid what he had done, leaving Plymouth still separate but the unlikely object of a new charter. Once convinced that their days of independence were over, most Plymouth people chose to be annexed to Massachusetts instead of New York.[32] But troubles with dissent and faction and particularly with tax collecting for revenue to support the war sapped the colony's strength, and for a time it did nothing but hope for the best. While Massachusetts' early proposals for settlement had included New Hampshire and Maine in the Bay Colony, nothing was said about Plymouth. The outcome in September was that the new charter annexed both Plymouth and Maine to the Bay but left New Hampshire to a separate existence as a royal colony.[33]

In the sudden change of Plymouth's fortunes, Ichabod Wisewall saw his colony's ruin, the "entail of our inheritance," he called it. The colony itself was partly to blame, but so was Increase Mather, whose "rashness and imprudence" had contributed to the colony's demise. Few wise men would rejoice at receiving their chains, he wrote, except those who sought honor and profit and were "wont to trot after the Bay horse." Wisewall might have added that there would probably be precious little of either honor or profit, since Plymouth would send only four out of the twenty-eight councillors to sit at Boston. The Old Colony's traditional struggle against its neighbors was over, and Plymouth, with no real chance to resist, was swallowed up by the Bay.

32. Cotton Mather to Hinckley, Boston, [Apr.?] 26, 1690, *Hinckley Papers*, pp. 248–49; John Walley to Wisewall [?], n.p., n.d., *ibid.*, 287; Hinckley to Increase Mather, Oct. 16, 1691, *ibid.*, 287–90; N. B. Shurtleff, *et al.*, eds., *Records of the Colony of New Plymouth* (12 vols., Boston, 1855–61), VI, 259.

33. For Plymouth's difficulties, see series of letters in *Hinckley Papers*, pp. 234–38, 239–42, 285–86, 287–90, 290–91, 296, 299–301. As late as August 1692, Cotton Mather could call Taunton's troubles a "filthy stir." *Diary of Cotton Mather* (2 vols., reprinted New York, 1957), I, 143; Richard LeBaron Bowen, "The 1690 Tax Revolt of the Plymouth Colony Towns," *Collected Papers, Armorial, Genealogical, and Historical* (Concord, N.H., 1959); Langdon, *Pilgrim Colony*, pp. 228–29.

Mather and Phips sailed for home with the charter in their baggage at the end of March 1692.[34]

And none too soon. Three years of anxiety and apprehension under a temporary and unstable government had taken its toll from Bay colonists. After tempering some of the exaggeration which appeared in reports by the colony's enemies and unsympathetic critics, who delighted in drawing the once proud commonwealth as a chaos and "labyrinth of Miserys," [35] one is left with the conclusion that even its friends could do little better than comment sadly on its confusion and distraction. In some instances normal institutions broke down wholly or functioned badly. Safeguards of the common law were abused when indictments occurred without grand juries, or as law officers seized property without warrants. Salem deputies protested a spring election and were libeled for their pains, while others nearer Boston ignored it, calling it a "Pretended Election." [36] The increase in taxes alone was enough to unsettle even a secure people—seven and a half rates were exacted in the first six months after rebellion according to Andros, while Joseph Dudley reported home that the people of Boston had paid as much in taxes by the spring of 1691 as they ought normally to pay for the next forty years, leaving them, of course, many thousands of pounds in debt. That Andros and Dudley exaggerated is possible, but doubtful in this case. Samuel Green and his brother were kept busy merely printing warrants for new taxes, six, sometimes ten, rates at a time, besides turning out orders repeatedly to "constibles to get in their Raits." Some colonists refused payment altogether, and a number went to jail as a result.[37]

Business fell off sharply except for those who traded illegally. Edward Randolph and John Palmer reported that there were plenty of these who needed no urging to return to their open trade with the Atlantic world, particularly importing European goods directly to Boston. But even illegal trade was not sufficient to sustain the economy.[38]

34. Wisewall to Hinckley, Sept. 5 and Nov. 5, 1691, *Hinckley Papers*, pp. 299–301; *CSPCol., 1689–1692*, #1731; Mather, "Autobiography," p. 344.

35. John Palmer, *An Impartial Account of the State of New England*, in *Andros Tracts*, I, 27.

36. "Bullivant's Journall," p. 104; C.O. 5/855, #94, p. 258; Hammond, "Diary," pp. 156–57.

37. "Andros' Report of his Administration, 1690," Andrews, ed., *Narratives*, p. 235; Dudley to Blathwayt, Mar. 17, 1691, BPCol. Wmsbg., v. IV; Samuel Green's Bill to General Court, Mass. Arch., Literary, 1645–1774, v. 58, 137–39; Benj. Bullivant's Journall, Feb. 27, 1690, C.O. 5/855, #94; Report Concerning New England to the King, Feb. 25, 1691, C.O. 5/855, #67.

38. One of the chief complaints against Massachusetts after the rebellion was violation of the Acts of Trade. See *A Particular Account of the Late Revolution at Boston* (1689), Andrews, ed., *Narratives*, p. 208; *New England's Faction Dis-*

Debts went unpaid, and many colonists suffered, particularly the poor who, Benjamin Bullivant claimed, were "ready to eat up one another, or turn Levellers." To add to their misery a smallpox epidemic broke out in February 1690 and lasted into June. It forced the temporary government out of Boston to Charlestown to carry on its business. In August fire swept Boston, gutting some twenty houses, and was stopped only by blowing up two or three more which lay in its path.[39]

Behind the apprehension which was apparent throughout the colony was still the paralyzing fear of the French and Indians. The toppling of Andros' government aggravated this fear, for once the Dominion crumbled, so did its defenses on the eastern frontier. Much as Bay colonists resented Andros' suspicious maneuvers in the wilderness, killing off the flower of their youth, they said, they gravely missed the protection he afforded. The French and Indians took advantage of the withdrawal and as part of Count Frontenac's master plan pushed their terrorism closer and closer to the Bay. Not long after their bloody assault upon Schenectady in early 1690, they swept down upon several Maine towns, Berwick, Salmon Falls, Casco, and Wells, murdering, capturing and carrying off colonists, plundering and burning.[40] Some estimates ran as high as a thousand dead and missing. Massachusetts had difficulty handling the crucial problem, since its troops were badly managed. Soldiers who had earlier marched to Maine with Sir Edmund had either mutinied before the revolution or were recalled and discharged by the Bay Colony's government once it was over. They were in a bad mood in the spring and summer of 1690, having not been paid for their earlier services, and they were not about to return to battle. In fact, their "ungovernableness" was one of the serious problems of the interim government; there was little chance of satisfying them without paying them, and the colony was in no position to do that, since the treasury was empty and the constables had great difficulty

covered . . . by C.D., _ibid._, p. 257; John Palmer, _An Impartial Account_, in _Andros Tracts_, I, 41; Randolph to [?], July 20, 1689, BPCol. Wmsbg., v. I; William Wallis to Henry Griffith, Plymouth, Feb. 4, 1690, C.O. 5/855, #62; Edward Randolph, A Short Account of the Irregular Trade . . . C.O. 5/855, #110; Randolph, List of Ships Trading Illegally, _ibid._; Cuthbert Potter, "A Journall and Narrative," Newton D. Mereness, ed., _Travels in the American Colonies_, p. 11; Nicholson to Lords of Trade, Nov. 4, 1690, C.O. 5/1385, 31–32.

39. Bullivant's Journall, C.O. 5/855, #94, p. 256; Hammond, "Diary," p. 152; William Milborne to Jacob Milborne, Boston, Feb. 17, 1690, _Doc. Hist. N.Y._, II (1849), 72; Sewall, _Diary_, I, 322–23, 326; Wait Winthrop to Fitz-John Winthrop, Boston, Aug. 11, 1690, _Winthrop Papers_, M.H.S. _Coll._, 5th ser., VIII, 495.

40. See letters in _Hinckley Papers_, pp. 203–5, 216–17, 219–23, 253–54; Hammond, "Diary," p. 153; Sewall, _Diary_, I, 315–16, 317, 321; "Bullivant's Journall," pp. 103–8; News from New England, C.O. 5/855, #17A.

collecting even arrears in taxes. The soldiers behaved insolently, God-blessed King William, even Sir Edmund, and publicly damned "all pumpkin states." Such blatant remarks were very unsettling to those who were attempting to keep the colony together and not really succeeding, according to a number of reports which played up the prevalent "divisions." Owing to the earlier abuses, it was doubtful that soldiers would obey orders even if they reenlisted, never mind march off to Maine to fight in the wilderness. Many who were ordered to muster shortly deserted; others hooted their captains. And the killing to the eastward continued; York in Maine was the target in January 1692, where, as a result, 140 colonists were missing, about forty of whom rescuers found dead and buried. Most of the town was burned.[41]

Distracted inhabitants in the "out parts" pled for help but got precious little. Ironically they blamed the revolution for their present danger, for it had ended their protection. Some from around the Piscataqua River petitioned the King directly for help, while others gave up altogether and sailed for Boston to throw themselves and what was left of their families on the mercy of the town whose people, they believed, were really responsible for their distress.[42]

The "I-told-you-so's" among the Tories were loud and clear. New England, strong and united under Andros, had now "devolved into about ten little independent kingdome's," none knowing a superior power, and "Every man a Governor." Vulnerable to the French and Indians who continued to strike, hopelessly in debt or so it seemed, with sharp differences and divisions among a people who had earlier prided themselves on their homogeneity, Bay colonists were close to demoralization. Tories prayed for the King's help and a strong royal governor to straighten them out. The Puritans prayed, too; in fact, they had continuously, but for Increase Mather's return with the old charter. The moderates, if they prayed at all, sought a compromise which would settle the government but at the same time give them sufficient independence to get on with the business of making money. The three-year period between revolution and settlement was doubtless as unpromising as any the colony had experienced. Tory, moderate, or old Puritan, they all agreed, the colony was indeed in a "sad con-

41. Petition of Christopher Pennington, etc., to King, Nov. [?], 1689, C.O. 5/855, #49; Bullivant's Journall, Mar. 1690, C.O. 5/855, #94 and M.H.S. *Proc.*, XVI, 103–9; Abstract of a Letter from Tho. Cooper to John Ellis, Boston, Apr. 2, 1690, C.O. 5/855, #78; Nicholson to Lords of Trade, Nov. 4, 1690, C.O. 5/1358, 31–32; Francis Foxcroft to Blathwayt, Boston, Apr. 16, 1691, BPCol. Wmsbg., v. V; Hammond, "Diary," p. 160; Sewall, *Diary*, I, 356.

42. Cooper to Ellis, Boston, Apr. 2, 1690, C.O. 5/855, #78; Petition from Inhabitants of Maine, *Andros Tracts*, I, 176–78; "Bullivant's Journall," pp. 107–8.

dičon." And if Trevor-Roper is right about seventeenth-century witch-craft having something to do with the need for scapegoats in time of intense stress, insecurity, and distraction, no wonder Increase Mather returned in the spring of 1692 to find Salem jail full of witches.[43]

43. Complaint from divers gentlemen and merchants, Jan. 25, 1690, C.O. 5/905, pp. 176–77; C.O. 5/855, #56; *CSPCol., 1689–1692*, #741; Address of Divers Merchants [Oct.] 1690, C.O. 5/855, #122; Extract from a Letter . . . from Mr Usher, July 10, 1689, C.O. 5/855, #16; *CSPCol., 1689–1692*, #242; *ibid.*, #311; Cooper to Ellis, Boston, Apr. 2, 1690, C.O. 5/855, #78; John Palmer, *An Impartial Account*, in *Andros Tracts*, I, 21–23; H. R. Trevor-Roper, *The Crisis of the Seventeenth Century* (New York and Evanston, Ill., 1968), ch. 3.

19 Resettlement II

Events in New York in the spring of 1691 were as unsettling to Bay colonists as the bloody Indian attacks in Maine. Leisler's arrest, imprisonment, and trial for treason and murder were events Massachusetts people watched with sickening fascination, and well they might. If New York's reward for rebellion against Andros' Dominion was trial of its leaders for treason, what about their own? In April and May of 1691 Mather's favorable charter was a year or more away, and if the King's new government in New York could revenge itself upon the rebels, why could not a new regime in Massachusetts do the same? Most Bay colonists had a "good opinion" of Jacob Leisler and saw little difference between his temporary administration and their own.[1]

Complicating Massachusetts' feelings for Leisler and his rebel victims was the presence in New York of Joseph Dudley. Early in January 1691 the former deputy governor, whom the Bay colonists had over-

1. C.O. 5/1081, 117.

thrown along with Andros, returned to Boston accompanied by a hardly less welcome figure, a new royal customs collector, Jahleel Brenton. While Brenton got down to business in Boston Harbor, Dudley moved on to New York, where, surprisingly, he took his seat at the head of Governor Sloughter's council. (It paid to be in England when governments were being formed.) And then when the governor commissioned a court of oyer and terminer to try Leisler and Milborne and the others, he made Dudley president of the court. Many Bay colonists had long since mistrusted Joseph Dudley even before he sold out to James II and Andros, and there he was about to decide the fate of a rebel in New York whose crime, if it were a crime, was hardly less than their own. After all, said even a Boston Tory, Leisler's doings were "soe like our own pattern we canot but love our own Bratt." For several weeks Massachusetts people kept a sharp eye on what went on at New York.[2]

Trial began the last of March and continued into the middle of April. The charges were rebellion and murder, or, as the warrant read: "traiterously levying war against" the King and Queen and "Felouniously murdering" Josias Brown, a "City Labourer," who was cut down in a skirmish during the final hours of resistance. Disturbing to Leisler's sympathizers in both New York and the Bay was the partisan nature of the proceedings. Dudley and Stephen Van Cortlandt were a majority of the committee which examined the prisoners before carrying them off to the common jail; the committee of Sloughter's council which prepared the evidence against the accused included Van Cortlandt, Nicholas Bayard, and William Nichols; two of the nine judges who sat at the trial—"gentlemen unconcerned with the late suffering"—were Joseph Dudley, president, and Major Richard Ingoldesby, Sloughter's military commander.[3] Leisler and Milborne refused to plead to the indictment. They claimed the court had no jurisdiction over them and that the power Leisler wielded as governor had never been "determined Judicially" illegal. The crux of the issue, then, was the packet of letters from William III which had arrived in the summer of 1689. The King had addressed his instructions to Francis Nicholson, or, in his absence, to those who then kept the peace in New York. It was these Leisler had seized after Nicholson fled, insisting that they were rightly his and not the old council's, made up of

2. Samuel Sewall, *Diary*, I, 340, Jan. 24, 26, 1691; William Nichols to Gov. Nicholson, May 7, 1691, BPCol. Wmsbg., v. XV; Graham to Blathwayt, May 5, 1691, *ibid.*, v. X; Francis Foxcroft to Blathwayt, Apr. 16, 1691, *ibid.*, v. V.

3. *Doc. Hist. N.Y.*, II (1849), 362, 363; Dudley to Blathwayt, Apr. 6, 1691, BPCol. Wmsbg., v. IV.

Bayard, Van Cortlandt, and Philips, who, Leisler charged, had refused to proclaim the new King. Dudley's court referred the matter for determination to Governor Sloughter and his new council, on which sat Dudley, Bayard, Van Cortlandt, Philips, Nichols, and Thomas Willett, Leisler's nemesis from Long Island. The council promptly concluded that the packet of letters addressed to Nicholson gave no "power or direction" for governing to Jacob Leisler.[4] Despite their refusal to plead, the prisoners were convicted as mutes by the jury, and the judges pronounced sentence a few days later. All told, the court tried ten of the rebels. Of these it acquitted two, found eight guilty, and sentenced them as traitors to hanging, disembowelment, decapitation, and quartering. A bill of attainder followed, and the government seized their estates.[5]

For a month New York was in as much "firment" as ever before. Governor Sloughter hesitated at the outset to act upon the sentences, preferring to lay the matter before the King and await his pleasure. But the council and Leisler's other enemies bombarded the governor with all manner of arguments for immediate execution. A strong example was needed, they claimed; delay, or heaven forbid, reprieve, could only encourage the rebels who were already "growing dayly very high and Insolentt." Failure to destroy the leaders could only build the rebels' confidence, already heartened by the court's clearing and releasing several of the guiltiest.[6] Joseph Dudley appeared to be the weak reed in the new government's campaign against Leisler. It was he who advised Sloughter to go slow and learn the King's pleasure before acting, and it was he, too, who was instrumental in freeing some of Leisler's henchmen. Dudley may very well have had an ear open to Bay colonists' comment on his role at New York, for no one doubted his ambition for high office in Massachusetts. Boston had called Leisler "Governor" for some time and fully expected Sloughter to let him off. Already there was talk there that it was Dudley and the

4. *Doc. Hist. N.Y.*, II (1849), 364–65; Graham to Nicholson, Apr. 6, 1691, BPCol. Wmsbg., v. X.

5. Graham to [Blathwayt], May 5, 1691, BPCol., Wmsbg., v. X; Dudley to Blathwayt, May 6, 1691, *ibid.*, v. IV; Dudley to Nicholson, May 7, 1691, *ibid.*, v. XV; Lawrence H. Leder, ed., "Records of the Trials of Jacob Leisler and his Associates," *New-York Historical Society Quarterly*, XXXVI (Oct. 1952), 431–57.

6. The best description of New York's problems between the trial and execution of Leisler is in the following letters: Graham to [Blathwayt], May 5, 1691, BPCol. Wmsbg., v. X; Graham to Nicholson, May 6, 1691, *ibid.*; Dudley to Blathwayt, May 6, 1691, *ibid.*, v. IV; Bayard to Nicholson, May 6, 1691, *ibid.*, v. VII; Van Cortlandt to Nicholson, May 7, 1691, *ibid.*, v. IV; Van Cortlandt to Blathwayt, May 7, 1691, *ibid.*, v. IX.

jury who ought to be hanged, not Leisler; in fact, said one, it was a pity Dudley had not been hanged in England. It was Joseph Dudley who dragged his feet after Leisler's trial, and as days of delay turned into weeks, the "firment" rose and swelled.[7]

Bayard, Van Cortlandt, Nichols, and Graham kept pressure directly on Sloughter for execution. They extracted at the very least his promise not to reprieve the rebels without consent of the council. This was little enough for Bayard's group, who openly claimed that if the decision were theirs, there would be no delay in exacting "Justice." Without it, Bayard confessed, none of his people felt safe in New York or the government secure.[8] Backing the council's strong stand was the new lower house—called into session on April 9—to which Leisler's friends were not admitted although elected. By the seventeenth, about the time the court passed sentence on Leisler, the assembly listed his crimes, including responsibility for the Schenectady massacre, and resolved that he and his government were arbitrary, illegal, tumultuous, and rebellious. By the middle of May Governor Sloughter could hold out no longer. He submitted, he said, to the "Clamour of the people," the opinion of a majority of the lower house, and a unanimous council. To ensure the "quiet and peace" of the colony, he ordered execution of Leisler and Milborne. Others under the same sentence were eventually released.[9]

They were hanged on May 16. To say that no part of Jacob Leisler's life became him like the leaving it, or that the moment he stood in the noose was his "finest," is sentimental nonsense. His speech, or sermon, on the gallows, although a moving piece, was typical of its genre; he forgave his enemies, claimed his innocence and loyalty, and defended the Protestant cause, besides espousing an almost fanatical trust in God. But it was the speech of a man who had failed to bring off a major change in New York politics against the power of an entrenched oligarchy, and he paid the prices his enemies set upon him. After a much shorter speech Jacob Milborne was turned off, not without a few unsettling words for "Mr Levingston." The government respited the rest

7. For Dudley's role, see Graham to Nicholson, Apr. 6, 1691, *ibid.*, v. X; Bayard to Nicholson, Apr. 26, 1691, *ibid.*, v. VIII; same to same, May 6, 1691, *ibid.*, v. VII; Nichols to Nicholson, May 7, 1691, *ibid.*, v. XV; Daniel Allin to Nicholson, Apr. 15, 1691, *ibid.*, v. IV; "Diary of Lawrence Hammond," M.H.S., *Proc.*, 1891, 1892, 2d ser., VII, 157.

8. Bayard to Nicholson, May 6, 1691, BPCol. Wmsbg., v. VII.

9. Graham to Nicholson, May 6, 1691, *ibid.*, v. X; *Doc. Hist. N.Y.*, II (1849), 366–67, 374; E. B. O'Callaghan, ed., *Calendar of Historical Manuscripts* [N.Y.], pt. II, 208; Memorial of Messrs. Jacob Leisler and Abraham Gouverneur to the Privy Council, Sept. 25, 1696, Hall, Leder, and Kammen, eds., *Glorious Revolution in America*, p. 126.

of the sentences except striking off their heads. Some New Yorkers may have remembered Masaniello.[10]

The New York assembly got busy setting straight the colony's affairs before the government was quite rid of Leisler. It met early in April, elected James Graham, one of Andros' close advisers, its speaker, and by the middle of May had enacted a good deal of legislation for "Quieting and Setling" the recent disorders. Besides establishing the government's revenue, it confirmed previous grants and patents of land, arranged for a colony militia, constructed a system of courts—modeled after an act passed in 1683 under the aborted assembly—and later approved a table of fees, thoughtfully including William Blathwayt's 5 percent as Auditor General of the Revenue.[11] And then on May 13, the day before Governor Sloughter ordered Leisler's execution, the assembly took a major step and declared by statute law "what are the Rights and Priviledges of their Majesties Subjects inhabiting within their Province of New York." [12]

This was a significant piece of legislation—the more so since the act was almost word for word a repetition of the Charter of Libertyes of 1683. The legislature's action revealed a good deal about the meaning of the Glorious Revolution in America and the colony's understanding of the imperial constitution. That the assembly felt the need to define again these rights for New Yorkers is prime evidence that its members believed neither the Revolution itself nor the settlement of government under Sloughter had done so. Unlike Massachusetts, whose new government rested on a royal charter, a perpetual grant of power from the King unless surrendered or revoked by court action, New York's new government and assembly were based only on the commission and instructions to the governor. And his office and authority were subject to the King's pleasure alone and therefore revocable.[13] New York government, then, still lacked the guarantees which colonists believed were absolutely necessary to assure them, as English subjects, Englishmen's rights in America. The Virginia government under Sir William Berkeley had attempted to secure the same kind of assurance by charter in 1675 but was equally disappointed.

10. "Dying Speeches of Leisler & Milborne," May 16, 1691, *Doc. Hist. N.Y.*, II (1849), 376–80. See also "Draft of a Letter to Mr. Blaithwayt," *ibid.*, p. 382.

11. Graham to Blathwayt, May 5, 27, 1691, BPCol. Wmsbg., v. X; Van Cortlandt to Blathwayt, May 7, 1691, *ibid.*, v. IX; *The Colonial Laws of New York*, I, 223–36; Paul M. Hamlin and Charles E. Baker, eds., *Supreme Court of Judicature of the Province of New York, 1691–1704* (2 vols., New York, 1959), I, 48.

12. *Colonial Laws of New York*, I, 244–48. The act is reprinted in Hall, Leder, and Kammen, eds., *Glo. Rev. in Am.*, pp. 121–23.

13. Leonard W. Labaree, *Royal Government in America*, pp. 8–9, 31, 36.

New Yorkers had a different plan. In its preamble to the new act, the first assembly under Governor Sloughter politely thanked William and Mary for their "gratious favour" in restoring the rights of Englishmen to New York colonists by permitting an assembly similar to those other American colonies enjoyed. What the assembly did not say, but what its actions made perfectly clear, was that William's "gratious favour" was not enough, that it was only a temporary grant of power and one the King could alter as he wished. In order that so necessary a right and other liberties might become permanent, the assembly asked that they be confirmed, that is, that the King approve the new statute which listed them in detail. For once the King officially approved of legislation, it was permanent and from that time beyond the Crown's control to revoke.[14] From here on it was a simple copying of the charter of 1683—omitting Duke James as proprietor, of course, and making several slight changes here and there.

According to the new statute the supreme legislative power in New York under the Crown was forever to reside in a governor, council, and the "people" through their representatives in a general assembly. After the Lords of Trade had scrutinized the charter of 1683, they severely questioned use of the word "people," for they found it a strange expression indeed, unlike that permitted in any other colonial charter or patent.[15] New Yorkers in 1691 continued its use; in fact, it appeared twice in their new document. At the same time the assembly limited somewhat its meaning by confining suffrage to freeholders, whom it defined, like the Massachusetts charter, as anyone having "fourty shillings per Annum in freehold." The representatives claimed several Parliamentary privileges for themselves, such as choice of meeting and adjourning, sole determination of their members' qualifications, an immunity to arrest for themselves and servants in coming to and fro. The governor enjoyed a veto power over the assembly's bills, as did the Crown, although all laws were effective until the King disapproved of them. While the earlier charter directed that the governor call the legislature triennially at least, the assembly of 1691 insisted upon annual meetings.

The declaratory law, like the Charter of Libertyes, boldly included for New Yorkers the personal liberties and property rights of Magna Carta and the Petition of Rights. It quoted again the pertinent paragraphs of each, noticeably the guarantees against arbitrary seizure and taxation without representation. It listed, too, other basic rights such as

14. Oliver M. Dickerson, *American Colonial Government, 1696–1765* (reprinted, New York, 1962), p. 225.
15. See ch. 9 above.

trial by jury, liberal bail, exemption from quartering of troops in private homes, protection from martial law. Again like the Charter of Libertyes, the new law guaranteed liberty of conscience for Christians but permitted no more freedom to Catholics in New York than the laws allowed them in England. The same assembly which condemned Jacob Leisler as a tyrant and rebel enacted this broad statute of liberties three days before the government hanged him.

The assembly's several actions were understandable. The government was again in the hands of the strong faction, really an oligarchy, which had called the turn in New York for several years and would for several more. Under the local leadership of the Bayards, the Van Cortlandts, the Philipses, and the Nichols, this group, with the help of proprietary and then royal governors, like Edmund Andros, Thomas Dongan, and Francis Nicholson, had directed the government and economy in their own behalf. The successful demand for a Charter of Libertyes in 1683 was no real threat to this domination, although it would have brought the government closer at least to some of the people. In fact, it was an advantage, for the faction, which spread through both assembly and council, had itself drafted the charter. While guaranteeing to New Yorkers the rights of Englishmen, it shored up its own people's opportunities for monopoly and control. When the charter failed in 1686 and Governor Dongan dissolved the assembly, there was little upheaval, since the faction, as always, kept its grasp on the council. Even New York's inclusion in the Dominion of New England caused little ripple, for Andros and Nicholson collaborated with the council to retain the same kind of control. Regardless of the type of government New York was subjected to, the same people, a well-to-do merchant-landowning clique, kept positions at the top. Their careers in public office had never demonstrated a devotion to the rights of Englishmen or government by consent except when control was in their hands.[16]

These were the people Leisler turned out by force in 1689. As part of the Glorious Revolution against James II and Catholicism, he and his rebels violently turned on James's counterparts in New York; they broke the oligarchy's grasp of government and distributed more widely political offices and economic opportunity, particularly among their own people. To give this government the sanction it needed Leisler exhumed the Charter of Libertyes as a basis for taxing New Yorkers and then for calling a representative assembly. And he was hated by

16. See ch. 6 above. David S. Lovejoy, "Equality and Empire: The New York Charter of Libertyes, 1683," *William and Mary Quarterly*, 3d ser., XXI (Oct. 1964), 507–8.

the former government for everything he did. But the power and connections of his enemies, with the help of Francis Nicholson, Joseph
Dudley, and William Blathwayt, were strong enough to defeat Leisler
in England and to secure for New York a new governor and an old
council already prejudiced against the rebels. Once the rebellion was
over, the old faction took up where it had left off, shortly reinstating
the trade monopolies to say nothing of customary offices. Retaliation
against Leislerians was effective, if not complete—Bayard would have
hanged the lot of them; at the outset thirty of the prominent rebels
were denied pardons.[17] And then the new government, with Bayard,
Van Cortlandt, Philips, and William Nichols in the council, proceeded
to reenact the Charter of Libertyes as statute law. It was a strong move
to protect their rights and ensure New York a basis for self-determination, but also to confirm their own power and gains. A guarantee of
the rights of Englishmen was a strong platform for colonial self-interest,
for enjoyment of Englishmen's rights meant freedom to pursue colonial needs as those in the saddle saw them. William Berkeley's people
in Virginia and John Coode's followers in Maryland had known this
for some time. Increase Mather and the Bay colonists came lately to
appreciate the relationship. Most of all, Leisler was aware of it, and
he had tried in the best way he knew to achieve it. But he attempted
too much in a colony where his opposition was strong and well connected in England. His agents had failed miserably to win support
among a ministry in London which, for example, was of a mind to
exonerate both Francis Nicholson and Edmund Andros and return
them as governors to America. They lacked the skill and sophistication
necessary to present Leisler's rebellion in England as an acceptable
counterpart of the Glorious Revolution. Increase Mather had deftly
drawn support from a dissenting clergy, Whig leaders, and nonconforming members of Parliament like Sir Henry Ashurst; he persuaded
William's regime to honor Massachusetts' distinctiveness with a liberal
royal charter. Again, John Coode was lucky; history was on his side.
He had little trouble in damning Baltimore's Catholic rule before a
new administration in England which had won a revolution on the
basis of its Protestantism. Furthermore, to rid Maryland of proprietary
government fitted nicely the plans of colonial policymakers like the
Lords of Trade and William Blathwayt who opposed all colonial governments which presented barriers to the Crown's control. But the
circumstances were stacked against Jacob Leisler, and he was hanged
as a rebel.

17. *Colonial Laws of New York,* I, 255–57; Petition to Gov. Benj. Fletcher,
Feb. 9, 1693, Hall, Leder, and Kammen, eds., *Glo. Rev. in Am.,* pp. 89–91.

The settlement of a new government and the death of Leisler hardly led to political peace in New York. Faction and mistrust in the 1690's were as deep as they had been during the heat of revolution. What Leisler's followers were unable to win by rebellion, they could only hope to secure through politics. But chances of success were meager under exclusive rule of the anti-Leislerians. Governor Sloughter died in the summer of 1691, only a few months after setting up the government. Without instructions the council presumptuously appointed Major Richard Ingoldesby to his place, and he, like Sloughter, sharply reflected Tory support in both New York and England. His vindictiveness against Leislerians had been apparent since his arrival. With solid Tory backing in England, Colonel Benjamin Fletcher arrived as royal governor in 1692. He early allied himself with the old council members and frustrated any chance for Leisler's followers—those not still in jail—to gain seats in the colony's assembly.[18]

By 1695 Tory ascendancy in Parliament had begun to fade. The change in political climate eventually made possible the recall of Fletcher but not before he had further ingratiated himself with Leisler's enemies by several notorious gifts of land. As Whig prospects improved, so, too, did those of Leislerians. Jacob Leisler, Jr., and Abraham Gouverneur, who had skipped bail in New York, commenced a campaign in England which soon resulted in a friendly Parliament's reversal of the convictions and attainders against both Leisler and Milborne. Massachusetts agents in London, particularly Sir Henry Ashurst, lent a helping hand. Richard Coote, Earl of Bellomont, soon to take Fletcher's place in New York, was a member of Parliament's committee which investigated the New York affair, and the inquiry convinced him that the two men were "barbarously murdered." [19]

While the Whig ascendancy had definite repercussions upon New York government, it did not have the same liberating effect upon colonial policy. A switch in English politics might easily reverse political decisions and replace governors in America; it did not alter English

18. Major Ingoldesby and Council to Lords of Trade, New York, July 29, 1691, *Doc. Hist. N.Y.*, II (1849), 386; *ibid.*, pp. 435–37; Jacob Leisler and Abraham Gouverneur to Privy Council, Sept. 25, 1696, Hall, Leder, and Kammen, eds., *Glo. Rev. in Am.*, pp. 126–27. See also excerpts from Bellomont's letters, *ibid.*, pp. 129–32.

19. "An Act for Reversing the Attainder of Jacob Leisler and Others," *Doc. Hist. N.Y.*, II (1849), 435–37; Mather to Dudley, Boston, Jan. 20 [?], *ibid.*, 437; Lawrence H. Leder, *Robert Livingston*, p. 103 n. For Fletcher's generosity in granting land, see Colonial Entry Book, Abstracts of Grants of Land, New York, C.O. 5/1134, *passim*. For circumstances surrounding Fletcher's recall, see James S. Leamon, "Governor Fletcher's Recall," *William and Mary Quarterly*, 3d ser., XX (Oct., 1963), 527–42.

attitudes toward colonies or change fundamental principles of the English empire. In 1696 the first batch of New York's laws surfaced in England for review before the new Board of Trade which William had recently commissioned in place of the old Lords of Trade. (A Whiggish Parliament had threatened to establish the Board itself, but William beat it to the draw in order to keep prerogative control over imperial affairs.) The new Board scrutinized the New York assembly's declaration of rights in 1696 with the same care the Lords of Trade had examined the Charter of Libertyes a dozen years before, and with the same results. After consulting with the Crown's law officers and a session with the assembly's agents, including councillor William Nichols, the Board firmly recommended the King's repeal of the declaratory act. Objecting first to the "great and unreasonable privileges" assumed by the assembly, it questioned specifically the exemption of the inhabitants from quartering soldiers, a privilege which might be very inconvenient to the King's service in New York. Moreover, the declaration contained several "large and doubtful expressions" which distinguished the government from others in America. William promptly accepted the Board's recommendation and vetoed the New York law. But to satisfy the uneasy minds of the colonists, the Board, in a very revealing move, suggested that the King grant New York a royal charter similar to the one Charles II sent to Virginia in 1676 after he had refused to approve the one presented by the colony's agents.[20] The Virginia model would have assured the colonists an "immediate dependence upon the Crown" and confirmed their land to them. But it would have offered them little more, since it was dead silent about the right of an assembly, laws of their own making, taxes only with consent, and all the other rights and privileges which the Charter of Libertyes and the New York act of 1691 had defined and sought to make permanent. However, the innocuous charter never materialized. William might instruct his governors to call assemblies and permit them to make laws and levy taxes, but the power to do so was still based on royal grace and favor and dependent upon the King's pleasure, and, of course, was revocable. In New York it was not the right of colonists. John Palmer had testily pointed this out to Bay colonists some time earlier.

Governor Bellomont disembarked in New York on April 1, 1698, and was "magnificently received." By October he had carried out fully the reversal of Leisler's and Milborne's convictions and attainders by which Parliament had sanctioned their seizure of the government and at the

20. *CSPCol., 1696–1697*, #846, #952, #1010, #1012; *N.Y. Col. Docs.*, IV, 263–65.

same time censured their executions. With the governor's blessing the two families exhumed the rebels' bodies from their shallow graves near the gallows and gave them a "Christian burial" in the Dutch Church on October 20. While the ghost of Masaniello rejoiced, twelve hundred solemn New Yorkers attended the grand funeral, and there would have been more had there not blown a "rank storm for two or three days together." The Bayards, Van Cortlandts, and Philipses sulked on their estates. A week later they conspicuously stayed home from services which marked a day of fasting and humiliation designed to quiet the "heats and differences" between parties. The new governor's activities drew him deeply into the Leislerian camp; it became the other faction's turn to howl, and howl it did. The bitter political struggle outlived Bellomont's few years in office, even Bellomont; conditioned by political events in England, it survived well into the eighteenth century.[21]

John Coode and his government were much luckier than Leisler and his. What he and his people sought, what they had rebelled for, they said, was to rid themselves of Baltimore and the proprietary so that the Crown might take over Maryland and protect them all from arbitrary government. Several circumstances which obtained in England after the Glorious Revolution tended to promote this kind of dependence upon the Crown. First was the solid Protestantism of William's government and its prejudice against the proprietor's religion. Furthermore, the new administration picked up where James's had left off and continued the hard look at colonies in America, primarily proprietaries, which were not directly under control of the Crown. Three months before Coode and his friends toppled Lord Baltimore's government, the Lords of Trade had scrutinized proprietary charters all along the line and asked thorny questions about how Maryland, Pennsylvania, and the Carolinas might be brought more closely under the thumb of the King. The imminence of war with France in the spring of 1689 persuaded many of the good sense of such a move, and then actual war in May made it imperative.[22] Back of all this, of course, were the policymakers at Whitehall, Blathwayt and his group of professionals, who were wholly opposed to any relaxation in colonial policy which might promote again independent attitudes in America. In fact, they

21. Samuel Sewall to John Wise, Boston, Apr. 12, 1698, *Letter-Book*, M.H.S., *Coll.*, 6th ser., I, 198–99 and 208; Excerpts from Letters of Bellomont, May 8– Oct. 27, 1698, Hall, Leder, and Kammen, eds., *Glo. Rev. in Am.*, pp. 131–32.

22. Lords of Trade to King, May 2, 1689, C.O. 324/5, pp. 46–47; *CSPCol.*, *1689–1692*, #102; *ibid.*, #123, #124.

were for a continuation of the Dominion, and would have thumped for it openly had it not been impolitic to push it owing to Whig popularity immediately following William's accession.[23] The Revolutionary philosophy, while constitutionally significant in England, did not make much of a dent in colonial policy in the long run. True, Increase Mather turned his back on the court for a time and pinned Massachusetts' hopes for a restoration of the charter on the Corporation Bill's success in Parliament, but the hope was short-lived. By early 1690 Parliament had dropped the bill and Mather returned to court where, in colonial affairs, prerogative power had declined little if any.[24] To be sure, during the Whig ascendancy the Crown showed some deference to Parliament in colonial matters and invited the legislature to join in the scrutiny of the proprietary relationship, particularly that of Baltimore's Maryland. But this, too, seemed short-lived. After the Lords of Trade suggested to William that members of the Privy Council who sat in the Commons persuade the House to consider the problem of Maryland, and after some consultation on the subject between the attorney general and the speaker, the Crown went ahead and made its own decision.[25]

While all this was going on, Lord Baltimore sought desperately to save his charter and regain his colony from the rebels. He offered compromises to the Lords of Trade, promised to appoint a Protestant governor, even pledged not to molest or prosecute John Coode—which must have been a reluctant concession. His agent, James Heath, colorfully testified to the rebels' plundering of Protestants and embezzling the proprietor's revenues, but the King's law officers were not persuaded to support the old government.[26] Meanwhile, John Coode and Kenelm Cheseldyne arrived in England in the fall of 1690, followed shortly by Henry Coursy and Richard Hill, both proprietary men who had managed to escape from St. Mary's. All the principals, including Baltimore, met face to face before the Lords of Trade, and there occurred a grand airing of Maryland's problems. Charges and answers were followed by countercharges and their answers. Coode seemed to have the last word when he claimed outright that the majority of Marylanders were on his side. The colony under Baltimore had never enjoyed a continuous peace, he said; the Catholics there were in league with the French and

23. See ch. 12 above.

24. Increase Mather, "Autobiography," A.A.S. *Proc.,* 71 (1961), pt. 2, pp. 342–43.

25. Lords of Trade to King, May 18, 1689, C.O. 324/5, pp. 50–51; *CSPCol., 1689–1692,* #124, #145, #656, #658. *Arch. of Md.,* VIII, 100–1.

26. Baltimore's Proposals to Lords of Trade, Jan. 11, 1690, *CSPCol., 1689–1692,* #708; *ibid.,* #947, #948; *Arch. of Md., VII,* 165–66; *ibid.,* VIII, 188–90.

Indians and had refused to proclaim William III.[27] After several legal maneuvers, some of them shabby enough, the attorney general decided that Catholic Baltimore was "incapacitated by Law to govern," and the King might send whom he pleased to direct affairs in Maryland. Other justifications for depriving the proprietor of control of his colony were based on the necessities of the case, it being the only means to preserve the colony which had fallen dangerously into disorder and confusion during a time of war. The only way to secure the safety of good subjects in Maryland was to take the government out of the proprietor's hands and annex it to the Crown. Baltimore retained his lands and rents, but he lost control of the government. Colonel Lionel Copley soon embarked for Maryland as royal governor, armed with a commission and instructions which blandly explained that there were several "curious Precedents for seizing of Governments in Cases of Defects in that Administration," hardly a precise explanation of Baltimore's loss.[28]

Coode's people and the proprietor had struggled for years over reconciling colonists' rights and Baltimore's absolute power. Depriving the proprietor of his government avoided any real decision about either claim. The seizure was made for necessity's sake, given immediate political circumstances in England: the proprietor's Catholicism, war with France, and a continuation of a colonial policy which sought centralization of control over the dominions. Copley's instructions provided for a typical royal government with a representative assembly, while the King named governor and council. Only freeholders might elect burgesses, a discrimination against freemen which the rebels earlier had complained about under Baltimore. Copley defended the restriction since it agreed with English customs, a kind of equality the rebels had hoped to avoid. The King warned Copley to permit Baltimore's agent and receiver, now Henry Darnall, to live peaceably among them and collect the proprietor's revenues. Although the new government disenfranchised Catholics, it permitted liberty of conscience to all Marylanders. If they could not vote, Catholics at least could go to church unmolested, and probably the rebels wanted no more or less.[29]

The King appointed Nehemiah Blackiston and several other Coode rebels to the royal council, much to the disgust of Edward Randolph,

27. Nicholson to Lords of Trade, Aug. 20, 1690, C.O. 5/1358/21; *Arch. of Md.*, VIII, 211–13, 215–18, 219–20, 225–28.

28. Abtracts of Commissions, etc., Add. Mss., 30372, f. 25b; *Arch. of Md.*, VIII, 185–86, 200–3, 204, 263; *CSPCol., 1689–1692*, #923.

29. Gov. Copley's Instructions, Nov. 2, 1691, C.O. 324/22, pp. 384, 387–400; *Arch. of Md.*, VIII, 264, 265, 272; L. W. Labaree, ed., *Royal Instructions to British Colonial Governors*, II, 494.

whom the Crown had returned to the colonies as surveyor general. Poking about as usual, Randolph managed to pass through St. Mary's in time for the sitting of the first meeting of the new assembly in the spring of 1691. He sneered at Blackiston's rise to power, now second to the governor. Still a knave, Blackiston was a poor attorney, said Randolph, not worth a hogshead of tobacco until he became collector of customs as a result of the revolution. Randolph found Henry Jowles "tolerable" enough. But once mellowed with wine and richer by a grant of 40,000 pounds of tobacco from the legislature, Jowles fell in with the rest of the "silly Animals" on the council. These, Randolph described as an Irish merchant, a "Scotch pedler," an English highwayman, and a "broaken London carpenter." He claimed he saw better men elected as burgesses than he found sitting on the council.

To ease the road ahead Maryland's first assembly presented Governor Copley with 100,000 pounds of tobacco. It was worth only £250 to £300 in real money, he quickly explained to William Blathwayt, whom he begged to ask the King if he could keep it. At the same time the assembly elected Kenelm Cheseldyne to his old place as speaker and presented him with an equal amount of tobacco. The gift was for the "extreame good service he has made them beleeve he did them," Copley jealously reported to Blathwayt.[30] When Coode arrived at St. Mary's, somewhat later than the rest, the new government voted him 100,000 pounds, too, which infuriated Randolph, as did all these gifts, since the colony was already dangerously in debt to the Crown for revenues, arrears Randolph was determined to collect. Rebellion may not have enfranchised all the freemen in Maryland, but it paid off some of the rebels, most of whom did very nicely under Governor Copley. Coode was soon up to his old tricks. Before the new governor was quite settled in the colony, Coode noised it about that Baltimore and Blathwayt in London were conniving to replace him with Francis Nicholson. Blathwayt vigorously denied the report and warned the governor that Coode's word was little to be depended upon when one considered "ye person and his moralls."[31]

Despite the squabbling, and there was plenty in the early years of royal government in Maryland, the new assembly got down to business in May and June of 1692. There followed a thoroughgoing reorganization of the colony's government with a batch of fresh laws which were

30. Randolph to Blathwayt, James Town, June 28, 1692, Toppan, ed., *Randolph*, VII, 373, 376–77; Copley to Blathwayt, Marieland, July 30, 1692, BPCol. Wmsbg., v. XVIII.

31. Randolph to Blathwayt, June 28, 1692, Toppan, ed., *Randolph*, VII, 379–80; Copley to Blathwayt and *verso*, June 20, 1692, Feb. 28, 1693, BPCol. Wmsbg., v. XVIII.

remarkable in demonstrating a shift of power from a proprietary oligarchy to a representative assembly. To be sure, the King appointed the governor and gave him a veto, but Lionel Copley exercised the power lightly. New laws regulated and adjusted in more equitable fashion a variety of governmental functions which the rebels earlier had listed as harsh grievances when in the hands of the proprietor. These included the manner of electing burgesses, methods of taxing, recording and publicizing laws, fees of all kinds, choosing sheriffs and determining their authority, land office practices, and significantly the administration of justice, which the assembly distributed more locally. Besides accommodating a number of former rebels by absorbing them into the new government, this new government by statute law lodged in the assembly a good deal of power which the rebels had claimed the proprietor abused at their expense. In Maryland, it appears, the revolution was a huge success.[32]

But was it? A final clout was missing. Granted William III had settled royal governments upon both New York and Maryland after the Glorious Revolution. Granted, also, he appointed governors over both colonies and permitted them to call representative assemblies. But to New Yorkers this was insufficient for Englishmen in America, as we have seen. When their new assembly met, it drafted a declaratory law which spelled out in detail colonists' rights as Englishmen and asked the King to confirm it, which would have guaranteed these rights forever—or so they hoped. The Maryland assembly was just as wary of the weak foundation upon which its new government rested, to say nothing of the laws it passed. The governor's authority to establish an assembly derived only from his commission and instructions, and he held this power, his commission, and his post, for that matter, at the Crown's pleasure. If the King could authorize the convening of an assembly and the vague rights it allegedly included under one governor, he as easily could omit the practice altogether under another governor in the future. The arrangement lacked a guarantee, a recognition of right. The Maryland assembly, like New York's a year earlier and Virginia's in 1675, attempted to extract this guarantee. But unlike New York and Virginia, its method was different and much more simple.

Governor Copley had come to Maryland with instructions to establish the Anglican Church there. After all, in royal colonies the King's Church won preferential treatment and usually establishment—except in Massachusetts. King William and Governor Copley expected the

32. *Arch. of Md.*, VIII, 312, 425–561, *passim;* Michael G. Kammen, "Causes of the Maryland Revolution of 1689," *Maryland Historical Magazine* (Dec. 1960), p. 330.

same in Maryland, as did the Bishop of London, who warmly pushed it. Whether Marylanders were generally agreeable to the idea is another question and not easily answered. That Maryland was overwhelmingly Protestant there can be no doubt, but how many colonists were actually Anglican and what support there was for an Anglican establishment among them is difficult to determine, if not impossible. Quakers, Baptists, Congregationalists, and Presbyterians, none of whom had much love for the King's Church, had settled in Maryland, too, and together they easily outnumbered the Anglicans. But the King and Bishop were determined to establish their church there, and so was the governor.[33]

To this pressure the assembly responded in 1692, but not in the manner one might expect. In its act "for the Service of Almighty God and the Establishment of the Protestant Religion," the assembly outlined a tenuous religious organization which reduced the governor's usual authority over the church and like Virginia played up the vestry as a strong body of laymen superior in power to the minister. Its loose structure hardly indicated a sincere intent to enhance the King's Church in Maryland. Moreover, buried in the act was a short but concise statement: "that the Great Charter of England be kept and observed in all points" within the colony. This must have come as a surprise to all who read it and probably was more important to those who drafted the law than establishing a church.[34]

For the next half-dozen years or more the assembly stubbornly included within its bill of establishment a clear statement guaranteeing Maryland colonists the rights of Englishmen. The King vetoed the first act, not because the church establishment was faulty, which it was, but because an extension of Magna Carta to America equated colonists with Englishmen and guaranteed them the same rights and liberties. This the King and his government refused to do. In 1694 the ubiquitous Francis Nicholson replaced Governor Copley, who had died the year before. Although he persuaded the assembly to amend its act by strengthening the clergy's role in the church administration, his lectures about colonial subordination and the inappropriateness of their bold demand were ignored. When in 1696 William vetoed two earlier attempts at establishment, Nicholson and the assembly tried again. Omitting this time reference to Magna Carta, the assembly inserted

33. *Arch. of Md.*, VIII, 276–77; Eugene R. Sheridan, "Maryland as a Royal Colony, 1689–1715," (unpubl. A.M. thesis, Univ. of Wisconsin, 1968), ch. II; Richard A. Gleissner, "Religious Causes of the Glorious Revolution in Maryland," *Maryland Historical Magazine* (Winter, 1969), 329.

34. *Arch. of Md.*, XIII, 425–30.

instead the claim that Maryland colonists enjoyed all the rights and liberties under England's "fundamental laws." Rather than a whittling of the original statement, the new one actually enlarged the claim. England's "fundamental laws" would necessarily include, besides Magna Carta and the Petition of Right of 1628, the recent Bill of Rights which emerged from the Glorious Revolution.

Governor Nicholson balked again and renewed his attempt to persuade the legislature that colonists were entitled only to rights the King was willing to give them. Curiously, the assembly declined the governor's invitation to draft a separate declaratory act of their rights despite his promise to approve it and recommend it to the King. A separate act, of course, was precisely what New York had attempted to push through in 1691 only to be met by a royal veto in the same year Maryland's more general acts were stopped, a fact the Maryland people may very well have known. While the burgesses adamantly refused to separate political from religious issues, they did alter their statement a third time, changing it to read "laws and statutes of England." But this was as objectionable in London as Magna Carta and the appeal to "fundamental laws," since the King's law officers interpreted it as a further challenge to the prerogative. The law provoked another royal veto besides a stiff reprimand to Governor Nicholson for approving and forwarding it. Only after the Privy Council had drafted a new law for them and strongly recommended its approval did members of the assembly knuckle under and pass an act of establishment in 1701. It contained no mention of the rights of Englishmen.[35]

The rights and liberties which Massachusetts people believed they achieved through a new charter after the Revolution, New York and Maryland attempted to grasp through statute law. New York's included a detailed listing, Maryland's a blanket statement about fundamental rights and laws of Englishmen. The King vetoed both and demonstrated the Crown's unwillingness to limit the prerogative in America. The Glorious Revolution may have liberalized the English constitution and permitted Parliament to clip the wings of the Crown, but the imperial constitution for overseas dominions had changed very little.

Boston turned out in style to greet Governor Phips and Increase Mather on May 14. When they disembarked after little better than six weeks from Plymouth, England, they found candles illuminating the Town House and eight companies of militia ready to escort them from the Boston wharves to their homes. Although under arms, the

35. Sheridan, "Maryland as a Royal Colony," ch. II; Gleissner, "Religious Causes of the Glorious Revolution in Maryland," pp. 332–41.

soldiers reluctantly refrained from the customary volleys since " 'twas Satterday night" and already the Sabbath. On Monday the militia re-formed as an honor guard for Phips's procession to the Town House, where the new commissions were read and the government established. Boston people learned that besides being governor of Massachusetts, William Phips was military commander of all New England, a legacy of the Dominion.[36]

Phips and Mather had their work cut out for them. Granted they returned with as liberal and favorable a charter as could be expected, convincing all Bay colonists that their new government was as good as if not better than the old was not an easy task. But Mather pitched into it with gusto, determined to paint the King's charter and the gov-ernment derived from it in all the acceptable colors of the old.

There were several obstacles in the way which made the campaign difficult. No doubt a majority of colonists thought Mather had done well enough, given the circumstances, but there was still a number of the old faction, reinforced by the return from England of Elisha Cooke and Thomas Oakes, who trusted God more than kings and the hell with the circumstances. Phips was the King's governor despite Mather's choosing him; he had a veto power, and colonists' votes could not turn him out the next spring even if they wished. Moreover, Mather's four years in London did not quite ring true in the ears of these people. He had left the colony as one of them, and here he was now immodestly bowing to the plaudits of the people for having accepted in place of the old a new charter which permitted the King and the powers-that-be in England a strong hand in Massachusetts' future. And then for Mather to tell the colonists that the new government was really an improvement upon the old, giving them now a splendid opportunity to take up where they had left off as custodians of the holy mission, this was difficult for the likes of Cooke and Oakes to swallow.[37] It was galling, too, for those of the old faction who had reluctantly accepted the moderates' help in getting rid of the Dominion in the first place, to find now these same moderates generously represented in the new government, although Mather had seen to it that there was a sprink-ling of the old guard among them.

Governor Phips reacted strongly to the opposition which centered on Cooke but now expanded to include William Stoughton, the deputy

36. Sewall, *Diary,* I, 360; Hammond, "Diary," p. 161; Phips's Commission, C.O. 324/22, pp. 401–07; Phips to Blathwayt, May 30, 1692, BPCol. Wmsbg., v. V.
37. Increase Mather, *A Brief Account concerning Several of the Agents* (Lon-don, 1691), Andrews, ed., *Narratives,* pp. 290, 291, 294; *Diary of Cotton Mather,* I, 148; Perry Miller, *The New England Mind: From Colony to Province,* p. 174.

governor, and Secretary Isaac Addington. When in London, he and
Mather had no idea these people were so bigoted to their "Idoll the
old charter," for had they known, they would never have nominated
any of them to offices. Although Mather and Phips had argued against
the governor's veto over the lower house's choice of councillors, they
were grateful for the power in 1693 when Phips used it to prevent
Cooke from becoming one. Even so the house replaced ten of Mather's
original nominees that year, and Massachusetts politics took on the
look of a struggle between a governor's or moderate party, geographically centered in the east, and an opposing group in the lower house
whose support was primarily rural. It was this opposition party or faction, although probably the smaller of the two, which Mather found
difficult to convince that the new charter and government were really
an improvement.[38]

Another annoying distraction to the government was the maneuver-
ings of Joseph Dudley. Despite his prestigious offices in New York,
Dudley left them for Massachusetts, managing to arrive just before
Phips's and Mather's elaborate reception. He had no role to play in the
new government, thanks to Mather, which left him free to scheme
against it. When he suddenly sailed to England in the summer of 1693,
the governor was understandably suspicious. Phips begged William
Blathwayt in London to keep an eye on Dudley and prevent at all
costs his return to Massachusetts, where he was generally hated, in
any public capacity whatever. So apprehensive was Phips's government
of Dudley's doings in London that he and his council and several
leading Boston merchants seriously considered sending Mather back to
London where, they hoped, he might frustrate Dudley's plans. But
nothing came of it, although Mather prayed over the prospect for
some time. Judge Dudley's hour had not yet come. A government in
London which shortly reversed Leisler's attainder and censured his
conviction and execution, and would soon replace Benjamin Fletcher
with Whiggish Lord Bellomont as governor of New York, was not
about to appoint Joseph Dudley to anything. But Bellomont soon died
and so did William III; Queen Anne's Tories found a place for Dudley,
and to the alarm of many, it was home in Massachusetts. But that is
another story.[39]

What Increase Mather had not been able to secure for Massachusetts

38. Phips to Blathwayt, Oct. 12, 1692, Feb. 24 or 27 [?], 1693, BPCol. Wmsbg.,
v. V; Miller, *The New England Mind: From Colony to Province*, pp. 174–76.

39. Hammond, "Diary," p. 160; Phips to Blathwayt, Sept. 11, Oct. 30, 1693,
BPCol. Wmsbg., v. V; Mather, "Autobiography," p. 345; Abstract of Governors,
1701, Add. Mss. 30372, f. 29.

in London, he and his party hoped to win through politics at home. And the new charter established a government which was as susceptible to politics as any on the Continent, if not more so. In the face of a liberty of conscience, any pious Massachusetts government worth its salt would see to it that colonists did not stray very far out of line in religious matters. The legislature soon enacted stiff laws making blasphemy and idolatry capital crimes. Since it represented overwhelmingly a Congregational population, the General Court lent the churches its willing support. It authorized salaries for orthodox ministers, permitting towns throughout the colony to maintain their churches through taxation of their people, Congregational, Anglican, Baptist alike.[40] At the outset even the new suffrage requirement, which outlawed religious qualifications, was whittled at in Charlestown when a majority of the town meeting voted down Thomas Graves's pointed inquiry into the right of some of his neighbors to vote. Townsmen, it was clear, "were not willing to question any present." Besides enacting a habeas corpus act, the legislature established a provincial court system which limited appeals to the Privy Council to actions exceeding £300, a restriction which would allow the colony to settle many of its own disputes without English interference.[41] Intensely eager that the King approve these laws, Mather assured William Blathwayt in London of the colony's "grateful acknowledgement" to him should they pass, while Governor Phips more realistically offered Blathwayt half interest in a new scheme for the peltry trade if the Crown confirmed them. Much to their disappointment, the King vetoed all the acts except that establishing ministerial salaries.[42] At least the public worship of God in the Congregational way would continue, which was, after all, part of the original mission.

Except for the defeat of Andros and the Dominion, the results of the Glorious Revolution in Massachusetts were not what the Puritan faction had expected. For revolution helped to lead Bay colonists away from their narrow, seventeenth-century perspective of colonists and colonies in the New World. It thrust them into an empire they had refused earlier to recognize, breaking down some of their prejudices toward life beyond New England. It forced them to adjust their politics and their trade to a larger world of the English empire where

40. Miller, *The New England Mind: From Colony to Province*, pp. 174–75.

41. Hammond, "Diary," p. 162; Samuel Sewall to Nathaniel Higginson, 1706, *Letter-Book*, M.H.S. *Coll.*, 6th ser., I, 337; Sewall to Thomas Cotton, Mar. 19, 1700, *ibid.*, 223 and n.

42. Mather to Blathwayt, July 6, 1694, BPCol. Wmsbg., v. V; Phips to Blathwayt, Sept. 30, Oct. 3, 1693, *ibid.*; Miller, *The New England Mind: From Colony to Province*, p. 174.

the Crown chose their governors and reviewed their laws, and a series of royal customs collectors kept them aware at least of the Acts of Trade. But Massachusetts' belief in its covenant and mission died hard. Religion remained prominent in Bay Colony life and continued to shape its people's view of themselves and their colony. Increase Mather and his son Cotton defended the new charter and government as God's way as long as they lived.

Conclusion

The results of the Glorious Revolution in America were not clear-cut, for the effects were as varied as the causes. If the chief goal of revolution was a shift of allegiance from James to William, as it was in England, then it was universally achieved, for it obtained in the colonies which did not revolt as well as in those which did. If a primary purpose of revolution was to smash a Catholic conspiracy (real or imagined) against Protestant Englishmen, then again, it was considered a successful affair. Further, if the acts of rebellion were simply the overthrow of arbitrary governments, the Dominion over New England, New York, and New Jersey and Lord Baltimore's regime in Maryland, then the Revolution was accomplished, for the Dominion was dissolved and the proprietor in Maryland lost control of his colony. If these were the heart of the Glorious Revolution in America, it was as successful there as it was in England. But to accept these consequences alone—all true—as a means to explain the rebellions of 1689 would be to write poor history and to gloss over what these people were about. Even a cursory reading of the preceding pages, I hope, would disprove such simplistic conclusions if left by themselves.

If, however, each of the rebellions was also a strike for supremacy by one or more groups of colonists over others, in order to satisfy self-interested needs, then the consequences fall less into a pattern. Viewed in this light, the upheavals were not one revolution at all but separate outbursts for distinct causes. Moreover, in Maryland the rebels' strike was victorious, while in New York it went down to bloody defeat. Among Bay colonists a large and small group collaborated to overthrow Andros' Dominion, after which their interests split. Results in Massachusetts were a mixture of success and failure on that score. Less important to the total picture were Connecticut and Rhode Island; each achieved eventually from rebellion precisely what it sought: a return to charter government with a built-in privilege, for the most part, of being left alone.

If, too, the revolutions in America were also an attempt by colonists to realize a conception of empire based on an equality between Englishmen at home and abroad, the results were diverse. Maryland achieved one primary purpose: a substantial shift of power from the hands of a proprietor to an elected assembly under royal government. But like Virginia in 1675, its legislature was unable to translate the Crown's grace and favor into a permanent right, or find a constitutional means to protect its dependent position from prerogative power. That this was the scheme of the antiproprietary party was as evident after the Revolution, when the prerogative was royal, as it had been before, when it was proprietary. New Yorkers had struggled for the same kind of guarantee, from the conquest of 1664, through Leisler's Rebellion, well into the 1690's, but they were defeated on all counts. Granted they won an assembly from the Revolutionary settlement, like that of Maryland it lacked the warranty which they had hoped to attach to it.

In Massachusetts the circumstances and the outcome were different, reflecting the peculiar character of that province. The chief difficulty in attempting to restore the godly community, which lived on in the minds of many Bay colonists, was the very nature of the Revolution and the King's settlement of the colony's government. And in this there was an unappreciated irony. In justifying revolt Massachusetts was forced off its usual foundation of old covenant and original charter, for such parochial sanctions had little appeal in the world of empire outside New England. Bay colonists had transcended their local and peculiar bases which long since had sustained them against royal commissions, Indian wars, Navigation Acts, and customs officers. In rebellion they greedily grasped the rights of Englishmen, a set of principles whose prospects the Glorious Revolution gave great promise to, or so

it seemed. Puritan settlers, who earlier had gloried in their holy isolation from Englishmen's rights and responsibilities had come suddenly
to see their value in relieving them from a nasty dilemma.

But curiously, the very rights granted them in the new charter, religious toleration, a more equitable basis for suffrage, a wider participation in lawmaking and tax levying, militated against a restoration of
the Bible State as Puritans had known it. Revolution and the new
charter made restitution of the ideal impossible. The principles on
which Massachusetts colonists rebelled forced the colony to accept a
place in the empire more like an equal and less a holy commonwealth.
This was humiliating, no doubt, to God's chosen people, but it defined
for the colony a broader, more secular role in an empire they had
come to believe lately and through necessity was based on the equality
of Englishmen in America and at home. It was this principle of equality which Increase Mather stood upon in London after William's victory and then by negotiation tried to improve upon in securing a charter. Once it was granted, Massachusetts colonists accepted the new
charter as a written constitution, not guaranteeing them all they
wanted, but more than either New York or Maryland had settled for.
They accepted, too, although less eagerly, the idea of empire the
charter defined.

A dependent but equal role for colonies was a contradiction in the
English empire of the seventeenth century. It was a conception which
had no currency in England during that century or the next. It denied
the superiority of the realm over the dominions and negated an uncon-
trolled prerogative in colonial affairs. A dependent people had no
business assuming rights reserved for subjects in the realm. Who are
colonists and what are colonies were questions Englishmen at home
answered vigorously in the latter half of the seventeenth century.
From these answers derived a colonial policy based primarily on the
economic and political needs of the realm.

Once imposed, the policy provoked colonists to ask the same questions, but their answers were very different, for their assumptions and
needs were different. From a conception of empire based on an equality of Englishmen in dominions and realm, colonists sought a colonial
policy which would honor Englishmen's rights in America. In these
rights, they believed, besides protection *from* arbitrary power and
troublesome "mutacons," lay sanction *for* government by law, equitable
justice, economic opportunity, and the rights of property—a combination of political principle and material advantage. Prevented from
realizing these guarantees before 1689, they championed the Glorious
Revolution as a means to that end. In this, too, they were disappointed.

Despite significant changes won by Englishmen in England, the lesson the Revolution taught colonies was that they were dominions of the Crown to be dealt with as the King wished, with no assurance of Englishmen's rights on permanent bases.[1]

What could not be extracted in written contracts gradually was assumed in practice as time went on. New York and Maryland joined Virginia and other colonies whose assemblies and inhabitants eventually took on the self-governing character, the rights and liberties the King had refused to guarantee them, while Massachusetts improved upon those it already enjoyed and added a few more. But this is the story of the eighteenth century. By 1765 these rights and liberties, a general assumption that colonists were as good as Englishmen at home and were entitled to equal treatment and respect from government, were pretty well fixed in the minds of English Americans. And well they might be, for their origins lay in the colonists' struggles of the seventeenth century.

1. Strong evidence of the inferior position colonists held in the empire was the imposition of admiralty courts after 1696 to try breaches of the Acts of Trade. These civil or maritime courts, presided over by crown-appointed judges, discriminated against colonists by denying them protection of the common law and trial by jury, rights which every Englishman at home enjoyed when accused of like offenses.

Bibliographical Essay

A detailed description of the sources examined in bringing together this study of the Glorious Revolution in America is impossible primarily for reasons of space. Anyway, it would doubtless go unread except by scholars who wished they had tackled the subject instead of me (and maybe should have) and a few indefatigable graduate students who hoped to discover what I have omitted. At the same time, a raw listing of the manuscripts, collections of documents, diaries, journals, and books and articles which are the bases for this book would probably leave both the author and his readers unsatisfied. Maybe something in between, a guide rather than an exhaustive and descriptive compilation, will be helpful to a variety of readers, if it does not suffice for all.

Manuscripts

If one took the time to sort out the footnotes in the preceding narrative (a tedious task at best), he would doubtless discover that nearly half of them cite manuscript sources. Of these the bulk came from three well-known repositories: the Public Record Office in London, the British Museum, and Colonial Williamsburg. Charles McLean Andrews in his *Guide to the Materials for American History, to 1783, in the Public Record Office of Great*

Britain . . . (2 vols., Washington, 1912–14, reprinted, New York, 1965) has best explained the P.R.O.'s overwhelming collections, and I leave the interested scholar in his worthy hands for description of the following Colonial Office categories cited by me: C.O. 1/47/103; C.O. 1/56/90; C.O. 1/57/81; C.O. 1/64/48; C.O. 1/65/97; C.O. 1/68/47; C.O. 1/68/108; C.O. 5/713/4; C.O. 5/785 (Sessional Papers, Council); C.O. 5/855, #94 (Bullivant's Journall); C.O. 5/896; C.O. 5/903–05; C.O. 5/1081; C.O. 5/1134 (New York Land Grants); C.O. 5/1135/114; C.O. 5/1371; C.O. 5/1385; C.O. 134/1; C.O. 309/1; C.O. 324/4–5; C.O. 389/1, 9; C.O. 391/6. To these C.O. categories, add Adm 1/5139; the Shaftesbury Papers in P.R.O. 30/24/49/26; and P.C. 6/14.

Many of these documents, but not all, are calendared, adumbrated, or the gist given—in modern prose—in the *Calendar of State Papers, Colonial Series, America and the West Indies*. But I found the originals invaluable, owing sometimes to overstrict condensation, even deletions of crucial statements, in the printed versions (C. M. Andrews more than once described certain documents as "inadequately calendared"). This is not to say that the *Calendars* are not useful; far from it, for I used them profitably, and gladly, when time and geography separated me from the originals.

At the British Museum I examined pertinent parts of the following collections: Additional Manuscripts 8133, 15487, 15898, 25120 (Coventry Papers), 28089, 30372, 34712, and 38144. (This last category contains James II's, Queen Mary of Modena's, and the Duke of Melfort's pleas to the Pope for help against Prince William.) Sloane Mss. 1008, 2902, 3339, 32681 (Henry Sidney); Harleian Mss. 1898; Egerton Mss. 2395, 2543; and the Stowe Mss. 746. The best explanation of these collections can be found in C. M. Andrews and Frances G. Davenport, compilers, *Guide to the Manuscript Materials for the History of the United States to 1783, in the British Museum, in Minor London Archives, and in the Libraries of Oxford and Cambridge* (Washington, 1908, reprinted, New York, 1965).

The Library of the Society of Friends provided Papers Relating to William Penn, Penn Manuscripts, Portfolio 31/95 and the London Yearly Meeting, Epistles Received, 1683–1706. Englishmen's help through their churches to Huguenot refugees is described in detail in pounds and shillings in the Ex-Guildhall Library Manuscripts, Miscellaneous Papers, Corporation of London Records Office, Guildhall, London.

In the United States I relied heavily upon the Blathwayt Papers of Colonial Williamsburg—half of a huge collection, the balance housed at the Huntington Library, San Marino, California—which I examined through microfilm at the Wisconsin State Historical Society. William Blathwayt, as secretary of the Lords of Trade and Auditor General of Plantation Revenues, administered an office which was a nerve center through which vibrated vital communications between the powers-that-be in London and the colonial governments and vice versa. His papers, I believe, are the single most important source of information which exists about the American colonies in the latter half of the seventeenth century—a statement which forces all interested scholars to wonder why this collection has never been published. For a splendid description of these papers, see Lester J. Cappon, "The Blathwayt Papers of Colonial Williamsburg, Inc.," *William and Mary Quarterly*, 3d ser., IV (July 1947), 317–31.

When one realizes the bulk of Massachusetts sources for the early period already in print, one is amazed at how much still remains in manuscript. At the Massachusetts Archives, State House, Boston, I found the following volumes particularly helpful: CVI Political; Ecclesiastical, 1679–1739; Literary, 1645–1775, vol. 58; and M.A. 1658–1751. Equally important were the Gay Transcripts, State Papers, II and III, and the Prince Collection, I, at the Massachusetts Historical Society, Boston.

For a number of letters and specific pieces of information about New York, I relied upon the Livingston Family Papers, particularly General Correspondence and Indian Affairs, in the Franklin Delano Roosevelt Library, Hyde Park, New York. I examined these on microfilm generously lent to me by Professor James S. Leamon of Bates College. Similarly for Pennsylvania I examined a collection called David Lloyd and Related Papers, Province of Pennsylvania, 1686–1731, from the Historical Society of Pennsylvania which I saw on microfilm at the Wisconsin State Historical Society.

Printed Sources

Following are the printed sources most heavily relied upon:

I. Records and Official Documents

N. B. Shurtleff, ed., *Records of the Governor and Company of the Massachusetts Bay in New England, 1628–1686* (5 vols., Boston, 1853–54); J. R. Bartlett, ed., *Records of the Colony of Rhode Island* (10 vols., Providence, R.I., 1856–65); J. H. Trumbull and C. J. Hoadly, eds., *Public Records of the Colony of Connecticut* (15 vols., Hartford, Conn., 1850–90); R. R. Hinman, ed., *Letters from the English Kings and Queens . . . to the Governors of Connecticut* (Hartford, 1836); E. B. O'Callaghan, ed., *Documentary History of the State of New-York* (4 vols., Albany, 1849–51); E. B. O'Callaghan and B. Fernow, eds., *Documents Relative to the Colonial History of the State of New-York* (15 vols., Albany, 1853–87); *The Colonial Laws of New York from the Year 1664 to the Revolution* (5 vols., Albany, 1894–96); W. H. Browne, *et al.*, eds., *Archives of Maryland* (69 vols., Baltimore, 1883–1962); W. W. Hening, ed., *Statutes at Large; Being a Collection of All the Laws of Virginia, from . . . the Year 1619 . . .* (Richmond, Va., 1819–23); H. R. McIlwaine, ed., *Journals of the House of Burgesses of Virginia, 1659/60–1693* (Richmond, Va., 1914); W. L. Saunders, ed., *Colonial Records of North Carolina, 1662–1776* (10 vols., Raleigh, N.C., 1886–90).

W. Noel Sainsbury, *et al.*, eds., *Calendar of State Papers, Colonial Series, America and the West Indies* (42 vols., London, 1860–1953); F. H. Blackburne Daniell, *et al.*, eds., *Calendar of State Papers, Domestic Series* (96 vols., London, 1856–1924). Early American historians tend to neglect this series. A number of reports, submitted locally, say, at one of the outports by ship captains, have shown up in the domestic series. W. A. Shaw, ed., *Calendar of Treasury Books, 1660–1718* (32 vols., London, 1904–57), explains a good deal about customs business, salaries, patronage, etc. See, too, W. S. Grant and J. Munro, eds., *Acts of the Privy Council of England, Colonial Series, 1613–1783* (6 vols., London, 1908–12).

Merely to list the two following works seems shameful, but among early American historians, they speak for themselves: Leo F. Stock, ed., *Proceedings and Debates of the British Parliaments Respecting North America, 1452–1727* (5 vols., Washington, 1924–41); and Leonard W. Labaree, ed., *Royal Instructions to the British Colonial Governors, 1670–1776* (2 vols., New York and London, 1935).

II. COLLECTIONS

W. H. Whitmore, ed., *Andros Tracts: Being a Collection of Pamphlets and Official Papers . . . of the Andros Government and the Establishment of the Second Charter of Massachusetts* (3 vols., New York, 1868–74), Publications of the Prince Society, vols. 5–7. Many of the important tracts and pamphlets pertaining to the Dominion and its overthrow are contained in these volumes. The bulk of the contents of C. M. Andrews, ed., *Narratives of the Insurrections, 1675–1690* (New York, 1915), has to do with the rebellions of 1689. M. G. Hall, L. H. Leder, and M. G. Kammen, eds., *The Glorious Revolution in America: Documents on the Colonial Crisis of 1689* (Chapel Hill, N.C., 1964). This excellent collection appeared after a good part of the research for this book in the United States was completed. Still, it was extremely helpful, printing several letters and documents for the first time. I have cited it frequently. Andrew Browning, ed., *English Historical Documents, 1660–1714,* vol. VIII (London, 1953); Merrill Jensen, ed., *English Historical Documents,* vol. IX, *American Colonial Documents to 1776* (London, 1955); C. C. Hall, ed., *Narratives of Early Maryland, 1633–1684* (New York, 1910); Peter Force, ed., *Tracts and Other Papers Relating Principally to the Colonies in North America* (4 vols., Washington, 1836–46).

Historical Manuscript Commission *Reports,* a hodgepodge often when it comes to finding specific information, these collections are loaded with vital material about the colonies. Most useful were the following papers: S. H. LeFleming, Dartmouth, Lindsey, Ormonde, Pepys, Westmoreland, Egmont, Leeds, Finch, Portland, Cowper, and the *House of Lords Manuscripts.*

III. TRACTS

In addition to the tracts and pamphlets found in the *Andros Tracts* and C. M. Andrews' *Narratives of the Insurrections,* the following were pertinent: Gershom Bulkeley, *Will and Doom, or the Miseries of Connecticut...,* Conn. Hist. Soc. *Collections,* III, 69–269; Beverly McAnear, ed., "Mariland's Grevances Wiy The Have Taken Op Arms," *Journal of Southern History,* VIII (1942); Philip Calvert, *A Letter From the Chancellour of Mary-Land to Col. Henry Meese* (London, 1682), John Carter Brown Library; Daniel Denton, *A Brief Description of New York . . .* (London, 1670), reprinted in Gowans' *Bibliotheca Americana,* 1 (New York, 1845); *At a Convention of the Representatives of the Several Towns* (Boston, 1689); *The Case of Massachusetts Colony Considered . . .* (Boston, 1689?); *A Short Account of the Present State of New-England. Anno Domini 1690,* by N.N. [London?, 1690], John Carter Brown Library; *The Cause of God and His People in New England* (Cambridge, Mass., 1663) in J. B. Felt, *Ecclesiastical History of New England* (2 vols., Boston, 1855–62), II, 303–14; *To the Parliament of England, the Case of the Poor English Protestants in Mary-Land . . .* [London, 1681], John Carter Brown Library; *From a Gentleman of Boston to a Friend in the Country,* by N.N. (Boston, 1689); [Nathaniel Byfield], *Seasonable Notices to our Duty and Allegiance . . .* (Philadelphia, 1689).

Somewhat different in nature are John Locke, *Two Treatises of Government,* ed. by F. I. Cooke (New York, 1947), and James Tyrrell, *Bibliotheca Politica* (n.p., 1694).

IV. LETTERS, JOURNALS, DIARIES, PAPERS, ETC.

At the top of this list is R. N. Toppan and A. T. S. Goodrick, eds., *Edward Randolph: Including His Letters and Official Papers . . . 1676–1703* (7 vols., Boston, 1898–1909), Publications of the Prince Society. The papers of this cantankerous and ubiquitous bureaucrat are a most significant source of information about the American colonies, particularly New England, for the last quarter of the seventeenth century.

For an inside look at Increase Mather's character, personality, and persistent negotiations, see his "Autobiography," ed. by M. G. Hall, A. A. S. *Proceedings,* 71 (1961), pt. 2. See, too, "The Diary of Increase Mather," M.H.S. *Proceedings* (1899, 1900), 2d ser., XIII.

Other helpful diaries and papers were: Benj. Bullivant's Journall, C.O. 5/855, #94, and printed in M.H.S. *Proceedings,* XVI (Boston, 1879), 103–8; *Calvert Papers,* No. 1, Fund-Publication, No. 28, Maryland Historical Society (Baltimore, 1889); "Clarendon Papers," New-York Historical Society *Collections* (1869); "Diary of Lawrence Hammond," M.H.S. *Proceedings* (1891–92), 2d ser., VII; *Hinckley Papers,* M.H.S. *Collections,* 4th ser., V (Boston, 1861); "Diary of John Hull," A.A.S. *Transactions and Collections,* III (1857); *Hutchinson Papers,* M.H.S. *Collections,* 3d ser., I (1825); *Diary of Cotton Mather* (2 vols., reprinted, New York, 1957); "Journall and Narrative of . . . Cuthbert Potter," Newton D. Mereness, ed., *Travels in the American Colonies* (New York, 1916); "Diary of Noahdiah Russell," *New England Historical and Genealogical Register,* VIII (1853); *Diary of Samuel Sewall,* M.H.S. *Collections,* 6th ser., vols. 5–7 (Boston, 1878–82); *Letter-Book of Samuel Sewall,* M.H.S. *Collections,* 6th ser., vols. 1–2 (Boston, 1886–88); *Wyllys Papers,* Conn. Hist. Soc. *Collections,* XXI (1924); *Winthrop Papers,* scattered through several volumes of M.H.S. *Collections,* 5th and 6th series.

E. S. De Beer, ed., *The Diary of John Evelyn* (London, 1959); William Hamper, ed., *Life, Diary and Correspondence of Sir William Dugdale* (London, 1827); Sir John Dalrymple, ed., *Memoirs of Great Britain and Ireland* (2 vols., London, 1773); John Lord Viscount Lonsdale, *Memoir of the Reign of James II* (London, 1857).

V. SECONDARY SOURCES

1. EARLY HISTORIES

Several seventeenth- and eighteenth-century histories added considerably to a picture of the times: Robert Beverley, *The History and Present State of*

Virginia, ed. by Louis B. Wright (Chapel Hill, N.C., 1947); Gilbert Burnet, *Bishop Burnet's History of His Own Time* (London, 1857); George Chalmers, *Political Annals of the Present United Colonies* (London, 1780), and *An Introduction to the History of the Revolt of the American Colonies* (2 vols. in one, Boston, 1845); Alexander Giraffi, *An Exact History of the Late Revolutions in Naples . . .* , trans. from the Italian by J[ames] H[owell] (London, 1664); Henry Hartwell, James Blair, and Edward Chilton, *The Present State of Virginia, and the College*, ed. by H. D. Farish (Williamsburg, Va., 1940); Thomas Hutchinson, *The History of the Colony and Province of Massachusetts-Bay*, ed. by L. S. Mayo (3 vols., Cambridge, Mass., 1936); Cotton Mather, *Magnalia Christi Americana* (2 vols., Hartford, Conn., 1820); Samuel Mather, *The Life of . . . Cotton Mather* (Boston, 1729); Daniel Neal, *The History of New England . . .* (2 vols., London, 2d ed., 1747); [John Oldmixon], *The British Empire in America* (2 vols., London, 1741).

2. NINETEENTH-CENTURY HISTORIES

Samuel G. Arnold, *History of the State of Rhode Island and Providence Plantations* (2 vols., Providence, R.I., 1894); John R. Brodhead, *History of the State of New York* (2 vols., New York, 1853, 1871); J. D. Burk, *History of Virginia . . .* (4 vols., Petersburg, Va., 1804–16), primarily the Appendixes. Bryan Edwards, *The History of the British West Indies* (4 vols., Philadelphia, 1806); J. B. Felt, *Ecclesiastical History of New England* (2 vols., Boston, 1855–62); Charles James Fox, *A History of the Early Part of the Reign of James the Second . . .* (London, 1808); Edward D. Neill, *Terra Mariae* (Philadelphia, 1867); E. B. O'Callaghan, *Origin of Legislative Assemblies in the State of New York* (Albany, N.Y., 1861), which appears also as "Historical Introduction" to *Journal of the Legislative Council of the Colony of New-York* [1691–1775] (2 vols., Albany, N.Y., 1861); John G. Palfrey, *A History of New England* (5 vols., Boston, 1858–90); Francis Parkman, *Count Frontenac and New France Under Louis XIV* (Boston, 1880, reprinted, 1966); J. Thomas Scharf, *History of Maryland, from the Earliest Period to the Present Day* (3 vols., Baltimore, 1879); Edgar A. Werner, *Civil List and Constitutional History of the Colony and State of New York* (Albany, 1889); Justin Winsor, *Narrative and Critical History of America* (8 vols., Boston, 1884–89). Winsor's critical bibliography is still an invaluable guide for the early American historian.

3. RECENT BOOKS AND ARTICLES

There is no single work devoted to the Glorious Revolution in America. The preceding pages are an attempt to satisfy this need. A number of recent books and articles, however, bear closely upon the subject, and several of them were indispensable to this study. Richard S. Dunn, *Puritans and Yankees: The Winthrop Dynasty of New England, 1630–1717* (Princeton, N.J., 1962), sheds much new light primarily on the latter half of the seventeenth century in a splendid treatment of Wait and Fitz-John Winthrop, whose careers symbolized what had happened to their grandfather's idea of a "Citty upon a Hill." Similarly Bernard Bailyn approaches Puritan Massachusetts from a fresh point of view in *The New England Merchants in the*

Seventeenth Century (Cambridge, Mass., 1955). In *Edward Randolph and the American Colonies, 1676–1703* (Chapel Hill, N.C., 1960), Michael G. Hall has epitomized in his protagonist the character of the colonial system in the last quarter of the same century. Although written more than forty years ago, Viola F. Barnes, *The Dominion of New England* (New Haven, Conn., 1923, reprinted, New York, 1960), has been the authority on Sir Edmund Andros and the Dominion. Somewhat one-sided, her work needs companion pieces to explain better the colonists' side of the story. One of the great biographies of an early American is Kenneth B. Murdock's *Increase Mather, Foremost American Puritan* (Cambridge, Mass., 1925). Murdock superbly handles his subject's amazing scope and ability as an intellectual leader, politician, and colony agent. Charles M. Andrews, *The Colonial Period of American History* (4 vols., New Haven, Conn., 1933–38), is continually indispensable, although its organization, even purpose, prevents his explaining the internal and external causes and consequences of the rebellions and their relationships with each other.

Lawrence H. Leder, in *Robert Livingston, 1654–1728, and the Politics of Colonial New York* (Chapel Hill, N.C., 1961), has devoted only one chapter to Leisler's Rebellion, but his interpretation is sophisticated and instructive, more so, I think, than Jerome R. Reich's in *Leisler's Rebellion, a Study of Democracy in New York, 1664–1720* (Chicago, 1953), which exaggerates its main theme but is still valuable for its bibliography and many facts, the latter, unfortunately, difficult to dig out owing to an almost useless index. The only recent attempt to explain the rebellion in Maryland is Michael G. Kammen's long article, "The Causes of the Maryland Revolution of 1689," *Maryland Historical Magazine* (Dec. 1960). His examination is broad and thoughtful, although hypothetical in parts. An article as good as this deserved better editing.

Philip Haffenden has placed the American colonies in proper perspective, demonstrating what they were up against respecting Crown policy during the Restoration, in an excellent article, "The Crown and the Colonial Charters, 1675–1688," *William and Mary Quarterly*, 3d ser., XIV (July 1958), 297–311, and (Oct. 1958), 452–66. A major treatment of Bacon's Rebellion is Wilcomb E. Washburn, *The Governor and the Rebel: A History of Bacon's Rebellion in Virginia* (Chapel Hill, N.C., 1957). Still helpful for an understanding of Virginia politics between Bacon's Rebellion and the Glorious Revolution is Thomas J. Wertenbaker, *Virginia Under the Stuarts, 1607–1688* (Princeton, N.J., 1914). Bernard Bailyn has put several of the problems discussed differently by Washburn and Wertenbaker in a new light in "Politics and Social Structure in Virginia," James Morton Smith, ed., *Seventeenth-Century America: Essays in Colonial History* (Chapel Hill, N.C., 1959).

Very helpful on several specific points was Leonard W. Labaree, *Royal Government in America* (New Haven, Conn., 1930). So, too, were two books by Wesley Frank Craven, *The Southern Colonies in the Seventeenth Century, 1607–1689* (Baton Rouge, La., 1949) and *The Colonies in Transition, 1660–1713* (New York, 1968).

On the English side several works provided needed background: George N. Clark, *The Later Stuarts, 1660–1714* (2d ed., Oxford, 1955); David Ogg,

England in the Reign of Charles II (2 vols., London, 1934, reprinted, 1963); J. P. Kenyon, *Robert Spencer, Earl of Sunderland, 1641–1702* (London, 1958); and J. H. Plumb, *The Origins of Political Stability: England, 1675–1725* (Boston, 1967). For more specific information I relied upon Stephen B. Baxter, *William III and the Defense of European Liberty, 1650–1702* (New York, 1966); Lucile Pinkham, *William III and the Respectable Revolution* (Cambridge, Mass., 1954); J. R. Jones, *The First Whigs: The Politics of the Exclusion Crisis, 1678–1683* (London, 1961); and of exceptional help, E. E. Rich, "The First Earl of Shaftesbury's Colonial Policy," *Transactions of the Royal Historical Society,* 5th ser., VII (London, 1957), 47–70.

4. THESES

John C. Rainbolt, "The Virginia Vision: A Political History of the Efforts to Diversify the Economy of the Old Dominion, 1650–1706" (unpubl. Ph.D. thesis, Univ. of Wisconsin, 1966); Theodore B. Lewis, Jr., "Massachusetts and the Glorious Revolution: A Political and Constitutional Study, 1660–1692" (unpubl. Ph.D. thesis, Univ. of Wisconsin, 1967); Maxine Neustadt Lurie, "Proprietary Purposes in the Anglo-American Colonies: Problems in the Transplantation of English Patterns of Social Organization" (unpubl. Ph.D. thesis, Univ. of Wisconsin, 1968); J. M. Neil, "Long Island, 1640–1691: The Defeat of Town Autonomy" (unpubl. A.M. thesis, Univ. of Wisconsin, 1963); Robert M. Bliss, Jr., "Connecticut, 1676–1708: The Institutionalization of the Organic Society" (unpubl. A.M. thesis, Univ. of Wisconsin, 1967); Eugene R. Sheridan, "Maryland as a Royal Colony, 1689–1715" (unpubl. A.M. thesis, Univ. of Wisconsin, 1968).

Index

72 73 74 75 10 9 8 7 6 5 4 3 2 1

Elizabeth Lovejoy

After receiving his doctorate in American Civilization at Brown University, David S. Lovejoy taught at Marlboro College, Brown and Northwestern Universities before going to the University of Wisconsin, where he is now a professor of history. As a Fulbright lecturer, he spent a year at the University of Aberdeen, Scotland; there and in London he continued his research for *The Glorious Revolution in America*. Later, he received a Guggenheim Fellowship which helped him complete the writing of the book.

Lovejoy's first book was *Rhode Island Politics and the American Revolution;* he is also editor of a collection of readings, *Religious Enthusiasm and the Great Awakening*. He lives in Madison, Wisconsin, with his wife, a painter.